Lecture Notes in Computer Science　　　9847

Commenced Publication in 1973
Founding and Former Series Editors:
Gerhard Goos, Juris Hartmanis, and Jan van Leeuwen

More information about this series at http://www.springer.com/series/7409

Muhammad Younas · Irfan Awan
Natalia Kryvinska · Christine Strauss
Do van Thanh (Eds.)

Mobile Web and Intelligent Information Systems

13th International Conference, MobiWIS 2016
Vienna, Austria, August 22–24, 2016
Proceedings

 Springer

Editors
Muhammad Younas
Oxford Brookes University
Oxford
UK

Irfan Awan
University of Bradford
Bradford
UK

Natalia Kryvinska
University of Vienna
Vienna
Austria

Christine Strauss
University of Vienna
Vienna
Austria

Do van Thanh
Telenor R&D
Fornebu
Norway

ISSN 0302-9743   ISSN 1611-3349 (electronic)
Lecture Notes in Computer Science
ISBN 978-3-319-44214-3   ISBN 978-3-319-44215-0 (eBook)
DOI 10.1007/978-3-319-44215-0

Library of Congress Control Number: 2016947187

LNCS Sublibrary: SL3 – Information Systems and Applications, incl. Internet/Web, and HCI

Printed on acid-free paper

This Springer imprint is published by Springer Nature
The registered company is Springer International Publishing AG Switzerland

Preface

This volume includes a collection of research articles presented at the 13th International Conference on Mobile Web and Intelligent Information Systems (MobiWis 2016), which was held in Vienna, Austria, during August 22–24, 2016.

With the universal application of 3G and 4G technologies, mobile Web and information systems continue to penetrate social lives, businesses, politics, economies, health care, and education among others. The number of mobile devices (such as smart phones, tablets, etc.) and their technical capacities have been increasing at an enormous rate. Mobile devices have now become one of the main portals for people to access the Web and millions of mobile Apps. People use mobile devices to carry out daily tasks such as checking the prices of grocery at supermarket, getting updates on road traffic conditions and weather, online shopping and banking, and communicating on social media networks such as Twitter, WhatsApp, Facebook, YouTube, etc.

The International Conference on Mobile Web and Intelligent Information Systems (MobiWis) aims to advance research on and practical applications of mobile Web, intelligent information systems, and related mobile technologies. It provides a forum for researchers, developers, and practitioners from academia, industry, and the public sector to share research ideas, knowledge, and experiences in the areas of mobile Web and information systems. The call for papers for MobiWis 2016 included new and emerging areas such as: smart and intelligent systems, mobile software systems, middleware/SOA for mobile systems, context- and location-aware services, data management in the mobile Web, mobile cloud services, mobile Web of things, mobile Web security, trust and privacy, mobile networks, protocols and applications, mobile commerce and business services, HCI in mobile applications, social media, and adaptive approaches for mobile computing.

MobiWis 2016 attracted 98 submissions from various countries across the world. All the papers were peer-reviewed by the members of the Program Committee. Based on the reviews, 36 papers were accepted for the conference – comprising 31 full and five short papers, with the acceptance rate of 36 %. The accepted papers covered a range of topics related to the theme of the conference. In addition to the research articles, MobiWis 2016 featured a distinguished invited talk delivered by Prof. Latif Ladid (University of Luxembourg), who is the Founder and President of the IPv6 FORUM and the Founding Chair of the 5G World Alliance. The invited talk was delivered in conjunction with the co-located conferences of the IEEE 4th International Conference on Future Internet of Things and Cloud (FiCloud 2016) and the Second International Conference on Open and Big Data (OBD 2016).

We would like to thank the invited speaker for delivering timely and visionary talks. We would also like to thank all authors for their contributions to MobiWis 2016. We also thank all the Program Committee members who provided valuable and constructive feedback to the authors and to the program chairs. We would like to thank Barbara Masucci (Workshop Coordinator), Jian Yu (Journal Special Issues

Coordinator), George Ghinea (International Liaison Chair), and Samia Loucif (Publicity Chair). We would like to thank the local organizing team of the University of Vienna, Austria, for their great help and support. Our sincere thanks also go to the Springer LNCS team, in particular Alfred Hofmann and Christine Reiss, for their valuable support in the approval and production of the conference proceedings.

August 2016

Muhammad Younas
Irfan Awan
Natalia Kryvinska
Christine Strauss
Do van Thanh

Organization

Mobiwis 2016 Organizing Committee

General Chair

Christine Strauss   University of Vienna, Austria

Program Co-chairs

Natalia Kryvinska   University of Vienna, Austria
Irfan Awan   University of Bradford, UK
Do van Thanh   Telenor Research and Norwegian University of Science
      and Technology, Norway

Local Organizing Co-chairs

Natalia Kryvinska   University of Vienna, Austria
Christine Strauss   University of Vienna, Austria

Publication Chair

Muhammad Younas   Oxford Brookes University, UK

Workshop Coordinator

Barbara Masucci   University of Salerno, Italy

Journal Special Issues Coordinator

Jian Yu   Auckland University of Technology, New Zealand

International Liaison Chair

George Ghinea   Brunel University, UK

Publicity Chair

Samia Loucif   ALHOSN University, UAE

Program Committee

Aneta Poniszewska-Maranda	Lodz University, Poland
Agnis Stibe	Massachusetts Institute of Technology (MIT), USA
Andrea Omicini	University of Bologna, Italy
Artur Niewiadomski	Siedlce University, Poland
Azzam Mourad	Lebanese American University, Lebanon
Boning Feng	Oslo and Akershus University College of Applied Sciences, Norway
Carlos Calafate	Technical University of Valencia, Spain
Chumming Rong	University of Stavanger, Norway
Christine Bauer	University of Cologne, Germany
Christophe Feltus	University of Namur, Belgium
Ciprian Dobre	Politehnica University of Bucharest, Romania
Dan Johansson	Umea University, Sweden
Do van Thuan	Linus AS, Norway
Dragan Stojanovic	University of Nis, Serbia
Fatma Abdennadher	National School of Engineering of Sfax, Tunisia
Florence Sedes	Paul Sabatier University, France
Grace Lewis	Carnegie Mellon University, USA
Hadi Otrok	Khalifa University, UAE
Harmidah Ibrahim	Universiti Putra Malaysia, Malaysia
Hong-Linh Truong	TU Wien, Austria
Ivan Demydov	Lviv Polytechnic National University, Ukraine
Janny Leung	Chinese University of Hong Kong, SAR China
Jeng-Wei Lin	TungHai University, Japan
Jianqiang Cheng	University of Paris Sud, France
Jingwei Li	The Chinese University of Hong Kong, SAR China
John Lindstrom	Luleå University of Technology, Sweden
Jorge Sa Silva	University of Coimbra, Portugal
Jozef Juhar	Technical University of Kosice, Slovakia
Jung-Chun Liu	TungHai University, Japan
Kamal Bashah Nor Shahniza	Universiti Teknologi MARA, Malaysia
Karl Andersson	Lulea University of Technology, Sweden
Kashif Mahmood	Telenor Research, Norway
Katty Rohoden	Jaramillo Universidad Técnica Particular de Loja, Ecuador
Lalit Garg	University of Malta, Malta
Lianghuai Yang	Zhejiang University of Technology, China
Lidia Ogiela	AGH University of Science and Technology, Poland
Lina Yao	The University of Adelaide, Australia
Lulwah AlSuwaidan	King Saud University, Saudi Arabia
Marek R. Ogiela	AGH University of Science and Technology, Poland
Maria Luisa Damiani	Università degli Studi di Milano, Italy

Contents

Security of Mobile Applications

Mobile and Wireless Networking

Mobile Applications and Wearable Devices

Mobile Web and Applications

Personalization and Social Networks

Mobile Web - Practice and Experience

An Android Kernel Extension to Save Energy Resources Without Impacting User Experience

Luis Corral[1], Ilenia Fronza[2(✉)], Nabil El Ioini[2],
Andrea Janes[2], and Peter Plant[3]

[1] ITESM/UAQ, E. Gonzalez 500, 76130 Queretaro, Mexico
lrcorralv@itesm.mx
[2] Free University of Bolzano, Piazza Domenicani, 3, 39100 Bolzano, Italy
{ilenia.fronza,nabil.elioini,andrea.janes}@unibz.it
[3] Vertical-Life, Guggenbergstrasse, 39042 Brixen, Italy
peter@vertical-life.info

Abstract. The autonomy of mobile devices is a requirement of utmost importance for end users. The autonomy is strongly related to the capacity of the built-in battery, in combination with the technical capabilities and the demand of energy of the diverse components of the device. As mobile equipment becomes more powerful and demanding, the need to find ways to optimize the overall energy consumption of the system grows as a critical research path. Software, as an instrumental component of a mobile system, is also an attractive target to deploy energy saving approaches. Several techniques of software-based energy aware strategies have been explored, including solutions placed at operating system, compiler and application level. In this paper, we present an energy saving strategy at operating system level. Our approach is implemented in the form of kernel extensions that assess the status of the device, and enable economic profiles without user intervention. Our experiments show that the power management kernel extension is able to significantly extend the battery runtime by 70 % to 75 %, at the expense of impacting user experience with an estimated performance degradation of 20 % to 30 %.

Keywords: Android · Energy · Kernel · Mobile

1 Introduction

Mobile devices have growth in capacity and power thanks to the integration of complex hardware. However, the autonomy of mobile technologies relies on the available power source and on its management. Therefore, it is important to research on power management strategies that may reduce power intake, thus extending the battery runtime. A possible approach is designing and implementing more efficient hardware. A second approach is to leverage the capacity of software as an instrumental component in the overall performance of the mobile device. This way, software running on a device is modified (at user space, application, or operating system level) to reduce energy consumption.

© Springer International Publishing Switzerland 2016
M. Younas et al. (Eds.): MobiWIS 2016, LNCS 9847, pp. 3–17, 2016.
DOI: 10.1007/978-3-319-44215-0_1

Android is a mobile operating system based on the Linux[1] kernel. Its layered architecture allows device-specific tailoring and customizations. Android's Linux kernel acts as the interface between user space and hardware components, operated through drivers. The device drivers controlling the hardware can be configured as modules, which can be loaded and unloaded while the system is running [3]. The so-called CPU governor controls how the CPU raises/lowers its frequencies according to the current workload [1].

In this study, we propose a low-level energy saving approach implemented in the form of a power management extension of the Android OS kernel[2], which monitors the battery level and, depending on the current power state, it applies pre-defined settings that lower the power demand of the device. The lower the current battery power is, the more restrictive the applied settings are. Moreover, this study analyzes how the energy-aware settings affect the performance of the mobile device. Our power saving system runs at the kernel level, avoiding the overhead associated to sending messages from user space all the way down to the modules that interface with the hardware. All the necessary settings to reduce power consumption of given hardware components can be directly set at kernel level; the settings will change to preserve more battery, especially at the lower charge stages. This allows extending the battery runtime at the moment the device is almost out of charge, at the expense of system performance. Since a way to preserve the energy of a mobile device is by inducing reductions in the performance of the involved hardware components, it is also important to measure the trade-off in terms of performance and usability.

The rest of the paper is structured as follows: Sect. 2 discusses the related work; Sect. 3 details our approach; Sect. 4 describes the experiments that analysed the impact of our solution on performance and battery runtime; Sect. 5 draws conclusions and provides directions for further research.

2 Related Work

Analyzing and improving the battery consumption of a mobile computing system at software level is a complex task, which resulted in a variety of approaches that have been extensively discussed and summarized [10, 14]. In general, this research field can be grouped in two directions: the first focuses on the measurement of the battery consumption with a focus on the different hardware components of a mobile device; the second, which is discussed in this Section, modifies the software to extend the battery runtime.

Kraiman et al. [9] designed an intelligent modular power management system suitable for any mobile platform. This system is based on the Advanced Configuration Power Interface (ACPI)[3] architecture and it includes mechanisms to define the most efficient power management strategy for a specific mobile device. The proposed system reduces the overall power consumption, and a testing

---

[1] https://www.linux.com/.

[2] https://www.android.com/.

[3] http://www.uefi.org/acpi/specs.

framework detects energy resource leaks in applications. Motlhabi [12] compares the built-in power saving mechanisms of the Android kernel (such as the ACPI used in [9]) with the ones of Linux, and describes different power saving mechanisms (e.g., wake-locks and ACPI). Bala and Garg [2] implemented a learning engine, which gets as input data about users behavior. The result is a customized power profile adapted to user's needs, allowing to save energy by reducing the minimum required resources. Datta et al. [5] applied the same concept and derived power saving profiles based on user contexts. This learning engine increases the overall battery runtime by 82 %. Ellis [6] focused on high level power management, through the implementation of a power-based API that allows a partnership between applications and system in setting the energy consumption policy. The approach [7] proposes app modifications to increase the device idle times and inform the operating system about the length of each upcoming period of idleness. This approach can reduce disk energy consumption, with a negative impact on performance of 8 %. Corral et al. [4] evaluated the impact of available Android kernel-based modifications on battery runtime. They performed 4 performance modifications as well as evaluation tests on each kernel, monitoring the battery consumption in background. In addition, a general performance test explored the impact of the applied kernel modifications to the overall performance of the optimized device. Kernel level enhancements improved battery runtime, showing in selected cases a positive impact in the performance of the device. The analyzed custom kernels can reduce the battery consumption up to 33 % for isolated tasks, improving the general performance of the device by up to 16 %. Finally, it is important to note that there are a number of energy-saving applications available in major app stores, like Google Play. However, it is difficult to have a deep study on commercial applications, as they are implemented at user space. Our approach is rather to discuss techniques for power management that can be implemented at different levels of the OS stack, in particular at Kernel space.

3 Implementing an Energy Aware Kernel Module for Android

This work proposes an Android kernel extension that monitors the battery level and, depending on the current power state, it applies pre-defined hardware settings that lower the power demand for device operation. The implementation was performed on a LG Nexus 5 (Hammerhead) device[4], operated by the Android Version 5.01 Lollipop OS (based on the 3.4 `lollipop-release` kernel).

As a first step, a power management system was implemented, running as a module at the kernel level. Since the Android Kernel source code is smaller than 1 GB, we decided to create patch files which can be applied directly to the kernel sources. Our system is composed of a set of modules, hardware drivers, and a power management module itself (not to be confused with the Android

---

[4] http://www.lg.com/us/cell-phones/lg-D820-Sprint-Black-nexus-5.

built-in power management engine). The power management module controls
the different involved device drivers by inducing specific settings, which aim to
reduce the performance of the controlled hardware component, pursuing a reduction in the battery consumption. As the battery level decreases, the settings are
continuously set to higher power preservation levels, which are aggressively economic and result in a progressive performance degradation. Figure 1 illustrates
the principle behind our power management module, which acts as the controlling unit of the power saving tool. The primary duties of this module are to
check periodically the energy level by communicating with the battery device
driver, and to activate a power class according to the current battery capacity.

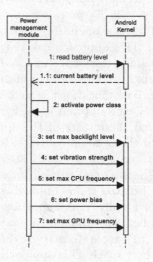

Fig. 1. Power management module communication.

Based on five settings, we defined ten power classes, which represent a range
of power levels (Table 1). A power class can be identified by the range it stands
for, e.g., power class P8 represents all battery levels ranging from 80 to 89. The
selection of ranges including 10 units, respectively 11 units for the 9th power
class should balance the number of updates done to the different parameters.
The choice of evaluating a power management module with ten power classes
was based on the following considerations. A too high number of power classes
results in frequent parameter updates: every time a new battery level is detected,
the new power class settings needs to be transferred to the different hardware
components. Considering that every update is associated to a cost in battery
consumption, it is advantageous to keep the number of power classes low. Nevertheless, a too low number of power classes results in inefficiencies, because
some values would need to be skipped. In addition to this, the procedure of how
to associate a given range to a power class would be more complex. Finally, the
limited amount of available frequencies for GPU and CPU settings reduces the
benefit of more than ten power classes.

Table 1. Settings for the different power classes.

	Max screen brightness (0–255)	Vibration (%)	Max CPU frequency (GHz)	Powersave bias (‰)	Max GPU frequency (0–6)
P9	Default	Default	Default	50	0
P8	150	Default	1958.4	50	1
P7	100	Default	1728.0	100	1
P6	40	30	1574.4	100	2
P5	30	30	1267.2	100	3
P4	20	30	1190.4	200	3
P3	10	0	1190.4	200	4
P2	5	0	1036.8	300	4
P1	3	0	1036.8	300	5
P0	1	0	960.0	300	5

The power saving system includes a set of device drivers that are already present in every stock Android kernel. Some of them were modified so that the configuration parameters become accessible from outside. The following drivers are part of the power saving system: the screen backlight driver, the vibration driver, the graphics processing unit (GPU) driver, and central processing unit (CPU) driver. The power saving system is composed of the following five components: (1) the overall Power management module controlling the other components; (2) the power module, reading the current battery level; (3) the backlight module (based on the Texas Instruments LM3630A Backlight driver chip[5]), to set the back-light level; (4) the CPU module setting the maximum CPU frequency and the power-save bias; and (5) the GPU module (based on the kernel graphics support layer provided by the Qualcomm Adreno GPU[6]), to set the maximum GPU frequency. Every component represents a kernel module which is either loaded into the kernel at run time or once at boot time. The power management module communicates with all other components by retrieving/providing values via function calls. The internal structure of the power management component includes a timer structure, which runs periodically to take the appropriate actions. Unfortunately, the native libraries used to build the kernel module do not provide timer structures that are able to run along a non-atomic environment that uses schedules, thread sleeps, and Mutex locks. Thus, a simple timer structure has been built, running in its own thread and calling the `read_battery_state()` function repeatedly. The delay of the function calls is achieved by a thread sleep of 2 min.

The power management module also defines all available power classes and the associated values of each class (Table 1). Each power class is represented by

---

[5] http://www.ti.com/product/lm3630a.
[6] https://developer.qualcomm.com/software/adreno-gpu-sdk/gpu.

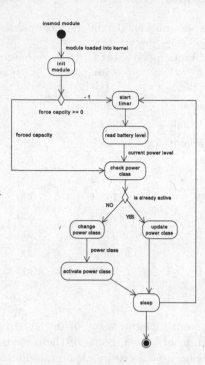

Fig. 2. Basic execution flow.

its own C file and has the same basic structure. The selection of the power class is done by a simple calculation on the basis of the current battery level, which is divided by 10. For example, the current battery level of a given smartphone is 55 %, when applying 50/10, we get 5, which defines P5 as the current power class. In contrast to the hardware driver modules, loaded into the kernel at boot time, the power management module can be loaded at any time once the system has booted. This way, the module can be modified during development without rebuilding the whole kernel, which can take up to 20 min.

Once the module has been loaded into the kernel, all data structures and variables that are used at a later point in execution time are setup. The kernel modules can be launched with parameters. In case a numeric value grater or equal than 0 has been passed, the periodic timer is not going to be started but the power class associated to the passed parameter value is directly activated (Fig. 2). Within a timer iteration, the battery level is read and passed to the routine that checks whether a new power class needs to be activated. In case the power class is already activated, the power class gets updated. After activation, the update is executed, and the timer thread is put to sleep for the defined amount of time. Once the thread wakes up again, a new timer iteration starts.

The power management module and the modified Android kernel are available on https://github.com/pplant/powerm_kernel. We built the kernel and the module on Ubuntu 14.10[7]. Before building the kernel and module code, it is required to setup the toolchain to build the code for an ARM processor architecture. The building toolchain we used is `arm-eabi-4.6`. The kernel building process creates the `zImage`, which contains the kernel executable. This file is embedded into the so-called `boot.img` file. To use the kernel, the previously created file needs to be flashed into the device by using the Android Bootloader and Fastboot (a tool that is part of the Android Software Development Kit[8]). Once the kernel is running in the device, the power management module can be built, which creates a kernel object file (with extension `.ko`). This is the file that is then transferred into the device using the Android Debug Bridge[9]. The last step is to load the `.ko` file into the kernel using the adb `push` command. Figure 3 illustrates the deployment diagram of our prototype.

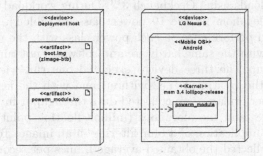

Fig. 3. Power management module deployment.

4   Evaluation

The developed power management system reduces the energy consumption by progressively decreasing the resources available to different hardware components, which, as a consequence, might reduce the performance of the smartphone. To investigate both aspects, we planned and executed two experiments using the "one factor with two treatments" structure [16]. We applied the principles of randomization, blocking, and balancing as follows: (1) we randomized the order of treatments; (2) we removed all applications except of the benchmark tools; and (3) we balanced the runs between the different devices, so that every device experiences the same number of executions. Moreover, both treatments were applied the same amount of times. We used three new LG Nexus 5 devices, all acquired at the same time, to minimize the source of variation induced by worn components. Before each experiment, we switched off the connectivity services such as radio, 2G, 3G, Bluetooth and GPS. Unfortunately,

---

[7] http://www.ubuntu.com/.

[8] http://developer.android.com/sdk/index.html.

[9] http://developer.android.com/tools/help/adb.html.

it was not possible to switch off the wifi, as the application that simulates workloads requires a working internet connection once a test has been completed. During the whole experiment the devices were connected to a power source to guarantee a constant power supply.

4.1   Experiment 1: Performance

This experiment investigates the impact on performance of our power management system. We focused on CPU and GPU performance, because they are related to the responsiveness and performance of the device, while features like vibration and screen brightness are related to the main I/O means that the device has to communicate with the user.

To measure the impact of the power management system on performance, we simulated workloads using Geekbench 3[10]. During workload simulations, we switched the mobile phone to the 10 power classes (Table 1). Then, we compared the measured performance on each power class with the values measured on a smartphone (with the same hardware and software) not running the power management system. The three devices executed one run without treatment and one run with the treatment (i.e., without and with the kernel extension). To measure CPU performance, we collected data throughput in MB/sec. during SHA1 encrypting [8] and the megaflops (million floating point operations per second) during the application of a blur filtering in an image. To measure GPU performance, we collected the obtained average frames per second as we played

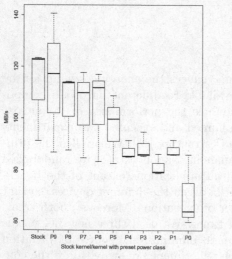

(a) Using SHA1 encrypting.

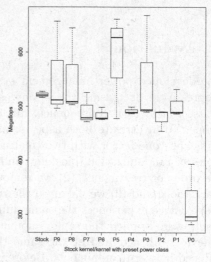

(b) Using blur filtering.

Fig. 4. Performance results for the CPU performance test.

---

[10] http://www.primatelabs.com/geekbench/.

an animation. Figure 4 depicts the results of the CPU performance experiment. Performance is negatively affected when the power management system is running: all observed variables except blur filtering show a downward trend with the simulated decreasing power level. Data resulting from the SHA1 encryption show that, at the beginning, the untreated and the treated device behave the same; afterwards, along with the decrease in hardware resources, the algorithm throughput decreases as well. Comparing the behavior of the algorithm throughput (Fig. 4a) along the different power classes, values seem to decrease slowly in the upper power classes (from P9 to P6). Even though the maximum available CPU frequency has changed from 2265.6 GHz in P9 to 1574.4 GHz in P6 and the power-save bias from 50 ‰ to 100 ‰, the algorithm seems to have enough resources to keep a rate over the 100 MB/s. The algorithm seems to be stronger affected between power class P6 and P4. The reason for this is a further reduction of the available resources (Table 1). The values of the power classes P3 and P1 are showing an abnormal behavior, by an increased value with respect to their predecessor. This phenomena can be retraced to the settings done in P3 and P1 which are not changing in comparison to their predecessor. The blur filtering algorithm does not reveal a clear trend: the results seem to vary independently of the decreasing battery level. The comparison of the power classes (Fig. 4b) shows a slight downward trend, including values which are breaking the order (P5, P3 and P1). Performance seems to decrease whenever the power-save bias is reduced (P7, P4 and P4). The reduction of the maximum CPU frequency seems not to impact directly the algorithm throughput.

Figure 5 shows the result of the GPU performance experiment. The power management system reduces the animation quality in terms of displayed frames per second. The comparison of the treatments observing the average frames per second shows a decreasing trend, whereas the values are constantly decreasing.

Results indicate that the application of the power management system decreases the performance of the device in terms of CPU and GPU. Among the different measurements, the performance reduction spans between 18 % and 30 %.

4.2   Experiment 2: Battery Runtime

This experiment investigates if the developed system has a positive effect on battery runtime and, if it has it, how longer a smartphone can run with one complete battery charge compared to a mobile device not running it.

To create a constant workload draining the battery, we built a small Android application to simulate different scenarios using the available phone resources. The benefits of using a battery draining application are: (1) the run times to completely discharge the device's battery are reduced; (2) shorter cycles lower the possibilities of confounding factors which could negatively affect the final results; and (3) such an application creates a constant workload over multiple runs that can not be achieved in a real world situation. The battery drainer application is composed of four tasks including three different 3D animations, a SHA1 encryption algorithm, a blur filter algorithm, and a vibration task.

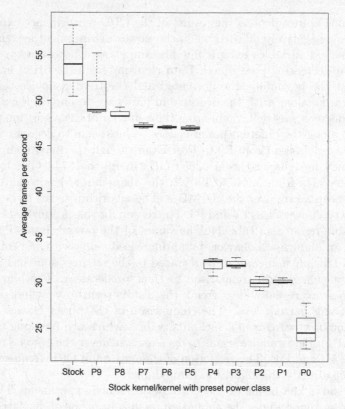

Fig. 5. Performance results for the GPU performance test.

This app targets to keep all those components busy, which are also included in the power management system. The three animations create an elevated workload mainly targeting the graphics processing unit (GPU). Each animation runs for two minutes, showing one or more objects with different surfaces, textures and details. The SHA1 algorithm and the blur filtering algorithm are for targeting the central processing unit. The first algorithm is taking as input a 150 MB text file containing random words. This file gets red line by line and encrypted by the SHA1 algorithm. The second algorithm continuously applies a blur filter to a 4000 × 4000 pixel image for about four minutes. The last task lets the device vibrate for one minute in intervals of one second. Running the sequence of all tasks creates a workload that increases the temperature of some hardware components. To avoid causing a reboot of the system, every task is followed by a one minute break. During the test runs of this experiment, we logged the time required to completely discharge the battery of a given device. This measurement allows to compare the different tests runs of different treatments, but also of the same treatment. Moreover, we also logged the current battery level every three minutes. This allows investigating the behavior of the battery consumption applying the two treatments. Moreover, it is possible to observe the discharging behavior influenced by the settings of the different activated power classes (Table 1) whenever the power management system is running.

Every run began by starting the battery drain application, which collected all the data. Depending on the treatment, the power management system needed to be started. After each test run, the resulting log files were transferred and archived, before the device was prepared for the next iteration. We performed 60 experiments in total, distributed between two treatments and two devices. Figure 6 shows the results of the obtained runtimes, with and without treatment. Run times ranges are: 28.300–29.000 s on device A, and 27.000–27.500 s on device B. Ranges of the cycles without treatment are: 15.500–17.000 s on device A, and 14.800–16.600 s on device B.

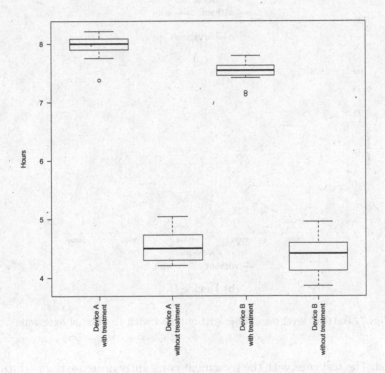

Fig. 6. Battery runtime (in hours) for the two tested devices with and without power management in hours.

Figure 7 shows the discharging processes of the different executions. In both the devices, test runs including the power management system initially behaves similar to the executions without the treatment. This trend continues until a battery capacity of 65 % is reached. At this point, the activated power classes include more restrictive settings that slow down the discharging process. In the meantime, the energy consumption of the executions not running the power saver tool proceeds to decay constantly until the energy resources are completely

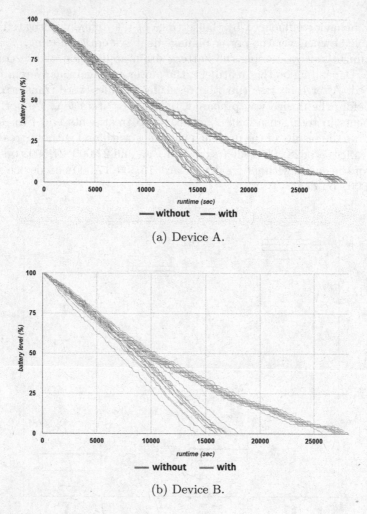

(a) Device A.

(b) Device B.

Fig. 7. Battery level over time, without and with the kernel extension.

exhausted. The test runs with the treatment constantly decrease the performance of the device which is progressively slowing down the discharging process. The performance settings reach their minimum level in the two lowest power classes.

We tested the normality of battery runtimes (i.e., with and without treatment for devices A and B) using the Shapiro-Wilk normality test [15]. The null hypothesis is that data are normally distributed; if the chosen alpha level is 0.05 and the p-value is less than 0.05, then the null hypothesis that the data are normally distributed is rejected. In three cases, results do not allow us to reject the null hypothesis that our samples come from a population which has a normal distribution (p-values = 0.02, 0.11, 0.15, and 0.58). We did not consider this result as an indication of normality distribution as, for small sample sizes, normality tests have little power to reject the null hypothesis [13]. Moreover, the variance of the populations is not equal. Thus, we used the Mann-Whitney-Wilcoxon Test [11] to decide whether the population distributions are identical. The null hypothesis is that data collected with and without treatment are identical populations. In both cases, at 0.05 significance level, we concluded that data originating from a device with treatment and data originating from a device without treatment are non-identical populations. Based on these results, we concluded that the implemented system is able to extend the battery runtime. However, even though the results seem to be promising, we can not generalize them to all Android devices, and especially not to smartphones running different operating systems. Experiments suggest that the collected data can be very fragile, in the sense that small side effects can affect negatively the validity of the results.

4.3   Threats to Validity

Internal Validity. The main problem is controlling unwanted background tasks. Even if the different treatments are executed multiple times, it is not possible to guarantee the complete absence of confounding factors. We tried to minimize this impact by uninstalling or deactivating all apps that were not involved in the experiments. Moreover, we deactivated all connectivity services.

Construct Validity. Battery of the used devices could be affected by a large number of experiments, e.g., recharging cycles or by the warming up of the device. We can not exclude the decreased energy consumption to be the result of unwanted side effects.

External Validity. The data we obtained are based on two devices of the same manufacturer and model. Therefore the results can not be generalized to all smartphones running the Android operating system. To enhance external validity, it is necessary to execute the developed system on different devices, covering the available devices on the market. Only one type of device was used, as our power management system implemented is based on a kernel which can only be used on specific devices such as the LG Nexus 5.

5   Conclusions and Future Work

In a world where business, entertainment, communication, and socialization rely upon the utilization of mobile devices, finding the right balance between performance and energy efficiency requires innovation, along with long lasting development, testing and measurement cycles, which set up a timely and challenging research area. This paper proposes a new approach to reduce the energy consumption of smartphones. Our approach extends the battery runtime by 70 % to 75 % with an estimated performance degradation of only 20 % to 30 %.

The results of this study are promising, and further work is worth in this direction, for example, to compare a user space power saving tool with the implemented system to study the different energy footprints caused by tools running on different layers. Another research path could inspect the selection of the settings defined in the power classes to optimize the ratio between performance tradeoffs and energy consumption. The comparison between the increase in battery runtime and the performance degradation suggests that the ratio does not behave in a linear fashion. Further study could examine the behavior of this ratio by changing the strength of the power saving settings. Moreover, there is a variety of possibilities to enhance the system proposed in this paper, for example including more components in the system such as the radio drivers. Additionally, evaluation could use a broader range of performance metrics, e.g., considering more human perception oriented metrics. Finally, user evaluation could contribute to evaluate our approach.

References

1. CPU Governors, Hotplugging drivers and GPU governors. http://androidmodguide.blogspot.it/p/blog-page.html. Accessed 29 Feb 2016
2. Bala, R., Garg, A.: Battery power saving profile with learning engine in Android phones. Comput. Appl. **69**(13), 38–41 (2013)
3. Bovet, D., Cesati, M.: Understanding the Linux Kernel. O'Reilly & Associates Inc., Sebastopol (2005)
4. Corral, L., Georgiev, A., Janes, A., Kofler, S.: Energy-aware performance evaluation of Android custom kernels. In: 2015 IEEE/ACM 4th International Workshop on Green and Sustainable Software (GREENS), pp. 1–7, May 2015
5. Datta, S., Bonnet, C., Nikaein, N.: Power monitor v2: novel power saving Android application. In: IEEE 17th International Symposium on Consumer Electronics (ISCE), pp. 253–254 (2013)
6. Ellis, C.: The case for higher-level power management. In: Proceedings of the Seventh Workshop on Hot Topics in Operating Systems, pp. 162–167 (1999)
7. Heath, T., Pinheiro, E., Hom, J., Kremer, U., Bianchini, R.: Code transformations for energy-efficient device management. IEEE Trans. Comput. **53**(8), 974–987 (2004)
8. Information Technology Laboratory, National Institute of Standards and Technology. Secure hash standard (2015). http://dx.doi.org/10.6028/NIST.FIPS.180-4
9. Kreiman, E., Emil, D., Lupu, C.: Using learning to predict and optimise power consumption in mobile devices (2010). http://www.doc.ic.ac.uk/teaching/distinguished-projects/2010/e.kreiman.pdf. Accessed 2 Sept 2015
10. Lewis, G., Lago, P.: Architectural tactics for cyber-foraging: results of a systematic literature review. J. Syst. Softw. **107**, 158–186 (2015)
11. Mann, H.B., Whitney, D.R.: On a test of whether one of two random variables is stochastically larger than the other. Ann. Math. Statist. **18**(1), 50–60 (1947)
12. Motlhabi, M.B.: Advanced Android Power Management and Implementation of Wakelocks (2013). http://www.cs.uwc.ac.za/~mmotlhabi/apm2.pdf. Accessed 2 Sept 2015
13. Öztuna, D.: Investigation of four different normality tests in terms of type 1 error rate and power under different distributions. Turk. J. Med. Sci. **36**(3), 171–176 (2006)

14. Procaccianti, G., Lago, P., Vetrò, A., Fernández, D.M., Wieringa, R.: The green lab: experimentation in software energy efficiency. In: Proceedings of the 37th International Conference on Software Engineering, ICSE 2015, vol. 2, pp. 941–942. IEEE Press, Piscataway (2015)
15. Shapiro, S.S., Wilk, M.B.: An analysis of variance test for normality (complete samples). Biometrika **52**(3–4), 591–611 (1965)
16. Wohlin, C., Runeson, P., Höst, M., Ohlsson, M.C., Regnell, B., Wesslén, A.: Experimentation in Software Engineering: An Introduction. Kluwer Academic Publishers, Norwell (2000)

Mobile Soundscape Mixer – Ready for Action

Kari Salo[1(✉)], Merja Bauters[1], and Tommi Mikkonen[2]

[1] Helsinki Metropolia University of Applied Sciences, Helsinki, Finland
{kari.salo,merja.bauters}@metropolia.fi
[2] Tampere University of Technology, Tampere, Finland
tommi.mikkonen@tut.fi

Abstract. Today, cultural organizations such as museums are seeking new ways to attract and engage audience. Augmented reality based applications are seen very promising. The target is to provide more interactive experiences for an audience with high familiarity of digital interaction. So far, visual presentation has been dominant in augmented reality systems. In contrast to this trend, we have chosen to concentrate on audio augmentation as user generated soundscapes. This paper discusses our approach, focusing on how to design and develop an easy-to-use and smoothly working Android application, which increases user interaction by developing soundscapes from building blocks stored in audio digital asset management system. We have successfully implemented applications for Android platform and evaluated their performance.

Keywords: Soundscape · Android · Audio Augmented Reality · Research-based design · Participatory design · User centered design · Performance profiling

1 Introduction

Interaction with environment increases and enhances each day. Augmented reality (AR) is one way to provide increasingly interactive experiences. Audio Augmented Reality systems have been used for navigation [1] and interacting with virtual objects [2]. Most previous projects have used extra devices such as a headphone-mounted digital compass or Kinect depth camera to track user's (head) location to produce sound that is modified according to user's movement.

As we believe that interaction and experiences are holistic using all senses, we have decided to concentrate to auditory presentation, focusing on the acoustic environment. To this end, a soundscape can be a musical composition, a radio program or an acoustic environment [3]. A soundscape is created out of multiple, time-varying sound sources [4]. Many of the soundscape systems – such as Klang.Reise [5] and the Sound Design Accelerator (SoDA) [6] – are either targeted to sound designers and need a lot of knowledge to operate, or require a dedicated space. We have combined these two concepts - soundscapes and audio AR. Our approach aims at ease-of-use and interaction without previous knowledge on sounds and soundscapes. Thus, the user is the active party and technology is in the supporting role either for searching relevant sounds with the help of mobile applications or producing the acoustic environment using her creativity and imagination. The user is not expected to be familiar with

M. Younas et al. (Eds.): MobiWIS 2016, LNCS 9847, pp. 18–30, 2016.
DOI: 10.1007/978-3-319-44215-0_2

acoustic terms or dependent on extra devices for tracking her head and hand movements, when creating soundscapes.

Our project, The Neighborhood Living Room, studies different methods how to create a more dynamic, participatory audience relationship with area residents (especially youth) and the Museum of Technology in Helsinki, Finland.

When developing audio AR and soundscape systems ease-of-use of the application and the backend service supporting these applications are two key aspects. Our target is to design and implement smoothly working mobile soundscape mixing application to increase user interaction by developing soundscapes from building blocks stored in audio digital asset management system.

The paper presents our results so far regarding the design of mobile applications. It is organized as follows. First we describe the overall system, design process, application development, and performance evaluation of the mobile applications. In the discussion we ponder on the outcomes we have achieved, and in conclusion we sum up the process and outline the need of further research.

2 System Overview

The overall system consists of an audio digital asset management system (ADAM), a management application, and mobile applications (Fig. 1). ADAM provides functionalities to manage assets and offers interfaces for both for management application and mobile applications over the Internet. The management application is more or less an administration console to manage assets and users. Mobile applications are for example audio augmented reality, soundscape design, audio story recording and listening, or audio memory sharing applications. This paper concentrates on a specific mobile application, soundscape mixer, represented as "the Mobile Apps" in the Fig. 1.

As pointed out above, the management application is used both for user management and asset management. The museum staff is able add new users, add audio file collections to users, and define which audio files belong to these collections. Users can be persons or devices. Sound designers as users can add new audio files, which are used as sound-scape building components. On the other hand a mobile device can be

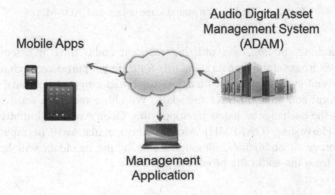

Fig. 1. System overview.

seen from the ADAM perspective as a user who would like to access audio files. To enable communication between ADAM and mobile applications three APIs were required: an authentication API, a search API, and an upload API. The authentication API is needed by the mobile users to receive a token, which in turn will be used with search and upload of APIs. The authentication is a security feature and ensures that only authorized users have access to token. The search API is a HTTP GET request containing token and predefined search parameters. The response given in JSON format contains audio files' metadata based on search parameters that are set along with the search request. Thus, the search API also enables downloading, as the link to audio file is a part of the metadata. The upload API lets users with a valid token upload their audio files along with metadata they choose to transmit to ADAM as a multi-part form using HTTP post. Metadata and token will be encoded in a part of the URL, and the audio file in the body of HTTP post (see Fig. 2).

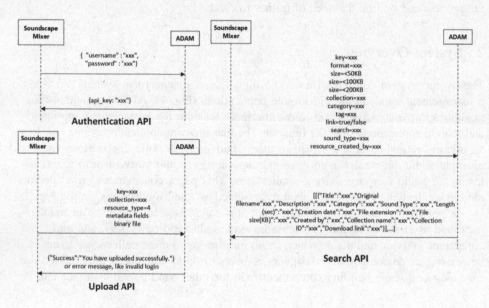

Fig. 2. APIs between soundscape mixer and ADAM

When searching, finding, and utilizing relevant audio files, it essential to use metadata. There are several metadata standards for different purposes, such as metadata exchange between systems, general metadata for broad range of domains, and audio specific structural and administrative metadata. We chose metadata set, which in the future enables the exchange of assets by supporting Open Archives Initiative Protocol for Metadata Harvesting (OAI-PMH). Most of the metadata will be input manually during the storage of audio files, although some of the metadata will be extracted automatically from the audio file properties [7].

3   Design Process of the Mobile Soundscape Mixer Application

For designing the mobile soundscape mixer applications, the research-based design approach [8] was used as a design process. It is an iterative process consisting of the following phases: contextual inquiry, participatory design, product design and prototype as hypothesis. The phases were executed in parallel. The emphasis of a phase changes during the process. The aim of the design was to design and implement a soundscape mixer application for mobile devices. Third year students from Helsinki Metropolia University of Applied Sciences, Helsinki, Finland carried out the design process. The students came from two courses (both of which lasted one semester, or three and half months): design-oriented course called Usability and Interface (28 students) and Android programming course called Android Advanced Application Development (19 students). Four sound design students created the sounds to be used in soundscape creations. We formed seven teams out of the design and programming courses. The teams were composed of 3–4 design students and 1–3 programmers. The design and programmer students had 5 organized meetings to present, organize, and test their intermediate outcomes. Between these joint meetings the sub-teams of designers and programmers were working on their own fields. In the end of the fifth iteration round a workshop was organized in the Museum of Technology. Each iteration included design in different levels of prototype granularity, ranging from low fidelity prototypes (see Fig. 3) to a running prototype (see Fig. 4).

The prototypes were tested in each of the iterations with users after which the students negotiated within their teams how the programming should continue, and how to prioritize features and functions of their applications [9, 10]. The aim was at creating a working mobile application for young museum visitors ready for the workshop.

The first phase of the design process was to familiarize with the context. The design students visited the Museum of Technology, discussed with the museum personnel, investigated the physical place and brainstormed on design [11]. The visit lasted three hours, and the students collected contextual material in the form of images and notes. The outcomes of the contextual inquiry were paper prototypes (see Fig. 3). The paper

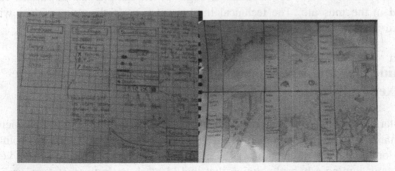

Fig. 3. Two different kinds of paper prototypes which were created after the visit to the Museum of Technology.

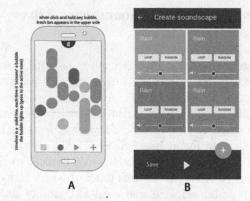

Fig. 4. (A) The left side screenshot displays an innovative idea on how to mix the sounds in a visuospatial manner. Each sound is represented as a colored bubble. The length of the bubble indicated the duration of the sound and the position of the bubble indicated when the sound is played in the timeline. (B) The right side displays an interface to mix the sounds in a more conventional orientation and interaction flow. Still, however, it achieves a clear interface for creating a soundscape. (Color figure online)

prototypes were discussed with the programmer students to construct a solution that is implementable with the teams' resources. The students, museum personnel, lecturers, and potential users listed out the first set of functional requirements [12], which were: listen, record, search files, save, delete and mix sounds for soundscape, login and out as well as sound file categories.

The created prototypes were tested with users belonging to the defined target group of 15–24 years old. Since the students themselves also belonged to the defined target group, they could pre-test their ideas with each other. The tests were video recorded and analyzed. Improvements were executed according to the test results for the next prototype (see Fig. 4).

The screenshot provides a glimpse over the multiple iterations that the students' teams performed. The screenshots are revealing since the idea of how to mix a soundscape is very different, but both are still easy and pleasant to use. In addition, one group implemented a QR code reader, through which sample sets of sounds can be retrieved in the museum. The technical implementation of the design ideas will be presented next.

4   Guidelines and Implementation for the Mobile Soundscape Mixer Application

When starting soundscape creation application (soundscape mixer) development we had to make a decision what smart phone platforms to support. As the Android platform is dominant at the moment, it was an obvious choice [13, 14]. Also an iOS version as well as designing a hybrid solution that would work on both platforms were considered, but we did not have any native iOS developers in the teams, and based on our previous experience on hybrid development [15], we ended up to selecting native Android application as web based audio APIs are not mature enough.

In order to coach programming teams towards the target, we provided some guidelines. From the development point of view these were the guidelines:

- Iterative/agile development process;
- Support Android 5.0 and newer version;
- Follow Google's material design guidelines;
- Support MP3 and/or PCM/Wave-format;
- Utilize Soundpool or Audiotrack classes for playing audio files;
- Utilize AudioRecord for recording.

Programming teams were given the following rough functional requirement specification:

- Login into Audio Digital Asset Management System (ADAM);
- Search content (audio files) in ADAM utilizing metadata;
- Download, save and play selected files either in MP3 or raw (PCM) format;
- If needed convert audio file format;
- Mixing, i.e. define combination of saved files that will played, possibility to loop, change volume, etc. of each audio file separately;
- Record audio file, convert the audio format and upload together with metadata into ADAM.

Following the guidelines and requirements, the design and programmer teams were able to implement mobile soundscape mixer applications according to iterative process described above. Four of the development teams were able to provide a fully working and tested application within the given timeframe. All of these four applications were in some respects different from each other. This was expected, as we were hoping to see each team use their imagination and creativity when designing and implementing the application. To test these applications with real users, we organized a workshop. For the workshop three applications were chosen for testing. These applications (Sound Bubbles, SoundSpace and SoundScape), were the most advanced applications. The UniChord application was left out because the Museum of Technology did not have the QR codes in their museum items or exhibition spaces.

The three remaining applications were implemented according to Android technical guidelines and best practices. As can be seen from the high level class diagrams (Fig. 5) object oriented approach was followed, multithreading was applied where required to avoid UI thread blocking, required functionalities were implemented, and recommended audio classes were used.

For security reasons, user identity and password were required when starting the application. In addition, also a collection identity was asked from the user. User identity and password are sent to backend service (ADAM), where they are checked and only authorized application will receive as a response security token, which will be used when sending search, download or upload requests to backend service. Each user identity could have several collections of audio files. Thus collection identity is used to limit which particular collection application is able to use. Implementation of this login

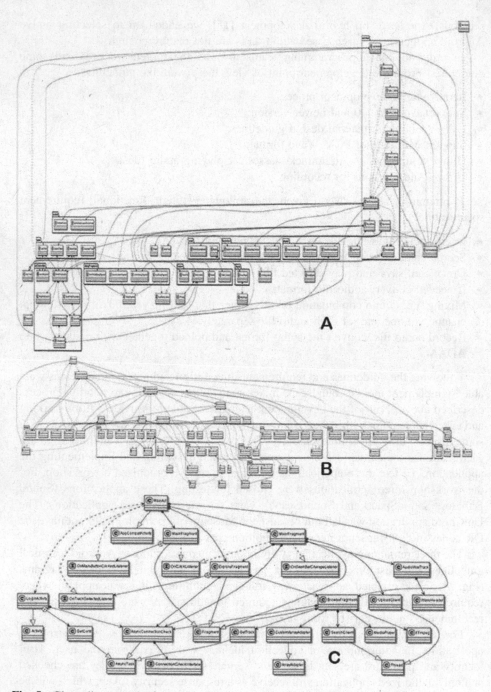

Fig. 5. Class diagrams describing the structure of applications. From top down there are A Sound Bubbles, B SoundSpace and C SoundScape applications.

functionality was similar in all applications, the only difference originating from the possibility to save credentials locally into phone's memory.

Searching audio files from ADAM was typically implemented either by providing a free search based on title or by asking user to select one of the four predefined categories (nature, human, machine and story) and then displaying as a scrollable list or grid all the titles. List and grid then provide a possibility to listen sounds before selecting them as a part of soundscape.

The possibility to record own audio files for using them as soundscape building components was found in all the applications. After recording these files, the files can be used locally or uploaded with metadata into backend service and thus shared with other users. Implementation of this recording and uploading functionality followed tightly the material guidelines being similar in all applications.

Finally, when all the soundscape components are available, the main functionality – mixing or creating the soundscape – can be described. Implementing mixing functionality differs from application to application. The applications implemented either time limitation or component limitation into their sound mixer. Sound Bubbles application is based on the idea of one minute soundscape and it can be divided into six parallel audio tracks. Each track can have zero or more audio files. SoundSpace and SoundScape applications, however, have limited the amount of audio files (Fig. 6). Looping either the whole soundscape or separately each audio file produces a longer soundscape than is possible with Sound Bubbles application.

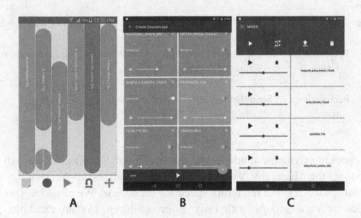

Fig. 6. Soundscape mixing functionality. From left to right there are A Sound Bubbles, B SoundSpace and C SoundScape applications

When the user is satisfied with her soundscape, she is able to save it either using digital audio recorder connected to Android phone's audio line-out, or in case of SoundScape (C) application, upload the soundscape file into ADAM. Testing the performance of these applications is described next.

5   Performance Evaluation

Application's performance has a vital impact on user experience. Testing the presence and effects of poor responsiveness is challenging due to non-existing testing strategies for exposing causes of poor responsiveness in Android applications. Some research has been done and approaches proposed [16, 17]. We decided to use tools available as a part of Android Studio, in particular the Android lint tool that checks Android project source files for potential bugs and optimization improvements. We run lint code analysis for all three applications to get an overall picture of potential problems. The following table (Table 1) describes the relevant findings. In addition, based on empirical study [17] we decided to mostly concentrate on GUI lagging type of performance bugs. Based on findings, it was necessary to check if there are problems with list scrolling (solution View Holder design pattern). As we are not heavily using long strings then potential StringBuffer problems do not have a major impact of performance.

Table 1. Static code analysis results.

Application	Lint category	Subcategory	Class name
Sound bubbles	Android lint	View holder candidates	• CategoriesAdapter • RecordingsAdapter • ServerFilesArrayAdapter
SoundSpace	–	–	–
SoundScape	Android lint	View holder candidates	• CustomArrayAdapter
	Performance issues	String Concatenation as argument to 'StringBuffer.append()'	• LoginActivity • SearchClient • WaveHeader
	Performance issues	'StringBuffer' can be replaced with 'String'	• WaveHeader

Before checking dynamic rendering of the frames of UI window we will use one more static tool, the Hierarchy Viewer. This tool visualizes application's view hierarchy and profiles the relative rendering speed for each view. We aimed to spot red dots in leaf nodes or view groups with only a few children. As an example, find the Hierarchy View tool's results for SoundScape (Fig. 7). As seen in the figure, there are no potential problem areas in leave nodes except in EditText, where the draw process could be slow. This EditText view refers to login screen's password field. When running on a device it seems to work smoothly. So far we have used static information. Next step was to use the GPU Monitor, which gives a quick visual representation of how much time it takes to render the frames of a UI window. It profiles the amount of time it takes for the render thread to prepare, process, and execute the draw commands.

As an example we have run the SoundSpace in Samsung Galaxy S5 and found some potential parts of the application where the user may see slower response than

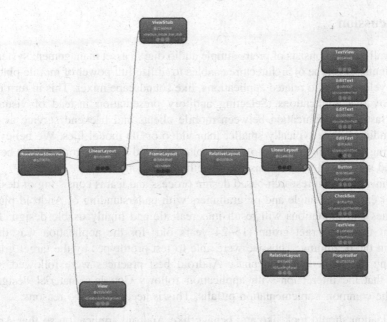

Fig. 7. SoundScape application's relative rendering speed for each view

expected (see Fig. 8). Adding audio components to soundscape is the main functionality of the application. The results are promising. Only few frames are exceeding 16 ms (green) line. This 16 ms frame duration is calculated from the recommended frame rate 60 frames per second, which ensures that user interactions with application are buttery smooth [18]. Saving soundscape project will happen very seldom, but it is pretty evident that user will see some slowness. We used GPU Monitor to test all three applications using Samsung Galaxy S5 and LG Nexus 5 phones. The results were similar to the above described SoundSpace results.

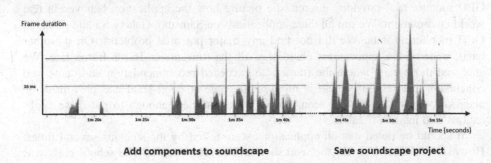

Fig. 8. SoundSpace GPU monitoring (Color figure online)

6 Discussion

Our overall system consists of pretty simple audio digital asset management system and smart clients. This type of architecture enables to utilize full power of mobile platforms when developing audio related applications, like soundscape mixer. This in turn results into innovative applications. Selecting auditory presentation instead of visual one enables faster communication between mobile clients and backend service as transmitted audio files are typically smaller than video or 3D model files. We believe that distributing main functionality to mobile platform and keeping traffic light between client and server will be the basis for smooth interaction.

We have seen that research-based design process and teams consisting of designers with user experience angle and programmers with understanding of Android platform capabilities and limitations will result into realistic and highly usable design. It was important that the target group (15–24 years old) for the application was defined already in the beginning. Thus we were able to test prototypes by the target group.

During the implementation phase Android best practices were followed, which ensured that the interaction with application follows Google's material design and avoids the common implementation pitfalls. This is needed for two reasons:

- Application should look like and behave like Android application so that Android phone owners will feel comfortable without any surprises;
- Most trivial performance bottlenecks will be avoided.

As application's performance has a vital impact on user experience it is important to evaluate performance before releasing applications. So far there are no (de-facto) standard testing strategies for exposing causes of poor responsiveness on Android applications. Thus we decided to utilize tools that are available as a part of the Android Studio. Static code analysis results confirmed that most of the common Android development pitfalls related to performance were avoided. As the GUI lagging is the most common performance bug we decided to check GUI performance. Hierarchy Viewer tool provides valuable information about potential rendering speed bottlenecks. In our case all three applications did not expose any major bottlenecks. Finally utilizing GPU monitor tool provided the realistic picture how the application behaves in real world environment. We run all three applications on Samsung Galaxy S5 and gathered GPU monitoring data. We did not find any major potential problems. On the other hand, none of the applications could stay all the time under 16 ms frame rate. We analyzed those parts where the frame rate exceeded recommendation and came into conclusion that responsiveness is most of the time at good level and only in some occasions slowness could be seen. So we were confident enough to put these applications into hands of real users.

It should be noted that all applications were tested by the students several times. However, the final test was the workshop with a school class. The school class was from secondary school in Helsinki, Finland and fitted well the target group. Based on the findings from the workshop we can state that the interaction with mobile soundscape mixer application was smooth and well appreciated [19]. This verified that our design and development process resulted into successful applications.

7 Conclusions

In this paper we have proposed how to develop an easy to use and smoothly working Android application to increase user interaction by developing soundscapes from building blocks stored in audio digital asset management system.

We have successfully designed and implemented four and tested three different sound mixer applications. Based on the performance testing we anticipated that the interaction with mobile mixer application is smooth. This was verified later from findings from the first workshop with real users. However, the outcomes that we draw are preliminary and require further testing. Next we will organize a similar workshop for adults in Museum of Technology. In addition, to prove that mobile mixer applications are versatile we will test applications in an outdoor city planning event together with our People's Smart Sculpture Project partner.

Acknowledgements. We thank media engineering and information technology students who participated into design and development of Android applications. In addition, we thank Aura Neuvonen and her sound design students for soundscape support. The work is co-funded by EU, Creative Europe Programme, The People's Smart Sculpture project (http://smartsculpture.eu). We thank the project partners for inspiring discussions.

References

1. Väänänen-Vainio-Mattila, K., Suhonen, K., Laaksonen, J., Kildal, J., Tahiroğlu, K.: User experience and usage scenarios of audio-tactile interaction with virtual objects in a physical environment. In: Proceedings of the 6th International Conference on Designing Pleasurable Products and Interfaces, DPPI 2013, pp. 67–76. ACM, New York (2013)
2. Heller, F., Krämer, A., Borchers, J.: Simplifying orientation measurement for mobile audio augmented reality applications. In: Proceedings of the SIGCHI Conference on Human Factors in Computing Systems, CHI 2014, pp. 615–624. ACM, New York (2014)
3. Schaefer, R.M.: The Soundscape: Our Sonic Environment and the Tuning of the World. Inner Traditions International/Destiny Books, Rochester (1993)
4. Jacucci, G., Oulasvirta, A., Salovaara, A.: Active construction of experience through mobile media: a field study with implications for recording and sharing. Pers. Ubiquit. Comput. **11**(4), 215–234 (2007). http://www.cs.helsinki.fi/u/oulasvir/scipubs/jacucci-etal_revised_print.pdf
5. Drechsler, A., Raffaseder, H., Rubisch, B.: Klang.Reise: new scientific approaches through an artistic soundscape installation? In: Proceedings of the 7th Audio Mostly Conference: A Conference on Interaction with Sound, AM 2012, pp. 44–46. New York, USA (2012)
6. Casu, M., Koutsomichalis, M., Valle, A.: Imaginary soundscapes: the SoDA project. In: Proceedings of the 9th Audio Mostly: A Conference on Interaction With Sound, AM 2014, Article No. 5. ACM, New York (2014)
7. Salo, K., Giova, D., Mikkonen, T.: Backend infrastructure supporting audio augmented reality and storytelling. In: Yamamoto, S. (ed.) HIMI 2016. LNCS, vol. 9735, pp. 325–335. Springer, Heidelberg (2016). doi:10.1007/978-3-319-40397-7_31
8. Leinonen, T.: Designing Learning Tools. Methodological Insights. Aalto University, Helsinki (2012). ISBN 978-952-60-0032-9

9. Snyder, C.: Paper Prototyping: The Fast and Easy Way to Design and Refine User Interfaces. Morgan Kaufmann, Burlington (2003). ISBN 9780080513508

10. Säde, S., Battarbee, K.: The third dimension in paper prototypes. In: Branaghan, R. (ed.) Design by People for People: Essays on Usability, pp. 203–212, Chicago, USA (2001)

11. Stappers, P.J.: Creative connections: user, designer, context, and tools. Pers. Ubiquit. Comput. **10**(2), 95–100 (2006)

12. Mullins, C.: Responsive, mobile app, mobile first: untangling the UX design web in practical experience. In: Proceedings of the 33rd Annual International Conference on the Design of Communication (SIGDOC 2015), Article 22, 6 p. ACM, New York (2015)

13. Smartphone OS Market Share, 2015 Q2. http://www.idc.com/prodserv/smartphone-os-market-share.jsp

14. Top 8 Mobile & Tablet Operating Systems in Finland from Oct 2014 to Oct 2015. http://gs.statcounter.com/#mobile+tablet-os-FI-monthly-201410-201510

15. Salo, K., Shakya, U., Damena, M.: Device agnostic CASS client. In: Marcus, A. (ed.) DUXU 2014, Part II. LNCS, vol. 8518, pp. 334–345. Springer, Heidelberg (2014)

16. Yang, S., Yan, D., Rountev, A.: Testing for poor responsiveness in android applications. In: Proceedings of 1st International Workshop on the Engineering of Mobile-Enabled Systems (MOBS), 25 May, pp. 1–6. IEEE, San Francisco (2013)

17. Liu, Y., Xu, C., Cheung, S.-C.: Characterizing and detecting performance bugs for smartphone applications. In: Proceedings of the 36th International Conference on Software Engineering, ICSE 2014, pp. 1013–1024. ACM, New York (2014)

18. Testing Display Performance. http://developer.android.com/training/testing/performance.html

19. Salo, K., Bauters, M., Mikkonen, T.: Mobile Soundscape Mixer Augmenting Reality in Museum. Manuscript submitted for publication

Onde Chiare: A Mobile Application to Mitigate the Risk Perception from Electromagnetic Fields

Katiuscia Mannaro$^{(\boxtimes)}$ and Marco Ortu$^{(\boxtimes)}$

Department of Electric and Electronic Engineering (DIEE), University of Cagliari,
Piazza D'Armi, 09123 Cagliari, Italy
`mannaro@diee.unica.it, marco.ortu@diee.unica`

Abstract. Nowadays, the increased exposure levels of electromagnetic
fields has generated in the public opinion a growing concern about the
perception of risks associated with mobile phones, base stations, and
other sources of electromagnetic fields to which the population may be
exposed daily. Given the widespread use of mobile devices with their
wireless technologies, the levels of public controversy about the risks and
benefits associated with different sources of electromagnetic fields, the
degree of scientific uncertainty, and the need to site new facilities appropriately in order to ensure the mobile phone users a more effective service,
a clear communication with the public is needed. On the basis of this
increased sensitivity to this issue both by citizens and local authorities,
resulting in requests for information and checks to guarantee the health,
we have developed Onde Chiare App, a mobile application enables to
reduce misunderstandings and improving trust through better dialogue
and improve the decision-making process by local governments.

Keywords: Mobile applications · Risk perception · Electromagnetic
fields

1 Introduction

Over the last few years we are witnessing an exponential technological innovation that is driving an increasing development of telecommunication systems.
Smartphones, tablets and other mobile devices with their wireless technologies
have become an integral part of everyday life. In many countries, over half the
population use mobile phones and the market is growing rapidly. According
to Gartner, Inc.[1], in the third quarter of 2015, the worldwide sales of smartphones to end users totaled nearly 478 million units, an increase of 3.7 % from
the same period in 2014. In its Mobility Report released in 2015, Ericsson[2]

---

[1] Gartner, Inc. (NYSE: IT) is the world's leading information technology research and
advisory company. Web site: http://www.gartner.com.
[2] The Ericsson Mobility Report is one of the leading analyses of mobile network data
traffic and shares forecast data, analysis and insight into mobile traffic, subscriptions,
and consumer behavior. Ericsson regularly performs traffic measurements in over 100
live networks in all major regions of the world. Available at http://www.ericsson.
com/mobility-report.

© Springer International Publishing Switzerland 2016
M. Younas et al. (Eds.): MobiWIS 2016, LNCS 9847, pp. 31–42, 2016.
DOI: 10.1007/978-3-319-44215-0_3

has declared advanced mobile technology will be globally ubiquitous by 2020, 70 % of the global population will be using smartphones and 90 % covered by mobile broadband networks. Moreover North America and Europe will continue to have highest data usage per smartphone. Todays users expect a high quality user experience and continual service improvement and so as to ensure it new mobile network functionalities for both data and voice are being required.

In order to ensure the mobile phone users a more effective service, from the development of UMTS to 4G, we assist on the global territory to a substantial increase in the number of installed base stations relative to the high frequencies for the cellular telephony and multiply this plant has helped to sharpen the attention of citizens on these sources of exposure, in particular creating a feeling on this issue very strong and widespread. If at this development we also associate a contextual expansion of urbanized areas, consequently we assist to an increase of the population potentially exposed to electromagnetic fields (EMF). As a matter of fact mobile phones communicate by transmitting radio waves through a network of fixed antennas called base stations, and radio-frequency waves are electromagnetic fields. In particular the increased exposure levels of electromagnetic fields generated in the public opinion a growing concern about the risk to which the population may be exposed daily. In some countries around the world the deployment of mobile network antenna sites has been opposed by local stakeholders due to potential health risks caused by the exposure to EMF. While many people recognize the personal benefits of mobile services, a poor understanding about radio signals perceived unfamiliar because unseen and unheard may lead to delays in acquiring new antenna sites or even to adopt further restrictions. Given the widespread use of technology, the levels of public controversy, the degree of scientific uncertainty, and the need to site new facilities appropriately, a clear communication with the public is needed. On the basis of growing demand for information about the risks arising from exposure to electromagnetic fields, resulting in requests for information and checks to guarantee the health, it is clear that being able to provide directly information to the people in effective and transparent way, is the main requirement.

Starting from this assumption we propose Onde Chiare App, a mobile application that could help to reduce misunderstandings and improving trust through better dialogue and consequently improve the decision-making process by local governments. In this work we refer particularly to practical guidance and support on good risk communications practice produced by GSMA and the MMF titled *Risk Communication Guide for Mobile Phones and Base Stations* [2]. In fact our research assumption is based on the fact that a dialogue, if implemented successfully, can help to establish an open and consistent decision-making process. As mentioned the majority of citizens have a smartphone connected to the Internet network, and they can share and receive information either with other citizens and with the government. Currently the environment, whether it is an urban or rural context, is evolving into an interconnected space where several distributed systems, such as measurement and monitoring points, allow to acquire and/or disseminate information of various kinds. The flow of this information may be arranged to feed a shared knowledge base and the environment itself through this distributed systems network becomes itself an integration platform. The mobile application we will present offers the possibility to every smartphone owner of becoming part of a network of distributed information made up of citizens interested in environmental issues and quality of life related to the urban area. The participation will take place through the active use by the user. So in addition to the involvement of experts that use monitoring technologies to read data and information related to the environmental status that surrounds us, the active participation of citizens and the individual citizen has a fundamental role. Data and signaling can generate active governance policies on the territory, resulting in the selection of actions to be taken within a given community. Data collected by experts and submitted to the institutional authority can be compared with reports from citizens, as happens in many cases for the weather information. This kind of activity, while not representing an environmental monitoring in the strictly scientific sense, are still very interesting for several reasons. This paper makes the following contributions: (i) We propose the conceptualization of an idea to fill the knowledge gap between the public and the experts about the effect of mobile phone radiation on human health, so the same mobile technologies are an opportunity for presenting different opinions and to help to understanding myths and realities; (ii) we propose a novel kind of mobile application as tool to reduce risk perception on EMF; (iii) we implement a proof-of-concept prototype of Onde Chiare and (iv) we evaluate Onde Chiare with case studies.

The paper is structured as follows: Sect. 1 provides an introduction and the motivation for the paper, Sect. 2 presents a general background information on Electromagnetic fields and public health and the perceived health risks of EMF are discussed.

Section 3 describes some design principles and the implementation of Onde Chiare App. A discussion of its implications and the conclusions are presented in Sect. 4.

2 Electromagnetic Fields and Public Health

As above mentioned 90 % of the worlds population was covered by mobile networks. Mobile and wireless communications networks use radio signals between the fixed radio transmitters, divided into geographic areas called cells each of which is served by a base station, and mobile devices to provide a range of voice, video and other data services. Base stations consist of different electronic components and antennas and can be located on masts, on rooftops, or on the outside or inside of buildings. Base stations emit high frequency (HF) fields in the range from several hundred MHz to several GHz. The exact frequency bands used differ between technologies (GSM, UMTS, CDMA2000, 4G) and between countries. The power of a base station varies (typically between 10 and 50 W) depending on the area that needs to be covered and the number of calls processed and this is low if compared to other transmitters such as radio and television [1]. Despite there are international safety recommendations and the mobile industry is subject to regulation, peoples perceptions about antenna sites or radio base stations are quite different: a common concern about base station and local wireless network antennas relates to the possible long-term health effects that whole-body exposure to the radio frequency (RF) signals may have. Mobile phone handsets and base stations present different exposure situations. Monitoring studies confirm RF exposure is far higher for mobile phone users than for those living near cellular base stations. Handsets transmit infrequent signals only to maintain links with nearby base stations and while a call is being made. Indeed base stations are continuously transmitting signals, although the levels from base stations in publicly accessible areas are 50 to 50,000 times below international safety recommendations, extremely small, even if they live nearby.

With respect to EMF exposure, these fields are imperceptible and unknown for the general public. This unawareness and imperceptibility can generate public distrust and rejection, which in turn can result in social conflicts and lead to delays in the deployment of new wireless technologies. Much of the public concern about base station and local wireless network antennas relates to the possibility of health hazards and if living near a base station can have some implications for the health.

Over the course of the past decade, numerous and several electromagnetic field sources, including most recently mobile phones, their base stations and local wireless network antennas, have become the focus of the growing public health concerns over possible health effects related to the possibility of health hazards from long-term exposures at low levels. A number of studies have investigated the effects of radio-frequency fields on brain electrical activity, cognitive function, sleep, heart rate and blood pressure in volunteers. In 1996, the World Health Organization (WHO), recognizing the rapid growth of public exposure to EMFs and increasing public anxiety and speculation, established a large, multidisciplinary International EMF Project to assess the potential hazards to health from ELF and RF fields. Extensive research has been conducted on the possible health effects of exposure to many types of radio signals. In [10] a background to research on the health impacts of electromagnetic fields and some examples of research projects funded by the Commission are described. The international consensus is that current limits are based on all the available scientific evidence, incorporate large safety factors and are highly protective of health [11]. To date, research does not suggest any consistent evidence of adverse health effects from exposure to radio-frequency fields at levels below those that cause tissue heating and WHO [3] has concluded: "Further, research has not been able to provide support for a causal relationship between exposure to electromagnetic fields and self-reported symptoms, or electromagnetic hypersensitivity. While no health effects are expected from exposure to RF fields from base stations and wireless networks, research is still being promoted by WHO to determine whether there are any health consequences from the higher RF exposures from mobile phones." As of January 2016, there were over 22,472 publications and 5,474 summaries of individual scientific studies on the effects of electromagnetic fields in the EMF-Portal[3] database.

---

[3] Available at http://www.emf-portal.de/.

The consensus scientific view is that there are no health risks from living near a base station. *"Considering the very low exposure levels and research results collected to date, there is no convincing scientific evidence that the weak RF signals from base stations and wireless networks cause adverse health effects."* [3]

Recent research on exposure from transmitters has mainly focused on cancer and symptoms and the data do not indicate health risks for the general public related to exposure to radio-frequency electromagnetic fields from base stations for mobile telephony, radio and TV transmitters, or wireless local data networks at home or in schools [12].

L' Health Council of the Netherlands in [14] declared ...*no evidence has been found that exposure to radio-frequency electromagnetic fields has a negative influence on the development and functioning of childrens brains, not even if this exposure is frequent.*

In January 2015, the Scientific Committee on Emerging and Newly Identified Health Risks (SCENIHR) published its final opinion on *Potential health effects of exposure to electromagnetic fields.* [9] whose purpose was to update previous SCENIHR opinions in the light of recently available information and to give special consideration to areas that had not been dealt with in the previous opinions. Information has primarily been obtained from reports published between 2009 and June 2014 in international peer- reviewed scientific journals in the English language and additional sources of information have also been considered, including web-based information retrieval and documents from governmental bodies. At the same time a complaint about the SCENIHR 2015 opinion on health effects from electromagnetic was sent to the European Commission from 20 organizations. In their opinion the experts behind the SCENIHR report are not representative of the scientific expertise in the field but they only represent the industry friendly single side of the expertise, in well known contrast to the opinion of a large and increasing number of scientists in the EMF scientific arena.[4] In such a context of scientific uncertainty the risk perception by the citizens is also influenced by conflicting sources of information. So improving risk communication on EMF exposure through systematic monitoring, common knowledge base and standards, as well as comparable exposure data and assessments, may help to better manage and accept it.

2.1   EMF Risk Perception

The term *risk perception* refers to what people perceive as risks and for definition any perception is subjective, so what one person perceives as a risk another might perceive not at all. Quoting Sjöberg et al. [5], *"Risk perception is the subjective assessment of the probability of a specified type of accident happening and how*

---

[4] IEMFA is the International Electromagnetic Fields Alliance, supported by an independent and growing global body of empirically-based scientific experts on living processes, with a multilevel, multidisciplinary health focus. Available at http://www.iemfa.org/wp-content/pdf/Complaint-to-the-European-Commission -SCENIHR-2015-08-31.pdf.

concerned we are with the consequences. To perceive risk includes evaluations of the probability as well as the consequences of a negative outcome. It may also be argued that as affects related to the activity is an element of risk perception" [5]. Base stations EMFs and cell phones are perceived differently [6]. In literature there are some empirical works on EMF risk perception available with regard to EMFs from cell phones and base stations.

In the context of base station EMFs risks, Siegrist et al. [7] showed that trust and confidence had a strong impact on the acceptance of a base station in one's proximity and may reduce opposition to mobile phone network antennas. In [6] the authors focus on people's understanding of their exposure to RF emitted by cell phones and base stations and how this understanding influences people's perceptions and preferences in regard to this technology. They examined the relevance of technical knowledge elements for people's exposure judgments and argued people's differing concerns in regard to cell phones and base stations could be due to laypeoples lack of knowledge, especially in regard to the exposure magnitude emitted by these devices.

Differences between experts and laypeoples perception of new technologies often lead to the assumption that the public simply needs to be better informed in order to accept new technologies.

In [8] the authors offer some works in the area of risk perception research on EMF across Europe, with special focus on RF EMF.

Results of the Eurobarometer 272a (European Commission 2007; cf. Rowley 2005) showed that citizens would like more information about the topic of mobile communication.

According to the U.S. National Research Council, risk communication is *an interactive process of exchange of information and opinion among individuals, groups and institutions. It involves multiple messages about the nature of risk and other messages, not strictly about risks, that express concerns, opinions, or reactions to risk messages or to legal and institutional arrangements for risk management* [13].

Scientists must communicate scientific evidence clearly; government agencies must inform people about safety regulations and policy measures; and concerned citizens must decide to what extent they are willing to accept such risk. In this process, it is important that communication between these stakeholders be done clearly and effectively [4].

The three underlying practicalities to address in risk communication are: (i) What information is being communicated (The Message); (ii) Who is delivering the information (The Messenger); (iii) How the information is being communicated (The means). Mobile applications are quickly becoming an useful tool for civic engagement and our scope is to design a new mobile application with underlying these three practicalities. In the following Sect. 3 we report some design principles and the implementation of our prototype of Onde Chiare app for Android, a mobile application of social nature with the objective to mitigate the risk perception by giving people detailed knowledge about EMF and means to involve them. Through the app citizens can report a problem or issues directly to government officials by snapping a photo and sending a report, and authorities receive the report and can send a response. This mobile application (the means) aims to make information (the message) accessible to the messenger, these are local stakeholders (for example, local residents) and public stakeholders (for example, local officials, leaders or politicians, decision makers), via a click. Stakeholders can be involved to different degrees with specific levels of participation.

3 Onde Chiare: Design and Implementation

In this section, the overall use cases, system design, and the mobile client application are described.

3.1 Use Case and Scenario

Onde Chiare aims to promote a proper form of active involvement of citizens and the real-time information sharing of electromagnetic field levels in a given geographical area.

The typical scenario is represented by users carrying a smartphone loaded with the Onde Chiare application and moving in a geographical area. For the sake of brevity in this scenario we implemented two use cases. The first use case starts when user launches the application, Onde Chiare opens a map view with an informative marker pointing the user's current position on the map. The marker shows a measure of estimated EMF in the current position, by taping other areas on the map the user can move a marker and can read EMF measures in the new location. In this view a user can to search for a specific location (by entering the address), the view map moves to the desired location, again an informative marker reports the EMF measure. In the second use case, the user is an active part of the system. This time, by taping a location in the map the user is able to send a report to the system. The following types of report are available: (i) A user-made measure of the EMF and (ii) An issue such as a broken device or antenna can be reported by users.

3.2 General Architecture

The application enables users with connected devices i.e., smartphone and tablets, to become part of a network of distributed information, made up of ordinary people (citizens) interested in environmental issues and quality of life related to the urban areas. The services that the application may manage are listed below:

- Measurement of environmental data;
- Geolocation of the measurements;
- Sending the geolocalized report (i.e. broken antennas);
- View geolocalized information on the map;

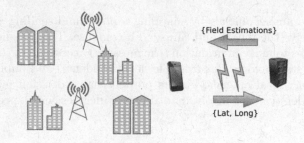

Fig. 1. General system schema.

Figure 1 depicts the general schema of the system. Here users are represented by a mobile device in an urban environment. The device communicate with a remote server sending geolocalized information, either provided by the user (when searching for a given area) or by the device's GPS module. The remote server's response contains information about the field measure (either real or estimated) in that area and the position of possible electromagnetic pollution sources in the surrounding area. In addition to the involvement of experts using tracking technologies to read data and information related to the environmental status, active participation of individual citizen has a fundamental role. As previously mentioned, users in this context are an active stakeholder of the system, they are able to send report that can be shared. Users' report may be a real measure of environmental data, i.e., an EMF measure, or more general report i.e., a broken antenna or apparatus. These report are validated by experts before being shared.

The data and reports can trigger active policies on the territory, influencing the decision making process of actions to be taken within an urban area community. Data collected by experts and submitted to the institutional authority, can be compared with reports from citizens, as happens in many cases for the weather information.

3.3 Server Side

The remote server is the part of the system demanded for the communication with the mobile application. It is responsible for processing the geolocalized point received from the application client. For example, by combining several information such as the number of building (area and height) in the surrounding area, the number of EMF sources and the number of report made by other users (citizens), the server may send back to the application its response. The server's response should contain the geolocalized EMF measures, the location of EMF sources in the surrounding area and other user's reports where available.

3.4 Android App

The design of the mobile application was oriented to the development of an effective tool enable to represent the EMF environmental data in a clear and

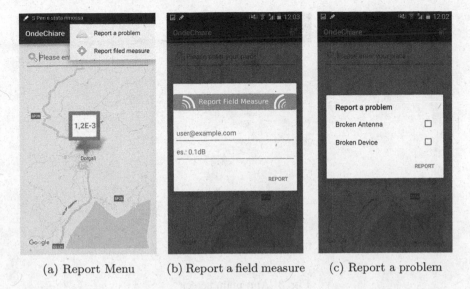

(a) Report Menu   (b) Report a field measure   (c) Report a problem

Fig. 2. Report a problem screens

concise way. The application allows a user to collect specific information directly from the system. As development environment of the mobile application, native Android has been choose has the default. The current asset for Android development is based on Java SDK 7[5] and Android 6.0. The application is developed using state of the art frameworks, such as RoboGuice[6] for dependency injection[7] and Roboletric[8] for automated testing.

In the first use case described, the application generates a map in real time, localized in the current device location, through the Google Maps Service[9]. The application places an informative marker on the user's current position on map as shown in Fig. 3. This marker contains the EMF measures, by clicking it more information are available.

The user can explore the area displayed in the map, moving and changing the zoom level by tapping the screen. When the user releases the tap the informative marker moves to the point just touched, showing the EMF measures obtained in the new point. As shown in Fig. 4 in the upper part of the App there is a textual search box.

By typing the name of a place the user activates an auto-complete system that suggests the possible location sought, then by pressing on the tip or the

---

[5] Software Developmet Kit for Java and Android.
[6] https://github.com/roboguice/roboguice.
[7] https://it.wikipedia.org/wiki/Dependency_injection.
[8] http://robolectric.org/.
[9] Google Maps is the reference application for geolocation and navigation on mobile devices with a spread that has no comparison with applications that have similar functionality.

Fig. 3. App main screen.

Fig. 4. App search feature.

ENTER button, the map moves in the selected location pointing the informative marker with the new EMF measures.

The second use case enables users to send a geolocalized report about a field measure provided by the user itself or an issue in the surrounding area such as a broken antenna or a service breakdown. Figure 2 shows, from left to right, the flow for sending a report. The user taps the *Report a problem* icon, in the upper right part of the screen, and chooses which kind of report he or she wants to send. Once a report category is selected, a contextual form is displayed, letting the user fill the required information. In particular as shown in Fig. 2b, in order to send a self-made measure the user must insert his email and the measure. Figure 2c shows how to send a report about a problem in the user's current position, i.e., a broken antenna or device.

4 Conclusion and Future Works

In the past few years, tablets and smarthphones became the main communication and entertainment devices for millions of people. It is assumed that lack of knowledge leads to misconceptions, and the benefit of using a technology is perceivable. Mobile applications are quickly becoming an useful tool for civic engagement and in this paper we have presented Onde Chiare that is a prototype for Android we tested internally at the University and we are working by testing with the aim of detecting usability and others functionalities. We described the initial phases of this mobile application design and at the moment Onde Chiare has been viewed as a valuable tool to enable community members to report specific information in the community and improve the communication efforts by local authorities. Risk perception research centred on the idea that if the public could access and understand all the facts of a issue, their evaluation about risk would tend to match those of the experts. To the best of our knowledge in the app store there are no similar mobile applications and they are not intended as tools of this type. Smartphones have become a necessity for everyone and their rapid adoption such a part of daily life makes us to foresee that mobile devices have a lot of power to reach people and can play an important role of communication channel about the interaction, not just information.

We also believe that increasing the communication and the interaction, will make it easier for policy makers to make decisions and for citizens to be informed on environmental issues.

Onde Chiare will make it easier for citizens to report public-facing issues, taking a picture, locate it, categorize it, quickly and conveniently to the appropriate parties for better response not only related to exposure to electromagnetic fields.

In conclusion, we are convinced that the scientific community as well as governmental and industrial organizations should increase their communication efforts about the potential health effects of the low frequency of electromagnetic fields. Only realistic expectations about the impact of risk communication together with careful planning and continuous evaluation of the results will help to improve risk communication and thus to provide a solid basis for further development of effective risk communication tools. Advancements in our mobile application are also expected to continue, in particular because this kind of mobile application may be adapted to other environmental issues.

Acknowledgments. This work is supported by the Regione Autonoma Sardegna, under the grant for project P.O.R FESR SARDEGNA 2007-2013 ASSE VI COMPETITIVITA LINEA DI ATTIVITA 6.2.2 "SOSTEGNO ALLA CREAZIONE E

SVILUPPO DI NUOVE IMPRESE INNOVATIVE." Asse I Ricerca, Sviluppo Tecnologico ed Innovazione; Determinazione RAS n. 33073 rep. N. 684 del 22/12/2014.

References

1. ICNIRP: Risk perception, risk communication and its application to EMF exposure. In: Proceedings of the International Seminar on Risk Perception, Risk Communication and Its Application to EMF Exposure, Vienna, Austria, 22–23 October 1997
2. GSMA and MMF: Risk Communication Guide for Mobile Phones, Base Stations. Practical guidance and support on good risk communications practice for the mobile. www.gsma.com
3. World Health Organization: Electromagnetic fields and public health: base stations and wireless technologies. Backgrounder, May 2006. http://www.who.int/peh-emf/publications/facts/fs304/en/
4. World Health Organization (WHO): Establishing a Dialogue on Risks from Electromagnetic Fields. Paperback, 31 December 2002
5. Sjöberg, L., Moen, B.E., Rundmo, T.: Explaining Risk Perception. An Evaluation of the Psychometric Paradigm in Risk Perception Research, vol. 84. Rotunde publikasjoner Rotunde (2004). http://doi.org/10.1080/135753097348447
6. Cousin, M.E., Siegrist, M.: The public's knowledge of mobile communication and its influence on base station siting preferences. Health Risk Soc. 12(3), 231–250 (2010). http://doi.org/10.1080/13698571003710332
7. Siegrist, M., Earle, T.C., Gutscher, H.: Test of a trust and confidence model in the applied context of electromagnetic field (EMF) risks. Risk Anal. 23(4), 705–716 (2003). http://doi.org/10.1111/1539-6924.00349
8. Pozo, C., Papameletiou, D.: European Information System on Electromagnetic Fields Exposure and Health Impacts, Country Reports on EMF and Health: Sources, Regulations, and Risk Communication Approaches. Joint Research Centre, European Commission, Ispra (2005)
9. SCENIHR: Potential health effects of exposure to electromagnetic fields (EMF) (2015). http://doi.org/10.2772/75635
10. European Commisson: EU-funded research into the impact of electromagnetic fields and mobile telephones on health. Health and Electromagnetic Fields, 1994, 14 (2006). http://www.tandfonline.com/doi/abs/10.1080/08870440701520973
11. Persson, T., Trnevik, C.: Mobile communications and health. Ericsson Rev. (English Ed.) 80(2), 48–55 (2003)
12. Swedish Radiation Safety Authority (SSM): Eighth report from SSMs Scientific Council on Electromagnetic Fields, March 2013
13. National Research Council: Improving Risk Communication, p. 21. National Academy Press, Washington, D.C. (1989)
14. Health Council of the Netherlands: Influence of Radiofrequency Telecommunication Signals on Childrens Brains. Health Council of the Netherlands, The Hague (2011). Publication no. 2011/20E

Ringtone Adaptation Based on Location and Surrounding Noise

Petr Mervart, Jan Dvorak, and Ondrej Krejcar[(✉)]

Center for Basic and Applied Research, Faculty of Informatics and Management,
University of Hradec Kralove, Rokitanskeho 62,
500 03 Hradec Kralove, Czech Republic
{petr.mervart.2,jan.dvorak}@uhk.cz,
Ondrej@Krejcar.org

Abstract. Although smart phones have many different functions nowadays, their primary function is calling. To answer calls successfully, ringtones are essential. The aim of this project is to create an application that would enable automatic adaptation of the ringtone to certain situations. The main task of the application will be adjusting the ringing based on the location of the phone. According to predefined locations set by the user, the application will change the ringtone based on where it is currently. The second task of the application will be adjusting the volume of the ringtone if the phone appears in a very noisy environment, so that it would minimize a chance that the incoming call would be overheard.

Keywords: GPS · Geofence · Location · Ringtone change · Volume · Surrounding noise · Noise measuring

1 Introduction

Smart phones are becoming a clearly natural part of our lives [8]. Apart from calling, they make our lives easier with many other functions, such as applications for making work tasks easier or applications for entertainment. With a gradual improvement of phones and applications, various sensors built in the phones started being used for improvements of the functions. Thanks to that, there is a wide range of different applications that bring us immense and unexpected possibilities.

However, due to all these new possibilities of the use of our phones, we might sometimes forget that their primary purpose is making calls. While trying to develop new applications that would improve our lives, although they do not necessarily need an improvement, there is not much attention given to the effort to enhance the quality and experience of calling. Specifically meaning, processing the ringtone that is supposed to notify people of their incoming calls. Here, the issue of making the experience more pleasant can be addressed and solved by a variety of ways, such as choosing a ringtone according to present situation, or an effort to minimize the number of missed calls by adjusting the volume of the ringtone based on the surrounding environment.

The current situation for choosing a suitable ringtone can be evaluated by the current location of the phone [13]. To determine the location, the modern sensors of the

© Springer International Publishing Switzerland 2016
M. Younas et al. (Eds.): MobiWIS 2016, LNCS 9847, pp. 43–55, 2016.
DOI: 10.1007/978-3-319-44215-0_4

phone can be employed. This way of improvement of applications is very popular and therefore frequent [1] (social media applications, photography applications, note pad applications, etc.), because it brings remarkable results and its implementation is not very demanding. The location can be determined using the GPS system, using the list of familiar Wi-Fi networks that the user assigns to certain locations or, alternatively, with the help of the GSM signal [2, 13]. This way we can ensure the phone ringing to be aptly set to home, work or otherwise specific environment.

There are relatively only few applications that would change different phone settings based on its location. Among the most popular ones belongs Llama or Trigger. However, these applications are very robust, often unnecessarily complicated and including such settings that an ordinary user can take advantage of very rarely.

In the effort to lower the number of missed calls, we may assess the noise of the surrounding environment and based on the ascertained information, temporarily raise the ringtone volume. That way, the probability of the user not overhearing the ringtone is increased. The main sensor that will be employed for this case is, naturally, the phone's microphone. However, it raises a problem of the accuracy of the obtained data of the surrounding noise with the microphone. According to Kardous [3], the microphones of different phones are very distinct, even within the same manufacturer or even the same series. For the process of measuring, the microphones in the phones from the company Apple are of a good use. On the contrary, the phones from different manufacturers with Android system have big problems with the accuracy of measuring and none of the measuring applications for the Android system met the requirements of the study [8].

There are surprisingly few applications for adaptation [9, 10, 12] of the volume to the surrounding noise and in addition to that, they are quite outdated. The most successful representatives are Intelligent Ringer and RingDimmer.

This project aims to create an application that will combine the two above mentioned approaches while maintaining simple and straightforward settings. The emphasis will be put on the most precise solution possible, real phone options, and the minimum possible source consumption, not on the purposeless and complicated effects.

2 Problem Definition

The aim of this project is to design an application that will enable the user [11] to pre-set different ringtones for certain locations, and it will also automatically raise the volume of the ringing in the case that the phone appears in a noisy environment. The application will be developed for the most widespread operating system, Android, namely from the 4.1 Jelly Bean version, which will enable to cover more than 90 % of devices working with this operating system [8].

The application, essentially, deals with two problems. The first problem is defining the phone's location, and based on that location, it has to set the ringtone chosen in advance [13]. The positioning of the phone is, nowadays, already part of different applications, whether it is in order to locate oneself on the map, to achieve more precise marketing aim, or to measure sporting performance. Then, there are various methods of determining the results for various purposes, and they differ in accuracy and battery consumption.

The basic and the widest spread method of determining the location is by the use of GPS coordinates. The article [1] describes this way quite thoroughly, and it adds also another method of positioning. This other method is tracking Wi-Fi networks that the phone connects to in certain locations. When reconnection to those certain networks occurs, it can be assumed that the phone is at the same place again. As distinct from the GPS approach, the big advantage is much lower battery consumption. Using Wi-Fi networks, the location can be determined very precisely, for example, because of algorithms from the article [4]. However, for the purposes of the application proposed here, this solution is too complicated. Also, the problem arises in the places where the user is not connected to any Wi-Fi network. In this case, the GPS has to be used again.

The GPS coordinates are then also used by geofencing [5]. It is a feature that determines the location using GPS coordinates, and then, consequently, creates a predefined radius around the coordinates. Any operations can be then done when entering the radius, in the radius and when leaving the radius. That means that this method is very suitable for delimitation of a certain area, and, therefore, it is widely used. Also, for the Android applications, there is a support available using Google GeofencingAPI, which enables to create and administrate geofences.

Another possibility of the current phone positioning is by Bluetooth or NFC tags. Both of these methods are employed in the applications, such as Trigger. They work similarly like localizing using Wi-Fi signal with the difference that the user connects to a Bluetooth device (e.g. transmitter connected to a personal computer), or to a NFC tag, instead of a network. With respect to their employment, both of these methods are interesting, however, currently still quite impractical. NFC tags are still not very commonly used in the general population and it is also necessary to be very close to them, which basically eliminates the idea of changing the ringtone settings without the user's direct participation [11]. Even though, Bluetooth signal has already wide reach, it is still not so widespread like Wi-Fi networks.

The last provided option is localization using GSM transmitters. The telephone signal coverage is provided by transmitters, and the phone is able to distinguish which transmitter is it connected to at the moment. This method could be convenient for a very general localization. However, it is not possible to discern more areas covered by one transmitter, which occurs very often in cities. Even though, it is possible to make the location more precise using the strength of the signal [2], it is not an attractive method for the purposes of this project.

From the above mentioned approaches, it seems that the most suitable method for the proposed application is the use of geofences and Wi-Fi networks. The combination of these two approaches guarantees the possibility of saving battery consumption in the town areas providing Wi-Fi networks, and, at the same time, it enables using GPS in the places where no Wi-Fi network is available.

The second problem is noise level measuring that serves for the application to react and raise the ringtone volume when the noise level rises. If positioning was a very frequently used and well charted function, surrounding noise level measuring is a complete opposite. Not only do every phone with Android system and every application with this system measure surrounding noise with different results [3], but also the perception of sound as such is a very complicated area. The article [6] shows that different people perceive sounds distinctly on different frequencies, and, therefore, it might not be possible to determine the accurate surrounding noise level with an appropriate ringtone volume level.

According to Google Play application catalogue, several applications attempted the functionality of this problem. The most successful one might have been the application Intelligent Ringer, and RingDimmer. However, according to the used ratings, both of these applications struggle with many problems and neither of these is significantly reliable.

One of the problematic approaches can be the intention to not only raise the ringtone volume in a noisy environment, but also lower the ringtone volume in a quiet environment. This property is very risky, because the user can go away from the phone in the quiet environment, and so, not to hear the low volume ringing. That is, naturally, against the purpose of the intelligent ringing. Therefore, the proposed ringtone application will only temporarily raise the volume and afterwards set it back to the original level.

Many of the user complaints are also directed on the big battery consumption, where in some cases it was cut in half. Here, the wrongly adjusted period of the surrounding noise level measuring, that does not probably react to surrounding conditions, might be to blame. Therefore, if it is connected with location tracking, it might mean that when the user stays longer in one place, it is supposed that the noise level does not change, and therefore, the measuring period can be extended.

The proposed application will mainly work with the most important factor for missed calls prevention, which means temporary volume adjustment. However, it will not try to adjust the volume to a quieter environment. This request might be substituted with the first part of the application, where for a certain location (e.g. church) it might be possible to turn off the ringing.

3   New Solution

For the description of the solution, we will maintain the division of the application into two parts indicated in the previous chapter.

Firstly, it is necessary to define ringtones for certain locality based on the location. The user adds a new item into the list of localities in the application. The item contains a name for the certain locality, a ringtone, GPS coordinates, and a radius (in meters) for geofence, possibly a name of the Wi-Fi network that will determine given location. There are two situations that might occur during the entering of a new locality. First, if the users save a location where they currently are, they can easily find out which Wi-Fi are they connected to (if there is such), and that network will be saved with the entry. That way, also the present GPS coordinates will be saved. On the other hand, if the users save location they are not currently in, they choose its GPS coordinates on a map that is accessible through the application. In that situation, Wi-Fi cannot be added to the entry.

Next, the detection of corresponding location can occur in two ways. In order to save energy, the user can disable GPS coordinates searching and rely only on Wi-Fi networks, which is convenient in the situation where in all the locations the user has a certainty of having a Wi-Fi connection (work, home, etc.). In this case, the location control for the ringtone change occurs with every Wi-Fi connection, and the possible return to default settings is done with every disconnection from the given network. This way, the location control can only fail if the user manually turns of Wi-Fi receiver in the phone.

In case that the user does not disable the GPS support, the application relies on geofence. Geofence creates a radius area around the given GPS coordinates and causes action when the device enters, stays in or exits the geofence. Google provides GeofencingAPI, which is part of Google Play Services, for an easier geofence administration.

For the most effective possible work with GPS sensors, it is convenient to use Location manager, which eases the work of a programmer, in communication with GPS phone module. Then, the Location listener is employed for positioning. In this case, the ringing is changed by entering the corresponding geofence and restored to the original settings by exiting the geofence.

In order to adjust the volume of the ringing to the surrounding noise, the microphone built in the phone is used. Since the Android system does not offer any help in the form of API, it is necessary to work with raw data collected through the microphone. The collected data can vary [14]. This application uses the method read() of the AudioRecord class, which returns value field representing the level of surrounding noise in a short audio recording. Another alternative is the method getMaxAmplitude() of the MediaRecord class, which returns only the highest recorded value in a determined measured interval.

As it has been mentioned in the previous chapter, the precise calculation of loudness is not practically possible [3] in the mobile phones with Android system, because the microphones of the individual devices differ in many areas. However, the relative increase of surrounding noise can be measured quite easily. First, it is necessary to calibrate the application in a regular noise environment. That way, the basic level of noise is obtained and is marked as p0. The data returned by the function from the previous paragraph is then inserted as p into the following formula [7]

$$x = 20 \cdot \log_{10}(\frac{p}{p_0}), \tag{1}$$

Thus, the approximate value of the current surrounding noise is acquired in decibels. Based on the fluctuation of the value, it can be estimated when the surrounding noise is significantly higher than in the regular environment, and therefore it is necessary to temporarily raise the volume of ringing. It should not be forgotten that the application will not lower the volume below the default settings; it will always only temporarily raise it.

Since this measuring will require a lot of the battery life, it needs to be done suitably and economically. In the ideal case, the surrounding noise should be measured only immediately before incoming call, however that is not possible. The incoming call cannot be predicted and the Android system does not allow changing the volume of an already ringing call. Then also, the ringing would have an influence on measuring of the surrounding noise. Therefore, the measuring has to be done periodically.

The ideal length of the measuring period will be a subject of a long-term testing and based on the results of the tests, it can be shortened or lengthened. There will also be an

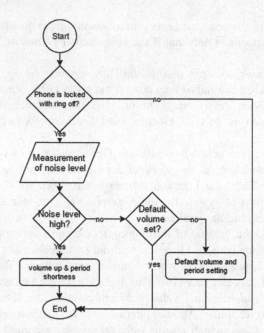

Fig. 1. Diagram describing periodical noise measuring

implemented possibility for the user to set this interval for the cases when the phone features extra-long battery life. The default time value was empirically set to a 30-s interval. In order to save more battery life, measuring will be done only in the time when the phone is locked. In the case of unlocked phone, it can be assumed that the phone is used and therefore any incoming call can be noticed.

The last mechanism for lowering the energy consumption is the possibility of connecting the noise measuring with positioning, which was introduced in the previous paragraphs. Provided that the user spends a longer period of time at the same place, it is probable that the current level of surrounding noise is not very often, or very significantly, changed. In that case, the measuring interval can be lengthened and therefore save battery life. This function can be turned on/off by the user.

In case that the phone detects raised level of surrounding noise, the application raises the volume of ringing and simultaneously shortens the period of measuring to 10 s. This is again a pre-set value that can be changed in the future based on a long-term testing. The interval is shortened to temporarily give more accuracy to the measuring and return the ringing volume to the default setting in the shortest time possible. As soon as the phone notices a return to the regular noise values, it sets the ringing volume to the default settings and lengthens the period of measuring again to the previous value.

The previous description of functioning is clearly depicted in a diagram in figure (Fig. 1). This process is then periodically performed according to the currently set interval length.

Lastly, it has to be noted that the application will follow the manual settings made by the user. Therefore, if the user manually turns off phone ringing (an unusual external situation that demands it can be supposed), the application will not violate this setting and it will not turn on the sounds, nor raise the ringing volume. On the contrary, it will apply this state to temporarily stop measuring, and that way it saves the valuable battery life. As soon as the user deactivates this mode, the applications will start again its periodical control of the surrounding noise level.

4 Implementation

The application is implemented on Android platform, specifically on the version 4.1 Jelly Bean, API 16. That covers approximately 90 % of users of this system. In the application implementation, the division into two parts that has been described in the previous chapters was kept. Therefore, the application has one part that deals with measuring surrounding noise and adjusting the ringing volume, and another part that tracks the position of the phone and modifies the ringtone.

The second part of the application employs some external solutions. Since it is necessary to store information of the entered locations by the user, it is necessary to use a database. Therefore, SQLite is employed for a simple database administration [11]. Its settings are described by the AreasDatabaseHelper class. As it has been mentioned previously in this paper, in order to operate geofences when GPS tracking is enabled, Google Play Services will be used, specifically, it will be GeofencingAPI for geofence administration and GoogleMapsAPI for the possibility of a simple area selection that will determine the geofence settings.

When the application is launched, the user sees the main screen, which works as a directory between the previously mentioned two parts of the application. The main screen is operated by the MainActivity class, which is a standard activity of the Android system. It contains two buttons that will direct the user to the corresponding part of the application. This class and the other important classes are shown in figure (Fig. 2).

The part of the application that deals with tracking the surrounding noise directs the user to the main screen of this part of the application. That presents another activity, this time NoiseCheckingActivity. The screen contains three buttons. The first two of them are for the start and the end of the surrounding noise checking, and based on that, raising and lowering the ringing volume. There is always only one of these buttons available, depending on the measuring. The third button serves for the initial calibration of measuring.

After pressing the button starting the measuring, a service created by Noise-CheckingService class is started. The service runs in the background until it is not stopped by the second button, or by the system when closing the application. Using the method scheduleAtFixedRate of the Timer class, there is a repeated cycle of measuring after the set time is created. In every cycle, it is controlled whether the user has not manually turned off ringing, and whether the display is locked. The measuring is only necessary under these conditions, otherwise does not run and the battery life is saved. Afterwards, an instance of the AudioRecord class is created and filled with corresponding values. Also, buffer is created and saves the measured values. The measuring is carried out by calling the measure method, that fills buffer with the data from the microphone, makes a calculation using the date, and after that, it compares them with

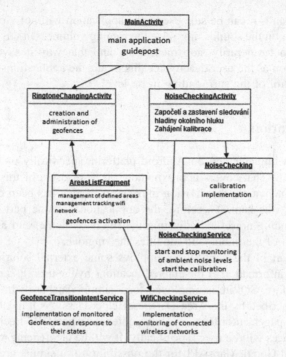

Fig. 2. Simplified class diagram

the calibrated noise value. If it detects a raised level, the volume of the ringing is changed using the corresponding methods, and with every change, the user is notified through a system notification. Also, the measuring period of time is shortened so that everything could be set to the default as soon as it is necessary.

The third button of the main screen of this part of application serves for calibration. This is carried out by the NoiseChecking class, which is a parallel to the above mentioned service. However, the calibration is run only once, measuring three times in a short succession and making an average. Then, the calibrated value is saved in the phone using SharedPreferences. After having tested more approaches to surrounding noise measuring, the method used in the application Splmeter proved to be the most suitable one. Therefore, it was slightly modified and used in this application.

The other part of the application, modifying the ringtone based on the location, can be accessed by tapping the button Ringtone on the main screen. The user is consequently redirected to a main screen of this part of the application that is represented by RingtoneChangingActivity. On the screen, there is an extract from the database listing all the saved areas by the user, using AreasListFragment. In ListView, there are individual items in the areas list that are represented by the Area class. Any given area in the list can activate its tracking by tapping on its name. The tracking method (GPS or Wi-Fi) is determined according to which item is chosen for the area. If both of them are chosen, the activation follows the fact, whether the application settings allow GPS tracking or not. By repeated tapping on one item, the tracking of that area is ended. The currently tracked area is highlighted in the list.

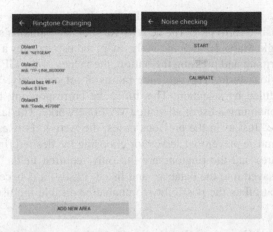

Fig. 3. Screen with a list of areas (left), and level of noise measuring (right)

If Wi-Fi tracking is activated, the WifiCheckingService is run. This service runs if at least one of the areas tracked by Wi-Fi is active. Using Broadcast Reciever it reacts to the changes of Wi-Fi connection status and it tracks which networks the phone is connected to. This is watched by the method checkConnection. If it connects to a network that is related to any of the tracked areas the corresponding ringtone for that area is set and the user is informed by system notification. The opposite process is run for disconnecting from this network (Fig. 3).

If tracking by GPS is activated, the RingtoneChaningActivity, which contains the code for geofence administration, is called again. The class is notified by calling the onAreaActivated method, which assumes control over the given area. The method then activates GPS sensor, saves default ringtone and creates Geofence from the received area. Furthermore, Geofence is added to the list of geofences, the launching GeofencingRequest is called, and the GeofenceTransitionIntentService using Pending Intent is created. In case of potential deactivation of geofence, the procedure is similar; however, there is a list of geofences that are being deactivated in onAreaDeactivated method, which is forwarded to the removeGeofences method. The above mentioned methods cooperate with GoogleApiClient, which connects when the activity is created, and disconnects when the activity is canceled. So geofence tracking runs in the mentioned GeofenceTransitionIntentService. The service code is inspired by a prime example and then edited for the needs of this application. If GeofencingApi detects a change at some of its active geofences, the onHandleIntent method is called, and it discovers which geofence the event happened in, and whether it was an event of entering or exiting the geofence. Based on the result, the ringtone is changed in the changeRingtone method, and consequently, the user is notified.

The last past of the application that has not been yet introduced is adding the areas into the list. That is included in the AddAreaActivity, which can be called using the button at the bottom part of the list. The activity contains a field for filling in the data about the requested area. The name field can be filled manually. To track the area using GPS, the user can use the button Open map to open a map that is processed as a fragment of a new activity called ActivityForResult. That secures the return of the values to the unfinished form [15]. The activity for the map contains standard methods for work with Google Maps. By tapping in the map, the user creates a geofence around the point. By confirming and pressing the button, the values of the GPS coordinates are filled into the previous form. The geofence radius is set manually. The name of the Wi-Fi network is filled by selection. This time, the corresponding button opens the WifiListActivity containing a list of all visited Wi-Fi networks. The last field serves for choosing a ringtone. Just as in the previous cases, the ActivityForResult is called and this time a default music player that serves for choosing the desired ringtone is opened. The name of the area and the ringtone are the only required fields. Pressing the last button, the area is saved into the database and listed. Lastly, it is necessary to mention SettingsActivity that offers the possibility to enable or disable the use of GPS.

5   Developed Application Testing - Solution

For reasons of clarity, both parts of the application will be tested individually. For the testing, two mobile phones were used: a mid-range phone Sony Xperia P with Android 4.1 system, and high-end Sony Xperia S with Android 4.2 system. These phones were chosen based on the availability to the author.

The testing of the location part of the application was carried out in 10 tests of positioning using Wi-Fi networks, and 10 tests using GPS geofences, always with a time limit of 20 s. In the first case, the ringing was successfully changed in all of the 10 tests, in the second case, one of the tests failed, most likely due to a bad GPS signal. In terms of accuracy, both of the methods are quite equal. The advantage of geofences is definitely the fact that they can be created anywhere (Table 1).

Table 1. Influence of positioning on battery life

Battery consumption in 8 h of regular use	Disabled application	Wi-fi detection	Geofence detection
Xperia P	42 %	45 %	66 %
Xperia S	34 %	39 %	67 %

In the second phase, the influence on battery life was tested. During 8 h of a regular daily regime of the tester, the battery consumption was tested first with disabled application, then with Wi-Fi detection turned on, and, in the end, with geofence detection turned on. On both of the tested phones, the detection of Wi-Fi networks had an influence on the battery life only by around few percent, which is quite insignificant. In case of geofence detection, the battery life was shortened by approximately 20 % to 30 %. For testing that part of application focusing on checking the noise level, the application Sound Meter was first downloaded into both of the phones. It is one of the most popular applications of surrounding noise measuring. After launching the application on both of the phones, there was a surprise in form of results differing in more than 20 dB. The reason for that are completely different microphones in Android phones, as it has been already mentioned in the previous chapter. However, such a big difference was not expected, since these phones are from the same manufacturer and made in the same year. Therefore, it was evident that all the measuring using our application would face problems.

A series of measuring was carried out in different locations and different situations.

Table 2 shows a list of several situations that the application was tested in. From the results, it can be said that the application is a useful assistant in many cases, however, its 100 % functionality cannot be guaranteed, especially if the phone's microphone is blocked in the pocket. Also, in the testing, the difference of the microphones mentioned already in [3] was reflected. The application on Xperia P was showing much smaller range of measured values (in the range approximately 36–48, 72 in the extreme, calibrated value 38). Xperia S had a bigger range of values (in the range 15–42, 81 in the extreme, calibrated value 21). For determining the volume rate, the breaking point based on empiric tests was set on 117 % from the calibrated value. The success rate of this value can be reviewed in Table 2. As it has been mentioned in [6], different frequencies of the sound have different impact on the microphones. Even this factor, as well as the factor of surrounding noise removal that the microphones use, has to be taken into account.

Just as with the previous part of the application, the influence of this part of the application on the battery life was measured. Both phones were left on a table in the living room for 15 h while the surrounding noise was changed from time to time. Having set a 30-s measuring interval in a quiet state and 5-s measuring interval in a noisy state, neither of the phones has shown any significant battery consumption. That was the reason for not connecting the noise measuring with the phone positioning from the first part of the application. The positioning uses significantly more energy for its run.

For any future attempts to improve this part of the application, it will surely be purposeful to test its functionality on a much larger sample of devices. Equally, it will be effective to refine the calculation formula, alternatively find a completely new method. However, as long as the Android phones have such a wide range of different microphones as it is today, the application for surrounding noise measuring will have big problems with measuring accuracy.

Table 2. Noise measuring in different situations

Situation	Xperia P	Xperia S
Living room, phones on the table, higher TV volume	Without reaction	Reacts
Train station, incoming train, phones outside/in the pocket	Reacts/reacts	Reacts/reacts
Small office, regular noise, phones outside/in the pocket	Reacts/without reaction	Reacts/without reaction
Public transport ride, phones outside/in the pocket	Reacts/without reaction	Reacts/reacts
Evening at a restaurant, phones outside/in the pocket	Reacts/without reaction	Reacts/reacts
Workshop with a sander running, phones in the pocket	Reacts	Reacts

6 Conclusions

In conclusion, the part of the application that was tracking the user's location met the expectations. Especially, while tracking only Wi-Fi networks, the application gave a satisfactory performance and it can be used in a daily life without any worries. The automatic ringtone setting is suitable for fixed locations and can save the user from socially uncomfortable situations. Unlike the competitor's solution, the big advantage of this application is its simplicity that does not force the user into long and complicated settings. Lastly, surrounding noise tracking confirmed the conclusions of the articles [3, 6], and also explained the lack of good quality applications of this sort. Still, it is an application that can be used, especially thanks to its very low battery consumption. For that reason, the not always accurate measuring and reacting to the current situation can be partly forgiven.

Acknowledgement. This work and the contribution were supported by project "Smart Solutions for Ubiquitous Computing Environments" FIM, University of Hradec Kralove, Czech Republic (under ID: UHK-FIM-SP-2016-2102). We also acknowledge the technical language assistance provided by Jirina Cancikova.

References

1. Lin, C., Hung, M.T.: A location-based personal task reminder for mobile users. Pers. Ubiquit. Comput. **18**, 303–314 (2014). doi:10.1007/s00779-013-0646-2
2. Arif, M.A., Ahsan, A.H.M.A., Hasan, M.K., Bhattacharya, C.: An operational design of indoor tracking system in the environment of GSM structure. Am. J. Comput. Sci. Eng. **1**(3), 18–24 (2014)
3. Kardous, C.A., Shaw, P.B.: Evaluation of smartphone sound measurement applications. J. Acoust. Soc. Am. **135**(4), 186–192 (2014)
4. Chirazi, H., Poston, T., Abd Razak, S., Abdullah, A.H., Salleh, S.: Local coverage measurement algorithm in GPS-free wireless sensor networks. Ad Hoc Netw. **23**, 1–17 (2014)
5. Oliviera, R.R., Cardoso, I.M.G., Barbosa, J.L.V., Da Costa, C.A., Prado, M.P.: An intelligent model for logistics management based on geofencing algorithms and RFID technology. Expert Syst. Appl. **42**(15–16), 6082–6097 (2015)
6. Moon, H., Han, S.H., Chun, J.: Applying signal detection theory to determine the ringtone volume of a mobile phone under ambient noise. Int. J. Ind. Ergon. **47**, 117–123 (2015)
7. Sound Pressure. [cit. 2015-12-27]. https://en.wikipedia.org/wiki/Sound_pressure
8. Behan, M., Krejcar, O.: Modern smart device-based concept of sensoric networks. EURASIP J. Wirel. Commun. Netw. **2013**(155), 13 pages (2013)
9. Behan, M., Krejcar, O.: Adaptive graphical user interface solution for modern user devices. In: Pan, J.-S., Chen, S.-M., Nguyen, N.T. (eds.) ACIIDS 2012, Part II. LNCS, vol. 7197, pp. 411–420. Springer, Heidelberg (2012)
10. Benikovsky, J., Brida, P., Machaj, J.: Proposal of user adaptive modular localization system for ubiquitous positioning. In: Pan, J.-S., Chen, S.-M., Nguyen, N.T. (eds.) ACIIDS 2012, Part II. LNCS, vol. 7197, pp. 391–400. Springer, Heidelberg (2012)

11. Kasik, V., Penhaker, M., Novák, V., Bridzik, R., Krawiec, J.: User interactive biomedical data web services application. In: Yonazi, J.J., Sedoyeka, E., Ariwa, E., El-Qawasmeh, E. (eds.) ICeND 2011. CCIS, vol. 171, pp. 223–237. Springer, Heidelberg (2011)
12. Machacek, Z., Hercik, R., Slaby, R.: Smart user adaptive system for intelligent object recognizing. In: Nguyen, N.T., Trawiński, B., Jung, J.J. (eds.) New Challenges for Intelligent Information and Database Systems. SCI, vol. 351, pp. 197–206. Springer, Heidelberg (2011)
13. Machaj, J., Brida, P., Majer, N.: Novel criterion to evaluate QoS of localization based services. In: Pan, J.-S., Chen, S.-M., Nguyen, N.T. (eds.) ACIIDS 2012, Part II. LNCS, vol. 7197, pp. 381–390. Springer, Heidelberg (2012)
14. Mashinchi, R., Selamat, A., Ibrahim, S., Krejcar, O.: Granular-rule extraction to simplify data. In: Nguyen, N.T., Trawiński, B., Kosala, R. (eds.) ACIIDS 2015. LNCS, vol. 9012, pp. 421–429. Springer, Heidelberg (2015)
15. Cimler, R., Matyska, J., Balík, L., Horalek, J., Sobeslav, V.: Security issues of mobile application using cloud computing. Adv. Intell. Syst. Comput. **334**, 347–357 (2015)

Loop Speed Trap Data Collection Method for an Accurate Short-Term Traffic Flow Forecasting

Sahraoui Abdelatif[1]([✉]), Derdour Makhlouf[2],
Philippe Roose[3], and Djamel Becktache[2]

[1] LAMIS Laboratory, University of Larbi Tebessi, Tébessa, Algeria
`s.abdelatif@univ-tebessa.dz`
[2] LRS Laboratory, University Badji-Mokhtar, Annaba, Algeria
`m.derdour@yahoo.fr,djamel_bektache@yahoo.fr`
[3] LIUPPA/UPPA, Anglet, 2 Allée du Parc Montaury, 64600 Anglet, France
`Philippe.Roose@iutbayonne.univ-pau.fr`

Abstract. Despite the growing trend in intelligent transportation systems applications, there are still many problems waiting for an accurate solution such as traffic flow forecasting. In this paper, based on real-time data provided by dual loop speed traps detectors at given slot of time, we propose a cloud-based data collection method which is aimed to improve prediction accuracy. To reach this level of accuracy, two traffic parameters were introduced, the average speed and the foreseen arrival time between two vehicles. By adopting Choquet integral operator, these parameters can subsequently aggregate to busiest traffic parameters. Afterwards, a simple linear regression is applied for a dual purpose, the first to predict the traffic flow, then prove that there is a relationship between derived busiest arrival time and the traffic flow. Moreover, the simulation charts demonstrates that the forecasts by the Choquet operator ensure an accurate results to the real-time data. In contrast, the forecasts using weighted average operator lead to low accuracy compared with real-time data.

Keywords: Short-term traffic flow forecasting · Cloud based-data collection method · Choquet integral operator · Weighted average operator · Simple linear regression

1 Introduction

The short-term and long-term traffic flow prediction horizons have long been considered since each one has concern in a particular period. Regardless to short-term forecasting horizon, no longer few minutes away for the traffic forecasts, where it has attracted various prediction methods including multivariate time series, kalman filtering method [5], non-parametric regression model [12], artificial neural model [7]. Furthermore, these methodologies can be categorized based on statistical models like linear regression or artificial models like neural models.

© Springer International Publishing Switzerland 2016
M. Younas et al. (Eds.): MobiWIS 2016, LNCS 9847, pp. 56–64, 2016.
DOI: 10.1007/978-3-319-44215-0_5

The predicted arrival time or foreseen arrival time delay and the traffic flow (q), are presents crucial traffic parameters which has attracted great attention in past few years. Whereas, the arrival time can usually use to assess the accuracy prediction of the traffic flow [6]. Indeed, prediction accuracy of these parameters can be performed by an effective data collection utilizing road detectors technologies. For traffic parameters forecasting purpose, many works which have been put forward enables aforementioned methods, but an accurate traffic forecasting using data collection has not been seen further. Feng et al. [4], propose real-time adaptive traffic control solution based on data collection from connected vehicles. Wherein, a set of multi-linear regression models [8] are devoted for arrival times prediction using data collected by automatic passenger counter (APC). Zhong et al. [14], used real-time traffic data were it continuously collected by inductive loop for enabling traffic flow output, while Kalman filtering method takes the advantage of traffic parameters forecasting based on historical models. From other perspective, traffic parameters prediction can be viewed as a complicated process affected by many factors. In which, Bai et al. [2], estimates baseline travel times from the historical bus trip data by utilizing Kalman filtering, where it consider three factors as inputs: day time, road segment and weighted average travel time. In this study, we deal with multi-factors influenced traffic flow on which they are in time and space related such as: road segment, safety distance, foreseen arrival time. In particular, the accuracy of the traffic flow is depending on utilized mathematical operator. Bachmann et al. [1] uses Choquet fuzzy integral operator to capture a complex relationship between sensors data measurements. Authors in [9,13], used weighted average speed in order to calculate the optimal speed estimation. Wherever, we support Choquet integral operator to capture an accurate traffic parameters.

The researches mentioned above treats the accuracy of the traffic parameters and its relationship with predicted vehicle arrival time, where it has not defined so far. For this reason, our contribution is not limited only on demonstrating the correlation between these two variables, but also proven that the foreseen arrival time aggregation factor has a great effect on traffic flow prediction.

In this paper, using dual loop speed traps detectors, we propose a cloud service-based data collection method aimed to add accuracy value to the short-term traffic flow forecasting. At first, we combine the dual loop speed traps and the cloud computing for significant improvements capability of this detector, provide an efficient processing for the proposed data collection method, provide higher bandwidth to tackle low reception rate problem. After that, by adopting Choquet integral operator on collected data speed after a slot of time, foreseen arrival time and busiest arrival time are introduced as two traffic parameters. Whereas, it is possible to deduce the traffic flow conditions thought the relationship between them. Also, we attempt incorporating these two parameters on the traffic flow forecasting process. To demonstrate the accurateness of the proposal, applied simple linear regression demonstrates high correlation between aggregated busiest arrival time and the traffic flow (q). This correlation proves that the foreseen arrival time could be considered as key parameter for short-term traffic forecasts. Moreover, simulation results indicate the proposed data collection method with Choquet integral is accurateness and closes to the real data compared with weighted average operator.

The remaining parts of this paper are arranged as follows. The Sect. 2 denotes our proposed cloud-service for short-term traffic flow forecasting. While the Sect. 3, dealt with our proposed real-time data collection method for traffic flow forecasting. Section 4, includes applied linear regression for the aforementioned process. While our conclusion work is given is Sect. 5.

2   Cloud Based-Service for Traffic Flow Forecasting

The deployment of the cloud computing technology with wireless sensor network (WSN) has the potential to be the most promising service for traffic detection applications. Through this deployment, a significant enhancement of WSN capability on data storage and processing are proven [10]. In this study, we are interesting by dual loop speed detectors to forecast short-term traffic flow, it used as an operated sensor to detect individual vehicle speed. From end to end combining cloud based-service with these detectors, an automatic offset of data can achieved through continues connection to the cloud service. Moreover, we deploy cloud computing technology in term of efficient computing and high bandwidth. The first characteristic aimed to bring more accuracy value to the traffic flow forecasting. Whereas the high bandwidth characteristic is to tackle the problem of low reception rate, insufficient bandwidth and network saturation.

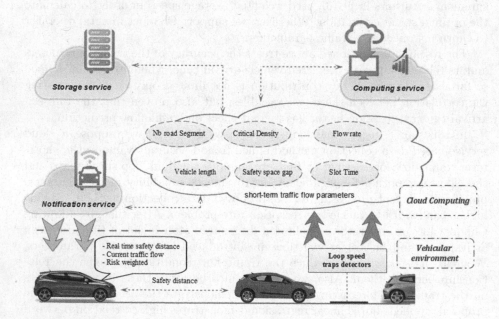

Fig. 1. Cloud based-service architecture for short-term traffic forecasting

The Fig. 1 outlines our proposed cloud based-service to forecast short-term traffic flow. As key feature, from real time data provided by dual loop speed detectors, the cloud service identify short-term traffic flow parameters such a safety space gap, average speed, critical road segment, entering rate, etc. At this level, three potential cloud based-services dealt with short-term traffic flow parameters: computing service, storage service and notification service. The computing service is usefull for data processing and performing intensive computing on short-time traffic data such for example: runs genetic algorithms for heuristic solutions, forecasting traffic flow using a linear regression as included in the next section. The storage service offers sustainable large storage capacity for real time traffic data and thus, further data analysis and decisions making to the transportation department. Furthermore, the cloud service has two communication interfaces with the vehicular environment. The first interface concern direct communication with dual loop speed detectors. While notification interface enables notifying all vehicles with real time traffic information such as: real time safety distance, current traffic flow and the risk weight.

Through an automatic identification of traffic parameters by the cloud service, our proposed architecture is intended to bring more advantages for emerged modern car applications like fleet management, pedestrians and queue safety. Where data notifications are relevant for all vehicles that are found in the cloud coverage area.

3   Real-Time Data Collection Method for Traffic Flow Forecasting

By assuming, that drivers on the road has a great interesting to know current traffic flow status (q) as well as the risk which may be subjected during their trips. For this, an installed dual loop speed detectors on road of 3 Km to record observed individual speed counts. Thus, we denote (Spi) to the vehicle speed at loop detector and (Lv) to the vehicle length (In this work we consider only the length of the light vehicles). After a slot of time, the proposed method operated microscopic parameters as inputs such as observed vehicle speeds, road length (d) and the vehicle length (Lv). On which the main purpose is to forecast an accurate traffic flow from observed speed counts. As key novelty, we introduce two traffic parameters called foreseen arrival time and busiest arrival time, which they are, warrants our intention to predict the traffic flow and highlight its impacts on safe driving.

3.1   Foreseen Arrival Time Parameter

Estimated arrival time, is defined as necessary time which must elapse between two consecutive vehicles. To determine its value, a safety distance and the average speed are needed. For more safety, a safety distance (Sd) should be determined because it describes required reaction time for a driver to react with a critical situation on the road [3]; this time is accurately close of 2 s. In addition, the vehicles must maintain this distance in order to avoid the risk of collision in case of sudden deceleration or sudden stop of ahead vehicles. The Eq. 1 in the following set the safety distance measured in meters which is closes to 5/9 of average speed:

$$Sd = AvgSpeed * 5/9 \tag{1}$$

After determining safety distance in accordance with the previous equation, the proposed method split the road length into segments. On which each segment length can be identified according to the Eq. 2:

$$SegLengh = Lv + Sd \tag{2}$$

At slot of time j, assume $Spj = \{Sp1, Sp2, ..., Spn\}$ represents a set of observed speed counts by utilizing speed trap detectors, and being aggregated as well. Where $\mu(\Delta Sp_{(i)})$ embodies a weight of importance which excludes two consecutive speeds since greatest difference speed between them. $Csp(Sp_1, Sp_2, ..., Sp_n)$ denotes determined busiest speed average at this slot by Choquet integral operator and further satisfying the following equation:

$$Csp(Sp_1, Sp_2, ..., Sp_n) = \sum_{i=1}^{n}(Sp_{(i)} - Sp_{(i+1)})\mu(\Delta Sp_{(i)}) \tag{3}$$

Now, we can compute foreseen arrival time (FArrT) between two vehicles by the following equation:

$$FArrT = SegLengh/Csp(Sp_1, Sp_2, ..., Sp_n). \tag{4}$$

3.2   Busiest Arrival Time for Safety Traffic Flow

Safer traffic flow reflects safety importance which is depending on observed traffic conditions in time and space, where it can lead to low-risk driving. For instance, two traffic conditions affect the traffic safety, maintaining safety distance by the vehicles and closer individual vehicle speed to the average speed. Indeed, it is crucial to aggregate observed arrival times between all vehicles for individual segment to busiest arrival time $\Delta t_{(p)}$ for all segments. After that, this busiest time will play an important role in identifying safer traffic flow level. By utilizing Choquet integral operator, compute $\Delta t_{(p)}$ parameter is giving by following equation:

$$\Delta t_p(t_1, t_2, ..., t_n) = \sum_{i=1}^{n}(t_{(i)} - t_{(i+1)})\mu(\Delta t_{(i)}) \tag{5}$$

Where $t_1, t_2, ..., t_n$ presents observed arrival times between pair of vehicles; $\mu(\Delta t_{(i)})$ implies a weight that eliminates two consecutive arrival times since greatest difference time between them.

Regardless to the Eqs. (4) and (5), a new real-time traffic conditions can be identified by comparing foreseen arrival time and busiest derived arrival time. In particular, if $\Delta t_{(p)}$ is greater than $FArrT$ that implies subjected vehicles in low risk driving. Otherwise, there is a significant weight of risk could be considered for current traffic flow. In contrast, traffic flow forecasts utilizing weighted operator can be attained through replacing Eqs. (3) and (5) by the Eqs. (6) and (7) respectively:

$$AvgSp(Sp_1, Sp_2, ..., Sp_n) = \sum_{i=1}^{n} Sp_{(i)}/N \tag{6}$$

$$\Delta t_p(t_1, t_2, ..., t_n) = \sum_{i=1}^{n} t_{(i)}/N \tag{7}$$

In summary, for an accurate traffic flow forecasts with the proposed method, the correlation between traffic flow (q) and busiest arrival time could be studied. In particular, a simple linear regression is applied in order to demonstrate high correlation between these two parameters. Extended details of applied simple linear regression analysis will be included in the next section.

4   Linear Regression for Traffic Flow Forecasting

In this section, we attempts to explore the relationship between the busiest arrival time and the traffic flow (q). Furthermore, positive correlation demonstrates a valuable traffic forecasts using the proposed busiest arrival time. To reach this purpose, a simple linear regression analysis was applied to explore the relationship between these two variables according to the following general equation:

$$Y_j = b_0 + \sum_{i=1}^{n} (b_i X_{ij}) + \epsilon \tag{8}$$

Where Y_j presents the traffic flow counts at slot of time j; b_0 denotes a constant; X_{ij} refers to busiest arrival time counts; ϵ are usually denotes the noise (error); b_i indicates the regression coefficient.

Traffic flow forecasting with our proposal was realized using $omnet++$ simulator [11]. For accuracy purpose, thanks to the supplied real time traffic data by department of transportation. These data are concern 3 Km of road length and it was recorded using loop speed detectors over 4 min of time, where the individual vehicle speed and the vehicle arrival times are recorded. With slot time of 20 s, the foreseen arrival times of all vehicles are computed and furthermore

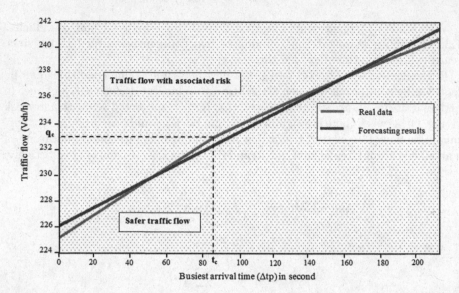

Fig. 2. Forecasting performance of the proposed method with Choquet integral operator.

assimilated for busiest arrival time aggregation. Nevertheless, we consider just one scenario that implements Choquet integral operator in one hand, weighted average operator in the other hand. Forecasting performance of our proposed method with Choquet integral operator is showed in Fig. 2.

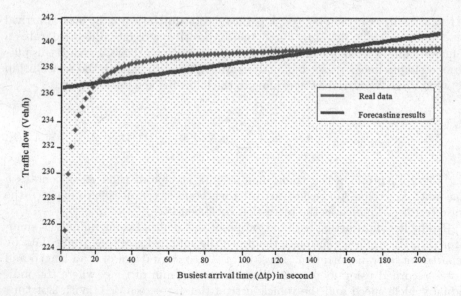

Fig. 3. Forecasting performance of the proposed method with weighted average operator.

As we can see, the forecasting results are high closes to the real time data. In addition, with Choquet integral operator, a critical foreseen arrival time (t_c) is corresponding to critical value of traffic flow (q_c). Positively, we can distinct safer traffic flow from traffic flow with likelihood of rear-end collision. This letter take us conclude that the safety distance between the vehicles are not respected while the traffic flow is greater than q_c. In contrast, the Fig. 3 shows the forecasting performance of our proposed method with weighted average. Which is remarkable is that the forecasting results are weak closes to the real time data comparing with forecasting performance in the Fig. 2. Moreover, the absences of critical point of the traffic flow make the distinction between the safer traffic flow and traffic flow with likelihood of rear-end collision very difficult.

5   Conclusion

In this paper, we have proposed a cloud service-based method treats with short-term traffic flow prediction accuracy. An efficient data collection mechanism is ensured by combining the cloud system and the speed trap detector. In this way, two traffic parameters were introduced, foreseen arrival time and busiest arrival time. By apply Choquet integral operator, the foreseen arrival times will be aggregated to the busiest arrival time. At the simulation stage, the simple linear regression demonstrates high coloration between busiest arrival time and the traffic flow (q). For more accuracy, Choquet integral operator offers an accurateness value to the traffic flow instead of weighted average operator. This take us concluded that the busiest arrival time is importantly and it has a great impact on the traffic flow prediction. Also, we argue that the Choquet integral utilization for data aggregation is appropriate for safety and future of traffic conditions. While in the future works, we attempt to propose hybrid model for short-term traffic flow estimation by incorporating real-time data and historical data.

Acknowledgments. This work is subscribed in the context of the thematic research project entitled "Integrated Road Traffic in Algeria", our objective is to develop VANETs applications that are "suspected" of spatiotemporal context, so to generalize the exchange of V2V information's (Vehicle-to-Vehicle), V2I information's (Vehicle-to-Infrastructure) and even V2X, and support all communication types (radio, internet, etc.) in their activities.

References

1. Bachmann, C., Abdulhai, B., Roorda, M.J., Moshiri, B.: A comparative assessment of multi-sensor data fusion techniques for freeway traffic speed estimation using microsimulation modeling. Transp. Res. Part C: Emerg. Technol. **26**, 33–48 (2013)
2. Bai, C., Peng, Z.R., Lu, Q.C., Sun, J.: Dynamic bus travel time prediction models on road with multiple bus routes. Comput. Intell. Neurosci. **2015**, 63 (2015)
3. Amended by Decree No: Article R412–12. Technical report

4. Feng, Y., Head, K.L., Khoshmagham, S., Zamanipour, M.: A real-time adaptive signal control in a connected vehicle environment. Transp. Res. Part C: Emerg. Technol. **55**, 460–473 (2015)
5. Ji, H., Xu, A., Sui, X., Li, L.: The applied research of kalman in the dynamic travel time prediction. In: 2010 18th International Conference on Geoinformatics, pp. 1–5. IEEE (2010)
6. Lindveld, C.D., Thijs, R., Bovy, P., Van der Zijpp, N.: Evaluation of online travel time estimators and predictors. Transp. Res. Rec.: J. Transp. Res. Board **1719**, 45–53 (2000)
7. Moretti, F., Pizzuti, S., Panzieri, S., Annunziato, M.: Urban traffic flow forecasting through statistical and neural network bagging ensemble hybrid modeling. Neurocomputing **167**, 3–7 (2015)
8. Patnaik, J., Chien, S., Bladikas, A.: Estimation of bus arrival times using APC data. J. Public Transp. **7**(1), 1 (2004)
9. Qian, J., Eglese, R.: Fuel emissions optimization in vehicle routing problems with time-varying speeds. Eur. J. Oper. Res. **248**(3), 840–848 (2016)
10. Savas, O., Jin, G., Deng, J.: Trust management in cloud-integrated wireless sensor networks. In: 2013 International Conference on Collaboration Technologies and Systems (CTS), pp. 334–341. IEEE (2013)
11. Varga, A., et al.: The omnet++ discrete event simulation system. In: Proceedings of the European Simulation Multiconference (ESM 2001), vol. 9, p. 65. (2001)
12. Williams, B., Durvasula, P., Brown, D.: Urban freeway traffic flow prediction: application of seasonal autoregressive integrated moving average and exponential smoothing models. Transp. Res. Rec.: J. Transp. Res. Board **1644**, 132–141 (1998)
13. Yasmin, S., Eluru, N., Lee, J., Abdel-Aty, M.A.: Ordered fractional split approach for aggregate injury severity modeling. In: Transportation Research Board 95th Annual Meeting (No. 16-6952) (2016)
14. Zhong, J.T., Ling, S.: Key factors of k-nearest neighbours nonparametric regression in short-time traffic flow forecasting. In: Qi, E., Shen, J., Dou, R. (eds.) Proceedings of the 21st International Conference on Industrial Engineering and Engineering Management 2014, pp. 9–12. Springer, Heidelberg (2015)

Advanced Web and Mobile Systems

Computational Thinking Through Mobile Programming
A Case Study in a Liberal Education Context

Ilenia Fronza[1(✉)], Nabil El Ioini[1], and Luis Corral[2]

[1] Free University of Bolzano, Piazza Domenicani, 3, 39100 Bolzano, Italy
{ilenia.fronza,nabil.elioini}@unibz.it
[2] ITESM/UAQ, E. Gonzalez 500, 76130 Queretaro, Mexico
lrcorralv@itesm.mx

Abstract. Computational Thinking (CT) is considered a fundamental skill for everyone. Therefore, research has focused on defining age and grade-appropriate curricula for teaching CT. In this context, mobile programming can be a good means to foster CT. Indeed, the growing adoption of mobile devices, also among females, minorities, and all economic groups, provides a powerful opportunity for engaging students. Nevertheless, further issues need to be addressed, in particular in the context of liberal education. For example, most of the students enroll in these schools because they have higher interest for liberal arts, and perceive programming as a very difficult task. Also, issues can emerge when trying to introduce new courses into schools. In this paper, we describe a course, which aims at creating a mobile application with students having no background in software development. The main strategy to accomplish this is to foster and evaluate CT, with the support of development tools that ease the learning and application of CT skills. We report the results and the evaluation of a case study conducted in a social-economic high school, with a total of 29 students of 8th and 9th grade.

Keywords: Mobile programming · Computational thinking · Case study

1 Introduction

In the last decades, Computer Science (CS) curricula have often aimed at teaching computer literacy, which resulted almost inevitably in the identification of the concept of CS with the concept of "ability to use technology" [8]. Nevertheless, "students should be able to use CS skills (especially computational thinking) in their problem-solving activities in other subjects" [19]. Computational Thinking (CT) is currently considered as "one of the fundamental skills" for everyone [1,27], which helps students recognizing their own potential to use technology in their professional career.

© Springer International Publishing Switzerland 2016
M. Younas et al. (Eds.): MobiWIS 2016, LNCS 9847, pp. 67–80, 2016.
DOI: 10.1007/978-3-319-44215-0_6

Research has recently focused on defining curricula for teaching CT. However, gaps still exist that call out for empirical inquiries, in particular in the K-12 context [13]. In this environment, mobile programming can be a good means to foster CT, for multiple reasons. First, mobile programming is a skill highly demanded in current labor market in many fields [5,16], including those not purely technical. This serves as an engagement factor, as students can have practical examples of the role of technology in their professional areas. Second, students learn best when learning objectives are contextualized with topics related to their daily activities [20]. Therefore, the growing adoption of mobile devices, also among females, minorities, and all economic groups, provides a powerful opportunity for engaging students to CS [7]. Third, the possibility to generate an economic profit by marketing mobile products across the various app markets represent an additional motivating factor [7].

If mobile programming courses seem to provide a good chance to foster CT in schools, further issues need to be addressed, in particular in the context of liberal education. For example, even if mobile programming is in general a motivating topic, most of the students get discouraged upfront as they perceive programming as a very difficult task. Also, issues can emerge when trying to introduce new courses into schools; for example, teachers might not be willing to add topics to their already intensive syllabus [11,29], especially if they do not see a direct linkage to their topic. Out-of-school venues are a good solution [11]; however, teaching mobile programming during school hours can ensure the engagement of the broadest audience possible, and an effective linkage to other subjects currently in progress.

In this paper, we describe a course, which aims at creating a mobile application (app) with students having no background in software development, in a liberal education context. The main strategy to accomplish this is to foster CT, with the support of development tools that ease the learning and application of CT skills. We report the results and the evaluation of a case study conducted in a social-economic high school[1], with a total of 29 students of 8th and 9th grade.

The paper is organized as follows: Sect. 2 provides background information; Sect. 3 details the structure of the course; Sect. 4 describes the case study; Sect. 5 discusses the results; and Sect. 6 draws conclusions and provides directions for further research.

2   Background

In 2011, the CS Teachers Association (CSTA) and the International Society for Technology in Education (ISTE) explained the implicit concepts of CT, in terms of nine skills: (1) data collection, (2) data analysis, (3) data representation, (4) problem decomposition, (5) abstraction, (6) algorithms and procedures, (7) automation, (8) simulation, and (9)parallelization [14]. In 2012,

---

[1] This type of high school combines liberal arts and social-economic sciences.

Brennan and Resnick developed an operational definition of CT that involves the following three key dimensions: computational concepts, computational practices, and computational perspectives [6].

Programming is a tool for supporting CT, the same as "performing does for music or going the lab for physics" [3], beside other practices that let students embrace all the CT skills. This consideration is particularly relevant during the design of activities to promote CT in liberal education environments, where programming itself can not be the main tool, since students are not inclined to programming or other "technical" activities.

Graphical programming environments are among the most popular tools to foster CT. Indeed, these tools allow problem driven learning [17], therefore they are good tools to teach CT [21]. During the early sessions, the simplicity and the intuitiveness of these tools help students to focus on design and construction, rather than dealing with traditional problems of programming, such as structural or syntax errors. Another part of current research deals with the need of evaluating the effectiveness of the educational techniques that promote CT, which remains a challenge [6,18,26]. This makes the introduction of CT in schools curricula difficult. An overview of the available techniques for the assessment of CT can be found in [13], where the author highlights the need for multiple measures that are complementary, encourage and reflect deeper learning, and contribute to a comprehensive picture of student learning. The possibility of using the Software Engineering process to teach CT is explored in [11], where each phase of the process is used to cultivate specific CT skills. Grover and Pea [13] highlight the need of empirical studies in schools.

3   Course Description

This Section introduces the goal of the course, and describes its rationale, structure, and assessment.

3.1   Motivation and Goal

As CT is recognized as a fundamental skill for everyone [1], it emerges a need to define curricula for teaching and assessing CT in schools of different types and levels. The goal is to leverage students' general curiosity for mobile programming to promote CT, and to convince them that with CT skills, creating a mobile app can be accessible to them. Beside teaching and evaluating the development of CT, this course aims at addressing organizational issues related to the introduction of such projects in schools [11].

The remaining part of this Section details the choice of the topic of the course, as well of the tools and strategies in order to ease the learning and application of CT skills.

3.2   Rationale

The idea of this course is to let students experience a practical example of the potential application of CS in their field, by working on a interdisciplinary project. In particular, the aim of the course is to create a mobile app that fulfills the requirements collected during liberal arts courses. This allows students perceiving the problem as well-connected to their path. Moreover, the creation of a mobile application allows to solve a problem by creating an actual product, which is generally motivating for students, since they can appreciate the usefulness and meaning of a mobile software application from the user point of view.

In order to enhance the analytical thinking skills needed to develop mobile applications, each phase of the software engineering process is used to promote the growth of CT skills, also using unplugged exercises [8]. Moreover, covering the entire software engineering process helps in experiencing that a good computational strategy can ease the technical part [11,25].

The choice of an interdisciplinary project helps addressing the issues related to running the course in school time. Indeed, in such a project teachers can cover some educational objectives of their subjects, therefore there is higher possibility for creating interest and engagement both from instructors and students.

3.3   Tools

As suggested in [23], our course pursues technology-independent learning outcomes. Indeed, in our course programming is not the main focus, but a tool to support the cognitive tasks involved in the creation of the mobile application (i.e., CT) [11]. The choice of the tools used in this course reflects this characteristic of the course: preference was given to tools that allow fostering CT.

App Inventor is a web-based application created by the Massachusetts Institute of Technology. It is a visual development environment for building Android apps, and it is composed of two main views: (1) the *designer view* allows users to drag-and-drop all the components needed to design their application (i.e., graphical interface and non visual components, such as sensors); and (2) the *blocks view* allows to attach actions and add behaviour to the components defined in the designer.

App Inventor is considered an attractive platform for engaging students at all levels in the computing curriculum [11,17]; therefore, a considerable effort has been spent in designing courses to teach programming using App Inventor [29]. Moreover, since it allows problem-driven learning, this tool is a good framework to teach CT [21]. As an additional strength of App Inventor, mobile apps can be tested, used, or run immediately. This gives a sense of practicality and reality in achievement, which can be very satisfying experiences in one's learning. Furthermore, the process of creation stimulates fun and creativity, and the products developed acquire practical use in real-life. Therefore, App Inventor was chosen for the liberal education contexts, where students are in general "scared" by programming tasks.

Table 1. CT skills fostered during each phase of the software engineering process.

	1	2	3	4	5	6	7	8	9
Requirements	✓	✓	✓	✓					
Design (high and low level)		✓	✓		✓	✓			
Data collection	✓	✓	✓						
Implementation			✓			✓	✓		✓
Testing (after each phase)		✓						✓	

R is a tool for statistics and data modeling, and also includes powerful graphics capabilities. Being a programming language, data analysis is performed by writing functions and scripts, not by pointing and clicking, therefore: (1) students learn that they can create their own objects and functions, (2) as scripts document all the work, it is much easier to re-run the analysis at any time, and (3) students can experience directly the advantages of automation. Moreover, as an interactive language, R encourages experimentation and simulation. All these characteristics make R a good tool to foster CT. As an additional benefit, R is open-source and platform-independent. Therefore, R can be used at school or at home without any restrictions.

3.4   Structure

At the beginning of the course, the concept of Software Engineering (SE) is introduced, with a strong emphasis on the need to take care also on other activities, beside programming [22]. Afterwards, we assist students on an interdisciplinary project, which covers the whole process from requirements elicitation till delivering a working product. Students work in pairs (trios when needed) to exercise parallelization [14]; moreover, previous studies have shown a positive effect of pair programming on CT assessment scores [26], and on novices' learning [10,12].

We adopted a V-shaped model, for the following reasons: (1) in this case, requirements are well defined before the implementation, the development direction is almost fixed, and reusability is not needed [15]; (2) each part of the V-shaped model comprises a phase of testing, which helps demonstrating the relationships between each phase of the development life cycle and its associated phase of testing [15]. As suggested in [11], all the phases of the SE process are used to grow specific CT skills (described in Sect. 2), as shown in Table 1. The length of the course is different for the two grades (Table 2); indeed, 9th graders need to learn the tool-set more thoroughly, which almost doubles the time needed for this phase. The remaining part of this Section details all the phases of the course.

Requirements and High-level Design. Teachers of liberal arts courses select a social-economic topic, and collect the requirements for the app that will be developed during the course. Afterwards, we assist students understanding

Table 2. Structure of the course, in 8th and 9th grade.

Phase	Hours	
	8th g.	9th g.
Requirements	2	3
High-level design	2	3
Data collection	Homework	
Learning the tool-set	6	10
Unit testing	4	4
Implementation	6	10
Total	20	30

whether the features they want to implement are possible or not. Also, features and their logical flow are analyzed. As a second step, students organize a high-level idea of the application based on the analyzed context. In our metaphore ("app as trees" [11]), the main menu of the application is the "trunk of the tree", and each menu option (i.e., each different screen) is called a "leaf". Each "branch" of the tree represents a condition under which the application is switching from screen to screen. Each node in the tree is a low-level component that incorporates an atomic functionality. The creation of this document is used to facilitate the interchange of ideas among the members of a team, and to ensure that all the participants speak and are listened to. Requirements are tested by looking at the final product and manually verifying that all the requirements have been implemented; the high level design is tested by checking that all the components are working correctly together. Output of this phase are: (1) the requirements document, which will be the basis for acceptance and system testing; (2) a pen-and-paper document, which represents the high-level design of the application and serves as a guide for the following phases.

Data Collection. As a homework, students collect all the data needed. Depending on the type of measures that have to be collected, data collection might be manual or computer assisted. This phase is tested manually by the instructor to verify the validity of the collected data.

Learning the Tool Set. App Inventor is introduced using a set of exercises of increasing difficulty; the training ends with the creation of a basic, functioning mobile application, which shows how to receive an input from the user, elaborate it internally, and produce an output. R is introduced through a tutorial, which covers the topics that are necessary for the applications that will be created during the course.

Low-level Design and Implementation. First, students design, with pen and paper, the visual aspects of the app. Afterwards, teams develop each feature by using the designer for the GUI and the non-visual components and using the blocks to connect actions to components. Also, they should provide the means to guarantee the interaction with the user; this is facilitated by the native controls that App Inventor provides for the management of the input means of the cellular phones. Low-level design is tested by checking the behavior of single nodes in the application; this is done manually by confronting a node design with its specification. During the development, students test their product (i.e., unit testing) by running the newly developed features either on the emulator or on a real phone and check whether the features behave correctly or not. A test is passed when the behavior of the implemented feature is the one reported in the requirements. Integration is needed when features are developed separately, while it is done during development if each feature is built on top of existing ones. User-level testing is performed by streaming the application to a real device or Android emulator, and executing it in a real context of use.

3.5   Assessment

At the end of the activities, we check that the final versions of the mobile applications do not show errors, and that the execution of the app follows a logical flow. Furthermore, we check each application to have a good level of accuracy with respect to its initial conception (i.e., the final app meets the high level requirements).

To assess the development of CT (i.e., practices, concepts, and perspectives), we adopt a framework [11] in which learners are engaged in a conversation about their progress, and at the same time their product is critically examined. These conversations are used to provide help and to check that all the members of the team are progressing, even if with their own pace. It is relevant to note that these interviews are useful to observe if students actually understand the meaning and the usefulness of following a precise process (i.e., SE process), with the creation of working products that are fundamental inputs for the following activities.

4   Case Study

A case study was conducted in a social-economic high school, with a total participation of 29 students (20 female and 9 male) of the 8th grade (12 participants, 8 female and 4 male) and the 9th grade (17 participants, 12 female and 5 male). The main issue in this context is that most of the teaching activities in the curriculum are dedicated to liberal arts: over the 5 years of school, CS is taught 2 h per week, Mathematics 4 hours per week, and Statistics only 1 hour per week, starting from the third year. This means that most of the students enroll in a such a curriculum because they have higher interest for liberal arts.

During the phase dedicated to *requirements and high level design*, two different topics were selected for the two grades. In the 8th grade, the goal was to create a mobile app that shows how we use and waste water. To this end, students and teachers decided to focus on two aspects of everyday life: (1) the water we waste while washing our teeth, especially if we do not close the tap while brushing, and (2) the amount of water that we use in our families compared to the minimum human right to water [24]. According to the requirements, in the desired applications, it is needed that the results are shown in the form of plots, with a short explanation or suggestions for improvement. In the 9th grade, it was decided to focus on "social networks" in order to show how users' data can be used for different purposes, such as marketing. To this end, students designed and created effective visualizations [9] using Facebook data to answer different questions, such as: (1) do friends know each other?; (2) where do friends live?; (3) what do friends like?; (4) when does the owner of the profile use Facebook during the day?; (5) which words are used the most in the status?; (6) what do friends think about 2014?; and (7) which music do friends like?. Figure 1a shows an example of the resulting document of the high-level design phase.

8th graders performed a manual *data collection*. Half of the students were in charge of reading the water counter at home every day for 8 days and to annotate also the number of people in the house in those days. The other students were in charge of putting a bowl in the sink while brushing their teeth and to measure the amount of water that was consumed in two cases: (1) closing the tap while brushing, and (2) leaving the tap open. 9th graders, instead, collected all the necessary data semi-automatically. They used existing web services to retrieve all the needed information, however, they had to integrate manually the collected data. For instance, to find Facebook friends of a particular user they used a specific web service that retrieves all the people connected with that user[2]; then, to find where the user's friends are located, a different web service had to be used[3]. Finally, data needed to be integrated manually using R. All the data collected as a homework were reviewed and approved by the instructors.

Data were imported in R, and subsequently, plots were created. In this phase, our role was to assist students selecting an effective visualization to convey the needed information.

During the *low-level design and implementation* phase, students designed and implemented each branch and node of the tree (i.e., each transition and screen of the application). Figure 1b shows an example of low-level design document. Students used the high-level design document during the implementation phase, and tracked possible changes. For example, the screen "nomi" (i.e., names) shown in Fig. 1a on the right side of the tree was removed, and for this reason it was cancelled in the tree. Each node was designed and implemented separately, then in the integration phase nodes were connected (i.e., the branches were designed and implemented) following the design document.

The testing phase was facilitated by App Inventor; indeed, the synchronization between the model (i.e., the code) and the view (i.e., the emulator) enabled the so-called "what you see is what you get" approach. Using the browser to interactively develop and test is an experience that many students describe as exciting, and that delivers more value both for the developmental and user point of views.

---

[2] https://developers.facebook.com/docs/graph-api/reference/v2.5/user/friends.
[3] https://developers.facebook.com/docs/graph-api/reference/v2.5/user/locations.

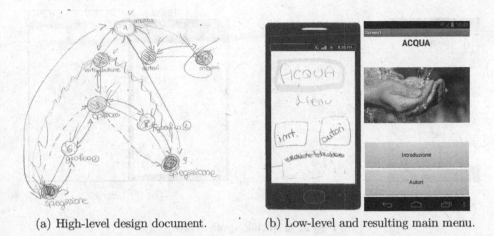

(a) High-level design document.   (b) Low-level and resulting main menu.

Fig. 1. High and low-level design, and resulting application.

The applications were intended to display information unidirectionally, with a minimal interaction with the user. After launching the applications, users can visualize an introductory page and information about authors, boosting the pride on the ownership and authorship of the final product. Afterwards, the applications allow to choose a visualization. Even providing such a limited functionality required to students to exercise a good command from the logic point of view, which can be quite challenging, in particular considering their liberal education context. The special attention dedicated to the design of the solution (i.e., following a precise Software Engineering process) and the usage of App Inventor facilitated students in focusing on the logic of their mobile applications.

The successful completion of the mobile applications shows that students were able to identify a problem, select the most effective solution taking as basis and inspiration from the introductory part, and finally create their own solution. For example, Fig. 2a shows that 8th graders used two buttons to open two different screens that contained the visualizations.

Also 9th graders, first, adopted this solutions; afterwards, as shown in Fig. 2b, they improved their design by using a "spinner" in order to avoid creating 7 similar buttons and keep the user interface as simple as possible. This idea represent a remarkable result, as the spinner was not explained in the "learning the tool set" phase; therefore, this shows that these students reached the higher part of Bloom's pyramid (i.e., remembering, understanding, and applying) [2,4] (Fig. 3).

The presence of specific blocks in the final applications can confirm that students were using the corresponding computational concept [6]. For this reason, we mapped computational concepts to App Inventor blocks, and we checked the presence of those blocks in the developed applications. Table 3 shows that students of the two grades used most of the computational concepts in their code. No block associated to loops and parallelism where found; nevertheless, code inspections revealed that there was no need to use those concepts.

(a) 8th grade.

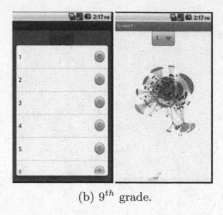

(b) 9th grade.

Fig. 2. Resulting applications.

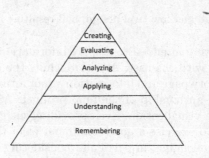

Fig. 3. Bloom's taxonomy [4].

Table 3. Blocks used in the applications mapped to computational concepts [6].

Concepts	Blocks
Sequences	Stacks of blocks
Loops	NA
Events	When...do
Parallelism	NA
Conditionals	If, if else
Operators	Math blocks
Data	Initialize, get, set, lists

5 Results

The quality and functionality of the final projects of the case study shows that the outcome of the course is clearly positive: 8th and 9th graders were able to implement their solutions without requiring specialized training on software development tools, which is an extremely important factor in the context of liberal education context.

Creating a mobile application helped to increase the interest and curiosity of students, as they belong to a range of age that makes strong use of devices like cellular phones or tablets. Moreover, even in a liberal education context, students could experience a practical example of the potential application of CS in their field. Those students that could be discouraged by the technical part (i.e., the programming part), understood that following a software engineering process and focusing on the design of the solution can ease the technical part.

At the end of the course, students of both grades were able to recognize their own potential to use technology in their path, which means that they proposed other examples of possible usages of CS and programming in their career.

Students took advantage of the assessment conversations to get help or solve issues, and they were happy to explain their work. Moreover, these conversations helped discovering conceptual gaps timely, and to provide feedback. Therefore, it is worth conducting more experiments to validate the framework [11] for formative assessment.

A third type of assessment for the proposed course is represented by data on participants' satisfaction and their feedback. According to students' feedback, they were happy of solving a problem by creating an actual product. Furthermore, they reported to be surprised by discovering that a developer does not only deal with coding, but she needs to work on different activities to create an application. In this sense, they were happy to discover that their knowledge and abilities can be spent in the Software Engineering process, even if they need to learn programming to create a product.

This course was multidisciplinary, as it blended mobile programming, CT, and liberal arts. In this context, teachers made some hours available, as some educational objectives of their subjects were covered during the course. This made possible to activate the course in school time, thus involving all the students.

6   Conclusion and Future Work

In this paper, we described a course at high school level in a liberal education context, which lets students experience a practical example of the potential application of CS in their field, by working on a interdisciplinary project. In particular, the aim of the course is to create a mobile app that fulfills the requirements collected during liberal arts courses. Thanks to this combination, students understood that they can build programs without being professionals, and at the same time they recognized their own potential to use technology in any professional path of their choice.

The accomplishments of the teaching program are reflected by the set of applications that students successfully developed, under the supervision of the teaching staff. Moreover, code inspections revealed that students were using computational concepts timely.

Following all the steps of the Software Engineering process helped in fostering CT skills, and allowed students understanding that a proper design of the solution can ease the programming part. Moreover, the utilization of a block-oriented development platform allowed for the development of the product based on the functionality of the product itself, overcoming traditional issues associated to coding. Courses ended with a working application, a product students were very proud of, and with a high sense of pride and ownership.

Beside achieving the educational objectives, the course presented in this paper shows that multidisciplinary courses have higher possibilities to be activated in schools, as most instructors agree on dedicating some hours to these sessions, since their covers educational objectives of a wider range, so more courses can benefit from this.

In general, results of case studies are difficult to generalize [28]. In our case, more analysis is required to generalize to other situations; therefore, further case studies should be conducted involving students of different (liberal) curricula. Moreover, other case studies would help in understanding the areas that require further development both from the conceptual and practical part. For example, the assessment framework could be validated; moreover, the effectiveness of the Software Engineering process in fostering CT could be proven. Current literature and the experience reported in this paper can recommend the development and empirical validation of an assessment framework of CT in a K-12 environment.

References

1. ACM and IEEE: Computer science curricula 2013. Technical report, Association for Computing Machinery (ACM) and IEEE Computer Society (2013)
2. Anderson, L., Krathwohl, D., Airasian, P., Cruikshank, K., Mayer, R., Pintrich, P., Raths, J., Wittrock, M.: A Taxonomy for Learning, Teaching, and Assessing: A Revision of Bloom's Taxonomy of Educational Objectives. Allyn and Bacon (Pearson Education Group), Boston (2001)
3. Bateman, K.: Let's not forget the computing curriculum's bigger picture: computational · thinking (2014). http://www.computerweekly.com/feature/Lets-not-forget-the-computing-curriculums-bigger-picture-Computational-thinking. Accessed 30 Nov 2015
4. Bloom, B., Krathwohl, D.R.: Taxonomy of Educational Objectives: The Classification of Educational Goals, by a Committee of College and University Examiners. Handbook I: Cognitive Domain. Longmans, Green, New York (1956)
5. Brandel, M.: 12 it skills employers cannot say no to (2007). http://www.computerworld.com.au/article/190963/12_it_skills_employers_can_t_say_no/. Accessed 25 Nov 2015
6. Brennan, K., Resnick, M.: New frameworks for studying and assessing the development of computational thinking. In: 2012 Annual Meeting of the American Educational Research Association (AERA 2012), Vancouver, Canada (2012)
7. Dabney, M.H., Dean, B.C., Rogers, T.: No sensor left behind: enriching computing education with mobile devices. In: Proceeding of the 44th ACM Technical Symposium on Computer Science Education, SIGCSE 2013, pp. 627–632. ACM, New York (2013)

8. Fronza, I., Ioini, N., Janes, A., Sillitti, A., Succi, G., Corral, L.: If i had to vote on this laboratory, i would give nine: introduction on computational thinking in the lower secondary school: results of the experience. Mondo Digitale **13**(51), 757–765 (2014)
9. Fronza, I., Janes, A., Sillitti, A., Succi, G., Trebeschi, S.: Cooperation wordle using pre-attentive processing techniques, pp. 57–64 (2013)
10. Fronza, I., Succi, G.: Modeling spontaneous pair programming when new developers join a team. In: Abrahamsson, P., Marchesi, M., Maurer, F. (eds.) Agile Processes in Software Engineering and Extreme Programming. LNBIP, vol. 31, pp. 242–244. Springer, Heidelberg (2009)
11. Fronza, I., El Ioini, N., Corral, L.: Students want to create apps: leveraging computational thinking to teach mobile software development. In: Proceedings of the 16th Annual Conference on Information Technology Education, SIGITE 2015, pp. 21–26. ACM, New York (2015)
12. Fronza, I., Sillitti, A., Succi, G., Vlasenko, J.: Understanding how novices are integrated in a team analysing their tool usage. In: Proceedings of the 2011 International Conference on Software and Systems Process, pp. 204–207. ACM (2011)
13. Grover, S., Pea, R.: Computational thinking in K-12. A review of the state of the field. Educ. Researcher **42**(1), 38–43 (2013)
14. ISTE, CSTA: Computational thinking. Teacher resources, 2nd edn. (2011). http://csta.acm.org/Curriculum/sub/CompThinking.html (2011). Accessed December 2014
15. Kumar, G., Bhatia, P.: Comparative analysis of software engineering models from traditional to modern methodologies. In: 2014 Fourth International Conference on Advanced Computing Communication Technologies (ACCT), pp. 189–196, February 2014
16. Kurkovsky, S.: Engaging students through mobile game development. In: Proceedings of the 40th ACM Technical Symposium on Computer Science Education, SIGCSE 2009, pp. 44–48. ACM, New York (2009)
17. Morelli, R., de Lanerolle, T., Lake, P., Limardo, N., Tamotsu, E., Uche, C.: Can Android app inventor bring computational thinking to K-12? In: Proceedings of the 42nd ACM Technical Symposium on Computer Science Education, SIGCSE 2011. ACM (2011)
18. Moreno-Leon, J., Robles, G., Roman-Gonzalez, M.: Dr. Scratch: automatic analysis of scratch projects to assess and foster computational thinking. RED-Revista de Educacin a Distancia **46**, 1–23 (2015)
19. Seehorn, D., Carey, S., Fuschetto, B., Lee, I., Moix, D., O'Grady-Cunniff, D., Owens, B.B., Stephenson, C., Verno, A.: CSTA K-12 computer science standards. Technical report, New York, NY, USA (2011). Revised 2011
20. Sherman, M., Martin, F.: Teaching for understanding: how to engage students in learning. Educ. Leadersh. **51**(5), 11–13 (1994)
21. Sherman, M., Martin, F.: The assessment of mobile computational thinking. J. Comput. Sci. Coll. **30**(6), 53–59 (2015)
22. Sommerville, I.: Software Engineering, 5th edn. Addison Wesley Longman Publishing Co., Inc., Redwood City (1995)
23. Sung, K., Samuel, A.: Mobile application development classes for the mobile era. In: Proceedings of the 2014 Conference on Innovation & Technology in Computer Science Education, ITiCSE 2014, pp. 141–146. ACM, New York (2014)
24. United Nations High Commissioner for Human Rights: The right to water (2010). http://www.ohchr.org/Documents/Publications/FactSheet35en.pdf. Accessed 19 Jan 2016

25. Vinayakumar, R.: Learning computational thinking with scratch programming, June 2014. http://scratched.gse.harvard.edu/sites/default/files/
26. Werner, L., Denner, J., Campe, S., Kawamoto, D.C.: The fairy performance assessment: measuring computational thinking in middle school. In: Proceedings of the 43rd ACM Technical Symposium on Computer Science Education, SIGCSE 2012, pp. 215–220. ACM, New York (2012)
27. Wing, J.M.: Computational thinking. Commun. ACM **49**(3), 33–35 (2006)
28. Wohlin, C., Runeson, P., Höst, M., Ohlsson, M.C., Regnell, B., Wesslén, A.: Experimentation in Software Engineering: An Introduction. Kluwer Academic Publishers, Norwell (2000)
29. Wolber, D., Abelson, H., Friedman, M.: Democratizing computing with app inventor. GetMobile: Mob. Comput. Commun. **18**(4), 53–58 (2015)

Realistic Offloading Scheme for Mobile Cloud Computing

Hamid Jadad[(✉)], Abderezak Touzene, Nasser Alzeidi, Khaled Day,
and Bassel Arafeh

Department of Computer Science, Sultan Qaboos University, Muscat, Oman
hamidjadad@gmail.com,
{touzene,alzidi,kday,arafeh}@squ.edu.om

Abstract. Nowadays, smartphone devices have become very important in our daily life. We carry them everywhere and anytime. This strong dependency has encouraged mobile application developers to develop a wide variety of mobile applications. However, the limitations of smartphone hardware, such as limited processing capacity and limited battery life have become a barrier in front of apps developers. On the other hand, cloud computing is changing the style of delivering IT services. Mobile cloud computing uses the cloud to overcome the mobile device limitations. Many works have been conducted to extend mobile capabilities by offloading intensive application codes to the cloud. However, they did not consider realistic data that dynamically changing in user environment such as processors load, battery level, network bandwidth, etc. in offloading decision. Therefore, this paper aims to propose a new approach that uses realistic data from the user real environment to decide at runtime whether to offload code or not. Our experimental results show that our approach reduces the execution time and battery consumption compared to other approaches that do not take into consideration mobile device condition data.

Keywords: Mobile cloud computing · Offloading · Smartphones · Battery life saving

1 Introduction

The rapid increase in the usage of mobile devices can be shown by the total number of mobile subscriptions that reached 3.6 billion at the end of 2014. This means, between every 10 persons, around 5 persons have mobile subscriptions [1]. Nowadays, Smartphones have become more popular and close to everyone due to improved computing services and mobility. This popularity of smartphones has encouraged rapid demanding on mobile applications. For example, in July 2015, Google Play stored around 1.6 million mobile apps, while Apple Store apps reached 1.5 million [2]. These mobile apps vary between many categories such as entertainments, business, health care, and education. On the other hand, applications like multimedia processing, video gaming, speech recognition, and natural language processing that demand high level of computing power are restricted by the limitations of mobile processing power and battery life of the mobile devices.

© Springer International Publishing Switzerland 2016
M. Younas et al. (Eds.): MobiWIS 2016, LNCS 9847, pp. 81–92, 2016.
DOI: 10.1007/978-3-319-44215-0_7

Recently, cloud computing has changed the way of delivering computing services. Where cloud providers can offer Infrastructure, Platform, and Software as services to the end user at lower cost. Cloud characteristics such as flexibility, reliability, and cost effectiveness are the major benefits to move to the cloud. The recent research in the cloud computing issues and challenges are discussed in [3–5].

Mobile cloud computing is a new paradigm that appeared from merging cloud computing and mobility. It allows the mobile users to utilize the cloud services on demand. It is envisioned that this paradigm will help to overcome mobile devices hardware limitations. Many researches explored how to utilize the cloud power to improve mobile resources limitations [6]. In [7], the authors proposed a taxonomy of mobile cloud computing based on the key issues and how they have been tackled in research. One of the key issues is job offloading which consists of migration of jobs (data or code) that take place from the resource constrained mobile device to the cloud. Issues related to the transfer through wireless communication channel and the storage of the user jobs to the cloud opens new problems of privacy and security. Cryptography tools might be used to solve user job's confidentiality [8].

Code offloading and code partitioning are common solutions that are used to overcome mobile hardware limitations. Code partitioning is more popular in current mobile cloud applications (e.g. Google Translator, Gmail, and Voice). The application is partitioned at design phase where all or most of the computational operations are designed to run in the cloud side, while the mobile device runs as a thin-client that displays received data from the cloud [9]. This approach extends mobile capabilities, but cannot work without connection to the cloud. Therefore, many works have been done based on the code offloading approach [10–12] due to the capability of an application to either run locally on a mobile device if there is no connection or to offload some of its computationally expensive code to be executed outside the mobile device when a connection is available. It is argued that, it is not convenient to offload the entire application code because some parts of the code need local sensors (e.g. GPS, camera). Moreover, the offloading cost (e.g. battery consumption, delay time) may outweigh the offloading benefits. Thus, deciding which part of the code to offload, where, when, and how are important questions for the code offloading approach.

A mobile application code can be partitioned at different code levels (e.g. methods [10], classes [13], threads [14]) either manually by programmer [10] or automatically [12] to identify the most computation intensive tasks to be migrated at runtime. Profiling certain mobile contexts (e.g. connection bandwidth, input data size, execution time, workload, and CPU load) helps to make an optimal decision regarding task offloading. There are two techniques of profiling: static (mobile contexts are stored in local database to be used in future offloading decision making) and dynamic (mobile contexts are captured at runtime and forwarded to the decision engine to make decisions). The latter makes better decisions because the mobile contexts (e.g. network bandwidth) are changing over time. It is true that dynamic profiling could cause additional overhead on mobile devices [11]. However, the saving of battery and execution time expected from making better offloading decisions may outweigh the overhead cost.

In this paper we present the design of a mobile cloud computing architecture with mobile and cloud cost prediction models. We develop an algorithm to make better offloading decisions.

The rest of this paper is organized as follows: Sect. 2 presents the system architecture. We provide cost prediction models in Sect. 3. In Sect. 4, we present realistic decision algorithm. Section 5 provides the evaluation of the system, following by a discussion. In Sect. 6, we discuss related work. Finally, we give a conclusion and future work in Sect. 7.

2   System Design Architecture

In this section we present the design of our system as shown in Fig. 1. The system is divided into two sides: mobile side and cloud side. Each side has its components as described in the following.

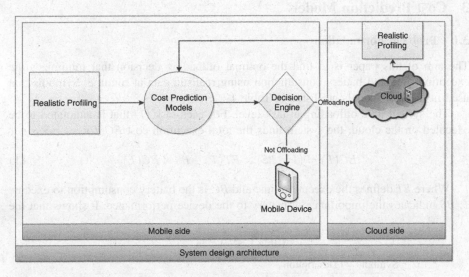

Fig. 1. System architecture

2.1   Mobile Side

- Realistic profiling: This profiler collects the realistic data of the mobile device at runtime. The gathered data is used as inputs of the cost prediction models. This profiler collects the mobile processor speed, and its utilization rate, mobile battery level, battery consumption per unit of time, task data size, task number of instructions, and wireless bandwidth.
- Cost prediction models: The realistic data that is collected by the realistic profiler is used here to calculate the total execution cost of a task on both the mobile device and on the cloud. Then, the costs are forwarded to the decision engine to make better decisions.

- Decision engine: this engine gets the costs from the cost prediction models and makes a decision to offload the execution of the task or not. The decision is made based on the minimum cost that will reduce the execution time and battery consumption.

2.2   Cloud Side

- Realistic profiler: This profiler gathers realistic data of the cloud. It collects cloud server processor speed and utilization rate and pushes them to the mobile device.

3   Cost Prediction Models

3.1   Problem Formulation

The aim of this paper is to find the optimal offloading decision that minimizes the execution time and battery consumption using realistic data at runtime. Symbols that used in the cost models are listed in Table 1.

The system uses offloading at task level. For each task (T) that is annotated to be executed on the cloud, the system finds the total execution cost $EC(T)$:

$$EC(T) = (1 - BS) \times ET(T) + BS \times BC(T) \tag{1}$$

Where ET defines the execution time and BC is the battery consumption to execute T. BS indicates the importance of battery to the device performance. It shows that the

Table 1. Notation.

Symbol	Description
Level	Battery level
BS	The importance of battery to the device performance
ET	Execution time of the task
BC	Battery consumption
W	Number of instruction of the task
CPI	Number of clocks per instructions
mCPU	Mobile CPU speed
mLoad	Mobile CPU load
BCU	A battery consumption amount per unit of time
Size	Size of task input data and operation code
Result size	Size of received data after processing in the cloud
cCPU	Cloud server CPU speed
cLoad	Cloud server load
uBW	Wireless upload bandwidth
dBW	Wireless download bandwidth

cost of battery consumption is very high when battery level is low. In [15, 16] authors proposed *BS* as a static value (0.5), which in reality should be dynamic to reflect the seriousness of how battery life affects the mobile performance. In our approach, we make *BS* dynamic which is more realistic to show the effect of the battery life on the mobile performance based on battery level. The following formula expresses how BS is obtained.

$$BS = \frac{100 - level}{100}. \tag{2}$$

3.2 Mobile Execution Cost Prediction

To find the mobile execution cost we consider multiple realistic data at runtime such as current CPU utilization, battery level and wireless traffic bandwidth. We consider that in a real mobile device, multiple processes run in the background. These processes consume device resources such as memory, CPU, and network bandwidth. Therefore, it is necessary to include them in the cost calculation to make better offloading decision.

From (1), the execution time of task $ET(T)$ in the mobile is defined as follows:

$$ET(T)_m = \frac{W(T) \times CPI}{mCPU \times (1 - mLoad)} \tag{3}$$

Where $W(T)$ defines the workload (number of instructions) of the task T. *CPI* defines the number of clocks per instruction. *mCPU* indicates the mobile CPU speed. The CPU utilization is shown in the *mLoad* parameter.

The prediction of the battery consumption on the mobile when the task T is executed locally is as follows:

$$BC(T)_m = B(T)_{proc} + B(T)_{Scr} \tag{4}$$

Where $B(T)_{proc}$ defines the battery consumed by the processor, and B_{Scr} the energy consumption by the mobile screen during the time of task T execution locally on the mobile. PowerTutor [17] shows that the $B(T)_{Scr}$ stays constant as the screen is ON. This means that $BC(T)_m$ depends mainly on the battery consumed by processing T. If we assume that *BCU* is a battery consumption amount per unit of time, then the battery consumption prediction will be the execution time multiplied by the battery consumption per unit of time:

$$BC(T)_m = BCU(ET(T)_m) \tag{5}$$

Therefore the total prediction cost of T on the mobile is defined as:

$$EC(T)_m = ET(T)_m + BCU(ET(T)_m). \tag{6}$$

3.3 Cloud Execution Cost Prediction

At the same time the system computes the execution cost of the task T if it is offloaded to the cloud. We start with the execution time prediction; that depends on:

$$ET(T)_c = t(T)_{tr} + t(T)_{pro} \tag{7}$$

Where $t(T)_{tr}$ indicates the transmission time of the task T and $t(T)_{pro}$ defines the processing time for T in the cloud.

$$t(T)_{tr} = \frac{Size(T)}{uBW} + \frac{Result\_size(T)}{dBW} \tag{8}$$

Where $Size(T)$ defines the task size that will be transferred including input data and task operation code. Also, $Result\_size(T)$ indicates the task result size after processing. uBW is the average uploading bandwidth, dBW defines average downloading bandwidth of wireless connection. The processing time of the task is shown as follows:

$$t(T)_{pro} = \frac{W(T) \times CPI}{cCPU \times cLoad} \tag{9}$$

Where $W(T)$ indicates the workload of the task as number of instructions, $cCPU$ defines the cloud server CPU speed, and $cLoad$ represents the usage percentage of the CPU of the cloud server. From 7, 8, and 9 the execution time of the task in the cloud will be as follows:

$$ET(T)_c = \frac{Size(T)}{uBW} + \frac{Result\_size(T)}{dBW} + \frac{W(T) \times CPI}{cCPU \times cload} \tag{10}$$

To predict the battery consumption of task T when offloading to the cloud, it depends on the battery consumed to transfer and receive T to and from the cloud, and the battery consumed by the device waiting the task T to be executed in the cloud. This is expressed as:

$$BC(T)_c = BC(T)_{tr} + BC(T)_{wait} \tag{11}$$

As we defined BCU to be the amount of battery consumption per unit of time, therefore, the battery consumed during transmitting and receiving T will be:

$$BC_{tr} = BCU(t_{tr}) \tag{12}$$

While the energy consumed during the waiting time of processing T remotely is defined as:

$$BC_{wait} = BCU(t_{pro}) \tag{13}$$

Thus, the total execution cost on cloud is defined as:

$$EC(T)_c = \left(\frac{Size(T)}{uBW} + \frac{Result_{size(T)}}{dBW} + \frac{W(T) \times CPI}{cCPU \times cload} \right) (BCU + 1). \qquad (14)$$

4 Realistic Decision Algorithm (RDA)

4.1 RDA Algorithm Description

RDA algorithm receives the task that is defined to be executed remotely with its data size and its number of instructions. Then, the algorithm checks the availability of wireless connection and the cloud server. If both are available, then a mobile cost prediction is calculated and a cloud cost prediction is calculated. The RDA algorithm compares both calculated costs and returns decision (OFFLOAD) if the cloud cost is lower than the mobile cost which means, the offloading is the best decision to this task because it will reduce the execution cost and battery consumption. Otherwise, the task will be executed locally in the mobile (NOTOFFLOAD).

Algorithm 1 Realistic Decision Algorithm RDA

1: **procedure** REALISTICDESCISION($T, Size, Inst$)
2:    **if** Wireless is Available AND Cloud is Available **then**
3:       $mEC \leftarrow MobileCostPrediction(T, Size, Inst)$
4:       $cEC \leftarrow CloudCostPrediction(T, Size, Inst)$
5:       **if** $cEC < mEC$ **then return** $OFFLOAD$
6:       **else return** $NOTOFFLOAD$
7:       **end if**
8:    **else return** $NOTOFFLOAD$
9:    **end if**
10: **end procedure**

4.2 RDA Algorithm Overhead

Dynamic offloading faces a challenge of a trade-off between profiling overhead on the mobile device and the accuracy of the offloading parameters to be taken into account for the offloading decision. RDA uses listeners that are registered with the system to track the device parameters such as battery level, connection level, and mobile CPU load only when it is needed and not periodically as in other algorithms. This will save energy cost on the mobile device.

5 Simulation Results

In this section, we implement the proposed algorithm and compare it with the a the most recently published algorithm [16] that we call it others algorithm. Note that we use the real value for most of the parameters in the simulation setup.

We use the following simulation parameters: There are 1000 tasks where, each task is assigned a random number of instructions between 1 and 10000. The battery level is

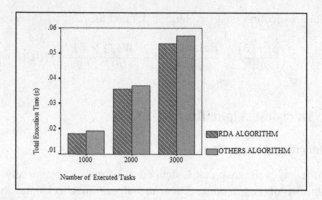

Fig. 2. Total execution time for workload under RDA and others algorithm

randomly chosen within range (5 % to 100 %) with assumption that applications cannot run when battery is less than 5 %. The size of data to be transferred to the cloud and data returned back are randomly selected from 1 KB to 2 MB. This range of data size represents virus scanning applications. For the WiFi connection, the average upload speed is randomly ranged from 2 Mbps to 5 Mbps, where, the average download speed is chosen randomly between 5 Mbps to 15 Mbps. Both mobile processor and cloud server processor loads are randomly selected for each task. The processor speed of mobile is 1 GHz and 3 GHz for cloud server virtual machine.

We evaluate the effectiveness of our algorithm by comparing it with others algorithm under four scenarios. In the first scenario we compare the total execution time and battery consumption of executing different number of tasks 1000, 2000, 3000 tasks under each algorithm.

Figure 2 shows the total execution time for different workloads 1000, 2000, and 3000 tasks in both algorithms RDA algorithm and others algorithm. We can notice that, the RDA algorithm gives better performance in all workloads compared to others algorithm. The improvement of performance is better for large number of tasks (3000).

Moreover, from Fig. 3 results, it is clear that, our algorithm RDA reduces the total of battery consumption at the different workloads. It saves around 5 % compared to others algorithm for the workload of 3000 tasks.

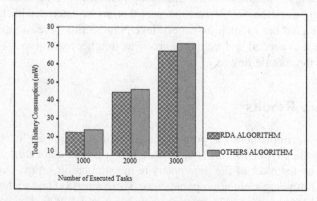

Fig. 3. Total battery consumption for different workloads under RDA and others algorithms

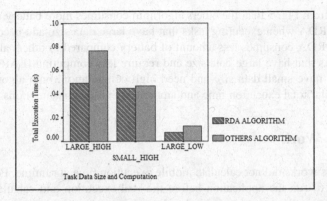

Fig. 4. Total execution time of different task data size and computation needs under RDA and others algorithm

We take a further step to investigate the efficiency of our approach. Where we compare our algorithm RDA and others algorithm for different type of tasks such as: data sizes and computation requirements. There are three scenarios here. The first one, when the size of task is large and it needs high computation (LARGE_HIGH), the second is (SMALL_HIGH) which defines the tasks of small data size and need high computation. In the third scenario (LARGE_LOW), tasks have large data size and require low computation.

The results of Fig. 4, show an improvement of the total execution time of RDA about 27 % compared to others algorithm for both cases where the tasks have large size which impact the network transfer (LARGE_HIGH, LARGE_LOW). This improvement is explained by taking the good decision of RDA based on the dynamic congestion level of the network. Where others algorithm is assuming no congestion at all. For tasks of small data size and require high computation (SMALL_HIGH), the RDA provides slight improvement in the execution time.

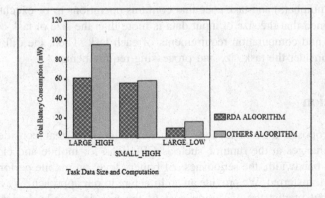

Fig. 5. Total battery consumption of different task data size and computation needs under RDA and others algorithm

It is clear from Fig. 5 that, the others algorithm consumes more battery (30 %) than our approach RDA when executing tasks that have large data size and need high computation. The RDA consumes less amount of battery compared to others algorithm for executing tasks that have large data size and require less computing (LARGE_LOW). For tasks that have small data size and need high computation, both algorithms have relatively similar total execution time and amount of energy consumptions.

6 Related Work

Many previous works did not calculate mobile execution time at runtime. For example, Zhou et al. [16] run the application before the real execution and calculate the execution time physically and store that in local database to be used in cost calculation at the next run time. Zhou et al. approach is similar to ThinkAir approach [10], they used last execution time in database to make the decision of offloading. In addition to that, Muai scheme [11] instrumented each method by running it on smartphone to measure method's duration time, and CPU cycles before the real execution. Estimating the mobile execution time of each task at runtime is crucial for optimal offloading solution. Because at real time, CPU utilization rate, Memory space, and battery level could be changed at every execution. The mobile could run other applications and the operating system that will affect definitely the task execution time at the mobile. This also could change the offloading decision. We used device profiler to collect CPU usage rate at runtime for both mobile and cloud server.

Zhou et al. [16] and Chen et al. [15] proposed the effect of how seriously can the battery life affect the mobile performance as a coefficient of a fixed value (0.5). We think that this coefficient should be dynamic to reflect the real cost of energy consumption. This coefficient could reflect the user preference of when to offload. For example, when user mobile battery level is full, the user preference for offloading maybe less, the cost of offloading could differ, while, when the battery level is low, the user would prefer the offloading if it will save energy. We used dynamic formula to represent the seriousness of the impact of battery level on the mobile performance.

Jade scheme [18] showed that a remote task divided into two parts, input data (e.g., images, texts, numbers) and task code that contains operations to be executed on input data. It mentioned that the size of input data is more than the size of task code. Due to different sizes and computation requirements of each task. Then, the offloading decision should consider the task size and processing requirements.

7 Conclusion

This paper proposed a realistic code offloading algorithm that considers the real environment changes at the runtime such as CPU load for mobile and cloud, battery level, network bandwidth, the seriousness of battery level on mobile performance, and data size to be transferred. We provide an architecture to our approach. We also provide cost models that predict the execution cost of the task in mobile device and in the cloud. Then these costs are forwarded to the decision engine where the algorithm makes the optimal offloading decision based on the minimum cost. We then design and implement our approach using simulation. We evaluate our algorithm RDA with others algorithm. The results showed that our approach provided minimum execution time and battery consumption compared to other algorithm. Where, it saved around 5 % of battery for workloads of 3000 tasks. That indicates the RDA algorithm can give better performance and save energy for those applications that large number of tasks. In addition of that, the RDA algorithm reduced the total execution time of tasks that have large data size and need high level of computation to 25 % compared to others algorithm. Not only that, the others algorithm consumes more battery (30 %) than our approach RDA when executing tasks that have large data size and need high computation.

As part of our future work, we plan to enhance our approach and doing more robust evaluation. Also we aim to include multiple wireless connections such as 4 G and Bluetooth and different cloud resources such as cloudlet, public cloud and mobile ad-hoc network. Another direction of our future work, is to implement the RDA algorithm in real mobile devices to determine its real effectiveness.

References

1. David, G., Jan, S., Mike, M., Pau, C.: The Mobile Economy 2015. GSMA Intelligence (2015). https://gsmaintelligence.com/research/2015/03/the-mobile-economy-2015/491/
2. Statista: Number of apps available in leading app stores as of July 2015 (2016)
3. Hashem, I.A.T., Yaqoob, I., Anuar, N.B., Mokhtar, S., Gani, A., Ullah Khan, S.: The rise of 'big data' on cloud computing: review and open research issues. Inf. Syst. **47**, 98–115 (2015)
4. Bera, S., Misra, S., Rodrigues, J.J.P.C.: Cloud computing applications for smart grid: a survey. IEEE Trans. Parallel Distrib. Syst. **26**(5), 1477–1494 (2015)
5. Rong, C., Nguyen, S.T., Jaatun, M.G.: Beyond lightning: a survey on security challenges in cloud computing. Comput. Electr. Eng. **39**(1), 47–54 (2013)
6. Lewis, G., Lago, P.: The journal of systems and software architectural tactics for cyber-foraging: results of a systematic literature review. J. Syst. Softw. **107**, 158–186 (2015)
7. Fernando, N., Loke, S.W., Rahayu, W.: Mobile cloud computing: a survey. Future Gener. Comput. Syst. **29**(1), 84–106 (2013)
8. Ustimenko, V., Touzene, A.: CRYPTALL: system to encrypt all types of data. Not. Kiev-Mohyla Acad. **23**, 12–15 (2004)
9. Flores, H., Srirama, S.N., Buyya, R.: Computational offloading or data binding? Bridging the cloud infrastructure to the proximity of the mobile user. In: Proceedings - 2nd IEEE International Conference on Mobile Cloud Computing, Services, and Engineering MobileCloud 2014, pp. 10–18 (2014)
10. Kosta, S., Aucinas, A., Hui, P., Mortier, R., Zhang, X.: ThinkAir: dynamic resource allocation and parallel execution in the cloud for mobile code offloading. In: Proceedings - IEEE INFOCOM, pp. 945–953 (2012)
11. Cuervo, E., Balasubramanian, A., Cho, D., Wolman, A., Saroiu, S., Chandra, R., Bahl, P.: MAUI: making smartphones last longer with code offload. In: MobiSys 2010, pp. 49–62 (2010)

12. Chun, B., Ihm, S., Maniatis, P.: Clonecloud: elastic execution between mobile device and cloud. In: EuroSys 2011, pp. 301–314 (2011)
13. Abebe, E., Ryan, C.: Adaptive application offloading using distributed abstract class graphs in mobile environments. J. Syst. Softw. **85**(12), 2755–2769 (2012)
14. Shivarudrappa, D., Chen, M., Bharadwaj, S.: COFA: Automatic and Dynamic Code Offload for Android. Bitbucket.Org (2011)
15. Chen, S., Wang, Y., Pedram, M.: A semi-Markovian decision process based control method for offloading tasks from mobile devices to the cloud. In: GLOBECOM - IEEE Globe Telecommunication Conference, pp. 2885–2890 (2013)
16. Zhou, B., Dastjerdi, A.V., Calheiros, R.N., Srirama, S.N., Buyya, R.: A context sensitive offloading scheme for mobile cloud computing service. In: 2015 IEEE 8th International Conference Cloud Computing, pp. 869–876 (2015)
17. Zhang, L., Dick, R.P., Mao, Z.M., Wang, Z., Arbor, A.: Accurate online power estimation and automatic battery behavior based power model generation for smartphones. In: Proceedings of Eighth IEEE/ACM/IFIP International Conference on Hardware/Software Codesign and System Synthesis, pp. 105–114 (2010)
18. Qian, H., Andresen, D.: Extending mobile device's battery life by offloading computation to cloud. In: Proceedings of Second ACM International Conference on Mobile Software Engineering Systems, pp. 150–151 (2015)

Model Driven Development Approaches for Mobile Applications: A Survey

Eric Umuhoza[✉] and Marco Brambilla[✉]

Dipartimento di Elettronica, Informazione e Bioingegneria, Politecnico di Milano,
Piazza L. Da Vinci 32, 20133 Milan, Italy
{eric.umuhoza,marco.brambilla}@polimi.it

Abstract. The usage and development of mobile applications (referred to as apps) are experiencing exponential growth. Moreover, the vastness and diversity of mobile devices and operating systems oblige the software companies, that want to reach a wide audience, to develop and deploy the same app several times, once for each targeted platforms. Furthermore, the dilemma between browser-based and native user interfaces remains relevant and challenges the capacity of organizations to meet the increasing demand for mobile apps. The adoption of model driven development (MDD) can simplify the development of mobile apps, reducing significantly technical complexity and development costs. Several researches have applied MDD techniques to address these challenges. In this paper, we define a set of criteria to assess the current model driven approaches to mobile apps development. We classify those approaches according the defined classification schema and present the current trends and challenges in this field. The survey shows a preference of code generation over model interpretation and of native apps over cross-platform ones.

1 Introduction

Nowadays, mobile devices are becoming the most common computing device. A vast array of features has been incorporated into those devices to address the different demands of users spanning from games to serious business. Mobile application usage and development is experiencing exponential growth. According to Gartner, by 2016 more than 300 billion applications will be downloaded annually. The number of apps that are available in the online markets has reached unseen numbers. In fact, by July 2015, the Google Play store counted 1.6 million of available apps while Apple's App Store counted 1.5 million [3]. In parallel with these numbers, the market also expects an increase in the number of global smart-phones users, which is expected to surpass 2 billion by 2016 [1] in comparison with 1.4 billion users estimated in 2013 [3]. From those statistics we can expect a healthy market of mobile apps that would be powered by a steady increase in the number of mobile device users, which as of today have, on average, 41 apps installed on their devices [2]. Furthermore, the motivation of the software development companies to continue producing more and better apps is supported by recent industry figures, according to which global mobile app

© Springer International Publishing Switzerland 2016
M. Younas et al. (Eds.): MobiWIS 2016, LNCS 9847, pp. 93–107, 2016.
DOI: 10.1007/978-3-319-44215-0_8

revenues are projected to surpass 76.52 billion US dollars in 2017. ABI research forecasts in 2018, app revenues will be worth 92 billion US dollars [25].

The mobile domain presents new challenges to software engineering. It is experiencing an intense competition among software and hardware providers who are continuously introducing innovative operating systems and increasingly powerful mobile devices into the market. Thus, in addition to an increasing request of mobile apps, developers must provide applications that work on all platforms, at least on the most popular ones (Android, iOS, and Windows Phone). Moreover, the dilemma between browser-based and native interfaces remains relevant and challenges the capacity of organizations to meet the demand for mobile apps.

So far, several authors have applied model driven techniques to the development of various aspects of mobile application. Model driven development (MDD) is a development paradigm that uses models as the primary artifact of the development process, with the aim of supporting as many phases as possible, covering also *executability*, i.e., the possibility of getting executable applications out of modeling efforts. Usually, in MDD the implementation is (semi) automatically generated from the models which allows for gains in productivity and quality of the software to be built [7]. This survey overviews the main state-of-the art model driven approaches to the development of mobile applications that support executability, and classifies them based on:

(i) *The phases of development process covered*: Requirements analysis, design, implementation, and testing;
(ii) *The aspects of mobile application covered*: App data, user interaction, user interface, and business logic;
(iii) *Model driven techniques applied*: Type of modeling language, model transformations, code generation or model interpretation;
(iv) *Mobile application developed*: Native, hybrid, or mobile web;
(v) *Supported mobile platforms*: Android, iOS, or Windows Phone.

The rest of the paper is structured as follows. Related work is studied in Sect. 2. Section 3 describes the classification criteria. Section 4 introduces the surveyed approaches and classifies them according to our classification schema. In Sect. 5 we present our analysis of the trends and evolutions. And Sect. 6 concludes.

2 Related Work

This research is the first one that attempts to assess various model-driven approaches to the development of mobile applications with aim of providing their classification and identifying current challenges and trends. In this work we surveyed only the approaches that apply model driven techniques to the development of mobile applications, covering the phases of development down to model execution either in terms of code generation or model interpretation. Thus, this section assesses the existing works that apply the model driven techniques to other concerns of mobile applications or that are not focusing their attention to executability.

Those works can be divided into two different clusters. On one hand we encounter a corpus of researches that apply model driven techniques to specify application interfaces and user interaction (in a broad sense) for multi-device UI modeling. Among them we can cite: TERESA (Transformation Environment for inteRactivE Systems representations) [6], based on a so-called *One Model, Many Interfaces* approach to support model based GUI development for multiple devices from the same ConcurTaskTree (CTT) model; MARIA [24], another approach based on CTT; UsiXML (USer Interface eXtended Markup Language) [33]; IFML (Interaction Flow Modeling Language) [8], a platform independent modeling language designed to express the content, user interaction, and control behavior of the front-end of software applications; and Unified Communication Platform (UCP).

On the other hand we find a collection of works that propose model driven solutions to address non functional requirements of mobile apps. In this cluster we encounter works that apply model driven techniques to automate mobile applications testing. Namely, MobiGUITAR (Mobile GUI Testing Framework) [5] is a model driven testing framework which uses the state machines to test Android apps. Also Ridene et al. [26] proposed MATeL (Mobile Applications Testing Language), a DSL allowing the modeling of test scenarios. Other researches apply model-driven approaches to address the issues of power consumption [22,29]. Thompson et al. [30] developed a model driven tool, SPOT (System Power Optimization Tool), which automates power consumption emulation code generation.

Few research works that use model driven approaches only for the purpose of modeling mobile apps can be found. Mobile IFML [9] is a PIM designed for expressing the content, user interaction, and control behavior of the front-end of mobile apps. Recently, a variant of Mobile IFML has been applied in the tool WebRatio Mobile Platform to model the user interactions of cross-platform mobile apps [4,31].

Currently, the hot debate in the research and the development community in general is whether to go down the native app route (developing mobile apps for a specific operating system) or cross-platform (developing apps that work across multiple platforms). Several works conducted research studies to compare the different development platforms using metrics such as complexity and user experience. For instance, Mesfin et al. [23] conducted a comparative evaluation of usability of cross-platform apps on the deployment platforms. They observed that the usability of crossword puzzle app developed with PhoneGap (for Android, Windows Phone, and BlackBerry) was unaffected when deployed on the respective native platforms. The research performed by Tor-Morten et al. [16] reviewed the mobile app development challenges and compared the issues and limitations of mobile platforms. Heitkötter et al. [17] evaluated the cross-platform development approaches for mobile apps. However, all these studies are comparing the different development platforms (native and cross-platform) at the programming level. This paper complements this discussion by offering a classification of model-based approaches for both native and web-based mobile applications development.

3   Dimensions of Analysis

In this section, we define a list of criteria for evaluating model-driven approaches to the development of mobile applications. This set of criteria will guide our discussion of the surveyed approaches in the next sections. For a better understanding, the list of criteria has been structured into perspectives: development process, aspects covered, techniques, and generated apps.

3.1   Development Process Phases

The development process dimension considers the main phases of the development process of the app: requirements analysis, design, implementation, and testing. The aim is to check which phases of the process are directly covered by each analyzed approach.

- **Requirements analysis.** This criterion examines whether the approach in question covers the requirements analysis phase.
- **Design.** This criterion examines whether the approach in question covers the application design phase.
- **Implementation.** This criterion examines whether the approach in question addresses the coding phase.
- **Testing.** This criterion examines whether the approach in question covers the testing phase.

3.2   Covered Mobile App Aspects

Aspects covered perspective sums up criteria relating to the layer of the app covered by the MDD approaches.

- **Content.** This criterion examines whether the approach in question covers the aspects related to the logical structure and operation to the data managed by the application.
- **Business logic.** This criterion examines whether the approach in question covers the aspects related to the internal behavior of the application.
- **User interaction.** This criterion examines whether the approach in question addresses the aspects related to the interactions between user and the application.
- **GUI.** This criterion examines whether the approach in question covers the graphical user interface of the application.

3.3   Model-Driven Development Techniques Applied

This dimension regroups the criteria related to the model-driven techniques used, e.g. visual modeling, code generation, or model-to-model transformations.

- **Modeling language.** This criterion assesses how the applications are modeled in the approach under exam. It indicates whether the approach uses a graphical and/or textual concrete syntax.

– **Multilevel code generation.** This criterion examines whether the approach in question uses intermediate models (e.g. platform independent model which maps to different platform specific models from which the code is generated) to describe the app requirements or produces the finally code directly from the initial models (e.g. final code generated from a platform independent model). This implies the use of model-to-model (M2M) transformations too.
– **Executability.** This criterion examines how the approaches addresses executability, i.e., it determines whether the approach relies on code generation or on model interpretation to execute the running apps. Notice that our analysis only focus on approaches that cover executability in some way.

3.4   Generated Apps Perspective

The generated apps dimension examines whether the approach generates native, hybrid (aka., cross-platform), or web apps. Native apps consist of applications developed for a specific target platform, using a programming language or framework provided by the platform itself (e.g., Objective C, or Java), and compiled as an executable software for that platform. Hybrid or cross-platform apps are designed and developed once and executed on multiple platforms, typically thanks to HTML-based code, that is wrapped inside some kind of Web browsing technology and delivered as executable applications. Finally, by web apps we mean actual web sites, developed on purpose to be consumed mainly from a mobile device (mobile-first development).

4   Overview of MDD Approaches

In this section we introduce the surveyed approaches based on the classification schema defined in Sect. 3. Those approaches are grouped into: researches approaches and commercial solutions.

4.1   Research Approaches

MD2. MD^2 [18] is a model-driven framework for cross-platform development of data-driven mobile apps. In MD^2, the application is firstly described in a platform independent model through a textual DSL. Then, a code generator (one for each platform of interest) transforms the PIM into source code, the business logic of the app along with necessary files to implement the the GUI, for the corresponding platform. The MD^2 framework provides in addition a code generator which creates a server back-end based on the data model of the application.

MobML. MobML is a collaborative framework for the design and development of data-intensive mobile apps [15]. The framework is composed of three components: modeling languages, synthesizers (code generators) and a collaboration tool. It offers four platform independent modeling languages each of which addressing a different concern of mobile application: (i) *Navigation*, which describes a mobile app as a collection of views and a set of navigation flows; (ii) *UI*, which describes the graphical interface of the app as a collection of graphic elements, which some extensions to represent the components of a particular target platform; (iii) *Content*, which models the data managed by the app; and (iv) *Business logic*, allowing the modeling of the internal operations of the app, and the interactions that occurs between the user and the app. A synthesizer receives as input the four different models of a mobile app and produces the source code for the targeted platform.

MobIle MultImodality Creator (MIMIC). MobIle MultImodality Creator (MIMIC) [13] is a model driven framework that enables the modeling and automatic code generation of multimodal mobile applications. MIMIC relies on the Mobile MultiModality Modeling Language (M4L), a language based on use of state machines to model input and output multimodal mobile interfaces. The M4L and its graphical editor have been specified through Obeo Designer[1]. The mobile interaction modalities supported by the framework include the tactile, speech, and proximity. The framework generates multimodal interfaces for Android, iPhone and Web.

Applause. Applause[2] is a toolkit for creating cross-platform mobile apps. It consists of a DSL to describe mobile apps and a set of code generators that use these models to generate native apps for iOS, Android, Windows Phone and Google App Engine. *Applause2*, the second version of the framework, is expected to cover all the aspects of a mobile app.

JUSE4Android. JUSE4Android [11] is a model driven tool that allows the automatic generation of business information systems (BIS) for Android. The apps are specified through annotated UML class diagrams from which the running code is generated.

Francese et al. Francese et al. [14] prose a model-driven approach for the development of multi-platform mobile apps based on finite-state machine. The proposed development environment provides a finite-state machine editor (an Eclipse plug-in) and a generator, which produces source code starting from the model (Data flow, control flow, and user interaction) of the mobile app. The business logic of the application is written in JS. The editor allows developers to call device native features accessed through PhoneGap.

MAG: Mobile Apps Generator. MAG is a model driven development approach to generate mobile apps for multiple platforms. The MAG approach is based on UML. The application requirements are modeled through use case diagrams, UML class diagrams are used to model the structure of the app while

---

[1] www.obeodesigner.com/.
[2] https://github.com/applause/applause.

UML state machine diagrams are used for behavioral modeling. The mobile domain specific concepts are included in the application models thanks to the mobile UML profile [32]. MAG allows the developer to automatically generate the business logic code of the app from those models while the GUI of the app is developed separately.

Vaupel et al. Vaupel et al. [34] propose a modeling language and an infrastructure for model-driven development of mobile business apps that support the configuration of user roles variants. Following this approach, different user roles are not combined in one app but lead to several app variants that may be configured after code generation. An app model consists of a data model defining the underlying class structure, a GUI model containing the definition of pages and style settings for the graphical user interface, and a process model which defines the behavior facilities of an app in form of processes and tasks.

Chi-Kien Diep et al. Chi-Kien Diep et al. [12] propose an online model-driven IDE which provides developers with a platform-independent GUI design for mobile apps. This approach consists on visually designing the GUI of the application once, as an abstract model, and transforming it several times targeting different specific platforms.

Mobl. Mobl [19] is a DSL based on standard web technologies for the development of mobile web applications. It integrates languages for user interface design, styling, data modeling, querying and application logic into a single, unified language.

Rule-Based Generation of Mobile User Interfaces (RUMO). RUMO [27] is a model driven development framework for multi platform user interface generation. The UI development in RUMO starts with the creation of a platform independent model which describes the basic structure of the user interface. Then, a set of rules has to be defined through a rule DSL in order to introduce application specific constraints such as usability or guidelines to guard the generation of the targeted user interfaces. Once the rules have been successfully checked, the PIM is finally transformed into target specific user interface (UI for Android, iPhone or for Win Phone). The platform specific ui generation involves the template mechanism which uses the predefined templates. Each template file is responsible of creating the source code for the desired platform. Furthermore, RUMO allows the creation of different versions of the template files as to address the issue of different versions of the same platform.

WL++. WL++ is a model driven code-generation framework for developing multi-platform mobile apps as clients to existing RESTful back-ends [28]. WL++ framework is based on IBM Workinglight platform, Backbone[3], and the WL++ app modeling plugin. WL++ inputs the specification of an existing back-end

---

[3] http://backbonejs.org.

service in the form of the APIs it exposes or the schema of the resource it serves, and infers the data model of the application. Then the developer enriches that application model by adding the proper views and the navigations among them. The source files are finally generated from those models through a set of pre-defined templates.

AXIOM. AXIOM [20] is a model-driven approach for the development of cross platform mobile apps. It uses Abstract Model Tree (AMT), a consistent model representation, as the basis for model transformations and code generation. In AXIOM, the requirements of the application are are firstly described in platform independent intent models (interaction and domain perspective) using AXIOM's DSL. Those intent models are then enriched with structural decisions and refined with platform-specific elements during a multi-phase transformation process to produce the source code for native apps: from requirements models to platform independent model (PIM), from PIM to platform specific models (PSMs), and finally from PSMs to running code.

4.2   Commercial Solutions

Mendix App Platform. The Mendix[4] App Platform enables business users and developers to build and deploy multi-channel apps with a MDD platform. The core library is offered as a set of standard services in the platform while specific libraries required for an optimal UI and user experience are built once and then offered as reusable widgets. In Mendix App Platform, the apps are built by defining visual models for the various app components such as the domain model, user interactions and business logic. Those models are then executed in a runtime environment. In addition, the platform provides core capabilities for non-functional application requirements, such as performance, scalability and security. Mendix combines model-driven development, the support of native device functions with the integration of Adobe PhoneGap to generate cross platform, hybrid apps.

IBM Rational Rhapsody. IBM Rational Rhapsody[5] integrates with Rational Team Concert to offer modeling capabilities for Android applications and the visual representation of the Android framework API that developers can reference from within Rational Rhapsody. The references are then generated into Java code to automate the manual coding task. Additionally, Rational Rhapsody can read the AndroidManifest.xml file to visualize activities, services, broadcast receivers, main activity and content provides specified for better understanding of the application. The Rational Rhapsody Debugger also enables runtime animation of the class diagrams created for an Android app.

---

[4] www.mendix.com.
[5] http://www.ibm.com/developerworks/.

WebRatio Mobile Platform. WebRatio Mobile Platform[6] is a model-driven development tool for the development of mobile applications [9]. The tool is based on the mobile-extended version of IFML standard [4]. WebRatio Mobile provides three integrated environment: (i) the modeling environment allowing the specification of user interactions through IFML diagrams and application content model through UML or ER diagrams; (ii) the development environment for supporting the implementation of custom components; and (iii) the layout template and style design environment, which allows the customization of UI through HTML 5, CSS and JavaScript. The code generated by the tool consists of ready-to-deploy cross-platform mobile apps, based on the PhoneGap.

Appian Mobile. Appian Mobile[7] is part of the integrated Appian BPM Suite designed for mobile applications following the *write-once, deploy anywhere* architecture. In Appian Mobile, application designers can simply drag-and-drop to design mobile process patterns in Appians Process Modeler. Using a graphical Business Process Modeling Notation (BPMN) modeler, even business users can model and orchestrate processes, define and update rules, create forms and enable them to render natively in mobile apps. The *User Experience* is powered by Appian Self-Assembling Interface Layer (SAIL) which allows designers to create a single user dynamic interface definition, then deploy to native mobile client applications on major device platforms and across major web browsers.

4.3 Classification

Table 1 summarizes the classification of the the surveyed approaches according to the classification schema defined in Sect. 3.

5 Trends and Outlook

Starting from the analysis we performed, this section identifies the current trends and suggests an outlook on the future of the Mobile MDD field.

5.1 Multilevel Code Generation Approaches

The surveyed approaches can be grouped into two clusters depending on whether they apply intermediate modeling (and thus model-to-model transformations) or not. When following multilevel code generation, the app is firstly specified in a platform independent manner, then the PIM is transformed into different PSMs, one for each platform of interest, from which the running code is generated. Only two approaches adopt this strategy: AXIOM (see Sect. 4.1) and the approach proposed by Chi-Kien Diep et al. (see Sect. 4.1). Therefore, despite the complexity of the mobile context and the number of possible target platforms, most of the approaches do not consider efficient to have some intermediate platform-specific models, which are in some sense seen as an excessive burden.

---

[6] www.webratio.com.
[7] www.appian.com.

Table 1. Model-driven approaches to the development of mobile applications and classification of their main characteristics.

Approach	Requirements	Design	Implementation	Testing	Content	Business logic	User interaction	GUI	Graphical lang. notation	Textual lang. notation	Multilevel code gen.	Code generation	Model execution	Native	Hybrid	Mobile Web	Android	iOS	Windows Phone	Black Berry	Web
Research Approaches																					
MD²		✓	✓	✓	✓	✓	✓	✓			✓		✓		✓			✓	✓		
MobML		✓	✓	✓	✓	✓	✓	✓			✓		✓		✓			✓	✓		
MIMIC		✓	✓				✓	✓	✓				✓		✓			✓	✓		✓
Applause		✓	✓			✓	✓	✓	✓				✓		✓			✓	✓	✓	✓	✓
JUSE4Android		✓	✓			✓	✓	✓	✓	✓	✓		✓		✓			✓			
Francese et al.		✓	✓				✓	✓	✓	✓			✓			✓		✓	✓		
MAG	✓	✓	✓				✓					✓			✓			✓		✓	
Vaupel et al.		✓	✓			✓	✓	✓	✓				✓		✓			✓	✓		
Chi-Kien Diep et al.		✓	✓				✓	✓	✓		✓	✓	✓		✓			✓	✓	✓	
Mobl		✓	✓			✓	✓	✓	✓				✓		✓			✓	✓		
RUMO	✓	✓	✓				✓	✓	✓	✓			✓		✓			✓	✓		
WL++		✓	✓			✓	✓	✓	✓	✓	✓		✓		✓			✓	✓		
AXIOM	✓	✓	✓	✓		✓	✓	✓	✓	✓	✓	✓	✓		✓			✓	✓		
Commercial Solutions																					
Mendix App Platform	✓	✓	✓			✓	✓	✓	✓	✓				✓		✓	✓	✓	✓	✓		✓
IBM Rational Rhapsody	✓	✓	✓	✓		✓	✓	✓	✓	✓	✓		✓		✓			✓			
WebRatio Mobile Platform		✓	✓			✓	✓	✓	✓	✓			✓			✓	✓	✓	✓			✓
Appian	✓	✓	✓			✓	✓	✓	✓	✓			✓			✓	✓	✓	✓		✓	✓

[a]The *Platforms* column reports the platforms actually supported by the approach, but in some cases those are only a subset selected to describe the approach.

5.2 Single Level Code Generation Approaches

This category groups the approaches which skip one or more levels of the model driven architecture. *Rhapsody* and *JUSE4Android* approaches specify directly the app in a platform specific models (PSMs) from which the android code is generated (PSM-to-Java Code). This is common when targeting a single platform since in that case there is no global model that can be reused across the target platforms. The remaining approaches like (MD², MobML, MIMIC, WebRatio, and Mobl) directly generate the code from the platform independent models PIMs skipping the PSM level. This is either obtained through actually generating cross-platform (hybrid) code, or through multiple generators of native code.

5.3 Development Process

All surveyed approaches apply MDD to Design and Implementation phases. Only 23 % of the approaches covers the testing phase, and only 35 % covers the requirements phase. However, it is interesting to note that 3 out of 4 analyzed commercial platforms cover requirements. This means that this is deemed a very important phase for production. Overall, only 11 % apply MDD to all phases of the development process.

5.4 Mobile App Aspects

Some approaches cover only few aspects of mobile applications. User interactions and GUI are the most covered aspects (94 %) while only 70 % of surveyed approaches address content and business logic aspects. This is explained by the fact that the most crucial points of mobile apps are related to user interaction. Therefore, the approaches specifically target these aspects with custom modeling solutions. Viceversa, more consolidated aspects like content and business logic can be covered with traditional modeling languages and approaches (E.g., UML, BPM and so on).

5.5 Executability

Model driven development approaches are commonly used to generate the final code either for a single concern or for all aspects of a mobile application. In fact, 94 % of surveyed approaches apply *code generation*: the running code is generated from the high level models, while only the 6 % relies on *model interpretation*. When following model interpretation, a generic engine is implemented and the model is interpreted by that engine, thus, model interpretation does not requires to generate the code to create a working application from a model. The code generation is preferred to model execution mainly for the following reasons:

(i) Code generation is easier to start with and allows reusing existing programming artifacts. The developers can start using code generation by turning existing code into templates and replacing parts of the code with tokens which will be replaced by model information;
(ii) The generated implementation is easier to understand. The generated code is produced in a standard programming language that any developer can understand, while for model interpretation one needs to understand the generic implementation of the interpreter and the semantics of the model;
(iii) A code generator is usually easier to maintain, debug, and track because it typically consists of rule-based transformations, while an interpreter has a generic and complex behavior to cover all the possible execution cases;
(iv) Code generation provides an additional check for errors since the generated code needs to be compiled.
(v) Generated apps are typically more easily accepted and integrated within an enterprise setting, because the generated code can be aligned with the company standards.

5.6   Native, Cross-Platform or Web Applications

Web apps are the less popular solution in MDD for mobile. Adoption of native and cross-platform apps is supported among others by the following advantages [10,21] with respect to mobile-accessible web applications:

(i) *Availability*. Users can easily find and download apps of their choice from the app stores and marketplaces;
(ii) *Offline*. With respect to web sites, apps have the ability to run offline;
(iii) *Safety and security*. Apps have to get the approval of the app store they are intended for.

More precisely, the model-driven community is focusing its attention on native apps development. In fact, 82 % of surveyed approaches target the development of native apps. The main reason of this is the perceived higher quality of the obtained applications, in terms of performance, usability, and capability of exploiting and integrating with the most advanced features of mobile devices.

This trend could be very interesting for the software development companies, especially to the SMEs. Indeed SMEs with limited resources, are currently obliged to go down the hybrid route, and thus, loosing some of the advantages of native apps in order to reach a large audience at a sustainable cost.[8] Adopting a MDD approach would allow these company to get the same benefit obtained through native development, but with the productivity of cross-platform development.

5.7   Cross Platform Development

When following MDD, with code generation, cross platform can be reached either by providing a code generator for each of targeted platforms or by generating the code required by the cross platform tool (like PhoneGap, Appcelerator Titanium, and Xamarin) to produce cross platform apps [31]. Basically, those code generators receive in input the same model describing the application and produce the code for the corresponding platforms. More than 88 % of surveyed approaches target the development of at least two platforms.

5.8   Lack of Standard Mobile Modeling Language

The modeling language is a fundamental building block of each model driven development approach. Almost each approach relies on its own DSL either defined from scratch [13] or from the existing standards [31,32]. However, no specific standard has been devised for the mobile domain. This means that the community looses all the advantages offered by the standards. This should be one direction to target in the near future.

---

[8] Gartner predicts that more than 50 % of mobile apps deployed by 2016 will be hybrid.

6   Conclusions

In this paper we presented the results of a survey on model-driven approaches to the development of mobile apps. We have classified those approaches based on the covered development phases, adopted MDD techniques, type of developed apps, and supported platforms. The current trends are in line with the ones of mobile apps, i.e., preference of native applications (more than 80 % of the cases), and prefer to apply code generation rather than model interpretation for the executability of apps.

References

1. eMarketer report, April 2016. http://www.emarketer.com/
2. Flurry, April 2015. http://www.flurry.com/
3. Statista, April 2015. http://www.statista.com/
4. Acerbis, R., Bongio, A., Brambilla, M., Butti, S.: Model-driven development of cross-platform mobile applications with web ratio and IFML. In: MOBILESoft 2015, pp. 170–171 (2015)
5. Amalfitano, D., Fasolino, A.R., Tramontana, P., Ta, B.D., Memon, A.M.: MobiGUITAR: automated model-based testing of mobile apps. IEEE Softw. **32**(5), 53–59 (2015)
6. Berti, S., Correani, F., Mori, G., Paternò, F., Santoro, C.: TERESA: a transformation-based environment for designing and developing multi-device interfaces. In: CHI Extended Abstracts, pp. 793–794 (2004)
7. Brambilla, M., Cabot, J., Wimmer, M.: Model-Driven Software Engineering in Practice. Synthesis Lectures on Software Engineering. Morgan & Claypool Publishers, San Rafael (2012)
8. Brambilla, M., Fraternali, P., et al.: The interaction flow modeling language (IFML), version 1.0. Technical report, Object Management Group (OMG) (2014). http://www.ifml.org
9. Brambilla, M., Mauri, A., Umuhoza, E.: Extending the interaction flow modeling language (IFML) for model driven development of mobile applications front end. In: Awan, I., Younas, M., Franch, X., Quer, C. (eds.) MobiWIS 2014. LNCS, vol. 8640, pp. 176–191. Springer, Heidelberg (2014)
10. Corral, L., Sillitti, A., Succi, G.: Defining relevant software quality characteristics from publishing policies of mobile app stores. In: Awan, I., Younas, M., Franch, X., Quer, C. (eds.) MobiWIS 2014. LNCS, vol. 8640, pp. 205–217. Springer, Heidelberg (2014)
11. da Silva, L.P., Brito e Abreu, F.: Model-driven gui generation and navigation for android BIS apps. In: MODELSWARD 2014, pp. 400–407, January 2014
12. Diep, C.-K., Tran, Q.-N., Tran, M.-T.: Online model-driven ide to design guis for cross-platform mobile applications. In: SoICT 2013, pp. 294–300 (2013)
13. Elouali, N., Le Pallec, X., Rouillard, J., Tarby, J.-C.: MoMM 2014, pp. 52–61 (2014)

14. Francese, R., Risi, M., Scanniello, G., Tortora, G.: Model-driven development for multi-platform mobile applications. In: Abrahamsson, P., Corral, L., Oivo, M., Russo, B. (eds.) PROFES 2015. LNCS, vol. 9459, pp. 61–67. Springer, Heidelberg (2015). doi:10.1007/978-3-319-26844-6_5

15. Franzago, M., Muccini, H., Malavolta, I.: MOBILESoft 2014, pp. 58–61 (2014)

16. Grønli, T.-M., Hansen, J., Ghinea, G., Younas, M.: Mobile application platform heterogeneity: Android vs Windows phone vs iOS vs Firefox OS. In: AINA, pp. 635–641 (2014)

17. Heitkötter, H., Hanschke, S., Majchrzak, T.A.: Evaluating cross-platform development approaches for mobile applications. In: Cordeiro, J., Krempels, K.-H. (eds.) WEBIST 2012. LNBIP, vol. 140, pp. 120–138. Springer, Heidelberg (2013)

18. Heitkötter, H., Majchrzak, T.A., Kuchen, H.: Cross-platform model-driven development of mobile applications with MD2. In: SAC 2013, pp. 526–533 (2013)

19. Hemel, Z., Visser, E.: Declaratively programming the mobile web with mobl. In: IOOPSLA 2011, pp. 695–712 (2011)

20. Jia, X., Jones, C.: AXIOM: a model-driven approach to cross-platform application development. In: ICSOFT 2012, pp. 24–33 (2012)

21. Jobe, W.: Native apps vs. mobile web apps. iJIM 7(4), 27–32 (2013)

22. Kelényi, I., Nurminen, J.K., Siekkinen, M., Lengyel, L.: Supporting energy-efficient mobile application development with model-driven code generation. In: Do, T., Thi, H.A.L., Nguyen, N.T. (eds.) Advanced Computational Methods for Knowledge Engineering. AISC, vol. 282, pp. 143–156. Springer, Heidelberg (2014)

23. Mesfin, G., Ghinea, G., Midekso, D., Grønli, T.-M.: Evaluating usability of cross-platform smartphone applications. In: Awan, I., Younas, M., Franch, X., Quer, C. (eds.) MobiWIS 2014. LNCS, vol. 8640, pp. 248–260. Springer, Heidelberg (2014)

24. Paternò, F., Santoro, C., Spano, L.D.: MARIA: a universal, declarative, multiple abstraction-level language for service-oriented applications in ubiquitous environments. ACM Trans. Comput.-Hum. Interact. 16(4), 19:1–19:30 (2009). doi:10.1145/1614390.1614394

25. ABI Research: ABI research (March 2013) application revenues coming from either smart phone or tablets, October 2013. http://mobithinking.com

26. Ridene, Y., Barbier, F.: A model-driven approach for automating mobile applications testing. In: ECSA 2011, pp. 9:1–9:7 (2011)

27. Schuler, A., Franz, B.: Rule-based generation of mobile user interfaces, pp. 267–272 (2013)

28. Stroulia, E., Bazelli, B., Ng, J.W., Ng, T.: WL++: code generation of multi-platform mobile clients to restful back-ends. In: MOBILESoft 2015, pp. 136–137 (2015)

29. Thompson, C., Schmidt, D.C., Turner, H.A., White, J.: Analyzing mobile application software power consumption via model-driven engineering. In: PECCS 2011, pp. 101–113 (2011)

30. Thompson, C., White, J., Dougherty, B., Schmidt, D.C.: Optimizing mobile application performance with model-driven engineering. In: Lee, S., Narasimhan, P. (eds.) SEUS 2009. LNCS, vol. 5860, pp. 36–46. Springer, Heidelberg (2009)

31. Umuhoza, E., Ed-douibi, H., Brambilla, M., Cabot, J., Bongio, A.: Automatic code generation for cross-platform, multi-device mobile apps: some reflections from an industrial experience. In: MobileDeLi 2015, pp. 37–44 (2015)

32. Usman, M., Iqbal, M.Z.Z., Khan, M.U.: A model-driven approach to generate mobile applications for multiple platforms. In: APSEC, pp. 111–118 (2014)

33. Vanderdonckt, J.: A MDA-compliant environment for developing user interfaces of information systems. In: Pastor, Ó., Falcão e Cunha, J. (eds.) CAiSE 2005. LNCS, vol. 3520, pp. 16–31. Springer, Heidelberg (2005)

34. Vaupel, S., Taentzer, G., Harries, J.P., Stroh, R., Gerlach, R., Guckert, M.: Model-driven development of mobile applications allowing role-driven variants. In: Dingel, J., Schulte, W., Ramos, I., Abrahão, S., Insfran, E. (eds.) MODELS 2014. LNCS, vol. 8767, pp. 1–17. Springer, Heidelberg (2014)

Fuzzy Ontology Based Model for Image Retrieval

Madiha Liaqat[1(✉)], Sharifullah Khan[1], and Muhammad Majid[2]

[1] School of Electrical Engineering and Computer Science,
National University of Sciences and Technology, Islamabad, Pakistan
{12phdmliaqat,sharifullah.khan}@seecs.nust.edu.pk
[2] Department of Computer Engineering,
University of Engineering and Technology, Taxila, Pakistan
m.majid@uettaxila.edu.pk

Abstract. Immense increase in digital images demands an efficient and accurate image retrieval system. In text based image retrieval, images are annotated with keywords based on human perception. On the other hand, keywords are included in a user query based on his/her requirements. Query keywords are matched with the annotated keywords for image retrieval. This process has been extended with ontology to resolve semantic heterogeneities. However, crisp annotation and querying processes could not produce the desired results because both involve human perception. To overcome this problem, we have proposed a fuzzy ontology based retrieval system that makes use of ontology for improving retrieval performance. For modeling the semantic description of image, it is divided into regions and regions are classified into concepts. The concepts are combined into categories. The concepts, categories and images are linked among themselves with fuzzy values in ontology. Retrieved results are ranked based on the relevancy between the keywords of a query and images. Experimental results show that the proposed system performs comparatively better than the existing systems in terms of retrieval performance.

Keywords: Image retrieval · Text based image retrieval · Fuzzy ontology

1 Introduction

Digital images are of great importance nowadays in every domain such as medical, education, astronomy, fashion and security [1, 2]. Everyday huge amount of images are generated by either military or civilian equipment that need to be organized for efficient and accurate retrieval [2]. Image retrieval is the science of finding images that fulfill a specified user need [3].

In text based image retrieval system [4], images are annotated with keywords based on human perception. On the other hand, keywords are included in a user query based on his/her requirements. Query keywords are matched with the annotated keywords for image retrieval [5]. The relationship between queries and images and the relevance of the retrieved images is considered as a foundation for image retrieval system. This process has been extended with ontology to resolve the problem of semantic heterogeneity. Ontology is a type of background knowledge. A complete description of

© Springer International Publishing Switzerland 2016
M. Younas et al. (Eds.): MobiWIS 2016, LNCS 9847, pp. 108–120, 2016.
DOI: 10.1007/978-3-319-44215-0_9

ontologies and their usefulness in image retrieval system have been mentioned in [6]. Ontological query language system: immense, has been proposed by Town et al. [7], for efficient image retrieval. Similarly ontology based systems such as OLYBIA and OntoPic have been proposed in [8, 9]. In the existing systems, the annotation of images with keywords is binary that is a keyword is either present or not in an image. However, annotation and the retrieval processes involve human perception that is mostly approximate or uncertain [10, 11]. We believe that the images cannot be precisely represented with keywords using binary model of annotation. Therefore existing systems could not produce the desired results. To overcome this problem fuzzy based retrieval systems are required as the relative importance of a particular keyword in annotation and retrieval process is different for different users and this information is essential for accurate satisfaction of a query.

In this paper we have proposed a fuzzy ontology-based model that makes use of ontology to improve the retrieval performance. Images are represented with concepts and a category. An image illustrates multiple concepts. A concept describes objects that the image contains. In order to annotate the image with all the possible concepts, it is divided into regions and regions are classified into concepts by adopting the technique proposed in [12]. The frequency of occurrence of the concepts inside an image determines the category. A category depicts a scene. This categorization allows for semantic comparisons of scenes and also helps in search space reduction while querying for specific concepts inside a category. Concepts, categories and images are linked among themselves with fuzzy values in the ontology. By adding a value for degree of membership to each concept and category, the retrieved images from ontology based search reflect the likely information need. For mapping the query terms and ontology concepts, fuzzy search mechanism is applied that search and rank the retrieved results based on the relevancy degree between the keywords of a query and images.

The remaining paper is organized as follows: Sect. 2 describes the related work. Section 3 describes the proposed methodology and image retrieval process. Section 4 contains the experimental results. The paper has been concluded in Sect. 5.

2 Related Work

Image retrieval systems are either content based or text based. In content based image retrieval systems (CBIR) low level features are extracted automatically and images are indexed by their visual content like color, shape, texture [1] but there is a gap between what image features, a system can recognize and what human perceives from the image. The focus of this research is on text based image retrieval systems so we will not discuss CBIR systems. Literature survey is categorized as: text based, ontology based and fuzzy ontology based retrieval systems.

2.1 Text Based Retrieval Systems

In text based image retrieval, images are annotated with text descriptors [4]. On the other hand, keywords are included in a user query based on his/her requirements.

Query keywords are matched with the annotated keywords for image retrieval [5]. Keyword and content based image retrieval has been proposed in [13]. The model is built for qualitative spatial relationships like before, after or more, less. In [14], text based image retrieval system has been combined with content based model for efficient search. First text based search was applied and then content based filtering was applied on the resulting set.

2.2   Ontology Based Retrieval Systems

Ontology is an explicit specification of the terms in a domain and the relations among them [5]. It defines a common vocabulary that can be shared among people and domain knowledge that can be reused [15]. In [16], author built and proved the ontologies in reducing the gap between low level features and high level semantics. Keyword and ontology based image retrieval has been compared by Wang et al. [17]. Result showed that ontology based system performed better as compared to keyword based system in terms of precision. A complete description of ontology's and their usefulness in image retrieval systems has been mentioned in [6]. In [12] a supervised learning system named OntoPic has been proposed that allows semantic searches. It has used DAML + OIL for domain knowledge but system performance was not mentioned. In [18], semantic based image retrieval system has been proposed. A domain specific, flower family, low level feature based ontology has been created. These low level features were set as a data property in OWL. Users can enter a text/image query. Features are extracted from a query image and matched with the ontology and matched images are retrieved and shown to the users. Semantic image representation model containing local and global categorization of scenes has been proposed in [19]. Ontology based image annotation (OLYBIA) system has been proposed in [8]. Low level features were extracted and were mapped to high level concepts through object ontology and inference rules. The experimental results have not been compared with any other model. In [20], content based image retrieval system has been proposed that has used ontology for object recognition. Retrieval algorithm has not been discussed and results were not compared with any other system. In [21], image annotation and retrieval through ontology has been discussed. Ontology was constructed for animal domain. Although the proposed work shows the benefits of using ontologies but the burden of manual annotation was still there.

2.3   Fuzzy Ontology Based Retrieval Systems

Document search using fuzzy set theory has been described in [22]. The proposed model considered the importance of text descriptors in search and the relevancy score between the query and the documents. Highly relevant documents were retrieved based on fuzzy set operations and shown to user. Information retrieval model based on ontology encoded with fuzzy relations has been proposed in [23]. When a user enters a query, composed of concepts, the system performs query expansion and may add new concepts based on the ontology knowledge. After expansion the similarity between the query and the documents is calculated by fuzzy operations. Author has compared his proposed model with Ogawa [24] and Horng [25] model. In Ogawa model, a keyword connection matrix has been proposed for computing the relevance of the document with the user keywords. Apart from it, users can enter compound queries containing operators: and, or, not. In Horng model, a multi-relationship fuzzy concepts network has been proposed that shows the fuzzy relations between the concepts and their relevance degree with the documents. Results show that the model proposed in [23] gives better retrieval accuracy as compared to Ogawa and Horng model. The above mentioned fuzzy based systems were tested for text documents retrieval.

3 Proposed Methodology

An overview of the proposed image retrieval system is shown in Fig. 1. Images are annotated with concepts and category by adopting the technique followed in [12]. Fuzzy knowledgebase and Fuzzy search are two main modules of the proposed system. An image with associated concepts and category are the inputs to the Fuzzy knowledgebase. To conceptually represent an image fuzzy ontology is constructed that utilizes the concepts and categories associated with the image. The fuzzy values in the ontology are then calculated by applying data mining approaches on the input images. For image retrieval, users are provided with an interface where they can input multiple keywords based on their requirements. Fuzzy search mechanism is applied and the retrieved images are ranked and shown to the user based on the relevancy degree between the image and keywords.

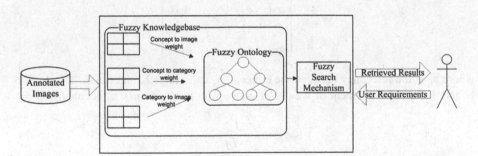

Fig. 1. The proposed image retrieval system

3.1 Fuzzy Ontology Construction

The fuzzy ontology is constructed based on the idea of [23] that was proposed for documents retrieval. The fuzzy ontology shows the relationship between the images and concepts, and concepts and categories and categories and images as a value between 0 and 1 (both 0 and 1 inclusive).

The steps followed for computing the fuzzy values in the ontology is as follows: Let I $\{I_1, I_2, I_3, \ldots, I_M\}$, A = $\{A_1, A_2, A_3, \ldots, A_N\}$ and B = $\{B_1, B_2, B_3, \ldots, B_O\}$ be a set of images, concepts and categories consisting of M, N and O number of elements respectively.

Let W_{CB} be the matrix representing binary weights of category to image and is written as:

$$W_{CB} = \begin{bmatrix} w_{11} & w_{12} & \cdots & w_{1M} \\ w_{21} & w_{22} & \cdots & w_{2M} \\ \vdots & \vdots & & \vdots \\ w_{O1} & w_{O2} & \cdots & w_{OM} \end{bmatrix}, \tag{1}$$

where $w_{kj} = 0$ or $w_{kj} = 1$, $1 \leq k \leq O$ and $1 \leq j \leq M$. Let W_{CI} be the matrix representing the frequency of concepts in images and is written as:

$$W_{CI} = \begin{bmatrix} f_{11} & f_{12} & \cdots & f_{1M} \\ f_{21} & f_{22} & \cdots & f_{2M} \\ \vdots & \vdots & & \vdots \\ f_{N1} & f_{N2} & \cdots & f_{NM} \end{bmatrix}, \tag{2}$$

where f_{ij} is the frequency of concept A_i in image I_j, and $1 \leq i \leq N$ and $1 \leq j \leq M$.

The image content is originally a crisp set as defined by W_{CB} and W_{CI} and is made fuzzy by proposed methodology. In our system, image content is represented by three matrices namely weight of the concept to image W_A, weight of the category to image W_B, and weight of the concept to category W_{CF} and are defined as:

$$W_A = \begin{bmatrix} a_{11} & a_{12} & \cdots & a_{1M} \\ a_{21} & a_{22} & \cdots & a_{2M} \\ \vdots & \vdots & & \vdots \\ a_{N1} & a_{N2} & \cdots & a_{NM} \end{bmatrix}, \tag{3}$$

where a_{ij} is the relevancy between the concept A_i and image I_j, and $0 \leq a_{ij} \leq 1$, $1 \leq i \leq N$ and $1 \leq j \leq M$. Element of weight of concept to image matrix a_{ij} is calculated as:

$$a_{IJ} = \frac{f_{IJ}}{T_J}, \tag{4}$$

where f_{ij} is the frequency of concept A_i in image I_j and T_j is the total number of concepts in image I_j. The weight of the concept to category is a matrix as shown below:

$$W_B = \begin{bmatrix} b_{11} & b_{12} & \cdots & b_{1O} \\ b_{21} & b_{22} & \cdots & b_{2O} \\ \vdots & \vdots & & \vdots \\ b_{N1} & b_{N2} & \cdots & b_{NO} \end{bmatrix}, \tag{5}$$

where b_{ik} is the relevancy between concept A_i and category B_k, and $0 \leq b_{ik} \leq 1$, $1 \leq i \leq N$ and $1 \leq k \leq O$. The proposed formula for calculating weight of the concept to category b_{ik} is as follows:

$$b_{ik} = \frac{\sum_{j=1}^{M} a_{ij} w_{kj}}{\sum_{j=1}^{M} w_{kj}}, \qquad (6)$$

The weight of the category to image is a matrix as shown below:

$$\mathbf{W}_{CF} = \begin{bmatrix} c_{11} & c_{12} & \cdots & c_{1M} \\ c_{21} & c_{22} & \cdots & c_{2M} \\ \vdots & \vdots & & \vdots \\ c_{O1} & c_{O2} & \cdots & c_{OM} \end{bmatrix}, \qquad (7)$$

where c_{kj} is the relevancy between category B_k and image I_j, and $0 \leq c_{kj} \leq 1$, $1 \leq k \leq O$ and $1 \leq j \leq M$. Element of weight of concept to image matrix $a_{i,j}$ is calculated as:

$$c_{kj} = \frac{\sum_{j=1}^{M} a_{ij} b_{ik}}{F_{ik}}, \qquad (8)$$

where F_{ik} is the number of concepts in a category.

3.2 Image Retrieval

A user query consists of keywords that can be concepts, categories or combination of concept and category. Table 1 shows the retrieval algorithm.

The detail of algorithm is illustrated below through example.

3.3 Walk-Through Example

Let I $\{I_1, I_2, I_3, I_4\}$, A = {Sky, Foliage, Grass, Water} and B = {Sky_Cloud, Field} be a set of images, concepts and categories. The matrix $\mathbf{W}_{CB}$ representing binary weights of a category to an image is defined as:

$$\mathbf{W}_{CB} = \begin{bmatrix} 1 & 0 & 1 & 0 \\ 0 & 1 & 0 & 1 \end{bmatrix}$$

The matrix $\mathbf{W}_{CI}$ representing the frequency of concepts in images is defined as:

$$\mathbf{W}_{CI} = \begin{bmatrix} 80 & 20 & 70 & 40 \\ 0 & 20 & 30 & 0 \\ 20 & 60 & 0 & 60 \\ 0 & 0 & 0 & 0 \end{bmatrix}$$

Table 1. Retrieval algorithm

Input: Single or combination of concepts, A_N,
    OR single or combination of categories, B_O,
    OR a combination of concepts and categories, $A_N B_O$, Retrieval size S,
    Database size Db
Output: A list of Ranked Images R
Basic Idea:
1. case 1: [query contains single or combination of concepts]
2.   [Use procedure 1.1 to retrieve images] Call RetrieveA(A_N, S, Db, R)
3. case 2: [query contains single or combination of categories]
4.   [Use procedure 1.2 to retrieve images] Call RetrieveB(B_O, S, Db, R)
5. case 3: [query contains combination of concepts categories]
6.   Split the query into two. Q1= A_N and Q2= B_O
7.   Call RetrieveA(A_N, S, Db, R), Call RetrieveB(B_O, S, Db, R)
8.   Take intersection of images returned by both the procedures and store it
        in R.
9. Show R to users.
10. Exit

Procedure 1.1: RetrieveA(A_N, S, Db, R)
1.   Repeat step 2 to 3 for k=1 to N [where N is the total number of concepts
        in Q]
2.   Repeat step 3 for p=1 to Db
3.   R2[A_k][p]= W_A[A_k][p]
4.   Rank each row of R2 in descending order. Take intersection of rows of
        R2 and store the result of intersection in R. Return R based on S.

Procedure 1.2: Call RetrieveB(B_O, S, Db, R)
1.   Repeat step 2 to 3 for k=1 to N [where N is the total number of
        categories in Q]
2.   Repeat step 3 for p=1 to Db
3.   R2[B_k][p]= W_{CF}[B_k][p]
4.   Rank each row of R2 in descending order. Take intersection of rows of
        R2 and store the result of intersection in R. Return R based on retrieval
        size.

The fuzzy weights in matrices W_A, W_B, and W_{CF} are computed according to the proposed formulas (4), (6) and (8) and are as follows:

$$W_A = \begin{bmatrix} 0.8 & 0.2 & 0.7 & 0.4 \\ 0 & 0.2 & 0.3 & 0 \\ 0.2 & 0.6 & 0 & 0.6 \\ 0 & 0 & 0 & 0 \end{bmatrix} \quad W_B = \begin{bmatrix} 0.75 & 0.3 \\ 0.15 & 0.1 \\ 0.1 & 0.6 \\ 0 & 0 \end{bmatrix}$$

$$W_{CF} = \begin{bmatrix} 0.31 & 0.08 & 0.285 & 0.18 \\ 0.18 & 0.15 & 0.12 & 0.24 \end{bmatrix}$$

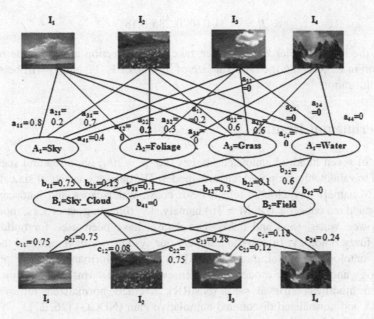

Fig. 2. Fuzzy ontology

Fuzzy ontology constructed according to the above computed weights is shown in Fig. 2.

The next step is to take user requirements and retrieval size and apply retrieval algorithm to get the list of retrieved images. If query contains concepts $Q = \{A1\}$. From W_A following vector is extracted against the given query:

$$R = [0.8\ 0.2\ 0.7\ 0.4],$$

The above vector is sorted in descending order $[0.8\ 0.7\ 0.4\ 0.2]$ and with the retrieval size of 3, images I_1, I_3, and I_4 will be shown to user.

When a query contains categories $Q = \{B1\}$. From W_{CF} following vector is extracted against the given query:

$$R = [0.31\ 0.08\ 0.285\ 0.18],$$

The above vector is sorted in descending order $[0.31\ 0.08\ 0.285\ 0.18]$ and with the retrieval size of 3, images I_1, I_3, and I_4 will be shown to user.

When query contains both the concepts and categories $Q = \{A1, B1\}$. The query is first split into two queries $Q1 = \{A1\}$ containing the concepts and $Q2 = \{B1\}$ containing the categories. $Q1$ will return following vector from W_A:

$$R = [0.8\ 0.2\ 0.7\ 0.4],$$

and $Q2$ will return following vector from W_{CF}:

$$R = [0.31\ 0.08\ 0.285\ 0.18]$$

Sort both the vectors in descending order, take the intersection and store the result of intersection in R. Keeping the retrieval size of 3, images I_1, I_3, and I_4 will be selected for user illustration.

4   Experimental Results

A dataset of seven hundred annotated images (i.e. N = 700) about natural scenes has been used to validate the proposed retrieval model. The dataset consists of six categories (i.e. O = 6) namely sky_clouds, forest, field, coast, waterscapes and landscape with mountains and ten concepts (i.e. M = 10) namely sky, foliage, grass, rocks, mountains, trunks, flower, water, sand and fields. The dataset have been used for building the proposed fuzzy ontology. In order to compare our system, we have selected the fuzzy relational ontological model proposed in [23]. The performance of the proposed methodology and reference model have been evaluated in terms of precision, recall, normalized modified retrieval rank (NMRR), average normalized retrieval rank (ANMRR), and normalized discounted cumulative gain (NDCG) [26, 27].

In order to evaluate the proposed methodology total of 167 queries have been used in which 122 queries are based on concepts, 11 queries are based on categories and 34 queries are based on combination of concepts and categories. Figure 3 shows the result of different queries against different evaluation measures. Higher precision values indicate that more relevant results are retrieved than irrelevant results; whereas higher values of recall indicate that most of the relevant results are retrieved. On the other hand, NMRR and ANMRR scores indicate the performance of algorithms based on the ranking of results; lower the value of NMRR and ANMRR better the algorithm ranked the results. NDCG measures the usefulness of images based on its position in a retrieved list. Higher NDCG indicates that the highly relevant images are retrieved at the top of the list.

Figure 4 shows the retrieved results for the proposed methodology and reference model against 3 different queries with retrieval size of 15. The first row shows the results of query-by-concept that is flower. Second row shows the results of query-by-category that is field. Third row shows the results of query-by-concept-and-category that is flower and field.

It is evident from the results that the proposed methodology outperforms the reference model. The proposed methodology shows better results in case of a query-by-concept and query-by-concept-and-category. However, the reference model shows slightly better result in the case of a query by category that is tolerable.

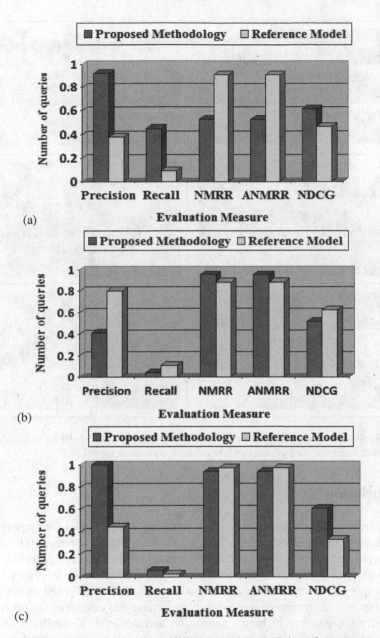

Fig. 3. Evaluation measure results against different queries consisting of concepts, categories and combination of concept and category. (a) Evaluation results against 122 different queries by concept. (b) Evaluation results against 11 different queries by category. (c) Evaluation results against 34 different queries by combination of concept and category.

Fig. 4. Retrieval output of the proposed methodology and reference model for retrieval size 15. Left column: Proposed methodology, Right column: Reference model [23]

5   Conclusion

In this paper, we have proposed a fuzzy ontology based model for improving the performance of image search results. First a fuzzy ontology is constructed by utilizing the concepts and categories associated with images. Then users are provided with an interface to input keywords. Search results are ranked based on the relevancy between the keywords of a query and images. The advantages of the proposed model are that relationship between an image and concepts and image and categories are fuzzy values that resolve the problem of binary annotation and retrieval. Secondly, it allows an image to belong to different categories with different degrees of membership. Experimental results showed that the proposed model achieves better results as compared to the reference model. Currently we are improving the ranking of the retrieved results where user requirements include multiple concepts and categories.

References

1. Liu, Y., et al.: A survey of content-based image retrieval with high-level semantics. Pattern Recogn. **40**(1), 262–282 (2007)
2. Rui, Y., Huang, T.S., Chang, S.-F.: Image retrieval: current techniques, promising directions, and open issues. J. Vis. Commun. Image Represent. **10**(1), 39–62 (1999)
3. Kaur, H., Jyoti, K.: Survey of techniques of high level semantic based image retrieval. IJRCCT **2**(1), 015–019 (2013)
4. Sivic, J., Zisserman, A.: Video Google: a text retrieval approach to object matching in videos. In: 2003 Proceedings of Ninth IEEE International Conference on Computer Vision. IEEE (2003)
5. Zheng, W., et al.: Ontology-based image retrieval. In: Proceedings of WSEAS MMACTEE-WAMUS-NOLASC (2003)
6. Avril, S.: Ontology-based image annotation and retrieval. Master of Science Thesis, University of Helsinki, May 2008
7. Town, C.: Ontological inference for image and video analysis. Mach. Vis. Appl. **17**(2), 94–115 (2006)
8. Park, K.-W., Jeong, J.-W., Lee, D.-H.: OLYBIA: ontology-based automatic image annotation system using semantic inference rules. In: Kotagiri, R., Radha Krishna, P., Mohania, M., Nantajeewarawat, E. (eds.) DASFAA 2007. LNCS, vol. 4443, pp. 485–496. Springer, Heidelberg (2007)
9. Schober, J.P., Hermes, T., Herzog, O.: Content-based image retrieval by ontology based object recognition. In: Proceedings of the KI-2004 Workshop on Applications of Description Logics (2004)
10. Galindo, J.: Handbook of Research on Fuzzy Information Processing in Databases, vol. 2. Information Science Reference, E-book, USA (2008)
11. Zadeh, L.A.: Fuzzy logic and approximate reasoning. Synthese **30**(3–4), 407–428 (1975)
12. Vogel, J., Schwaninger, A., Wallraven, C., Bülthoff, H.: Categorization of natural scenes: local versus global information and the role of color. ACM Trans. Appl. Percept. **4**(3), 19:1–19:21 (2007)
13. Sarwar, S., Qayyum, Z.U., Majeed, S.: Ontology based image retrieval framework using qualitative semantic image descriptions. Proc. Comput. Sci. **22**, 285–294 (2013)
14. Luo, B., Xiaogang, W., Xiaoou, T.: World Wide Web based image search engine using text and image content features. In: Electronic Imaging 2003. International Society for Optics and Photonics (2003)
15. Natalya, N.F., McGuinness, D.L.: Ontology development 101: A guide to creating your first ontology (2001)
16. Liu, S., Chia, L.-T., Chan, S.: Ontology for nature-scene image retrieval. In: Meersman, R. (ed.) OTM 2004. LNCS, vol. 3291, pp. 1050–1061. Springer, Heidelberg (2004)
17. Wang, H., Song, L., Liang-Tien, C.: Does ontology help in image retrieval? A comparison between keyword, text ontology and multi-modality ontology approaches. In: Proceedings of the 14th Annual ACM International Conference on Multimedia. ACM (2006)
18. Minu, R.I., Thyagharajan, K.K.: Semantic image description for ontology based image retrieval system. Int. J. Appl. Eng. Res. **9**(26), 9332–9335 (2014)
19. Vogel, J., Schiele, B.: Semantic modeling of natural scenes for content-based image retrieval. Int. J. Comput. Vision **72**(2), 133–157 (2007)
20. Schober, J.-P., Thorsten, H., Otthein, H.: Content-based image retrieval by ontology-based object recognition. In: Proceedings of Workshop on Applications of Description Logics, Ulm, Germany (2004)

21. Schreiber, A.Th.G, et al.: Ontology-based photo annotation. IEEE Intell. Syst. **3**, 66–74 (2001)
22. Radecki, T.: Fuzzy set theoretical approach to document retrieval. Inf. Process. Manag. **15** (5), 247–259 (1979)
23. Pereira, R., Ricarte, I., Gomide, F.: Fuzzy relational ontological model in information search systems. Capturing Intell. **1**, 395–412 (2006)
24. Ogawa, Y., Tetsuya, M., Kiyohiko, K.: A fuzzy document retrieval system using the keyword connection matrix and a learning method. Fuzzy Sets Syst. **39**(2), 163–179 (1991)
25. Horng, Y.-J., Shy-Ming, C., Chia-Hoang, L.: Automatically constructing multi-relationship fuzzy concept networks in fuzzy information retrieval systems. In: The 10th IEEE International Conference on Fuzzy Systems, 2001, vol. 2. IEEE (2001)
26. Järvelin, K., Jaana, K.: IR evaluation methods for retrieving highly relevant documents. In: Proceedings of the 23rd Annual International ACM SIGIR Conference on Research and Development in Information Retrieval. ACM (2000)
27. Wenyin, L., et al.: A performance evaluation protocol for content-based image retrieval algorithms/systems. In: Proceedings of the CVPR Workshop on Empirical Evaluation in Computer Vision, vol. 232 (2001)

Face-Based Difficulty Adjustment for the Game Five in a Row

Jan Novotny, Jan Dvorak, and Ondrej Krejcar[✉]

Faculty of Informatics and Management, Center for Basic and Applied Research,
University of Hradec Kralove, Rokitanskeho 62,
500 03 Hradec Kralove, Czech Republic
jan.novotny.17@uhk.cz, dvorakj@gmail.com,
ondrej@krejcar.org

Abstract. History of the logic games like chess, checkers or five in a row as is old as humanity itself. Primary goal of these games is to train the human brain with a thinking on the future moves. Idea is that the winner is that one with the most successfully predicted moves. Any help for this goal is more than welcome. In current day there is trend to brings all games to our SmartPhones to fill the free time by a possibility of play at any place anytime. There is a many existing solutions, application and ideas how design graphical user interface of these game applications, where the actual trend is to make an intelligent computer opponent with some intelligence which has no standard (all time same) strategy or starting parts. The goal of this paper is to use some standard algorithms like Minimax or Alpha-Beta with the help of user/player face detection usable for difficulty level adjustment. This is described in whole paper step by step as design as well as implementation issues related to appropriate parts of solution. Face detection is used to indicate meta-info of the player by the help of front camera of SmartPhone. This meta-info as age, sex or mood is evaluated and is taken as input for difficulty adjustment not only at start of every game, and even in every move, what make a playing this game amazing.

Keywords: Android · Five in a row · Minimax · Alpha-Beta pruning · Genetic algorithms · Face recognition

1 Introduction

Actual trend in western society is that every people above 15 own one SmartPhone (exclude old people). Many of these holder use it not only for general purposes (make a call or text messages), but also for performing some applications and games as well. One example of such game is known as school desk game – five in a row. Playing five in a row on the smartphone has a big advantage, that the user doesn't need a real opponent. The opponent can be some algorithm of an artificial intelligence.

For the best possible enjoyment of the game it is important that the user can choose the opponent to play with the equable emulator possible. And even better is, if the suitable opponent for the user is set automatically and the user can simply enjoy the experience of the game with the opponent and does not have to deal with any application settings.

© Springer International Publishing Switzerland 2016
M. Younas et al. (Eds.): MobiWIS 2016, LNCS 9847, pp. 121–134, 2016.
DOI: 10.1007/978-3-319-44215-0_10

For the automatic selection of the opponent's level can be used the data from the smartphone front camera. Presently there exist a number of algorithms of computer vision, which are able not only to identify a human faces (face-detection), but also to analyse the found face and gain different specifications (face-recognition), such as sex, age, race etc.

The main goal of this work is the conception of the suitable opponent algorithm in the game five in a row that can intelligently change its difficulty according to the front camera data. Thus the work handles with two main topics:

(1) *formation of the algorithm for the opponent in the game five in a row with a possibility to modify its difficulty*
(2) *work with the image from the front camera and application of the computer vision algorithms with the purpose of recognition the shot faces*

The formation of the new algorithm for recognition of the shot faces is beyond the scope of this work. It is a difficult problem, which is well described in an article [1]. Though, this work resumes information about currently used technologies. Consequently, the technologies are used and compared.

In this work there is suggested the algorithm of the artificial intelligence for the opponent in the game five in a row. The paper does not contain explanation of the game rules. Concretely there are considered game rules of Gomoku with a playing field sized 15×15, see [6].

According to [2] there generally exist two types of algorithms for five in a row (and similar games such as chess) – no-searching and searching.

- The first, easier of them, is mostly based on several rules that result from experience of the algorithm's author. This way in contrary to the other does not use any searching.
- The second way is more sophisticated and uses space searching of all the possible rolls into a certain depth. Principally it comes from already existing algorithms such as Minimax or its enhancement – Alpha-Beta pruning. These algorithms are described in detail for example in articles [3] and [4] and in the work they will be represented in the next section. For this work it is more suitable to use the second way with searching, because it is possible to easily change the performance of the algorithm by customizing the searching depth. The concept of the evaluating function is a subject of next sections.

2   Problem Definition

Problem described in introduction section can be seen in two main areas, algorithm development and image processing from camera source respectively. This section contains both of the problems.

2.1   Genetic Algorithms - Minimax

One goal is to suggest the suitable artificial intelligence algorithm for the opponent in the game while one suitable algorithm is minimax. This algorithm uses a "game

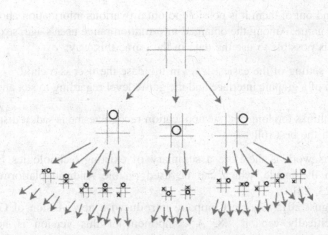

Fig. 1. Minimax algorithm [7]

tree" [5]. The algorithm calculates with the game tree limited by a certain pre-set depth, because the whole tree would be huge. Minimax evaluates every tree leaf using the evaluating function. The evaluation of each node is defined as the best value of its successor. The best value is defined different way in the case of odd and even tree levels [5]. The principal of minimax method is shown in the figure (Fig. 1).

An article [8] suggests total of 6 methods to implement the evaluating function. Through a tournament it was found out, that in a competition stands the best an algorithm called "Simple (Line Based)". It evaluates every unblocked tuple of a specific player with value 4n and again every unblocked tuple of an opponent with value −4n. Then the function result becomes a sum of these values.

Evaluating function by author [9] searches for every quadruplet, triplet and couple on the playing field and to these values it assigns a certain weight, whereas the weight of the quadruplet is the highest and the weight of the couple is the lowest. Generally, it applies, that the more of such consecutive quadruplets, triplets and couples the player has, the bigger is his chance to win.

Next author [10] mentions an evaluating function based on searching models. Every model is evaluated by a certain value; the result afterwards becomes a sum of these values. The models are being searched in all possible different directions.

Next evaluating function was designed by author [11]. The principal is to locate all the quintuples of consequent fields, whereas every quintuple is evaluated according to its content [11]. This work utilizes the last mentioned algorithm of the evaluating function and tries to improve it. Unfortunately the numbers suggested by the author [11] are not supported by any objective analysis. Therefore, this paper try to find out the optimal values for this evaluating function.

2.2 Face-Based Difficulty Adjustment of the Game According to the Shots from the Front Camera

As it was mentioned in the first section, for setting the difficulty of the five in a row it is possible to use the shots from the front camera on the mobile device. These shots can be analysed and out of them it is possible to obtain various information about the user, who plays the game. Among the obtained information range user's age, sex and mood. Concretely it is possible to use the data in the game this way:

- Automatic setting of the easiest level in the case the user is a child.
- Adaptation of a graphic interface and the game level regarding to sex and age of the user [17].
- If the user thinks too long and the application recognizes he is sad, it displays a help option with the best roll.

Part of this work is therefore a summary of existing technologies for the face recognition in the image, which can be used on the Android platform, and their comparison [23, 24].

In the August 2015 Google Company introduced a new version of Google Play services, specifically version 7.8. A component of this version is new Mobile Vision API, which contains a support for the face recognition in the image and a real-time [20] recognition of the barcodes. The new API for the face recognition in the image has 4 functionalities for now [14]: (1) Face detection in the image; (2) Face tracking; (3) Discovering areas of concern in the face; (4) Classification. Unfortunately, Google Play services are not able to guess sex, age and race etc. But it is possible to find various web services available on the internet.

The first one from Microsoft Company is a "Face APIs" [15]. This service can classify information about the found person listed below: (1) Different facial landmarks – many times more than Google Play services (total 27); (2) Age and sex. Though the Microsoft service is free, but unfortunately it is limited by up to 20 requests in a minute and 5000 requests in a month, what is reachable in a hour unfortunately.

Next service (free with no limits), is called Face++ [16]. It can classify following data about the identified person: (1) Various facial landmarks – less then Microsoft service (total 6); (2) Probability of smile; (3) Sex – including its probability; (4) Race – including its probability; (5) Age – including from-to range.

There are also some other web services, but majority of them is charged, while they don't bring something new in regarding the purposes of this game project.

3 New Solution

This section concerns with suggesting the new opponent algorithm in the game five in a row and results from the algorithm described in the second section. To find a suitable quadruplet of aforementioned values there are used genetic algorithms in the work. Genetic algorithms are inspired by natural evolution process in the nature. The fundamental is Darwin's theory of natural selection and Mendel's genetics theory. The intention of the genetic algorithms is seeking through the space and discovering the optimal solution of the specific function, for which doesn't exist (or is too difficult) an exact algorithm. Every possible solution is represented by an individual in a population. The population then is a set of individuals – a set of possible solutions. Over time the population evolves. The poor individuals die out; better individuals appear and replace them.

Such algorithm can be written in pseudo code this way:

```
k = 0
Initialization P(k)
Evaluation P(k)
Repeat
    k = k+1
    Selection P(k) from individuals in P(k-1)
    Recombination P(k)
    Evaluation P(k)
Until the terminal condition is fulfilled
```

The step Recombination P(k) means executing two genetic operators – crossing and mutation. Evaluation P(k) is realized by fitness function calculation, which evaluates each individual in the population according to his quality [12].

The selection in the genetic algorithms may be realized using several selection methods. These include for example different alternatives of roulette selection and a tournament selection. In this work it is used the tournament selection that picks the best individuals from the population on the base of an arranged tournament between the individuals.

3.1   Design and Realisation of Tournament Selection

Within this work it was arranged a tournament between algorithms for five in a row. Every individual was represented by a quadruple of values (a, b, c, d), where

- a represents number of points for one sign in a quintuple
- b represents number of points for two signs in a quintuple
- c represents number of points for three signs in a quintuple
- d represents number of points for four signs in a quintuple

in the evaluating function described supra.

The tournament was realized using all-play-all method. The matching rivals were algorithms with different values (a, b, c, d) in the evaluating function with scanning of the minimax tree into depth 2. In every match of two individuals:

- the winner gained 1 point
- the loser gained 0 points
- both players gained ½ point in the case of draw (filling the whole playing field 15 × 15)
- Further tournament specification:
- In every round total 10 individuals matched each other; in that round they competed each other two times; every time different player started the match.
- Total 21 rounds of the tournament were arranged.
- In every round there were played total 90 matches.
- Fitness function of an individual means a sum of points gained during a specific tournament round.
- Into the next round principally progressed:
- 2 individuals with the highest fitness function (without crossing and mutation),

- 5 individuals originated by mutation of an individual with the highest fitness function,
- 3 randomly generated individuals
- In the zero generation there were generated ten individuals by a generator of pseudorandom numbers.

4 Implementation Issues of Developed Game

4.1 Implementation of the Game Algorithm

The whole application is implemented in Java language and is intended for Android platform [23]. The main logic of the algorithm is divided into two classes [18].

The most important class is the class GomokuMiniMaxEngine with the method play, which receives as an input a two-dimension field of values representing an actual game position and also a numeric value, which represents the specific symbol (a cross or a circle). The method returns coordinates of the best found roll. The second considerable class is GomokuGame, which represents a certain game position. The class includes a method checkGameEnd, which returns value 0 in the case that it's not end yet, 1 in the case the cross wins, 2 in the case the circle wins and 3 in the case of draw (filling the whole playing field).

The basic minimax algorithm was improved in this work with the alpha-beta pruning, which is very well described for example in the article [2]. This algorithm accelerates the slow minimax by pruning the minimax tree by redundant branches. This way it gives the same result with a shorter calculation time. For easier imagination the calculation with the classic minimax algorithm with searching into depth 3 took approximately 1.5 min on a common laptop.

Using alpha-beta pruning the calculation was reduced to ca. 6 s. With alpha-beta pruning it depends on an order of searching the rolls, in which they are being searched through – therefore in the work it was implemented also simple sequencing of the rolls. With this sequencing of the rolls the calculation was reduced from 6 s to ca. 1 s, which is already an acceptable calculation time.

4.2 Implementation of the Technologies for the Face Recognition

The technologies applicable for the face recognition in the image were mentioned in the second section. This section handles with their practical use.

(1) *Google Play services*

The first technology applicable for the Android platform is Faces API in Google Play services. A fundamental class of this API is a class FaceDetector. While creating the class it is possible to set how much the API shall recognize in the detected face [18]. Concretely:

- setTrackingEnabled turns on/off tracking the face in the shots sequence
- setLandmarkType – when a value ALL_LANDMARKS is set, there are detected the facial landmarks, with NO_LANDMARKS there aren't detected any of them

- setMode regulates a velocity (and therefore also accuracy) of the calculation. The possible variants are FAST_MODE and ACCURATE_MODE
- setProminentFaceOnly estimates, if the service shall look for all the faces in the image, or just the most distinctive one
- The concrete values can be then obtained from the concrete instances of the class called Face, which contains methods such as *getIsSmilingProbability()*, *getIsLeftEyeOpenProbability()*, *getIsRightEyeOpenProbability()*, or *getLandmarks()*.

(2) *Face APIs (Microsoft)*

For the API by Microsoft [15], it is possible to set demanded parameters similarly as with Google Play services. Furthermore, while requesting the web service it is necessary to use a key (subscription-key), which can be generated while registration on the web. Afterwards the web service returns the calculated values in the JSON format [18].

(3) *Face++*

To simplify the use of API Face++ in the Java language there exist an elementary library directly from authors of Face++, which can be downloaded at the project web site [16]. While creating an instance httpRequests of the class HttpRequests it is required to enter the generated key, similarly as with the Microsoft product.

4.3 Implementation Issues of Face-Based Difficulty Adjustment

Computing of the AI is time consuming, therefore it is necessary that the calculation is made in the background by using an IntentService.

The playing field of size 15 × 15 is realized in the GUI by 225 instances of an ImageView class. If the square is empty, then empty white area is selected, if the square isn't empty, image of a cross or a circle is selected. For each square it is applied an onClickListener, which operates a certain event (a click).

After game is started, GUI show the selection option for New Game and Option, where some selection as well as modification of game are available (Fig. 3, left). After the press of "New Game" button, the code is checking whether is selected option "Intelligent adjustment of complexity" (Fig. 2 left) or not. Application was designed mainly for the purpose of testing this options, so this is one of the key point of this article as well as whole project. Code is checking firstly user face detection by the help of face recognition APIs (Sect. 4.2). This option takes approximately 7–8 s depending on actual light disposition and user/player face and used HW SmartPhone as well (see Sect. 5.3). Other options like a detection of smile, left and right eye are showed immediately after the GUI is showed, so immediately after "New Game" button is pressed. After age is detected (Fig. 2) the exact age is returned with a correctness of this fact. E.g. number 35 ± 10 or 40 ± 8 years. This value is taken as an input value for the selection of difficulty level, where option easy, 2nd, 3rd and 4rd (most difficult) is available. If face detection fail, there is an option to manual selection of difficulty level (as a standard way in normal games). This problem of fail selection of age can be also verified by shading of front camera. If player unfortunately allow front camera, the

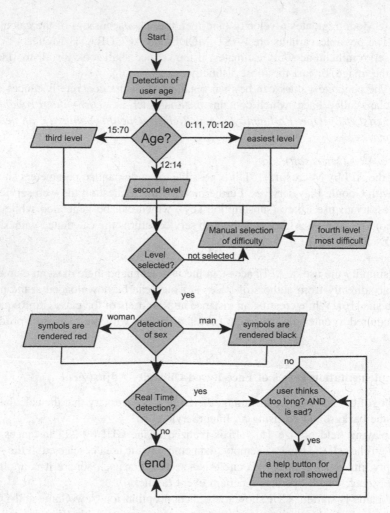

Fig. 2. Algorithm of game initialization

selection of appropriate opponent is changed immediately based on detected face and returned value (see Fig. 2 at right bottom corner with an option of real-time detection).

Second intelligent adjustment option lay in the selection of sex (man or woman), where real comparison of both types is a not a contribution of this paper and is set in the code based on study [19].

The last part of algorithm (Fig. 2) describe an option for real-time which allow to provide a sequential executing of parallel thread of face detection based intelligent adjustment of game difficulty.

Real-time execution of face detection is a very time consuming operation which consume a high power of the device. This is the reason why there are implemented two possibilities of use in the option. Detection of face on the start of a new game or real-time execution of face detection. In this case it is displayed the user's face below

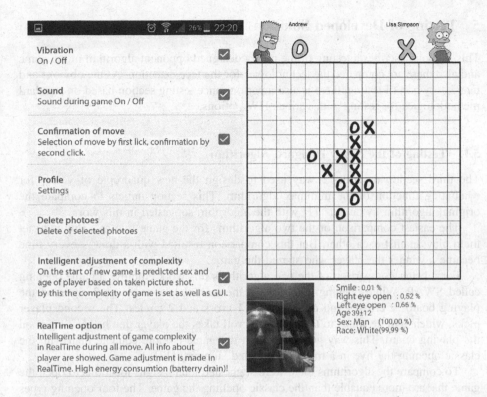

Fig. 3. GUI of developed testing application – game (left). Settings menu (right).

the playing board to him and there are showed the detected information in real-time. See figures (Figs. 2 and 3).

4.4 Implementation Issues of Real-Time Option for Artificial Intelligence

GUI of the developed application is showed in figure (Fig. 3 right). In the top left corner, there is a visualization of the actual player (a person) with a name and a symbol for which he plays. In the right top corner there is the opponent (computer player) with his symbol. This opponent is selected based on player age and sex or set manually.

The whole game is thanks to the real-time option (Fig. 3 left) providing an amazing game entertainment thus the selection of appropriate level can be for each move different. The best essence is added by the smile option, where user can be sad or smile what have an effect to a final selection of game difficulty. For example, if the user going to win with the sad smile strategy and is one or two moves before the win and make a smile, difficulty option is immediately changed to harder level while user can lose whole game in several moves! This fact is one of the key points in the sense of user experience.

5   Testing of Developed Solution

This section describes a testing of the newly designed opponent algorithm in the game and also there are compared the technologies for the face detection. As the obvious and mandatory part of testing, there is also a performance testing section based on standard methodologies for testing with various HW options.

5.1   Testing of the Newly Designed Algorithm

The third section describes a way used to design the new quadruple of values for evaluating function of the minimax algorithm. This section targets to compare the original algorithm by author [11] with the algorithm suggested in this work.

The easiest comparison of the two algorithms for the game five in a row is to let them play against each other. But this comparison resulted with a draw – every time became a winner the player who started the game.

For a better comparison of the two algorithms this work employs a game opening called SWAP. While opening with SWAP the starting player places 3 signs on the playing board; 2 crosses and one circle or 1 cross and 2 circles. The second player picks, which sign he wants to take. The first roll takes the player that has less signs on the playing board. This way guarantees that the game is more equable than with the classic opening the five in a row game (called surewin) [13].

To compare the algorithms there were suggested total 4 signs locations to open the game that are more equable than the classic opening the game. The four opening types are visualized on the figure (Fig. 4).

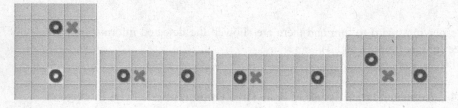

Fig. 4.   Opening for test no. 1, 2, 3, 4

The test consisted of 8 games of the algorithms mentioned supra. Every algorithm played each opening type two times – ones with crosses and for the second time with circles. The game results are displayed in table (Table 1).

Table 1.   The results of the comparison

	(1, 73, 511, 1751)	(1, 4, 193, 1079)
Opening 1	0 wins	2 wins
Opening 2	0 wins	2 wins
Opening 3	0 wins	2 wins
Opening 4	1 win	1 win

The original algorithm [11] with the quadruple (1, 73, 511, 1751) made it only once to win - in the fourth opening. Concretely in that case the algorithm played with circles (that is two signs in the SWAP opening). This result approves that the new suggested solution is better than the original one.

5.2   Comparison of the Technologies for the Face Detection in the Image

In the second section there were mentioned existing technologies for the face detection in the image. This section brings their comparison by concrete examples. For the testing there were used total 10 pictures of people taken from public web servers. The information detected using Face++ (F++), Face API by Microsoft (MS) and Google Play services (G) are showed in table (Table 2).

Table 2. Technologies comparison

Sex (M/F)			Age			Smile (%)		
R	F++	MS	R	F++	MS	F++	MS	G
F	F	F	18	23	20	88	–	45
M	M	M	24	35	39	3	–	0
F	F	F	26	25	27	95	–	98
M	M	M	29	21	31	1	–	1
F	F	F	31	30	27	5	–	1
F	F	F	32	30	23	1	–	1
F	F	F	34	34	38	4	–	12
M	M	M	39	36	35	0	–	27
M	M	M	62	65	71	58	–	10
M	M	M	76	52	67	94	–	98

From testing results it was recognized, that both of the web services (Face++ and Microsoft Face API) successfully managed to recognize sex of the photographed people in all the cases. The person's age estimation was also very good in all the cases; the largest diversion from the real age was made by Face++ service in the last photo (diversion of 24). An average diversion was similar for both of the services: Face++ 5.8 years and the Microsoft service 5.9 years.

Considering the probability of the certain person's smile is a subjective matter. The measured values are only informative. But taken subjectively we can say that both of the algorithms work very well. The largest difference between the algorithm values is within the penult person, though neither a human would say if this person does smile or not.

5.3   Speed Performance Testing

The mandatory part of testing is a performance of whole designed and developed application. Our solution was tested on two HW SmartPhones:

- Xperia Z1 Compact with Android 5.1.1 (further Z1)
- Samsung Galaxy Note 4 with Android 6.0.1 (further Note 4)

Z1 has Qualcomm Snapdragon 800 2.2 GHz quad-core CPU with 2 GB of RAM and display with resolution at 1280×720 pixels.

Note 4 SmartPhone is setup by processor Exynos 7 Octa, with a technology ARM big.LITTLE. It has four cores on 1.9 GHz (Cortex-A57) and four green cores on 1.3 GHz (Cortex-A53). Graphical acceleration provides with Mali-T760 on 695 MHz. Display with 2560×1440 pixels' resolution.

GUI of developed solution were showed on both models with no problem. Game play ground was rendered up to all corners. Camera preview was also targeted to right place at left bottom corner with correct display of green rectangle around face (Fig. 3 right) all time with defined frequency of 30 FPM (Frame Per Second) [21, 22].

The most CPU drained part of the application running is the real-time mode option when enabled every move (algorithm with minimax and alpha-beta) is computed after face detection (age, smile, eyes) which select appropriate level of difficulty for every move. For both testing devices the time of "thinking" was not disturbing as it was all time under the two second limit, which is defined as the maximum limit for which user (player) is able to wait and watch the display without any loss of concentration [25].

6 Conclusions

The main goal of this project was to confirm an idea if it is possible to develop an application of some game with the intelligent (artificial intelligence) adjustable difficulty of computer opponent during the play. This goal was evaluated by the partial results from face detection evaluation and comparison of three APIs as well as development of game algorithm with implementation of minimax and alpha-beta pruning trees.

Side goal of this project to compare the new developed algorithm with existing one. Also this goal was successfully evaluated while the newly developed one beat his predecessor.

As a next result we can mention the evaluation of actual trendy technology of face detection in real usage where results are very good (Table 2) and the CPU drain is not a big disadvantage in the case of modern SmartPhone devices, like we used in the testing process.

Future development of game application will be directed to show thinking time of each computer move as well as number of computed iterations. Also option for limited thinking for both side is going to be implemented as to put for both player's same conditions.

Acknowledgement. This work and the contribution were supported by project "Smart Solutions for Ubiquitous Computing Environments" FIM, University of Hradec Kralove, Czech Republic (under ID: UHK-FIM-SP-2016-2102). We also acknowledge the technical language assistance provided by Pavla Simkova.

References

1. Yang, M.H., Kriegman, D.J., Ahuja, N.: Detecting Faces in Images: A Survey (2002). http://vision.ai.illinois.edu/publications/pami02a.pdf. Accessed 11 Nov 2015
2. Fialka, L.: Advanced environment for playing board games), Bachelor thesis, Czech Technical University in Prague, Praha (2006). https://dip.felk.cvut.cz/browse/pdfcache/fialkl2_2006bach.pdf. Accessed 11 Nov 2015
3. Pearl, J.: The Solution for the Branching Factor of the Alpha-Beta Pruning Algorithm and its Optimality. Programming Techniques and Data Structures (1982). http://wiki.cs.pdx.edu/wurzburg2009/nfp/abavg.pdf. Accessed 11 Nov 2015
4. Knuth, D.E., Moore, R.W.: An Analysis of Alpha-Beta Pruning. Artificial Intelligence (1974). http://www-public.tem-tsp.eu/~gibson/Teaching/CSC4504/ReadingMaterial/KnuthMoore75.pdf. Accessed 11 Nov 2015
5. Kuhr, T.: Algorithm minimax, Palacky University Olomouc, Olomouc. http://www.inf.upol.cz/downloads/studium/PS/minimax.pdf. Accessed 27 Nov 2015
6. Gomoku: Game Rules (2009). http://gamerulesguru.com/gomoku.shtml. Accessed 27 Nov 2015
7. Eppstein, D.: Strategy and board game programming (1997). https://www.ics.uci.edu/~eppstein/180a/970417.html
8. Kulev, V., Wu, D.: Heuristics and Threat-Space-Search in Connect 5 (2009). http://isites.harvard.edu/fs/docs/icb.topic707165.files/pdfs/Kulev_Wu.pdf. Accessed 27 Nov 2015
9. Kim, J.: Gomoku agent using Minimax/Alpha-beta pruning, Gomoku (2013). https://github.com/janecakemaster/gomoku. Accessed 27 Nov 2015
10. Loos, A.: Machine Learning for k-in-a-row Type Games Using Random Forest and Genetic Algorithm, University of Tartu, Tartu (2012). http://comserv.cs.ut.ee/forms/ati_report/downloader.php?file=5D52AF13A55F51ADB1F03E3C1EEAF628BA1BC580. Accessed 27 Nov 2015
11. Description of the five in a row algorithm, Trixi blog, 27 November 2015. http://blog.trixi.cz/2013/02/popis-piskvorkoveho-algoritmu/. Accessed 27 Nov 2015
12. Posik, P.: Genetic algorithms, Czech Technical University in Prague, Praha (2000). http://labe.felk.cvut.cz/~posik/pga/theory/ga-theory.htm. Accessed 27 Nov 2015
13. The five in a row rules. The tutorial center of five in a row and renju (2015). http://www.vcpr.cz/napoveda-a-pravidla/pravidla-piskvorek/. Accessed 27 Nov 2015
14. Mobile Vision. Google developers: Find objects in photos and video, using real-time on-device vision technology (2015). https://developers.google.com/vision/. Accessed 28 Nov 2015
15. Face APIs. Microsoft Project Oxford (2015). https://www.projectoxford.ai/face. Accessed 28 Nov 2015
16. Face++ API. Face++: Leading Face Recognition on Cloud, 28 November 2015. http://www.faceplusplus.com/. Accessed 28 Nov 2015
17. Krejcar, O.: Human computer interface for handicapped people using virtual keyboard by head motion detection. In: Katarzyniak, R., Chiu, T.-F., Hong, C.-F., Nguyen, N.T. (eds.) Semantic Methods for Knowledge Management and Communication. SCI, vol. 381, pp. 289–300. Springer, Heidelberg (2011)
18. Novotny, J., Dvorak, J., Krejcar, O.: User based intelligent adaptation of five in a row game for Android based on the data from the front camera. In: De Paolis, L.T., Mongelli, A. (eds.) AVR 2016. LNCS, vol. 9768, pp. 133–149. Springer, Heidelberg (2016)
19. Howard, R.W.: Are gender differences in high achievement disappearing? A test in one intellectual domain. J. Biosoc. Sci. 37(3), 371–380 (2005)

20. Krejcar, O., Tucnik, P., Adamec, O.: Evaluation of aJile aJ-80 real time embedded platform for RT-Java parameters. Measurement **44**(7), 1253–1260 (2011). doi:10.1016/j.measurement.2011.03.030

21. Machacek, Z., Slaby, R., Hercik, R., Koziorek, J.: Advanced system for consumption meters with recognition of video camera signal. Elektronika ir Elektrotechnika **18**(10), 57–60 (2012). ISSN 1392-1215

22. Machacek, Z., Hercik, R., Slaby, R.: Smart user adaptive system for intelligent object recognizing. In: Nguyen, N.T., Trawiński, B., Jung, J.J. (eds.) New Challenges for Intelligent Information and Database Systems. SCI, vol. 351, pp. 197–206. Springer, Heidelberg (2011)

23. Behan, M., Krejcar, O.: Modern smart device-based concept of sensoric networks. EURASIP J. Wireless Commun. Netw. **2013**(155), 13 pages (2013)

24. Behan, M., Krejcar, O.: Adaptive graphical user interface solution for modern user devices. In: Pan, J.-S., Chen, S.-M., Nguyen, N.T. (eds.) ACIIDS 2012, Part II. LNCS, vol. 7197, pp. 411–420. Springer, Heidelberg (2012)

25. Krejcar, O.: Problem solving of low data throughput on mobile devices by artefacts prebuffering. EURASIP J. Wireless Commun. Netw. **2009**, 1–8 (2009). doi:10.1155/2009/802523. Article ID 802523

Security of Mobile Applications

Adaptive Trust Scenarios for Mobile Security

Şerif Bahtiyar[✉], Orhan Ermiş, and Mehmet Ufuk Çağlayan

Computer Networks Research Laboratory, Department of Computer Engineering,
Boğaziçi University, Bebek, 34342 Istanbul, Turkey
{serif.bahtiyar,orhan.ermis,caglayan}@boun.edu.tr

Abstract. Mobile systems interact with many autonomous entities and multiple services that provide a ubiquitous environment for societies. In this environment, trust to security is a challenging issue. Entities and services have unpredictable behaviors therefore conventional trust models have limited accuracy for security related computations due to static nature of the models. Adaptive trust computations are needed to make accurate trust decisions. In this paper, we propose an adaptive approach to compute trust for mobile security. We evaluate the approach with different scenarios and comparisons to show the adaptive property.

Keywords: Security · Mobile · Trust · Adaptive

1 Introduction

The increasing amount of mobile systems with autonomous entities has made societies connected more than ever. Such systems provide an open communication environment for social interactions. People interact with their relatives, friends, and colleagues by using intelligent systems over mobile devices. Financial operations, health care services are some of other significant relations that have become popular with the ubiquitous access opportunities provided by mobile systems. The diverse number autonomous entities and services running on mobile systems has made trust based decision making about security a significant research challenge [2,4].

The concept of trust has been widely used in various contexts since it provides diverse decision-making opportunities under different subjective expectations of entities [11]. This makes a trust model highly context dependent and only suitable for specific conditions. On the other hand, mobile systems are highly personal so each user may have different expectations when a mobile system moves. Moreover, mobile systems provide new security vulnerabilities. Therefore, different models are needed when a mobile system has changed its state, location, or interactions to have precise trust based decisions. However, existing trust approaches use only one computation model, where models are not adaptive or have limited adaptive properties. Having an adaptive trust based decision-making approach related to security is a significant issue for mobile systems that is our motivation in this paper.

© Springer International Publishing Switzerland 2016
M. Younas et al. (Eds.): MobiWIS 2016, LNCS 9847, pp. 137–148, 2016.
DOI: 10.1007/978-3-319-44215-0_11

The contribution of this paper is an adaptive computation approach for decision-making based on trust in mobile systems. It ensures a mobile system to use many trust and information gathering models to have more accurate trust computation results. We have also explained the proposed approach with six scenarios by showing how the approach may be applied to the scenarios with four existing models.

The rest of the paper is organized as follows. Section 2 is a brief overview of trust. Section 3 describes the adaptive trust computation approach with six scenarios and four models. The paper is concluded in Sect. 4.

2 Trust in Mobile Systems

Generally, cryptographic methods are used to establish trust in mobile systems. Trusted Computing Group (TCG) has specifications to measure, store, and monitor hardware and software integrity through root-of-trust, which is a hardware platform called Trusted Platform Module (TPM) and Core-Root-of-Trust Measurement (CRTM). CRTM measures the boot loader of a system before it runs and then it stores measurements into the TPM. Then, the image of operating system is loaded and executed. A detailed survey regarding trust and security for mobile devices is given in [6,13].

Trust is a significant research area in mobile ad-hoc networks [16]. It enables users in such networks to cope with uncertainty. Moreover, assessing the trust of information received from network security services is essential to have secure resource sharing among entities and services [7]. A detailed survey regarding trust computations and trust dynamics in mobile ad-hoc networks is given in [3].

Recently, there are significant research efforts on trust to security of services in information systems. For instance, security as a service in relation to trust is investigated in [9]. In a more specific study, privacy of trust negotiations is achieved with an ontology-based approach [14]. The number of trust models has rapidly increased, but they are for specific contexts and not adaptive.

3 Scenarios for Adaptive Trust

In this section, we present the adaptive trust computation approach and six scenarios for mobile systems, where an entity can dynamically change its trust computation model to have more accurate trust computation results. Moreover, we show how four known computation models, namely EigenTrust [8], FIRE [5], PeerTrust [17], and TrustInfo [1] can be applied in proposed scenarios.

Trust is highly context sensitive and information varies in each context. Therefore, there are two significant components of trust based decision making, the information gathering model and the trust computation model. In existing trust computation approaches, trust is computed according to a specific model with a fixed information gathering approach. On the other hand, mobile systems are dynamic. This means that the systems may contain many applications which interact with different services temporarily, such as smart phones. Thus, mobile systems should have different information gathering and trust computation models to cope with dynamic security requirements. In this paper, we propose an adaptive approach for trust based decisions about mobile security with different scenarios.

In our approach, a mobile system may use different information gathering and trust computation models according to changing conditions to have more accurate trust based decisions. Assessing the trust of security related to a particular application in specific conditions and then making decisions about the application according to the trust assessments is an instance for adaptive trust based decision making.

Our approach considers data obtained from environment with its communication interfaces and sensors, such as wi-fi interface, which we call data from outside. The configuration and the number of software and hardware components provide data for information extraction regarding trust computations, which we call data from mobile system. For example, a mobile system can extract information from security systems with the model presented in [1]. Additionally, the proposed approach considers prior trust computations and trust based decisions for subsequent trust computations.

Since obtaining information is one of the two conditions, a mobile system may use different models to obtain information depending on changing conditions. An optimal model is another condition required for adaptive trust computations. The remaining of the algorithm is similar to many other trust based decision making approaches in literature.

Adaptive trust based decision making, which we call AdaptiveTrust, for mobile systems works according to assessed trust with a condition that is used to determine the result of the decision. Since the trust assessment may be done with different trust models depending on moves of the mobile system, each trust model may use different information. Therefore, the accuracy of the decision depends on the success of context and environment representations related to trust assessment model. Equation 1 shows adaptive trust based decision making $\Theta(T(t), \Xi(t), t) \in \{0, 1\}$, where $\Theta(T(t), \Xi(t), t) = 1$ and $\Theta(T(t), \Xi(t), t) = 0$ mean accept and reject respectively. $\Theta(T(t)$ represents assessed trust whereas $\Xi(t)$ is trust threshold, which is used for decision making.

$$\Theta(T(t), \Xi(t), t) = \begin{cases} 1 & \text{if } T(t) \geq \Xi(t) \\ 0 & \text{if } T(t) < \Xi(t) \end{cases} \tag{1}$$

Context is a significant factor for trust computations. In this paper, we focus on security context of mobile systems therefore the scenarios are constructed accordingly.

3.1   S1: Based on System Configuration

A mobile system simply consists of hardware and software that may change time to time. For example, an external speaker may be attached to a smart phone or a memory card may be removed from the phone. On the other hand, the user may install or remove some applications, such as a game application or an anti-virus program.

Configurations of hardware and software components are important to meet the requirements of a mobile system user. Mobile systems like smart phone are highly personal so a user is free to configure hardware and software components of its mobile system. This makes some mobile systems prone to various attacks, such as security attacks and physical thefts.

In this scenario, the initial state of the configuration of a smart phone has a hardware component and two software components, *state 1*. The hardware component is a GSM communication interface. Software components are a conversation component and a game application. Let us assume that the user removes the game application and installs a social networking application. Moreover, the user updates the configuration of GSM interface to connect cheaper but less secure GSM networks, *state 2*. Furthermore, since the smart phone now has a social networking application which supports Bluetooth communication, the user has enabled the Bluetooth interface for social networking with its application in a cheaper way. The user knows that recent updates make its phone vulnerable to security attacks so she installs an additional security application to the smart phone, *state 3*.

In this scenario, different trust computation and information gathering models may be used due to changes in information sources and trust computation parameters. Specifically, the game application is removed and a social networking application is installed, where the user may receive information from peers in its social network via the networking application. On the other hand, having a new communication interface may also necessitate updating parameters of information gathering and computation model. Thus, specific models for information gathering and trust computation are needed to have more accurate trust metrics. The proposed approach supports the change of models.

3.2 S2: Communication Interface Diversity

Mobile systems may contain many communication technologies, such as wi-fi, Bluetooth, and NFC. Additionally, each communication technology has different properties so different information gathering models are needed to compute trust metrics. On the other hand, people trust mobile systems more than conventional communication systems because mobile systems are considered to be more personal. This makes people careless. For example, 44 % of adults access personal emails via free or unsecured wi-fi connections [12,15].

Consider scenario S1. Assume that the smart phone has a secure access solution to entities and services from GSM interface. All entities accessed from a secure interface are honest. On the other hand, the phone has no secure access to entities and services from Bluetooth interface. Moreover, there are both honest and fraudulent entities, where malicious activities may occur. Furthermore, the user can enable the USB interface of the phone and then connects it to a personal computer. Here, the USB connection is assumed insecure. Actually, when the number of active communication interfaces increases in a mobile system, the total number of vulnerabilities in a system increases for both secure and insecure interfaces. Therefore, a trust computation approach should consider information gathering differences between secure and insecure interfaces with the total number of different communication interfaces.

The mobile system may use the same information gathering and trust computation models during the execution of this scenario. However, parameters of the information gathering model need to be updated to cope with the effect of changing communication interface. This scenario shows that an adaptive trust computation solution may be provided with updating the parameters of information gathering and trust computation models for some cases.

3.3   S3: In Secure Environment

The mobile system moves in a secure environment, where many security solutions are applied. Additionally, all connections of the mobile systems are considered secure whereas there may be dishonest entities. In a secure environment, determining dishonest entities is a significant issue due to relatively high trust to the environment.

Assume that the smart phone in scenario S1 communicate only with wi-fi interface and it is connected the internal network of a financial company. The network has many wi-fi access points and the mobile system can connect any of them according to move. The company has strong security policies and periodic security assessments are carried on by security experts. In this paper, such kinds of networks are considered to be a secure environment.

In this scenario, the mobile system moves in a secure environment. If there is no change in the system, the mobile system may not update information gathering and trust computation models. Otherwise, such models may be updated according to changes in the mobile system, such as configuration updates. This scenario shows that different models may be needed either in secure environments.

3.4   S4: In Open Environment

A mobile system may move only in a secure environment or an insecure environment. If there is no change in the system, the mobile system may not update its information gathering and trust computation models in any environment.

Here the mobile system moves in an open environment that is considered to be insecure. There are different kinds of entities and services that may have malicious behaviors in such environments. Moreover, open environments are highly dynamic. Thus, trust based decision making in dynamic environments, where malicious events occur, necessitate adaptive approaches to have accurate decisions. In our approach, the mobile system changes trust and information models according to its needs and dynamic condition of the environment. Specifically, the mobile system replaces its information gathering and trust computation models when it changes connections to wi-fi access points and updates interactions with entities and services.

This scenario shows that adaptive trust based decision approaches are needed to have precise decisions in open environments. Our approach supports such needs by combining many trust computation and information gathering models in an adaptive manner.

3.5   S5: Move Along Environments

Contemporary pervasive communication opportunities ensure mobile systems to traverse many environments without losing their connections. Since a mobile system may move among different environments and within an environment, trust based decisions should consider all the conditions mentioned in scenarios S2, S3, and S4. Additionally, moving between two environments may need to change trust computation and information gathering models considerably.

Consider scenario S2. Assume that the user has a meeting in a foreign country and she attended the meeting after a journey with her smart phone. Initially, the user was in her office and connected to internal network via wi-fi to access the Internet. Then, she left the office and went to airport with a taxi, where she was connected to the office database via a UMTS connection. In airport of her country, she had a secure connection to a special network dedicated for premium passengers only. She used the insecure network connection of the airplane during the fight. In the foreign airport, she made a payment by using a mobile payment service of her smart phone via NFC. Finally, she connected to a network in meeting point. In this scenario, the mobile system traverses many environments with different security levels. If the mobile system was applied our approach, then it would have more accurate trust based decisions because of adaptive property of our approach.

3.6   S6: Having Connections with Many Entities

Mobile systems may interact with many other entities simultaneously that have honest, dishonest, or malicious behaviors. Trust based decisions may be highly inaccurate if trust computation approaches are constructed according to specific types of entities with a single trust computation model. An adaptive trust based decision making approach should consider as much as possible types of entities and so it should be able to integrate different kinds of trust computation models.

In scenario S5, the mobile system moves along many different environments. Assume that the user has new connections with many new peers in these environments and she keeps going these connections either she moves from one environment to another. Moreover, the mobile system continues to interact with entities from different environments. This makes the trust computation process of the mobile system highly vulnerable to security attacks [10]. An entity can update its trust computation and information gathering models in such cases to cope with different kinds of entities. In this scenario, our adaptive trust computation approach can update models according to interacted entities.

3.7   Applying Trust Models to the Scenarios

We show four computation models that may be used for adaptive trust computations based decision making. We have compared the models with respect to the scenarios in Table 1.

Table 1. Adaptive trust computations for the scenarios with four trust models.

Trust model	S1	S2	S3	S4	S5	S6
EigenTrust [8]	−	+	+	+	−	+
FIRE [5]	−	−	+	+	−	+
PeerTrust [17]	−	+	+	+	+	+
TrustInfo [1]	+	+	+	−	−	−

PeerTrust is a reputation based trust model for peers in P2P networks [17], where peers communicate directly with each other. The significance of PeerTrust is that it has two adaptive factors in computing trustworthiness of peers. However these factors do not represent all changes in a mobile system, such as context changes explained in S1.

PeerTrust model uses Eq. 2 to compute trust $T(u)$ of peer u, where $I(u,v)$ represents the total number of transactions performed by peer u with v, $I(u)$ denotes the total number of transactions performed by peer u with all other peers. $p(u,i)$ is the ith transaction of other participating peer and $S(u,i)$ is the normalized amount of satisfaction peer u receives from $p(u,i)$ in its ith transaction. $Cr(v)$ is the credibility of the feedback submitted by v and $TF(u,i)$ is the adaptive transaction context factor for peer us ith transaction. The last parameter $CF(u)$ represents the adaptive community context factor for peer u.

$$T(u) = \alpha \sum_{i=1}^{I(u)} S(u,i) \, CR(p(u,i)) \, TF(u,i) + \beta CF(u). \tag{2}$$

Another reputation based trust computation model is FIRE [5]. It combines interaction trust $T_I(a,b,c)$, role-based trust $T_R(a,b,c)$, witness reputation $T_W(a,b,c)$, and certified reputation $T_C(a,b,c)$ with Eq. 3 to have trust $T(a,b,c)$, where ω_k is an importance coefficient. FIRE is an important model to assess the performance of a peer but it is not adaptive and needs models for information gathering to provide accurate trust assessments.

$$T(a,b,c) = \frac{\sum_{k \in \{I,R,W,C\}} \omega_k T_k(a,b,c)}{\sum_{k \in \{I,R,W,C\}} \omega_k}. \tag{3}$$

EigenTrust model uses histories of peers in a file sharing system to compute a global trust value for each peer [8]. Local trust of peer i about peer j is computed with Eq. 4, where $sat(i,j)$ is the number of satisfactory transactions with peer j of peer i and $unsat(i,j)$ is the number of unsatisfactory transactions. The normalized values of local trust are computed with Eq. 5.

$$s_{i,j} = sat\,(i,j) - unsat\,(i,j)\,. \tag{4}$$

$$c_{i,j} = \frac{\max\,(s_{i,j}, 0)}{\sum_j \max\,(s_{i,j}, 0)}\,. \tag{5}$$

$$t_{i,k} = \sum_j c_{ij}c_{jk}. \tag{6}$$

Global trust is computed with the aggregation of normalized local trust values. EigenTrust model has a version for distributed environments. The model deals with some security attacks, such as Sybil attack; therefore it is a useful model for P2P environments. However, the model does not consider internal configurations of systems and entities.

Security information is a significant factor to have accurate trust computation results related to the security of a mobile system. However, there is a lack of information gathering model in some prominent trust computation models, such as FIRE [5]. TrustInfo [1] may provide detailed information about security of mobile systems according to needs of a specific entity by extracting trust information from the security systems of a service. Extracted information can be represented with a set according to the granularity need of the computation model to ensure adaptive trust computations. Trust information related to atomic unit p_j is represented with $ta_j\,(t) \in [0,1]$ and is computed with Eq. 7. Moreover, extracted trust information related to an atomic unit consists of all trust information extracted from the security system of a service based on needs an entity. Specifically, *extracted trust information* is a combination of information extracted from the security policy of a service and the security system of the service. Additionally, it depends on the perception of the entity. Extracted trust information from service c in an entity related to atomic unit p_k is represented with $\iota_k\,(t) \in [0,1]$ and is computed Eq. 8.

$$ta_j\,(t) = \begin{cases} 1 & ,\, stp_j\,(t) + h_j\,(t) > 1 \\ 0 & ,\, stp_j\,(t) + h_j\,(t) < 0 \\ stp_j\,(t) + h_j\,(t) & ,\, otherwise \end{cases} \tag{7}$$

$$\iota_k\,(t) = \pi_{k,j}\,(t)\,ta_j\,(t)\,. \tag{8}$$

A model may be a convenient model for a specific scenario whereas it may be an inconvenient one for another one as shown in Table 1. Specifically, all computation models in the table can be used in scenario S3 whereas some of them may be convenient only for some scenarios. For instance, EigenTrust and PeerTrust models are convenient for scenarios S2 and S6. Thus, these scenario and trust models show that emerging mobile systems necessitate adaptive trust computation approaches regarding security of mobile systems to have accurate trust based decisions. Our approach provides an adaptive trust computation for security of mobile systems.

3.8   Numerical Evaluation

We evaluate the adaptive trust based decision making according to the presented scenarios and trust models compared in Table 1 numerically. We used adaptive factors in each model to determine the accuracy of trust computations so the accuracy of the adaptive trust based decision making for mobile systems were done accordingly. EignTrust has one adaptive factor. FIRE, PeerTrust, and TrustInfo have four, two, and three adaptive factors in sequence. We selected TrustInfo for scenarios S1 and S2, FIRE for scenarios S3 and S4, PeerTrust for scenario S5, and EigenTrust for scenario S6 according to the adaptive trust computation based decision making. Moreover, we set $\Xi(t) = 0.5$ for decision makings.

We simulated ten updates of trust assessments for EigenTrust, FIRE, PeerTrust, and TrustInfo according to boundaries shown in Table 2. Since the trust models use different factors to compute trust, assessed trust results are inconsistent among the models for a specific time as shown in Fig. 1. In Figs. 1, 2, and 3, time may represent a second, a minute, or any other time interval. The time interval depends on computing power of the mobile device. Inconsistent behaviors of trust models may lead to inaccurate trust decisions. For this reason, the trust based decision making for a mobile system should consider the inconsistency and the decision making should use adaptive trust computations.

In the numerical analysis, we computed trust based decisions according to each individual model and $\Xi(t) = 0.5$ as shown in Fig. 2. Similar trust assessment results to trust decisions may be consistent or inconsistent for specific times. For instance, trust decisions are *accept* in all models for time 4 and 5 as shown in Fig. 2. In contrast, trust decisions based on EigenTrust and TrustInfo for time 1 are *accept* whereas FIRE and PeerTrust based decisions are *not accept* for the same time as sown in the figure.

We selected one of the four models for each scenario according to the properties of the scenarios as described in the first paragraph of this sub section. Since all trust based decisions are *accept* according to all trust modes and the threshold for time 4 and 5, decisions based on the adaptive trust computations are also *accept* for time 4 and 5 as shown within the ellipse in Fig. 3. This means that any of the four trust models provides the same decisions for all scenarios with values of factors for time 4 and 5. On the other hand, only PeerTrust provides the correct decision for scenario S5 in time 6 as shown with the arrow in Fig. 3. These results show that mobile systems should have adaptive trust computation approaches depending on their dynamic circumstances that here we explained with different scenarios.

Table 2. Boundaries of models for trust assessments.

Trust model	EigenTrust [8]	FIRE [5]	PeerTrust [17]	TrustInfo [1]	AdaptiveTrust
Min	0.1	0.45	0.3	0.4	0.1
Max	0.9	0.7	0.6	0.8	0.9

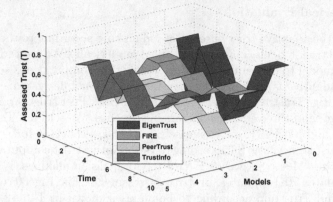

Fig. 1. Trust assessments for the models.

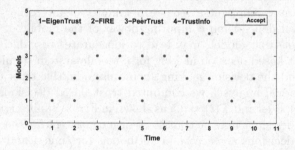

Fig. 2. Trust based decisions for EigenTrust, FIRE, PeerTrust, and TrustInfo.

We analyzed the adaptive trust based decision making by using a single trust model for each scenario yet. This provides accurate trust based decisions instead of using a single trust model for all scenarios. However, many trust computation models may be used to have more accurate trust assessments so we may have more precise decisions. For instance, we selected PeerTrust for scenario S5. Assume that the mobile system uses three trust models for each scenario when there is a decision change and it updates the decision according to the weighted average of the trust assessments by considering the three models. For example, the decision for scenario S5 goes from *not accept* to *accept* when time goes from 2 to 3 and it goes from *accept* to *not accept* when time goes from 7 to 8 as shown in Fig. 3. In this case, if the new approach is applied the decision changes may not occur.

These analysis show that more grained adaptive trust assessments will provide more accurate trust based decisions. Using trust models simultaneously will provide more accurate results but this may consume more computing resources of mobile systems. Performance evaluation regarding computing resources of the adaptive trust assessment based decision making is beyond the scope of this paper.

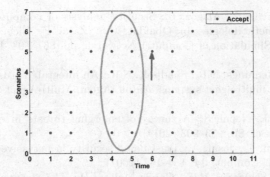

Fig. 3. AdaptiveTrust based decision making for the scenarios.

4   Conclusion

Adaptive trust computation related to security is a significant challenge for trust based decision-makings in mobile systems because they may be highly personal and move along dynamic environments. There are also many autonomous entities with different behaviors that complicate trust computations in such environments. In this paper, we proposed an adaptive trust computation approach for decision-makings based on trust results about security of mobile systems. The approach was illustrated with six scenarios to show its diverse applicability in different circumstances. Additionally, we compared the scenarios according to four existing models to clarify the adaptive property of our approach.

Our contribution in this paper is the adaptive trust computation approach for security of mobile systems. It can adaptively select an information gathering model and/or a trust computation model to provide more accurate decisions based on trust results. Such decisions will help societies to be more connected by doing some critical transactions and operations over mobile systems.

Acknowledgments. This work is supported by the Turkish State Planning Organization (DPT) under the TAM Project, number 2007K120610.

References

1. Bahtiyar, Ş., Çağlayan, M.U.: Extracting trust information from security system of a service. J. Netw. Comput. Appl. **35**(1), 480–490 (2012)
2. Conti, M., Das, S.K., Bisdikian, C., Kumar, M., Ni, L.M., Passarella, A., Roussos, G., Tröster, G., Tsudik, G., Zambonelli, F.: Looking ahead in pervasive computing: challenges and opportunities in the era of cyber-physical convergence. Pervasive Mobile Comput. **8**(1), 2–21 (2012)
3. Govindan, K., Mohapatra, P.: Trust computations and trust dynamics in mobile adhoc networks: a survey. IEEE Commun. Surv. Tutor. **14**(2), 1–20 (2012)

4. Gür, G., Bahtiyar, Ş., Alagöz, F.: Security analysis of computer networks: key concepts and methodologies. In: Obaidat, M.S., Zarai, F., Nicopolitidis, P. (eds.) Modeling and Simulation of Computer Networks, pp. 861–898. Elsevier, Amsterdam (2015)

5. Huynh, T.D., Jennings, N.R., Shadbolt, N.R.: An integrated trust and reputation model for open multi-agent systems. Auton. Agent. Multi-Agent Syst. **13**(2), 119–154 (2006)

6. Jang-Jaccard, J., Nepal, S.: A survey of emerging threats in cyber security. J. Comput. Syst. Sci. **80**, 973–993 (2014)

7. Kagal, L., Finin, T., Joshi, A.: Trust-based security in pervasive computing environments. IEEE Comput. **34**, 154–157 (2001)

8. Kamvar, S.D., Schlosser, M.T., Garcia-Molina, H.: The eigentrust algorithm for reputation management in P2P networks. In: Proceedings of the 12th International Conference on World Wide Web, pp. 640–651. ACM, Budapest, Hungary (2003)

9. Kaufman, L.M.: Can a trusted environment provide security? IEEE Secur. Priv. **8**(1), 50–52 (2010)

10. Mármol, F.G., Pérez, G.M.: Security threats scenarios in trust and reputation models for distributed systems. Comput. Secur. **28**(7), 545–556 (2009)

11. Massa, P.: A survey of trust use and modeling in real online systems. In: Song, R., Korba, L., Yee, G. (eds.) Trust in E-services: Technologies, Practices and Challenges, pp. 51–83. Idea Group Inc., Calgary (2007)

12. Norton: 2012 norton cybercrime report. Technical report, Symantec (2012)

13. Polla, M.L., Martinelli, F., Sgandurra, D.: A survey on security for mobile devices. IEEE Commun. Surv. Tutor. **15**(1), 446–471 (2013)

14. Squicciarini, A.C., Bertino, E., Ferrari, E., Ray, I.: Achieving privacy in trust negotiations with an ontology-based approach. IEEE Trans. Dependable Secure Comput. **3**(1), 13–30 (2006)

15. Trustwave's SpiderLabs: Global Security Report (2013). https://www2.trustwave.com/2013GSR.html

16. Xia, H., Jia, Z., Li, X., Ju, L., Sha, E.H.M.: Trust prediction and trust-based source routing in mobile ad hoc networks. Ad Hoc Netw. **11**(7), 2096–2114 (2013)

17. Xiong, L., Liu, L.: Peertrust: supporting reputation-based trust for peer-to-peer electronic communities. IEEE Trans. Knowl. Data Eng. **16**, 843–857 (2004)

Access Control Approach in Development of Mobile Applications

Aneta Poniszewska-Maranda$^{(\boxtimes)}$ and Aneta Majchrzycka

Institute of Information Technology, Lodz University of Technology, Lodz, Poland
aneta.poniszewska-maranda@p.lodz.pl

Abstract. Recent tendencies in the field of application development indicate the more and more significant role which mobile applications fulfil in everyday live of the rapidly growing number of smartphone users. It is important to establish new standards of data management as well as create mobile applications extending the functionalities of their existing systems to enable the users to benefit from the newest technological advances. Addressing these tendencies the paper presents the secure development model to overcome the existing threats faced by mobile application developers with particular emphasis on access control and proposed access control model.

1 Introduction

In order to assess and find flaws in the security of any mobile application it is worth determining what are the possible points of interest for the potential attacker. The most obvious reasons for breaking into the application are stealing the confidential data like passwords, account or credit card numbers and other personal data. Sometimes also capturing the multimedia data like videos or photos, data contained in the address book, mail or location info may be the target of the attack. Among other reasons one may also distinguish the will to omit some licensing issues or simply doing this "for fun".

Basing on these potential aims that the attackers want to gain an access to one can deduce that the most vulnerable parts of the application will embrace the data storage points, the permission management policy, the application file system and any kind of configuration files that may be stored within the device. Even if we do not want to use external configuration files and some configuration data are just stiffly hard coded in the code of the application one has to remember that there exist numerous reverse engineering techniques which may enable to extract such data. It would require more effort however still it is possible.

While assessing the potential risks in mobile application development a common term of privacy violation by unauthorized access to sensitive data is frequently used. At this point it is worth to specify what is meant by *sensitive data*. According to [1] the term sensitive data refers to a wide range of information which embraces "ethnic or racial origin, political opinion, memberships, health details, personal life, (...) information that relates to you as a consumer, client,

© Springer International Publishing Switzerland 2016
M. Younas et al. (Eds.): MobiWIS 2016, LNCS 9847, pp. 149–162, 2016.
DOI: 10.1007/978-3-319-44215-0_12

employee, patient or student, (...) contact information, identification cards and numbers, birth date".

The increase in mobile Internet traffic is mainly due to the increasing possibilities of mobile devices offered to the users. Nevertheless, these possibilities would not be achievable if it wasn't for the enhanced development features represented by the newest versions of operating systems. iOS owes its popularity both to the luxurious brand status as well as to its reputation of being more secure and less prone to external attacks than any other system. However, the intuitiveness and ease of use of Android applications make it comparably attractive despite its known drawbacks in the area of security. Any developer of mobile application for these platforms should be aware of the threats and vulnerabilities that each of them carries and should adjust the development strategies in such a way so that the optimal level of security is assured especially when interaction with confidential or sensitive data is required.

The problem presented in the paper concerns the known mobile application vulnerabilities for two most popular mobile platforms – Apple's iOS and Google's Android, and proposes the secure development model to overcome the existing threats faced by the mobile application developers with particular emphasis on access control and proposed access control approach.

The presented paper is structured as follows: Sect. 2 gives the outline of possible security risks in the development of iOS and Android applications, presenting the existing solutions to prevent the security treats in such development. Section 3 deals with the concept of security model which aims to facilitate the work of mobile application developers by enabling the usage of a range of security mechanisms. Section 4 presents the access control model approach for mobile applications while Sect. 5 describes the unified framework incorporating security procedures at different levels of application operations.

2   Mobile Security - Treads and Vulnerabilities

Preventing the threats connected with development of iOS applications and vulnerabilities characterizing the platform is not a task which can be realized by a single targeted solution. Some attempts have been made to establish the policy of securing the iOS applications each of them embracing different regions of security breaches.

The popularity of Android and lack of the *vetting* process makes it the most frequent aim of attacks, therefore its developers make every effort to increase the security of their system and as a result the security of applications created for their platform.

2.1   Security Risks in iOS Application Development

According to the Apple's security report the design ore of the iOS architecture is its security [3]. And it is beyond doubt that a lot care has been taken to assure proper level of security by incorporating such mechanisms as data encryption, code-signing and sandboxing.

Encryption is a standard mechanism and should prevent any unauthorized party from decoding information even if they are captured. *Code-signing* is connected with a strict procedure reserved for any application to be published in the AppStore which assures that only applications conforming to the Apple's standards, using allowed API's methods and submitted by registered distributors will let to be published. *Sandboxing* is a well-known mechanism for running programs separately from other system resources so that there is full control over the permissions and allowed access that the application requires. Sandboxing is frequently used with untrusted programs which have to be run on the device but here it is used to prevent downloaded application to use the resources of other application or the system or accessing the kernel resources that they are not allowed to.

All these internal platform security measures seem to be more than sufficient to feel secure while starting to use any new application from the AppStore. Nevertheless, this is not entirely true. The iOS platform implements sandboxing at the kernel level which means that privileges are granted basing on a set of predefined sandboxing profiles. The sandboxing profiles are assigned to all mobile applications admitted for distribution. During runtime an application invokes certain system calls and the process of granting appropriate privileges to such application i.e. whether it can perform desired operation run as a validation mechanism when a system call is invoked. The operating system itself has however no knowledge on the Objective-C runtime and it allows any installed third party application to invoke system calls and use the public resources. This makes all public resources vulnerable to attacks as well as creates the opportunity to manipulate the initial set of privileges and gaining more control than allowed access rule enable [5].

One of the most frequently used features provided by Apple is the possibility to use the *key-chains* as a storage for sensitive data. Key-chains enable to store string data outside of the application sandbox, which also makes it more vulnerable to be captured by third party applications. Apple itself uses key-chains to store the data such as passwords to Wi-Fi or VPN networks. Many developers also choose it as a definitely more secure and convenient alternative to *NSUserDefaults*. Data stored in key-chains enable the user to be constantly logged in and he is not required to input credentials every time he opens the application.

The aforementioned examples seem to be controllable if a sensible approach to data storage and access is assured. Some actions of the potential attackers cannot be however predicted and avoided. There exist numerous jailbreaking tools available widely through the Internet. They require some deeper knowledge on the architecture of the system itself and skill in mastering them however they can be used to break into the application in many ways and therefore to gain an access to its code. By gaining access to the code it is meant the access to the information about the structure of the application, data and control flow within it through the reversed binaries of the application.

2.2   Major Vulnerabilities of Android Applications

Compared with iOS applications, Android ones more frequently become the target of attacks of malicious software [4]. Even though they have been reported as more vulnerable is terms of security. This may derive from the fact that unlike Apple, Google is not performing a strict *vetting* process i.e. it does not check the compliance of the applications published on Google Play with the company's standards. Therefore more malicious software may be slipped through on to the market.

Android applications are commonly written in Java which makes them more easily reversible than iOS ones. As it was mentioned in Sect. 2 reversing any application allows to gain the information on its structure, data flow and control flow. Thus, the security risks for Android applications are in this case corresponding to the ones encountered when dealing with iOS ones. Although the changes that can be done to the application are a lot further-gone as after reversing an Android application it is possible to change the obtained byte-code and repackage the application. The target of such repackaging may be for instance an XML file containing permission configuration – *AndroidManifest.xml*. Among others the information which permissions the application has to store: Internet access permission, sharing location, accessing contact list, etc. By altering this file, doing which in fact does not require the changing of byte-code, one may easily increase the range of permissions available for an application. Reversing Android applications is the first step in finding all the information the potential attacker would have in his list. As proven by [6] anything starting from configuration files, database files, certificates, keystores with the use of proper and available tools can be recovered from the byte-code of the application and altered.

Going further, another visible threat which can be used by malicious software is connected with *activities* that Android applications contain. *Activity* is a component of Android application which defines the user interface and specifies what the user can to do. Activities return the results which can be easily captured by other activities and they are the consequence of the interaction with the user. The values returned by activities maybe for instance passwords, logins or card numbers which the user would rather leave unknown to others. Normally the activities are fired one by the other as the components of the application interact sequentially. Firing the activities can be performed by malicious software applications. Also each activity has to be defined in *AndroidManifest.xml* file where its permissions for other components and applications are specified.

3   Secure Development Model

The field of security of mobile applications requires the elevated attention because of the privacy issues of millions of users of smartphones and the lack of adequate solutions to assure the security of data. Having this in mind it is worth to think about more ways of how to reduce the risks connected with the mobile security in the context of the development process itself [7–10].

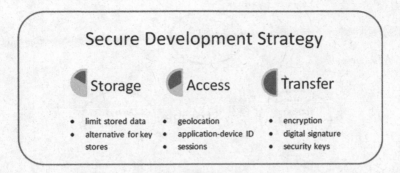

Fig. 1. Pillars of Secure Development Strategy for mobile applications

The developed model called *Secure Development Strategy (SDS)* was introduced for building mobile applications so that they would be less vulnerable to external attacks and leaks of sensitive data (Fig. 1).

The existing approaches to mobile application security focus mainly on the transmission of sensitive data to external services, whereas using the SDS approach equal focus is put on all aspects of the sensitive data management. Safe data transfer between mobile and external devices is undoubtedly a crucial link in the process of securing the applications, however not the only one.

The idea of *Secure Development Strategy* assumes that application should conform to predefined security standards embracing three main areas: *storage* (of sensitive data on the mobile device), *access* and *transfer* of sensitive data. Conformation to the standards should be achieved by implementing threefold security pattern for each of the mentioned areas. The model specifies the assumptions on how to achieve a proper level of security in each field and provides necessary details on the implementation of mechanisms which will allow achieving desired security effects.

3.1 Data Storage Security Model

The first pillar of the SDS storage concerns solely the client-side of the system i.e. the mobile application. The major assumptions of data storage pattern embrace sensitive data encryption, limitation and restricted access (Fig. 2).

While designing mobile applications the developer has two possibilities on where to store application data. He can choose external server where data will be stored in databases and special firewall mechanisms will block access to it. On the other hand some of the information which the application uses are necessary to be stored on the device. The most common reason for this, is application working in an offline mode when there is no communication with the server and the external database and login mechanisms with "remember me" feature.

The first option seems to be a better solution as it eliminates the risk of losing data when the device is damaged. Nonetheless, it requires a large amount of data traffic between the application and the server. In that light the second option comes in handy – it reduces the amount of data transfer. However it

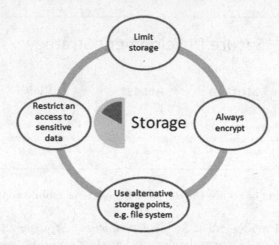

Fig. 2. Assumptions of data storage model

seems to be less practical, as the data to be valid need to be updated. Moreover, the storage space of the device is also limited. Thus, the combination of both solutions comes from the need of keeping the data up-to-date and accessible by many devices at any time simultaneously giving the possibility to store a little number of crucial information on the device.

The storage mechanisms depend on the place of where the data is saved on the device. Two places for data storage which are also a potential risk points can be discussed for SDS: key-chain and device file system. Three rules regarding the data storage can be formulated as follows:

- sensitive data should never be stored as plain text, but they should always be encrypted and stored as such in key-chains and any other storage places,
- sensitive data could be stored within the application database files and encrypted using encryption keys stored in the external server databases to limit the risk of reading the data,
- access to the internal database objects should be restricted only to the privileged functions (function calls).

3.2   Data Access Security Model

The second pillar of SDS strategy concerns the access to data. This comes from the fact that mobile applications need to communicate with external services and other applications. The major assumptions of this area of security embraces three mechanisms which aim to enable identification of the user requesting access to application resources (Fig. 3).

The access to the application resources can be controlled at different levels. Firstly, one may consider an access to the resources by application functions which is vital in case if anyone tries to modify the behaviour of the application

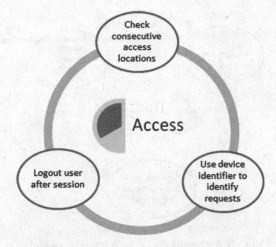

Fig. 3. Assumptions of data access models

by for instance swizzling method. This issue was partially addressed in the previous section regarding permission-based model to the database objects which may contain vital information. The other point of view is an access to data by unprivileged services or remote calls to the server from parties impersonating valid devices. The SDS strategies for such threats include the use of the *geolocation* and the *device identifier* as means of distinguishing suspicious behaviours.

The fundamental SDS rules for the data access are:

- the mobile application should inform about the current location of the device every time it requires an access to sensitive data,
- the mobile application should always present itself with a digital signature composed of unique device identifier,
- server should always check whether the device session is open before it realizes any requests.

3.3 Data Transfer Security Model

Data transfer pattern refers to all mechanisms which involve the exchange of data between the mobile application and the external services. These mechanisms should incorporate in their action flow the additional security procedures – data encryption, the use of security keys and the verification of the requests integrity (Fig. 4).

Data transfer seems to be the weakest link in the entire process of the mobile application development. It comes from the fact that the requests are travelling over the Internet in an unprotected space and they are prone to a special kind of attacks called the "man in the middle".

This attack means that between the mobile device and server application a third-party may be listening and waiting for the exchange of information. There exist three types of attacks for "man in the middle" scenario:

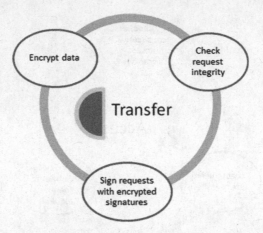

Fig. 4. Assumptions of data transfer model

- attack on the privacy of data – stealing confidential information,
- attack on the integrity of data – changing the content of the message,
- impersonation – impersonating other device/user.

4   Access Control Model Approach

Currently, traditional access control models, such as Discretionary Access Control (DAC) model [14], Mandatory Access Control (MAC) model [14], Role-Based Access Control (RBAC) model [11] or even Usage Control model [15], are not sufficient and adequate in many cases for information systems, especially modern, dynamic, distributed information systems, which connect different environments by the network. The same situation exist in the aspect of mobile applications and mobile platforms. It caused the creation of new access control model for mobile applications that can encompass the traditional access control ideas and solutions and allow to define the rules for mobile applications and systems, containing both static and dynamic access control aspects. Therefore, to ensure the functionality of the second pillar of SDS strategy, i.e. data access security model, the new access control model approach for mobile applications was proposed.

Actual applications and information systems can contain or work with many different components, applications, located in different places in a city, in a country or on the globe. Each of such components can store the information, can make this information available to other components or to different users. The authorized users accessing the information can change this information, its status, role or other attributes at any time. These changes can cause the necessity of modifications in security properties of accessed data at access control level.

Therefore, there is the need to have the access control approach that will describe the organization of mobile application/system that should be secured, their structure in proper and complete way, and on the other hand it will be appropriate and sufficient for dynamic application/system.

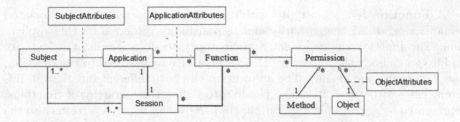

Fig. 5. Elements of mobile Application-based Access Control model

The proposed mobile access control approach was named *mobile Application-based Access Control (mABAC) model*. The core part of mABAC approach essentially represents the basic elements of access control, such as *subjects*, *objects* and *methods* (Fig. 5). We distinguished two main types of subjects in mABAC: user (*User* and mobile device (*Device*). These two elements are represented by the element **Subject** that is the superclass of User and Device. *Subjects* hold and execute indirectly certain rights on the objects. Mobile applications are working on behalf of users who execute them on devices directly or indirectly.

Subject permits to formalize the assignment of users and mobile devices to different functions. Subject can be viewed as the base type of users and mobile devices in mobile system. It can be presented as an abstract type, so it can not have direct instances – each subject is either a users or a devices. A mobile application **Application** is a mobile program executed on a device by a user. It needs to obtain an access to the desired data in order to realize the tasks asked by a user, so it represents the system entity, that can obtain some access rights in a system. A **User** is a human being, a person or a process in a system, who can also indirectly obtain some access rights in a system or on the device.

The **Session** element represents the period of time during which the user is logged in a system and can execute its access rights or represents the period of time during which the application is working on the device and can also execute its access rights. In our model the *Session* is assigned to the *Subject*, i.e. a user is login on the device during a single session. On the other hand a session is connected with the *functions* and this association represents the functions that can be activated during one session.

The association relation between the subjects and applications is described by the association class **SubjectAttributes** that represents the additional subject attributes (i.e. subject properties) as in usage control. *Subject attributes* provide additional properties, describing the subjects, that can be used in taking decision about granting or revoking the subject an access to certain object – especially *Location* and *Device ID*, but also for example an identity, role, credit, membership.

Location, L is expressed by IP address of the device. It is used to determine whether the request is valid (or should be handled) by checking the privileges pursuant to incoming IP address.

A **Function** is a job-activity within the application with some associated semantics regarding the authority and responsibility conferred on this application. The function can represent a competency to do a specific task-activity and it can embody the authority. The applications are assigned to the function, based on their functionality. The application can have different functions in different cases/situations. It is also possible to define the hierarchy of functions, represented by aggregation relation *FunctionHierarchy*, which represents also the inheritance relations between the functions. The function of the part end of the relation inherits all privileges of parent function.

The association relation between applications and functions is described by the association class **ApplicationAttributes** that represents the additional applications attributes (i.e. application properties) that can be used in taking decision about granting or revoking the application an access to an object. *Application attributes* provide additional properties, describing the applications, especially *Security Level* and *Application-Device ID*.

Security level, Sl is the ability to set different levels of security for different methods/objects or at the level of entire application. It is necessary therefore, that not all applications require such extensive control and security. There are three levels of security: Ignore, Warn, Block. It is used especially when detected no permission for the request.

Application-Device IDentifier, ADID is combined string of unique application ID (the same for all devices using the application, 16 characters, alpha-numeric) and device UDID. Application ID is stored in the configuration file of the server and the configuration of application (*XML config file*). UDID is transmitted during the first application use and stored in the database (encrypted).

Each function can perform one or more operations, so it needs to be associated with a set of related permissions **Permission**. A function can be defined as a set or a sequence (depending on particular situation) of permissions. The access to required object is needed to perform an operation, so necessary permissions should be assigned to corresponding function. Therefore, all the tasks and required permissions are identified and they can be assigned to the application to give it the possibility to perform the responsibilities involved when it realize its functionality. Due to the cardinality constraints, each permission must be assigned to at least one function to ensure the coherence of the whole access control schema.

The permission determines the execution right for a particular method on the particular object. In order to access the data, stored in an object, a message has to be sent to this object. This message causes an execution of particular method **Method** on this object **Object**. Very often the constraints have to be defined in assignment process of permissions to the objects. Such constraints are represented by the authorizations and also by the obligations and/or conditions. Therefore, the *permission* can be presented as a function $p(o, m, Cst)$ where o is an object, m is a method which can be executed on this object and Cst is a set of constraints which determine this permission.

Taking into consideration the subjects attributes (Location and DeviceID) *SubjectAttr* = {*L, DID*} and application attributes (Security level and ADID) *AppAttr* = {*Sl, ADID*}, the *permission* can be presented as a function *p(o, m, SubjectAttr, AppAttr, Cst)* or more precisely as *p(o, m, {L, DID}, {Sl, ADID}, Cst)*.

Authorization (A) is a logical predicate attached to a permission that determines the permission validity depending on the access rules, object attributes and subject attributes. **Obligation (B)** is a functional predicate that verifies the mandatory requirements, i.e. a function that a user has to perform before or during an access. They are defined for the permissions but concerning also the subjects – *Subject* can be associated with the obligations which represent different access control predicates that describe the mandatory requirements performed by a subject before (*pre*) or during (*ongoing*) an access. **Conditions (C)** evaluate the current environmental or application status for the usage decision concerning the permission constraint. They are defined also for the permissions but they concern the session – *Session* can be connected with the set of conditions that represent the features of a system or application.

A constraint determines that some permission is valid only for a part of the object instances. Taking into consideration a concept of authorization, obligation and condition, the set of constraints can take the following form *Cst* = {*A, B, C*} and the permission can be presented as a function *p(o, m, {L, DID}, {Sl, ADID}, {A, B, C})* . According to this, the permission is given to all instances of the object class except the contrary specification.

The **objects** are the entities that can be accessed or used by the applications. The objects can be either privacy sensitive or privacy non-sensitive. The relation between objects and their permissions are additionally described by association class **ObjectAttributes** that represents the additional object attributes (i.e. object properties) that can not be specified in the object's class and they can be used for usage decision process. The examples of object attributes are security labels, ownerships or security classes. They can be also mutable or immutable as subject attributes do.

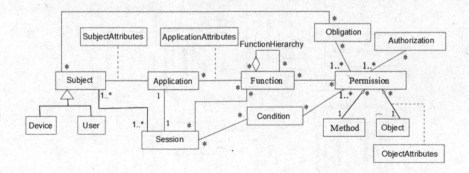

Fig. 6. Meta-model of mABAC model

The **constraints** can be defined for each main element of the model presented above (i.e. subject, session, application, function, permission, object and method), and also for the relationships between the elements. The concept of constraints was described widely in the literature [12,13,16]. It is possible to distinguish different types of constraints, static and dynamic, that can be attached to different model elements. Detailed view of presented mobile Application-based Access Control (mABAC) model with the set of all elements and relationships is given in Fig. 6.

5   iSec Framework as the Implementation of SDS Model

The aforementioned model for building the secure mobile applications specifies the guidelines which should be taken into consideration while creating such applications by developers. They were used to created *iSec framework* (Fig. 7).

The implementation of the ready-to-use classes and methods which would assure security of any mobile applications seems to suit the current needs for simultaneous time-efficiency and security. That is why in the scope of this research the prototype framework *iSec* was developed. Its main components correspond to three pillars of the security model presented in the previous section: storage, access and transfer. Additionally, addressing a practical need for a fast login mechanism, the component generating classes and controllers indispensable while creating login views was designed and incorporated as a part of this framework. This mechanism enables also the use of roles, which are frequently applied for the mobile applications.

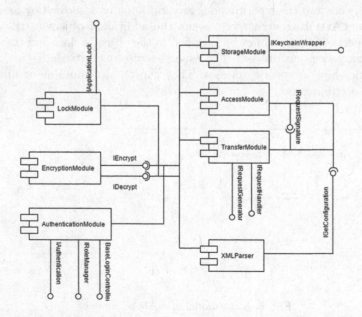

Fig. 7. Components of the *iSec* framework

All the major components of the framework use the *encryption module* which provides basic and complex encryption methods gathered together for the simplicity of use. Its user will be able to specify the default encryption algorithm to be used or he will use different ones for different purposes. Another component common for others is the *XMLParser* which will enable to read and write the security configuration stored in an external XML file. This configuration refers to the variables set from all three basic modules, with the most significant usage of function privilege information.

6 Conclusions

The presented Secure Development Strategy for mobile applications introduces three pillars which should be taken into consideration while designing and implementing the mobile applications and their security aspects. All these pillars: data storage, data access and data transfer should be treated as equally significant throughout the entire development process. The SDS provides details on its assumptions and mechanisms which should be implemented within the application framework in order to provide the mobile security.

The mobile Application-based Access Control (mABAC) model presented in the paper allows to define the access control policy based on access request, as traditional access control models, and the access decision can be evaluated while the access to information to which we want to control the usage. All the elements of mABAC approach form fairly complex model to present the features of mobile applications/systems at the access control level. On the other hand, it expresses more then simple authorizations but also the interdictions or obligations that have to be fulfilled in order to obtain the access to dynamic applications/information systems.

The practical implementation of the components of SDS strategy has shown weaker points of the assumptions made initially. It also enabled to look deeper into the structures of the applications and find other possible areas where security can be breached and the breaches could be avoided. The possibilities include especially the data access control mechanisms. The further research on data storage model will be conducted in order to provide an easy to use way for developers to securely store indispensable data directly on the device.

References

1. Felt, A.P., Finifter, M., Chin, E., Hanna, S., Wagner, D.: A survey of mobile malware in the wild. In: Proceedings of 1st ACM Workshop on Security and Privacy in Smartphones and Mobile Devices, pp. 3–14 (2011)
2. Souppaya, M.P., Scarfone, K.A.: Guidelines for Managing the Security of Mobile Devices in the Enterprise. NIST Special Publication 800-124, June 2013
3. Apple: iOS Security (2016). https://www.apple.com/business/docs/iOS_Security_Guide.pdf
4. Zhou, Y., Jiang, X.: Dissecting android malware: characterization and evolution. In: Proceedings of 33rd IEEE Symposium on Security and Privacy (2012)

5. Werthmann, T., Hund, R., Davi, L., Sadeghi, A., Holz, T.: PSiOS: Bring Your Own Privacy & Security to iOS Devices (2013)
6. Benedict, C.: Under the Hood: Reversing Android Applications. Infosec Institute, Elmwood Park (2012)
7. Seriot, N.: iPhone Privacy (2010)
8. Enck, W., Octeau, D., McDaniel, P., Chaudhuri, S.: A study of android application security. In: Proceedings of 20th USENIX Security Symposium (2011)
9. Alhamed, M., Amir, K., Omari, M., Le, W.: Comparing privacy control methods for smartphone platforms. In: Engineering of Mobile-Enabled Systems (2013)
10. Michalska, A., Poniszewska-Marada, A.: Security risks and their prevention capabilities in mobile application development. Inf. Syst. Manag. **4**(2), 123–134 (2015). WULS Press
11. Ferraiolo, D., Sandhu, R.S., Gavrila, S., Kuhn, D.R., Chandramouli, R.: Proposed NIST role-based access control. ACM TISSEC **4**(3), 224–274 (2001)
12. Ahn, G.-J., Sandhu, R.S.: Role-based authorization constraints specification. ACM Trans. Inf. Syst. Secur. **3**(4), 207–226 (2000)
13. Poniszewska-Maranda, A.: Modeling and design of role engineering in development of access control for dynamic information systems. Bull. Pol. Acad. Sci. Tech. Sci. **61**(3), 569–580 (2013)
14. Sandhu, R.S., Samarati, P.: Access control: principles and practice. IEEE Commun. **32**(9), 40–48 (1994)
15. Park, J., Sandhu, R.: The UCONABC usage control model. ACM Trans. Inf. Syst. Secur. **7**(1), 128–174 (2004)
16. Strembeck, M., Neumann, G.: An integrated approach to engineer and enforce context constraints in RBAC environments. ACM Trans. Inf. Syst. Secur. **7**(3), 392–427 (2004)

Using Mobile Technology in National Identity Registration

Thanh van Do[1,2], Clark Swafford[3], Loc H. Khuong[3], Van Thuan Do[4],
and Boning Feng[5(✉)]

[1] Telenor ASA, Snarøyveien 30, 1331 Fornebu, Norway
thanh-van.do@telenor.com
[2] Norwegian University of Science and Technology, 7031 Trondheim, Norway
[3] Keller Graduate School of Management,
DeVry University, Irving, TX 75063, USA
{cswafford,lkhuong}@devry.edu
[4] Linus AS, Martin Linges vei 15, 1364 Fornebu, Norway
t.do@linus.no
[5] College of Applied Sciences, Oslo and Akershus University,
Pilestredet 46, 0167 Oslo, Norway
Boning.Feng@hioa.no

Abstract. To increase the low birth registration rate in Pakistan a Mobile Identity concept is proposed and used in a pilot project in Punjab and Sindh provinces in Pakistan. This paper explains thoroughly the Mobile Identity concept, which makes use of mobile technology, i.e. mobile networks, mobile handsets and mobile application in the birth registration and establishment of civil identity for children. The paper also clarifies how Mobile Identity can surpass the obstacles to the current birth registration. The value propositions to the citizens, government and mobile operators are presented. A social benefit analysis is also depicted showing that Mobile Identity is more beneficial to the society than the current birth registration.

Keywords: Mobile Identity · Citizen identity · Civil identity · Mobile Birth Registration · Birth registration

1 Introduction

In the last two decades mobile communication has evolved from a pure communication system providing only voice and message communication services to be a mobile computing system which makes use of mobile communication, mobile hardware, and mobile software to offer uncountable useful and fancy services to users. But, the potential of mobile communication does not stop there. In fact, the usefulness of mobile communication can be extended further in the development of the society. In developing countries where the fixed telecommunication is not sufficiently deployed mobile communication can play a central role in the development and improvement of the societal infrastructure such as health, education, housing, civic, etc. In this paper, we present an initiative called Mobile Identity, carried out by Telenor [1] and UNICEF [2]

© Springer International Publishing Switzerland 2016
M. Younas et al. (Eds.): MobiWIS 2016, LNCS 9847, pp. 163–172, 2016.
DOI: 10.1007/978-3-319-44215-0_13

within the GSMA [3] Mobile Identity Programme [4], which aims at contributing to the establishment of civil identity. More specifically, the goal of the initiative is to improve the birth registration rate in Pakistan by using the mobile communication system.

The goal of this paper is to shed light on the concept of Mobile Identity, which proposes to use mobile communication as enabler for the establishment of citizen identity and hence paving the way for other societal and public services. The paper is aiming at showing that the Mobile Identity is both a technically feasible and a social economically beneficial concept rather than a technology or scientific contribution to mobile technologies. The paper starts with reviewing the notion of identity, citizen identity and digital, which are essential to understand the Mobile Identity concept. The central part of the paper is the description and clarification of the Mobile Identity concept. The values propositions for governments and mobile operators are also presented. Last but not least, a social benefit analysis is also explained.

2   Definition of Identity

As defined in [5, 6] an identity is a set of permanent or long-live permanent attributes and personal identifiers associated with an entity such as an individual. With an identity, it must be possible to recognize an individual.

As shown in Fig. 1 an identifier is an attribute that is most representative for an entity within a context. An identifier is also referred to as name, label and designator.

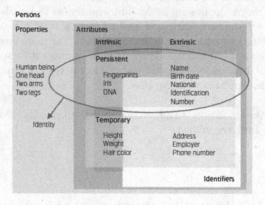

Fig. 1. Definition of identity

Related to identity there are three different processes that need to be clarified as follows:

- **Identification** is the association of a personal identifier with an individual presenting certain attributes. For example, accepting the association between a physical person and claimed name, or determining the association with a medical record and a patient using physical attributes.

- **Authentication** is proving an association between an identifier or attribute, and the relevant entity. For example, an automobile is identified by its license place, and that is authenticated as legitimate by the database of cars that are being sought for enforcement purposes.
- **Authorization** is a decision to allow a particular action based on an identifier or attribute. Examples include the ability of a person to make claims on lines of credit, the right of an emergency vehicle to pass through a red light or a certification of a radiation-hardened device to be attached to a satellite.

In most of countries, in order to ensure the rights and obligations of citizens governments wish to establish a national identity used in the identification and authentication of their citizens.

A **national identity** includes quite often the following attributes:

- Full name (i.e. First, Middle and Last Name)
- Birth Date
- Gender
- Place of Birth
- Parent Names
- National identification number (e.g. social security number, national number, personal identification number, personal number)
- Religion
- Ethnic

However, an identity with only the mentioned extrinsic attributes is very difficult to verify since extrinsic attributes can be copied, falsified and mistaken easily. Intrinsic attributes like face, fingerprints, iris, etc. must be used to ensure the authenticity of a person. In addition, these attributes must be stored in databases that are available and accessible for authentication when requested.

To facilitate identity authentication additional credentials or identification document or identity card are introduced.

A **credential** is an attestation of qualification, competence, or authority issued to an individual by a third party with a relevant de jure or de facto authority or assumed competence to do so.

An **identification document or identity card** is a credential designed to verify aspects of a person's identity. Information present on the document might include the bearer's full name, a portrait photo, age, birth date, address, an identification number, profession or rank, religion, ethnic or racial classification, restrictions, and citizenship status. New technologies could allow identity cards to contain biometrics such as photographs, face, hand or iris measurements, or fingerprints.

A **digital identity** is a representation of a human individual's identity in a computer network system like Internet, Corporate Intranet, Home networks, etc. A person does not really exist in the cyber world. Moreover, the communications and interactions in the cyber world are not face to face. People do not see who they are dealing with. Consequently, the physical intrinsic attributes like face, hair colour, fingerprint, etc. cannot be used to identify the user. Extrinsic attributes and identifiers like name, pseudonym, etc. are required. Unfortunately, they can be easily copied and duplicated.

A credential must hence be introduced as an additional attribute to prevent theft of identity. This credential is a secret that only each individual and the corresponding authentication authority know. In its simplest and weakest form, this credential is a password. For higher level of security, encryption keys and algorithms are used to realize this credential.

3   The Mobile Identity Concept

There is no unanimous and clear definition of Mobile Identity. According to [7] *"Mobile Identity is an extension of the digital identity which may be divided into three classes (and their combinations): device-to-device, location-to-location, and context-to-context."* Mobile Identity is intended for the authentication and authorisation to resources when moving and changing devices, locations or contexts. Another different definition is from the Estonian government in their e-Estonia programme [8] which defines Mobile-ID as a service that allows a client to use a mobile phone as a form of secure electronic ID.

With the focus on developing countries we adopt a broader definition for Mobile Identity that will be elucidated as follows:

In every society, establishing the identity of the individual is the cornerstone for development and prosperity. Indeed, a government can only provide services like health, education, security, financial, etc. to its citizen with the existence of a sound identity system. Unfortunately, this is not always the case in developing countries.

Mobile Identity is defined as the concept of making use of mobile communication in the establishment, development and protection of civil identity.

Hence, Mobile Identity includes the following features:

- Use of mobile communication including mobile network, infrastructure and distribution chain in:
  - The establishment of citizen identity.
  - The distribution, authentication and verification of citizen identity.
  - The provision of governmental, public and social services.
  - The provision of financial, private and enterprise services.
- Use of mobile phone as an identification and authentication token.

The Mobile Identity concept will now be illustrated with some concrete use cases.

3.1   Establishment of Citizen Identity – Birth Registration

In developing countries today, people living in poverty in rural areas do not have any kind of identification e.g. social security number, driving license, military ID, etc. and identity verification systems are not functioning properly. Every year, 51 million babies remain invisible and are being denied their right to an identity, to the fulfilment of additional rights and to protection as citizens.

Statistical analysis [9] show that children under five years old whose births have not been registered, tend to:

- Being poor, living in rural areas, having limited access to health care.
- Not attending early childhood education.
- Having higher levels of malnutrition and a higher mortality rate.

The consequences of the lack of birth certificates are very severe as follows:

- Difficulty in enrolling at school or taking exams.
- Access denial to health services such as vaccination programmes.
- Problems in being reunited with the right family after being trafficked or separated from families due to conflict or natural disaster.
- Child headed households are often denied inheritance.
- Problems accessing bank accounts, financial products, passports, ID cards, voting.
- Problems accessing telecommunication services and mobile money services (e.g. M-Pesa).

3.2 Obstacles to Birth Registration in Pakistan

According the Pakistani national statistics, nearly 60 million children in Pakistan, in which approximatively 3 million are added every year, can simply not prove their legal existence due to non-registration. This shows that just over a quarter of birth or more precisely 27 % are registered, with 32 % in urban areas and 24 % in rural areas. Currently, births are registered to the Civil Registration Management System (CRMS) managed by the National Data·base and Registration Authority (NADRA) through local governmental basic unit, Union Councils (UC) offices. Although there are 6550 Union Councils only 2,233 UCs have been made operational with varying degrees of effectiveness. Still more than 70 per cent of children are not registered at birth, especially girls, children belonging to a religious or minority group, refugee children and children living in rural areas.

The low rate of birth registration is due to the following reasons:

- **Long distance and lack of transportation means:** Parents have often to travel long distances to registration office to register their children's birth and several trips may be required to obtain the birth certificate. This can be costly time consuming and impractical if they have to use public transportation. The level of effort required can appear disproportionate especially as the importance of birth registration is not always well understood.
- **Lack of awareness:** In many cases, the rural population is unaware of the importance of birth registration. Literacy remains low in many rural areas of Pakistan and legal documents are often not clearly understood by citizens.
- **Administrative delays and inefficiency:** According to field research in Pakistan, it is quite common for registration offices to run out of official registration forms. In other cases, offices refuse to register people if they do not pay for the certificate at the same time. Such problems contribute to undermine people's willingness to register new-born babies.
- **Cost and poverty:** Quite often, birth registration is free as in Thailand or rather cheap in Pakistan when it is done on time. However, associated travel expenses can

be discouraging, though it is important to note that families often travel much greater distances to inform friends and family of a birth (and incur greater cost). Combined with the time required to complete a registration, the low level of awareness of its importance, and the other financial priorities of families on extremely low incomes, the perception of the cost of registration serves to further reduce participation.

Taking into consideration the mentioned obstacles the usage of the mobile telephone and network could contribute to improve the current birth registration.

3.3   Mobile Birth Registration in Pakistan

To address the main obstacles of the current birth registration in Pakistan, namely the long travel for birth registration and the awareness of the parents, and to drive up birth registration, the Mobile Birth Registration process proposes the introduction of trusted, reliable and community based '**gatekeepers**' who make use of mobile phones to carry out birth registration.

These gatekeepers can help leapfrog the natural adoption and acceptance of birth registration as a must practice. While the citizens and households will take a long time to reach the literacy and awareness levels to proactively get births registered among the various societal issues and bias, gatekeepers can help increase birth registration rates.

Two types of gatekeepers are proposed:

- **Mobile gatekeepers:** will comprise of government officials/field staff that have regular interaction with households in the communities and are well aware of any births happening.
  The potential primary gatekeepers in this category are:
  - **Lady Health Workers/Supervisors/Visitors** who are the agents of maternal and child health advisory especially in rural areas.
  - **Teachers** who are aware of community dynamics by virtue of their respected role in the social settings and interactions with children in school.
  - **Nikah Registrars** (Marriage Licensing Registrars) who are the only agents registering marriages in a community and are connected to the Union Council as part of their legal authority.
- **Stationary gatekeepers:** will serve as an intermediary facilitation improving access of households to get births registered. Instead of interacting with only one UC office, presence of multiple stationary gatekeepers will not only help reduce the travel time and cost but also streamline the process stages by gatekeepers serving as process facilitators.

  Typically, private sector partners who have a ready distribution network equipped with technology systems can serve as the ideal fit. Telenor Pakistan, being a partner for this pilot, has offered to use their 'Sahoolat Ghar' distribution network of retailers as stationary gatekeepers.

Gatekeepers will be equipped with handheld devices and a custom application to digitize the standard birth registration application form. As shown in Fig. 2 all inputs

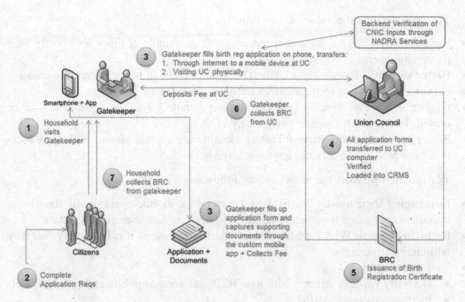

Fig. 2. Mobile Birth registration process

necessary for birth registration will now be entered into this mobile application and saved as unique applications.

All necessary documents (CNIC[1], hospital certificate etc.) will be scanned and/or pictured through the device to serve as an electronic copy. The CNIC details will be verified through NADRA (National Data base and Registration Authority) online/Short Message services to ensure the data entered is credible. Once the form has been duly filled, gatekeepers will also collect the stipulated fee and issue a receipt through a pre-printed book.

The digital forms along with supporting digital documents will then be transferred to the respective UC along with the fee collected for onwards birth registration through the NADRA CRMS (Civil Registration Management System). The mobile application will be designed to shake hands with the NADRA CRMS and enable import of data.

The UC Secretary, can then review applications address any queries and process the registration. Once registered, the gatekeepers will be issued Birth Registration Certificate (BRC) for their respective households for onward delivery.

To ensure security stronger encryption is carried out using a ciphering key generated by the SIM card.

4   Value Proposition

The Mobile Identity is undoubtedly valuable to the people in rural areas but it is nevertheless quite compelling both the governments and mobile operators.

---

[1] Computerized National Identity Card.

For governments the values are as follows:

- **Cost efficient:** Digital document management is usually 6 times less costly than paper equivalents
- **Better security:** Potentially, mobile ID on the phone can be more secure because it is protected by a pin or is stored securely on the SIM or servers
- **Higher flexibility:** Identity can be managed remotely (mobile certificates can be erased, forwarded to another party easily etc.)
- **Better services to the citizens:** Putting identities on mobile phones will allow users to access places and services anytime, anywhere

For mobile operators the values are as follows.

- **Leveraging their assets:** The SIM card own by the mobile operator will have more important role since it carries in addition to service data user personal data.
- **Reducing churn:** With the SIM strongly tied to the users, it is less likely that they will change operators.
- **New revenues:**
  - Diversify revenue streams with new B2B solutions to public and private clients
  - Increase customer ARPU
- **Extended reach and improved image:**
  - Facilitation of ID registration means more citizen will be able to access mobile operator services
  - Improving operator's image
- **Best defense against Internet players:** Big players such as Apple, Google or Facebook are entering the identity field with their Over-the-top services like Google Authenticator, Facebook Connect, etc.) and Mobile Identity is the operator's best weapon.

5 Social Benefit Analysis

To show the social benefits brought by the Mobile Identity concept, a comparison between mobile birth registration and the traditional fixed registration was carried out. The obvious value of Mobile Identity is to increase the registration rate from around 27 % to 100 %. The project is obviously beneficial since it will bring a better future to a lot of children but the challenge here is how to monetize the outcomes of mobile birth registration and how to prove that it is better than the fixed birth registration. In fact it is very difficult or almost impossible to put a value on a child's life. To avoid this, a Cost-Effectiveness Analysis (CEA) [10] is proposed.

The Cost-Effectiveness is defined as the ratio of Cost to Outcome. Lower CE will yield high effectiveness.

According to the Pakistani national statistic, 60 million of children i.e. around 73 % are not registered.

Let the current birth registration cost be C_o and the outcome be the birth registration percentage.

The current Cost-Effectiveness is:

$$CE_o = \frac{C_o}{27} = \frac{100C_o}{27 \times 100}$$

Let C_M the cost of introducing Mobile Identity and if the goal is to achieve 100 % birth registration the outcome will be 100.

The Mobile Identity Cost-Effectiveness is:

$$CE_M = \frac{C_o + C_M}{100} = \frac{27C_o + 27C_M}{27 \times 100}$$

If Mobile Identity is more beneficial than the current fixed birth registration we have:

$$CE_M \leq CE_o \leftrightarrow 27C_o + 27C_M \leq 100C_o$$
$$\leftrightarrow 27C_M \leq 73C_o$$
$$\leftrightarrow C_M \leq \frac{73C_o}{27}$$
$$\leftrightarrow C_M \leq 2,7C_o$$

In general it is difficult to find statistics and we propose to concentrate on the costs for one Union Council instead of the whole country.

According to the figures from The Telenor Mobile Identity pilot project in Pakistan the total implementation cost of Mobile Identity in two Union Councils in Sindh and two other in Punjab is 30 592 800 Rs.

The average cost for one Mobile Identity is hence:

30 592 800 Rs.: 4 = 7 648 200 Rs.

Regarding the cost of the current birth registration we are not able to find any documentation. Since the current birth registration is executed by the Union Councils (UC) we propose to use part of UC's total expenditure, for instance a quarter of the expenditures as the birth registration cost.

According to Tehsil Municipal Administration Kasur [11] the total expenditure of Tehsil Kasur in 2012–13 is 729 546 800 Rs.

The average expenditure of a UC is:

729 546 800 Rs.: 55 UC in Kasur = 13 263 487 Rs.

The estimated birth registration cost is:

13 263 487 Rs.: 4 = 3 315 872 Rs.

Consequently:

C_M = 7 648 200 Rs. < 2,7 C_o = 2,7 × 3 315 872 Rs. = 8 952 854 Rs.

This shows that:

$CE_M < CE_O$

This proves hence at Mobile Identity is more beneficial for the society than the current birth registration.

6 Conclusion

In this paper the usability and usefulness of Mobile Computing in the development of the society. In fact, mobile computing with its ubiquity and agility is by far a superior solution to the fixed infrastructure, which is not sufficiently installed in developing countries. A typical example is Mobile Identity which makes use of the mobile networks, mobile handsets and mobile application in the birth registration and establishment of civil identity. This is a compelling concept that could help increasing the birth registration rate due to its flexibility and reachability. Indeed, it reaches people in rural areas that the current birth registration is not capable of. Mobile Identity brings values not only to the citizen user but also to the governments, the intermediary gatekeepers and mobile operators. A preliminary social benefit assessment shows also that Mobile Identity is more beneficial than the current birth registration. A pilot project is currently executing at 4 Union Councils in Sindh and Punjab regions in Pakistan and statistics will be collected to enable the execution of a complete financial feasibility study that will be useful for a full scale deployment of Mobile Identity in Pakistan. The experiences and lessons learned can be then used in other countries in the benefit of the children in the world.

References

1. Telenor ASA. http://www.telenor.com
2. UNICEF. http://www.unicef.org/
3. The GSM Association. http://www.gsma.com/
4. van Thanh, D., Huy, N.P., Khuong, L.H.: Mobile identity as social economic enabler. In: Proceedings of the 7th International Conference on Computing and Convergence Technology 2012 (ICCCT 2012), IEEE PDF files. ISBN: 978-89-94364-22-3
5. van Do, T., Jørstad, I.: The ambiguity of identity. Telektronikk 103(3/4), 3 (2008). 20057 – Identity Management - ISSN 0085-7130
6. van Do, T., et al: Mobile identity as a tool to develop society. In: Proceedings of 5th 2015 International Conference on IT Convergence and Security, ICITCS 2015 IEEE Catalog Number: CFP1591W-ART (Article), CFP1591W-USB (USB), ISBN 978-1-4673-6537-6
7. Papadopouli, M. (ed.): European Network and information Security Agency (ENISA): Mobile Identity Management, University of Crete, Greece, 13 April 2010
8. E-Estonia Mobile ID. http://e-estonia.com/components/mobile-id
9. UNICEF: The 'Rights' Start to Life: A statistical analysis of birth registration. ISBN 92-806-3858-0, February 2005
10. Wholey, J.S., Hatry, H.P., Newcomer, K.E.: Twenty-one cost-effectiveness and cost benefit analysis. In: Cellini, S.R., Kee, J.E.: Handbook of Practical Program Evaluation. Jossey-Bass, A Wiley Imprint, San Francisco. ISBN 978-0-470-52247-9 (hardback)
11. Tehsil Municipal Administration Kasur. http://tmakasur.com/Budget.html

Strengthening Mobile Network Security Using Machine Learning

Van Thuan Do[1], Paal Engelstad[2],
Boning Feng[2], and Thanh van Do[3,4]([✉])

[1] Linus AS, Martin Linges vei 15, 1364 Fornebu, Norway
t.do@linus.no
[2] College of Applied Sciences, Oslo and Akershus University,
Pilestredet 46, 0167 Oslo, Norway
{paal.engelstad,boning.feng}@hioa.no
[3] Telenor ASA, Snarøyveien 30, 1331 Fornebu, Norway
thanh-van.do@telenor.com
[4] Norwegian University of Science and Technology, 7031 Trondheim, Norway

Abstract. Lately, several episodes of tapping and tracking of mobile phones in Europe including Norway have been revealed, showing the vulnerabilities of both the mobile network and mobile phones. A better protection of the user's confidentiality and privacy is urgently required. This paper will present an innovative mobile network security system using machine learning. The paper will start with a vulnerability and threat analysis of the evolving mobile network, which is a fusion of mobile wireless technologies and Internet technologies, complemented with the Internet of Things. The main part of the paper will concentrate on clarifying how machine learning can help improving mobile network security. The focus will be on elucidating what makes machine learning superior to other techniques. A special case study on the detection of IMSI Catcher, the fake base station that is used in mobile phone tracking and tapping, will be explained.

Keywords: Mobile network security · Mobile privacy · Cyber security · Cyber attacks

1 Introduction

Until lately the mobile network was perceived as quite secured compared to the Internet since the users benefit of stronger encryption provided by the SIM card [1]. Unfortunately, the recent phone tapping incidents revealed by the former CIA agent Snowden have shocked the whole world and raised doubt about the security of the mobile network [2]. In fact, the reduced prices of hardware equipment resulting from advances in microelectronics combined with the availability of open source mobile communication software have made the attacks on mobile networks both easier and more affordable. The need for better protection of user security and privacy is more urgent than never. The biggest challenge is, however, due to the fact that the mobile network resulting from a fusion of mobile and Internet technologies, inherits the weaknesses of both parties and worst suffers also of the unknown ones born by the marriage.

© Springer International Publishing Switzerland 2016
M. Younas et al. (Eds.): MobiWIS 2016, LNCS 9847, pp. 173–183, 2016.
DOI: 10.1007/978-3-319-44215-0_14

This paper will present an innovative mobile network security system using machine learning. The paper will start with an overview of the vulnerabilities and threats of the modern mobile network, which is a fusion of mobile wireless technologies and Internet technologies, complemented with the Internet of Things. The main part of the paper will concentrate on clarifying how machine learning can help improving the mobile network security. The focus will be on elucidating what makes machine learning superior to other techniques. A special case study on the detection of IMSI Catcher, the fake base station that is used in mobile phone tracking and tapping, will be explained. A machine learning based IMSI catcher detection is described. The paper ends with suggestions of future works in the area of Machine Learning and mobile network security.

2   Related Works

Mobile network security has attracted more attention lately but the research activities are still limited to the ones of a few communities that will be briefly described in the coming sections.

2.1   Security Research Labs (SRLabs)

The SRLabs [3] in Berlin led by the famous German Cryptographer and security researcher Karsten Nohl has considerable activities related to detection of mobile phone tapping. SRLabs has a collection of tools for the assessment of mobile network security.

2.2   P1 Security

P1 Security (Priority One Security) [4] is a company led by Philippe Langlois, a well-known security expert, which is dedicated to providing top security products and services for high-expertise security areas. P1 Security has a Telecom Security Task Force, which is a research think tank and consulting network in Telecom sector.

2.3   SBA Research

SBA Research [5] is an Austrian research center for Information Security funded by the national initiative for COMET Competence Centers for Excellent Technologies and consisting of 25 companies, 4 Austrian universities and several international research partners. The center is focusing on challenges ranging from organizational to technical security and has recently a few activities on mobile network security including the implementation of the IMSI catcher.

All the mentioned communities do have activities on mobile network security yielding valuable results, which are used in our research. However, none of them proposes to use machine learning in the protection of the mobile network.

3 Threats and Vulnerabilities in the Mobile Network

Although compared to the Internet the mobile network is still much more secured it is now more exposed. Designed and built as a walled garden system the mobile network has evolved to become an open system, which is in nature much more vulnerable to attacks. Further, a lot of changes have been happening since the introduction of mobile communication and reshaping the landscape dramatically. First, deregulation was removing the monopoly of telecom operators at the same time as opening the market for less trusted parties. Next, in order to pave the way for innovative services in addition to voice and short message, mobile operators have to adopt IP technology, which brought with it a series of weaknesses. Third, advances in microelectronic have made possible the production of lower price hardware equipment that could be used in the attacks against mobile networks. Last but not least, the emergence of open source mobile communication software such openBTS [6], openBSC [7], Open Source GSM Baseband software, etc. has enabled the construction of base station of a few hundred dollars, which can be used as fake base station, aka IMSI catcher [8–10] to impersonate the users.

Figure 1 shows the vulnerable entry points where attacks have been launched against the mobile network as follows:

- **Mobile phone:** mobile phones are exposed to viruses and could be crashed by attacks such as SMS of Death. OsmocomBB [11] a free Open Source GSM Baseband software implementation can be used to build hostile phones that are used in the attacks against subscribers and mobile networks.

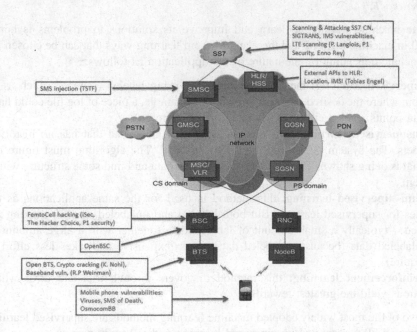

Fig. 1. Vulnerabilities in the mobile network

- **BTS (Base Transceiver Station):** Open source openBTS can be used to build fake base station aka IMSI catcher. Crypto cracking (by Karsten Nohl), Baseband vulnerabilities (by Weinman) show that the encrypted radio channel between the BTS and the mobile phone could be cracked.
- **BSC (Base Station Controller):** Fake BSC can be built using OpenBSC. Femtocell hacking can be used to penetrate the mobile core network.
- **SMSC (Short Message Service Center):** SMS injection can be used to attack SMSC.
- **HLR (Home Location Register):** Location tracking, IMSI capture (by Tobia Engel) can be launched using the HLR's external APIs
- **SS7 (Signalling Signal 7):** Scanning & attacking SS7 CN, SIGTRANS, IMS vulnerabilities, LTE scanning (by Langlois) show the vulnerabilities of SS7 networks.

4 Briefly About Machine Learning

Before examining how machine learning can contribute to securing mobile network it is worth to revise the definition of machine learning. According to Mitchell [12]:

"The field of machine learning is concerned with the question of how to construct computer programs that automatically improve with experience"

He provides also a short formalism as follows:

"A computer program is said to learn from experience E with respect to some class of tasks T and performance measure P, if its performance at tasks in T, as measured by P, improves with experience E."

The machine's ability to learn and improve its solutions to problems is hence central in machine learning and there are different learning ways that can be chosen for the machine depending on the nature of the application as follows:

- **Supervised learning:** the machine is trained using labeled examples, such as an input where the desired output is known. For example, a piece of log file could have data points labeled either "A" (attack) or "B" (benign).
- **Unsupervised learning:** this method is used against data that has no historical labels. The system is not told the "right answer." The algorithm must figure out what is being shown. The goal is to explore the data and find some structure within them.
- **Semi-supervised learning:** this method is used for the same applications as the ones for supervised learning. But both labeled and unlabeled data for training are used – typically a small amount of labeled data together with a large amount of unlabeled data (because unlabeled data is less expensive and takes less effort to acquire).
- **Reinforcement learning:** this method discovers through trial and error which actions yield the greatest rewards.

Two of the most widely adopted machine learning methods are supervised learning with around 70 percent and unsupervised learning with 10 to 20 percent.

5 How Can Machine Learning Improve Mobile Network Security

5.1 Zero Day Attacks

As stated previously, the mobile network has considerable vulnerabilities but the worst is that not all the vulnerabilities are identified and there are probably other unknown vulnerabilities.

In addition to attacks that exploit older, more commonly known vulnerabilities that have not yet been patched, or make use of basic poor security practices, there are **Zero day attacks**.

Zero day attacks are attacks on zero day vulnerabilities, i.e. vulnerabilities that become publicly known (zero-day) on the same day of the attack or more generally, vulnerabilities which have not been patched or made public. Once known the vulnerability is not called zero day anymore but known vulnerabilities and a race for protection solutions begins.

A zero-day attack starts when a flaw or software or hardware vulnerability is exploited and attackers release malware before a developer has an opportunity to create a patch to fix the vulnerability — hence "zero-day."

Vulnerabilities may be discovered by hackers, by security companies or researchers, by the software or hardware suppliers themselves or by users. If discovered by hackers, the vulnerabilities will be exploited and kept secret for as long as possible. Hackers will circulate only through the ranks of hackers, until software or security companies become aware of it or of the attacks targeting it. These types of attacks are defined by some as 'less than zero-day' attacks.

Lately, although not yet common, attacks exploiting multiple zero day vulnerabilities has emerged. Further, in order to extend the attack window the attackers modify their tools just enough to evade detection a little bit longer. Polymorphism and metamorphism are obfuscation techniques that are used to evade detection.

Consequently, zero day attacks and their mutations are quite difficult to parry and this is where Machine Learning can come to help. It can help building a variety of profiles such as user profile, network traffic, service usage, access activities, etc. which define normal situation or normal behavior. Any deviation indicates anomalies that can trigger an alarm resulting to intervention of experts.

5.2 Challenges in the Construction of Conclusive Attack Signatures

To detect known attacks on their networks mobile operators could use signature based IDS (Intrusion Detection System). There exist several definitions of attack signature which are slightly different depending on the focus and detail level. In this paper, an attack signature is defined as a characteristic or distinctive pattern that can be searched for or that can be used in matching to previously identified attacks [13]. Unfortunately, some serious known attacks on the mobile networks do not have sufficiently distinctive patterns that can be used to distinguish them from regular benign actions. The usage of such patterns in the detection of abuses in the mobile network leads to both unacceptably high false positive rate and high false negative rate i.e. while the usage of insufficiently distinctive patterns trigger a lot of false alarms, real abuses can still go unobserved. This situation will be illustrated with the case study IMSI catcher in the next section.

6   Case Study: The IMSI Catcher

6.1   Short About IMSI Catcher

According to [14] An IMSI catcher is a device for intercepting GSM mobile phones. It subjects the phones in its vicinity to a Man-In-The-Middle (MITM) attack by pretending to be the preferred base station in terms of signal strength. Actually, it is a fake base station that lures mobile phone to attach to it instead of legal ones. As its name tells, the IMSI catcher logs the IMSI numbers of all the mobile phones in the area, as they attempt to attach to the base station, and can determine the phone number of each individual phone. It also allows forcing the mobile phone connected to it to revert to A5/0 for call encryption (in other words, no encryption at all), making the call data easy to intercept and convert to audio. The phone calls can hence be tapped and recorded by the IMSI Catcher.

6.2   Challenges in the Detection of IMSI Catcher

IMSI catchers constitute undoubtedly a substantial threat to the users since they can be used in the invasion of the user's privacy i.e. they can be used in the surveillance of the users, in the interception of calls and short messages. However, they do not cause any harm to the mobile network neither in terms of availability and performance nor revenues and reputation. Further, they do not leave real trace since they do actually not intrude into the mobile network. This is probably the reason for that most of the IMSI catcher detection solutions are device based, i.e. a dedicated handheld device such as a GSMK CRYPTOPHONE [15] or an app like to be installed on a smartphone like Android IMSI-Catcher Detector (AIMSICD) [8], Snoopsnitch [16]. In fact, according to our knowledge there is currently no IMSI catcher detection solution that is on the network and operated by mobile operator for the protection of the users. In this case study, we are proposing a network-based IMSI catcher which is using Machine Learning to detect the presence of IMSI catcher.

6.3   Challenges in the Establishment of IMSI Catcher Signature

To detect the presence of IMSI catcher in the mobile network it is necessary to have a signature which does not exist since no detection system exists in the mobile network. Therefore, we have to build a signature by composing several indicators i.e. characteristics that could together indicate a probable presence of an IMSI catcher. A thorough study of the mobile network architecture, network elements and network interfaces has been carried out to identify the relevant indicators that are successively described in the coming sections.

6.3.1   Handover from 3G to 2G

The current mobile network is usually a composition of 2G (GSM) and 3G (UMTS) mobile networks in order to provide ubiquitous mobile coverage and support of all types of mobile phones. However, most of current mobile phones in use support both 2G, 3G and a series of frequency bands. When the mobile phones are moving around handover i.e. shift between cells of same technology, i.e. 2G-2G or 3G-3G or between cells of different technologies, i.e. 2G-3G or 3G-2G can be executed depending on:

- Signal strength variation
- Signal quality
- Load balancing between cells
- Distance between cells

Indicator HO1: Abnormal high handover from 3G to 2G in an area where 3G coverage is good could indicate the presence of an IMSI catcher jamming 3G signal and forcing mobile phones to downgrade to 2G for call tapping.

- *Dependency:* Must be used together with other indicators
- *Limitation:* 3G-2G handover is quite usual because 2G usually has better coverage than 3G
- *Quality:* High level of false positives
- *Confidence:* Low

Indicator HO2: Changes in the 2G-2G handover patterns could also indicate the arrival of an IMSI catcher.

- *Dependency:* Must be used together with other indicators
- *Limitation:* Influenced by changes in the network such as network optimalisation, errors in neighbor cells, traffic variations, atmospheric variation, etc.
- *Quality:* Very high level of false positives because 2G-2G can occur due circumstances mentioned in limitation
- *Confidence:* Low

Indicator HO3: Increase in unsuccessful handovers could also be due to the signal jamming of an IMSI catcher.

- *Dependency:* Must be used together with other indicators
- *Limitation:* Influenced by changes in the network such as network optimalisation, errors in neighbor cells, traffic variations, atmospheric variation, etc.
- *Quality:* Very high level of false positives because unsuccessful handovers can occur due circumstances mentioned in limitation
- *Confidence:* Low

6.3.2   Location Update

In the mobile networks, cells are grouped into *Location Area* (LA) for 2G networks, *Routing Area* (RA) for 3G networks. These areas are identified by an area code such as

Location Area Code (LAC), Routing Location Code (RAC). When a mobile phone moves and changes location areas it will perform a location update to inform the mobile network about the new location area such that calls can be delivered to the mobile station. A mobile terminal can change areas between 2G and 3G network without changing geographical locations. Changes in LAC or RAC can be used in the detection of IMSI catcher because they can show abnormal location areas or abnormal location update patterns due to the presence of IMSI catcher.

Indicator LU1: Increase in LAC updating can be a sign of an IMSI catcher

- *Dependency:* Must be used together with other indicators
- *Limitation:* Influenced by changes in the network such as network optimalisation, errors in neighbor cells, traffic variations, etc.
- *Quality:* High level of false positives because the increase in LAC updating can be due to circumstances stated in limitation
- *Confidence:* Medium

Indicator LU2: Sequence of last visited LAC can also indicate the presence of an IMSI catcher

- *Dependency:* Must be used together with other indicators
- *Limitation:* If the IMSI catcher is configured as a 3G base station covering the same area as the 2G cell this indicator will not be able to detect it.
- *Quality:* High level of false positives because the mobile phones can be switched off or run out of battery
- *Confidence:* Medium

6.3.3   Relation Between IMSI and IMEI

Every mobile subscriber gets assigned from her mobile operator a universal unique identity called IMSI (International Mobile Subscriber Identity), which, installed in the SIM card is used in the identification of the subscriber at connection to the mobile network. The mobile phone itself has also a unique identity called IMEI (International Mobile Equipment Identity). Normally the relation IMSI-IMEI is quite stable and recorded in mobile network. A change of the IMSI-IMEI relation can be used in the detection of IMSI catcher.

Indicator II1: Multiple IMSI One IMEI can indicate that one IMSI catcher is impersonating multiple subscribers

- *Dependency:* Relies on the database storing the relation IMSI-IMEI
- *Limitation:* This indicator can be used to detect only active IMSI catchers that are monitoring calls or intercepting SMS but fails to detect passive IMSI catchers that track the location of the user. More advanced IMSI catchers can also clone the IMEI of their target and remain invisible. Of course, this indicator fails totally when a large number of phones does not have IMEI or use the same fake IMEI as it is the case of many developing countries.

- *Quality:* medium quality to detect less advanced IMSI catchers but low quality for advanced IMSI catchers
- *Confidence:* Medium

Indicator II2: One IMSI Multiple IMEI can indicate that a particular subscriber is exposed for attack by one or more IMSI catchers.

- *Dependency:* Relies on the database storing the relation IMSI-IMEI
- *Limitation:* This indicator has the same limitations as indicator II1. In addition, the user may also have multiple devices and move her SIM card between them.
- *Quality:* medium quality to detect less advanced IMSI catchers but low quality for advanced IMSI catchers
- *Confidence:* Medium

By examining all the indicators we can conclude that none of the indicators can be used alone by itself and more importantly, by using all the indicators together it is still not sufficient to determine the presence of an IMSI catcher. Therefore, a signature based IMSI catcher detection is proved to be insufficiently efficient.

6.4   A Machine Learning Based IMSI Catcher Detection

Although the indicators described in the previous sections are not sufficient to compose a signature usable in the detection of IMSI catchers they can be used in a Machine Learning based IMSI catcher detection.

As shown in Fig. 2 the online-detection part contains different anomaly detectors, each of which uses an indicator i.e. HO1, HO2, HO3, LU1, LU2, II1 and II2 to define normal and abnormal behavior. A simplest form of the ensemble model is the majority voting between the different detectors but a weighted voting may also be considered in later phases. Several machine-learning algorithms, such as one-class Support Vector Machines [17] and Neural Networks, can be used as anomaly detectors.

Following the suggestions from the ensemble detector, security experts would then look at suspicious places to verify if there any true IMSI catchers at a point in time. The feedback from the security experts is then given back to off-line learning part to update the models where the normal behavior was defined.

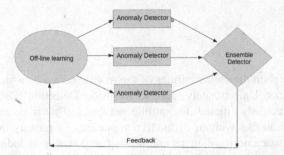

Fig. 2. The proposed Machine Learning based IMSI catcher detection

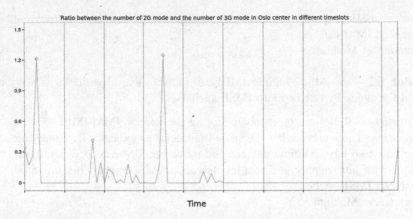

Fig. 3. Experiments on 2G/3G modes with Aftenposten data set

At the present stage of our project no real data set has been yet collected from the mobile network and for illustration sake we did some experiments on the public available data set related to IMSI catcher detection from Aftenposten [18]. The data came from a handset while interacting with the mobile network and possibly with the IMSI catchers as well, and we cannot show the advantages of machine-learning in correlating different events from many different devices. However, the main objective of this experiment is to show that there is a potential of applying machine learning techniques to facilitate the detection process.

For our simple experiment, from the data set we were interested in the frequency of the mode change between 2G and 3G. Our hypothesis is that the high value of the frequency would indicate abnormality in an area.

We split the data by equal time slots and calculate the ratio between the number of 2G and 3G in each time slot. We applied the anomaly detection algorithm named S-H-ESD from Twitter [19] to detect abnormalities for those obtained ratio values. The result is shown in Fig. 3. The three high spikes, which denote the abnormalities, indicate the possible presence of IMSI catcher.

In the next stage, we will deploy an IMSI catcher that we are building using openBTS in a test mobile network. We will collect data and feed them into the anomaly detectors. The results from the Ensemble Detector will be used to train the off-line learning.

7   Conclusion

In this paper we explain the vulnerabilities of the mobile networks which can exploited by malicious attacks. Unfortunately, current Intrusion Detection Systems using signature are not sufficiently efficient for mobile networks. This is because of zero-day vulnerabilities and attacks without distinctive signature. To remedy the situation, we propose to adopt machine learning technique that makes use of indicators to define normal and abnormal situation. Such detection could be much more efficient than existing solutions. The paper presents an IMSI catcher detection as a case study and a pilot Machine Learning based IMSI catcher Detection is elaborated for verification. As further, we will establish a test mobile network and an IMSI catcher by using openBTS such that experiments can be carried out and data collected for the Machine Learning detection.

References

1. van Thanhe, D., Jørstad, I., van Thuan, D.: Strong authentication for web services with mobile universal identity. In: Younas, M., Awan, I., Mecella, M. (eds.) MobiWIS 2015. LNCS, vol. 9228, pp. 27–36. Springer, Heidelberg (2015). ISSN 0302-9743, ISSN 1611-3349 (electronic), ISBN 978-3-319-23143-3, ISBN 978-3-319-23144-0 (e-book)
2. Foss, A.B., Johansen, P.A., Hager-Thoresen, F.: Secret surveillance of Norway's leaders detected; Aftenposten, 16 Dec 2014. http://www.aftenposten.no/nyheter/iriks/Secret-surveillance-of-Norways-leaders-detected-7825278.html
3. Security Research Labs. https://opensource.srlabs.de/
4. Priority One Security. http://www.p1sec.com/corp/
5. SBA Research. https://www.sba-research.org/
6. Openbts.org. http://openbts.org/
7. The Osmocom (Open Source Mobile Communication) project. http://openbsc.osmocom.org/trac/wiki/OsmocomOverview
8. Android IMSI-Catcher Detector (#AIMSICD). https://secupwn.github.io/Android-IMSI-Catcher-Detector/
9. Dabrowski, A., Pianta, N., Klepp, T., Mulazzani, M., Weippl, E.R.: IMSI-catch me if you can: IMSI-catcher-catchers. In: Annual Computer Security Applications Conference (ACSAC). ACM 978-1-4503-3005-3/14/12 (2014)
10. Daehyun Strobel: IMSI Catcher, Chair for Communication Security, Ruhr-Universität Bochum, 13 July 2007
11. The Osmocom (Open Source Mobile Communication) project – OsmocomBB. https://osmocom.org/projects/baseband
12. Mitchell, T.M.: Machine Learning. Mcgraw-Hill Companies Inc., New York (1997). ISBN ISBN-0-47-042807-7
13. Yegneswaran, V., Giffin, J.T., Barford, P., Jha, S.: An architecture for generating semantics-aware signatures. In: Proceedings of the 14th USENIX Security Symposium, pp. 97–112 (2005)
14. van Do, T., Nguyen, H.T., Momchil, N., Do, V.T.: Detecting IMSI-catcher using soft computing. In: Berry, M.W., Mohamed, A.H., Yap, B.W. (eds.) SCDS 2015. CCIS, vol. 545, pp. 129–140. Springer, Heidelberg (2015). ISSN 1865-0929 ISSN 1865-0937 (electronic)
15. GSMK CRYPTOPHONE. http://www.cryptophone.de/en/
16. Security Research Labs: SnoopSnitch app. https://play.google.com/store/apps/developer?id=Security+Research+Labs&hl=no
17. Vert, R., Vert, J.-P.: Consistency and convergence rates of one-class SVMs and related algorithms. JMLR **7**, 817–854 (2006)
18. Aftenposten data set. http://www.aftenposten.no/meninger/kommentarer/Derfor-publiserer-Aftenposten-hele-datagrunnlaget-for-mobilspionasje-sakene-7849555.html
19. Anomaly Detection algorithm from Twitter. https://github.com/twitter/AnomalyDetection

Secured Authentication Using Anonymity and Password-Based Key Derivation Function

Mohd Izuan Mohd Saad[(✉)], Kamarularifin Abd Jalil,
and Mazani Manaf

Faculty of Computer and Mathematical Sciences,
UiTM Shah Alam, Shah Alam, Selangor, Malaysia
mdizuansaad@gmail.com,
{kamarul,mazani}@tmsk.uitm.edu.my

Abstract. In cloud environment, security is a vital issue that will bring major impact to business operation. Cloud service provider has to ensure that data storage and communication medium is highly secured. In recent years, password-based authentication method has gained attention because of its simplicity, its capability in providing a secured process and its resistance from vulnerabilities. Nevertheless, there still have an issue on providing user identity protection and integrity of data from being abused by an adversary. Most of the current scheme involved third party in verification process and some of the scheme expose user's identity during authentication process. These can lead to the trust and transparency concern to the user. By exposing user identity will make a chance to the adversary to perform impersonate attack by impersonating legitimate user. Thus, strong cryptography algorithm with secure key exchange protocol is needed to further enhance the authentication process. This paper proposed an enhancement of password-based authentication scheme with anonymity features and key derivation function. The proposed scheme uses the Secure Remote Password (SRP) protocol and Password-Based Key Derivation Function 2 (PBKDF2) to enhance the authentication process. This paper also presents the anonymity description in authentication process which preserves user's identity information from being exposed. Anonymity is one of imperative feature that could hide identity of users during the authentication process. This is then followed by discussion of comparison of using password-based authentication scheme with other methods of authentication. Finally, this paper presents the flow of the proposed scheme which involved some algorithm modification. This research significantly enhances security level in password-based authentication using anonymity features and PBKDF2 to preserve user's privacy and to resist from any attack vulnerabilities.

Keywords: Authentication · Anonymity · Privacy · Trust · Key derivation

1 Introduction

Cloud computing provides dynamic and flexible infrastructure in order to serve multi-tenancy and multiple domain. Sharing equipment (hardware, software, application, etc) requires security assurance for protection of assets and data. Trust relationship

© Springer International Publishing Switzerland 2016
M. Younas et al. (Eds.): MobiWIS 2016, LNCS 9847, pp. 184–197, 2016.
DOI: 10.1007/978-3-319-44215-0_15

between cloud service provider and cloud user becomes important when all the resources are disseminated beyond their control perimeter [1]. Trust achievement between both parties will encourage the growing of cloud services with the guarantee of security control.

Most of the information is linked together with a user's identity information. Information leakage usually relates to exposure of user's identity information which leads to privacy issue. There have been many studies that propose solution to overcome the identity thief issue [2]. Most cases are associated with authentication and authorization process to protect from unauthorized user. Authentication process is an essential element to control and filter legitimate user to access important information via application system. Weak authentication scheme will cause vulnerability to malicious attacks [3]. Hence, strong and flexible authentication scheme is needed to support heterogeneous independent cloud platforms. It also has to preserve user's privacy by protecting the user's identity information during authentication process.

Anonymization of user's identity in authentication scheme will protect user's credential by hiding the user ID and password. Cloud users often exposed their users' credential in the cloud domain and some of them using the same user ID and password for multiple applications thus are highly exposed to adversary attack. User anonymity is n important requirement for information privacy and it has critically becoming a challenge for cloud security. Applying anonymity in authentication scheme can conceal user identity and at the same time could preserve user privacy from unauthorized party. User does not have to worry whether they communicate in a secured network or otherwise. The strong anonymous authentication should be able to protect user credential in both circumstances. Anonymity can improve trustworthy of the computer system and will eventually enhance the level of trust among the cloud users to utilize the cloud services [4].

There are many types of authentication scheme which can provide solution for a secured communication system [5, 6]. However, there is no single solution that could serve for all types of environment and application systems. System developers should study the overall process of the system before they can come out with the solution. Password-based authentication is a basis authentication scheme which is commonly in use until now. Although there are many new solutions proposed in the current market, password-based authentication still receives much of attention in recent years. It is a simple method (using user ID and password), does not require any complex infrastructure and also easy to deploy. Therefore, password-based authentication scheme is still relevant and suitable for use in a dynamic and big scale environment. This research uses SRP as a zero knowledge proof protocol with enhancement on key derivation using PBKDF2. This paper will further discuss details in providing strong anonymous password-based authentication scheme to enhance the trust relation as well as user's privacy in cloud environment.

This paper is organized in the following sections. Section 2 presents the background of study including authentication scheme comparison and anonymity in authentication scheme. Section 3 presents the proposed scheme which introduces PBKDF2 workflow and details description of the protocols. Section 4 describes the security analysis of the possible attack and its solution. Finally, Sect. 5 concludes the proposed scheme and future works.

2 Background

Authentication and authorization is considered as one of the most important key issue in cloud security issue. The weakness of authentication will allow room for vulnerability from malicious attack to get into cloud resources. It could lead to issues of transparency, integrity, privacy and may also cause security breach. Therefore strong authentication is needed to preserve user's privacy as well as to ensure secured communication among the cloud users. Nevertheless, there are still loopholes in the current studies that require further research and improvement.

2.1 Authentication Scheme Comparison

The selection of authentication scheme is associated with possible attacks that will cause vulnerability in the user business process. Some users are communicating using secured network infra while some of them are not. Thus, the best solution is authentication scheme that could accommodate with both environments. There are several types of authentication scheme that provide solution for the users to enhance their security control in order to verify legitimate user before they can access to resources. Authentication process act as a frontline protection in the communication system to verify and authorize only legitimate user can gain access to the resources.

The classic authentication paradigm described that authentication type is based on three factors such as something you now (password), something you have (token) and something you are (biometric) [7]. Based on this classic paradigm, three main authentication techniques that are commonly in use are password-based authentication, biometric authentication (finger print, voice, face) and smart-card authentication. There is no standard set of security properties which can be widely adopted for all types of system development. Each of this authentication schemes have their own strength and weakness. Thus system developers should consider and understand business requirement in order to adapt with user need.

A. Password-based authentication

Password-based authentication is a basic authentication scheme which are widely used because of its convenience, simplicity and easy to deploy. User need to memorize user ID and password for verification process without any requirement for additional devices. Users have to ensure that their passwords are not being exposed to prevent them from being stolen. Password stealing has always been one of critical issues in security because it could happen due to internal attack, external attack, website spoofing or key logging on public terminal [3]. It is also vulnerable to malicious attack such as man-in-the-middle attack, dictionary attack and eavesdrop attack. To overcome these issues, the cryptographic secret key is introduced to secure the session key exchange in the authentication process. Key establishment in the authentication process is a fundamental procedure to enhance the security level in network communication over an insecure platform [8]. The user will exchange secret key over the network for verification during the authentication process.

A classic model for key exchange is the Diffie-Hellman Key Exchange [9]. Diffie-Hellman protocol is a method that enables two users to share a secret key and agree to exchange the information over insecure network. However, this protocol is vulnerable to the man-in-the-middle attack because it allows user's credential to be transmitted via network communication. Password-Authenticated Key Exchange (PAKE) has been introduced key exchange protocol in password-based authentication technique to enhance their security in the communication [10]. This scheme uses one-way function to generate verifier and all party involved to compute the secret key. However, this scheme suffers in protecting the verifier from malicious attacker and the corresponding secret password is still needed. Lamport's scheme [11] has been introduced to allow authentication over insecure network infrastructure. However, this scheme also faced many problems including password management, storage capacity, hash computation overhead and necessity of counter resetting. It was also vulnerable to many attacks such as reply attack, dictionary attack, eavesdropping and Man in the Middle attack.

B. Smart card authentication (Two-factor authentication)

Smart card authentication scheme seems to be the most convenience way to provide two-factor authentication because of its efficiency in providing the cryptographic method together. It is a secured user credential with complex intelligent computation capability. It [12] was mentioned that smart card provide multi-functional and is easy to adapt with any of devices physically or logically. It will also cover a wide range of application deployment at affordable cost. Chang and Wu have used the Chinese Remainder Theorem (CRT) as a basis method to propose a remote password authentication scheme using a smart card [13]. This scheme resists replay attacks and does not require verification table in the server. Nevertheless, this scheme does not allow users to determine and change their own passwords freely. It is also not suitable in a dynamic and big scale environment such as cloud.

According to the [14], there is possibility that the smart card is vulnerable to the attack if the adversary manage to obtain secret information or some intermediate computational results from the smart card. Smart card is also vulnerable to impersonation attack, stolen smart card attack, offline password guessing attack and server masquerading attack. Additionally, smart card has some limitation on deployment process because not all computer and devices could support the smart card reader. They cannot utilize the smart card technology in public application system such as airport, bus station and hotel. Due to this limitation and constraints, thus smart card is difficult to be used in a wide range of dynamic and flexible environment.

Apart from using a smart-card as alternative solution for two-factor authentication (2FA), there is another alternative solution by using mobile phone for the second factor authentication. Mobile phone 2FA is widely use particularly involving financial institution and others well known organization such as Google, Amazon, Facebook, Microsoft and many more. In order to enable 2FA using mobile phone, users have to sacrifice their some personal information such as mobile phone number to enable 2FA in securing their account. It's actually expose their another personal secret information to the application owner and lead to the privacy issues. Another issue is some of the application cannot be used in certain platform (android or iOS). This constraint will lead to inefficient and useless. The integration is needed to close the gap between computer and mobile devices. However, in order to increase efficiency and usability, it's jeopardized 2FA with synchronization vulnerabilities and can cause the security breach [15]. Synchronization vulnerabilities is use a usability feature to blurs the gap which can potentially open the attacker (man-in-the-middle attack) to intercept One-Time-Password sent via mobile phone and bypass the chain of 2FA mechanism.

C. Biometric authentication

A biometric authentication is mechanism that use human body features as a unique and immutable measurement such as finger print, voice, face, etc. Biometric provide non-repudiation element and is more reliable in handling confidential and classified information. The characteristics are very difficult to counterfeit, cannot be lent or stolen, the person have to present himself to the point of authentication [16]. It is very hard to break a biometric key since it cannot be copied, shared or distributed [17]. The range of biometric signal is from hundred bytes to over a megabyte which is higher than password phrase that makes it more complicated and complex. The use of bio-metric authentication could solve a few limitation of password-based and smart card scheme. Nevertheless, biometric also have some limitation to the users. The following are limitations of using biometric authentication:

- **Additional devices** – Require additional device such as finger print reader, facial recognition system, speaker and voice recorder to authenticate the features of human body. It also requires technical expert to install and troubleshoot.
- **Cost overhead** – Additional devices to set up the biometric technology will increase the cost project. It does not only prepare the reader but also storage for logging data (PC) and also requires more storage capacity in the server.
- **Location of devices** – Installation of device have to consider a few things such as lighting (face recognition), background noise (voice recognition), temperature and air pressure, etc. Bad lighting and noise will cause major problem because it will interrupt the reader to capture the right input for authentication process.
- **Interference of Devices** – Injury like cut or burns on physical body (finger) will disrupt the reader and most probably fail to read the finger print. Similar problem for face recognition if the users cut have a haircut or increase their weight would result to failure in identifying the captured images.
- **Fake biometric** – It is possible that the adversary to reproduce the same biometric technology and will use fake finger, copy of signature and fake mask to assault the system application.
- **Accuracy** – If someone stole or copy a user identity, the user cannot change the record. It is because the users cannot change their finger, voice or face easily to replace their stolen or duplicated user identity.

Based on the discussion above, there are pros and cons for all types of authenti-cation scheme. The selection of authentication scheme should be wisely chosen. The key security issue for all authentication mechanism is to bind the user credential using the security method that you have. The strength of authentication mechanism can be measured as follows:

- The complexity of entropy of the mechanism
- Exploitation of vulnerabilities
- Procedural and human interaction

Table 1 shows the comparison of authentication mechanism based on the above measurement. Following the discussion, password-based authentication is still significant to be implemented with further enhancement to achieve the research objective. This research will be using Secure Remote Password (SRP) protocol as a basis of password-based authentication scheme. Secure Remote Password (SRP) [18] is a password-based protocol that provides zero-knowledge proof and it is a popular choice by the IETF for strong password protocols. The advantages of this protocol are as follows [8]:

Table 1. Authentication scheme comparison

Item	Password-based	Smart card	Biometric
Complexity of entropy	High entropy (depend on the length of password)	High entropy	Medium entropy
Exploitation of vulnerabilities	- Vulnerable to social engineering attack	- Reverse engineering of the chip - Flaw in design/ implementation	- Lack of secrecy - Biometric trait cannot replace - External attack
Procedural and human interaction	- Forgot password - Easy to guess - Short password make easy for adversary to guess	- Lost smart card - Theft - Can distribute or sharing	- Fake machine - Cannot change/update if fingerprint copy by someone else - Accuracy of reader may cause problem

i. **Not Require Password Table** - The protocol does not require password table in the server to store any information of password equivalents. In this protocol, the password will be computed together with random number known as salt number to generate the verifier value. Therefore, the attacker will not be able to guess or even if they can gain access to the server they still fail to predict or capture the real password. It also protects the server from dictionary attack.

ii. **Verifier-based** - Its verifier is values that replace the password for verification purpose during the login process. This is what they called as "verifier-based" which protect password from being stolen if there is any hacking or attack attempt. The server will use verifier value to prove knowledge of the legitimate user. Thus, the password will never be sent via network. If the attackers get access to the server, they cannot use verifier value to authenticate because it requires both sides to verify the process known as mutual authentication process.

iii. **Strong key establishment** - The protocol provides strong session key establishment without revealing the key in public. Both user and server will establish new session key every each login session. Thus, the key is not useful to eavesdropper because the session key is different for each processing task.

iv. **Mutual authentication** - Both parties have to verify each other before they can begin communicate. This is what they called "mutual authentication" by sending the evidence message for verification purpose. The advantage of mutual authentication is to allow the user to communicate with the server even in an unsecured network.
v. **Not require trusted third party** - It does not involve any third party for verification or identification of user credential. It can also avoid overhead that is equivalent with the PKI-based scheme.

2.2 Anonymity in Authentication Scheme

Anonymity is a fundamental right and very important to protect information privacy in all aspect especially related to finance, crime and terrorism. User's privacy protection is one of the most challenge issues because once it is breached, it will affect the whole system communication. User's privacy is associated with classified information that should be protected and located in secured environment. Anonymity in authentication process is to preserve user credential from being exposed over the network communication. Some of the applications called it anonymous authentication. The exposure of user credential will affect security process in daily business operation and lead to security breach [19]. Many researches were carried out to accommodate with this requirement [20, 21]. Vulnerability from malicious attack can intercept and manipulate user's identity to gain access to sensitive data of users in the cloud storage.

Implementation of anonymity is not only to protect from external intruder but also to protect from internal intruder especially intruders who are using a third party service as an entity to authorized the legitimate user. This is important for the user to control and monitor their privilege especially in cloud environment since they do not know exactly where the server and storage is located. Therefore, there is a need for strong cryptography mechanism to secure the authentication process to verify and control the communication system. The mechanism should be capable to hide user credential from being exposed to prevent from adversary impersonating as legitimate user. In this research, the proposed scheme is secured with anonymity feature which does not transmit the plaint-text of user ID and password across the network. The mutual authentication process takes place without any involvement of third party will make the proposed scheme become stronger.

2.3 Password-Based Key Derivation Function 2 (PBKDF2)

PBKDF2 is a pseudorandom function to derive a secret key and it is part of RSA Laboratories' Public-Key Cryptography Standards (PKCS) series - PKCS#5 v2.0. It is also published as Internet Engineering Task Force's RFC 2898. PBKDF2 use password together with large value of random salt and iteration count to compute stronger key value. The password is never sent across the network during the process of generating the key and only available during the active session. Although the password is not stronger enough but the key can reasonably be generating strong key due to

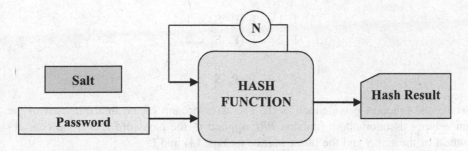

Fig. 1. PBKDF2 process flow

combination of random salt value and iteration count. Figure 1 below shows the flow of PBKDF2 to derive the key.

This function is using symmetric encryption key which can be generated only in active session and what is more the password is not stored in the server. By adding large iteration count, it will make password cracking much more difficult and will take a longer time, it is also called key stretching. Having random salt added to the computational function will reduce the chance of pre-computed hashes for attacks. Both random salts and iteration count will ensure that the key derivation process is secured against brute-force attack and dictionary attack. Here are the steps on how to derive a key using PBKDF2 [22]:

$$Derived\,Key\ =\ PBKDF2\,(P,\ S,\ c,\ dkLen)$$

Where:

PRF	pseudorandom function of two parameters with output length hLen (e.g. a keyed HMAC)
P	password, an octet string
S	salt, an octet string
c	iteration count, a positive integer
dkLen	desired length of the derived key
DK	derived key, a dkLen-octet string

Steps:

i. If $dkLen > (2\wedge 32 - 1) * hLen$, output "derived key too long" and stop.

ii. Let l be the number of *hLen*-octet blocks in the derived key, rounding up, and let r be the number of octets in the last block as Eqs. (1) and (2):

$$l\ =\ CEIL\,(dkLen/hLen) \tag{1}$$
$$r\ =\ dkLen - (l - 1) * hLen \tag{2}$$

iii. For each block of the derived key apply the function F defined below to the password P, the salt S, the iteration count c, and the block index to compute the block as Eq. (3):

$$T\_1 = F\ (P,\ S,\ c, 1)$$
$$T\_2 = F\ (P,\ S,\ c, 2)$$
$$\cdots \tag{3}$$
$$T\_l = F\ (P,\ S,\ c,\ l)$$

where the function F is defined as the exclusive-or sum of the first c iterates of the underlying pseudorandom function PRF applied to the password P and the concatenation of the salt S and the block index i as Eqs. (4) and (5):

$$F\ (P,\ S,\ c,\ i) = U\_1 \backslash xor\ U\_2 \backslash xor\ \cdots \backslash xor\ U\_c \tag{4}$$

where

$$U\_1 = PRF\ (P,\ S\ ||\ INT\ (i))$$
$$U\_2 = PRF\ (P,\ U\_1)$$
$$\cdots \tag{5}$$
$$U\_c = PRF\ (P,\ U\_\{c-1\})$$

iv. Concatenate the blocks and extract the first *dkLen* octets to produce a derived key *DK* as Eq. (6):

$$DK = T\_1\ ||\ T\_2\ ||\ \cdots ||\ T\_l < 0..r - 1 > \tag{6}$$

v. Output the derived key *DK*.

3 The Proposed Scheme

This section will describe the detail process of proposed scheme. It includes the anonymity features in SRP and also the enhancement of key derivation using PBKDF2. This scheme is mutual authentication scheme which provides zero-knowledge proof using verifier value to validate the process.

3.1 Protocol Description

The main goal of this paper is to preserve user's privacy in order to establish trust in a secured communication. It also protects user's credential vulnerability from malicious attack. It will use SRP protocol as a basis on developing the proposed protocol. In this proposed scheme, it consists of two phases; client registration phase and authentication phase.

The flow of client registration phase is shown in Fig. 2. The value of (n) and (g) is assumed as known value. This phase is normally done once for each user during

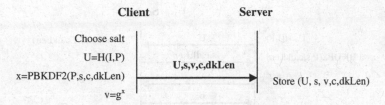

Fig. 2. Client registration phase

account setup. In this phase, anonymous identification (U) and password verifier (v) is computed based on Eqs. (7), (8) and (9). Descriptions of this phase are as follows:

i. Client input username (I) and password (P);
ii. Select salt (s) randomly;
iii. Compute anonymous identity (U) as Eq. (7) by using Secure Hash Algorithm (SHA-1) as a one-way hash function which produce 160-bit hash value (H);

$$U = H(I, P) \tag{7}$$

An practical example of the calculation of U can be the following, using SHA-1 as the hash function H:

$$U = SHA1(I \mid P)$$

iv. Compute password verifier (v) as Eqs. (8) and (9) by using PBKDF2;

$$x = PBKDF2(P, s, c, dkLen) \tag{8}$$

$$v = g^x \tag{9}$$

v. The value of anonymous identity (U), verifier (v) and salt (s) send to server;
vi. Server stored all the value received into its database.

The actual username and password is not sent over the network or even stored in the database. This will preserve the user ID to be exposed during the authentication phase. Attackers have suffered to identity the user ID is belonging to whom before they can try to breach a password.

Once the registration phase is completed, the client will then proceed with authentication process by providing anonymous identifier (U). Both client and server will calculate public key (A) and (B) by choosing random ephemeral private key (a) and (b). All these value will be exchanged to calculate Session Key (S) as Eq. (10). Finally, they will exchange evidence messages M1 and M2 to proof each other. The cryptographic strong key session (K) will be generated after successfully proof the secret knowledge as Eq. (11).

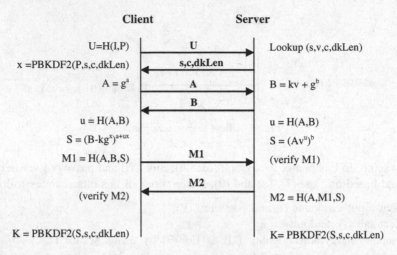

Fig. 3. Client authentication phase

$$S_{client} = (B - kg^x)^{a+ux}$$
$$= (kv + g^b - kg^x)^{a+ux} = g^{ab+uxb} = (g^a g^{xu})^b \qquad (10)$$
$$= (Av^u)^b = S_{server}$$

$$S_{client} = S_{server} = > PBKDF2(S_{client}) = PBKDF2(S_{server}) = K \qquad (11)$$

Figure 3 shows the workflow of the client authentication process between client and server. Both side required four roundtrip by exchanging the public key (A and B) and message evidence (M1 and M2) before establishing cryptographic strong key session (K).

4 Vulnerabilities and Security Analysis

4.1 Cloud Vulnerabilities

Cloud services require a mechanism to manage identity management for control and filter the access from cloud user. To a certain extent, compromising the authentication process will lead to primary vulnerability in the cloud services and cause security breach [20]. Cloud computing provides convenient, on-demand, dynamically scalable, highly available, interoperable and can be provisioned with minimal management efforts [23]. Following are examples of vulnerabilities with root causes in one or more of these characteristics [24]:

- **Unauthorized access to physical machines** – One of the cloud characteristics is resource pooling among the multiple users. All resources are sharing the same device to pool all the resources. Cloud service provider has full authority to access and monitor to the physical server activities. It is possible that vulnerability may come from internal attack. This issue will bring impact and put the cloud services at high risk.

- **Internet protocol vulnerabilities** – Cloud computing is on-demand and ubiquitous network access which can be accessed via web application. Some of the users access from a trusted network but there are some who access from an untrusted network. Web application protocol (HTTP) is vulnerable to session-hijacking, session-riding and man-in-the-middle attack.
- **Data recovery vulnerability** – Broad network access characteristic provide heterogeneous platforms which allow for multiple platform sharing and communicate in the same cloud domain. In some cases, this characteristic needs to recover data from different platform and need to allow access to the devices. The process of data recovery gives possible chances to adversary to penetrate into the network communication.

4.2 Possible Attacks

Proposed authentication scheme provide protection against different types of attacks such as dictionary, man-in-the-middle, impersonation, replay, stolen verifier attack and other feasible attacks. The scheme is secure against possible attack as follows:

- **Dictionary Attack** – Attacker using this technique to defeating and trying to determine decryption key or user ID and password offline or online. In proposed scheme, private key (a) and (b) compute at both side (client and server) and does not exposed in public. Furthermore, it's use PBKDF2 to derive the key, so it is very hard for attacker to break a key.
- **Impersonate Attack** – The adversary will assume one of the legitimate user in the system communication to perform an attack. It's very hard to assume because this scheme will not exposed user ID or password and do not transmitted user credential over the network. The session key (K) also not exposed in public so attacker cannot compute the evidence message (M1) and (M2) to prove that they are a legitimate user.
- **Replay Attack** – This attack is a form of network attack by adversary to intercept the valid data and repeatedly retransmitted. This scheme use a random 'salt' value (s) to generating secret key and keep changing for every login session. So the attacker cannot use a same value to retransmit because it keeps changing at every session.
- **Man-in-the-Middle Attack** – This attack is an interception the communication between two parties. The adversary secretly relays in between two parties and try to alter the communication path for them to capture the conversation and information. It's only possible if the adversary can capture the user ID (I) and password (P) for them to authenticate as a legitimate user. But, in proposed scheme, user ID (I) and password (P) are not transmitted over the network. So, it is impossible to masquerade as a client or server.
- **Stolen Verifier Attack** – This attack performing to steal a user's verifier *s* in the database when they gain access to the server. In order to perform an authentication

process or to generate a verifier value, they still required a user's password which not stored in the server. So, it is hard to break the communication even though they got the verifier value because the value of (x) is computed based on value (I) and (P).

- **Anonymity Protection** – This attack is to steal user credential including user ID and password to impersonating as a legitimate user to get an access to the system application. Proposed scheme are not exposed user ID and password to preserve user's privacy by replacing it as a anonymous identity using one-way hash function.

5   Conclusion

Cloud security can be achieved through high level of trust and privacy of information in system application. Authentication is a major issue in order to achieve trustworthy in cloud services. Password-based authentication with secure key exchange protocols has offer better solution in handling vulnerability from malicious attack. Vulnerability in the operating system application requires new approach and method to overcome weakness in the operating system which could lead to high risk of data integrity. Providing anonymity in an authentication scheme will hide user's credential from being exposed to any feasible attack.

This paper has proposed a password-based authentication scheme using secure key exchange protocols with some enhancement on derivation key and applying anonymity element. SRP provide strong mutual authentication password-based authentication which provides zero-proof knowledge based. PBKDF2 is used to enhance the process of derivation private key (x) and cryptographically strong key session (K) in the SRP protocols. Anonymity element is applied to hide user ID during registration and authentication process to prevent from adversary attack.

For future work, the proposed scheme will be evaluate and verify by performing the attack model to proof of concept of the proposed scheme. It also be measure the performance of the proposed scheme by compute the response time and latency during authentication process. Furthermore, it will also put under study to enhance it with certificate pinning method to reduce computation overhead and roundtrips communication steps. It is an effective method to reduce latency in computation cost.

Acknowledgment. The authors would like to thank Public Service Department (JPA) for their financial support in funding this research paper.

References

1. Abbadi, I.M.: A framework for establishing trust in cloud provenance. Int. J. Inf. Secur. **12** (2), 111–128 (2013)
2. Sengupta, S., Kaulgud, V., Sharma, V.S.: Cloud computing security–trends and research directions. In: 2011 IEEE World Congress on Services, October, pp. 524–531, July 2011
3. Sood, S.K., Sarje, A.K., Singh, K.: Cryptanalysis of password authentication schemes: current status and key issues. In: Proceedings of International Conference on Methods and Models in Computer Science, ICM2CS 2009 (2009)

4. Khattak, Z.A., Manan, J.A., Sulaiman, S.: Analysis of open environment sign-in schemes-privacy enhanced & trustworthy approach. J. Adv. Inf. Technol. **2**(2), 109–121 (2011)
5. Sumitra, B., Pethuru, C.R., Misbahuddin, M.: A survey of cloud authentication attacks and solution approaches. Int. J. Innov. Res. Comput. Commun. Eng. **2**(10), 6245–6253 (2014)
6. Chen, N., Jiang, R.: Security analysis and improvement of user authentication framework for cloud computing. J. Netw. **9**(1), 198–203 (2014)
7. Thomas, M.V., Dhole, A., Chandrasekaran, K.: Single sign-on in cloud federation using CloudSim. Int. J. Comput. Netw. Inf. Secur. **7**(6), 50–58 (2015)
8. Izuan, M., Saad, M., Jalil, K.A., Manaf, M.: Preserving user privacy with anonymous authentication in cloud computing. ARPN J. Eng. Appl. Sci. **10**(23), 17937–17944 (2015)
9. N. Co-investigator: Password-authenticated key (PAK) Diffie-Hellman exchange. J. Chem. Inf. Model. **53**, 1689–1699 (2013)
10. Bellovin, S.M., Merrit, M.: Encrypted key exchange: password-based protocols secure against dictionary attacks. In: IEEE Computer Society Symposium on Research in Security and Privacy (1992)
11. Lamport, L.: Password authentication with insecure communication. Commun. ACM **24**(11), 770–772 (1981)
12. Taherdoost, H., Sahibuddin, S., Jalaliyoon, N.: Smart card security; technology and adoption. Int. J. Secur. (IJS) (15), 74–84 (2011)
13. Chang, C.-C., Wu, T.-C.: Remote password authentication with smart cards. IEEE Trans. Consum. Electron. **139**(4), 91–98 (2000)
14. Wang, D., Ma, C.G., Zhang, Q.M., Zhao, S.: Secure password-based remote user authentication scheme against smart card security breach. J. Netw. **8**(1), 148–155 (2013)
15. Konoth, R.K, van der Veen, V., Bos, H.: How anywhere computing just killed your phone-based two-factor authentication. In: Proceedings of the 20th International Conference on Financial Cryptography and Data Security (2016)
16. Uludag, U., Pankanti, S., Prabhakar, S., Jain, A.K.: Biometric cryptosystems: issues and challenges. Proc. IEEE **92**(6), 948–960 (2004)
17. Li, C.-T., Hwang, M.-S.: An efficient biometrics-based remote user authentication scheme using smart cards. J. Netw. Comput. Appl. **33**(1), 1–5 (2010)
18. Wu, T.: The secure remote password protocol. In: Network and Distributed System Security Symposium, NDSS 1998, pp. 97–111 (1998)
19. Huang, J., Nicol, D.M.: Trust mechanisms for cloud computing. J. Cloud Comput. Adv. Syst. Appl. **2**(1), 1–14 (2013)
20. Yassin, A.A., Jin, H., Ibrahim, A., Qiang, W., Zou, D.: Cloud authentication based on anonymous one-time password. In: Han, Y.-H., Park, D.-S., Jia, W., Yeo, S.-S. (eds.) Ubiquitous Information Technologies and Applications. LNEE, vol. 214, pp. 423–431. Springer, Netherlands (2013)
21. Mishra, R.: Anonymous remote user authentication and key agreement for cloud computing. In: Pant, M., Deep, K., Nagar, A., Bansal, J.C. (eds.) SocProS 2013. AISC, vol. 258, pp. 899–913. Springer, Heidelberg (2014)
22. Contini, S.: Method to protect passwords in databases for web applications. IACR Cryptology ePrint Achieve, 387 (2015)
23. Tim Mell, P.G.: NIST definition of cloud computing. Natl. Inst. Stand. Technol. **53**, 50 (2009)
24. Grobauer, B., Walloschek, T., Stocker, E.: Understanding cloud computing vulnerabilities. IEEE Secur. Priv. **9**(2), 50–57 (2011)

Mobile and Wireless Networking

Optimal Resource Allocation for Non-Real Time Visible Light Communication Networks

Fabián Seguel, Pablo Adasme$^{(\boxtimes)}$, Ismael Soto, and Belarmino Nuñez

Departamento de Ingeniería Eléctrica, Universidad de Santiago de Chile,
Avenida Ecuador, 3519 Santiago, Chile
{fabian.seguel,pablo.adasme,ismael.soto,belarmino.nunez}@usach.cl

Abstract. In this paper, we consider the optimal joint resource allocation problem of subcarrier and power for non-real time wireless networks
that use visible light communication (VLC) technology. VLC has been
recognized as a promising technology as it allows to transmit data in
considerably higher orders of magnitude compared to traditional radio
frequency (RF) methods [3]. Therefore, it is expected that most of the
current existing protocols for resource allocation using traditional RF
technologies will adapt to VLC technology in the near future. We model
the resource allocation problem by means of a mixed integer nonlinear
optimization problem that we further linearize using a piecewise linear
approximation method. The latter allows to compute optimal and near
optimal solutions for the problem. Optimal solutions can be obtained as
long as the number of line segments is sufficiently large. Subsequently,
we propose a variable neighborhood search based decomposition procedure that allows to compute, in average, tight near optimal solutions in
less than one second compared to the high CPU time required by the
piecewise linear model.

Keywords: Visible light communications · Mixed integer nonlinear
programming · Piecewise mixed integer linear programming · Variable
neighborhood search

1 Introduction

Wireless Networks is becoming an active research field due to the innumerable
real life applications including medicine, transportation, agriculture, industrial
processes, environmental monitoring, battlefield surveillance, smart buildings
and cities, and military applications [1, 3, 15, 16, 19]. In this paper, we consider
the optimal joint resource allocation problem of subcarrier (subchannel) and
power for non-real time wireless networks that use visible light communication
(VLC) technology. VLC has been recognized as a promising technology as it
allows to transmit data in considerably higher orders of magnitude compared
to traditional radio frequency (RF) methods [3]. Therefore, it is expected that
most of the current existing protocols for resource allocation using traditional
RF technologies will adapt to VLC technology in the near future.

© Springer International Publishing Switzerland 2016
M. Younas et al. (Eds.): MobiWIS 2016, LNCS 9847, pp. 201–212, 2016.
DOI: 10.1007/978-3-319-44215-0_16

We model the resource allocation problem by means of a mixed integer non-linear optimization problem that we further linearize using a piecewise linear approximation method. The latter allows to compute optimal and near optimal solutions for the problem. Optimal solutions can be found as long as the number of line segments used in the piecewise linear model is sufficiently large. In practice, the number of line segments is enough when the objective function values found with the piecewise linear model do not further increase while incrementing the line segments. Piecewise linear methods allow to transform nonlinear programming problems into pure mixed integer linear programming problems which can be efficiently solved with specialized solvers [2,12]. We refer the reader to [6,8,14,17,20] for a deeper understanding on piecewise linear methods.

The proposed model aims to maximize the total bandwidth channel capacity of a wireless network subject to a quality of service constraint on the maximum signal to interference noise ratio (SINR) allowed in the system while simultaneously scheduling users in time. The SINR is mainly generated due to subchannel reuse which is caused by the different users [3]. In general, notice that the nodes are continuously interchanging information with a base station in the network. Therefore, the resource allocation problem must be solved dynamically in time in order to assign different subsets of subcarriers to users. As such, the proposed model is best suited for non-real time applications where signals can be transmitted at different time slots without further restrictions. The latter allows the fact that sub-channel multiuser diversity can be further exploited simultaneously in frequency and in time domains. As far as we know, joint subcarrier and power allocation transmission schemes for wireless networks have not been investigated so far for non-real time applications using RF and VLC technologies [5,13,18]. Moreover, there has been no attempt yet to solve this problem to optimality using piecewise linear models and variable neighborhood search (VNS for short) based metaheuristic procedures. We propose a VNS based decomposition procedure that allows to compute tight near optimal (and possibly optimal) solutions in significantly less computational effort compared to the piecewise linear model. The decomposition approach solves within each iteration a convex optimization problem which is characterized by its Karush Kuhn Tucker (KKT) conditions leading to the optimal solution.

The paper is organized as follows. Section 2 briefly introduces the system description and presents the nonlinear mathematical formulation of the problem. Next, we present the equivalent piecewise linear model. In Sect. 3, we sketch the VNS procedure. Subsequently in Sect. 4, we conduct preliminary numerical experiments in order to compare the piecewise linear model with the VNS procedure. Finally, in Sect. 5 we give the main conclusions of the paper.

2   System Description and Problem Formulation

In this section, first we give a brief system description of a wireless VLC network and then, we present the mathematical formulation of the resource allocation problem.

2.1 System Description

We consider a radial transmission area composed by a base station placed at the center and several mobile users randomly placed inside this area that simultaneously interchange information with the base station. The interchange of information generates interference and degrades the quality of wireless channels. In general, the interference phenomena is a major concern in wireless networks. One of the most used strategy to overcome interference is to make an efficient use of bandwidth channel capacity. This can be performed by dividing the bandwidth channel into several parallel subcarriers which allows to assign different subset of subcarriers to different users in the network. This allows to exploit the so-called multi-user diversity which in turn allows to increase the overall capacity of the system [4]. We consider a wireless VLC based network composed by a set of $\mathcal{N} = \{1, \ldots, N\}$ subcarriers, a set of $\mathcal{K} = \{1, \ldots, K\}$ users and a set of $\mathcal{T} = \{1, \ldots, T\}$ time slots within a given transmitted frame. A frame is a packet in which the data to be transmitted is placed. Each frame is composed by T time slots and N subcarriers.

2.2 Problem Formulation

We propose the following nonlinear formulation for this problem

$$P: \quad \max_{\{x,p\}} \sum_{t=1}^{T} \sum_{k=1}^{K} \sum_{n=1}^{N} x_{kt} \log_2 \left(1 + \varphi_{kn}^t p_{kn}^t \right) \tag{1}$$

$$\text{s.t.} \quad \sum_{k=1}^{K} \sum_{n=1}^{N} H_{kn}^t p_{kn}^t \leq \Gamma, \quad \forall t \in \mathcal{T} \tag{2}$$

$$\sum_{t=1}^{T} x_{kt} = 1, \quad \forall k \in \mathcal{K} \tag{3}$$

$$p_{kn}^t \geq 0, \quad \forall k, n, t \tag{4}$$

$$x_{kt} \in \{0, 1\}, \quad \forall k, t \tag{5}$$

where $\varphi_{kn}^t = \frac{R_{PD} H_{kn}^t}{\sigma_{kn}^t + \eta}$. Variables p_{kn}^t for all k, n, t and x_{kt} for all k, t are the decision variables. The variable p_{kn}^t denotes the amount of power to be assigned for user k in subcarrier n if scheduled to be attended on time slot t. Similarly, the variable $x_{kt} = 1$ if and only if user k is scheduled to be attended on time slot t and $x_{kt} = 0$, otherwise. The nonnegative condition on variable p_{kn}^t and the binary condition on variable x_{kt} are imposed in the constraints (4)–(5), respectively. Notice that whenever $x_{k't'} = 0$ for a particular k' and t', this implies that $p_{k'n}^{t'} = 0$ for all $n \in \mathcal{N}$ since the objective function (1) equals zero. The objective function computes the maximum capacity of the network [1,3,16]. The parameters R_{PD}, H_{kn}^t, σ_{kn}^t and η denote the photo-detector response, channel gain associated to subcarrier n for user k in time slot t, the Additive White Gaussian Noise (AWGN) and the accumulated AWGN power, respectively [3]. Constraint (2) ensures that the optimal solution cannot be larger than a predefined maximum SINR threshold denoted by Γ. Finally, constraint (3) schedules each user to be attended on a unique time slot $t \in \mathcal{T}$.

2.3 Piecewise Linear Formulation

We note that problem P is formulated as a binary nonlinear optimization problem which is hard to solve directly. Instead, we propose an equivalent piecewise mixed integer linear programming model. It turns out that each log-term in the objective function (1) is an increasing concave univariate function of the variable p_{kn}^t. Besides, we can remove the variable x_{kt} from the objective function (1) and add the following constraints $p_{kn}^t \leq x_{kt} M \; \forall k, n, t$ where M is a bigM positive value. These constraints ensure the facts that $p_{kn}^t = 0$ when $x_{kt} = 0$ and $p_{kn}^t > 0$ when $x_{kt} = 1$. Finally, we let $\theta_{kn}^t = \varphi_{kn}^t p_{kn}^t$ and introduce the nonnegative continuous variables $\phi_{k,n}^t$ for all k, n, t to bound from below each log-term in (1). This leads us to write the following model

$$\text{MP}: \quad \max_{\{x,p,\phi,\theta\}} \; \sum_{t=1}^{T} \sum_{k=1}^{K} \sum_{n=1}^{N} \phi_{k,n}^t \tag{6}$$

$$\text{s.t.} \quad \phi_{k,n}^t \leq a_m \theta_{kn}^t + b_m, \quad \forall k, n, t, m \tag{7}$$

$$p_{kn}^t \leq x_{kt} M, \quad \forall k, n, t \tag{8}$$

$$\theta_{kn}^t = \varphi_{kn}^t p_{kn}^t, \quad \forall k, n, t \tag{9}$$

$$\sum_{k=1}^{K} \sum_{n=1}^{N} H_{kn}^t p_{kn}^t \leq \Gamma, \quad \forall t \in \mathcal{T}$$

$$\sum_{t=1}^{T} x_{kt} = 1, \quad \forall k \in \mathcal{K}$$

$$p_{kn}^t \geq 0, \quad \forall k, n, t$$

$$x_{kt} \in \{0, 1\}, \quad \forall k, t$$

where the index "m" represents the line segments used for the piecewise linear approximation in constraint (7). The parameters a_m and b_m are obtained with the points we evaluate in the logarithm function. Clearly, the higher the number of line segments, the better the accuracy of the model. Although, the computational cost to solve the problem will certainly increase since we add more constraints in the model. So far, we consider MP as an alternative approximation method to compute near optimal solutions to be compared with our VNS approach.

3 VNS Decomposition Procedure

Metaheuristics are simple algorithmic procedures often used to find suboptimal (or near optimal) solutions for combinatorial optimization problems. In practice, they have proven to be highly effective when solving many of these hard problems [9]. Especially when the dimensions of the problem increase rapidly which is often the case in real world applications and where no solver is available yet to solve these large size instances to optimality. The most frequently utilized metaheuristics are: Genetic Algorithms, Tabu Search, Ant Colony Optimization, Particle Swarm Optimization, Variable Neighborhood Search, Simulated Annealing, just to name a few. For a detailed explanation on how these metaheuristics work, we refer the reader to the book in [9]. Basically, any metaheuristic approach would serve to compute feasible solutions for P. However, we propose a VNS approach due to its simplicity and low memory requirements. In particular, we adopt a reduced VNS approach which drops the local search phase of the basic VNS algorithm as it is the most time consuming step [10,11].

In order to compute feasible solutions for MP using a VNS approach, we randomly partition the set of users into T disjoint subsets of users within each iteration of the VNS approach. Denote by Ω_t the set of users for each $t \in \mathcal{T}$. In this case, we should solve T small size convex optimization subproblems, one for each subset of users assigned to time slot $t \in \mathcal{T} = \{1, \ldots, T\}$. In fact, this is a keystone of our proposed VNS approach since the subproblems we solve are convex and thus, we compute the optimal solutions for each one of them within each iteration of the VNS approach. More precisely, for each $t \in \mathcal{T}$ and for a fixed assignment of variable $x = \bar{x}$, problem P reduces to solve the following convex optimization problem

$$Q: \quad \max_{\{p\}} \sum_{k \in \Omega_t} \sum_{n=1}^{N} \log_2 \left(1 + \varphi_{kn}^t p_{kn}^t\right) \tag{10}$$

$$\text{s.t.} \quad \sum_{k \in \Omega_t} \sum_{n=1}^{N} H_{kn}^t p_{kn}^t \leq \Gamma \tag{11}$$

$$p_{kn}^t \geq 0, \quad \forall k \in \Omega_t, n \tag{12}$$

In principle, notice that each subproblem can be solved to optimality in sequential or in parallel order using any algorithmic procedure. Also notice that there are T^K feasible assignments for variable $\bar{x}$. A simple strategy to solve problem Q can be obtained as follows. First, we can intuitively relax the nonegative power constraints as we maximize on the continuous variable p_{kn}^t. Next, notice that the constraint (11) will always be active, i.e., $\sum_{k \in \Omega_t} \sum_{n=1}^{N} H_{kn}^t p_{kn}^t = \Gamma$ since the variable p_{kn}^t is continuous. Consequently, the Lagrangian function of problem Q can be written as

$$L(p, \lambda) = \sum_{k \in \Omega_t} \sum_{n=1}^{N} \log_2 \left(1 + \varphi_{kn}^t p_{kn}^t\right) + \lambda \left(\Gamma - \sum_{k \in \Omega_t} \sum_{n=1}^{N} H_{kn}^t p_{kn}^t\right) \tag{13}$$

The derivatives $\frac{\partial (L(p_{kn}^t, \lambda))}{\partial p_{kn}^t}$ for each $k \in \Omega_t, n \in \mathcal{N}$ are calculated as

$$\frac{\partial (L(p_{kn}^t, \lambda))}{\partial p_{kn}^t} = \frac{\ln(2)\varphi_{kn}^t}{(1 + \varphi_{kn}^t p_{kn}^t)} - \lambda H_{kn}^t \tag{14}$$

By equating to zero these derivatives, it is easy to see that

$$\frac{\varphi_{kn}^t \ln(2)}{H_{kn}^t(1 + \varphi_{kn}^t p_{kn}^t)} = \frac{\varphi_{11}^t \ln(2)}{H_{11}^t(1 + \varphi_{11}^t p_{11}^t)} = \lambda \tag{15}$$

for each $k \in \Omega_t, n \in \mathcal{N}$ where $(k \neq 1)$ or $(n \neq 1)$. Thus, we arrive at the following explicit power formula

$$p_{kn}^t = \left[\frac{H_{11}^t(1 + \varphi_{11}^t p_{11}^t)}{\varphi_{11}^t H_{kn}^t} - \frac{1}{\varphi_{kn}^t}\right]^+ \tag{16}$$

where $[\cdot]^+ = \max\{\cdot, 0\}$. The latter ensures that each power p_{kn}^t is nonnegative. By replacing this power formula in the active constraint $\sum_{k \in \Omega_t} \sum_{n=1}^N H_{kn}^t p_{kn}^t = \Gamma$ allows one to compute

$$p_{11}^t = \frac{1}{H_{11}^t |\Omega_t| N}\left(\Gamma + \sum_{k \in \Omega_t} \sum_{n=1}^N \frac{H_{kn}^t}{\varphi_{kn}^t}\right) - \frac{1}{\varphi_{11}^t} \tag{17}$$

We mention that in our numerical results, none of the found solutions violates the active constraint $\sum_{k \in \Omega_t} \sum_{n=1}^N H_{kn}^t p_{kn}^t = \Gamma$ which means that all the solutions found are optimal solutions for problem Q.

VNS is a metaheuristic approach that uses the idea of neighborhood change during the ascent toward local optimal solutions in order to avoid being trapped. The aforementioned decomposition approach allows us to propose the VNS procedure depicted in Algorithm 1. It works as follows. It receives an instance of problem P as input and provides a near optimal solution for it. We denote by $(\bar{x}, \bar{p}, \bar{f})$ the final solution obtained with the algorithm where $\bar{f}$ represents the objective function value of P. In Step 0, we initialize all the required variables. Then, in Step 1 we obtain an initial feasible solution for the problem. For this purpose, we use the optimal power allocation formulas (16) and (17). Finally, during the execution of the while loop in Step 2, the algorithm performs a variable neighborhood search by randomly switching $\{0, 1\}$ values in $\mathcal{H}$ entries of variable x. Initially, $\mathcal{H}=1$ and it is increased by one unit when there is no improvement after new β_1 solutions have been evaluated. On the other hand, if a new current solution is better than the best found so far, then $\mathcal{H} \leftarrow 1$, the new solution is recorded and the process goes on. Notice that if "β_1" solutions have been evaluated without improvement and if $\mathcal{H} = \beta_2$, then we set $\mathcal{H} \leftarrow 1$. This gives the possibility of exploring in a loop manner from small to large zones of the feasible space. The whole process is repeated while the cpu time variable "$Time$" is less or equal than the maximum available "$maxTime$".

4   Numerical Results

In this section, we present our preliminary numerical results in order to compare the piecewise linear model MP with the VNS procedure. For this purpose, we

---

Algorithm 1. VNS approach

Data: An instance of problem P

Result: A near optimal solution $(\bar{x}, \bar{p}, \bar{f})$ for P

Step 0: $Time \leftarrow 0; \mathcal{H} \leftarrow 1; count \leftarrow 0; x_{kt} \leftarrow 0, \forall k, t; p_{kn}^t \leftarrow 0, \forall k, n, t;$

Step 1: **foreach** $k \in \mathcal{K}$ **do**

> Choose randomly $j \in \mathcal{T}$;
>
> $x_{kj} \leftarrow 1$;

Compute the optimal power allocation using the formulas (16) and (17);

Let (x, p, f) be the initial solution found for P with objective function value f;

Step 2: **while** *(Time $\leq$ maxTime)* **do**

> **for** $i = 1$ *to* $\mathcal{H}$ **do**
>
> > Choose randomly $i \in \mathcal{K}$;
> >
> > Choose randomly $j \in \mathcal{T}$;
> >
> > $x_{it} \leftarrow 0, \quad \forall t \in \mathcal{T}$;
> >
> > $x_{ij} \leftarrow 1$;
>
> Compute the optimal power allocation using the formulas (16) and (17);
>
> Let (x^*, p^*, g^*) be a new feasible solution found for P with objective function value g^*;
>
> **if** *($g^* > f$)* **then**
>
> > $\mathcal{H} \leftarrow 1, (x, p, f) \leftarrow (x^*, p^*, g^*); Time \leftarrow 0; count \leftarrow 0$;
>
> **else**
>
> > Keep previous solution; $count \leftarrow count + 1$;
>
> **if** *(count $> \beta_1$)* **then**
>
> > $count \leftarrow 0$;
> >
> > **if** *($\mathcal{H} \leq \beta_2$)* **then**
> > > $\mathcal{H} \leftarrow \mathcal{H} + 1$;
> >
> > **else**
> > > $\mathcal{H} \leftarrow 1$;

$(\bar{x}, \bar{p}, \bar{f}) \leftarrow (x, p, f)$, Return $(\bar{x}, \bar{p}, \bar{f})$;

---

generate the input data randomly as follows. Each entry in the channel gain matrix $H^t = H_{kn}^t$ for each $t \in \mathcal{T}$ is computed as [3]

$$H_{kn}^t = \frac{A}{d_{kt}^2} I * cos(\psi_{kn}^t)$$

where A is the surface capacity of the receiver. We assume that each receiver has an area of $A = 1\,cm^2$. The distance between the base station and each user is denoted by d_{kt}^2 and is randomly generated in the interval $[3, 10]\,ms$ whilst the angle of incidence of light at the receiver ψ_{kn}^t is randomly generated in the interval $[15^0, 45^0]$. Finally, I is a Lambertian radiant intensity profile and models light emitting diode radiation. We set this value to $I = 500$ [3]. Finally, the entries in the matrices $\sigma^t = (\sigma_{k,n}^t)$ are drawn from the interval $(0, 1]$ while the values of $\eta = 1, R_{PD} = 0.55$ and $\Gamma = 100$, respectively. These are realistic input data values for direct line of sight (LOS) VLC networks [3].

In Fig. 1, we plot for a fixed time slot, the distribution of the received power (dBm) for users in a room of dimensions $10*10\,\mathrm{ms}^2$ with height equal to 3 ms. In particular, in this figure we consider only four subchannels in order to show the existence of interference in an indoor environment while using VLC networks with direct LOS [7].

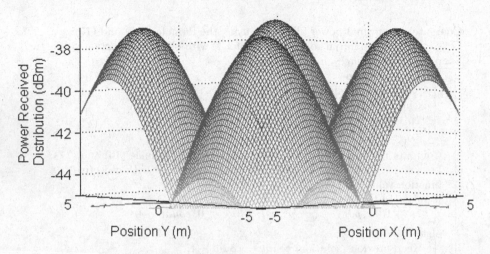

Fig. 1. Power distribution in a room of $10*10\,\mathrm{ms}^2$ with height equal to 3 ms in four subchannels where interference is present.

The input parameters of the VNS algorithm are set to $\beta_1 = 50$, $\beta_2 = 5$ and $maxTime = 10\,\mathrm{s}$, respectively. In MP, we set the bigM value to $M = 1000$. We implement a Matlab program using CPLEX 12.6 [12] to solve MP and the VNS Algorithm 1. The numerical experiments have been carried out on an Intel(R) 64bits core(TM) with 2.6 GHz and 8 GoBytes of RAM.

In Table 1, columns 1–3 present the instance dimensions. Column 4–7 presents the optimal solution found with MP, the number of branch and bound nodes, its CPU time in seconds, and the real objective function value of P obtained with the optimal solution of MP. This allows to observe how tight is the piecewise linear model with respect to the real objective function values. In columns 8–10, we present the initial solution found with VNS, the best solution found and its CPU time in seconds. Finally, in columns 11–13, we present gaps we compute as $\left(\frac{|MP-RObj|}{RObj}\right)*100$, $\left(\frac{|VNS-VNS_I|}{VNS_I}\right)*100$ and $\left(\frac{|VNS-RObj|}{RObj}\right)*100$, respectively. Without loss of generality, we set the maximum available CPU time for CPLEX to solve MP to one hour. Additionally, we calculate the maximum value $\bar{\theta} = \max_{\{k,n,t\}}\{\theta_{k,n,t} = \varphi_{k,n,t}p_{k,n,t}\}$ for MP and consider the interval $[0,\bar{\theta}]$ while divided into equally spaced subintervals of length one in order to generate the piecewise linear segments. In order to give more insight with respect to the numerical results obtained, in Fig. 2 we plot averages for 10 samples with the same dimensions of each instance in Table 1.

Table 1. Numerical results for MP and for VNS Algorithm 1

K	N	T	MP	$B\&Bn$	CPU(s)	RObj	VNS_I	VNS	CPU	Gap_1 (%)	Gap_2 (%)	Gap_3 (%)
4	16	4	114.1260	144	9.72	114.1673	70.2843	114.5032	0.03	0.04	62.91	0.29
8	16	4	149.0225	31	9.92	149.0961	136.9480	150.4059	0.15	0.05	9.83	0.88
10	16	4	157.6509	276	18.43	157.7854	139.9098	160.6967	0.07	0.09	14.86	1.85
12	16	4	161.9502	21	12.96	162.0643	124.4928	167.5892	0.51	0.07	34.62	3.41
4	32	4	146.5794	13	9.26	146.7490	114.5512	148.7284	0.10	0.12	29.84	1.35
8	32	4	170.5687	14	14.33	170.6914	132.9067	177.9621	0.34	0.07	33.90	4.26
10	32	4	179.1046	486	48.09	179.2365	144.5489	187.9955	0.07	0.07	30.06	4.89
12	32	4	184.0684	17	19.76	184.3013	190.4371	194.2784	0.19	0.13	2.02	5.41
4	16	7	116.7848	215	22.45	116.8431	113.8818	117.1993	0.01	0.05	2.91	0.30
8	16	7	209.8958	8258	517.91	210.0034	162.8886	210.8523	0.22	0.05	29.45	0.40
10	16	7	224.8082	60419	3600	224.9441	192.9419	226.2670	0.07	0.06	17.27	0.59
12	16	7	244.2483	41342	3600	244.4127	181.6533	246.6191	0.15	0.07	35.76	0.90
4	32	7	147.3715	1595	115.12	147.4217	114.7067	149.1415	0.01	0.03	30.02	1.17
8	32	7	262.8989	2525	358.49	263.1283	200.5413	267.1121	0.03	0.09	33.20	1.51
10	32	7	276.8499	15406	2082.54	277.1304	238.1528	284.0400	0.24	0.10	19.27	2.49
12	32	7	289.3150	8804	1674.89	289.5962	254.1204	299.6867	0.27	0.10	17.93	3.48
4	16	10	117.7056	342	34.88	117.7458	114.1273	118.1262	0.09	0.03	3.50	0.32
8	16	10	231.9223	29370	3600	231.9960	184.9788	232.8376	1.17	0.03	25.87	0.36
10	16	10	291.3993	2212	578.95	291.5066	179.6399	291.9474	10.61	0.04	62.52	0.15
12	16	10	306.3240	32012	3600	306.4276	214.1476	307.7926	0.12	0.03	43.73	0.45
4	32	10	146.2666	8844	910.86	146.3518	146.0650	147.7009	0.06	0.06	1.12	0.92
8	32	10	295.0916	11070	3600	295.2685	231.4539	298.4896	0.23	0.06	28.96	1.09
10	32	10	366.6056	1474	866.93	366.8600	268.0650	370.3158	2.63	0.07	38.14	0.94
12	32	10	383.3237	9332	3600	383.7929	317.0072	389.9256	0.66	0.12	23.00	1.60
Min. values			114.12	13	9.26	114.16	70.28	114.50	0.01	0.03	1.12	0.15
Max. values			383	60419	3600	384	317	390	11	0	63	5
Ave. values			215.6	9759.2	1204.4	215.7	173.7	219.2	0.8	0.1	26.3	1.6

From Table 1, we observe that the objective function values obtained with the piecewise linear model are very tight when compared to the real objective function values of P. This can be confirmed by the gaps reported in column 11 which are in average 0.1 %. This suggests that MP is a tight approximation for P. Consequently, the solutions obtained with MP are near optimal solutions for P. Next, we observe that the number of branch and bound nodes increase significantly with the instance dimensions. This is also illustrated by the amount of CPU time required by CPLEX to solve the large size instances with MP. Notice that for some instances, we cannot solve MP to optimality in 1 hour. The remaining instances are solved to optimality in less CPU time. The average CPU time for all the instances is 1204.4 s.

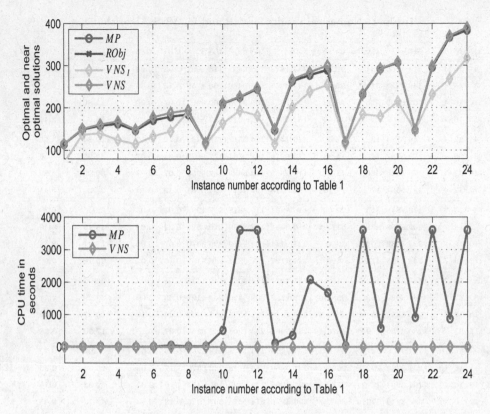

Fig. 2. Average numerical results for the optimal and near optimal solutions and for the CPU time in seconds of MP and VNS algorithm.

Regarding VNS Algorithm 1, we see that the average of the initial feasible solutions found is 173.7. Whilst the average for the best solutions found is 219.2. This means that VNS improves upon the initial feasible solutions obtained in about 27 %. This shows the effectiveness of the proposed algorithm. Concerning the CPU time required by VNS, we observe that the average is below 1 s which is a remarkable numerical result. Notice that only 3 out 24 instances require less than 11 s. All the remaining instances require less than 1 s. Finally, we observe that the objective function values obtained with the VNS approach are slightly better than the real objective function values of P obtained with the optimal solutions of MP. More precisely, these values report an average improvement of 1.6 %. This last observation can be verified by the gap column 13 in Table 1. The average curves in Fig. 2 confirm all our observations in Table 1. More precisely, we observe that VNS Algorithm 1 allows to obtain near optimal solutions in remarkably less CPU time compared to the piecewise linear model. Finally, we observe that the average initial solution found with VNS algorithm improves significantly in less than one second of CPU time.

5 Conclusions

In this paper, we consider the optimal joint resource allocation problem of subcarrier and power for non-real time wireless networks that use visible light communication technology. We model the resource allocation problem by means of a mixed integer nonlinear optimization problem that we further linearize using a piecewise linear approximation method. The latter allows to compute optimal and near optimal solutions for the problem. Finally, we propose a variable neighborhood search based decomposition procedure that allows to compute tight near optimal solutions in remarkably less computational effort compared to the solutions obtained with the piecewise linear model. Moreover, the decomposition approach allows to obtain slightly better solutions than the piecewise linear model.

Our future research will be focussed on other variants of the proposed model as well as on other metaheuristic approaches for different configurations of visible light communication networks.

Acknowledgments. The authors acknowledge the financial support of the Center for multidisciplinary research on signal processing (Project Conicyt/ACT1120) and Projects USACH/Dicyt Number 061413SG and 061513VC_DAS.

References

1. Amzallag, D., Armarnik, T., Livschitz, M., Raz, D.: Multi-cell slots allocation in OFDMA systems. In: 16th Mobile and Wireless Communications Summit (IST), pp. 1–5 (2007)
2. Bixby, R.: Solving real-world linear programs: a decade and more of progress. Oper. Res. **50**(1), 1–13 (2002)
3. Bykhovsky, D., Arnon, S.: Multiple access resource allocation in visible light communication systems. J. Lightwave Technol. **32**, 1594–1600 (2014)
4. Cao, Z., Tureli, U., Liu, P.: Optimum subcarrier assignment for OFDMA uplink. In: IEEE International Conference on Communications, pp. 11–15 (2003)
5. Chang, Y., Chien, F., Kuo, C.: Cross-layer QoS analysis of opportunistic OFDM-TDMA and OFDMA networks. IEEE J. Sel. Areas Commun. **25**, 657–666 (2007)
6. Dantzig, G.: Linear Programming and Extensions. Princeton University Press, Princeton (1963)
7. Ghassemlooy, Z., Popoola, W., Rajbhandari, S.: Optical Wireless Communications. Taylor and Francis Group, London (2013). 1–497
8. Lee, J., Leyffer, S. (eds.): Mixed Integer Nonlinear Programming. The IMA Volumes in Mathematics and its Applications, vol. 154. Springer, Berlin (2012)
9. Gendreau, M., Potvin, J.-Y. (eds.): Handbook of Metaheuristics. International Series in Operations Research & Management Science, vol. 146. Springer Science+Business Media, Berlin (2010)
10. Hansen, P., Mladenovic, N.: Variable neighborhood search: principles and applications. Eur. J. Oper. Res. **130**, 449–467 (2001)
11. Hansen, P., Mladenovic, N., Perez Brito, D.: Variable neighborhood decomposition search. J. Heuristics **7**, 335–350 (2001)

12. IBM ILOG CPLEX Optimization Studio Information Center. http://pic.dhe.ibm.com/infocenter/cosinfoc/v12r4/index.jsp
13. Katoozian, M., Navaie, K., Yanikomeroglu, H.: Optimal utility-based resource allocation for OFDM networks with multiple types of traffic. In: IEEE Vehicular Technology Conference, pp. 2223–2227 (2008)
14. Keha, A., de Farias, I., Nemhauser, G.: Models for representing piecewise linear cost functions. Oper. Res. Lett. **32**(1), 44–48 (2004)
15. Keller, T., Hanzo, L.: Adaptive multicarrier modulation: a convenient framework for time frequency processing in wireless communications. Proc. IEEE **88**, 611–640 (2000)
16. Kim, I., Lee, H.L., Kim, B., Lee, Y.H.: On the use of linear programming for dynamic subchannel and bit allocation in multiuser OFDM. In: IEEE GLOBECOM 2001, vol. 6, pp. 3648–3652 (2001)
17. Markowitz, H., Manne, A.: On the solution of discrete programming-problems. Ecometrica **25**, 84–110 (1957)
18. Navaie, K., Yanikomeroglu, H.: Optimal downlink resource allocation for non-realtime traffic in cellular CDMA/TDMA networks. IEEE Commun. Lett. **10**, 278–280 (2006)
19. Stankovic, J.: When sensor and actuator networks cover the world. ETRI J. **30**, 627–633 (2008)
20. Vielma, J., Nemhauser, G.: Modeling disjunctive constraints with a logarithmic number of binary variables and constraints. Math. Program. **128**, 49–72 (2009)

On Information Sharing Scheme for Automatic Evacuation Guiding System Using Evacuees' Mobile Nodes

Nobuhisa Komatsu, Masahiro Sasabe[✉], and Shoji Kasahara

Graduate School of Information Science, Nara Institute of Science and Technology,
8916-5 Takayama-cho, Ikoma, Nara 630-0192, Japan
{komatsu.nobuhisa.kg1,sasabe,kasahara}@is.naist.jp
http://www-lsm.naist.jp/index.php/top-e

Abstract. We have proposed an automatic evacuation guiding scheme based on cooperation between evacuees and their mobile nodes. In the previous work, we assume that information about blocked road segments is shared among mobile nodes through Epidemic routing, which is a Delay Tolerant Network (DTN) routing protocol. In this paper, we propose an information sharing scheme called On-Demand Direct Delivery, which can reduce the network load compared to Epidemic routing. Since each evacuee moves to a safe place, he/she will require the information about blocked road segments in the region from the current position to the safe place. The proposed scheme selectively retrieves the information about blocked road segments in that region, through Direct Delivery. Through simulation experiments, we show the proposed scheme can keep the effectiveness of evacuation guiding with reduction of network load to about 1/36, compared to Epidemic routing.

Keywords: Automatic evacuation guiding · Mobile nodes · On-Demand Direct Delivery

1 Introduction

The 2011 Great East Japan Earthquake highly damaged communication infrastructures. As a result, disaster victims and rescuers could not smoothly collect and distribute important information, e.g., safety information, evacuation information, and government information, even though they carried their own mobile nodes, e.g., smart phones [10] When disasters occur, disaster victims have to evacuate quickly to near safe places for their own safety. Although they can acquire static information, e.g., map and locations of safe places, in usual time, they cannot grasp dynamic information, e.g., damage situations, in advance.

To tackle this problem, we have developed an automatic evacuation guiding system based on implicit cooperation between evacuees and their mobile nodes [9]. In [9], each mobile node tries to navigate its evacuee by presenting

© Springer International Publishing Switzerland 2016
M. Younas et al. (Eds.): MobiWIS 2016, LNCS 9847, pp. 213–221, 2016.
DOI: 10.1007/978-3-319-44215-0_17

an evacuation route. At the same time, it can also trace the actual evacuation route of the evacuee as the trajectory by measuring his/her positions periodically. Thus, it can automatically estimate a road segment, which yields the difference between recommended route and actual evacuation route, as a blocked road segment. As a result, it can recalculate an alternative evacuation route, which does not include blocked-road-segments discovered. In addition, mobile nodes also share such information among them, with the help of Delay Tolerant Network (DTN) [3].

In [9], we evaluated the effectiveness of evacuation guiding in terms of average/maximum evacuation time, but did not consider network load caused by information sharing. As in [4,5], the evacuation guiding scheme in [9] applies Epidemic routing for information sharing. In Epidemic routing, when two mobile nodes can directly communicate with each other, one tries to send information about blocked road segments that the other does not possess, and vice versa. Thus, the network congestion will occur with the increase in the target region and/or in the population of evacuees. Since each evacuee moves to the safe place, he/she will improve his/her own evacuation by the information about blocked road segments in the region, called *view*, which spreads over before him/her. Note that the view of each evacuee keeps changing during his/her evacuation. In such situations, DTN routing will not work effectively because the information to be shared between mobile nodes will change per meeting.

In this paper, we propose an information sharing scheme, called On-Demand Direct Delivery. When a mobile node can communicate with other node, i.e., a mobile node or a server on the cloud system, it tries to obtain necessary information based on its view from the node. Actual data transfer among nodes can be achieved by Direct Delivery [6]. Through simulation experiments, we evaluate the effectiveness of the proposed scheme in terms of both evacuation time and network load.

The rest of this paper is organized as follows. Section 2 gives related work. After introducing the overview of automatic evacuation guiding system in Sects. 3 and 4 describes the proposed scheme. In Sect. 5, we show the simulation results. Finally, Sect. 6 provides conclusions and future work.

2   Related Work

It has been expected that Information and Communications Technology (ICT) can effectively support evacuation guiding [4,5,7,9]. Iizuka et al. propose an evacuation guiding system using an ad hoc network, which can present evacuees with both evacuation routes and timing to avoid crowds of evacuees [7]. When a large-scale disaster occurs, it may be difficult to maintain an ad hoc network, which tries to keep connectivity among mobile nodes. There are several studies [4, 5,9], which try to support evacuation guiding even in such poor communication environments, with the help of DTN.

In [4,9], when evacuees and mobile nodes newly discover blocked road segments, they try to broadcast the corresponding information using Epidemic routing. Note that the mobile nodes can automatically (resp. manually) discover information about blocked road segments in [9] (resp. [4]). Gorbil and Gelenbe propose a scheme that collects emergency information, i.e., hazard points and their discovered times (time stamps), from three kinds of sources: (1) fixed nodes, mobile nodes, and social networks among evacuees [5]. They also apply Epidemic routing but additionally introduce a prioritization mechanism based on the time stamps. The newer the time stamp is, the higher the priority becomes.

If network resources are abundant, Epidemic routing is effective in terms of bundle (message) delivery ratio and bundle delivery delay. Epidemic routing, however, also lays heavy burden on the network, because of its nature of broadcast. To alleviate the network load while keeping high bundle delivery ratio and short bundle delivery delay, there exist many studies on DTN routing protocols [2]. They are generally based on store-carry-forward paradigm where mobile nodes carry stored information and forward it to other nodes through direct wireless communication. Each DTN routing protocol tries to control the balance between bundle delivery ratio, bundle delivery delay, and network load.

In this paper, we focus on the fact that the necessary information for evacuees changes during their evacuations as mentioned above. In such situations, when two mobile nodes can communicate with each other, it is reasonable for them to share only the necessary information. For this purpose, we propose On-Demand Direct Delivery in the next section.

3   Automatic Evacuation Guiding System

In this section, we give the overview of automatic evacuation guiding system proposed in [9]. $G = (\mathcal{V}, \mathcal{E})$ denotes a graph representing the internal structure of the target region, where $\mathcal{V}$ is a set of vertices, i.e., intersections, and $\mathcal{E}$ is a set of edges, i.e., roads in the map. There are K ($K > 0$) evacuees in the region and each of them has a mobile node. $\mathcal{K} = \{1, 2, \ldots, K\}$ denotes the set of all the nodes. Each node $k \in \mathcal{K}$ measures its own locations by using Global Positioning System (GPS) at a certain interval of I_M ($I_\mathrm{M} > 0$).

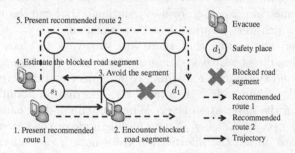

Fig. 1. Flow of evacuation guiding

Figure 1 illustrates the flow of guiding one evacuee to a safe place. Note that the evacuee has to pre-install an application for evacuation guiding into his/her mobile node before disasters occur. The application obtains the surrounding map of the target region and the location information of the safe places in usual time. When disasters occur, the evacuee initiates the applications on his/her node. The application first finds out the nearest safe place d_1 from the location s_1 of node k, which was recorded on start-up. Next, it calculates an evacuation route $\widehat{p}^k_{s_1,d_1}$ and presents him/her the route as a recommended route. (Step 1 in Fig. 1.)

The evacuee tries to move along the recommended route. When the evacuee discovers a blocked road segment during his/her evacuation along the recommended route $\widehat{p}^k_{s_1,d_1}$ (Step 2 in Fig. 1.), he/she will take another route by his/her own judgment. (Step 3 in Fig. 1.) The application can trace his/her actual evacuation route as the trajectory by measuring his/her positions periodically. Thus, the application can detect the road segment $e \in \mathcal{E}$, which yields the difference between the recommended route and the actual evacuation route. The application adds the road segment e to the set $\mathcal{E}^k_{\mathrm{NG}}$ of blocked road segments. (Step 4 in Fig. 1.) After that, the application recalculates the nearest safe place d_2 from the current location s_2. Next, it also recalculates a new evacuation route, which does not include blocked road segments ($\forall e \in \mathcal{E}^k_{\mathrm{NG}}$), and presents him/her the route. (Step 5 in Fig. 1.) The succeeding flow is the same as that for the first recommended route $\widehat{p}^k_{s_1,d_1}$. (Note that $s_2 = s_1, d_2 = d_1$ in Fig. 1.) Evacuation guiding finishes when the evacuee reaches the safe place or the application cannot find out any evacuation route to any safe place.

In addition, the evacuee may encounter other evacuees and get a chance to communicate with infrastructures during his/her evacuation. Under these situations, the application will obtain new information about blocked road segments. (See the details in Sect. 4.) Then, it recalculates a new recommended route and present it to him/her.

4   Proposed Scheme

As mentioned above, the application of each mobile node $k \in \mathcal{K}$ automatically obtains the information about blocked road segments $\mathcal{E}^k_{\mathrm{NG}}$ on the way to the safe place. Evacuees may improve their own evacuation if they can share blocked road segments $\mathcal{E}^k_{\mathrm{NG}}$, which were acquired by other evacuees.

In this paper, we assume that there are two ways to share the information among nodes: direct wireless communication among nodes and communication with the cloud system via remaining communication infrastructures. As we stated in Sect. 3, mobile node k maintains the information about blocked road segments $\mathcal{E}^k_{\mathrm{NG}}$ on the application layer. When mobile node k can communicate with other node j ($k, j \in \mathcal{K}^+, k \neq j$), i.e., mobile node or the server on the cloud system, it tries to obtain the information from node j on demand. Note that $\mathcal{K}^+ = \mathcal{K} \cup \{0\}$ and the server's ID is set to be 0. In this section, we propose an information sharing scheme, called *On-Demand Direct Delivery*, which consists of two procedures: (1) selecting blocked road segments that evacuees may need, and (2) sending the selected information through DTN routing.

In what follows, we give the detail of On-Demand Direct Delivery.

4.1   Selection of Blocked Road Segments Based on Evacuees' Views

Information sharing without any restriction will cause network congestion with the increase in the target region. Since each evacuee moves to the safe place, he/she will require the information about blocked road segments in the region from the current position to the safe place. Although there may be several ways to define that region, we apply the concept of *view* [1] because of its simplicity. Specifically, we define evacuee k's $(k \in \mathcal{K})$ view $v^k(l^k, l^d)$ as a rectangle whose diagonal vertices are current coordinates of evacuee k's location, $l^k = (x^k, y^k)$, and coordinates of his/her destination, $l^d = (x^d, y^d)$, as shown in Fig. 2.

Evacuee k basically tries to retrieve the information about blocked road segments in set $\mathcal{E}^k_{\text{view}}(l^k, l^d)$, which consists of the blocked road segments whose one (both) of the end points is (are) included in view $v^k(l^k, l^d)$. The current/future route, however, will be out of the view, depending on the locations of blocked road segments and the graph structure. To tackle this problem, we extend the range of view by adding margin ν $(\nu \geq 0)$ to both x-axis and y-axis. Let $v^k(l^k, l^d, \nu)$ and $\mathcal{E}^k_{\text{view}}(l^k, l^d, \nu)$ denote evacuee k's view with the margin and the corresponding set of blocked road segments, respectively. Whenever mobile node k can communicate with other node j $(k, j \in \mathcal{K}^+, k \neq j)$, it calculate $\mathcal{E}^k_{\text{view}}(l^k, l^d, \nu)$.

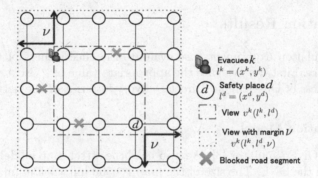

Fig. 2. Selection of blocked road segments based on evacuees' views

4.2   Communication Through DTN Routing

When large-scale disasters occur, conventional TCP/IP may not work well due to the damage of communication infrastructures. In such situations, DTN, which is based on store-carry-forward routing, is expected to be a promising technique. Mobile nodes store and carry bundles (data), which are originally generated or received from others. When mobile nodes meet others, they first exchange summary vectors, which are lists of their possessing bundles. Then, the mobile nodes send part/all of others' unpossessing bundles to them, depending on DTN routing protocols.

One of the most typical DTN routing protocols is Epidemic routing [11]. Since Epidemic routing is a kind of flooding schemes, it achieves high reachability together with heavy network load. In our scenario, we assume that each bundle includes information about a blocked road segment. This also causes wasteful transfer of bundles, which are generated by different mobile nodes but include the information about the same blocked road segment. In addition, each evacuee requires the information about blocked road segments, depending on their current position and destinations, as mentioned in Sect. 4.1.

Taking account of these points, we propose the following information sharing scheme. When mobile node k can communicate with other node j ($k, j \in \mathcal{K}^+$, $k \neq j$), i.e., a mobile node or a server, it sends node j coordinates l^k of the current position, coordinates l^d of its destination, and margin ν. Then, mobile node j calculates $\mathcal{E}_{\text{view}}^k(l^k, l^d) \cap \mathcal{E}_{\text{NG}}^j$ and sends it back to mobile node k. For this direct communication, we can use Direct Delivery [6], which is a DTN routing protocol where source nodes send their own bundles only to their destination nodes.

If node j is a mobile node, j can also obtain its necessary information from mobile node k in the same manner. On the other hand, if node j is a server, it sends mobile node k two coordinates, which describe the whole region, and $\nu = 0$, such that it can retrieve the information about blocked road segments in the whole region.

5   Simulation Results

Through simulation experiments, we evaluate the effectiveness of On-Demand Direct Delivery. First, we evaluate the appropriate value of ν. Next, we evaluate the effectiveness of On-Demand Direct Delivery in terms of the network load.

5.1   Simulation Model

We used the ONE simulator [8]. We also used the street map of Helsinki, which is included in the ONE. The size of the map is 4500 [m] × 3400 [m]. We assume that one hundred evacuees with their own mobile nodes start evacuating from initial positions, each of which is randomly chosen from the points on the streets of the map. In addition, we set one safe place near the center of the map. We set the simulation time to be 7200 [s]. When the simulation starts, a disaster occurs and all evacuees start evacuating from their initial positions to the safe place at moving speed of 4 [km/h].

We set I_M to be 10 [s]. Mobile nodes can directly communicate with other nodes through Wi-Fi Direct whose transmission range is 100 [m], and communicate with a server in the cloud system through Wi-Fi access points whose transmission range is also 100 [m]. We set Wi-Fi access points in a 5 × 5 grid manner, which can cover about 7 % area of all road segments. We made a disaster scenario as follows. We randomly set a certain number of edges on graph G to be blocked such that the probability that evacuation routes exist from arbitrary points to the safe place becomes 0.6.

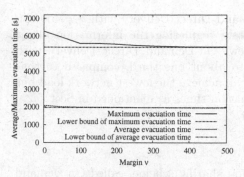

Fig. 3. Impact of ν on average and maximum evacuation times.

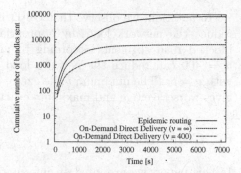

Fig. 4. Cumulative number of bundles sent.

We use *average/maximum evacuation time* and *network load* as evaluation criteria. The evacuation time of an evacuee is the time interval from the evacuation start to the evacuation completion. We define the network load as the cumulative number of bundles sent by all mobile nodes. The succeeding results are the average of 100 independent simulation experiments.

5.2 Appropriate Margin of View

Figure 3 illustrates average and maximum evacuation times of On-Demand Direct Delivery, when changing the value of ν. In addition, we also show the lower bounds of average and maximum evacuation times, which are given by On-Demand Direct Delivery with $\nu = \infty$. We observe that both average and maximum evacuation times monotonically decrease with ν and almost converge to their lower bounds when $\nu = 400$. Thus, we use $\nu = 400$ as an appropriate value. Note that the appropriate value of ν may change depending on the map structures and disaster scenarios. As future work, we plan to propose a scheme to determine the appropriate value of ν.

5.3 Network Load

Figure 4 illustrates the cumulative number of bundles sent. Note that the scale of the vertical axis is logarithmic. We observe that On-Demand Direct Delivery with $\nu = \infty$ can reduce the network load to about one twelfth compared to Epidemic routing. In Epidemic routing, when different mobile nodes discover an identical blocked segment, they generate their own bundles. These bundles include the same information but any DTN routing protocols in Bundle layer, e.g., Epidemic routing, cannot inspect the content of them and finally treat them as different bundles. This cause wasteful transfer of bundles. On the other hand, On-Demand Direct Delivery can avoid this problem. In On-Demand Direct Delivery, mobile nodes generate bundles on demand when they can communicate with other nodes. The bundles are generated according to the information about blocked road segments, which they have at that time.

In addition, we observe that On-Demand Direct Delivery with $\nu = 400$ can reduce the network load, by appropriately regulating the information about blocked road segments according to view. On-Demand Direct Delivery with $\nu = 400$ can reduce the network load to about one third, compared to that with $\nu = \infty$. The minimum ν, i.e., zero, can achieve the lowest network load but gives worse average and maximum evacuation times as mentioned in Sect. 5.2.

6   Conclusions

In this paper, we proposed an information sharing scheme, called On-Demand Direct Delivery, for the automatic evacuation guiding system. When two mobile node can communicate with each other, they try to obtain the information about blocked road segments in their own view, which are possessed by the opponent. Through simulation experiments, we showed that On-Demand Direct Delivery with appropriate ν can reduce the network load to about 1/36, compared to Epidemic routing. As future work, we plan to propose a scheme to determine the appropriate value of ν.

References

1. Bai, Y., Guo, Y., Meng, X., Wan, T., Zeitouni, K.: Efficient dynamic traffic navigation with hierarchical aggregation tree. In: Proceedings of the 8th Asia-Pacific Web Conference on Frontiers of WWW Research and Development, pp. 751–758 (2006)
2. Cao, Y., Sun, Z.: Routing in delay/disruption tolerant networks: a taxonomy, survey and challenges. IEEE Commun. Surv. Tuts. **15**(2), 654–677 (2013)
3. Fall, K.: A delay-tolerant network architecture for challenged internets. In: Proceedings of SIGCOMM 2003, pp. 27–34 (2003)
4. Fujihara, A., Miwa, H.: Disaster evacuation guidance using opportunistic communication: the potential for opportunity-based service. In: Bessis, N., Dobre, C. (eds.) Big Data and Internet of Things: A Roadmap for Smart Environments Studies in Computational Intelligence, pp. 425–446. Springer, Heidelberg (2014)
5. Gorbil, G., Gelenbe, E.: Disruption tolerant communications for large scale emergency evacuation. In: Proceedings of 2013 PERCOM Workshops, pp. 540–546 (2013)
6. Grossglauser, M., Tse, D.: Mobility increases the capacity of ad hoc wireless networks. IEEE/ACM Trans. Netw. **10**(4), 477–486 (2002)
7. Iizuka, Y., Yoshida, K., Iizuka, K.: An effective disaster evacuation assist system utilized by an ad-hoc network. In: Stephanidis, C. (ed.) Posters, Part II, HCII 2011. CCIS, vol. 174, pp. 31–35. Springer, Heidelberg (2011)
8. Keränen, A., Ott, J., Kärkkäinen, T.: The ONE simulator for DTN protocol evaluation. In: Proceedings of the 2nd International Conference on Simulation Tools and Techniques, pp. 55:1–55:10 (2009)
9. Komatsu, N., Sasabe, M., Kawahara, J., Kasahara, S.: Automatic evacuation guiding scheme using trajectories of mobile nodes. In: Proceedings of MobiWis 2015, pp. 3–14 (2015)

10. Ministry of Internal Affairs and Communications: 2011 WHITE PAPER Information and Communications in Japan. http://www.soumu.go.jp/johotsusintokei/whitepaper/eng/WP2011/2011-index.html
11. Vahdat, A., Becker, D.: Epidemic routing for partially connected ad hoc networks. Technical report CS-200006, Duke University (2000)

Cognitive Downlink Interference
LTE Femtocell

Nahla NurElmadina, Ibtehal Nafea[(✉)], and Nuha Bihary

Computer Science and Engineering College, Taibah University, Medina,
Saudi Arabia
nahlla.awadnoor@gmail.com, nuhabeh@gmail.com,
inafea@taibahu.edu.sa

Abstract. The next generation of cellular networks is based on the concept of autonomous infrastructure deployment. Deploying femtocells inside a macrocell in a cellular network can significantly increase the macrocell's capacity in terms of network optimization. However, the deployment of many femtocells within a macrocell's coverage area causes severe femto-femto interference, or macro-femto interference, which may have an impact on the overall performance of femtocells. Avoiding interference is very important for co-tier or cross-tier femtocells and macrocells. In this paper, we propose a femtocell resource allocation scheme to alleviate the problem of co-tier or cross-tier interference. In the proposed scheme, orthogonal avoid interference with other femtocells. This paper studies a framework for autonomous network optimization based on the method of cognitive interference management to decrease the system's capacity. Results showed improvement in femtocell QOS.

1 Introduction

Currently, more than 20 cellular operators worldwide, representing together more than 1.8 billion of the total 3.5 billion mobile subscribers in the world, have already stated a commitment to LTE, and more than 32 million LTE subscribers are expected by 2013 [4]. Figure 1 shows LTE traffic growth from 2013 and expected growth until 2017. Therefore, many researchers have concentrated their efforts on the study of LTE systems, proposing new solutions in order to analyze and improve their performance.

LTE has developed a new technology in order to enhance indoor coverage. This new technology is called femtocells (short distance) and is achieved with the use of access points installed by home users; however, interference problems between femtocells and the macrocells decrease the system's capacity. Femtocells are one sufficient solution to increase the capacity and coverage to meet the high demand of the next generation of services on broadband wireless access. This paper focuses on femtocell technology and studies a framework for autonomous network optimization based on the method of cognitive interference management to decrease the system's capacity. Femtocells are not only a good solution for users but also for vendors. E-UTRAN Node B (eNodeB) is the base station in the Long Term Evolution/System Architecture Evolution (LTE/SAE) network [3]. It has many functions, such as radio resource management, radio mobility, and routing user plane data towards SAE gateway,

© Springer International Publishing Switzerland 2016
M. Younas et al. (Eds.): MobiWIS 2016, LNCS 9847, pp. 222–231, 2016.
DOI: 10.1007/978-3-319-44215-0_18

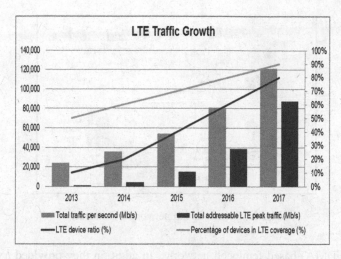

Fig. 1. LTE Traffic growth

internet protocol (IP) header compression and encrypting of data streams. eNodeBs are connected via X2, and to the SAE gateways (S-GWs) via the S1 interface. An access gateway in the radio network design connects eNodeBs together.

The paper is organized as follows. The first section presents related works. The next section defines the key issues regarding interference between femtocells and macro-cells, and one possible solution to the problem is shown. Next, the principle of cognitive channel allocation is explained. The last section presents simulation frame and performance results for capacity and coverage increase scenarios.

2   Related Works

The idea of project a vision for (LTE) 4G cellular networks based on the concept. [1] Femtocell is a low-power cellular base station designed primarily to provide the best coverage inside buildings in the commercial and small business office. It is affordable and it can be connected to an existing operator's network via broadband, such as DSL or cable, without the need for expensive towers. In addition, it is a limited user support to eight users. A call that begins from a handset equipped with a femtocell base station would start at a cellphone and then be sent to the femtocell, which would then go from the femtocell to the internet via a broadband connection and end up at the cellular network, as represented in Fig. 2 [5, 6].

As shown in Fig. 2, a femto network consists of a femtocell and various elements supporting a network which provides communication security, network provisioning, network management and integration. Home Node B (HNB) is the device that is installed to the user's premises serving as a femtocell. This operator has no exact control of the location.

In [8], they provided a survey of the different state-of-the-art approaches for interference and resource management in orthogonal frequency-division multiple

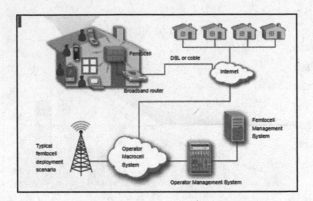

Fig. 2. Generic femto network architecture

accesses (OFDMA)-based femtocell networks. In addition they provided a qualitative comparison of the different approaches. They concluded that with efficient interference management schemes, the network capacity and coverage can be increased to benefit both the subscribers and the operators.

In [9] the author employed the colouring algorithm concept to mitigate the interference of the femtocell. The developed algorithm works by creating the interference graph by using the colouring algorithm, and once the graph is produced, the colouring algorithm is applied to that. The chromatic number of that graph is found, that chromatic number leads to a number of zones being created in the femtocell region, and once the zones are divided, the users are sent to a particular zone depending upon the SINR value. Meanwhile we allocate the number of channels to that particular user. They concluded that the proposed system algorithm reduces interference and increases the performance by more than 5 %, and in some scenarios it reaches up to 10 %.

3   Problems

The femtocell which operates at the same frequency band as the existing macrocell system would induce interference between femtocells or macrocell to femtocell, leading to these problems seriously affecting their performance [10]. Note that the term macrocell is used to describe the broadest range of cell sizes, and they are found in rural areas or along highways.

Co-channel interference is more critical in the femtocell network. There are two types that can thus be divided into tiers: themacrocell tier with femto interference and femto-femtocell tier interference [10] (see Fig. 3).

LTE cellular networks based on the concept of autonomous infrastructure deployment, cellular base station or femtocell access points are deployed by network users without being constrained by the conventional cell planning process from the network operator. Figure 4 explains the cognitive channel allocation procedure.

As seen in Fig. 4, cognitive channel allocation starts to process a femtocell access point by constantly sensing the radio environment (step one) and characterizes the

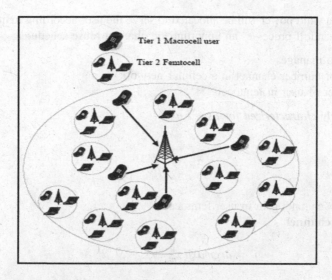

Fig. 3. A femtocell based two-tier OFDMA network [2, 7, 11]

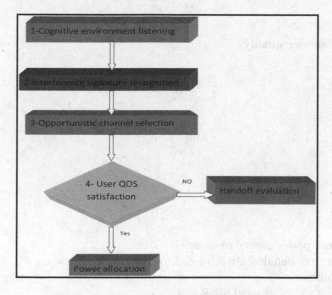

Fig. 4. Cognitive channel allocation procedure

interference signature from its neighbour (step two), then the condition channel information can be exchanged between femtocell and macrocell.

This process is supposed to run as a loop according to a particular control period (opportunistic channel scheduler is implemented) (step three). The scheduler works to always pick the best channel for reuse in which the inverse causes low interference to other cells. The user's Quality of Service (QOS) requirement will be evaluated based on the selected channel condition. If the channel can satisfy the target service requirement, a valid power will be allocated to serve the user according to the equation, otherwise a handoff processes an opportunistic channel reuse scheduler.

m = femto manages
j = total of number channel in a cellular network
i = number of user in femtocell

Cognitively characterized for user I as

$$\alpha_{m,i}^{j} = \frac{h_{m,i}^{j}\,^2}{I_{m,i}^{j}}$$

H and I = channel gain in user femtocell
Optimal channel

$$j^* = argmaxj(\alpha_{m,i}^{1}, \alpha_{m,i}^{2}, \ldots, \alpha_{m,i}^{j})$$

$$\alpha_{m,i}^{j*} = \frac{h_{m,i}^{j*}\,^2}{I_{m,i}^{j*}}$$

Equation service quality

$$\frac{p_{m,i}(t)h_{m,i}^2}{I_{m,i} + N_{m,i}} \geq \gamma_{m,i}$$

$$\text{Min} \sum_{i=1}^{Nm} P_{m,i}$$

$$P_{m,i} * \alpha_{m,i}^{j*} \geq \gamma_{m,i}$$

$$P_{m,i} \geq 0$$

P(t) transmit power control of channel
H = channel amplitude from femtocell to user inside coverage
j* = best channel
$\gamma_{m,i}$ = user QOS of channel SINR
$N_{m,i}$ = noise level
$I_{m,i}$ interference from neighbor femto and macro cell

4 Simulation

Design macrocell scenario system is model one cell macro contains many femtocell we will main simulation assumption of study can be draw macrocell and user generation distribute in macrocell with femtocell.

Table 1. Simulation parameters.

Parameter	Value
Macrocell radius	500 m
Femtoocell radius	40 m
Carrier frequency	2 GHZ
Bandwidth (BW)	5 MHz
Tx power fmtocell	20 mw
Tx power macrocell	20 w
White noise (thermal noise)	−174 dB/Hz
Pathloss	$38.4 + 20\log(d), d$ = distance (meter)
Data rate	$R = BW(1 + SINR)$

The Matlab program is used for the simulation of macrocells. The system is modelled on one macrocell as four femtocells.

The main simulation assumptions of the study are shown in Table 1. The simulation is used to evaluate the performance of the cognitive channel allocation procedure.

Subscribers Generation. The system-level simulators are used to generate a random distribution of users as shown in Fig. 5. A total of 500 users are generated in a macrocell and contain four femtocells. (0–8) users in a femtocell serving base station of a given subscriber are taken as the one that is associated with the path loss.

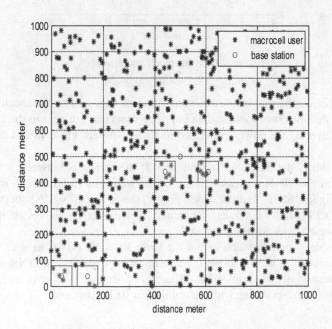

Fig. 5. Distribution of random subscribers

5   Results and Discussion

Figure 6 shows an estimation of the Signal to Interference plus Noise Ratio (SINR) (mobile terminate or user) level at any given position of the user's macrocell and user femtocell; it also shows the minimum improvement in SINR of the user's macrocell because of the high interference. This fact increases the experienced SINTR maximum level corresponding with the minimum distance requirement to preserve the SINR level.

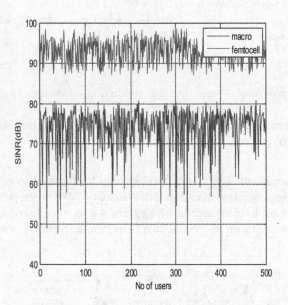

Fig. 6. SINR macrocell and femtocell

Figure 7 shows the maximum achieved data rate values. The femtocell users' data rate is higher than macrocell users' data rate. The users that are near to the centre of the femtocell receive higher power compared to those who are close to the centre of the base station.

Figure 8 shows the SINR for a femtocell. If the power is between p = 5mw, the performance of the SINR decreases. If the power transmits (femtocell) a maximum of 20 mw, the highest SINR, but decreases power, the femtocell's SINR decreases. This means high QOS (SINR) femtocell avoidance, so the interference between femtocells achieves the best signal for the femtocell.

Figure 9 shows an estimation of the Bit Error Rate (BER) of the user's macrocell and user's femtocell. It is also shows the minimum improvement in SINR of the user's macrocell because of the high BER. This fact increases the experienced SINTR maximum level corresponding with the minimum BER femtocell.

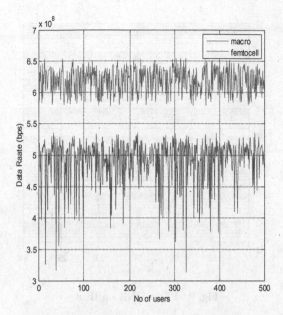

Fig. 7. Achieved data of macrocell and femtocell

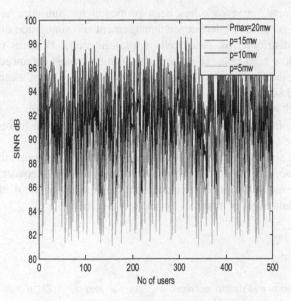

Fig. 8. Effect the power on SINR femtocell

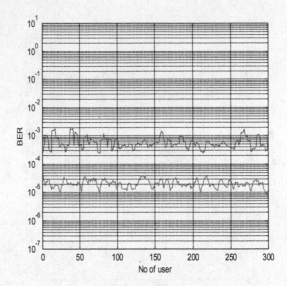

Fig. 9. Effect SINR on BER

6 Conclusion

In this paper a new framework has been proposed for autonomous network optimization based on cognitive interference management and simulation of macrocells and user generation distributed in macrocells with femtocells. Features covered by this simulator will allow both researchers and practitioners to test enhanced techniques for improving 4G cellular networks, such as decreasing the system's capacity and high performance, and so on.

The proposed system algorithm improves QOS of femtocells in next generation LTE and reduces interference. In addition, the proposed system increases the performance of femtocells by achieving more data.

Future works aims to study network capacity based on different strategies for user access i.e. open access, closed access or hybrid access. Other network factors will be considered in the model for power management, such as the traffic distribution in cells and mobile handoff between macrocells and femtocells.

References

1. Khan, A.: Macro and femto network aspects for realistic LTE usage scenarios. Royal Institute of Technology (KTH), Stockholm, Sweden (2011)
2. Li, Y.: Cognitive interference management in 4G Autonomous femtocell. University of Toronto, Toronto (2010)
3. Deva, B.: LTE vs. Wimax-next generation Telecommunication Network (2011)
4. McQueen, D.: The momentum behind LTE adoption. IEEE Commun. Mag. **47**(2), 44–45 (2009). Appendix: Springer-Author Discount

5. Femto 802.16 m Base Stations; IEEE 802.16 Presentation Submission Template(V 9)
6. Femtocell Networks: A Survey Vikram Chandrasekhar and Jeffrey G.Andrews, the University of Texas at Austin Alan Gatherer, Texas Instruments; 23 June 2008
7. Chandrasekhar, V., Andrews, J.G.: Uplink capacity and interference avoidance for two-tier cellularnetworks. In: Proceedings IEEE GLOBECOM (2007)
8. Saquib, N., et al.: Interference management in OFDMA femtocell networks: Issues and approaches. IEEE Wirel. Commun. **19**(3), 86–95 (2012)
9. RenukaRajendra, B.: Controlling the interference between femto cell and macro cell in LTE. Int. J. Electron. Commun. Eng. **6**(1), 111–118 (2013)
10. Ismail, I., Baba, M.D.: Assigning cognitive radio to the femtocell in lte based network: a solution for interference mitigation. In: IEEE 6th Control and System Graduate Research Colloquium, Malaysia (2015)
11. Jiang, C.: Optimal pricing strategy for operators in cognitive femtocell networks. IEEE Trans. Wirel. Commun. **13**, 5288–5301 (2014)

Correlation Properties of QOCCC Based on 1D-CCC with Parameters (N, N, 2N) and (N, N, N)

Monika Dávideková[1,2(✉)] and Michal Greguš ml.[3]

[1] Institute of Telecommunication, FEI, Slovak University of Technology,
Bratislava, Slovakia
davidekova@ut.fei.stuba.sk
[2] Vysoká škola Manažmentu/City University of Seattle, Bratislava, Slovakia
[3] Department of Information Systems, FM, Comenius University,
Bratislava, Slovakia
michal.gregus.ml@fm.uniba.sk

Abstract. Researchers focusing on code division multiple access devote significant attention to complete complementary codes. The reason for the interest on these codes lies in the unique ideal overall correlation properties of these codes that no other codes dispose of. These ideal overall auto-correlation and cross-correlation allow concurrent transmission of communicating users without interference. However, there is a significant limitation in the given number of users for given length. Quasi orthogonal complete complementary codes enable trade-off between ideality of overall correlation and the number of users. These non-ideal codes allow higher number of users for a slight loss of ideality of these properties. This paper provide analysis of identified changes of the correlation properties of these quasi orthogonal complete complementary codes related to the changes in element dimension and provides recommendation in further use.

Keywords: Code Division Multiple Access (CDMA) · Complete Complementary Codes (CCC) · Quasi Orthogonal Complete Complementary Codes (QOCCC) · Ideal correlation properties

1 Introduction

Communication technology enables fast communication over distant places for a large number of users. Technology that allowed to become truly mobile (communicating whilst travelling) is the mobile wireless technology. The number of communicating users and devices is increasing with time. For this reason, new technological approaches that would allow higher number of communicating users or higher efficiency of the communicating channels are being researched and developed.

The Code Division Multiple Access (CDMA) allow differentiation of concurrently communicating users by unique code sequences and transmits the user transmissions concurrently. Among the codes used for several purposes, among those also the differentiation of concurrently transmitting users is, belong complete complementary codes that dispose of unique correlation properties.

© Springer International Publishing Switzerland 2016
M. Younas et al. (Eds.): MobiWIS 2016, LNCS 9847, pp. 232–245, 2016.
DOI: 10.1007/978-3-319-44215-0_19

Golay introduced unique binary sequence pairs in 1961 [1] that disposed of unique auto-correlation properties in his studies. Since this important discovery, several researchers devoted their efforts to this area and introduced sequence pairs and later sequence sets with ideal auto- and cross-correlation properties [2–14]. These codes became called Complete Complementary Codes (CCC).

The CCCs dispose of ideal overall auto- and cross-correlation properties. Ideal auto-correlation property denotes the property when the aperiodic auto-correlation function equals zero value for all possible shifts except the zero shift. Ideal cross-correlation property denotes the property when the aperiodic cross-correlation function equals zero value for all possible shifts. It was proven, that is it not possible to maintain ideal auto- and cross-correlation properties for more than two individual sequences [5, 6]. To maintain these ideal properties, a set/collection of sequences has to be composed [5, 6]. The word overall denotes the fact, that this property is maintained only for the set/collection as whole and not for each single sequence. These unique properties are very special and enable applications of these codes in several scientific areas [10]: physics, mathematics, combinatorics, as well as in the area of digital processing: image processing, radar technology, and telecommunication technology. These codes found their application also in eHealth and evacuation guiding system or disaster prevention. Further information about the versatile application of these codes can be found in [10].

These codes found their widest application in telecommunication where the ideal overall cross-correlation property enables interference free concurrent communication of several users [11]. The ideal overall auto-correlation property enables fast recognizing of the given user transmission using a matched filter on receiving end [11]. These two correlation properties of CCCs attracted the researchers attention and promise wide use in telecommunication technology.

Until 1988, these collections of sequences were identified by brute force. In 1988, Suehiro and Hatori introduced first automated generating algorithm [9] that enabled a systematic generating of these codes without exhausting computational complexity of the search. Since then, several researchers devoted their endeavors to this research field and introduced several construction algorithms and introduced CCCs with shorter and shorter sequence length. We consider among most important construction algorithms those, which introduced codes with shorter sequence length what is considered to be advantageous for some mobile applications [11]. These most interesting constructions that allowed shorter sequence length were: sequence length N^2 introduced in 1988 [9], $2N$ introduced in [12] and the most recent construction allowing the shortest possible length N introduced in 2011 [13] where N denotes number of sequences in a collection and is the power of two. The last mentioned construction algorithm denotes the shortest sequence length published so far.

The discovery of CCC become spread to two-dimensional case by Farkaš and Turcsány in 2003 [14] who introduced construction algorithm that generated codes based on one-dimensional CCCs with length N^2 from 1988 [9]. This construction was generalized later by Dávideková, Farkaš and Ružický in 2013 [15]. This generalized construction allowed use of newer one-dimensional CCCs with shorter sequence length [12, 13] on input.

However, the ideal CCCs allow the concurrent communication of only a very limited number of users. This is why, the researchers Turcsány and Farkaš developed Quasi Orthogonal Complete Complementary Codes (QOCCC) in 2003 [16] that used a trade-off between ideal overall correlation properties and the number of concurrently communicating users. Dávideková published the generalized construction of this algorithm in 2013 [17, 18] to allow newer CCCs on input, similarly to the previous generalization. These codes promise to keep the number of communicating channels low when enabling higher number of communicating users. Therefore, these codes denote a very interesting field with significant importance for the development of the communication technology.

This paper analyzes the properties of these newer QOCCC and identifies the changes in the correlation properties that are related to the changes of sequence length. It identifies the shifts of broken ideality of these unique properties and describes the parameters of these codes. This analysis contributes to the analysis results of QOCCCs based on one-dimensional CCCs with parameters (N, N, N^2) from 1988 [9] and (N, N, N) from 2011 [13] published in [20].

This paper is organized as follows: Sect. 2 provides basic definitions of CCCs for the convenience of the reader including the construction algorithms of analyzed codes. Section 3 provides research results of the analysis and proposes solutions of detected issues. The conclusion gives a brief summary of the research carried out and its results.

2 CCC Definitions

In this section, the basic brief definitions on CCC are given for the convenience of the reader. This section includes also the construction algorithms of analyzed CCC and QOCCC constructions.

2.1 One-Dimensional CCCs

For better understanding, the terms used in this paper are given first and followed by mathematical definitions.

A *signature* denotes a sequence set or collection of sequences that disposes of ideal overall auto- and cross-correlation properties and is assigned to one user [10].

Ideal overall auto-correlation property denotes the property for which the aperiodic auto-correlation function (1) equals zero for all shifts except the zero shift, computed through all sequences [15].

Ideal overall cross-correlation property denote the property for which the aperiodic cross-correlation equals zero for all possible shifts computed through all sequences [17, 18].

Two signatures are called *mutually orthogonal* if every two sequences in the collections are mates of each other [20].

Each signature consists of sequences called *elements* [19]. An element consist usually of complex numbers with absolute value equal to one. For the convenience of the reader, in this paper, the elements will consist of binary symbols +1 and −1 denoted as + and − in this paper.

The *aperiodic correlation function* $\rho_{\mathbf{c}^{(i)},\mathbf{c}^{(j)}}(\tau)$ [16] for L long sequences $\mathbf{c}^{(i)} \in C$ and $\mathbf{c}^{(j)} \in C$ is defined as:

$$\rho_{\mathbf{c}^{(i)},\mathbf{c}^{(j)}}(\tau) = \sum_{l=0}^{L-1} \mathbf{c}^{(i)}(l).\left[\mathbf{c}^{(j)}(l+\tau)\right]^* \tag{1}$$

where τ denotes the shift. For $i = j$ (1) denotes auto-correlation and for $i \neq j$ (1) denotes cross-correlation function.

Then, an i-th signature in a set C of N signatures can be denoted as follows:

$$\mathbf{c}^{(i)} = \left(\mathbf{c}_1^{(i)}\mathbf{c}_2^{(i)}\ldots\mathbf{c}_E^{(i)}\right); \quad i = 1, 2, \ldots N \tag{2}$$

where k-th element of it of length L is denoted as follows

$$\mathbf{c}_k^{(i)} = \left(\mathbf{c}_{k,1}^{(i)}\mathbf{c}_{k,2}^{(i)}\ldots\mathbf{c}_{k,L}^{(i)}\right); \quad k = 1, 2, \ldots E \tag{3}$$

Each element denotes a vector in one-dimensional CCC (1D-CCC) case, consisting of complex numbers (in this paper, binary +1 and −1 were used for the convenience of the reader).

Ideal overall aperiodic correlation property denotes the case for which (1) equals to zero for any shift for cross-correlation and for any shift except the zero shift for auto-correlation.

Elements have to be transmitted via independent channels in Multi-Carrier CDMA architecture [11]. This allows the computation of the correlation functions independently for each channel on the receiving end and then to sum up all independent results to obtain the overall correlation [19].

The generating algorithms of analyzed constructions are noted in following manner:

(*number of signatures, number of elements of one signature, element length*)-CCC
$$(M, N, L)\text{-CCC}$$

where the parameter N denotes power of 2. As it is advantageous for some applications to use the shortest possible elements, only the CCCs with maximal number of signatures (M) and the shortest possible element length (L) are considered.

Both analyzed constructions are based on unitary-like matrices where a unitary-like matrix is defined as follows:

$$\mathbf{U}_N.\mathbf{U}_N^H = \mathbf{U}_N^H.\mathbf{U}_N = \alpha\mathbf{I}_N \tag{4}$$

where $\mathbf{I}_N$ denotes a $N \times N$ identity matrix, $\mathbf{U}_N^H$ denotes a Hermitian transpose of $\mathbf{U}_N$, $\alpha > 0$ denotes a scalar and N denotes the power of 2. $\mathbf{U}_N$ denotes a unitary matrix if $\alpha = 1$.

The construction of $(M, N, L = 2 N)$-CCC from 2005 [12] is composed of 2 steps: the construction of generation matrix Δ and the cross-concatenation.

The generation matrix is composed of two unitary-like matrices **A** and **B** defined as follows:

$$
\mathbf{A} = \begin{bmatrix} \mathbf{a}_0 \\ \mathbf{a}_1 \\ \cdots \\ \mathbf{a}_{N-1} \end{bmatrix} = \begin{bmatrix} a_0^0 & a_0^1 & \cdots & a_0^{N-1} \\ a_1^0 & a_1^1 & \cdots & a_1^{N-1} \\ \vdots & \vdots & \ddots & \vdots \\ a_{N-1}^0 & a_{N-1}^1 & \cdots & a_{N-1}^{N-1} \end{bmatrix} \tag{5}
$$

$$
\mathbf{B} = \begin{bmatrix} b_n^m \end{bmatrix} \tag{6}
$$

where $|a_n^m| = 1$, $|b_n^m| = 1$, $0 \leq n, m \leq N-1$.

The submatrices $\Delta_0, \Delta_1 \ldots \Delta_{N-1}$ of the generation matrix Δ are:

$$
\Delta_i = \mathbf{B}.diag(\mathbf{a}_n) \tag{7}
$$

where the *diag* operator for a vector $\mathbf{a} = (a_0, a_1, \ldots a_{N-1})$ is:

$$
diag(\mathbf{a}) = \begin{bmatrix} a_0 & 0 & \cdots & 0 \\ 0 & a_1 & \cdots & 0 \\ \vdots & \vdots & \ddots & \vdots \\ 0 & 0 & \cdots & a_{N-1} \end{bmatrix} \tag{8}
$$

The generation matrix is then constructed:

$$
\Delta = \begin{bmatrix} \Delta_0 \\ \Delta_1 \\ \cdots \\ \Delta_{N-1} \end{bmatrix} \tag{9}
$$

The one-dimensional CCC is generated by the cross-concatenation as follows:

$$
\mathbf{D} = cross^j(\Delta) = \begin{bmatrix} \Delta_0 \circ + \Delta_1 \\ \Delta_0 \circ - \Delta_1 \\ \Delta_2 \circ + \Delta_3 \\ \Delta_2 \circ - \Delta_3 \\ \cdots \\ \Delta_{N-2} \circ + \Delta_{N-1} \\ \Delta_{N-2} \circ - \Delta_{N-1} \end{bmatrix} \tag{10}
$$

The maximum case for this construction is for $M = N$ and $L = 2N$.

The construction of $(M, N, L = N)$-CCC from 2011 [13] is generated in one step from following equation:

$$C = \left\{ \left\{ \mathbf{c}_n^m \right\}_{n=0}^{N-1} \right\}_{m=0}^{M-1} = \left\{ \left\{ \mathbf{u}_N^m \odot \mathbf{u}_N^n \right\}_{n=0}^{N-1} \right\}_{m=0}^{M-1} \tag{11}$$

where $\odot$ is the Hadamard product, $\mathbf{u}_N^m$ is m-th row of unitary-like matrix $\mathbf{U}_N$ of order N and $\mathbf{c}_N^m$ is the coordinate of n-th element of m-th signature and $M = N$. The maximum case for this construction is for $M = N = L$. In other words, the maximum number of signatures equals the number of elements and the element length L.

2.2 Two-Dimensional CCCs

An element represents a matrix $\mathbf{C}$ of order P in two-dimensional space, where the element consists of complex numbers c_{ij} with absolute values $|c_{ij}| = 1$:

$$\mathbf{C} = \begin{bmatrix} c_{11} & c_{12} & \cdots & c_{1P} \\ \cdots & & & \\ c_{P1} & c_{P2} & \cdots & c_{PP} \end{bmatrix}. \tag{12}$$

Then the 2D-CCCis composed of M_{2D} sets of N_{2D} matrices

$$\left\{ \mathbf{C}_1^{(1)}, \mathbf{C}_2^{(1)}, \ldots, \mathbf{C}_{N_{2D}}^{(1)} \right\}, \ldots, \left\{ \mathbf{C}_1^{(M_{2D})}, \mathbf{C}_2^{(M_{2D})}, \ldots, \mathbf{C}_{N_{2D}}^{(M_{2D})} \right\}, \tag{13}$$

with the ideal overall correlation properties. The two-dimensional auto- and cross-correlation functions can be found in [14] in the appendix. A set of N_{2D} matrices $\left\{ \mathbf{C}_1^{(i)}, \mathbf{C}_2^{(i)}, \ldots, \mathbf{C}_{N2D}^{(i)} \right\}$ is called i-th signature and a matrix $\mathbf{C}_j^{(i)}$ is called the j-th element of i-th signature.

The construction [17, 18] generates i-th line of n_{2D}-th element of a k_{2D}-th signature of the $(N_{ID}.M_{ID}^2, N_{ID}, L_{ID}xL_{ID})$−QOCCC as follows:

$$\mathbf{c}_{n_{2D,i}}^{k_{2D}} = \mathbf{c}_{n_{2D}}^{([(k_{2D}-1)\mathrm{mod}M_{1D}]+1)} \times c_{v,i}^{(f)} \tag{14}$$

$$f = [(k_{2D} - t) \bmod M_{1D}] + 1 \tag{15}$$

$$v = \left[\left(\left\lfloor \frac{k_{2D} - 1}{M_{1D}} + 1 \right\rfloor - 1 \right) \bmod N_{1D} \right] + 1 \tag{16}$$

$$t = t + 1 \text{ for } (k_{2D} - 1) \bmod M_{1D}^2 = 0 \tag{17}$$

$$-N_{1D} + 1 \leq t \leq 0 \tag{18}$$

$$k_{2D} = 1, 2, \ldots, M_{1D}^2 \cdot \left(\frac{L_{1D}}{N_{1D}} \right) \tag{19}$$

$$n_{2D} = 1, 2, \ldots, N_{1D} \tag{20}$$

where $\lfloor x \rfloor$ is the greatest integer, which is equal or smaller than x, M_{1D} and N_{1D} denote the number of signatures and the number of elements of the inputted 1D-CCC, respectively.

3   QOCCC Properties

The properties of the analyzed QOCCCs of given underlying 1D-CCCs are described and discussed in this section.

3.1   Parameters

As it can be seen, the parameters of analyzed QOCCCs are as follows:

$$\left(\left(\frac{L_{1D}}{N_{1D}} \right) . M_{1D}^2, N_{1D}, L_{1D} \times L_{1D} \right) \text{-QOCCC} \tag{21}$$

where

$$\left(\frac{L_{1D}}{N_{1D}} \right) = 2 \text{ for } [12] \tag{22}$$

$$\left(\frac{L_{1D}}{N_{1D}} \right) = 1 \text{ for } [13] \tag{23}$$

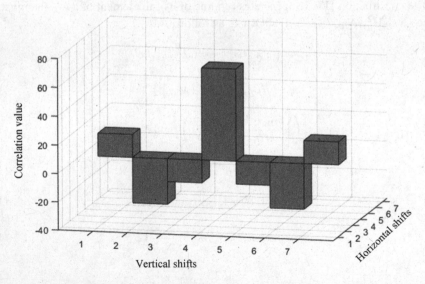

Fig. 1. Example of auto-correlation properties of (16,4,4 × 4)-QOCCC constructed by [17, 18] based on [13] where only non-zero values are displayed

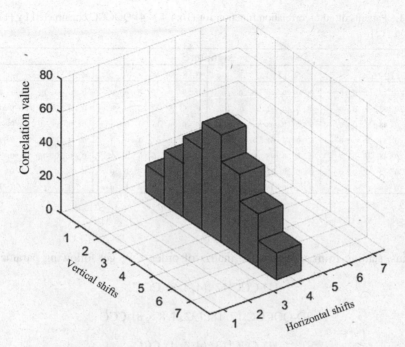

Fig. 2. Examples of auto-correlation properties for $(16,4,4 \times 4)$-QOCCC constructed by [17, 18] based on [13] where only non-zero values are displayed

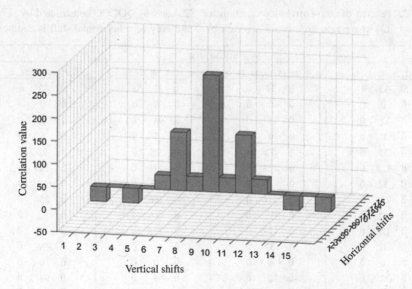

Fig. 3. Examples of auto-correlation properties for $(32,4,8 \times 8)$-QOCCC constructed by [17, 18] based on [12] where non-zero values and zero values for horizontal zero shift are displayed

Table 1. Patterns of auto-correlation function for $(16,4,4 \times 4)$-QOCCC constructed by [17, 18] based on [13]

signature			
1., 6., 11., 16.	2., 5., 12., 15.	3., 8., 9., 14.	4., 7., 10., 13.
0 0 0 16 0 0 0	0 0 0 -16 0 0 0	0 0 0 -16 0 0 0	0 0 0 16 0 0 0
0 0 0 32 0 0 0	0 0 0 32 0 0 0	0 0 0 -32 0 0 0	0 0 0 -32 0 0 0
0 0 0 48 0 0 0	0 0 0 -48 0 0 0	0 0 0 16 0 0 0	0 0 0 -16 0 0 0
0 0 0 64 0 0 0	0 0 0 64 0 0 0	0 0 0 64 0 0 0	0 0 0 64 0 0 0
0 0 0 48 0 0 0	0 0 0 -48 0 0 0	0 0 0 16 0 0 0	0 0 0 -16 0 0 0
0 0 0 32 0 0 0	0 0 0 32 0 0 0	0 0 0 -32 0 0 0	0 0 0 -32 0 0 0
0 0 0 16 0 0 0	0 0 0 -16 0 0 0	0 0 0 -16 0 0 0	0 0 0 16 0 0 0

Thus, starting from a unitary-like matrix of order 4 we get following parameters:

$$1\text{D-CCC}[12]:(4,4,8)\text{-CCC} \tag{24}$$

$$2\text{D-QOCCC}[17,18]:(32,4,8 \times 8)\text{-CCC} \tag{25}$$

$$1\text{D-CCC}[13]:(4,4,4)\text{-CCC} \tag{26}$$

$$2\text{D-QOCCC}[17,18]:(16,4,4 \times 4)\text{-CCC} \tag{27}$$

Table 2. Patterns of auto-correlation function for $(32,4,8 \times 8)$-QOCCC constructed by [17, 18] based on [12] where zero vectors are depicted by $\bar{0}$ and only zero horizontal shift is enumerated

signature			
1., 6., 11., 16., 18., 23., 28., 29.	2., 5., 12., 15., 19., 22., 25., 32.	3., 8., 9., 14., 20., 21., 26., 31.	4., 7., 10., 13., 17., 24., 27., 3.
$\bar{0}$ -32 $\bar{0}$	$\bar{0}$ 32 $\bar{0}$	$\bar{0}$ 32 $\bar{0}$	$\bar{0}$ -32 $\bar{0}$
$\bar{0}$ 0 $\bar{0}$	$\bar{0}$ 0 $\bar{0}$	$\bar{0}$ 0 $\bar{0}$	$\bar{0}$ 0 $\bar{0}$
$\bar{0}$ -32 $\bar{0}$	$\bar{0}$ 32 $\bar{0}$	$\bar{0}$ -96 $\bar{0}$	$\bar{0}$ 96 $\bar{0}$
$\bar{0}$ 0 $\bar{0}$	$\bar{0}$ 0 $\bar{0}$	$\bar{0}$ 0 $\bar{0}$	$\bar{0}$ 0 $\bar{0}$
$\bar{0}$ 32 $\bar{0}$	$\bar{0}$ -32 $\bar{0}$	$\bar{0}$ 96 $\bar{0}$	$\bar{0}$ -96 $\bar{0}$
$\bar{0}$ 128 $\bar{0}$	$\bar{0}$ 128 $\bar{0}$	$\bar{0}$ -128 $\bar{0}$	$\bar{0}$ -128 $\bar{0}$
$\bar{0}$ 32 $\bar{0}$	$\bar{0}$ -32 $\bar{0}$	$\bar{0}$ -32 $\bar{0}$	$\bar{0}$ 32 $\bar{0}$
$\bar{0}$ 256 $\bar{0}$	$\bar{0}$ 256 $\bar{0}$	$\bar{0}$ 256 $\bar{0}$	$\bar{0}$ 256 $\bar{0}$
$\bar{0}$ 32 $\bar{0}$	$\bar{0}$ -32 $\bar{0}$	$\bar{0}$ -32 $\bar{0}$	$\bar{0}$ 32 $\bar{0}$
$\bar{0}$ 128 $\bar{0}$	$\bar{0}$ 128 $\bar{0}$	$\bar{0}$ -128 $\bar{0}$	$\bar{0}$ -128 $\bar{0}$
$\bar{0}$ 32 $\bar{0}$	$\bar{0}$ -32 $\bar{0}$	$\bar{0}$ 96 $\bar{0}$	$\bar{0}$ -96 $\bar{0}$
$\bar{0}$ 0 $\bar{0}$	$\bar{0}$ 0 $\bar{0}$	$\bar{0}$ 0 $\bar{0}$	$\bar{0}$ 0 $\bar{0}$
$\bar{0}$ -32 $\bar{0}$	$\bar{0}$ 32 $\bar{0}$	$\bar{0}$ -96 $\bar{0}$	$\bar{0}$ 96 $\bar{0}$
$\bar{0}$ 0 $\bar{0}$	$\bar{0}$ 0 $\bar{0}$	$\bar{0}$ 0 $\bar{0}$	$\bar{0}$ 0 $\bar{0}$
$\bar{0}$ -32 $\bar{0}$	$\bar{0}$ 32 $\bar{0}$	$\bar{0}$ 32 $\bar{0}$	$\bar{0}$ -32 $\bar{0}$

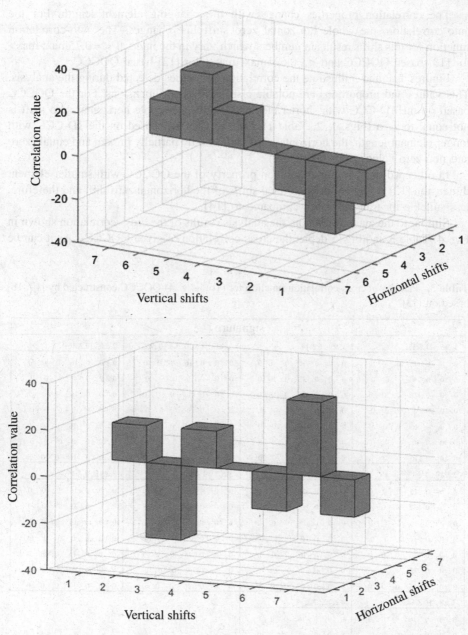

Fig. 4. Examples of cross-correlation properties for (16,4,4 × 4)-QOCCC constructed by [17, 18] based on [13] where non-zero values and zero values for horizontal zero shift are displayed

The correlation properties change with the changing element length. For the auto-correlation, the whole horizontal zero shift line changes. The auto-correlation function for this shifts results in numbers which vary in the interval $< -0.75max; max>$ for [13] based QOCCC and $< -0.625max; max>$ for [12] based QOCCC.

Figures 1, 2 and 3 illustrate the correlation properties detected during the analysis. This values and proportions are notable also for higher dimensions. For the QOCCC based on the 1D-CCC with shorter element length, the whole horizontal zero shift is not equal to zero (Figs. 1, 2, Table 1). For the QOCCC based on the 1D-CCC with longer element length, the horizontal zero shift is only partially broken and equals zero and non-zero values (Fig. 3, Table 2).

In other words, the auto-correlation property of the QOCCC with smaller element dimension [12] is broken for all vertical shifts of the horizontal zero shift and therefore, less suitable for transmission if compared to [14].

Similar to the auto-correlation, the analysis results of the cross-correlation shown in Fig. 4, Table 3 and Fig. 5 depict the cross-correlation of given QOCCCs. As it can be

Table 3. Patterns of cross-correlation function for (16,4,4 × 4)-QOCCC constructed by [17, 18] based on [13]

signature			
1.&5., 11.&15.	**1.&9., 6.&14.**	**1.&13.,4.&16.,6.&10.,7.&11.**	**2.&6., 12.&16.**
0 0 0 -16 0 0 0 0 0 0 0 0 0 0 0 0 0 0 -16 0 0 0 0 0 0 0 0 0 0 0 0 0 16 0 0 0 0 0 0 0 0 0 0 0 0 0 16 0 0 0	0 0 0 -16 0 0 0 0 0 0 -32 0 0 0 0 0 0 -16 0 0 0 0 0 0 0 0 0 0 0 0 0 16 0 0 0 0 0 0 32 0 0 0 0 0 0 16 0 0 0	0 0 0 16 0 0 0 0 0 0 0 0 0 0 0 0 0 -16 0 0 0 0 0 0 0 0 0 0 0 0 0 -16 0 0 0 0 0 0 0 0 0 0 0 0 0 16 0 0 0	0 0 0 16 0 0 0 0 0 0 0 0 0 0 0 0 0 0 16 0 0 0 0 0 0 0 0 0 0 0 0 0 0 -16 0 0 0 0 0 0 0 0 0 0 0 0 0 -16 0 0 0
2.&10., 5.&13.	**2.&14.,3.&15.,5.&9.,8.&12.**	**3.&7., 9.&13.**	**3.&11., 8.&16.**
0 0 0 16 0 0 0 0 0 0 -32 0 0 0 0 0 0 16 0 0 0 0 0 0 0 0 0 0 0 0 0 -16 0 0 0 0 0 0 32 0 0 0 0 0 0 -16 0 0 0	0 0 0 -16 0 0 0 0 0 0 0 0 0 0 0 0 0 16 0 0 0 0 0 0 0 0 0 0 0 0 0 16 0 0 0 0 0 0 0 0 0 0 0 0 0 -16 0 0 0	0 0 0 16 0 0 0 0 0 0 0 0 0 0 0 0 0 -48 0 0 0 0 0 0 0 0 0 0 0 0 0 48 0 0 0 0 0 0 0 0 0 0 0 0 0 -16 0 0 0	0 0 0 16 0 0 0 0 0 0 32 0 0 0 0 0 0 16 0 0 0 0 0 0 0 0 0 0 0 0 0 -16 0 0 0 0 0 0 -32 0 0 0 0 0 0 -16 0 0 0
4.&8., 10.&14.	**4.&12., 7.&15.**		
0 0 0 -16 0 0 0 0 0 0 0 0 0 0 0 0 0 48 0 0 0 0 0 0 0 0 0 0 0 0 0 -48 0 0 0 0 0 0 0 0 0 0 0 0 0 16 0 0 0	0 0 0 -16 0 0 0 0 0 0 32 0 0 0 0 0 0 -16 0 0 0 0 0 0 0 0 0 0 0 0 0 16 0 0 0 0 0 0 -32 0 0 0 0 0 0 16 0 0 0		

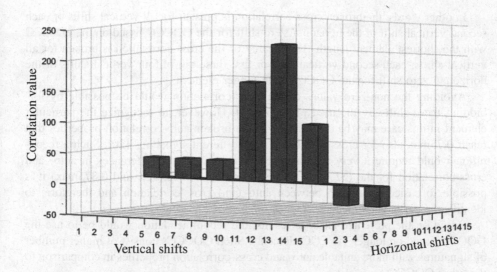

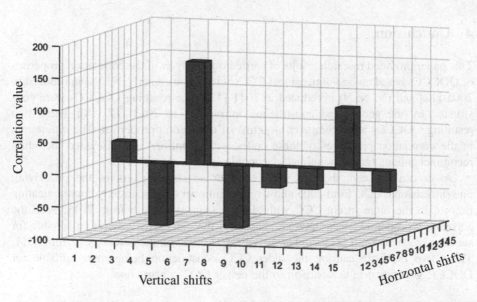

Fig. 5. Examples of cross-correlation properties for (32,4,8 × 8)-QOCCC constructed by [17, 18] based on [12] where non-zero values and zero values for horizontal zero shift are displayed

seen, the cross-correlation of the QOCCC based on shorter sequences [13] reaches values in interval < − 0.75max; 0.75max>. The QOCCC based on longer sequences [12] the cross-correlation achieves < −0.875max; 0.875max>. The table with cross-correlation patterns for (32,4,8 × 8)-QOCCC is left out due to its size. Please, contact the authors for retrieving it in case of need.

In other words, the broken cross-correlation is present for all vertical shifts or each second vertical shift of the horizontal zero shift for the QOCCC based on the 1D-CCC with the shortest element length. The ideality of the cross-correlation is broken for all vertical shifts, each second vertical shift or first three out of four vertical shifts of the horizontal zero shift for the QOCCC with longer element.

Avoiding the non-zero values of the cross-correlation would be possible by forbidding these shifts by the used protocol [14]. However, to recognize the particular element in this case may be difficult due to the broken auto-correlation properties that reach 0.75max also for cross-correlation with different signatures [20]. Such a recognition would require a very accurate measurements. As the differences in auto- and cross-correlation for the $(32,4,8 \times 8)$ are measurable (0.625max and 0.875max) it is possible to easier distinguish between auto- and cross-correlation and therefore, to identify the particular signature.

Based on the presented analysis results, the recommendation would be to use the QOCCC based on longer 1D-CCC elements. Such QOCCCs consist of higher number of signatures with more suitable auto- and cross-correlation properties in comparison to the other QOCCC.

4   Conclusion

This paper provided research results of carried out analysis of the correlation properties of QOCCCs based on one-dimensional CCCs with parameters (N, N, 2N) introduced in 2005 [12] and (N, N, N) introduced in 2011 [13]. The resulting QOCCCs were constructed by the generalized construction introduced in 2013 [17, 18]. These two resulting QOCCCs were compared in terms of correlation properties. The differences in the correlation properties of these codes were identified and discussed including recommendations for the solutions of possible issues.

As it can be seen, the CCCs with longer sequence length of the underlying one-dimensional CCC from 2005 allow higher number of concurrently communicating users than the more recent CCC with shorter sequence length from 2011. Also the correlation properties of the QOCCC based on the older CCCs are more suitable for sequence recognition if compared to the QOCCC based on the newer CCC from 2011. These two facts are causing the older CCC construction being more suitable for QOCCC generation in comparison to the newer CCC construction.

Acknowledgment. This work was supported by Slovak Academy of Sciences under contract VEGA 1/0518/13 and by the Department of Information Systems, Faculty of Management of the Comenius University in Bratislava.

References

1. Golay, M.J.E.: Complementary series. IRE Trans. Inf. Theor. IT **7**, 82–87 (1961)
2. Turyn, R.: Ambiguity function of complementary sequences. IEEE Trans. Inf. Theor. IT **9**, 46–47 (1963)

3. Taki, Y., Miyakawa, H., Hatori, M., Namba, S.: Even-shift orthogonal sequences. IEEE Trans. Inf. Theor. IT **15**, 295–300 (1969)
4. Tseng, C.C., Liu, C.L.: Complementary Sets of Sequences. IBM Thomas J. Watson Research Center Report, RC 3397 (1971)
5. Tseng, C.C., Liu, C.L.: Complementary sets of sequences. IEEE Trans. Inf. Theor. IT **18**, 652–664 (1972)
6. Sivaswamy, R.: Multiphase complementary codes. IEEE Trans. Inf. Theor. IT **24**, 546–552 (1978)
7. Frank, R.L.: Polyphase complementary codes. IEEE Trans. Inf. Theor. IT **26**, 641–647 (1980)
8. Suehiro, N.: Complete complementary code composed of N-multiple shift orthogonal sequences. Trans. IEICE **J65-A**, 1247–1255 (1982)
9. Suehiro, N., Hatori, M.: N-shift cross-orthogonal sequences. IEEE Trans. Inf. Theor. IT **34**, 143–146 (1988)
10. Dávideková, M., Greguš ml., M., Farkaš, P., Rákus, M.: Applications of complete complementary codes and propositions for future research areas of these codes. Proc. Comput. Sci. **83**, 592–599 (2016)
11. Hsiao-Hwa, C., Jun-Feng, Y., Suehiro, N.: A multicarrier CDMA architecture based on orthogonal complementary codes for new generations of wideband wireless communications. IEEE Commun. Mag. **39**, 126–135 (2001)
12. Zhang, C., Chenggao, H., Liao, Y., Lin, X., Hatori, M.: Iterative method for constructing complete complementary sequences with lengths of 2mN. Tsinghua Sci. Technol. **10**, 605–609 (2005)
13. Chenggao, H., Suehiro, N., Hashimoto, T.: A systematic framework for the construction of optimal complete complementary codes. IEEE Trans. Inf. Theor. **57**, 6033–6042 (2011)
14. Farkaš, P., Turcsány, M.: Two-dimensional orthogonal complete complementary codes. In: Joint 1st Workshop on Mobile Future and Symposium on Trends in Communications (SympoTIC 2003), pp. 21–24. IEEE Press, New York (2003)
15. Dávideková, M., Farkaš, P., Ružický, E.: Generalized construction of two-dimensional complete complementary codes. In: 36th International Conference on Telecommunications and Signal Processing (TSP), pp. 747–750. IEEE Press, New York (2013)
16. Turcsány, M., Farkaš, P.: Two-dimensional quasi orthogonal complete complementary codes. In: Joint 1st Workshop on Mobile Future and Symposium on Trends in Communications (SympoTIC 2003), pp. 37–40. IEEE Press, New York (2003)
17. Dávideková, M.: Generalized construction of two-dimensional quasi complete complementary codes. In: The 8th International Doctoral Seminar (IDS 2013), pp. 46–52. University of Zagreb, Zagreb (2013)
18. Dávideková, M.: Generalized construction of two-dimensional quasi complete complementary codes. Research papers Faculty of Materials Science and Technology, Slovak University of Technology in Trnava 21 SI, pp. 12–17 (2013)
19. Dávideková, M., Farkaš, P.: On the cross-correlation properties of complete complementary codes of different families (N, N, N^2) and (N, N, N). In: 1st Biannual CER Comparative European Research Conference, pp. 117–120. Sciemcee Publishing, London (2014)
20. Dávideková, M., Farkaš, P., Greguš ml., M.: Analysis of the correlation properties of QOCCC. In: The 23rd International Conference on Systems, Signals and Image Processing (IWSSIP 2016). IEEE Press, New York (2016, in press)

Heterogeneous Traffic Modeling and Analysis for Wireless Sensor Networks

Hamida Qumber Ali$^{(\boxtimes)}$ and Sayeed Ghani

Institute of Business Administration, Karachi, Pakistan
{hali,sghani}@iba.edu.pk

Abstract. Traditional wireless sensor networks (WSNs) face power limitation which is mainly caused due to inter-node data transfer. Multi-sensor nodes, in which multiple sensors are mounted on a single radio board, are becoming popular to counter this issue. However, these sensor nodes may require handling heterogeneous traffic in terms of different bandwidth demand, traffic load and packet sizes. A single traffic based model cannot provide a tractable performance analysis of heterogeneous traffic. In this paper, we propose a heterogeneous traffic-based model to analyze the performance of WSNs. The proposed model is capable of handling traffic of variable bandwidth requirements, load and packet sizes. Our results indicate that heterogeneity of traffic affects the performance of individual traffic and overall network efficiency.

1 Introduction

The advancements in CMOS (Complementary Metal-Oxide Semiconductor) technology has given rise to low cost cameras, microphones, biosensors, bio-potential Electrode Sensors and chemical sensors which together with the enhanced processing capabilities and memory have changed the face of the traditional sensor networks [1, 2]. This new class of sensors has improved the monitoring and control systems by embedding real-time analysis and interpretation with the controlled environment. Examples of such systems include multimedia surveillance systems, traffic monitoring systems, industrial process control, smart grids, smart home building, and smart healthcare systems. These WSN applications generate traffic that may vary in bandwidth requirement, packet sizes and traffic loads.

Today's sensor networks are quiet effectively using multi-sensor based sensor nodes in which a set of non-intrusive sensors are mounted on a single sensor board [3–7]. The rapid evolution of the sensing technologies, MEMS (Micro-Electro-Mechanical Systems) and WSNs has contributed to the development of multi-sensor nodes. A number of applications that are potentially using multi-sensor platforms are listed in Table 1. These multi-sensor nodes are gaining popularity for minimizing the inter-node data transfers and improving its power efficiency.

In this paper we propose a heterogeneous traffic-based CTMC (Continuous Time Markov Chain) model for WSNs. The proposed model assumes that each device is capable of generating heterogeneous traffic. To the best of our knowledge, our proposed model is unique in its approach of analyzing the performance of multi-sensor

© Springer International Publishing Switzerland 2016
M. Younas et al. (Eds.): MobiWIS 2016, LNCS 9847, pp. 246–255, 2016.
DOI: 10.1007/978-3-319-44215-0_20

Table 1. Multi-sensor devices and applications

Year	Multi-sensor platform	Sensed data	Communication network	Application
2007	Mica Weather Board [3]	Photoreceptive, digital temperature, humidity, digital pressure, thermopile (infrared detector)	WSN	Habitate and microclimate monitoring
2009	APOLLO (Air POLLutants mOnitoring system) [4]	CO, CO2, NO2, (PM), volatile organic compounds (VOCs), temperature/humidity sensor	WSN	Monitor air pollution
2009	PIR Sensors [5]	Pedestrian Monitoring, Traffic Monitoring, vehicle detection, travel direction, vehicle classification and speed estimation	WSN	Human and vehicle activity monitoring
2015	STEVAL-IDI003V2 [6]	MEMS accelerometer, pressure sensor, humidity sensor, and microphone	Contiki and 6LoWPAN	Develop applications for IoT,
2015	SmartSense, MSP430 MCU & TI CC2420 [7]	Movement, vibration, orientation or angle, and temperature	Zigbee, IEEE802.15.4	Zigbee applications

based WSNs. By keeping track of the type of traffic in our model we have made our performance analysis more tractable.

2 Applications

In order to appreciate the applicability of this model this section presents an example use case of a smart healthcare system.

2.1 Smart Healthcare System

In a smart healthcare system remote monitoring of patients can be performed via medical sensors such as audio sensors, location sensors and motion and activity sensors. These patients wear various sensors to monitor parameters such as body temperature, blood pressure, pulse oximetry, ECG (Electrocardiogram) and breathing activity [8]. The process flow chart in Fig. 1 represents a patient health monitoring system. A data collection and processing unit is the central entity of this system. A request for patient's ECG may be sent to the control unit. The request can be either internal or by external sources such as by the authorized nursing staff. The system periodically observes the patient's pulse rate. The internal alert is caused after an abnormal pulse value from the pulse reading sensors. If an internal request is received

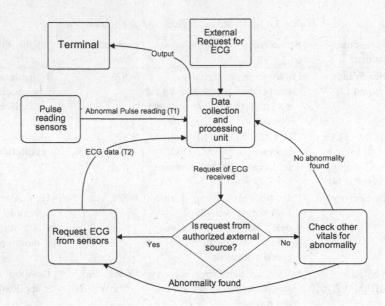

Fig. 1. Smart healthcare system

at the control unit, the system will check for other vitals such as patient's blood pressure, fever, oximeter reading to evaluate the case further against a set of predefined rules. For this purpose a set of sensors will be implanted on patient's body to monitor major vitals. For abnormal vitals, the request for ECG is approved and the ECG sensors capture and transmit the ECG images to the central control unit. When the central control unit receives a request for patient's ECG from the external source the request is entertained instantly.

The system will instantly request the ECG sensors for the patient's current ECG. In this example the abnormal pulse reading data is termed as T1 traffic while the images of ECG is termed as T2 traffic. It can again be seen here that both the traffic types have different arrival rates, traffic load and different QoS (Quality of Service) requirements such as bandwidth, reliability and delay bounds.

3   Related Work

Modeling of heterogeneous traffic has been widely done for Internet and cellular networks. However, to the best of our knowledge, little work has been done to model heterogeneous traffic for WSNs. Shrestha et al. in [9] model WSN in which different devices can generate heterogeneous traffic. The model takes into account the heterogeneity of traffic in terms of variable bandwidth requirement and packet size by different devices. In this work the authors have proposed a general discrete time Markov chain model for the hybrid communication system of IEEE802.15.4. The model, however, does not consider multi-sensor nodes capable of collecting heterogeneous traffic from the environment.

An extensive research has been done to evaluate the performance of WSNs through simulations. Kan [10] proposes a multi-hop activity aware delay analysis of WSNs. The paper suggests that by optimizing the data rate along a multi-hop path the transmission delay can be minimized. Sung et al. [11] proposed an efficient request handling mechanism that ensures that each sensor mote's queue is stable. This scheme is based on a compressed sensing mechanism that achieves near contention free transmission. Fallahi et al. [12] proposed a channel reservation scheme that can effectively reduce packet loss and improve network local channel efficiency in multi-hop wireless networks.

However relatively sparse work has been done on the performance modeling of contention-free and contention-based sensor networks. In a contention-based network nodes compete for the channel to get the right to transmit. Das and Abouzeid [13] obtained a closed form solution for the average end-to-end delay of packets and throughput of nodes in an opportunistic secondary cognitive radio network that co-exist with a primary network. In another work Lin and Weitnauer [14] proposed a model based on a Markov Decision Process (MDP) framework. The model analyzes the life-time of multi-hop sensor networks. The authors incorporate the dynamics of MAC (medium access layer) layer link admission, routing layer queuing and energy evolution issues into their model. Similarly Kempa in [15] models the performance of WSNs using a mathematical model. The model derives the time-dependent queuing delay by using the idea of embedded Markov chain to derive the queuing delay distribution of nodes at fixed time period. Liu et al. in [16] proposed an infinite queuing model to study the tradeoff between network performance and power consumption in contention-based sensor networks. The model considers active/sleep states of a sensor node and an infinite buffer. Luo et al. in [17] has done similar work for a finite buffer size. In [18] similar authors have developed a finite queuing model of contention-based WSNs with the synchronous wakeup patterns. Jun et al. in [19] proposed an analytical model to analyze the impact of active-sleep dynamics and node buffer size on the performance of SMAC-enabled network. Yang and Heinzelman in [20] proposed a Markov model to describe the behavior of SMAC with variable number of nodes, queue capacities, contention window sizes and data arrival rates. Liu and Lee [21] present an infinite queuing model of sensor nodes and analyze the network performance in contention-free WSN. In [22] the tradeoff between network performance and power consumption in contention-based sensor networks using an infinite queuing model has been discussed. None of these models, however, have addressed heterogeneity of traffic.

4   System Model and Assumptions

Consider N sensor nodes in a contention-based sensor network. Nodes may be randomly deployed in geographically dispersed area. Nodes are connected to the sink node through multi-hop multi-path topology. Each node can collect two types of traffic and transmit to the sink. Traffic of both types is independent and identically distributed. It is assumed that every node follows periodic active and sleep cycles for energy conservation. As the active period starts, nodes turn on their radio transceivers for communication with other nodes. In the sleep period nodes turn off their radios. In sleep state nodes can locally generate packets but they can neither receive any traffic from other nodes nor initiate any transmission. During the sleep cycle all pending packets are stored in a local node buffer to be sent in the upcoming active period.

4.1 Heterogeneous Traffic Model

In order to design a model based on heterogeneous traffic we will make some simplifying assumptions to make the model tractable. Following are some of the assumptions we shall make:

i. We represent type of traffic by k such that $1 \leq k \leq R$, where R is total number of types of traffic.
ii. Assume traffic stream arrives as independent Poisson process with average arrival rate λ_k.
iii. The model does not sustain the type information of packets inside the buffer. We keep track of the type of packet at the head of the queue.

Sensor nodes are modeled as periodically transitioning between active (A) and sleep (S) states according to predefined fixed value of duty cycle. As the model assumes that the traffic generated by sensing the environment ($\lambda_{g,k}$) as Poisson process we make a simplifying assumption that the relayed traffic ($\lambda_{r,k}$) to a node is also Poisson process. Now we can define the average arrival rate of packets when the node is in active state λ_k^a by using the additive property of Poisson process such as $\lambda_k^a = \lambda_{g,k} + \lambda_{r,k}$. The average arrival rate of packets when the node is in sleep state is $\lambda_k^s = \lambda_{g,k}$.

4.2 Sensor Node Queuing Model

We have assumed the duration of the active and the sleep period are exponentially distributed with mean T_a and T_s respectively. We made this assumption to simplify analysis. Therefore the sensor node's active and sleep states can be modeled using a CTMC as shown in Fig. 2. The node transitions from state A to state S with rate $a = \frac{1}{T_a}$ and from S to A at rate $s = \frac{1}{T_s}$.

The multi-sensor node in Fig. 3 can transmit traffic of R different types with average arrival rate λ_k^a in active state and λ_k^s in sleep state. μ_k is the transmission rate of packet of type k. We assume that the system capacity is limited to a maximum of M packets.

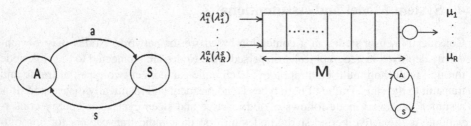

Fig. 2. Active/sleep model of sensor   **Fig. 3.** Sensor node queuing model

5 Traffic Model of a Sensor Node

In this section we model a single node by a CTMC as shown in Fig. 4. Let $P^a_{k,m}$ denote the probability that a node is in active state with m number of packets in the system. The subscript k represents the type of packet being served. Correspondingly, $P^s_{k,m}$ denotes the probability that a node is in sleep state with m number of packets in its buffer. In sleep state the node does not transmit data therefore the subscript k represents the type of packet at the head of queue. The state space of a heterogeneous sensor node in Fig. 4 is defined as State (t, k, m).

Where
t $\in$ (A, S) or t = active/sleep state of a node,
k $\in$ (1−R) or k = type of packet
R = total number of types of traffic and
m $\in$ (0−M) or m = current number of packets in system and M = Capacity of the system.

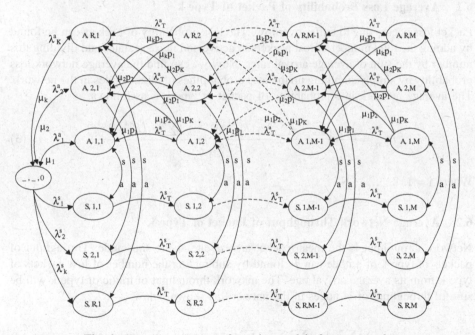

Fig. 4. Transition diagram of queuing model of a sensor node

In Fig. 4 λ^a_T represents the average arrival rate of packets of all types. The rate of forward transition between two states for m ≥ 1 is equal to λ^a_T. This is because we do not keep track of type information inside the buffer. Therefore an average of all arrival rates has been used to show the transition rate of a packet from the buffer to the server. Similarly λ^s_T is the transition rate of a packet to the head of a queue when the node is in sleep state. The equations for λ^s_T and λ^a_T are as follows:

$$\lambda_T^a = \sum_{k=1}^{R} \lambda_k^a p_k^a, \qquad \lambda_T^s = \sum_{k=1}^{R} \lambda_k^s p_k^s \tag{1}$$

In the equation above p_k^a is the probability that the next packet that gets service is of type k given that the node is in active state as shown in equation below.

$$p_k^a = \frac{\lambda_k^a}{\sum_{i=1}^{K} \lambda_i^a} \tag{2}$$

6 Network Performance Estimation

We derive the performance of WSN in terms of average packet loss probability, average latency and average power consumption as given below:

6.1 Average Loss Probability of Packet of Type k

Packet loss occurs due to buffer overflow. The loss probability of packets can be found by adding the total number of lost packets in active and in sleep states and dividing this number by the sum of average arrival rates. Now we can find the average network loss probability by simply summing up the loss probabilities of all the nodes in the network. The average network loss probability of packet of type k is as follows:

$$\bar{P}_{loss}^k = \frac{\sum_{i=1}^{N} \sum_{k=1}^{R} [(\sum_{k=1}^{R} (P_{k,M}^{a,i})) \lambda_k^{a,i} + (\sum_{k=1}^{R} (P_{k,M}^{s,i})) \lambda_k^{s,i}]}{N \sum_{k=1}^{K} \lambda_g^k} \tag{3}$$

Where i = 1, 2, ..., N.

6.2 Average Network Throughput of Packet of Type k

Network throughput is the mean packet arrival rate at the sink node. Throughput of packets of type k of a node can be found by subtracting the number of lost packets of type k from its average arrival rate. The network throughput of traffic of type k will be sum of throughput of N nodes in the network as shown below:

$$C_k = N \sum_{k=1}^{R} \lambda_g^k - \sum_{i=1}^{N} \sum_{k=1}^{R} [(\sum_{k=1}^{R} (P_{k,M}^{a,i})) \lambda_k^{a,i} + (\sum_{k=1}^{R} (P_{k,M}^{s,i})) \lambda_k^{s,i}] \tag{4}$$

6.3 Average Network Delay of Packets of Type k

The average network delay of packets of type k can be found by using Little's law [23]. According to which the average number of packets of type k in the buffer of a node can be calculated by the following equation:

$$\bar{m}_k = p_k^a \sum_{m=1}^{M} m_k P_{k,m}^a + p_k^s \sum_{m=1}^{M} m_k P_{k,m}^s \qquad (5)$$

Hence by applying Littile's law we can find the average network delay for packets of type k is as follows:

$$\bar{D}_{net,k} = \frac{\sum_{i=1}^{N} \bar{m}_k^i}{C_k} \qquad (6)$$

7 Network Performance

We implemented our model in Matlab and derived the performance of heterogeneous traffic in WSN. The system parameters used for our theoretical analysis are as follows: N = 10, W = 64, Pw_{tran} = 17 mA, Pw_{recv} = 16 mA, Pw_{idle} = 16 mA, E_{tr} = .025 mJ. The average arrival of T_1 and T_2 traffic are λ_g^1 = 1 packets/s (pps) and λ_g^2 = 0.5 pps. Mean service rates for T_1 and T_2 traffic are 45.5 pps and 35.5 pps respectively.

Figure 5 shows packet loss probability and power consumption for different values of duty cycles. Our result shows that as duty cycle increases nodes remain active for longer which causes packets loss to reduce. The fall in loss probability is higher for T1 traffic due to the higher arrival intensity and faster service rate compared to T2 traffic. However this reduction in loss probability comes with a cost of increased power consumption. Figure 6 shows the impact of different values of duty cycles on the average end-to-end delay. It is observed that the delay decrease gradually as duty cycle increases for both types of traffic. This happens because at lower duty cycles nodes remain active for short time hence fewer packets can be transmitted. This increases end to end delay significantly. While at higher duty cycles nodes remain active most of the time and can transmit more packets while in active state.

Hence packets do not remain inside the buffer for long which results in reducing the network delay. This reduction in delay, however, comes with a cost of increased power consumption.

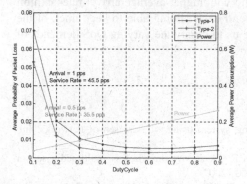

Fig. 5. Average packet loss, power consumption and duty cycles

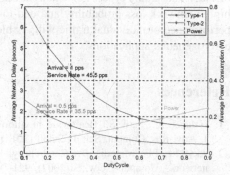

Fig. 6. Average network delay, probability, power consumption and duty cycles

In Fig. 7 we observe that probability of loss decreases as system capacity increases. The higher loss of T_1 traffic is due to its higher arrival rate. Power consumption increases initially. However when the value of M is higher than 12, the loss curve and the mean power consumption level out to a fixed value. We can conclude that the buffer size of 12 may be a good choice for better performance. Figure 8 shows that the delay for T1 is higher than T2 due to the fact that it has higher arrival rate. It is also observed that increasing system capacity will increase the average network delay. This might be due to the fact that at very small values of M both types of packets get dropped almost equally. However as M increases the number of T_1 packets in the system increases significantly that broadens the delay gap between the two types. Like the previous experiment initially the mean power consumption increases with increasing system capacity. However when the value of M is higher than 12, the curve of the mean power consumption levels out to a fixed value.

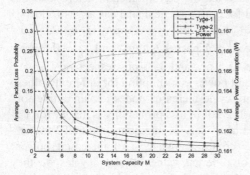

Fig. 7. Average packet loss and system capacity

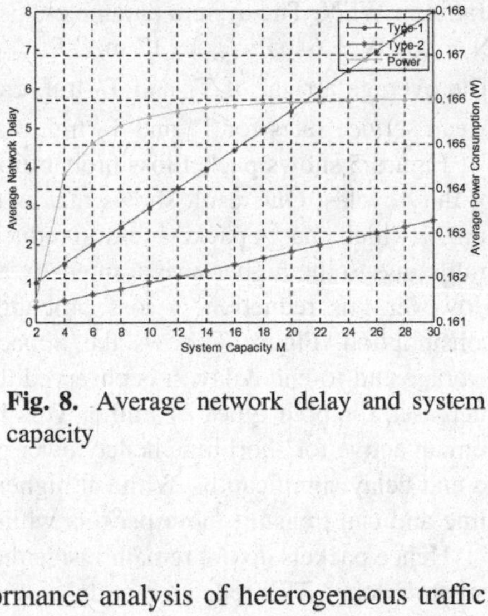

Fig. 8. Average network delay and system capacity

8 Conclusion

In this paper we presented a model for performance analysis of heterogeneous traffic based WSNs. Our results indicate that heterogeneity of traffic impacts the performance of individual traffic types. For example traffic with higher average arrival rates exhibit higher network loss probability and end-to-end delay. Being able to keep track of the performance of individual traffic will enable us to satisfy the varying QoS demands of heterogeneous applications.

References

1. Halapeti, P., Patil, S.: Healthcare monitoring system using wireless sensor networks. Int. J. Adv. Res. Comput. Sci. Technol. (2014)
2. Akyildiz, I.F., Melodia, T., Chowdhury, K.R.: A survey on wireless multimedia sensor networks. Comput. Netw. **51**(2007), 921–960 (2007)
3. Raghavendra, C.S., Sivalingam, K.M., Znati, T.: Wireless Sensor Networks, Software edn. Springer, New York (2006). ISBN 0-387-35269-4

4. Choi, S., Kim, N., Cha, H., Ha, R.: Micro sensor node for air pollutant monitoring: hardware and software issues. Sensors (Basel) **9**(10), 7970–7987 (2009). Published online 12 October 2009
5. Hungt, P., Tahir, M., Farrell, R., McLoone, S., McCarthy, T.: Wireless sensor networks for activity monitoring using multi-sensor multi-modal node architecture. In: ISSC 2009, UCD Dublin, 10–11 June 2009
6. Multi-sensor RF platform 6LoWPAN & NFC interface board. User Manual, November 2015
7. Nguyen, C.M., Mays, J., Plesa, D., Rao, S., Nguyen, M., Chiao, J.C.: Wireless sensor nodes for environmental monitoring in Internet of Things. In: IEEE MTT-S International Microwave Symposium (IMS) (2015)
8. Ghayvat, H., Mukhopadhyay, S., Gui, X., Suryadevara, N.: WSN and IOT-based smart homes and their extension to smart buildings. Sensors **15**(5), p. 10350 (2015). MDPI, Switzerland
9. Shrestha, B., Hossain, E., Camorlinga, S.: A Markov model for IEEE 802.15.4 MAC with GTS transmissions and heterogeneous traffic in non-saturation mode. In: IEEE International Conference on Communication Systems (ICCS) (2010)
10. Kan, B.Q.: Towards minimizing delay in MHWN based on activity estimation. In: Military Communications Conference - MILCOM 2012 (2012)
11. Sung, C.K., Egan, M., Chen, Z., Collings, I.B.: Performance of wireless nano-sensor networks with energy harvesting. In: IEEE 79th Vehicular Technology Conference (2014)
12. Fallahi, A., Hossain, E., Alfa, A.S.: QoS and energy trade off in distributed energy-limited mesh/relay networks: a queuing analysis. IEEE Trans. Parallel Distrib. Syst. **17**(6), 576–592 (2006)
13. Das, D., Abouzeid, A.A.: Delay analysis of multi-hop cognitive radio networks using network of virtual priority queues. In: IEEE Wireless Communications and Networking Conference (WCNC) (2014)
14. Lin, J., Weitnauer, M.A.: A Markovian approach to modeling the optimal lifetime of multi-hop wireless sensor networks. In: IEEE Military Communications Conference (2013)
15. Kempa, W.M.: On queuing delay in WSN with energy saving mechanism based on queued wake up. In: 21st International Conference on Systems, Signals and Image Processing, May 2014
16. Liu, J., Jiang, X., Lee, T.T.: Analysis of random sleep scheme for wireless sensor networks. Int. J. Sens. Netw. **7**(1/2) (2010). Inderscience Publishers, Geneva, Switzerland
17. Luo, J., Jiang, L., He, C.: Finite queuing model analysis for energy and QoS tradeoff in contention-based wireless sensor networks. In: IEEE International Conference on Communications (2007)
18. Luo, J., Jiang, L., He, C.: Performance analysis of synchronous wakeup patterns in contention-based sensor networks using a finite queuing model. In: IEEE GLOBECOM (2007)
19. Jun, L., LingGe, J., He, C.: An analytical model for SMAC protocol in multi-hop wireless sensor network. Sci. China Inf. Sci. **53**(11), 2323–2331 (2010). Science China Press, China
20. Yang, O., Heinzelman, W.: Modeling and throughput analysis for SMAC with a finite queue capacity. In: 5th International Conference on Intelligent Sensors, Sensor Networks and Information Processing (2009)
21. Liu, J.M., Lee, T.: A framework for performance modeling of wireless sensor networks. In: IEEE International Conference on Communications, vol. 2, pp. 1075–1081 (2005)
22. Chiasserini, C.F., Garetto, M.: Modeling the performance of wireless sensor networks. In: IEEE Infocom, vol. 1, pp. 7–11, March 2004
23. Chhajed, D., Lowe, T.J.: Building Intuition: Insights from Basic Operations Management Models and Principles. Springer Science + Business Media, LLC, New York (2008)

Duco - Hybrid Indoor Navigation

Can Surmeli[✉] and Tacha Serif

Yeditepe University, 26 Ağustos Yerleşimi İnönü Mah. Kayışdağı Cad.,
34755 Ataşehir, İstanbul, Turkey
can@cansurmeli.com, tserif@cse.yeditepe.edu.tr

Abstract. This paper proposes an application especially designed for
indoor navigation, Duco. A hybrid approach at trying to find a solution
to the problem of indoor navigation by mainly utilising pedestrian dead-
reckoning (PDR) along with the aid of iOS wireless location determination systems to aid the process. Using merely the digital accelerometer
and compass sensors of modern smartphones, PDR can reflect location
changes in real-time with high-precision while retaining battery life at
maximum. An algorithm is utilised to analyse the data from these noisy
sensors to enable high success rate of detecting step count. Duco also
makes use of wireless location determination systems to retrieve the initial location where PDR falls short or iBeacons to get around problematic
places inside an indoor venue like stairs, elevators or signal dead-zones. ·

Keywords: Indoor navigation · Positioning · Pedestrian dead-
reckoning · Smartphone inertial sensor · iBeacon · CoreLocation

1 Introduction

While outdoor navigation unfolds at full-speed, indoor navigation remains mar-
ginal. People are losing time and energy when they are inside an indoor environment since a viable solution is not available to retrieve precise location information continually as GPS does for outdoors.

Due to the lack of line of sight to satellites, GPS usage in an indoor environment is not plausible. To fill in this gap, various other researches focuses
on utilising wireless signals such as Wi-Fi or Bluetooth Low Energy (BLE), e.g.
[1–3], to provide a location determination infrastructure in indoors. Through the
years, researches in this manner made headway that even though still not precise
enough as a GPS solution, such infrastructures can yield sufficient results [4,5].
Although their major downside is that their precision is not continuous that
it gets affected by various indoor environment elements, such as signal reflections [2] from various indoor materials or signals being absorbed by humans,
and therefore return fluctuating results [6]. Another downside is that, it's not
cost efficient to deploy and maintain such a network to operate at it's highest
accuracy [7]. Even then, constant usage of such a network requires a lot energy
usage on the smartphone (receiver) end ([8]) which is problematic since smartphones have a limited battery capacity along with various other tasks going on
as todays smartphones are getting more capable.

© Springer International Publishing Switzerland 2016
M. Younas et al. (Eds.): MobiWIS 2016, LNCS 9847, pp. 256–267, 2016.
DOI: 10.1007/978-3-319-44215-0_21

The proposed system in this paper, namely Duco which means to lead in Latin, aspires to solve the problem of indoor navigation in a two-fold manner: (1) retrieve the initial location of the user via the underlying operating system's location estimation framework. (2) Once the initial location is determined, start navigating the user with pedestrian dead-reckoning.

Most indoor environments already have Wi-Fi coverage available with a proper network. This infrastructure yields information of value and therefore should be utilised to retrieve the initial location as PDR lacks on this subject. If location determination using Wi-Fi signals used continuously, the returned results may not be satisfactory. Although for an initial fix, they should be sufficient.

The technique of PDR merely relies upon using the accelerometer and the digital compass. These low-cost sensors practically found on every smartphone provide noisy data, although the algorithm proposed can cope with the analysis and provide accurate step count. This allows Duco to operate with high precision while making minimal energy usage.

Another advantage of Duco is it's usage of Bluetooth Low Energy devices; more specifically beacons operating with Apple's BLE beacon protocol: iBeacons. Because of their signal specifications, iBeacons provide highly accurate results in a short range. Due to this short range, they can't cover physically large areas but they can be successfully used to provide location data in specific places such as stairs, elevators or Wi-Fi dead zones.

2   Background

An indoor navigation solution's fundamental requirement is getting an initial fix on the user's location. The approach for location determination mostly relies on utilising various wireless signals (cellular, Wi-Fi or Bluetooth) either in a stand-alone or a cumulative manner and afterwards interpreting them with different techniques [9].

A popular technique is trilateration. In broad terms, trilateration (or triangulation) measures the distances (or angles) to a set of access points at known locations (at least three points required) and calculates the position of the receiver as a set of linear mathematical equations [10]. A notable use of trilateration is done by GPS systems [11].

In terms of indoor navigation, [12] uses trilateration collectively with Bluetooth and Wi-Fi signals. First, since Bluetooth signals are better at accuracy than Wi-Fi [13], they propose the methodology to find the propagation of Bluetooth signals and then combine it with the propagation model of Wi-Fi signals. Finally, an algorithm determines the receiver location through these models. The interesting part of this study is that they observed that the RSSI values of transmitters, either Bluetooth or Wi-Fi, vary in huge amounts over time. Therefore, the researchers conducting the study opted for using the RSSIs of the receivers, in this case, the smartphones. In their evaluations, their results were satisfactory, 0.5 m precision. However their testbed was not a large scale crowded indoor environment with complex paths where a lot of signal interferences occur but a straight line at the ground floor of a house (Fig. 1).

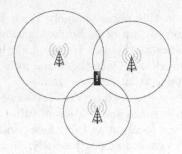

Fig. 1. Trilateration using wireless access points [10]

Another approach at location determination is fingerprinting which consists of two phases: offline and online. In the offline phase, a receiver device gets moved inside the selected venue by an expert, measures the RSSIs of the access points and notes them in a database; also known as database training. At the online phase, a device is able to determine it's location by taking real-time RSSI measurements and comparing them against the database. The complication is that various environmental effects distorts the signals and changes the RSSI values at the premises. Therefore the measurements in the database does not match with the ones taken by the receiver at the online phase and the database requires periodic retraining. Moreover, covering a large scale environment is time-consuming; therefore makes fingerprinting impractical.

[8] utilises Wi-Fi fingerprinting. Their purpose is to make use of the ubiquitous Wi-Fi networks but at the same time be able to minimise it's energy usage footprint. For this reason, they propose making use of the device's sensors to provide information about minimal user movements and disregard fingerprinting at that moment. One other proposed idea to reduce the energy consumption from the authors was to make most of the computation on device rather than transmitting it to a server. In line with their proposed idea, their findings showed that a transmission between a Wi-Fi network and a receiver uses five times more power compared to just connecting to that same access point. As a result, they achieve a usage of 14 h with a precision of 4.75 m.

[6] study Bluetooth and Wi-Fi signals coexisting at the same environment. The researchers utilise the technique of fingerprinting. The principal notion is that as Bluetooth and Wi-Fi signals both operate at the same unlicensed 2.4 GHz frequency spectrum, they experience a lot interference. Therefore they propose methods to improve the signal quality by tuning the receivers to minimise interference. A tuning they propose for the Wi-Fi terminals is changing their broadcasting channels. And for Bluetooth signals, they suggest spread-spectrum frequency hopping to avoid interference. Their evaluations have shown that Wi-Fi positioning performed the worst while Bluetooth devices were online at the same time.

So far we have discussed location estimation and indoor navigation using signal strength and beacons. Another approach at indoor navigation is the use of pedestrian dead-reckoning (PDR) which is already being used by ship and aircraft navigation systems [14]. In broad terms, PDR is the technique of determining one's current position via a previously determined position, and advancing that position based upon known or estimated speeds over elapsed time and course [15]. PDR is subject to errors although it performs well with inertial navigation systems where a computer aids in the process. Then again, the downside of PDR is that as it requires the previous location in every step, it's unable to get a fix on the initial location. For PDR to function, the initial location must have been established as precise as possible. However, some researches came over this by the method of pattern matching. [16] initially retrieves a rough estimate about where the user is located using Assisted Global Positioning System (AGPS), as their solution is for outdoors, and forms a perimeter as to where the user might be. Following the initial step, they match the user's walking patterns with the paths available in that perimeter. The results of their study show that they can estimate the user's position by an error rate of 11 m. [17] takes this approach a step further. They leave out the usage of AGPS and fully rely on pedestrian dead-reckoning by applying string matching algorithms from the field of bioinformatics to be able to initially determine the user. As their field of usage is for indoors, they cut the usage of an additional network infrastructure and become fully self-contained with no additional network costs. When errors accumulate during navigation, the system resets itself by turns in the path or when it detects elevator like patterns. A downside of this study is that the system require the user to walk before determining his/her location. Therefore instantaneous location determination is not possible.

3 Implementation

Duco, in order to perform, requires two facets of processing: offline and online. Offline phase, which is a one-time routine for any selected venue that entails the creation of the indoor map. Whereas the online phase consists of 2-steps: (1) determining the location of the user and (2) navigating the user from the identified location to the selected destination.

3.1 Indoor Map Graph Generation

Since outdoor navigation has been around and used for a long period of time, outdoors have been mapped pretty meticulously over the years and navigation maps are available for almost every geographical area [18]. Also, there are various local providers sharing their map data for outdoors and most of those providers constantly update their data even upon a minor change.

As indoor navigation is still at it's infancy and has not been widely accepted commercially, indoor venues aren't fully covered by these map providers [19,20].

One of the map providers, Google, displays indoor maps in it's map solution by letting venue owners submit their floor plans. Although the submitted floor plans are not capable of navigation, such as route determination, they provide detailed explanation on the indoor environment. As a result, even though indoor routing graph creation is out of the scope of this research paper, to compensate for this shortcoming, Duco employs a rudimentary graph creation approach. Accordingly, it employs a simple graph creator app, namely Cartographer, which can create routing graphs that can be superposed on the existing indoor map views.

More specifically, Cartographer allows the user to visually create the indoor map graph data structure. The user drops the nodes by making the long press gesture to the touchscreen and afterwards connects those nodes by selecting them. Accordingly, the Cartographer app records the positions of the nodes and edges in geographic coordinate system. As soon as the map graph data collection is finished, it is then exported out of Cartographer and imported into Duco (Fig. 2).

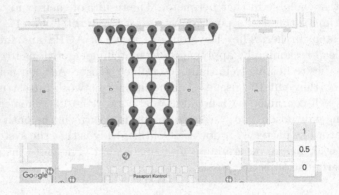

Fig. 2. Graph creation inside Cartographer

The graph over the map view represents a grid structure. A grid arrangement is chosen to be able to systematically determine the location and paths. As so, the nodes of the graph represents the possible locations a user can be at and the edges are the paths available to the user.

Duco only makes use of the cardinal directions and hence the grid system is designed accordingly since human movement is complex and sharps turns provide clarity to the PDR algorithm.

When the map graph creation process finishes, Duco is able to parse the indoor floor plan; that is it can identify possible user locations along with the routes available.

3.2   Initial Location Determination

In order for the navigation process to start, Duco is required to establish the initial location of it's user. The navigation methodology being used by Duco, pedestrian dead-reckoning, is only capable of getting the user from point A to point B. For this reason, the starting point is of utmost importance to provide precise navigation.

Duco utilises the underlying operating system's (iOS) location services framework, CoreLocation, which provides the following capabilities: location determination, interaction (ranging or region monitoring) with iBeacons and compass updates. All aspects of CoreLocation are controlled through a manager object which can start/stop the location updates at any given moment. This manager also has parameters regarding the precision returned, which are set to be the highest. Although this precision level consumes a lot battery power, as soon as the initial location is identified, all location updates are stopped to preserver battery. Duco uses two methods to retrieve the location information. It either acquires location information from CoreLocation's location estimation or, if possible, uses an iBeacon in range to assign the user to a location (Fig. 3).

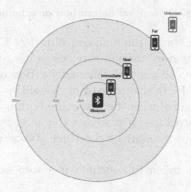

Fig. 3. iBeacon ranging

CoreLocation's location estimation occurs by utilising a combination of GPS, cellular, Wi-Fi and Bluetooth signals though since it works as a blackbox, it's specific implementation details are unknown.

iBeacons are deployed to places such as stairs, elevators or Wi-Fi dead-zones. If Duco captures a signal from one of the iBeacons, it assigns the user location to a location in range of that iBeacon.

3.3   Navigation

After the initial location estimation process, Duco is ready to accept the target destination. Hence, at this stage, the app is ready to accept a target destination from the user. Following the user's destination input, it by taking under consideration the user's current location and the target destination, Duco uses Dijkstra's shortest path algorithm on the indoor map graph to find the shortest path between the given two points.

Once the path is determined, Duco calculates the step count required to complete the path along with the directions of each step. After these processes are completed, Duco is ready to route and navigate the user to the destination via pedestrian dead-reckoning (Fig. 4).

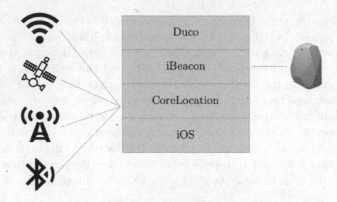

Fig. 4. Location determination scheme

When the navigation starts, the manager object of CoreLocation receives a message to stop all location estimation services as it's requirement is complete and to reserve battery life. Although the manager's iBeacon ranging and compass update (required for the PDR algorithm) functionalities, are still in effect.

The existing PDR algorithm in the literature [2] has been enhanced so that it performs with more precision. It analyses the accelerometer data to classify the user's walking pattern into one of the three states: static, slow walking or fast walking.

The actions that are taken to conclude if a step occurred or not are the following:

1. Retrieve the raw x-y-z axis accelerometer data,
2. Apply a low-pass filter of 15 % to each axis,
3. Calculate the Euclidean Norm,
4. Measure the variance in a window length of 1 s,
5. Compare the variance against the two threshold values (T_{static}, $T_{slowWalking}$):

- $V_a \leq T_{static}$: user static
- $T_{static} < v_a \leq T_{slowWalking}$: user slow walking
- $T_{slowWalking} < v_a$: user fast walking

Empirical study by [2] shows that the best results are obtained when the thresholds T_{static}, $T_{slowWalking}$ are set to be $0.008\,g^2$ and $0.05\,g^2$ respectively. Their test device was a Nokia N95. Duco was implemented on an Apple iPhone 5. Due to this change with the hardware, after empirical analysis, the thresholds were found to be $0.013\,g^2$ and $0.05\,g^2$ respectively.

Each individual exhibits a unique pattern of acceleration. Even though Duco does not make real-time threshold analysis and adjust the thresholds on-the-fly, the above thresholds are found to be suitable as an average for most people.

If the analysis of the user's acceleration using the above procedure is found to be between T_{static} and $T_{slowWalking}$, it is considered as a single step. Otherwise, if the acceleration is accounted to be higher than $T_{slowWalking}$, then it is assumed as two steps.

The above step detection system only properly functions while holding the phone parallel to the floor a little above the waist line. This holding position can also be defined as holding the phone at the state where it's possible to use it standing up (Fig. 5). The main reason for requiring this specific walking posture is due to the threshold points used in the development of the step detection algorithm described above. Therefore the activity of sliding the hand or placing the phone into a pocket/bag will provide additional acceleration data and hence will result in extra unwanted step detection.

Fig. 5. The norm walking state

As each step is detected, Duco also retrieves the current heading (measured in degrees) relative to true north. This heading value is then used to assign a cardinal direction (up, down, left and right) to the user's movement relative to the venue.

Finally, the detected real-time step count along with the heading information is checked against the direction required by the route. If they both match, the user's movement is reflected to the map view with the number of steps taken.

4   Evaluation

4.1   Evaluation Environments

Duco is intended for large venues like airports, hospitals or shopping malls. However, due to availability and logistical reasons, initially it was evaluated in a home environment as a proof-of-concept in a small environment, which is $133.64\,\mathrm{m}^2$.

As the second test bed, TAV Istanbul Atatürk Airport was chosen as a real life test environment, that is $179,000\,\mathrm{m}^2$ (all three floors of the international terminal). The reason for choosing Atatürk Airport is that their indoor floor plans are already available on Google Maps since they were recently been uploaded

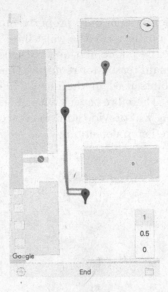

Fig. 6. Ongoing navigation at the airport

by the airport authorities. Both environments have Wi-Fi coverage and where supplied with six iBeacons (Fig. 6).

4.2   Evaluation Hardware

Duco is developed for iOS 9.1 and above with Swift 2.2. Mainly is was tested using an Apple iPhone 6 64 GB housing a 1.4 GHz dual-core 64-bit ARMv8-A with 1 GB LPDDR3 RAM.

The smartphone includes a wide range of sensors available but the ones related to Duco were the 3-axis gyroscope, 3-axis accelerometer and digital compass.

In the evaluation of the Duco navigation system, Estimote iBeacons were deployed because of their high range capabilities compared to other iBeacons, i.e. 70-m signal broadcasting range instead of the usual 50 m.

4.3   Small Environment Test - Home Scenario

Even though CoreLocation is not a part of the development process in this study but merely used as a blackbox for providing the initial location, it was tested to see how well it was performing. For this reason, five different spots were chosen and made measurements for two times to check the location fix CoreLocation displayed inside the map view against the real location. Table 1 represents the results regarding CoreLocation being tested in the home scenario.

The rest of the home scenario evaluation was concerning the PDR algorithm. To measure how well step detection performs, 9 people were chosen to take thirty

Table 1. Home scenario CoreLocation test results

	Trial 1	Trial 2
Spot 1	4 m	3.5 m
Spot 2	0.5 m	0.5 m
Spot 3	1 m	2 m
Spot 4	4 m	4 m
Spot 5	0.5 m	1 m

steps twenty times in a predetermined route. The subjects were instructed to perform their regular walking patterns. Figure 7 represents the average steps detected for each subject.

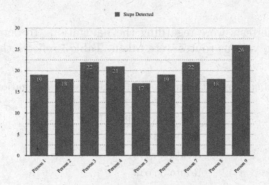

Fig. 7. Step detection results

There were cases where the algorithm captured all thirty steps for subjects with an average of more than 20 steps. It was observed that if the subject exhibited a dynamic walking pattern, that is the upper body moving with the phone as well, it captured enough acceleration to account for a step. If the subject was walking with the upper body mostly staying intact, the algorithm was unable to retrieve enough acceleration to detect a step. Another aspect of these tests was that sharp turns immensely helps the algorithm to detect a step due to the evident change in acceleration.

4.4   Large Environment Test - Istanbul Atatürk Airport Scenario

In accordance with the home scenario, initially, CoreLocation was tested before hand. Table 2 represents the results obtained by trying CoreLocation in ten different spots for three times. As mentioned in the table, some of the spots had GPS line-of-sight (LOS).

Table 2. Airport scenario CoreLocation test results

	GPS LOS	Trial 1	Trial 2	Trial 3
Spot 1	Yes	6 m	11 m	11 m
Spot 2	Yes	3 m	6 m	4 m
Spot 3	No	3 m	1 m	0.5 m
Spot 4	No	2 m	2 m	1 m
Spot 5	No	1 m	3 m	4 m
Spot 6	No	5 m	9 m	14 m
Spot 7	Yes	0.5 m	4 m	1 m
Spot 8	Yes	5 m	2 m	1 m
Spot 9	Yes	2 m	2 m	4 m
Spot 10	No	6 m	6 m	5 m

The rest of the tests were regarding the navigation. To determine how well it was performing, various routes were taken. Table 3 reflects these results.

Table 3. Misplacement from the destination when navigation finished

	Misplacement
Route 1	4 m
Route 2	6 m
Route 3	5 m
Route 4	1 m
Route 5	7 m
Route 6	6 m

5   Conclusion and Discussion

The growing popularity of location based services calls for greater localisation, better ubiquity, higher precision and lower energy usage. Therefore indoor navigation is a popular subject attracting many people. It has been researched for a long period of time and it is still an actively researched area. Although that may be the case, indoor navigation still remains an immense challenge. Through the years, it made headway in terms of acquiring greater success although the factors presented by indoor environments makes it difficult to provide a decent solution.

Wireless technologies are a crucial part of an indoor navigation solution although it's also plausible to utilise different approaches such as pedestrian dead-reckoning to achieve the navigation process. Duco evaluates this approach. Trying to achieve a better precision while conserving battery life.

References

1. Faragher, R., Harle, R.: An analysis of the accuracy of bluetooth low energy for indoor positioning applications. In: Proceedings of the 27th International Technical Meeting of the Satellite Division of the Institute of Navigation (iON gNSS+2014) (2014)
2. Liu, J., Chen, R., Pei, L., Chen, W., Tenhunen, T., Kuusniemi, H., Kroger, T., Chen, Y.: Accelerometer assisted robust wireless signal positioning based on a hidden Markov model. In: Proceedings of IEEE/ION PLANS, pp. 488–497 (2010)
3. Jung, S.-H., Lee, S., Han, D.: A crowdsourcing-based global indoor positioning and navigation system. Pervasive and Mobile Computing (2016)
4. Altintas, B., Serif, T.: Improving RSS-based indoor positioning algorithm via k-means clustering. In: European Wireless, 27–29 April 2011, Vienna, Austria (2011)
5. Altintas, B., Serif, T.: Indoor location detection with a RSS-based short term memory technique (KNN-STM). In: Tenth Annual IEEE International Conference on Pervasive Computing and Communications, PerCom, 19–23 March 2012, Lugano, Switzerland, Workshop Proceedings, pp. 794–798 (2012)
6. Pei, L., Liu, J., Guinness, R., Chen, Y., Kröger, T., Chen, R., Chen, L.: The evaluation of WIFI positioning in a bluetooth and WIFI coexistence environment. In: Ubiquitous Positioning, Indoor Navigation, and Location Based Service (uPINLBS), 2012, pp. 1–6. IEEE (2012)
7. Mannings, R.: Ubiquitous Positioning. Artech House, Norwood (2008)
8. Yao, D., Yu, C., Dey, A.K., Koehler, C., Min, G., Yang, L.T., Jin, H.: Energy efficient indoor tracking on smartphones. Future Generation Comput. Syst. **39**, 44–54 (2014)
9. Liu, H., Darabi, H., Banerjee, P., Liu, J.: Survey of wireless indoor positioning techniques and systems. IEEE Trans. Syst. Man Cybern. Part C (Appl. Rev.) **37**, 1067–1080 (2007)
10. Evrendilek, C., Akcan, H.: On the complexity of trilateration with noisy range measurements. IEEE Commun. Lett. **15**, 1097–1099 (2011)
11. Brain, M., Harris, T.: How GPS receivers work (2011)
12. Galván-Tejada, C.E., Carrasco-Jiménez, J.C., Brena, R.F.: Bluetooth-WiFi based combined positioning algorithm, implementation and experimental evaluation. Proc. Technol. **7**, 37–45 (2013)
13. Bekkelien, A., Deriaz, M., Marchand-Maillet, S.: Bluetooth indoor positioning. Master's thesis, University of Geneva (2012)
14. Nebot, E.: Sensors used for autonomous navigation. In: Tzafestas, S.G. (ed.) Advances in Intelligent Autonomous Systems, pp. 135–156. Springer, Heidelberg (1999)
15. Wikipedia: Dead reckoning. https://en.wikipedia.org/wiki/Dead_reckoning
16. Constandache, I., Choudhury, R.R., Rhee, I.: Towards mobile phone localization without war-driving. In: 2010 Proceedings of IEEE INFOCOM, pp. 1–9. IEEE (2010)
17. Link, J.A.B., Smith, P., Viol, N., Wehrle, K.: FootPath: accurate map-based indoor navigation using smartphones. In: IPIN, pp. 1–8. Citeseer (2011)
18. Wikipedia: List of online map services. https://en.wikipedia.org/wiki/List_of_online_map_services
19. Google: Indoor maps availability. https://support.google.com/maps/answer/1685827?hl=en
20. OpenStreetMap: Indoor mapping. http://wiki.openstreetmap.org/wiki/Indoor_Mapping#Places

Mobile Applications and Wearable Devices

Persuasive Cities for Sustainable Wellbeing: Quantified Communities

Agnis Stibe[(⊠)] and Kent Larson

MIT Media Lab, Cambridge, USA
{agnis,kll}@mit.edu

Abstract. Can you imagine a city that feels, understands, and cares about your wellbeing? Future cities will reshape human behavior in countless ways. New strategies and models are required for future urban spaces to properly respond to human activity, environmental conditions, and market dynamics. Persuasive urban systems will play an important role in making cities more livable and resource-efficient by addressing current environmental challenges and enabling healthier routines. Persuasive cities research aims at improving wellbeing across societies through applications of socio-psychological theories and their integration with conceptually new urban designs. This research presents an ecosystem of future cities, describes three generic groups of people depending on their susceptibility to persuasive technology, explains the process of defining behavior change, and provides tools for social engineering of persuasive cities. Advancing this research is important as it scaffolds scientific knowledge on how to design persuasive cities and refines guidelines for practical applications in achieving their emergence.

Keywords: Persuasive technology · Socially influencing systems · Wellbeing · Sustainability · Urban design · Health behavior change · Quantified communities

1 Motivation

Quality of life and the health of the individual and communities are important subjects that can be studied and improved through the creation of persuasive cities, streets, buildings, homes, and vehicles [16]. Information technology and computer systems are increasingly designed to support everyday routines and advance user experience in multiple ways [6]. Novel computer systems can be also intentionally designed to influence how users think and behave. Theories of persuasion [18] and social influence [4] provide various strategies for the developers of such systems to facilitate desired effects on users.

Research on persuasive cities seeks to advance urban spaces to facilitate societal changes. According to social sciences [2], any well-designed environment can become a strong influencer of what people think and do. There is an endlessly dynamic interaction between a person, a particular behavior, and an environment in which that behavior is performed. This initiative leverages this knowledge to engineer persuasive environments and intervention for altering human behavior on individual and societal levels. This research is primarily focused on socially engaging environments for supporting

© Springer International Publishing Switzerland 2016
M. Younas et al. (Eds.): MobiWIS 2016, LNCS 9847, pp. 271–282, 2016.
DOI: 10.1007/978-3-319-44215-0_22

entrepreneurship and innovation, reshaping routines and behavioral patterns in dense urban districts, intelligent outdoor sensing for shifting mobility modes, enhancing environmentally friendly behaviors through social norms, interactive public feedback channels for affecting attitudes, engaging residents through socially influencing systems, exploring methods for designing persuasive neighborhoods, testing agent-based models and simulations of persuasive interventions, and fostering adoption of novel urban systems.

2 Perspective

This research aims at tackling an area that is currently underestimated, but at the same time, bears extremely high importance for mankind to prosper. The world's population grows exponentially, especially in cities, so the architecture and design of future urban places are going to have the dominant impact on human behavior. The proposed research agenda is highly important, as it will directly influence everyone living in future cities. Environmental, personal, and behavioral factors are locked into triadic reciprocal determinism [2], meaning that all three are strongly interconnected and continuously reshaping each other. Thus, environmental design, including persuasive urban systems, is strong influencer on human behavior and attitude. In other words, quite often it is merely sufficient to improve urban spaces to help people become healthier and to create sustainable communities. This is a very powerful vision as it encompasses transformation of human behavior and urban environments at scale.

The proposed research reflects on novel ways of how socially influencing systems [20, 21] enable mechanisms to perpetually support motivation of individuals comparing to conventional methods, such as those that are based on the principle of carrots and sticks. Earlier research on motivation discusses methods that have substantial limitations. For example, monetary incentives are mostly effective only as long they are provided, so people tend returning to their earlier behavior after the motivators are taken away. Instead, persuasive urban systems harness social influence from crowd behavior to craft influential messaging aimed at shifting behavior and attitude of an individual, who naturally is an integral part of the same crowd. Such continuous interplay can ultimately result in an ongoing process that reshapes communities and societies without any other incentives.

3 Emergence of Persuasive Cities

Ongoing research streams focus on *sensitive cities* (researching sensing technologies to read human behavior in urban spaces) [12] and *smart cities* (analyzing big data to classify groups of people based on their distinct behavioral patterns) [3, 5], however there is a lack of knowledge about perspective ways to achieve persistent behavioral changes at scale. Therefore, the proposed research extends an ecosystem of future cities (Table 1) by introducing the notion of *persuasive cities* that aims to advance and refine influential strategies designed for intentionally reshaping how people think and act in urban environments.

Table 1. Ecosystem of future cities

Role	Character	Technology
Persuasive		
Change	Care	Socially influencing systems
Smart		
Classify	Understand	Big data analytics
Sensitive		
Read	Feel	Sensor networks

Each *layer* of future cities has its *role*, *character*, and supportive *technology*. Sensitive cities employ sensor networks to read crowd behaviors. In other words, these cities feel human movements. These crowd behaviors further serve as an input for big data analytics that smart cities apply to classify groups of people according to similar behavioral patterns (profiles). When that is accomplished, the groups having better routines can be exemplified to other underperforming groups through intentionally designed socially influencing systems, which are at the core of persuasive cities.

3.1 Susceptibility to Persuasive Technology

People generally can fall into one of the three generic categories depending on their susceptibility to persuasive technology (Fig. 1). *Self-contained* people (the red circle) most likely are not open for changing anything in them. They are fully satisfied with who they are and what they do on daily basis, thus many behavioral interventions might fail in attempts to influence this group of individuals. *Self-driven* people (the green circle) typically have comparatively high levels of motivation and can achieve everything that they have envisioned. Thus, these people most likely are not looking for additional sources of encouragement, and therefore persuasive technologies might become unnecessary for this group.

However, there is another group of people that oftentimes would like to change their routines, but rarely succeed in doing so. That reminds of New Year's resolutions

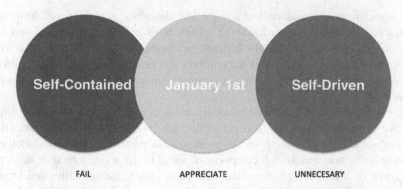

Fig. 1. Susceptibility to persuasive technology (Color figure online)

that in many cases end around February. Therefore, this group is entitled as January 1st (the yellow circle) and seem to be the most welcoming towards technology supported behavioral interventions designed to help achieving target behaviors. Although, Fig. 1 presents all three groups as equal circles, in reality the size of each group might significantly vary depending on the context and particular behavior.

3.2   Defining Behavior Change

To achieve an envisioned target behavior, the process and components of behavior change have to be well understood and clearly defined. In the process of defining behavior change, there are three main components, namely the target group, its present behavior, and its envisioned future behavior (Table 2).

Table 2. The three main components for defining behavior change

Target group	Current behavior	Future behavior
Description		
A group of people currently having an unsatisfactory behavior. It is important to narrow down the target group as precise as possible	A certain behavior of the target group that currently is not in line with an envisioned future behavior in a given context	An ultimate future behavior of the target group that is envisioned to be more beneficial for everyone
Example		
There are MIT faculty members	Who currently commute alone in their private cars	They could commute by bicycles instead whenever possible
Example		
There are other people in our residential building	Who use regular light bulbs in their apartments	They would change the regular light bulbs to energy efficient ones

3.3   Tools for Social Engineering

Earlier research on persuasive technology [8] describes several ways how social dynamics can influence human behavior, which have been further refined and structured as a framework for Socially Influencing Systems (SIS) [20, 21], see Fig. 2. The SIS framework is a useful tool for scholars and practitioners aiming at improving future cities by introducing persuasive urban interventions targeted to support wellbeing.

The framework describes seven socially influencing principles that can support persuasive urban interventions. The principles are interlinked and have potential to exert stronger effects depending on the context of a particular behavioral challenge. Normative influence and social comparison seem to be more effective to achieve involvement of the target group as the two principles focus on attitudinal changes. Cooperation and social facilitation seem to be more effective to make individuals

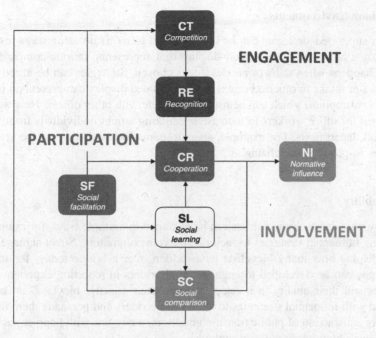

Fig. 2. Socially Influencing Systems (SIS) framework

participate and do the envisioned future behavior even without a formed attitude towards it. Competition and recognition seem to be more effective in engaging the target group to do the future behavior as the principles focus on both attitude and behavior simultaneously. For example, the effects several socially influencing principles have already been studied in the context of urban mobility, e.g. bicycling [24].

4   Contexts of Future Persuasive Cities

To achieve substantial behavior changes at scale, the persuasive cities research agenda is focused on reshaping and redesigning three main urban areas: outdoor environments, indoor environments, and mobility in cities.

4.1   Outdoor Environments

Public spaces can be advanced in many ways, e.g. supermarkets can project a portion of how many healthy products have been purchased that day, week, or month. Responsive environments can use ambient lights to provide feedback about behavioral patterns of crowds. For example, streetlights can change color depending of how many joggers have been on that street on that morning. The window frames of residential buildings can be illuminated for those apartments, which have changed regular light bulbs to energy-efficient ones.

4.2 Indoor Environments

Computer-supported strategies can be implemented to motivate using stairs instead of an elevator. For example, a situated display that represents various comparisons of what can happens when stairs or an elevator is chosen. Strategies can be introduced to increase water intake in offices. For example, a situated display can present an increase of water consumption, which can be used to compete with other offices. New ways can be designed for office workers to increase socializing among individuals from various groups and departments. For example, specific game-like activities can be set up for employees to promote socializing.

4.3 Mobility

Mobility within dense urban districts can be reshaped in multiple ways, for example, by introducing influential strategies to facilitate bicycle commuting. Street signage can be used to display how many bicyclists have ridden over a bridge today, for instance. Mobile apps can be developed to engage bicycle riders in reporting experiences with bike lanes and their quality in a selected urban area. Electric bicycles can be complemented with influential strategies to attract more riders and persuade them to pedal. To care for satisfaction of public transit commuters, a city bus with happier passengers on board can obtain more colorful outlook.

5 Application to Bicycling in Cities

Besides investing in road infrastructure, cities can work on shifting mobility patterns towards bicycling as one the most sustainable and healthiest forms of individual transportation. It also has several major advantages as compared to conventional motorized transport, e.g. bicycling is carbon neutral, provides major health and financial benefits, and requires less space than private motorized transport. Therefore, it is necessary to design interventions for promoting bicycling, experience the enjoyment from this activity, and develop new mobility patterns [9].

Previous research points out that interventions to promote modal shift can be effective, however most of these follow traditional policy approaches like publicity campaigns, engineering measures or financial incentives [17] leaving a blind spot for behavior oriented soft-policy measures [19]. Persuasive cities have potential to significantly contribute to this effort, for example, through publicly displayed street signage with interactive social comparison [22] on how quickly bicycles move as compared to the speed of cars on the same street.

5.1 Biking Tourney

In a recent Biking Tourney study [23], a socially influencing system [21] was engineered and implemented to provoke competition between and cooperation [7] within organizations. In that study, the participating organizations were ranked under four different categories related to their performance related to bicycling. The categories were designed to reflect the goals of the Biking Tourney, that is, to encourage employees to ride bicycles instead of choosing high-energy means of transportation for their daily commutes.

The hypothesis of the study was that the competition between organizations would provoke cooperation among employees in each of the organizations. Furthermore, the use of publicly displayed rankings in common areas of the companies should raise awareness of the tourney and facilitate [10] commuting by bicycles. Out of the total number of 239 registered participants, 127 people filled out the ex post survey that contained intentionally designed set of questions for assessing their engagement in the Biking Tourney.

5.2 Assessing Engagement

We used partial least squares structural equation modeling (PLS-SEM) to analyze factors influencing participants' engagement in the Biking Tourney. Based on the relevance to this study, five factors were included as constructs in the research model (Fig. 3). Three of them were derived from the framework of socially influencing systems [21], namely social facilitation [10], competition, and cooperation [7]. Rankings and public display were added, as they were fundamental components of the study design. The indicators for main constructs (Appendix A) were adopted from Stibe [20] for this particular study.

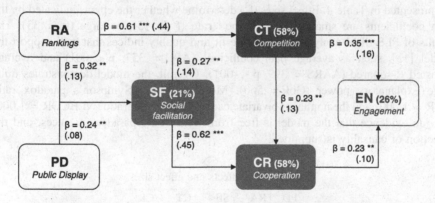

Fig. 3. The structural model with the results of PLS-SEM analysis

All constructs of the research model demonstrate good internal consistency, as evidenced by their composite reliability scores, which range from .85 to .98 (Table 3), and the fact that they share more variance with own indicators (AVE) than with other constructs.

The research model (Fig. 3) was built upon the framework for socially influencing systems [21] and shaped by the strongest correlations between the constructs (Table 3). Further, it was analyzed using PLS regression algorithm [13] and the results provide

Table 3. Latent variable coefficients and correlations

	COR	CRA	AVE	VIF	PD	RA	SF	CT	CR	EN
PD	.98	.97	.95	1.2	**.97**					
RA	.90	.83	.75	2.1	.20	**.86**				
SF	.87	.78	.70	2.3	.33	.36	**.84**			
CT	.85	.74	.66	2.6	.34	.71	.51	**.81**		
CR	.90	.83	.75	2.5	.38	.32	.73	.53	**.86**	
EN	.92	.87	.80	1.3	.18	.34	.39	.38	.42	**.89**

COR = Composite Reliability; CRA = Cronbach's Alpha;
VIF = variance inflation factor (full collinearity); Bolded
diagonal = square root of Average Variance Extracted (AVE)

substantial support for the research model. The β-values demonstrate the strength of relationships between the constructs and the asterisks mark their statistical significance, while the R-squared contributions are presented in brackets.

The five influencing factors are intricately interconnected and altogether they explain 26 % of the variance in engagement in the Biking Tourney. The main direct contributors to explain the variance in engagement were competition (16 %) and cooperation (10 %). Social facilitation (45 %) and competition (13 %) together explain 58 % of the variance in cooperation. Rankings (44 %) and social facilitation (14 %) together explain 58 % of the variance in competition. Rankings (13 %) and public display (8 %) together explain 21 % of the variance in social facilitation.

For a more elaborate view of the model, total effects and effect sizes for total effects are presented in Table 4. Effect sizes (f^2) determine whether the effects indicated by the path coefficients are small ($f^2 \geq .02$), moderate ($f^2 \geq .15$), or large ($f^2 \geq .35$). The results of PLS-SEM analysis also provide fit and quality indices that well support the model [13], such as average path coefficient (APC = .357, p < .001) and average adjusted R-squared (AARS = .399, p < .001). Overall, the model demonstrates quite large explanatory power (GoF = .560). Moreover, both Sympson's paradox ratio (SPR = 1.000) and the nonlinear bivariate causality direction ratio (NLBCDR = 1.000) provide evidence that the model is free from Sympson's paradox instances, and the direction of causality is supported.

Table 4. Total effects and effect sizes.

	PD	RA	SF	CT	CR
SF	.24** (.08)	.32*** (.13)			
CT	.06 (.02)	.69*** (.50)	.27** (.14)		
CR	.16** (.06)	.36*** (.11)	.68*** (.50)	.23** (.13)	
EN	.06 (.01)	.32*** (.11)	.25** (.10)	.40*** (.19)	.23** (.10)

***p < .001; **p < .01; *p < .05;
(f^2) = Cohen's f-squared

The results of PLS-SEM analysis illustrate how competition and cooperation [7] made employees feel engaged in the Biking Tourney. Although social facilitation [10] and rankings are not directly pointed to engagement, both contributed with strong and significant indirect effects on it. Interestingly, public display exerted also a significant indirect effect on cooperation, which emphasizes the importance of ubiquitous feedback channels in facilitating social dynamics.

6 Future Research Opportunities

This section describes several potential applications of how the previously introduced concepts of persuasive cities can be designed and introduced in various urban contexts to support wellbeing.

6.1 Sedentary Behavior

Recent reports show that a growing number of students are becoming obese not just because of their lack of exercise, poor diet, and excessive screen time but simply because they do not stand up during the active hours of their day. Even when they get enough daily exercise, students who spend the rest of the day seated suffer from a greater risk of obesity as well as of diabetes, cardiovascular disease, and even some cancers than students who stand. Thereby, the more stand-biased furniture there is, for example, installed in classrooms, the more likely students are to stand more than sit and gradually come to like or at least expect that behavior as the norm.

When implemented, socially influencing systems supported by a technologically enabled built environment may have a more sustainable impact on behavior change than stand-biased furniture alone. Therefore, a behavioral intervention can be designed for the built environment of the classroom with a technologically enabled seating system that serves as a persuasive change agent [8] even when students are not directly using it.

6.2 Water Conservation

A large component of urban water is attributed to residential use, which includes water for drinking, bathing, clothes and dish washing, toilet flushing, and landscaping. Use of persuasive technology [11] paves the way to new channels of influencing behavior towards sustainability, e.g. better access to quick and frequent feedback, personalization and two-way interaction, optimized information source for feedback, and ability to scale amongst others. The power of persuasive technology lies in its customizability and opportunity for scale.

Persuasive cities research takes advantage of digital platforms to influence impact to the individual. By taking this one step further and sharing the tool among users, the concept of "environmental feedback" can harness the benefits of normative influence among crowds. This can prove to be very powerful when considering tenants of an apartment building, or local residents of a neighborhood, or even a city. Thus, by first using a platform customized to the user, the data among a larger network can be aggregated and then re-shared to a group of users on situated displays.

6.3 Walking

There are modifications that city planners can potentially make, and have made, to the urban environment to promote walking. For instance, walkability can be improved through the provision of clean, well-lit and safe sidewalks, shelter from rain and sun, an attractive urban environment and so on. However, while these are all important elements, they alone do not seem to be sufficient to bring about the behavior changes that could be so beneficial to health. In addition to meeting the basic requirements of safe and navigable walking conditions, there are proven methods of causing attitudinal change through social influence [4] that can promote sustained behavior change. Through persuasive changes to the environment, barriers to walking such as normative influence [14], social learning, and social facilitation [10] can change the way people think about walking and lead to increased physical activity. Recognition [15], competition [7], and cooperation [1] can be leveraged to build on the initial activity of walking and promote sustained adoption.

Persuasive cities can make walking experience more engaging by combining a mobile phone app that interacts with retrofitted traffic light junctions. To participate, users will have to download a mobile app and provide information on where they live, in order to be placed into a team that corresponds to their address. When waiting at traffic light junctions, users obtain riddles either through a small screen attached to the junctions or directly messaged to their phones. They would input their answers into the mobile app, and correct answers win points for the team. When playing outside own neighborhood, or when teaming up with other users, the user gets additional points, for example. An interactive color strip could be placed on each traffic light, which would display the top three teams with the highest points scored that day at each light.

7 Conclusions

Fundamentally new strategies must be found for creating the places where people live and work, and the mobility systems that connect these places, in order to meet the profound challenges of the future [16]. Novel models for urban architecture and personal vehicles should be more responsive to the unique needs and values of individuals though the application of disentangled systems and smart customization technology. Future research should be directed towards exploring how urban design might be combined with persuasive technology and socially influencing systems to encourage healthy behaviors at scale.

Future computer-supported innovations should be designed with intent to understand and respond to human activity, environmental conditions, and market dynamics. The design of future cities requires optimal combinations of automated systems, just-in-time information for personal control, and interfaces to persuade people to adopt sustainable behaviors. Drawing on socio-psychological theories and integrating them with new concepts for urban design and technology, the proposed persuasive cities research will advance the livability in future cities.

Acknowledgements. We gratefully acknowledge Matthias Wunsch, Alexandra Millonig, Katja Schechtner, Ryan C.C. Chin, Stefan Seer, Chengzen Dai, Felipe Lozano-Landinez, Francesco Pilla, Rosalind Picard, Pattie Maes, Kevin Slavin, Liz Voeller, Christiana von Hippel, Leo Brown, Shin Bin Tan, Austrian Institute of Technology, and the Schoeller Research Center, for their support and contribution to this research.

Appendix A: Measurement Items and Combined Loadings

Constructs	Indicators	Load
Social facilitation	I noticed that my colleagues were participating in the Biking Tourney	.880
	I noticed how other coworkers rode bikes as part of the Biking Tourney	.826
	I recognized that there were other people from my organization biking to work during the Biking Tourney	.799
Cooperation	I noticed that my colleagues cooperated during the Biking Tourney	.897
	I noticed how my co-workers encouraged each other to ride during the Biking Tourney	.843
	I observed that my colleagues are collaborating during the Biking Tourney	.853
Competition	I was able to follow my organization in standings of the Biking Tourney	.826
	I followed how organizations were competing during the Biking Tourney	.852
	I noticed how competitive my organization was in the Biking Tourney	.755
Public display	My organization had a public screen which displayed the Biking Tourney standings	.983
	I noticed the rankings of Biking Tourney on a public screen in my organization	.962
	There was a public screen in my organization for everyone to see the Biking Tourney activity	.977
Rankings	I noticed the ranking of organizations based on total miles ridden	.823
	I noticed the ranking of organizations depending on average miles ridden	.910
	I noticed the ranking of organizations based on number of employees biking to work	.856
Engagement	The Biking Tourney encouraged me to commute by bike to work	.937
	The Biking Tourney motivated me to continue riding my bike to work	.917
	I felt engaged in riding to work during the Biking Tourney	.818

References

1. Axelrod, R.: On six advances in cooperation theory. Anal. Krit. **22**(1), 130–151 (2000)
2. Bandura, A.: Social Foundations of Thought and Action: A Social Cognitive Theory. Prentice Hall, Englewood Cliffs (1986)
3. Batty, M., Axhausen, K.W., Giannotti, F., Pozdnoukhov, A., Bazzani, A., Wachowicz, M., Ouzounis, G., Portugali, Y.: Smart cities of the future. Eur. Phys. J. Spec. Top. **214**(1), 481–518 (2012)

4. Cacioppo, J.T., Petty, R.E., Stoltenberg, C.D.: Processes of social influence: the elaboration likelihood model of persuasion. In: Kendall, P.C. (ed.) Advances in Cognitive-Behavioral Research and Therapy, pp. 215–274. Academic Press, San Diego (1985)
5. Caragliu, A., Del Bo, C., Nijkamp, P.: Smart cities in Europe. J. Urban Technol. 18(2), 65–82 (2011)
6. Chatterjee, S., Price, A.: Healthy living with persuasive technologies: framework, issues, and challenges. J. Am. Med. Inform. Assoc. (JAMIA) 16, 171–178 (2009)
7. Deutsch, M.: A theory of cooperation-competition and beyond. Handb. Theor. Soc. Psychol. 2, 275 (2011)
8. Fogg, B.J.: Persuasive Technology: Using Computers to Change What We Think and Do. Morgan Kaufmann, San Francisco (2003)
9. Forester, J.: Bicycle Transportation: A Handbook for Cycling Transportation Engineers. MIT Press, Cambridge (1994)
10. Guerin, B., Innes, J.: Social Facilitation. Cambridge University Press, Cambridge, England (2009)
11. Ham, J., McCalley, T., Midden, C., Zaalberg, R.: Using persuasive technology to encourage sustainable behavior. In: 6th IEEE International Conference on Pervasive Computing, Sydney, pp. 83–86. IEEE (2008)
12. Hancke, G.P., Hancke Jr., G.P.: The role of advanced sensing in smart cities. Sensors 13(1), 393–425 (2012)
13. Kock, N.: WarpPLS 5.0 User Manual. ScriptWarp Systems, Laredo, TX (2013)
14. Lapinski, M.K., Rimal, R.N.: An explication of social norms. Commun. Theory 15(2), 127–147 (2005)
15. Malone, T.W., Lepper, M.: Making learning fun: a taxonomy of intrinsic motivations for learning. In: Snow, R.E., Farr, M.J. (eds.) Aptitude, Learning and Instruction: III. Conative and Affective Process Analyses, pp. 223–253. Erlbaum, Hillsdale (1987)
16. Mumford, E.: A socio-technical approach to systems design. Requir. Eng. 5(2), 125–133 (2000)
17. Ogilvie, D.: Promoting walking and cycling as an alternative to using cars: systematic review. BMJ 329, 763 (2004)
18. O'Keefe, D.J.: Theories of persuasion. In: Nabi, R., Oliver, M.B. (eds.) Handbook of Media Processes and Effects. Sage Publications, Thousand Oaks (2009)
19. Richter, J., Friman, M., Gärling, T.: Soft transport policy measures: gaps in knowledge. Int. J. Sustain. Transp. 5, 199–215 (2011)
20. Stibe, A.: Socially influencing systems: persuading people to engage with publicly displayed Twitter-based systems. Acta Universitatis Ouluensis (2014)
21. Stibe, A.: Towards a framework for socially influencing systems: meta-analysis of four PLS-SEM based studies. In: MacTavish, T., Basapur, S. (eds.) PERSUASIVE 2015. LNCS, vol. 9072, pp. 172–183. Springer, Heidelberg (2015)
22. Wood, J.V.: What is social comparison and how should we study it? Pers. Soc. Psychol. Bull. 22(5), 520–537 (1996)
23. Wunsch, M., Stibe, A., Millonig, A., Seer, S., Chin, R.C.C., Schechtner, K.: Gamification and social dynamics: insights from a corporate cycling campaign. In: Streitz, N., Markopoulos, P. (eds.) DAPI 2016. LNCS, vol. 9749, pp. 494–503. Springer, Heidelberg (2016). doi:10.1007/978-3-319-39862-4_45
24. Wunsch, M., Stibe, A., Millonig, A., Seer, S., Dai, C., Schechtner, K., Chin, R.C.: What makes you bike? Exploring persuasive strategies to encourage low-energy mobility. In: MacTavish, T., Basapur, S. (eds.) PERSUASIVE 2015. LNCS, vol. 9072, pp. 53–64. Springer, Heidelberg (2015)

H-Plane: Intelligent Data Management for Mobile Healthcare Applications

Rahul Krishnan Pathinarupothi[1]([⊠]), Bithin Alangot[2],
Maneesha Vinodini Ramesh[1], Krishnashree Achuthan[2], and P. Venkat Rangan[1]

[1] Amrita Center for Wireless Networks and Applications (AmritaWNA),
Amrita School of Engineering, Amritapuri,
Amrita Vishwa Vidyapeetham Amrita University, Clappana, India
pprahul@gmail.com
[2] Amrita Center for Cybersecurity Systems and Networks,
Amrita School of Engineering, Amritapuri,
Amrita Vishwa Vidyapeetham Amrita University, Clappana, India
https://www.amrita.edu

Abstract. We present an intelligent data management framework that can facilitate development of highly scalable and mobile healthcare applications for remote monitoring of patients. This is achieved through the use of a global log data abstraction that leverages the storage and processing capabilities of the edge devices and the cloud in a seamless manner. In existing log based storage systems, data is read as fixed size chunks from the cloud to enhance performance. However, in healthcare applications, where the data access pattern of the end users differ widely, this approach leads to unnecessary storage and cost overheads. To overcome these, we propose dynamic log chunking. The experimental results, comparing existing fixed chunking against the H-Plane model, show 13 %–19 % savings in network bandwidth as well as cost while fetching the data from the cloud.

Keywords: Cloud computing · Healthcare IoT framework · Log storage system

1 Introduction

Remote monitoring of patients through the use of wearable sensors and smartphones is becoming an effective tool for quality healthcare delivery. If scaled up, it can reduce the load on hospitals as well as the need for patients to visit the hospitals multiple times.

Technologies such as low cost body attached sensors, powerful smartphones which can act as Internet of Things (IoT) gateways for these sensors, cheap and easily deployable cloud solutions and many other innovations have become enablers for remote monitoring applications. Most of the current applications leverage cloud for storage and analytics of data. The cloud also acts as an entity, which helps the globally distributed and highly mobile IoT devices to interconnect. However, as the edge devices (such as IoT gateways and smartphones) are

© Springer International Publishing Switzerland 2016
M. Younas et al. (Eds.): MobiWIS 2016, LNCS 9847, pp. 283–294, 2016.
DOI: 10.1007/978-3-319-44215-0_23

becoming powerful, the cloud is also moving closer to the edge as discussed in [1]. This has helped to build IoT infrastructure which delivers low latency response for applications and reduce network cost of sending large amount of unfiltered data to the cloud.

Based on these developments, we present a 3-tier architecture for remote healthcare applications. We call this architecture as H-Plane, which stands for Healthcare-Plane. It consists of a modified log abstraction for data management that can facilitate location unaware routing and scalable storage. We also present a user access pattern based log prefetch model that can highly improve the efficiency of data reads from the cloud, compared to other systems such as Bolt [2] and Global Data Plane (GDP) [3].

In H-Plane, the log is the fundamental storage abstraction for transferring and managing data. The logs are divided into segments and distributed across different nodes to meet quality of service (QoS) needs. Even though the logs are divided into segments and distributed, the applications have a single logical view of Log. The segments are again divided into logical chunks. A chunk constitutes a contiguous sequence of records and it is the basic unit of data access. Accessing data from the cloud as chunks helps to prefetch data, which in turn reduces the number of requests and round trip delay [2]. However, the method of fixed size chunking in GDP, Bolt and other log based systems, leads to unnecessary storage and cost overheads due to unused prefetch data. In order to overcome this, we present a method for dynamic chunking of the logs based on the user access patterns.

The rest of the paper is arranged in the following way. Section 2 describes the background and related work. The H-Plane architecture, log data abstraction and different log operations are discussed in Sect. 3. We introduce dynamic chunking models in Sect. 4, followed by the evaluation and cost benefits in Sect. 5. The future direction of the research and conlusion is presented in Sect. 6.

2   Related Work

Earlier IoT and cloud architectures as summarized in [4–6] considered the IoT devices connected to each other through the cloud. As the edge devices gained more capabilities, the concepts such as Fog computing [1] gained prominence, which enabled the use of edge devices as storage and processing nodes. As IoT and cloud infrastructures are increasingly used for various applications, scalability becomes a big factor. It is argued in the work of Zhang et al. [3] that the current architecture would not scale to the needs of future applications and hence a data level abstraction, including a log data structure was suggested. The need for a log based storage for numeric time series data such as EEG and ECG is also well studied by Shafer et al. [7]. One of the research work by Gupta et al. [2] leveraged these ideas and implemented the same for connected home devices. Global Data Plane [3] was proposed to overcome the challenges in Bolt [2]. It utilizes the data management capabilities of Bolt such as time-series append-only log, chunking of logs for performance, policy-based storage, data confidentiality and integrity. In order to meet the scalability needs, they have used OceanStore [8], which is a highly scalable distributed storage system. To provide location independent routing, concepts from Named Data Network (NDN) [9] were also incorporated in GDP. Since this is a new concept, we do not know of any applications that have used or tested this framework. Our previous experience [10] with remote monitoring healthcare applications provided the impetus to adapt GDP like architectures for healthcare applications. We feel that it is going to highly simplify the application development and at the same time ensure data integrity.

Many of the existing healthcare applications have been using various cloud and IoT architectures. As the ground realities are changing, the applications need to move towards a more scalable architecture, that is both secure and at the same time ensures certain QoS that are specific to healthcare applications. In this paper, we have enhanced the data management capabilities of healthcare applications using H-Plane. Though it is only in the early stages of conceptualization, we have built upon GDP to design H-Plane as a framework for deploying healthcare applications.

3   H-Plane

3.1   Architecture

In this section, we describe the architecture for H-plane and explain how we have tailored data management for healthcare applications. We consider an extended cloud architecture where there are various body sensors connected to the patient. Usually, these sensors send the data to an IoT gateway, which could be the patient's smartphone or another kind of high-end device. These high-end devices have the capability to perform minimal computation and real-time processing. There could be multiple high-end devices which are in the neighbourhood. These high-end devices could have varying capabilities and could be linked over a heterogeneous network, such as WiFi or Bluetooth. It may be noted that the patient's high-end device could also be connected to another patient's device or to a health service personnel (HSP), such as that of a doctor or a clinician. The high-end devices are connected to the cloud (private or public) over different media and networks. The cloud has higher capabilities for batch processing as well as large storage space for long term archival of data. The public and private parts of the cloud are also connected through proper interfaces. In the following part of the paper, the sensors, the devices and the cloud are referred to as nodes in general. This is depicted in Fig. 1.

Here, the edge devices can communicate with each other and share their processing and storage capabilities, independent of the cloud. The patient's data could be routed to the doctors high-end device skipping the cloud, thereby reducing the upstream traffic to the cloud. The data archival in the cloud could be done at a later time when the cost of transmission is less. This architecture allows the high-end devices to go offline from the cloud and then join in later through a different network. The connectivity of the devices and location unaware routing are managed using NDN [9].

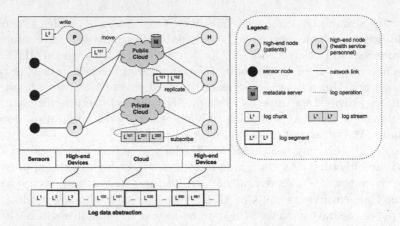

Fig. 1. The H-plane architecture.

Figure 1 also shows a global logical log, which has multiple physical log segments that are located in different nodes. A detailed discussion on logs, chunks, segments and log operations follows in the next section.

3.2 Logs

In H-Plane, a single-writer append-only log is the basic storage abstraction for the healthcare applications. The application gets a single logical view of the log, although it is physically divided into different segments. These segments could be placed at different nodes (cloud, gateways etc.) in the infrastructure to meet various Quality of Service (QoS) requirements as shown in Fig. 2(b). In a log, only the head segment is mutable and all other segments are immutable. The segments are

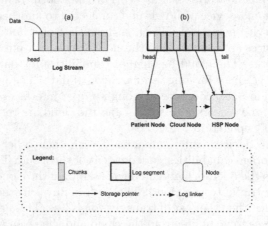

Fig. 2. The H-Plane log abstraction. (a) Data is written to the head of a log segment. (b) Log segments are placed in a distributed manner across different nodes.

divided into different logical chunks. A chunk is the basic unit of data access in our infrastructure and helps in batching data during a read operations which improves the system performance. In the below discussion on logs and log operations, we assume constant chunk size for the sake of clarity. We introduce the concept of dynamically deciding the chunk size based on the readers access pattern, and is explained in a later section. The healthcare applications can use this log abstraction to store and move data between different nodes. H-Plane provides few basic operations to enable applications to effectively use log data structure. These may be further extended based on future needs.

3.3   Log Operations

We define a set of basic log operations that can be used by the applications using API function calls to the H-Plane.

- **Log Creation.** An application can create a new log by calling the following API functions:

  create (user_id, sensor_id=none, sensor_type=none, segment_size=default)

  Using the above, a new log stream is created and a locally generated log_id is returned. The log_id is a unique identifier assigned to a log from a 256-bit address space. The details of the newly created log is then sent to the metadata server. The segment_size can either default to a preset value or could be assigned according to the type of sensor used. This flexibility would allow in optimizing performance of the log management for different kinds of sensors.
- **Log Write.** The medical data received from the sensors are appended into a log in the form of data record; a time-tag-value pair, which may be changed according to the requirements of the application. The append() API function is provided to write data to the log. This API function is initiated with the following parameters:

  append (log_id, value, tag, timestamp)

  The append operation identifies the mutable segment corresponding to the log and then adds the new data record to its head. Once the append operation is complete, it returns the file offset of the data record. The offset is added to the segment's chunk index which is stored along with the segment.
- **Log Read.** A single log has multiple readers, which enables data sharing amongst different applications or users. A user is able to retrieve the data within a particular timeframe using the read API function. It has the following parameters:

  read (patient_id, log_id, start_time, end_time)

  To retrieve data record from the log for a specific time window, the application identifies the location of the segments, which is stored in the segment index (SegmentIdx) in the metadata server. It has the details such as the location, segment_id and time_window. After identifying the segment location, it downloads the corresponding chunk index (ChunkIdx) from the remote device that has the segment. The chunk index contains entry for each data item in the segment. The application queries the chunk index locally to identify the offsets related to the chunk. It then sends a request to the remote device for the chunk and retrieves the data.

We present a special use case that makes use of logs extensively. Suppose a user, such as an HSP or patient needs to retrieve a part of the data. The application can request for log chunks, either from the same log stream or from different log streams. For example, if the doctors want to see all the sensor readings from a patient during a time frame, then the system can retrieve the log chunks from different sensors, which have those timestamps. Another utility is that we can create a critical log stream, that contains only the log chunks which are flagged as critical. This will help in better management of critical data across the cloud infrastructure.

- **Log Subscribe.** The users can subscribe to a log stream to get instant updates from a particular IoT device. When an application calls a subscribe API, the corresponding user id is added to the subscribers list associated with a log stream, which resides in the metadata server. This list is updated when the user moves to another location or when he switches his device. The following parameters are passed to the subscribe API:

subscribe (log_id)

Once a user is added to the subscriber's list, the mutable segment of the log is asynchronously replicated to the node associated with the user. A cloud backup node can be made, by default, a subscriber to all the log streams. If a subscriber node goes offline, the data from the source node need to be temporarily stored and sent at a later time, when the node restores the network connection. This storage may be done locally or in the cloud or in the neighbouring nodes.

- **Log Replication.** The reliability and availability of medical data is of utmost priority. Hence, we can make use of the storage capabilities of the neighbouring nodes as well as the cloud, viewing them as a shared storage space. A log segment can be replicated by using the following API call:

replicate (log_id, segment_id)

This will inturn send the segment to all the subscribers as well as the neighbouring nodes. The number of neighbouring nodes, time of replication and medium selection are all chosen by the application according to the data management policy as well as the user preferences. In case of replicating a mutable segment, the application will need to send the data records to the subscribers and neighbouring nodes as and when the data is written.

As seen above, the log abstraction model forces the applications to access the data as chunks. Since the log data is time series in nature and the users generally tend to access near by data, chunking is an effective method to prefetch data from the cloud. However, in most of the healthcare applications, the end users are of different categories. For instance, the doctors, technicians, clinical assistants and patients access the log in different ways. Also, the temporal variability in access patterns can also be seen even among the same user group. Suppose the doctor requests a one minute ECG data for a particular patient. The downloaded chunk contains two minutes of extra data which may not be accessed later. It would be inefficient in downloading that chunk into his smartphone. However, in case of a technician, he might use all the three minutes of data. Thus, a constant chunk size leads to inefficient prefetch of data from the cloud, resulting in cost and bandwidth overheads.

We identified that the log writer cannot decide the chunking size since the log reader preferences are varying even on the same segment of data. In order to overcome this challenge, we propose a dynamic log chunking model based on the reader access pattern.

4   Dynamic Log Chunking Model

In this section, we elaborate our approach towards chunking the log segment based on user or reader access patterns. As shown in the Fig. 3, a log chunk, requested by a reader, consists of two parts: requested data - R_{size} (data that is requested for current use by the reader) and extra data - R_{ed} (data that is prefetched along with the requested data). Extra data can be classified as unused data - D_{un} (extra data that is not used by the reader for succeeding requests even though it is stored locally) and used data - D_u (extra data that is used in the succeeding requests). Our aim is to reduce the unused data by dynamically deciding the chunk size for each reader based on access pattern. In order to achieve this, we analyze the amount of D_{un} and D_u for each chunk request. The relationship between D_{un} and D_u is a direct measure of the readers access pattern, and hence we can change the chunk size C_{size}, for the next request based on these. Suppose C_{size}^n is the current chunk size and C_{size}^{n+1} is the chunk size for the $(n+1)^{th}$ request, then we formulate it as:

$$C_{size}^{n+1} = C_{size}^n - D_{un}^n, \ if \ D_{un}^n > 0. \tag{1}$$

$$C_{size}^{n+1} = C_{size}^n + \alpha * D_u^n, \ if \ D_{un}^n = 0 \ and \ D_u^n > 0. \tag{2}$$

$$C_{size}^{n+1} = C_{size}^n + \beta * R_{size}^n, \ if \ D_{un}^n = 0 \ and \ D_u^n = 0. \tag{3}$$

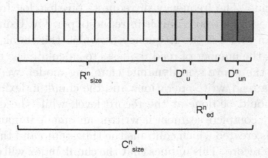

Fig. 3. Representation of a log chunk showing the requested, extra, used and unused data sizes.

Equation (1) is used when there is unused data in the current chunk and it effectively reduces the unused data from the succeeding chunk size. Equation (2) is used when there is no unused data in the current request. This implies that all the prefetch data was useful. Hence, we can slowly increase the prefetch size by using a growth rate α. The value of α is decided by the application to control the growth rate of chunk size. Equation (3) is used when both the used and the unused data in the chunk is zero. It means that the request size was equal to the chunk size, thereby leaving no space for any prefetch data. Hence, we can increase the chunk size by a factor β of the current request size. Once again, the value of β is decided by the application based on how it wants to control the growth rate of chunks. The update of the chunk size could be done after each request or after multiple requests. In H-Plane we have used two different models to update the chunk size.

- **Dynamic Chunking 1 (DC 1).** The Eqs. (1) to (3) are applied based on the average of D_{un}, D_u and R_{size} over n requests. Accordingly a new chunk size C_{size} is calculated and used for the next n requests.
- **Dynamic Chunking 2 (DC 2).** C_{size} is calculated after each request but not updated until a predefined number of requests, n, are completed. The average of C_{size} over n requests is calculated and then used as the new chunk size for the next n requests.

The frequency of updation of chunk size must be based on the frequency of reader access. If the logs are accessed with high frequency, then we can learn for larger number of requests and then use that. On the other hand, if the reader accesses the logs less frequently, then we may use those few access history to learn and calculate the new chunk size. In both cases, the goal is to learn and calculate new chunk sizes faster. This also implies that the frequency of changing chunk sizes is inversely proportional to the frequency of read requests. Hence, we formulate the update frequency parameterized by the frequency of requests and is written as follows:

$$n = \gamma * f. \tag{4}$$

In Eq. (4), n is the number of requests to be used for learning the new chunk size. The value of γ is used to control the update frequency, and it is up to the application to decide. The frequency of requests on that log from a particular reader is represented by f, whose unit is in requests per day. Using this equation, the application can find out the frequency at which the chunk sizes should be updated as well as the number of read requests to calculate the new chunk sizes.

To implement the above said dynamic chunking model, we propose modifications to the data read/write operations and the chunk indexing methodology. The data write should be done at the record level, while the data read at the chunk level. Once a complete segment is written and made immutable, an associated chunk index is created which contains the timestamp and the corresponding offset for each data record. This implies that the chunk index will contain as many entries as the number of data records in that segment. When a reader requests for data from a segment, the application downloads this chunk index locally on that device. For every request of size R_{size}, the corresponding offsets are identified from the chunk index. Based on the current chunk size C_{size}, the prefetch size is calculated and an offset is identified accordingly. The final request will thus have the requested data as well as the prefetch data size added together. The remote device, which has the segment, will retrieve the data according to the C_{size} and send it back. It may be noted that for the first read request on a log, a default chunk size may be used.

5   Evaluation

To evaluate the performance of the proposed model, we compared the D_{un} that gets downloaded while using dynamic chunking versus fixed size chunking models. We used 384 KB for fixed chunk size. This is equivalent to about two minutes of standard 3-channel ECG data. The request sizes R_{size} was picked up from normally distributed data request sizes, with mean as 230 KB and standard deviation of 40 KB. The used prefetch data D_u also varied with a mean of 60 % of the extra data R_{ed} and standard deviation of 10 %. A total of 100 requests, totalling to around 35 MB of data (equivalent to four hours of three channel ECG data) were considered for the evaluation.

The frequency of updation of chunk size, for dynamic chunking, was fixed at n = 10. This was done based on a sample usage scenario. Suppose there are 100 request/day, we considered $\gamma = 0.1$. Hence, the latest ten requests are used to calculate the log chunk size. After every ten requests, the chunk size was updated based on both the updation methodologies listed in the above section. The values used for the growth rate α was 0.3 and that of β was 0.1. Though we experimented with these values, different values of α, β and γ could be used based on the application requirements. Figure 4 shows R_{ed}, D_u and D_{un} as a percentage of the chunk size while using the fixed chunking method and two approaches of the dynamic chunking model. In both models the chunk size was updated after every

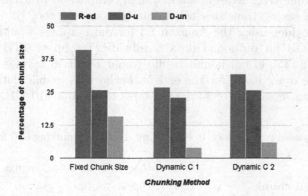

Fig. 4. Comparison of percentage of used data, unused data, and the extra data while using dynamic chunking and fixed chunking models.

10 requests. On an average about 15 % of all the chunk data that is prefetched is not getting used in subsequent requests (as expected according to our mathematical modelling of used data sizes). However, in such cases, the dynamic chunking method 1 decreases the unused data to less than 5 %. Along with this decrease, a slight decrease in the used data is also seen. Using the second dynamic chunking model, the unused data percentage stays at 6 % while the used data percentage is same as that of the fixed chunking method. This reduction in the unused data without affecting the percentage of used prefetch data is considerable and can lead to savings in both costs and bandwidth for the service providers as well as the end user.

5.1   Benefits

Bandwidth Benefits. We notice that on an average about 15 % of all the chunk data that is prefetched is not getting used in subsequent requests (as expected according to our mathematical modelling of used data sizes). However, in such cases, when we use the dynamic chunking method 1, the unused data percentage decreases to less than 5 %. Along with this decrease, a slight decrease in the used data is also seen. Using the second dynamic chunking model, the unused data percentage stays at 6 % while the used data percentage is same as that of the fixed chunking method. This reduction in the unused data without affecting the percentage of used prefetch data is considerable and can lead to savings in both costs and bandwidth for the service providers as well as the end user. The fact that DC 2 has relatively higher D_u also suggests that the reduction in chunk size has not reduced the used prefetch data in absolute terms.

Cost Benefits. The reduction of unused prefetch data also reduces the overall data download and upload requirements, both at the cloud as well as at the end user nodes. Table 1 compares the data downloaded from 100 requests for fixed and dynamic chunking models, given the same request size. DC 1 gives around 20 % savings while DC 2 saves around 14 % in comparison to fixed chunking.

These data saving translates to similar cost savings too. For instance, an application provider using the Amazon S3 for data storage would be charged around \$0.09/GB for outbound data bandwidth for up to 1TB per month. A reduction of 14 % in out-bound traffic would result in savings of \$126 per month. On the other hand, for the end user who uses mobile data for accessing patient data, a savings of 14 % translates to around \$10/GB. Apart from

Table 1. Data usage comparison (in KB) using dynamic chunking and fixed chunking

	R_{size}	R_{ed}	Total data	Savings %
Fixed chunk	22,546	15,854	38,400	-
Dynamic chunking 1	22,546	8,304	30,850	19.7
Dynamic chunking 2	22,546	10,584	33,130	13.7

the cost perspective, the dynamic chunking could result in much efficient use of bandwidth across the entire IoT infrastructure as well.

6   Conclusion and Future Work

The H-Plane architecture for remote monitoring healthcare applications provides a data centric abstraction using logs and related log operations, thereby viewing the entire IoT infrastructure including the cloud, the edge devices and the sensors as a single storage, processing and routing infrastructure. Our experience with using fixed chunking of logs in healthcare applications presented a particular problem of unnecessary prefetch from the cloud and remote devices. The proposed solution was found to improve the performance of log systems by around 15 % translating into cost and bandwidth savings for the cloud user as well as the end users. We envisage that the use of dynamic chunking would be explored further in other domains as well and that other models would be developed that could further enhance the performance.

Acknowledgments. We deeply appreciate the help of our colleagues and friends who reviewed the paper. A special mention to Uma Gopalakrishnan who provided important suggestions for this work. We are grateful to the Chancellor of Amrita University, Sri Mata Amritanandamayi Devi, for constant support and encouragement in conducting research that has direct societal impact.

References

1. Bonomi, F., Milito, R., Zhu, J., Addepalli, S.: Fog computing and its role in the internet of things. In: Proceedings of the first edition of the MCC Workshop on Mobile Cloud Computing, pp. 13–16. ACM (2012)
2. Gupta, T., Singh, R.P., Phanishayee, A., Jung, J., Mahajan, R.: Bolt: data management for connected homes. In: Proceedings of the 11th USENIX Conference on Networked Systems Design and Implementation, pp. 243–256. USENIX Association (2014)
3. Zhang, B., Mor, N., Kolb, J., Chan, D.S., Lutz, K., Allman, E., Wawrzynek, J., Lee, E., Kubiatowicz, J.: The cloud is not enough: saving IoT from the cloud. In: 7th USENIX Workshop on Hot Topics in Cloud Computing (HotCloud 2015) (2015)
4. Gubbi, J., Buyya, R., Marusic, S., Palaniswami, M.: Internet of Things (IoT): a vision, architectural elements, and future directions. Future Gener. Comput. Syst. **29**(7), 1645–1660 (2013)
5. Dinh, H.T., Lee, C., Niyato, D., Wang, P.: A survey of mobile cloud computing: architecture, applications, and approaches. Wirel. Commun. Mob. comput. **13**(18), 1587–1611 (2013). Wiley Online Library
6. Bui, N., Zorzi, M.: Health care applications: a solution based on the internet of things. In: Proceedings of the 4th International Symposium on Applied Sciences in Biomedical and Communication Technologies, pp. 131. ACM (2011)
7. Shafer, I., Sambasivan, R.R., Rowe, A., Ganger, G.R.: Specialized storage for big numeric time series. In: 5th USENIX Workshop on Hot Topics in Storage and File Systems (2013)

8. Kubiatowicz, J., Bindel, D., Chen, Y., Czerwinski, S., Eaton, P., Geels, D., Gummadi, R., Rhea, S., Weatherspoon, H., Weimer, W., Wells, C.: Oceanstore: an architecture for global-scale persistent storage. ACM Sigplan Not. **35**(11), 190–201 (2000)
9. Zhang, L., Afanasyev, A., Burke, J., Jacobson, V., Crowley, P., Papadopoulos, C., Wang, L., Zhang, B.: Named data networking. ACM SIGCOMM Comput. Commun. Rev. **44**(3), 66–73 (2014)
10. Dilraj, N., Rakesh, K., Rahul, K., Maneesha, R.: A low cost remote cardiac monitoring framework for rural regions. In: 5th EAI International Conference on Wireless Mobile Communication and Healthcare - "Transforming healthcare through innovations in mobile and wireless technologies" (MOBIHEALTH). ACM (2015)

Mobile Health Devices for Aging Population Groups: A Review Study

Blanka Klimova[(✉)]

University of Hradec Kralove, Rokitanskeho 62, Hradec Kralove,
Czech Republic
blanka.klimova@uhk.cz

Abstract. At present the demographic changes cause a gradual, but permanent growth of older generation groups. This trend of aging results in serious problems such as incidence of aging diseases, social and economic burden. Therefore there is considerable effort to maintain this population group active and healthy as long as possible. One of the ways of doing this is the exploitation of the so-called mobile health devices which can provide people with information on their health, reminders for scheduled visits, medication instructions, or consulting a doctor at a distance. The purpose of this review study is to explore mobile health devices which are effectively used by older people for the enhancement or maintenance of their state of health. In addition, the author of this review study lists the main benefits and limitations of mobile health devices for older people. The methods used for the discussion of this topic include a method of literature search, a method of comparison and evaluation of the selected sources.

Keywords: Mobile health devices · Older people · Randomized clinical trials · Benefits · Limitations

1 Introduction

Currently, due to the demographic changes, there is a gradual, but permanent growth of older generation groups. In 2013 there were 44.7 million people aged 65+ living worldwide. By the year of 2020 it is estimated that the number of elderly aged 65+ will reach 98 million [1]. For example, in Europe, the proportion of elderly aged 65+ is expected to rise from 18.2 % in 2013 to 28.1 % in 2050 [2]. This trend of aging causes serious problems such as incidence of aging diseases, social and economic burden [3–5]. Therefore there is considerable effort to maintain this population group active as long as possible. For example, governments all over the world try to establish strategic plans aimed at aging population groups. They look for sustainable sources of retirement incomes to support retirement living; emphasize the importance of the need for positive individual and community attitudes to aging; building up age-friendly infrastructure and community support (including housing, transport and communications), to enable elderly to participate in and remain connected to society; and stress the importance of healthy aging to enable a greater number of older people to remain healthy and independent for as long as possible [6], which can be maintained by using new modern

M. Younas et al. (Eds.): MobiWIS 2016, LNCS 9847, pp. 295–301, 2016.
DOI: 10.1007/978-3-319-44215-0_24

communication and information technologies, particularly the Internet, in order to improve older people's health. This concept is called electronic health (e-Health) [7].

At present e-Health has a big potential for elderly because it can enable easier access to better and more effective healthcare. Moreover, most of older people now own and know how to use a mobile device which can provide such an e-Health or more precisely, mobile health (m-Health) service. According to de Veer et al. [9], older people start to be open-minded towards the use of eHealth applications. As Fiordelli et al. [8] state, the use of mobile devices can improve diagnosis and compliance with treatment guidelines, patient information and administration efficacy. At present, elderly use selected eHealth services which include, for example, obtaining information on their health, receiving reminders for scheduled visits, medication instructions, or consulting a doctor at a distance. Furthermore, they use Internet for searching health information about the right nutrition, exercise or weight issues, diseases such as cancer, heart disease, or arthritis, high cholesterol, and health providers (cf. [10]).

The purpose of this review study is to explore mobile health devices which are effectively used by older people for the enhancement or maintenance of their state of health. In addition, the author of this review study lists the main benefits and limitations of mobile health devices for older people.

2 Methods

The methods used for this review study include a literature search in the world's acknowledged databases such as Web of Science, Scopus, PubMed, and Springer. The search was based on the key words: mobile health devices/technologies for older people; mobile health devices/technologies for elderly; and mobile health devices/technologies in healthcare in the period of 2013 till present. In addition, methods of comparison and evaluation of the findings from the selected studies were applied. The studies included in this review comprise only randomized clinical trials conducted among the older population groups and those written exclusively in English. Furthermore, the studies had to match the corresponding period, i.e., from 2013 up to the present time; the period is limited to these years only since till 2013 several review studies on this topic were written. This analysis was conducted by identifying the key words and checking duplication of available sources in the databases mentioned above. Afterwards, the studies were assessed for their relevancy, i.e. verification on the basis of abstracts whether the selected study corresponds to the set goal. After the exclusion of such studies, 29 sources were analysed and 21 eventually excluded. In addition, older studies were used for the comparison of the findings in the part of Discussion, as well as in the Introductory part to discuss the topic.

3 Results and Discussion

Altogether eight randomized controlled clinical trials were identified and their overview is presented in Table 1 below. The studies include both healthy and ill older individuals aged on average 60 years.

Table 1. Selected randomized controlled clinical trials

Study	Number of subjects	Age of subjects	Period of the trial	Type of mobile devices	Benefits
Fontecha et al. [11]	20	65+ years	1 year	Accelerometer-enabled mobile devices	Development of an objective method of assessment of frailty
Goldstein et al. [12]	60	Mean age 69 years	1 month	Electronic pill box application on a smartphone	Patients preferred m-health approach
Knight et al. [13]	45	Mean age 63 ± 5 years	3 months	mHealth technology kit (smartphone, blood pressure monitor, glucometer, pedometer)	Prevention of lifestyle-related chronic diseases among the elderly
Martin et al. [14]	48	Mean age 58 ± 8 years	5 weeks	Smartphone	An automated tracking-texting intervention increased physical activity
Muller et al. [15]	43	55–70 years	6 months	Mobile phone	SMS text messaging may promote exercise in older adults.
Nyman et al. [16]	8	60–87 years	62 days	Pedometer	Self-monitoring increased walking in 7 out of 8 individuals
Petrella et al. [17]	149	Mean age 57 ± 10 years	6 months	mHealth technology kit (smartphone, blood pressure monitor, glucometer, pedometer)	An assistive tool for interested patients or for patients in need of monitoring for control of other diseases such as hypertension or pre-diabetes
Piette et al. [18]	331	67.8 years	1 year	Smartphone	Improvement of patients' medication adherence and caregiver communication

As the findings in Table 1 show, majority of these studies include mobile health devices (e.g. smartphones or pedometers), which should help increase physical activity among older individuals (cf. [13–16]). Two studies [12, 18] show a positive effect of mobile health devices, such as electronic pill box application on a smartphone, on the improvement of patients' medication adherence. In addition, mobile health devices assist in monitoring of patients' diseases, for example, diabetes or hypertension [17]. Specific features of mobile health devices, such as accelerometer sensors, can contribute to the development of enhanced methods for diagnosing different diseases older people may suffer from [11].

Thus, as other research studies state, elderly people are generally in favour of mobile health devices since they can assist them in reminding them of their hospital appointments, or monitoring their health (cf. [19–21]). Furthermore, these mobile health services seem to motivate them in raising their daily physical activities (cf. [22, 23]) and contribute to the improvement of quality of their life. In addition, mobile health technologies are also beneficial for diagnostics (cf. [24]).

The findings indicate that there have been so far modest benefits of mobile technologies for elderly (cf. [25]). However, it is becoming evident that with the growth of aging population worldwide, there will be a higher incidence of chronic diseases, frailty, and disability and therefore the mobile technologies will be suitable intervention tools for elderly [2]. In fact, they can provide them with real-time, long-term, nonintrusive assisted living and care services, tailored to their personal health condition [26]. The mobile health technologies also enable easier and faster access to healthcare to for elderly living in remote areas [27]. In addition, these technologies are also more economical since they can contribute to the reductions of costs of treatment [28].

Although, there are clinical trials in progress [29], the findings show that there should be more high quality longitudinal randomized controlled clinical trials with larger size samples of subjects (cf. [25]) since most of the clinical trials in Table 1 included small samples of subjects (cf. [11–16]). In addition, the trial period should last at least for six months.

Table 2 below then summarizes the main benefits and limitations of mobile health technologies for older people.

Table 2. Key benefits and limitations of mobile health technologies for elderly

Benefits	Limitations
• Very suitable and stimulating intervention and diagnostic tools for elderly • Enhanced access to healthcare for elderly living in remote areas • Improvement of elderly people's quality of life • Cutting potential costs of treatment and care on elderly people • Ecological approach	• Lower awareness of the benefits of mobile health applications among elderly • A lack of longitudinal, randomized controlled clinical trials with large size samples of subjects • A lack of motivation among elderly to use mobile health technologies

4 Conclusion

Overall, with the enhancement of new technologies, mobile devices can assist elderly both in the prevention and in the treatment since they offer unique opportunities for monitoring their progress, providing them and their family members (usually informal caregivers) with education materials, receiving personalized prompts and support, collecting ecologically valid data, and using self-management interventions when and where they are requested [30]. However, elderly people must be motivated in order to understand the magnitude of the health problem and the benefits of the mobile application [21].

Acknowledgments. This review study is supported by SPEV project No. 2103, Faculty of Informatics and Management, University of Hradec Kralove, Czech Republic.

References

1. AoA (2016). http://www.aoa.acl.gov/aging_statistics/index.aspx
2. Bujnowska-Fedak, M.M., Grata-Borkowska, U.: Use of telemedicine-based care for the aging and elderly: promises and pitfalls. Smart Homecare Technol. TeleHealth **3**, 91–105 (2015)
3. Klimova, B., Maresova, P., Kuca, K.: Non-pharmacological approaches to the prevention and treatment of Alzheimer's disease with respect to the rising treatment costs. Curr. Alzheimer Res. (2016, in press)
4. Klimova, B., Maresova, P., Valis, M., Hort, J., Kuca, K.: Alzheimer's disease and language impairments: social intervention and medical treatment. Clin. Interv. Aging **10**, 1401–1408 (2015)
5. Maresova, P., Mohelska, H., Dolejs, J., Kuca, K.: Socio-economic aspects of Alzheimer's disease. Curr. Alzheimer Res. **12**, 903–911 (2014)
6. National Strategy for an Ageing Australia (2001). http://www.ifa-fiv.org/wp-content/uploads/2012/11/062_Australia-2001-National-Strategy-for-an-Ageing-Australia.pdf
7. Bujnowska-Fedak, M.M., Pirogowicz, I.: Support for e-health services among elderly primary care patients. Telemed. J. E-Health **20**(8), 696–704 (2014)
8. Fiordelli, M., Diviani, N., Schulz, P.J.: Mapping mHealth research: a decade of evolution. J. Med. Internet Res. **15**(5), e95 (2013)
9. de Veer, A.J.E., et al.: Determinants of the intention to use e-Health by community dwelling older people. BMC Health Serv. Res. **15**(103), 1–9 (2015)
10. Kaiser Family Foundation: e-Health and the elderly: how seniors use the Internet for health information. Key findings from a national survey of older Americans (2013). https://kaiserfamilyfoundation.files.wordpress.com/2013/01/e-health-and-the-elderly-how-seniors-use-the-internet-for-health-information-key-findings-from-a-national-survey-of-older-americans-survey-report.pdf
11. Fontecha, J., Hervas, R., Bravo, J., Navarro, F.J.: A mobile and ubiquitous approach for supporting frailty assessment in elderly people. J. Med. Internet Res. **15**(9), e197 (2013)
12. Goldstein, C.M., Gathright, E.C., Dolansky, M.A., Gunstad, J., Sterns, A., Redle, J.D., Josephson, R., Hughes, J.W.: Randomized controlled feasibility trial of two telemedicine medication reminder systems for older adults with heart failure. J. Telemed. Telecare **20**(6), 293–299 (2014)

13. Knight, E., Stuckey, M.I., Petrella, R.J.: Health promotion through primary care: enhancing self-management with activity prescription and mHealth. Phys. Sportsmed. **42**(3), 90–99 (2014)

14. Martin, S.S., Feldman, D.I., Blumenthal, R.S., Jones, S.R., Post, W.S., McKibben, R.A., Michos, E.D., Ndumele, C.E., Ratchford, E.V., Coresh, J., Blaha, M.J.: mActive: a randomized clinical trial of an automated mHealth intervention for physical activity promotion. J. Am. Heart Assoc. **4**, e002239 (2015)

15. Muller, A.M., Khoo, S., Morris, T.: Text messaging for exercise promotion in older adults from an upper-middle-income country: randomized controlled trial. JMIR **18**(1), e5 (2016)

16. Nyman, S.R., Goodwin, K., Kwasnicka, D., Callaway, A.: Increasing walking among older people: a test of behaviour change techniques using factorial N-of-1 trials. Psychol. Health **31**, 313–330 (2015). doi:10.1080/08870446.2015.1088014

17. Petrella, R.J., Stuckey, M.I., Shapiro, S., Gill, D.P.: Mobile health, exercise and metabolic risk: a randomized controlled trial. BMC Publ. Health **14**, 1082 (2014)

18. Piette, J.D., Striplin, D., Marinec, N., Chen, J., Trivedi, R.B., Aron, D.C., Fisher, L., Aikens, J.E.: A mobile health intervention supporting heart failure patients and their informal caregivers: a randomized comparative effectiveness trial. JMIR **17**(6), e142 (2015)

19. Goh, G., Tan, N.C., Malhotra, R., Padmanabhan, U., Barbier, S., Allen, J.C., Østbye, T.: Short-term trajectories of use of a caloric-monitoring mobile phone app among patients with type 2 diabetes mellitus in a primary care setting. J. Med. Internet Res. **17**(2), e33 (2015)

20. Arora, S., Burner, E., Terp, S., Nok Lam, C., Nercisian, A., Bhatt, V., Menchine, M.: Improving attendance at post-emergency department follow-up via automated text message appointment reminders: a randomized controlled trial. Acad. Emerg. Med. **22**(1), 31–37 (2015)

21. Mena, L.J., Felix, V.G., Ostos, R., Gonzalez, J.A., Cervantes, A., Ochoa, A., Ruiz, C., Ramos, R., Maestre, G.E.: Mobile personal health system for ambulatory blood pressure monitoring. Comput. Math. Methods Med. **2013**, 598196 (2013)

22. Casey, M., Hayes, P.S., Glynn, F., O'Laighin, G., Heaney, D., Murphy, A.W., Glynn, L.G.: Patients' experiences of using a smartphone application to increase physical activity: the SMART MOVE qualitative study in primary care. Br. J. Gen. Pract. **64**(625), e500–e508 (2014)

23. King, A.C., Hekler, E.B., Grieco, L.A., Winter, S.J., Sheats, J.L., Buman, M.P., Banerjee, B., Robinson, T.N., Cirimele, J.: Harnessing different motivational frames via mobile phones to promote daily physical activity and reduce sedentary behavior in aging adults. PLoS ONE **8**(4), e62613 (2013)

24. van Hooff, R.J., Cambron, M., van Dyck, R., de Smedt, A., Moens, M., Espinoza, A.V., van de Casseye, R., Convents, A., Hubloue, I., de Keyser, J., Brouns, R.: Prehospital unassisted assessment of stroke severity using telemedicine: a feasibility study. Stroke **44** (10), 2907–2909 (2013)

25. Free, C., Phillips, G., Watson, L., Galli, L., Felix, L., Edwards, P., Patel, V., Haines, A.: The effectiveness of mobile-health technologies to improve health care service delivery processes: a systematic review and meta-analysis. PloS Med. **10**(1), e1001363 (2013)

26. Lv, Z., Xia, F., Wu, G., Yao, L., Chen, Z.: iCare: a mobile health monitoring system for the elderly. In: Proceedings of the 2010 IEEE International Conference on Green Computing and Communications, pp. 699–705 (2010)

27. Klimova, B., Simonova, I., Poulova, P., Truhlarova, Z., Kuca, K.: Older people and their attitude to the use of information and communication technologies – a review study with special focus on the Czech Republic (older people and their attitude to ICT). Educ. Gerontol. **42**(5), 361–369 (2015). doi:10.1080/03601277.2015.1122447

28. Maresova, P., Klimova, B.: Investment evaluation of cloud computing in the European business sector. Appl. Econ. **47**(36), 3907–3920 (2015)
29. Amorin, A., Pappas, E., Simic, M., Ferreira, M.L., Tiedeman, A., Jennings, M., Ferreira, P. H.: Integrating mobile health and physical activity to reduce the burden of chronic low back pain trial (IMPACT): a pilot trial protocol. BMC Musculoskelet. Disord. **17**, 36 (2016)
30. Sun, J., Guo, Z., Wang, X., Yeng, Q.: mHealth for aging China: opportunities and challenges. Aging Dis. **7**(1), 53–67 (2016)

Sensors in Your Clothes: Design and Development of a Prototype

Kristine Lorentzen[2], Tor-Morten Grønli[2(✉)], Gheorghita Ghinea[1,2], Muhammad Younas[3], and Manoranjan Satpathy[4]

[1] Brunel University, London, UK
george.ghinea@brunel.ac.uk
[2] Faculty of Technology, Westerdals Oslo ACT, Oslo, Norway
{sunkri, tmg}@westerdals.no
[3] Oxford Brookes University, Oxford, UK
m.younas@brookes.ac.uk
[4] Indian Institute of Technology, Bhubaneswar, India
nuapatana@gmail.com

Abstract. Wearable computing is fast advancing as a preferred approach for integrating software solutions not only in our environment, but also in our everyday garments to exploit the numerous information sources we constantly interact with. This paper explores this context further by showing the possible use of wearable sensor technology for information critical information systems, through the design and development of a proof-of-concept prototype.

Keywords: Wearables · Sensors · Design and development · Smart clothing

1 Introduction

The topic of wearable computing and smart garments have been researched and developed for several decades (Mann 1996), but has only in recent years become a popular research field. Gartner first introduced *Wearable User Interfaces* into their Hype Cycle for Emerging Technologies in 2013, two years after introducing *Internet of Things* (Fig. 1). Since its introduction, it has stayed on the Peak of Inflated Expectations, but is showing a trend of moving into the Trough of Disillusionment. According to Gartner, when a technology transitions into the Trough of Disillusionment, it is expected to see an increase in failed experiments and implementations within the field, and a struggle to satisfy the early adopters of, and investors for the technology (Gartner 2016). Because of this, it is important that research on this field focuses not only on simple prototypes and single-case studies, but also on how it can be integrated with existing business practices.

For this paper, we will use Sonderegger's (2013) definition of smart garments:

"Smart garments are clothes containing technology such as sensors, processors, communication equipment, displays or input devices that are integrated into a textile-based garment structure and provide some additional functionality compared to the classical physical and socio-cultural functions of clothing."

© Springer International Publishing Switzerland 2016
M. Younas et al. (Eds.): MobiWIS 2016, LNCS 9847, pp. 302–312, 2016.
DOI: 10.1007/978-3-319-44215-0_25

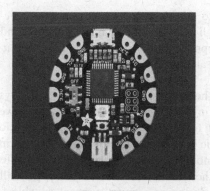 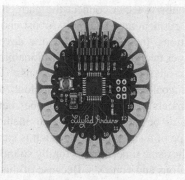

Fig. 1. Arduino processors

We also make a clear distinction between the term wearables and the term smart garments, as the term wearables also includes smart watches and other similar technologies that can be worn, but does not fill the requirements of a garment.

According to Karrer et al. (2011), current smart garment systems consist of DIY approaches, textile music controls and specialized systems for health and sports. It has also recently been embraced by the fashion industry, predominantly with use of LEDs, and other sources of light, that enhance the visual impact of the garment (Rossi et al. 2011; Ashford 2014a, 2015; Cochran et al. 2015). Several companies are working to make this technology more accessible for everyone, and Adafruit is a company one of these companies. They focus on both providing hardware and easy-to-use electronic components, but also on providing guidance and extensive learning for their users. Included in their product line is a set of sow able components, with custom pads made for use with conductive thread, headlined by their electronics platform named Flora (Adafruit 2016a). Another very similar product is the Lilypad Arduino (Fig. 1), originally developed to be a kit for schoolchildren and adults to learn how to build and program their own wearable computers (Buechley et al. 2008), and is now a part of Arduino's own product line (Arduino 2016).

Although these examples far from indicate a widespread adoption of this tech- • nology, it does demonstrate the fact that the smart garment industry is not just catering those with existing knowledge about the technology, but also people competent in other areas, such as fashion. Because cooperating with the fashion industry is instrumental to developing successful smart garments (Jacob and Dumas 2014; Silina and Hadaddi 2015; Cochran et al. 2015), this trend of making wearable technology easy to use and develop may be instrumental to a successful, widespread adoption of smart garments.

According to Perera et al. (2014), most of the research done on IoT during the last two decades has been focused around prototypes, systems and solutions with a limited number of data sources. However, as the technology develops, a need to be context-aware and able to utilize a large number of sensors arises, and with this, the need to develop solutions which implement a strong core architecture, and is flexible and modular enough to be combined with other IoT solutions (Perera et al. 2014). One way of exploring how this would apply to the development of a smart garment, is to look at how we can connect the garment to other context sources, and how we can make a garment architecturally robust enough to be utilized by many different kinds of applications. In addition to this, the development of smart garments poses particular challenges tied to wearability, fashionability and durability (Karrer et al. 2011) not seen in many other technological solutions.

Our goal for this paper is to look at how both the architectural- and physical requirements of the garment can be met, in a way which is flexible and powerful enough to be context aware. Our method for exploring this will be to develop a prototype of a smart garment which is simple enough to be worn as a normal garment, but at the same time, architecturally sound enough to support being utilized by different applications and contexts. Because of this, the research question for this paper will be:

What considerations are needed when designing a smart garment suitable for a range of unknown applications?

To answer this, we will present a prototype of a smart garment in the form of a jacket containing both input, output and networking devices, and how this garment can be used with different contexts.

2   Background

To provide a robust solution, we have done a thorough literary search on similar projects and solutions. This includes topics relating both to placement and configuration of the hardware and the garment, as well as architecture and context management.

A reoccurring trend with smart garments is the development of products placed on the user's chest or arms (Davide et al. 2014; Karrer et al. 2011; Pailes-Friedman et al. 2014; Jacob and Dumas 2014; Koo 2014; Pailes-Friedman 2015; Mann 1996; Todi and Luyten 2014; Bian et al. 2011; Randell and Muller 2000). Several of these include research and testing which supports this being the ideal placement for smart garment technology as it is now (Pailes-Friedman et al. 2014; Karrer et al. 2011; Gemperle et al. 1998). From their user tests, Karrer et al. found that, for placement of an input device where the user pinches a piece of fabric, they found that the forearms, upper arms and .area around the collar bone as most popular. The testing also revealed that the chest may not be suitable for interaction, both because it was seen as possibly socially unacceptable, and also because it may not be compatible with the use of, for instance, a low-cut top (Karrer et al. 2011). Because of this, a jacket with an open front has been chosen for the prototype for this project.

As previously mentioned, Karrer et al. (2011) highlight wearability, fashionability and durability as challenges when designing, engineering and manufacturing smart garments. To make sure we meet the challenges tied to wearability, we will be following the set of design guidelines for wearability presented by Gemperle et al. (1998). The guidelines including the following listing, from simple to more complex: Placement (where on the body it should go); Form language (defining the shape); Weight (as its spread across the human body); Accessibility (physical access to the forms); Aesthetics (perceptual appropriateness); Long-term use (effects on the body and mind).

These guidelines have been used to dictate the design of the garment, and will be used as a benchmark to evaluate whether or not the solution meets the challenge of wearability. Regarding the challenge of fashionability, Karrer et al. (2011) suggest that the electronics in the garment, if possible, should be completely hidden. However, we would argue that fashion is about much more than just whether or not the electronics are visible, but also how the garment reflects the societal impact the garment has. In general, clothing can have two distinguished functions: the physical and socio-cultural function (Sonderegger 2013). Not only do clothes keep us protected from the elements, but it can also reflect the wearer's individual, sexual, cultural or religious characteristics and social status (Sonderegger 2013). When looking more specifically at wearables, the solutions can generally be divided into *responsive and emotive wearables* (Ashford 2014b). Responsive wearables are a term which describes a wearable technology that reacts to the user's social environment, or one which intercepts, processes and displays data from other devices and context sources (Ashford 2014b). Emotive wearables on the other hand are technologies which amplifies physiological data associated with non-verbal communication, reflecting, for instance, the user's emotions or mood (Ashford 2014b). This indicates that smart garments may use electronics not only to make a hidden computer, but also to open up new avenues for self-expression, being able to adapt itself to the needs and wants of the user continually. In some cases, it can even assist users who have problems expressing themselves due to mental conditions such as autism (Koo 2014).

Finally, regarding durability, Karrer et al. (2011) state that in order to truly function as a regular garment, the smart garment must be able to be stained, washed and dried repeatedly. According to Berglund et al. (2015), solutions utilizing conductive thread may be suitable for machine washing, however, it seemed that tumble-drying should be avoided. Although this test is quite limited in the materials tested, it does indicate that it would be possible to treat garments containing conductive thread and fabrics just as you would any other delicate garments. Using solder points on components is however more fragile to stochastic, high-intensitivity wear conditions (Berglund et al. 2015). Testing also indicates that using lines of conductive thread is more advantageous than conductive fabrics with woven conductive yarn, as the fabric is harder to isolate, and often enforces an orthogonal, constrained trace layout (Berglund et al. 2015). Their research also suggests that having many, short stitches may me more reliable than few and long ones.

The functions of the garment must also, naturally, be user-friendly and easy to use. In their paper, Holleis et al. (2008) test and evaluate input on smart garments in the form of capacitive touch. They conclude that, for project using similar input methods, four main aspects are important:

- Finding an input design which is compatible with a large array of people;
- Having the controls be easy to find;
- That it supports one-handed interaction;
- Ensures that the feedback from the action is immediate.

Usability also includes challenges such as connecting the garment to other devices, the different kinds of output devices it can use and what components the user has access to. Being able to connect the garment to other devices and the internet is essential to classifying the garment as smart, and essential to the success of the product (Gubbi et al. 2013; Henfridsson and Lindgren 2005). To ensure that the garment truly is user friendly, rigorous user testing is needed. To mitigate the halo-effect, an effect which indicates that users correlate the attractiveness of the product with its usability, it is necessary to do long-term testing, over several hours or days (Sonderegger 2013).

In the context of a garment not tied to a specific application, a scalable and robust architecture is a necessity. According to Perera et al., a modular architecture, with no single control point, is the best way to achieve this. They list 12 design principles they consider to be most important when designing the architecture of an Internet of Things device: Components and layering, scalability and extensibility, easy-to-use API, debugging mechanisms, automatic life cycle management, context model in-dependency, extended, rich and comprehensive modelling, multi-model reasoning, mobility support, sharing information, resource optimization and monitoring and detecting events.

These are design principles on which the design of a possible application for the garment are based, and will be measured by.

3   Design and Implementation

Based on the previously mentioned research by Karrer et al. (2011) and several others, we have chosen to use a jacket as the choice of garment for this prototype, in order to make the implementation of this application feasible and related to the cases (See Fig. 2).

Fig. 2. Smart garment

3.1   Garment

The garment itself is a blazer, made out of a fabric with little to no stretch. This is to ensure that the conductive thread used will not stretch and lose its connection during use (Fig. 3). The jacket also has an inner lining which allows access to the interior of the garment by just opening a few stitches in one seam. The garment contains an Adafruit Flora (Adafruit 2016a), connected to a Bluetooth module (Adafruit 2016a) that is placed directly beside the Flora. These two components do most of the logic handling in the garment, the Flora doing all the computational tasks, and the Bluetooth module securing the connection between the garment and other devices. Bluetooth was chosen because of its compatibility with many different devices and easy connection and setup.

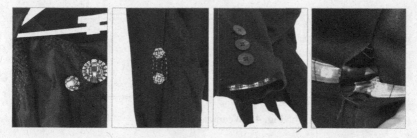

Fig. 3. Close-ups of the prototype

From the Flora, 4 lines of 3-ply conductive thread (Adafruit 2016a) is sown into the lining of the garment, following the garment's natural seams to ensure maximum stability, ensuring that they won't budge around. Initial testing indicates that this connection is stable, but further user testing is needed to verify that this configuration is stable enough for use. The conductive thread runs down the right arm of the garment, connecting to the Lux light sensor (Adafruit 2016a), and is further used to chain this sensor to the color sensor. Both of these sensors are located on the right forearm. Because of the chainable nature of the sensors, adding additional sensors poses little to no additional challenge.

The garment also contains two separate LED strips, one located on the exterior of the garment on the left upper arm, meant to be used for situations where you would want high visibility, and one located on the inside of the left wrist, giving a subtle lighting effect to notify the user. Because the LED strips used in this project do not include sowable pads, the strips had to be connected through wires soldered to pads on the strips, and on the Flora. For this a flexible, silicon coated wire has been chosen, and any areas where the solder or wire is exposed, is covered by shrink tubing to insulate it. The wires are drawn along the inside of the jacket, between the lining and the outer fabric layer. Because the LED strips can be chained in a similar fashion to the sensors, the 5 V and GND connections have been chained from the high-visibility lights to the subtle lights. The data line to the subtle lights, however is drawn directly to the Flora, to

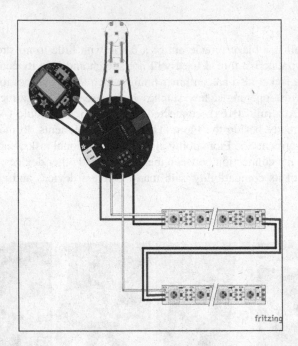

Fig. 4. Wearable schematics

make it more easy to address and program (Fig. 4). The testing done during implementation indicated that the jacket is still fully functional as a piece of clothing, and that the hardware does not contribute to any significant discomfort.

3.2 Application

The example application we have chosen for this project is one which demonstrates the combination of different contexts with the garment, and how all the components can be given different instructions according to the needs of the user's environment. The app is designed for use with conferences and similar indoor places where the user wants to locate points of interest. The following scenarios are given:

Scenario 1: The user, Alice, is going to a large conference venue, and has a particular set of booths that she would like to visit and companies to speak to during the conference. All the businesses have their own stand at the conference, and the organizers of the event has fitted each stand with a beacon, and made an API tying each beacon to a specific business. This API is used in an application which Alice uses, and connects to the garment. She plots the businesses she's interested in, into the application.

Her friend, Johnny, is meeting her there. Unfortunately, he cannot find her in the crowd of people, so Alice activates her high-visibility lights, which she previously had set to light up with the same color as her top with the color sensor. She is now clearly distinguishable, and Johnny locates her. They both go into the conference.

The application registers when she enters the location, and when she goes near a point of interest, the LEDs at her wrist start shining dimly. As she walks nearer the stand, her wrist shines brighter, to help her find the right stand.

Scenario 2: A fire breaks out in the cellar of the conference, causing the fire alarm to activate, and, because of damage to electrics, makes the lights of the location go out. When the fire alarm is triggered, the application goes into emergency mode, and the high visibility lights are turned on. Several other participants are also wearing the garment, and the LEDs of those closest to the emergency are brighter than others, using the location data from a battery-driven beacon. The garment has automatically adapted the brightness of the lights according the light of the dark room by using the light sensor, to ensure that the LEDs are clearly visible without being obtrusive. Using the brightest lights are a guide, she quickly finds her way out of the building and into safety.

These two scenarios demonstrate use of the same components used by two different contexts, the high visibility lights, being used both to make the user visible, and to guide the user to the nearest exit. It also demonstrates the combination of several different devices and context, by including both the beacon system and the fire alarm system.

3.3 Software Architecture

Based on the two previously mentioned scenarios, we have made a graphical model representing a preliminary software design architecture, using the guidelines presented by Perera et al. (2014) as a foundation (Fig. 5).

It shows a modular setup, where each service has a very limited and tightly defined role. From top to bottom, we first see development and debugging services, acting as a middle layer between the developer and the garment, providing a data model and services specifically modelled for development and debugging. Further we see the software on the garment itself just contains methods to read from and write to the components. Little to no data modelling is done on this layer, as the modelling may be context specific. The context acquisition for the garment itself is therefore based on responsibility, where acquisition happens through pull- and push methods (Perera et al. 2014). From there the data is sent to the user's device through Bluetooth, and the application on the device handles routing to the correct data modeler and combining the data from the garment with other contexts.

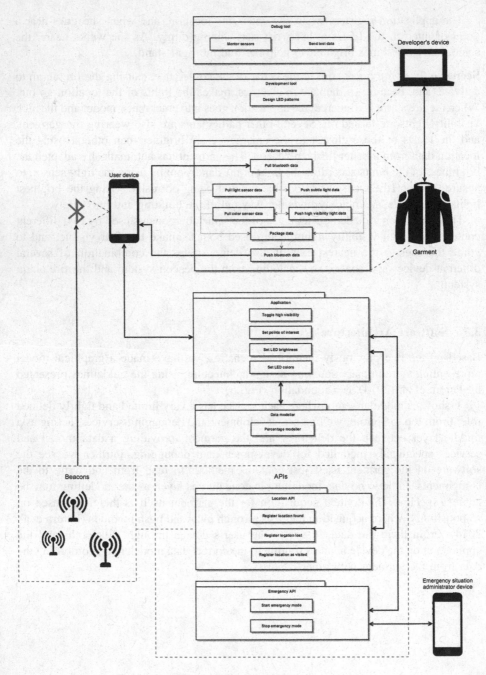

Fig. 5. Software architecture

4 Conclusions and Future Work

This research highlights the novelty of wearable computing for information critical purposes. Through design, prototype development and architectural blueprints a novel approach for sensor integration in clothing is shown. The approach is low cost, feasible and solves real world challenges. Further work will include a large scale user test and evaluation to harvest data from the actual use of the garment. We will further pursue continuous development of wearable computing as an answer to ubiquitous computing and a full user test will enable rigorous testing of sensor based clothing for innovative user activities.

References

Adafruit: About Us (2016a). https://www.adafruit.com/about. Accessed 5 Apr 2016

Arduino: Lily Pad Arduino Main Board (2016). https://www.arduino.cc/en/Main/ArduinoBoard LilyPad. Accessed 1 Apr 2016

Ashford, R.: Baroesque barometric skirt. In: Proceedings of the 2014 ACM International Symposium on Wearable Computers: Adjunct Program, pp. 9–14 (2014a). http://doi.acm.org/10.1145/2641248.2641271

Ashford, R.: Responsive and emotive wearables. In: Proceedings of the 2014 ACM International Symposium on Wearable Computers Adjunct Program - ISWC 2014 Adjunct, pp. 99–104 (2014b). http://dl.acm.org/citation.cfm?doid=2641248.2642731

Ashford, R.: ThinkerBelle EEG amplifying dress. In: Proceedings of the 2015 ACM International Joint Conference on Pervasive and Ubiquitous Computing and Proceedings of the 2015 ACM International Symposium on Wearable Computers - UbiComp 2015, pp. 607–612 (2015). http://dx.doi.org/10.1145/2800835.2801673, http://dl.acm.org/citation.cfm?doid=2800835.2801673

Berglund, M.E., et al.: Surface-mount component attachment for e-textiles. In: ISWC 2015 Proceedings of the 2015 ACM International Symposium on Wearable Computers, pp. 65–66 (2015)

Berglund, M.E., et al.: Washability of e-textile stretch sensors and sensor insulation. In: Proceedings of the 2014 ACM International Symposium on Wearable Computers - ISWC 2014. ACM Press, New York, pp. 127–128 (2014). http://dl.acm.org/citation.cfm?doid=2634317.2634326. Accessed 7 Apr 2016

Bian, L., Yao, L., Hirsch, M.: Queen's new clothes. In: Proceedings of the 8th International Conference on Advances in Computer Entertainment Technology - ACE 2011, p. 1 (2011). http://dl.acm.org/citation.cfm?doid=2071423.2071531

Buechley, L., Eisenberg, M., Catchen, J.: The LilyPad Arduino: using computational textiles to investigate engagement, aesthetics, and diversity in computer science education. In: CHI 2008 Proceedings of the Twenty-Sixth Annual SIGCHI Conference on Human Factors in Computing Systems, pp. 423–432 (2008). http://dl.acm.org/citation.cfm?id=1357123

Cochran, Z., Zeagler, C., McCall, S.: Addressing dresses: user interface allowing for interdisciplinary design and calibration of LED embedded garments. In: ISWC 2015 Proceedings of the 2015 ACM International Symposium on Wearable Computers, pp. 61–64 (2015)

Davide, B., et al.: Jackit: power generating jacket. In: Proceedings of the 2014 ACM International Symposium on Wearable Computers: Adjunct Program, pp. 27–32 (2014). http://doi.acm.org/10.1145/2641248.2641274

Gemperle, F., et al.: Design for wearability. Digest of papers. In: Second International Symposium on Wearable Computers (Cat. No. 98EX215), pp. 116–122 (1998). http://ieeexplore.ieee.org/lpdocs/epic03/wrapper.htm?arnumber=729537

Gubbi, J., Buyya, R., Marusic, S.: Internet of things (IoT): a vision, architectural elements, and future directions. Future Generation Comput. Syst. **29**(7), 1645–1660 (2013)

Henfridsson, O., Lindgren, R.: Multi-contextuality in ubiquitous computing: investigating the car case through action research. Inf. Organ. **15**(2), 95–124 (2005)

Holleis, P., et al.: Evaluating capacitive touch input on clothes. In: Proceedings of the 10th International Conference on Human Computer Interaction with Mobile Devices and Services - MobileHCI 2008, p. 81 (2008). http://portal.acm.org/citation.cfm?doid=1409240.1409250

Jacob, C., Dumas, B.: Designing for intimacy: how fashion design can address privacy issues in wearable computing. In: Proceedings of the 2014 ACM International Symposium on Wearable Computers, pp. 185–192 (2014). http://dl.acm.org/citation.cfm?id=2641353

Karrer, T., et al.: Pinstripe: eyes-free continuous input on interactive clothing. In: Proceedings of the 2011 Annual Conference on Human Factors in Computing Systems - CHI 2011, pp. 1313–1322 (2011). http://dl.acm.org/citation.cfm?doid=1978942.1979137

Koo, H.: "TellMe": therapeutic clothing for children with autism spectrum disorder (ASD) in daily life. In: Proceedings of the 2014 ACM International Symposium on Wearable Computers: Adjunct Program, pp. 55–58 (2014). http://dl.acm.org/citation.cfm?id=2641278

Mann, S.: Smart clothing: the shift to wearable computing. Commun. ACM **39**(8), 23–24 (1996)

Pailes-Friedman, R.: BioWear: a kinetic accessory that communicates emotions through wearable technology. In: UbiComp 2015/ISWC 2015 - Adjunct Proceedings of the 2015 ACM International Joint Conference on Pervasive and Ubiquitous Computing and the 2015 ACM International Symposium on Wearable Computers, pp. 627–633 (2015)

Pailes-Friedman, R., et al.: Electronic-textile system for the evaluation of wearable technology. In: ISWC 2014 Adjunct, pp. 201–207 (2014)

Perera, C., et al.: Context aware computing for the internet of things: a survey. IEEE Commun. Surv. Tutorials **16**(1), 414–454 (2014)

Randell, C., Muller, H.: The shopping jacket: wearable computing for the consumer. Pers. Ubiquit. Comput. **4**(4), 241–244 (2000)

Rossi, M., Cinaz, B., Tröster, G.: Ready-to-live: wearable computing meets fashion. In: Proceedings of the 13th International Conference on Ubiquitous Computing, pp. 609–610 (2011). http://doi.acm.org/10.1145/2030112.2030238

Silina, Y., Haddadi, H.: " New Directions in Jewelry ": a close look at emerging trends and developments in jewelry - like wearable devices. In: ISWC 2015 Proceedings of the 2015 ACM International Symposium on Wearable Computers, pp. 49–56 (2015). http://dl.acm.org/citation.cfm?id=2808410

Sonderegger, A.: Smart garments – the issue of usability and aesthetics. In: Proceedings of the 2013 ACM Conference on Pervasive and Ubiquitous Computing Adjunct Publication - UbiComp 2013 Adjunct, pp. 385–392 (2013). http://www.scopus.com/inward/record.url?eid=2-s2.0-84885205848&partnerID=tZOtx3y1

Todi, K., Luyten, K.: Suit up!: enabling eyes-free interactions on jacket buttons. In: Conference on Human Factors in Computing Systems - Proceedings, pp. 1549–1554 (2014). http://www.scopus.com/inward/record.url?eid=2-s2.0-84900550993&partnerID=40&md5=fb4fc9a9e5b3fc19b8cc4d9cba3b2f9a

Utilizing Multiple Interaction Styles to Collect Installed Base Information Using Wearable and Mobile Devices

Markus Aleksy(✉) and Nicolaie Fantana

ABB Corporate Research, Wallstadter Str. 59, 68526 Ladenburg, Germany
{markus.aleksy,nicolaie.fantana}@de.abb.com

Abstract. Excellent service is a key component of making industrial plants work without unexpected shutdowns and safety hazards to workers. Especially, up-to-date information regarding installed base is crucial to support the entire life cycle of systems and products as well as to provide tailored service offerings. However, the myriad and variety of industrial equipment and systems manufactured throughout various periods increase the effort related to the collection of corresponding installed base data. Moreover, organizational changes, such as corporate mergers or company take-overs can introduce additional complexities, such as intersecting serial numbers or the existence of heterogeneous identification plates. In addition, the time related to collecting installed base data is critical since it is often done during customer visits by well trained service engineers that have to focus on solving time-critical problems. Thus, the corresponding data is often processed slowly because of time consuming media conversion and paper work before and after the actual service work.

In this paper, we present an approach to collect installed base data utilizing wearable and mobile devices. Here, we use different interaction styles at the same time. The proposed approach falls back on using existing hardware components, voice commands, and QR codes in parallel.

1 Introduction

Instant availability of up-to-date information is a vital prerequisite in today business for decision making and the execution of any job task. Especially in service business, which is to a high degree based on expertise, experience, skills and judgement of a human expert, tailored information support is the key factor to deliver services efficiently and with high quality. This includes knowledge about customers, products, application domains, the history of installed equipment and service procedures and processes. This knowledge is prerequisite to diagnose and fix problems fast and reducing the impact on the rest of the plant at the same time. In global operating enterprises, this knowledge is in people's heads, but also stored as electronic information in many databases of the enterprise information technology infrastructure. ServIS - ABB's installed base information system [6] - is an example for such an enterprise information system which provides the basic

M. Younas et al. (Eds.): MobiWIS 2016, LNCS 9847, pp. 313–320, 2016.
DOI: 10.1007/978-3-319-44215-0_26

infrastructure to support the entire life cycle of industrial systems and products as well as to provide lean and preventive service to ensure best conditions for the installed base. "*A product's installed base (IB) is the total number of products currently under use ...*" [4]. An extended definition of IB that also covers systems can be found in [1]. ServIS allows keeping track of all ABB products and systems information at a customer site, including technical and project details. It is integrated with other ABB information systems, such as ABB Product that provides detailed information regarding available products.

Utilizing mobile and wearable systems to access installed base information provides an opportunity for more efficient service delivery and execution including:

– Finding the location of industrial equipment
   Finding equipment that needs to be serviced might be a challenge if the plant is large. Augmented reality can be used to overlay real world view of the plant with information related to the location of the equipment. The current location of the worker can be obtained via the GPS sensor of a mobile device. The GPS position of the equipment can be loaded from an installed base management system, such as ServIS. Afterwards, the field service worker can be guided to the proper equipment.
– Identification of industrial equipment
   Advanced identification and labeling techniques, such as bar codes and NFC- or RFID-based tags respectively, can be used for efficient identification of the equipment. The camera of a mobile or head-mounted device can be used to read the bar code. Moreover, many smart phones are already equipped with a NFC reader, thus facilitating device identification based on radio technology. The data read from the bar code or tag can be used to request further information from backend systems, such as the aforementioned ServIS system.
– Access to information
   Field service workers often need to access various types of information, such as prior service reports, technical drawings, manuals, and checklists to perform proper actions. Field personnel could also access to a process control system of a plant to view real-time values of different process devices. Mobile and wearable devices can be used to access this information without being constrained to a single location. Moreover, augmented reality features can be used to overlay real world images with work instructions [2] or equipment- or safety-related information. Moreover, utilizing wearable devices, such as head mounted displays, eyeglasses, or contact lenses enables hands-free operations while accessing this information.
– Situational awareness
   Recent environmental changes or updates affecting service-execution can be directly pushed to the service worker via wearable devices in an non-intrusive way. Here, besides the aforementioned wearable displays technologies, wristwatch displays can be used to ensure that the worker can still use his both hands to proceed with his work while getting recent information updates. The number of wristwatch displays and smart watches, such as Pebble and I'm Watch is steadily increasing. Moreover, the provided functionality is improving.

– Work quality monitoring and documentation
Person-mounted cameras and microphones can be used for continuous collection of surrounding plant state. The collected multimedia information, such as sound recordings or movies can be used for documentation purposes, e.g., to provide proofs and audit trail of correct actions as well as for plant analysis. Video records of executed work and supervision of correct execution of mechanical work by monitoring body movements [3,5] can help to improve the work quality.
– Seamless integration of the worker
Mobile and wearable solutions provide the opportunity for seamless integration of mobile field service workers into service processes avoiding media breaks often introduced by paper based work. Thus, asset information can be retrieved and updated instantly. Moreover, they enable service workers to connect to remote diagnostics and optimization applications or expert systems hosted by backend systems or in a cloud environment. That way, he can fix the problem fast and properly as well as use the opportunity to optimize asset's configuration. Additionally, such devices facilitate remote collaboration with peers and remote experts.

However, capturing and keeping installed base information up to date are time consuming and error prone activities. Mobile and wearable devices can support field personnel in plants by providing equipment identification techniques and simplified data collection capabilities.

The proWiLAN project (http://www.industrialradio.de/Projects/Home/PROWILAN) is addressing the development of an innovative wireless communication technology for industrial applications with focus on low latency, high bandwidth and a set of inevitable features required by industrial systems. The corresponding functionality covers safety and security features, an integrated positioning system providing high accuracy as well as object identification and tracking techniques. Moreover, new interaction styles and workflow support for industrial processes are addressed by the project. The latter are in focus of this paper.

2   Utilizing Mobile and Wearable Devices to Collect Installed Base Information

Recent advances in information and communication technologies make it feasible to collect, track, and access installed base information anytime and anywhere. We used Vuzix smart glasses and an Android smart phone in our approach.

Using smart glasses as the main device for collecting installed base information requires new considerations regarding the interaction styles. In contrast to smart phones and tablet devices, it is not possible to touch objects presented on the display or use gestures, such as sliding. In this case, one can fall back on the user interface elements provided by the human machine interdace (HMI) of smart glasses, that is operating small buttons or utilizing speech-recognition to determine the corresponding actions. The usage of the small buttons is often limited in the daily business since service workers have to wear gloves. Thus, speech-enabled operation can be used to control the application. However, a number of industrial environments are characterized by a high noise level. Therefore, we decided to utilize an approach that supports mixed interaction styles in parallel. In our approach, the user can perform some actions using the buttons of the smart glasses, execute actions via voice control, and fall back on quick response (QR) codes to start actions. The QR codes can be visualized on a smart watch or a smart phone (see Fig. 1). Afterwards, if the QR code is recognized by the camera integrated in the smart glasses, the corresponding action is started automatically.

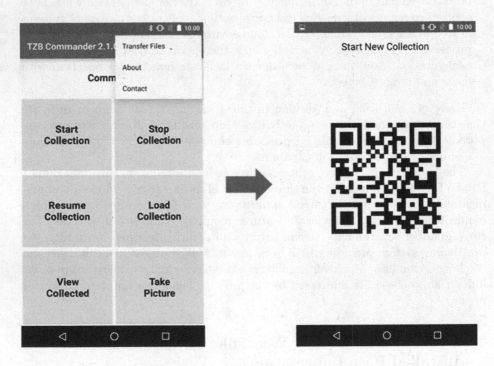

Fig. 1. App providing QR commands.

Utilizing smart watches fosters an almost hand-free operation while using smart phones or tablets helps to reuse exiting hardware since service personnel often is already equipped with corresponding devices. Either way, a seamless transition between the device types is easily feasible.

2.1 Collecting Installed Base Information

The procedure starts either by creating a new collection or by continuing an existing collection. Here, a collection is a set of installed base items. In the case that an existing collection is used, the user can either decide to resume the procedure using the last collection or to select and load one of the previously stored collections. The application also stores the corresponding location information of the collection as well as the included items. Figure 2 presents the general procedure.

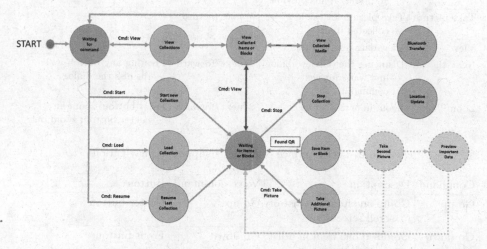

Fig. 2. Procedure to collect installed base information.

We tried to foster an almost hand-free solution in our approach. Besides, using QR codes for commands, we utilized them for the identification of industrial devices. The collection of industrial devices is done by scanning QR codes attached to them. Here, the smart glasses scans the environment and automatically recognizes QR codes. Therefore, no user interaction is needed. Once a QR code has been detected by the device, it parses the information included in the code and creates an installed base element. The type of the identified element can be either an item or a block depending on the identified information regarding the serial number of the industrial device. In case that the application was able to identify a serial number within the scanned element, it is typed as an item. Otherwise it is typed as a block that have to be followed up in the back office. Scanning already collected items or blocks are raising a message informing the user that the element already exists. Should GPS signal be available, an approximate location will be added to the collected item or block.

We defined a set of *commands* that represent a particular action but can be started in a different way, e.g. by pressing a button, voice control, or scanning a QR code to enable different interaction styles. Table 1 provides an overview of the commands used in our approach. Additionally, we introduced some commands to

Table 1. Commands related to installed base data collection

Command	Description	Voice command	Button
Start	Start new collection	1	
Close/stop	Stop collecting items and close collection	2/stop	
Resume	Reload last collection to continue work	3	
Load	Select and load an existing collection. Adding additional items possible	4	
Take picture	Take picture for the last collected item	5/take picture	-
View	View data and pictures	6	
Next	Dismisses the preview dialog and waits for next command	7/next/forward	Pressing any button will dismiss the dialog
Zoom	Zoom in or zoom out	8/next/forward	Front button: zoom in; center button: zoom out

Table 2. User interface commands supporting navigation

Command	Description	Voice command	Button
Go up	Go up one item in a list or scroll screen up	Go up	Center button
Go down	Go down one item in a list or scroll down	Go down	Front button
Go back	Go back to previous screen	Go back	Long pressing rear button
Select	Select items/press buttons	Select	Read button

support the navigation within the application, e.g., to navigate between different items in a list or screens (see Table 2 for details).

2.2 Commands

As already mentioned, our approach utilizes multiple interaction styles. Therefore, we used the concept of *commands*. A command executes a particular action. However, it can be started using in a different way, e.g., by pressing a button, voice operation, or scanning a QR code.

– Start
  The *start* command is used to create new collections. The collection is automatically created using the system's time and date. When the command is accepted a message notifies the user that he is ready to collect elements.

- View

  This command allows the user to see the already created collections. Afterwards, the user can select one of the available collections and use it to collect further elements.
- Resume

  The *resume* command loads the last collection allowing the user to continue working using the last collection. Afterwards, he can add elements to the collection.
- Load

  This command enables the user to access any collection previously stored on the device by selecting it from a list. Thereafter, he can add elements to this collection.
- Take picture

  This command adds an additional picture to the last collected element. It gives a 5 s count down before taking the picture.
- View

  The *view* command shows collected elements or pictures depending on the application mode.
- Next

  This command dismisses the preview dialog and waits for next command.
- Zoom

  The *zoom* command enables zooming (in- and out).
- Stop

  The *stop* command tells the application that the user is done with a collection and that he wants to exit the collecting mode. When the command is accepted the user will return to the standby mode (*waiting for command*).
- Navigation Commands

  Finally, we defined a set of commands that will help the user to navigate within the lists or screens. They enable the user to go up/down an item in a list or switch between different application's screens, or to select an element.

3   Conclusion

In this paper, we have presented an approach that combines different interaction styles to improve the collection of installed base information. The proposed approach utilizes existing hardware UI elements, voice commands, and QR codes to start actions. The different interaction styles support the process of collecting installed base information in various industrial environments taking into account corresponding restrictions. These restrictions can limit the usage of existing user interface elements, such as hardware buttons due to regulations that direct wearing safety gloves or the utilization of voice commands due to a high level of noise in an industrial plant.

Acknowledgments. This research was supported by the German Federal Ministry of Education and Research (BMBF) under grant number 16KIS0244. The responsibility for this publication lies with the authors.

References

1. Borchers, H.W., Karandikar, H.: A data warehouse approach for estimating and characterizing the installed base of industrial products. In: 2006 International Conference on Service Systems and Service Management (ICSSSM 2006), Troyes, France, October 2006. IEEE (2006)
2. Henderson, S., Feiner, S.: Exploring the benefits of augmented reality documentation for maintenance and repair. IEEE Trans. Vis. Comput. Graph. **17**(10) 1355–1368
3. Naya, F., Ohmura, R., Takayanagi, F., Noma, H., Kogure, K.: Workers' routine activity recognition using body movement and location information. In: 10th IEEE International Symposium on Wearable Computers (ISWC 2006), Montreux, Switzerland, October 2006. IEEE (2006)
4. Oliva, R., Kallenberg, R.: Managing the transition from products to services. Int. J. Service Industry Management **14**(2), 160–172 (2003)
5. Roggen, D., Tröster, G., Lukowicz, P., Ferscha, A., Millan, D.R.J., Chavarrigiara, R.: Opportunistic human activity and context recognition. IEEE Comput. **46**(2) 36–45
6. Stich, C.M., Petersen, H.: ServIS managing the installed base. ABB Research Center Germany - Annual Report, ABB (2007)

Mobile Web and Applications

Shopping Furniture and Appliances Using FAV Mobile Application

Samia Loucif$^{(\boxtimes)}$, Dena Ahmed, Reem Salem, and Nasra Ali

Software Engineering Department,
ALHOSN University, Po. Box: 38772, Abu Dhabi, UAE
{s.loucif,d.ahmed}@alhosnu.ae,
{rsmohammed01,naobaid01}@students.alhosnu.ae

Abstract. Smartphones are becoming an essential tool in our daily life. Numerous mobile applications have been developed to make people life easier. In the field of shopping, for instance, choosing the right piece of furniture that fits in a room or even matches the other existing furniture is a tedious task. Therefore, there is a need for an application that helps users to make the right decision before purchasing items, especially when some stores do not have refund, return, or exchange policy. This paper proposes a Furniture and Appliances Virtualizer mobile application that uses the augmented reality technology. With this application, users can visualize furniture items and electrical appliances, changing their attributes, their location to see how they look like in a particular location. The application allows users to visualize more than five items at the same time with a single mobile device, share the captured picture, order furniture and electrical appliances, locate the nearest store branch. A maximum of five target markers is used for any number of items to visualize.

Keywords: Furniture virtualizer · Augmented reality · 3D modelling

1 Introduction

Smartphones are multicore systems, equipped with advanced computing features, sensors, and wireless Internet connectivity [12]. The most popular smartphone devices are Samsung and IPhone. Furthermore, Android is the most dominant operating system in the mobile market [2, 10], and this is due to the fact that Android is an open source operating system compared to iOS. Smartphones are becoming an essential tool in our daily life. This has resulted in the emergence of numerous mobile applications targeting almost all fields and sectors such as banking, education, entertainments, health care, social media, shopping, and much more [5, 6].

Augmented Reality (AR) is an old technology used in the past but its application was very limited. Now with the advent of smartphones, several applications using AR have emerged. AR can be defined as a technology that adds the virtual content to the reality around us [8]. Depending on the method used to connect the three-Dimensional (3D) objects to the real physical world, several methods are possible [11]. The most popular AR methods are marker and marker-less tracking. Marker tracking uses a physical object such as an image target that the system's AR camera is trained to track. When the

© Springer International Publishing Switzerland 2016
M. Younas et al. (Eds.): MobiWIS 2016, LNCS 9847, pp. 323–333, 2016.
DOI: 10.1007/978-3-319-44215-0_27

image target is recognized by the AR application's camera, an action will take place; such as displaying 3D object on top of that image target. Markerless tracking can be implemented by user defined locations. Instead of using an image target, markerless tracking lets users choosing any area from the world around them and then the application augments and displays the required 3D object on that specified area. Markerless tracking is much more versatile, but also less reliable than marker tracking.

Shopping is a necessity in our life. A recent study conducted in USA on purchasing furniture [13] has shown that most people who participated in the survey purchase furniture because they need it. Moreover, only thirty percent of respondents like replacing some of their furniture frequently. Hence, people need to take the right decision before purchasing furniture or electrical appliances, especially when furniture or electrical appliance stores have a no return, refund, or exchange policy. In this paper, we propose an AR-based mobile application: Furniture & Appliances Virtualizer (FAV for short) that serves as an important tool to assist customers to make the right decision when purchasing items.

The remainder of the paper is organized as follows. Section 2 discusses related research work. Section 3 introduces the proposed application with its architecture, database system, functions and features, and an illustrative example using FAV. Finally, Sect. 4 concludes this paper.

2   Related Work

As mentioned earlier, numerous mobile applications have been developed in various fields. Very few furniture or appliances stores have developed their own AR mobile applications. Below is a summary of these applications.

Augment [1] is an AR application created by the company Augment. This application allows customers to have custom 3D models specially designed for their industry's purpose. This includes furniture items virtualization, visualizing real-estate architectural models, grocery merchandises for planning the structure of a supermarket by visualizing 3D objects of merchandise before actually placing them.

IKEA Catalogue [7] is an AR mobile application from IKEA, the world's largest furniture store. It offers users several services for browsing IKEA catalogue. With AR, the application gives users the ability to view how a piece of furniture will look like in their homes using a smartphone or a tablet. They can either view the item with or without the printed IKEA catalogue as an image target. Also, users can rotate the item to view it from different angles, take a picture of the 3D object shown in a selected location and save it in their device gallery.

MEview3D [9] is another AR mobile application from Mitsubishi Electric Corporation. It enables users to view an electrical appliance in a selected location at home before purchasing it. The MEView3D application has most of the features found in IKEA Catalogue. But in addition to that, it shows the 3D object with its actual size, which is not the case of IKEA Catalogue.

Direct Furnishing Supplies Sofa and Room Planner (DFSS & RP) [3] is an application that features AR for rendering furniture items and products. This application shares similar features with the applications presented earlier. Similar to Augment, DFS Sofa and Room Planner provides users the ability to see more than one 3D object at the same time and gives users the choice of either using image targets or not at all. In addition, with this application user can find and contact their nearest store. Also, it allows users to take pictures of the room showing 3D objects, and to share them with people from the application.

Dare Gallery [4] is provided by a furniture store in Australia. Users can choose the furniture item, take a picture of their room, and then add the 3D model on the picture. They can share the pictures taken with other people directly from the application.

Although all these applications have several nice features, they still miss interesting ones. Except from the DFSS & RP application, in all other applications, the user cannot view multiple items simultaneously. This can be difficult for users who want to see how different items will look like together in a room. The Dare Gallery application seems to offer less features and services compared to the other applications. The tracking of the 3D models is not done live from the camera. Instead, users have to take a picture of the room, and then view the 3D model from the picture. This limits the experience of users, since they cannot see the 3D model live from the camera in front of them. In addition, users cannot view the 3D model from different angles.

Moreover, IKEA Catalogue, Augment, and MEview3D do not provide the ability to share pictures taken for the 3D objects directly from the application. This means users have to exit the application, and open the gallery from which they can share pictures. More importantly, all the aforementioned applications do not support the feature of ordering items directly from the application. This feature could save users time and effort.

This present paper proposes FAV, a mobile application that assists users in making decisions before purchasing any furniture item or electrical appliance. This application helps users to visualize furniture and electrical appliances in any location they want without having to physically place the items there. Users can visualize up to five items at the same time with a single smart device. They can take picture of the items visualized, share, and place order through the application. More details are found in the following section.

3 The Proposed Application- FAV

FAV is based on the AR technology and runs on smart devices (phone/tablet) that operate the Honeycomb version of Android (3.1) or higher. It helps users to visualize furniture items or electrical appliances in a desired location by displaying 3D objects of these items. By simply pointing the smart phone's camera to a special printed image to be tracked, FAV recognizes the image tracked and renders a 3D model of the selected object to be viewed. Users visualize the exact size of the real product, decide upon the best color that matches the other pieces of furniture in the room, see the 3D items from different angles, order the items from their selected stores, display history of ordered products and locate the nearest store branch.

3.1 FAV Architecture

The architecture of the proposed application is shown in Fig. 1. It adopts the client-server three tier architecture: presentation, business logic, and data layers. The presentation layer contains the set of interfaces through which customers can perform several tasks such as browse items' categories, view 3D objects of the required furniture or electrical appliance, capture 3D objects, and other functions detailed later. The business logic layer has the Java code (Android) that interacts with the XML layouts to display and get data to and from users. It represents stores' business rules and FAV system's logical constraints. In addition, the data layer contains the entire users, products, and customers' orders database and interacts with business logic layer to retrieve/store data from/and to the database. The database server has all of the PHP files that allow the application to fetch and alter the data in the database. The FAV database consists of the entities: User, Category, Product, Branch, Order, 3DObject, ImageTarget, Texture, and Material. The User entity is added to enable users to register, login/logout, change the password to secure the ordering and purchasing operations, edit profile, receive purchase receipts by email, contact the store or send feedback, have his own log of orders that he can actually refer to anytime. Also, users' information can be used by stores to inform them in case of sales promotions. Additionally, FAV uses directories to store the 3D objects of the products. These directories are resource folders of the 3D objects stored in users' mobile devices.

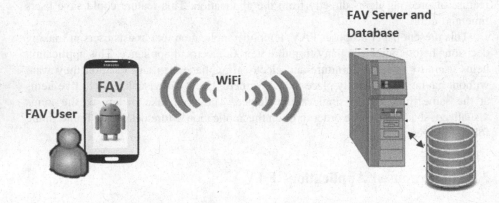

Fig. 1. FAV architecture

3.2 FAV Features

The following summarizes the FAV functions:

1. Register/Login/Logout: users register, login, or logout from the FAV application. Also, FAV permits users to change their passwords if they were previously registered in the system, or reset the password in case it is forgotten.
2. Browse items' categories: users browse the items' categories, furniture and electrical appliances.

3. Visualize 3D objects: users view 3D object(s} of the furniture item(s)/electrical appliance(s) using the application's AR camera.
4. Change attributes of 3D objects: users change the attributes of the viewed 3D object, such as color.
5. Capture 3D objects: users capture a picture of the 3D object(s) and save the captured picture in the device gallery. In addition, users can share these pictures directly from FAV application using any photo sharing application installed on the mobile device.
6. Order products: users order selected item (s) directly from FAV application. The order can be using credit card or cash payment method. In the latter case, the user selects the nearest store branch to collect the purchased items.
7. Show history of ordered items: users can access to the list of all the items they purchased with all details.
8. Locate Nearest Store Branch: this assists users in utilizing the GPS built into the mobile device to find the nearest store branch to their location.

Once the user login, s/he can then browse items' categories. There are two main categories of FAV products: furniture and electrical appliances. The user can browse products to know more about their detailed information such as products' name, quantity, height, width, weight, price, etc. The user can view the categories of products by selecting the category then the product(s) of that category. The user then can view 3D object for any selected product(s) by projecting it (them) on the image target. The user can change the color, location, viewing from different angles. The user can then order any product(s) from that list by adding it (them) to the cart. Two options are possible for the payment: cash or credit card. In case the payment method is cash, the user can select the closest store branch using the GPS built into the mobile device and a maximum of three days is given to the customer to collect the ordered item (s); here three days are seen reasonable time otherwise, the purchase order will be cancelled. In both cases, the user receives the order/receipt by email with all the details (products, quantity, price, total, etc.). The user can access to the history of all orders made in the past and can save them.

FAV is not only an important tool for customers by helping them in making decisions in purchasing furniture and appliances, but it is an important application for furniture and electrical appliances stores as well. FAV provides an engaging, useful, and interactive environment for customers and concerned stores. In addition, FAV can boost sales and marketing for furniture and electrical appliances stores since it can attract a large number of potential users and customers. Moreover, FAV architecture is flexible to deal with many stores, because its architecture does not enforce stores' systems to apply dramatic changes in order to use FAV mobile application. The only changes will be within the database of the FAV system, which is a huge advantage for many stores that want to escape system configuration problems. The benefits of FAV are summarized as follows:

- Help users (customers) to visualize products in a given place in a room.
- Give customers the opportunity to experiment with products before buying them.
- Enhance customers' creativity of home decoration.
- Reduce the risk customers buy inappropriate products.

- Reduce the risk customers return back purchased products.
- Reduce the risk customers lose money.
- Save time and effort for customers to visit stores.
- Increase the communication and collaboration between customers and stores.
- Boost stores' sales and marketing.

As said beforehand, FAV allows users to visualize up to five items simultaneously with a single mobile device. This allows users to experiment with the products and use their imagination to create different decorating styles and designs. Other applications, such as IKEA Catalogue, only allow users to visualize one 3D item at a time. Additionally, compared to the aforementioned applications, FAV has reduced the number of image targets used to a maximum of five. With our application, users can use five image targets to visualize any large number of products they want, which will reduce the number of papers used. Other applications that use image targets such as MEview3D have a predefined image target for each type of product. This can be tedious for users since they have to print out each image target not to mention the negative effects on the environment.

3.3   An Illustrative Example

In this section an illustrative example is given to show how FAV works and the interfaces that result from user interaction with the system. Note that not all interfaces are shown here due to the space limitations.

When the user first launches the FAV app, the login screen appears. The user can then login or register in case s/he is not registered yet. In case the password is forgotten, the system takes the user to another interface to reset the password. Once the user login successfully, the home screen appears as shown in Fig. 2. There are four main options:

Fig. 2. The FAV main screen

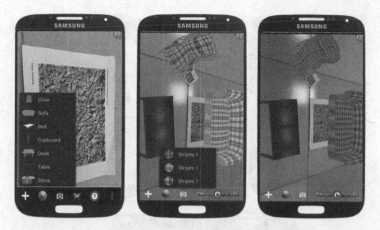

Fig. 3. Virtualize products

"Browse Items Categories", "Virtualize Products", "History of Ordered Items" and "Locate Nearest Store Branch". By pressing the "Virtualize Products" button, the user will be directed to the screen shown in Fig. 3. It is the app AR Camera and a toolbar of six icons that appears at the bottom of the screen: "+", color palette, camera, cart, help, and more options icon. With the "+" icon the user can add items to virtualize as 3D objects. When selected, a menu appears with the list of all the available products for virtualization. The user first places the image targets then adds the furniture items or electrical appliances by clicking the "+" button, then the 3D object of the corresponding item will be displayed on the screen. The user can add up to five items simultaneously on the same screen. By clicking the color palette icon, a list of available colors will appear to allow the user to select the desired color of the objects to virtualize. The camera icon is used to capture a scene with all selected 3D objects on the display, and the captured scene can be shared directly from FAV using any photo-sharing app installed on the device. The cart icon allows the user to order the selected items. The more options icon includes settings, help, edit profile, change the language (in our case Arabic and English are the two options.)

The selection of the option "Browse Items Categories" results in the screen shown in Fig. 4(a). The navigation drawer shows the list of the furniture and electrical appliances available in the store as two sub-categories. For example, if the user selects "Chairs" from the list, the screen shown in Fig. 4(b) will appear, showing all the chairs available in the store. From the action bar, the user can sort the products displayed in ascending/descending order by branch, name, or price. The search icon helps the user to search for an item by typing full word or using wildcard characters. If any of the items, result of the search, is selected then the corresponding product screen will appear, Fig. 4 (c). It shows all the details about the product including name, price, whether it is available in stock or not, available colors, etc. The user can select any color from the available colors for that product, the required quantity by pressing the button "+" or "−". If the user selects a quantity that exceeds the available quantity in the stock, the system will notify the user. When the user presses the button "Add to Cart", the item (s) will be

Fig. 4. Browse items categories

added to the cart. The user can add more items to the cart, and by pressing the button Cart found at the top of the screen, the list of all items in the cart with their respective details will be displayed in addition to the grand total shown at the bottom of the screen, Fig. 4(d).

In case the user decides to proceed to the checkout phase, a new screen appears prompting the user to choose the preferred payment method either credit card or cash. In case credit card option is selected, the user selects the type of credit card with the necessary information, and the preferred date of delivery. However, in case the cash payment method is selected, the user has to select the nearest store branch using the mobile device built-in GPS. Once the user places an order, an email will be sent to the customer with all details of the purchase done as shown in Fig. 4(e). In case the payment method is cash, an extra message is sent to the user about the selected store branch from where to pick up items, and a maximum of three days to collect the items otherwise the order will be automatically cancelled.

Additionally, the user can access to the history of all ordered items from the option given in the main menu of Fig. 2. The application displays all the orders made by the user with details as shown in Fig. 5. Selecting one of these orders, the application

Fig. 5. History of ordered items

shows all the details about the items, their prices, etc. in that particular order. Also, the user can sort the list by payment method, date, or price in ascending/descending order.

The option "Locate Nearest Store Branch" in Fig. 2 will open the Google Map app and using the mobile device built-in GPS shows the closest store branch.

FAV has many other interesting features; users can select the preferred language; the current implementation of FAV allows user to use either Arabic or English. Users can share the scenes taken with the app AR camera with people directly from FAV using any of the photo sharing app installed on the mobile device, these features are found on the settings screen, Fig. 6.

Usability is an important factor to consider when designing any interactive application, principles that supports usability have been taken into account. Our application

Fig. 6. Settings screen

is robust, it has user-friendly interfaces, multiple languages are offered to the users where they can select from the settings the preferred language (English or Arabic), the users can customize the results based on their choices.

4 Conclusion

This paper has proposed an AR mobile application to facilitate the visualization of furniture items and electrical appliances. It is an important tool to assist users to make the right decision before purchasing any furniture or electrical appliances, especially when stores do not have return, refund, or exchange of items policy. Also, this application can be used in the field of interior design improving customers' creativity in decorating homes. Unlike other applications, FAV allows users to visualize up to five different items simultaneously using one single mobile device, and using a maximum of five image targets which saves users' time and effort and protecting the environment. With FAV users can also order the items from their selected stores, display and save history of ordered products, share captured picture directly from the application using any photo sharing application installed on the mobile device, and locate nearest store branch. Last but not least, FAV architecture is flexible to deal with many stores, because its architecture does not enforce stores' systems to apply dramatic changes in order to use FAV mobile application. The only changes will be within the database of the FAV system, which is a huge advantage for many stores that want to escape system configuration problems.

References

1. AUGMENT, 30 March 2016. http://augmentedev.com/how-augmented-reality-works.php
2. Butler, M.: Android-changing the mobile landscape. Pervasive Comput. **10**(1), 4–7 (2011)
3. Direct Furnishing Supplies Sofa and Room Planner, 30 March 2016. http://www.dfs.co.uk/content/inspiration-and-help/faqsandcontactus
4. Fenech, S.: TechGuide Dare Gallery Augmented Reality App, 30 March 2016. http://www.techguide.com.au/reviews/apps/dare-gallerys-augmented-reality-app-can-visualise-furniture-in-your-home/
5. Gavalas, D., Economou, D.: Development platforms for mobile applications: status and trends. IEEE Softw. **28**(1), 77–86 (2011)
6. Holzer, A., Ondrus, J.: Trends in mobile application development. In: Hesselman, C., Giannelli, C. (eds.) Mobilware 2009 Workshops. LNICST, vol. 12, pp. 55–64. Springer, Heidelberg (2009)
7. IKEA, 30 March 2016. http://www.ikea.com/ms/en_CA/mobile/mobile_splash.html
8. Madden, L.: Professional Augmented Reality Browsers for Smartphones: Programming for Junaio, Layar and Wikitude. Wiley, Chichester (2011)
9. MEview3D, 30 March 2016. http://www.mitsubishi-aircon.ru/news/news.php?id=153
10. Mobile/Tablet Top Operating System Share Trend, 30 March 2016. https://www.netmarketshare.com/operating-system-market-share.aspx?qprid=9&qpcustomb=1
11. Mullen, T.: Prototyping Augmented Reality. Wiley, Indianapolis (2011)

12. Nick, T.: Did You Know How Many Different Kinds of Sensors Go Inside a Smartphone? 30 March 2016. http://www.phonearena.com/news/Did-you-know-how-many-different-kinds-of-sensors-go-inside-a-smartphone_id57885
13. Pander, N.: Consumer Attitudes and Buying Behavior for Home Furniture, 30 March 2016. www.ffi.msstate.edu/pdf/consumer_attitudes.pdf

A Measurement Tool to Track Drones Battery Consumption During Flights

Luis Corral[1], Ilenia Fronza[2(✉)], Nabil El Ioini[2], and Aristea Ibershimi[2]

[1] ITESM/UAQ, E. Gonzalez 500, 76130 Queretaro, Mexico
lrcorralv@itesm.mx
[2] Free University of Bolzano, Piazza Domenicani, 3, 39100 Bolzano, Italy
{ilenia.fronza,nabil.elioini,aristea.ibershimi}@unibz.it

Abstract. The autonomy of mobile systems depends greatly on the capability of the power source that supplies the necessary energy. Typically these sources are limited batteries that cannot keep up with the functionality and services that modern mobile equipment features. This situation motivates researchers and practitioners to develop strategies to promote efficient energy usage on mobile platforms. However, to reduce the energy consumption it is required to have reliable means to measure the devices behavior and its relationship to the battery discharge. This problem is relevant in platforms that depend strongly on batteries like cellphones, tablets, wearables, or drones. This paper focuses on drones, introducing a software system that acquires data during a drone mission, featuring an online battery discharge analyzer. The goal of this software is to provide a means to identify the operations that spend more energy and, as consequence, deliver the necessary information to avoid energy expensive movements and extend the battery lifetime for improved drone autonomy.

Keywords: Autonomy · Battery · Drone · Energy · Mobile

1 Introduction

Mobile computing systems had unfolded in a variety of applications that support many aspects of daily life. From smartphones and tablets to wearables and drones, the autonomy of mobile devices is of paramount importance for the accomplishment of their goals, since they are designed to perform the majority of their functions away from a power source. Moreover, the capabilities and features of the most modern mobile devices boost a high demand of power that traditional batteries cannot sustain. For example, mobile phones have vibrators, sensors and antennas that are power consuming, or drones have small prop engines or built-in video-cameras that take an important toll from the available battery. This situation triggers the need of strategies to promote efficient energy usage to reduce the power demand on mobile platforms, with the goal of guaranteeing the capacity of these devices to complete their functions properly.

The fast development and diffusion of the new generation of unmanned aerial vehicles, more popularly known as drones, has brought a number of needs and

© Springer International Publishing Switzerland 2016
M. Younas et al. (Eds.): MobiWIS 2016, LNCS 9847, pp. 334–344, 2016.
DOI: 10.1007/978-3-319-44215-0_28

opportunities for different research paths. The drone industry has been a very relevant object of study both for researchers and practitioners. In the last decade, the discussion on drones has spanned in different aspects: applications, handling, management, airworthiness, autonomy, and energy efficiency.

Although there has been extensive research about designing software for autonomous, energy-efficient mobile devices (for instance, smartphones, tablets, or wearables) [17], there is a very limited body of research or experience reports about applying the energy-aware computing approach in drone platforms. To create drones that offer an improved performance with respect to energy consumption and battery usage, there is much need of techniques that facilitate the design and development of energy aware software. However, to accomplish this goal an important requisite raises first: to suggest approaches to reduce the consumption of energy in a given target, it is of utmost importance to have the ability to understand the way in which the energy is invested and spent. To contribute to address this issue, in this paper we outline a strategy to measure the energy consumption of commercial quad drones. We developed Green Flight, a software system that provides a means to identify the behavioral patterns that spend more energy and, as consequence, supply the necessary intelligence to avoid energy expensive maneuvers. This knowledge can be of great importance for strategic actions like identifying and monitoring power-relevant characteristics of drones; propose metrics to evaluate the energy performance; and establish baselines to manage energy consumption and identify energy relevant faults.

The rest of the paper is organized as follows: Sect. 2 covers the related work on energy aware software design for non-stationary platforms; Sect. 3 shows the project environment and solution approach; Sect. 4 describes two prototypical analyses that were performed to assess the suitability of our approach, and to determine if it is worth pursuing the approach further; Sect. 5 sets directions for future work; Sect. 6 draws conclusions.

2 Related Work

2.1 Literature Review

The problem of energy-awareness in non-stationary devices has been discussed since the introduction of mobile target computers, like primitive smartphones or hand-helds [8]. The analysis of the state of the art in the field of non-stationary devices shows that the existing strategies are mostly based on common, autonomous devices such as smartphones, tablets or wearables. As battery technology and other hardware-based innovations run at a slow pace, a common approach is the design and implementation of software-based energy aware techniques [3]. These techniques include: understanding the way in which the battery is invested in the target [16,21]; strategies to save energy at operating system level, implementing extensions for economic profiles [6,20], distributing the computing power to stationary resources [7,12], and in general, trying to reduce the energy footprint of software executed away from a power source [2].

Many of these strategies have been implemented and validated in targets like smartphones and tablets [19]. Nonetheless, just like smartphones or wearables, drones have to rely on their battery capacity which represents one of the most important limitations to their operation; similarly, drones have to perform the majority of their functions far from a power source. However, this constraint becomes much more relevant as a key operative attribute is airworthiness, which includes "sufficient power to maintain movement, to implement the controls, and to operate sensors and data-feeds, for the duration of the flight" [5]. Moreover, the potential usefulness of drones in many mission critical applications (such as emergency relief, surveillance, defense) is prevented by the battery life constrain. This limitation is increased in those cases where power resources are needed not only to fly successfully, but also to power on-board facilities such as a camera.

2.2 Operative Target

Drones are a particular mobile target. Unlike smartphones or tablets, that are commonly operated by an operating system (e.g., Android, iOS, etc.) the operative platform of a drone is embedded software or a software stack that can be accessed through a Software Development Kit (SDK). Moreover, the interaction between the user and the target varies in many ways from smartphones and similar devices. Due to their functional nature, drones do not have a screen, input/output means or buttons or keyboard. Instead, as aircraft that have no on-board, human pilot, *remote pilot* is the term that is commonly used to refer the person handling the device is at a certain distance, but in full control of the drone using a radio-control or mobile device.

Small commercial drones are subject to a range of limitations in relation to load capacity, flight duration (maximum autonomy of about 15 min), power supply, and other technical features. Drones share with other mobile targets the fact of being energetically limited, although from the software point of view they are simpler. However, the limitations of energy supply and the high power consumption of the drone poses important constraints to the duration of a mission. The power demand of drones is satisfied commonly using a battery, but the increasing intake of power and high requirement of autonomy on drones increases the need of a strategy towards efficient power consumption. In addition, the operational standard of drones should be aware of the most important quality requirement of this target: airworthiness. This term is used to refer to an aircraft's suitability for safe flight. A drone is considered airworthy if it is able to take off, conduct its mission and land safely [9]. As an unyielding requirement to perform its function, energy efficiency techniques must support airworthiness.

3 A Tool to Measure Drones Energy Consumption

3.1 Proposed Architecture

The objective of this work is to design and build a software-driven solution that contributes to improve the energy consumption of drones by establishing a tool

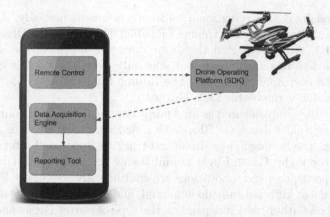

Fig. 1. Proposed architecture.

to measure the energy consumption of commercial quad drones. The software system shall monitor the action of the drone, measure the consumed battery and the overall flight time while the drone is flying, deliver data about how the drone is consuming the energy, and permit future analysis for the user. To this end, we developed a software system called *Green Flight*, composed by the following architecture (Fig. 1):

- an API-accesible operative software of the drone;
- a software enabled remote controller that allows to pilot a commercial small drone;
- a software engine that tracks the behavior of the drone to characterize the energy consumed by the execution of each maneuver during the flight, based on the readings of the battery level of the drone;
- a reporting tool that can expose energy-oriented suggestions to operate the drone, based on the collected data.

To control the drone, the application shall allow to pilot the drone, with the usual commands: taking off and landing; rolling left, right, forward and backward; and yawing, that is, rotating either to the left or to the right side. Then, to characterize the power consumption of the device, the software system shall measure with high granularity the power spent by the drone while it is flying. Afterwards, the measurement engine shall analyze the acquired data, to map them to the actions performed by the drone. Finally, the analyzed data shall activate the suggestions mode (i.e., a battery saving mode) once a critical battery level is reached. This mode shall consist of suggestions for the user in order to take fullest advantage of the remaining flight time.

3.2   Selected Target

The drone used for implementing Green Flight and collecting data throughout the necessary experiments is a Parrot Rolling Spider[1]. This drone is designed

---

[1] http://www.parrot.com/usa/products/rolling-spider.

and commercialized for recreational and entertainment use only. The Rolling
Spider is controlled by a smartphone or tablet that supports Bluetooth Low
Energy (BLE). This means that the drone does not appear in the usual list of
Bluetooth devices in smartphones, but it is only visible and able to connect to
it through the host application [15]. The Rolling Spider weights 55 g, and relies
on a 550 mA, 1.1 V removable LiPo battery.

Green Flight is implemented as an Android application which connects to the
Parrot Rolling Spider drone via Bluetooth Low Energy (BLE). This application
allows piloting the Rolling Spider drone and tracking the drone battery consumption during the flight; Green Flight is built using the Parrot ARSDK3[2]. As the
topic is still pretty new and innovations are continuously added, the Parrots software development kit is not fully documented, and only some sample applications
are provided on Github, which depend on the type of Parrot Drone and OS of the
piloting device. Since the target is a Parrot Rolling Spider drone, Green Flight
was built by customizing one of the sample Android applications that let pilot the
device. These customizations measure the energy spent by the drone and associate
this consumption to the maneuver performed and to its duration.

In order to improve accuracy, during the flight, whenever a button (which
commands a maneuver) is pressed, the event is logged together with the current
battery state and current timestamp. The same happens even when the button
is released, which means that the maneuver is completed. Figure 2 shows an
example of the log file. The first line says that the maneuver performed is Roll
Right (RR), and that it started at 14:12:301 with battery level of the drone
of 98 %. The second line instead tells us that the current maneuver finished at
14:12:356, therefore it lasted 1 second and 55 milliseconds, with a battery level
of 97 %, therefore it consumed 1 % of battery.

```
1 RR    P 98% 14:12:301
2 RR    R 97% 14:13:356
```

Fig. 2. Two example lines of a log file.

4   Sample Applications

To assess the suitability of our approach, we have performed two prototypical
analyses intended to determine if it is worth pursuing the approach further. To
this end, we collected data about the energy consumption (indoor). All the performed experiments started with fully-charged battery and went on doing combined movements (i.e., up - down, back - forward, roll left - roll right, yaw left -
yaw right) until battery percentage went down to 3 % (time when the drone automatically shuts down). Data were collected as follows: action (pressed/released),
battery percentage (for action pressed and released) and time (for action pressed
and released). In total, energy consumption was measured 75 times for each
maneuver.

---

[2] https://github.com/Parrot-Developers/ARSDKBuildUtils.

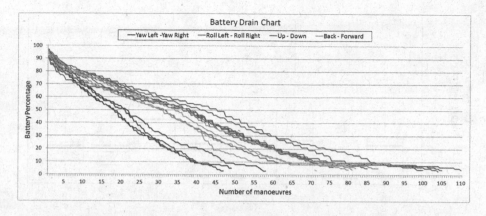

Fig. 3. Data collected allow to visualize the battery drain.

4.1 Battery Drain

Battery drain can be analysed using data collected by our measurement tool. The SDK does not expose any class or API to have an accurate knowledge about the distance when the drone moves; therefore, each manoeuvre range was performed for 1.5 m. This means that in the example shown in Fig. 2, the energy consumption of manoeuvre results to be 0.66 %, which is the battery consumed for rolling 1 m to the right. For example, Fig. 3 shows that, during experiments, battery was draining faster for some combinations of movements, such as yaw left - yaw right. Moreover, battery seems to be consumed faster after it reaches a level of about 40 %.

A graphic like Fig. 3 is built on top of direct detection of drone movements, and may help to create a model able to provide a characterization of how a drone invests its energy resources and therefore, how the user should expect the battery discharge cycle based on the actual operation of the unit. Green Flight surveys the status of the system, and illustrates the impact that each movement has in the overall power consumption of the drone. Its software-based approach fosters a less hardware-dependent analysis, and its maneuver-based strategy makes it extendible to diverse product families, since most common small commercial drones can perform the same operations than the Parrot. However, it will be necessary as well to implement and test the Green Flight architecture in drones of different models, to ensure that similar results are obtained in different product lines.

4.2 Characterizing Each Type of Maneuver in Terms of Energy Consumption

While making use of a smartphone, there are certain activities that consume more energy than others: Wi-fi and Bluetooth connection, screen brightness, Global Positioning System (GPS) and 3G are included among the most common battery drainer actions [14]. In order to optimize battery consumption,

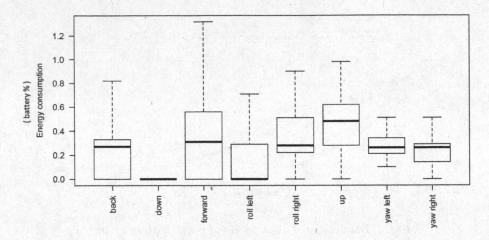

Fig. 4. Energy consumption of each maneuver.

many manufactures provide the so-called *power-saving mode* which manages for the user the most power-exhausting features of the smartphone [14]. Normally, this mode is activated when the battery level drops to 20–30%. Essentially, this mode turns off almost all the features except the necessary ones for making and receiving phone calls and sending text messages. For drones, there is no such knowledge. Therefore, the identification of the most energy consuming drone maneuvers can represent a first step towards drone energy consumption optimization. Our measurement tool provides a means to achieve this goal.

Figure 4 compares the energy consumption of all the maneuvers. The maneuver "down" has almost no cost from the energy consumption point of view. The same holds for the maneuver "roll left". This means that these maneuvers will be always possible for the user, even with a very low battery level. Therefore, we excluded them form the following analysis.

The normality of the obtained values of battery consumption was tested for the 6 types of maneuvers using the Shapiro-Wilk normality test [18], which is recommended as the best choice for testing the normality of data [11]. The null hypothesis for this test is that data are normally distributed; if the chosen alpha level is 0.05 and the p-value is less than 0.05, then the null hypothesis that the data are normally distributed is rejected. In all cases, results allow us to reject the null hypothesis that our samples come from a population which has a normal distribution (i.e., all the p-values are less than 0.05).

Based on these results, we used the Mann-Whitney-Wilcoxon test [13], which does not assume the population distribution to follow a normal distribution. The null hypothesis is that energy consumption of maneuver i and energy consumption of maneuver j are identical populations, where i and j are 2 of the 6 analysed maneuvers. When p-value is lower than 0.05 the null hypothesis can be rejected, at 0.05 significance level. P-values were higher that 0.05, therefore we could not reject the null hypothesis, when running the test for the following maneuvers:

– yaw right and yaw left;
– yaw left and roll right;
– yaw left and back;
– yaw left and forward;
– roll right and forward.

Therefore, from the energy consumption point of view, the following clusters of maneuvers are revealed by this sample application of our approach: (1) down and roll left, having almost no cost from the energy consumption point of view; (2) up, the most expensive maneuver; and (3) back, forward, roll right, yaw left and yaw right, which are identical maneuvers from the energy consumption point of view.

With this knowledge, we can envision the development of a real-time suggestion mode. As discussed, with drones we do not have economic modes like smartphones, and on top of that, it is difficult to choose what functions to disable, since many of them contribute to the goal of airworthiness. Therefore, as a first approach towards drone energy consumption optimization, we can suggest a *suggestion mode*, based on our previous identification of the most energy consuming maneuvers. The suggestion mode shall works as follows:

– the suggestions mode starts after detecting a critical battery level, which can be determined by analysing battery drain charts (such as Fig. 3);
– the software provides suggestions based on flights analysis (Fig. 5), that is, it instructs the remote pilot what maneuvers to do, avoiding those that resulted as being energy expensive from the previous analysis;
– by reaching a given very low battery level, the suggestion mode may directly send a command to the drone to perform and immediate landing.

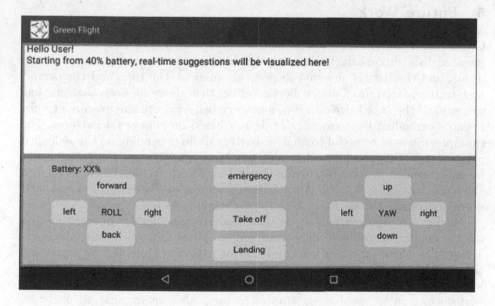

Fig. 5. Possible UI of an application with suggestions.

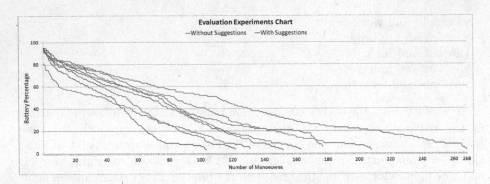

Fig. 6. Battery drain of the experiments with and without the suggestion mode.

To have better notion of the suggestion mode, we created a prototype that can be used to understand if the suggestions mode approach is useful for diverse drone models. We implemented an outline of the tool and we were able to note a slight but noticeable improvement, for the same flight mission, in the energy performance of the Parrot drone (Fig. 6). However, implementing the same suggestions mode with a different drone model (Bebop), we were not able to notice any improvement. This allows us to conclude that the suggestions have to be built in model by model basis, as different maneuvers may have different effects depending on the drone. For this reason, it is necessary to conduct additional experiments with a variety of drone models to obtain patterns and suggestions that can be generalized.

5   Future Work

Green Flight contributes towards a better understanding on how the energy is invested in a drone target, exposing a relationship between operation of the drone, and the battery invested during the mission. The tool, and the overall architecture, facilitates a data collection effort that allows for deep analysis that can expand the knowledge on drone's battery behavior, opening research tracks towards extending the autonomy of drones based on behavioral patterns. For example, it would be useful to analyse battery drain depending on the sequence of movements that precede a particular one. Moreover, different algorithms could be experimented in order to provide Green Flight with the possibility to predict the next movement [1,4,10]. Also, furhter experiments could inspect how well users understand the GUI and if users find suggestions to be useful.

Having a tool suggestions mode that analyzes and suggests in real time the most economic operations, will permit remote pilots to perform only the operations that allow to extend the duration of missions. Moreover by extending the capacity of Green Flight, we may have the ability to learn data of different kinds (height, speed, etc.) in a way that we can also characterize the energy performance in terms of these kind of factors. Also, smart analysis could be implemented based on user's actual goal, in order to provide suggestions that allow achieving a goal more efficiently. Finally, deeper analysis can also shed light on the energy impact of combinations of maneuvers.

6   Conclusions

In this paper we show the first software-based approach towards the reduction of energy consumption of commercial quad drones: Green Flight, an Android application built on top of the Parrot ARSDK3. To assess the suitability of our approach, we describe a prototypical analysis intended to determine if it is worth pursuing the approach further.

An important constraint in the implementation of this project was imposed by the software development kit of the Parrot platform, since it is not well documented, and it does not allow APIs to access to the drone hardware. Without these constraints, we could have been able to implement a more accurate solution. This is an open issue that can be solved by new releases of the SDK, and by research works that follow up the present one. Additionally, a clear next step in this research roadmap is to utilize the data collected and analyzed by Green Flight to create tools that leverage this knowledge to suggest economic modes to be automatically inducted to the drone.

With the results obtained, we can conclude that having a system that collects in real time relevant data from the drones, helps to identify the behavioral patterns that spend more energy. As consequence, the software system can supply the necessary intelligence to avoid energy expensive maneuvers, leading to an operation-oriented efficient energy consumption. By having energy-aware drone operating software, pilots could extend the duration of missions, be aware of risky conditions created by the lack of battery, and promote the use of drones on critical missions or in scenarios that demand extended autonomy and drone dependability.

References

1. Abrahamsson, P., Fronza, I., Moser, R., Vlasenko, J., Pedrycz, W.: Predicting development effort from user stories, pp. 400–403 (2011)
2. Balan, R.K., Satyanarayanan, M., Park, S.Y., Okoshi, T.: Tactics-based remote execution for mobile computing. In: Proceedings of the 1st International Conference on Mobile Systems, Applications and Services, pp. 273–286. ACM (2003)
3. Bornholt, J., Mytkowicz, T., McKinley, K.S.: The model is not enough: understanding energy consumption in mobile devices. Power (Watts) 1(2), 3 (2012)
4. Cao, L.: Support vector machines experts for time series forecasting. Neurocomputing 51, 321–339 (2003)
5. Clarke, R.: Understanding the drone epidemic. Comput. Law Secur. Rev. 30(3), 230–246 (2014)
6. Corral, L., Georgiev, A., Janes, A., Kofler, S.: Energy-aware performance evaluation of Android custom kernels. In: IEEE/ACM 4th International Workshop on Green and Sustainable Software (GREENS), pp. 1–7, May 2015

7. Corral, L., Georgiev, A.B., Sillitti, A., Succi, G.: Method reallocation to reduce energy consumption: an implementation in Android OS. In: Proceedings of the 29th Annual ACM Symposium on Applied Computing, SAC 2014, pp. 1213–1218. ACM (2014)

8. Flinn, J., Satyanarayanan, M.: Energy-aware adaptation for mobile applications. SIGOPS Oper. Syst. Rev. **33**(5), 48–63 (1999)

9. Fronza, I., El Ioini, N., Corral, L.: The Future of Energy-Aware Software: The Case of Drones. Cutter Information Corp., Arlington (2015)

10. Fronza, I., Sillilti, A., Sued, G., Vlasenko, J.: Failure prediction based on log files using the Cox proportional hazard model, pp. 456–461 (2011)

11. Hj, T.: Testing for Normality. Marcel Dekker, New York (2002)

12. Lewis, G., Lago, P.: Architectural tactics for cyber-foraging: results of a systematic literature review. J. Syst. Softw. **107**, 158–186 (2015)

13. Mann, H.B., Whitney, D.R.: On a test of whether one of two random variables is statistically larger than the other. Ann. Math. Statist. **18**(1), 50–60 (1947)

14. Martin, J.: How to improve smartphone battery life: 10 tips and tricks to make your phone's battery last longer - is facebook to blame for poor battery life? October 2015. http://www.pcadvisor.co.uk/how-to/mobile-phone/how-improve-smartphone-battery-life-facebook-3284240/. Accessed 25 Feb 2016

15. Parrot Rolling Spider: Rolling spider user guide UK (2015). www.parrot.com/support/parrot-rolling-spider/

16. Pathak, A., Hu, Y.C., Zhang, M.: Where is the energy spent inside my app?: fine grained energy accounting on smartphones with eprof. In: Proceedings of the 7th ACM European Conference on Computer Systems, EuroSys 2012, pp. 29–42. ACM (2012)

17. Procaccianti, G., Lago, P., Vetro, A., Fernández, D.M., Wieringa, R.: The green lab: experimentation in software energy efficiency. In: Proceedings of the 37th International Conference on Software Engineering, vol. 2, pp. 941–942. IEEE Press (2015)

18. Shapiro, S.S., Wilk, M.B.: An analysis of variance test for normality (complete samples). Biometrika **3**(52), 591–611 (1965)

19. Vallina-Rodriguez, N., Crowcroft, J.: Energy management techniques in modern mobile handsets. IEEE Commun. Surv. Tutorials **15**(1), 179–198 (2013)

20. Yoon, C., Kim, D., Jung, W., Kang, C., Cha, H.: Appscope: application energy metering framework for android smartphones using kernel activity monitoring. In: Proceedings of the 2012 USENIX Conference on Annual Technical Conference, USENIX ATC 2012, p. 36. USENIX Association (2012)

21. Zhang, L., Tiwana, B., Qian, Z., Wang, Z., Dick, R.P., Mao, Z.M., Yang, L.: Accurate online power estimation and automatic battery behavior based power model generation for smartphones. In: Proceedings of the Eighth IEEE/ACM/IFIP International Conference on Hardware/Software Codesign and System Synthesis, CODES/ISSS 2010, pp. 105–114. ACM (2010)

Speed Up Native Mobile Form Development

Armin Engesser[1]([✉]), Mike Groezinger[2], and Ralf Schimkat[1]

[1] HTWG Konstanz, Brauneggerstr. 55, Konstanz 78462, Germany
armin.engesser@htwg-konstanz.de
[2] Siobra GbR, Kaltbrunner Str. 24, Allensbach 78476, Germany

Abstract. The development of native user interface components is a time consuming and repetitive process, especially for quite simple components like text fields in a form. In order to save time during development an approach is presented in this paper, abstracting the description of the elements into separate files independent from the source code. With aspects from generative and model-driven approaches this leads to simple reusable UI components without the need of deep knowledge in native programming languages.

1 Introduction

Native mobile apps have been developed for use on a particular mobile platform in the associated development language. In comparison to that cross-platform frameworks like PhoneGap [9] or Cordova[1] mostly make use of a WebView to present the content to the user. This obviously leads to multiple implementations of the same task if more than one mobile platform should be supported, which means the required development time for mobile apps increases analogous to the number of platforms, followed by higher development costs. About 56 % of the development and deployment processes for a mobile app take at least seven months while the average costs are about 270 000 $ [7].

To address this issue a lot of effort has already been put into approaches and development paradigms which reduce code replication. One of these is called *Generative Development* (GD) which allows automatic creation of software depending on configuration knowledge [4]. Another paradigm is the so called *Model-Driven Engineering* (MDE) which is used since the early 1980's and where software is generated from an abstract model description [12].

In the following a short overview about related work is given before the typical complexities in mobile application projects are discussed. Then it is shown how these techniques are used to produce mobile user interfaces (UI) – more concrete, mobile forms for collecting data, similar to the one shown in Fig. 1 – in a fraction of the time needed otherwise. After that the method and the results of a small evaluation are presented. The main purpose of this work was to develop a solution allowing a software developer to save time by abstracting the repetitive process of UI design and implementation into a separate library leading to a significant

---

[1] https://cordova.apache.org.

© Springer International Publishing Switzerland 2016
M. Younas et al. (Eds.): MobiWIS 2016, LNCS 9847, pp. 345–352, 2016.
DOI: 10.1007/978-3-319-44215-0_29

simplification of the development itself. Another important aspect was to make the form description part of the solution platform independent while the results are still native UI elements.

2   Related Work

This work is related to approaches from the model-driven software engineering and generative programming.

Botterweck [3] describes how multiple UI's for desktop applications, websites and mobile devices can be transformed from one abstract UI model through concrete, platform-specific UI models. He shows that model-driven approaches can be a solution for the problem of redundancy and variance of multiple interfaces with the same functionality.

Eisenstein et al. [6] a hypothetical software with multiple device dependent UI's which point out the challenges a developer is confronted with during UI design and implementation. Even if the devices they used to show the problems are outdated nowadays, the main problems are still the same: Implementing UI's for each device type separately is repetitive, time-consuming and error-prone. Rather than developing a whole application, the presented approach integrates in other applications as a separate library focused on mobile devices.

Fig. 1. Example form

Schlee [11] described the transformation process with which dialogue based desktop UI's can be generated from an XML description using GD.

In his work Vanderdonckt [12] evaluates different principles of model-driven UI design and the methods used in general.

Using some of these techniques a couple of industrial companies (e.g. [5,8]) developed mobile apps. While they built high level applications in which they handle different forms and the outcome of these, the presented solution here can be integrated in existing apps rather addressing developers than customers. With Angular Schema Form [1] there is a solution to be used in modern web browsers. Meanwhile others (e.g. [2,9,10]) built cross-platform frameworks for the development of whole apps. Therefore they need to address a lot of issues in different contexts[2]. The presented solution however concentrates on the form aspect of an app, trying to handle this as simple and best as possible.

3 Complexities of Form Driven Mobile Applications

To show how time needed for development of mobile forms can be reduced, first the typical development process is described, second the complexities of such a development are identified and afterwards the new approach is presented.

3.1 Typical Development Cycle

There are a couple of steps required to develop a mobile app which can be seen in Fig. 2, where the steps with thick border generally require more time. First the requirements need to be specified, especially if it is a customer's order. After that the screenflow and mockups are developed and result in a prototype which then is discussed with the customer again. Following the prototype comes the actual implementation. In the implementation process the controller, the layout files and the validation code need to be adjusted before a running version could be presented to the customer. After the presentation the customer usually will provide feedback regarding the produced app or ask for changes which will lead to another round in this development cycle.

This per screen development cycle of Mockup – Implementation – Feedback is repeated as long as the developer respectively the customer is completely satisfied. Not to mention the time necessary for meetings with the customer it is fair to say that this is a tedious process.

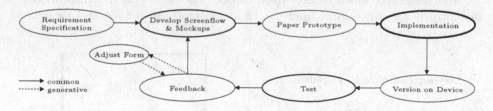

Fig. 2. Possible development cycle

3.2 Identify the Complexities

Forms on mobile devices need to appear simple in the first place even if they might be quite complex. They might consist of a mixture of different input types requiring different approaches of validation.

The complexities can be categorized into the layout, meaning where to place which field, and its styling as part of the UI design. Another aspect concerns the

---

[2] E.g. Push Notification, File Handling, etc.

validation of the data entered in the fields requiring different types of validation rules. For example, a value for a field has only to be present, but another value has to be in a specific range. Because a normal app in general has more than only one view, some navigation concept needs to be thought of. This might even include some validation before allowing a transition to be made. The last complexity is the implementation itself, so all the nicely specified elements look and behave as they are expected to.

3.3 Reducing Complexity

The number of complexities[3] is decreased through a few steps. Firstly, the number of attributes required to define a UI component like a text field is decreased to a minimum. With only three attributes ("id", "title" and "type") a usable component can be defined. This results in a default component without big customizations like adjusting colour or exact text size, but with the defined input type. But for sure there is more than simple text fields. Let's think about a field which displays some values to the user between which they have to choose, this requires only a few more attributes like it is shown in Listing 1. Afterwards it has to be initialized with a few lines of code which can be seen in Listing 2. This results in a text field with a modal view attached which is shown in Fig. 3.

The valid attribute fields are described in a simple JSON-Schema[4], which can be easily extended by custom implementations. The complete schema in its current version is available on BitBucket[5].

As the form description is completely independent from the platform itself, it can be reused without modification for the same form on another platform, making this part cross-platform available.

Another aspect which reduces the complexity is the provided domain model. It abstracts away the form from the technical platform details and therefore

Listing 1. Simple Field Definition

```
{
 "id": "status-id",
  "title": "Status",
  "type": "enum",
  "values": [
   "Pending", "Approved",
   "Rejected"
  ]
}
```

Fig. 3. Resulting modal view

---

[3] Complexity hereby means the amount of attributes, how they are nested and the amount of knowledge required to implement such a form.

[4] http://json-schema.org.

[5] https://bitbucket.org/snippets/siobra/b4gqg.

Listing 2. Integration in App

```
@InjectForm("create_project.json")
public LinearLayout linearLayout;

@Override
protected void onCreate(Bundle state) {
    ...
    FormGen formGen = new FormGen(this);
    formGen.init();
}
```

reduces the programming to the facets needed for form development. This simplifies and speeds up development. Treating the form aspects as data enables the generic handling of form processing which simplifies the change life cycle as no new app is required in case the form or data model changes.

After defining the form itself, the data entered in the fields usually need some validation. A typical approach is to retrieve the values from each separate field and manually check them. In comparison to that, this generative approach allows to define validation rules in a separate file and reference them where needed.

3.4 Generative Development

In comparison to the development cycle described in Sect. 3.1 the generative approach looks slightly different. Even if the same steps may have to be completed, not all of them need to be repeated like in the previous cycle. Because the form is independent and can be changed without touching the implementation of the mobile app, the feedback can be followed directly without the need to produce a new app version, shortening the "distance" between customer and developer. This shortened path is indicated in Fig. 2 with the dashed arrows. Obviously a later update of the form does not automatically require a new app version.

After setting up the project with the required dependencies, only the parent view has to be configured, cleaning up the native layout field almost completely. The form needs to be described in a JSON file according to the provided schema, same counts for the validation rules. Data entered in the generated form can be validated and extracted at once, querying all the fields separately is not necessary.

4   Measure the Improvement

In the following section the methods used to evaluate this solution and the improvements themselves made possible through the presented approach are shown, always with the comparison to native development in mind.

4.1   Validation of the Solution

Trying to validate the usability and especially the time-saving aspect of the approach an – admittedly small – number of test users has been asked to evaluate the solution and to provide feedback.

The Test Users for the validation have been software developers with at least basic experience in developing applications for mobile platforms, most of them with focus on the Android platform. They rated their knowledge on a scale from 1 to 10, with 10 as "most experienced". The results can be seen in Table 1.

The Test Cases the users had to complete included the project setup of an Android app, the integration of the library of the presented approach and the definition of a given form. This form contains different input types and styling challenges, with each field having a label and a placeholder, displayed in Fig. 1. The same task had then to be accomplished with a pure native approach and compared to the previous results.

Afterwards the testers were asked for feedback regarding usability and differences in their time needed for implementing the requested features.

4.2   How Much Time Could Be Saved?

The feedback of the test users was that even if the initial project setup and the first few parts of the form description took slightly longer, in the long run they saved a significant amount of development time while implementing the form. This is shown in Table 1. So it could be said that the implementation time of the form took only around 20–25 % of time compared to the native implementation, meaning it sped up development at least by factor 4.

The gathered data indicates that especially rather inexperienced developers can save a good amount of time using the presented library approach.

5   Benefits

The presented solution requires the developer to implement a form only once in a very shortened, code independent and human-readable JSON syntax, making it available on different platforms with less effort.

As the form description is processed at runtime, it can be changed from outside without requiring an update of the app. It can even be stored on a remote server, completely independent from the app itself. So the traditional development cycle mentioned in Sect. 3.1 can be brought down to only redefine the form description instead of the whole mobile app. The "Mockup" phase might even be neglected using the prototype itself instead. As it requires far less knowledge this can even be done by someone with only basic knowledge in the matter of mobile application development. This leads to reduced development costs and is less time-consuming (Fig. 4).

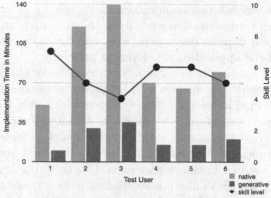

Table 1. Implementation time (in Minutes)

Test user	1	2	3	4	5	6
Native	50	120	140	70	65	80
Generative	10	30	35	15	15	20
Experience	7	5	4	6	6	5

Fig. 4. Test results compared

Another benefit of this solution is its cross-platform awareness. Without modification the form could be reused on another platform simplifying the development of that part even more. For the solution does not use a WebView as a wrapper for the form but only native elements instead, it looks just like any normal native developed app regarding performance and behaviour.

5.1 Covered Input Types

While the concept itself works for most input types, by default a few of frequently used input fields are implemented. These fields can be easily extended or overridden by custom implementations. At the moment the supported and probably most common input types are `Text`, `Integer` and `Number`, `Date`, `Time` and – as already shown in Sect. 3.3 – `Selection`.

For sure there remain input types where this concept would not work. But rather than covering all possible types it is covering the default ones in a very simple way.

5.2 Supported Platforms

Currently this project is a work in progress and the approach is only implemented for Android KITKAT (19) and above. Support of Apple iOS and a web presentation are planned for the near future. Nevertheless, the concept behind the abstract form definition is applicable to other platforms as well.

6 Conclusion and Future Work

Summarizing it can be said that due to the reduced complexity of forms in the simple JSON format, according to our first empirical study the development of forms on mobile devices can be sped up at least by factor 4. Even more as soon as this solution is implemented for other platforms than Android. As the forms can be described in a few lines, the implementation tasks do not necessarily have to be done by developers. They can therefore concentrate on more complex tasks of the application development process.

For the future a couple of extensions for this generator approach are planned. To make the solution working platform independent, the generator will be implemented at least for Apple's iOS and the web, leading to a significant amount of saved time during development. Also it will soon be possible to create forms with navigation aspects with nested or multiple forms, reducing the need for custom implementation code and therefore the development complexity more and more. To reduce the knowledge needed for the form design even more a graphical editor for the JSON files is scheduled, making it possible to create the form descriptions via a simple UI, which therefore should speed up the development even more. Besides the technical extensions, a more detailed study with a larger number of developers is planned to get a better understanding of the approaches value.

References

1. AngularJS: Angular Schema Form, 31 March 2016. http://schemaform.io
2. Appcelerator Titanium: Mobile App Development & MBaas Products, 12 June 2016. http://www.appcelerator.com/mobile-app-development-products/
3. Botterweck, G.: A model-driven approach to the engineering of multiple user interfaces. In: Kühne, T. (ed.) MoDELS 2006. LNCS, vol. 4364, pp. 106–115. Springer, Heidelberg (2007)
4. Czarnecki, K., Eisenecker, U.W.: Generative Programming: Methods, Tools, and Applications. Addison-Wesley, Boston (2000)
5. Device Magic: Use mobile forms on your Android iPhone, or iPad, 31 March 2016. http://www.devicemagic.com/features/mobile-forms-app
6. Eisenstein, J., Vanderdonckt, J., Puerta, A.: Applying Model-Based Techniques to the Development of UIs for Mobile Computers (2001)
7. Kinvey Inc.: State of Enterprise Mobility Survey 2014, December 2014. http://resources.kinvey.com/docs/State+of+Enterprise+Mobility+Survey+2014+-+Kinvey.pdf
8. Kizeo Mobile Solutions: Kizeo Forms: Forms for iPad, iPhone & Android, 31 March 2016. http://www.kizeo.com/kizeo-forms/
9. PhoneGap: How PhoneGap Works, 15 June 2016. http://phonegap.com/about
10. RhoMobile: About RhoMobile, 15 June 2016. https://developer.zebra.com/community/rhomobile-suite/about
11. Schlee, M., Vanderdonckt, J.: Generative programming of graphical user interfaces. In: Proceedings of the Working Conference on Advanced Visual Interfaces AVI 2004 (2004)
12. Vanderdonckt, J.: Model-driven engineering of user interfaces: promises, successes, failures, and challenges. In: Proceedings of the National Conference on Human-Computer Interaction, pp. 1–10 (2008)

Location Based Services Used in Smart Electronic Wallet Mobile Application

Jan Kozlovsky, Jan Dvorak, and Ondrej Krejcar[✉]

Faculty of Informatics and Management, Center for Basic and Applied Research,
University of Hradec Kralove, Rokitanskeho 62,
500 03 Hradec Kralove, Czech Republic
{Jan.Kozlovsky,Jan.Dvorak.2}@uhk.cz,
ondrej@krejcar.org

Abstract. The article deals with the project of electronic wallet that would serve to keep record of personal financial activity, especially for cash payments, which are the most frequent types of transactions in an ordinary life. Smart phone that every person carries around would be used for the evidence of the financial activity, thus it would serve as a wallet. There are many applications that offer keeping record of finances and transactions. This proposed solution has an added value which is the fact that every payment is tied to a location where it was executed. Then, it is possible to group together the different types of financial activity based on the location and also predict them when the user comes back to the same location where a payment has already been made. The users of smart electronic wallet do not have to worry that they will not find their incomes and expenses retrospectively if they forget to enter them into the electronic wallet because it will remind the users to do that. Based on testing of this proposed solution, a relatively high location and suggestion accuracy was reached. Generally speaking, the proposed solution that calls the user to action based on the found location connected to the existing history can be used in a wider area of work, for example, to keep record of tasks and other events of normal life.

Keywords: Smart wallet · Electronic wallet · Personal wallet · Finance control · Expense evidence · Expenses under control

1 Introduction

These days, it is very easy to spend money. At the same time, it is very important to keep track of the finances. The current growth of mobile technologies changed the way of the mobile phone use and extended it from the mere GMS (Google Mobile Services) services onto using the internet connection, web applications [13, 14], internet banking and others. Mobile phone, respectively "smart phone" is therefore an adequate tool for realizing online payments [1, 18]. These electronic payments are securely documented [2] because it is an intentional and well secured online transaction. Thus, we keep a good track of these electronic transactions. Which way should we control the cash payments that are in an ordinary life often the most frequent form of payments? The possibility of simply but conscientiously recording our everyday cash expenses opens a space for us to evaluate our finances on the long term basis and then alternatively optimize them.

© Springer International Publishing Switzerland 2016
M. Younas et al. (Eds.): MobiWIS 2016, LNCS 9847, pp. 353–362, 2016.
DOI: 10.1007/978-3-319-44215-0_30

Nowadays, everyone carries around a smart phone as their wallet and for this evidence it is an ideal means [15, 16, 18]. There is a set of applications that behave like an electronic wallet. They allow keeping record of income and expenses and segment them into their corresponding categories, they display the current "budget", generate the statistics of the expenses, etc. However, the disadvantage of these applications is that the user has to remember to enter manually every financial activity into the application. If the user does not do that, the information about the financial activity stays unrecorded; in the worst case it is forgotten. These financial activities have to be then retrospectively searched and sometimes their tracing is not possible so the generated statistics are not accurate. The whole use of the application in this case loses its sense.

This project or more precisely an application in the form of a smart electronic wallet focuses on it being as autonomous as possible. That means that in the ideal case, the application itself should offer the user to record the financial activity and estimate which category the financial activity should go to.

2 Problem Definition

In this modern age, we pay attention to the automation of processes and elimination of the intervention of the user. This trend is especially present in mobile technologies. However, the competing solutions of electronic wallets rarely comply with this requirement.

An example of this can be an electronic wallet WalletApp [3], My wallets [4], or My Wallet – Expense Manager [5]. All these above mentioned electronic wallet applications belong into the top solutions in this field and can be freely downloaded on Google Play. Their advantages are a wide scale of information that we can enter and well-arranged statistics that serve as their output. The finances can be easily divided accordingly to the type (income, expense), category (food, car, fuel, personal) etc. Based on the categories, it is possible to see weekly or monthly reports about the remaining budget, etc. This is the way these previously mentioned applications are very useful and actually function as electronic banking for cash payments.

However, these applications in no way disengage their users from the responsibility to note the transaction into the application immediately if such a transaction is made. The user has to remember to regularly enter the transaction. And if they do not enter them immediately, these transactions can be irretrievably forgotten. Nevertheless, the mere short-term omission of a regular, almost everyday evidence of financial activity could be the cause for the whole system of financial control to fall apart – because the user would be discouraged by the subsequent search of missing records.

A similar principle of the use of long-term monitoring of the current location, so called "real-time", was used in the proposal of the application, for example, in civil engineering where it can be used to find optimization of work and costs based on the worker's location when working on the construction of the dam [6], alternatively to track the current location of the individual carrier vehicles for optimization of logistics in the planning of their routes [7].

3   New Solution

Smart mobile phones as opposed to real wallets can also ascertain the current location of the user [17–19]. The location can be traced in more ways, either directly using GPS sensors or by using GMS services from the operator. This fact creates the added value of the proposed smart electronic wallet solution.

The proposed solution consists in establishing financial activities in a specific GPS location. It means that if the user makes a financial transaction, a specific location of this transaction is saved. The requirement for the best use of this added value is that the financial transaction would be made in these usual places. For example, the user buys food regularly in the same shopping centre, eats in the same restaurants or buys fuel for their car in the nearby petrol station, etc.

Since the user spends money in the same places repeatedly and the expenses belong into the same category (i.e. expenses for lunches in their favourite restaurant, the purchase of fuel in the nearby petrol station, etc.), it is possible to sort and predict the financial activity. Specifically, there are two advantages that the application offers:

(1)   When the user enters a new financial activity into the application, the current location is traced and if there has already been another financial activity in this location, the application suggests a category (food, car, fuel, personal, or other) and the amount of the financial activity. That can but does not have to be changed. See (Fig. 1)

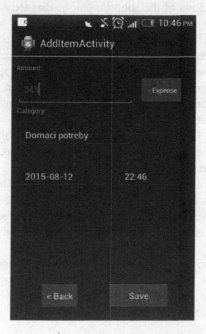

Fig. 1. Suggestion of the expense that the user is just saving if the location was found as already known.

(2) In regular intervals, the application automatically runs a control of the current location of the mobile device. If the mobile device is in a location where the user has previously saved a financial activity, the smart wallet automatically saves this event. That happens even if the user does not try to enter any financial activity into the application. Later, at the nearest opportunity when the user looks into their smart electronic wallet, it invites them to take action. So the user either marks these accumulated events (in case there are more) as a real financial activity or just ignores them.

In order for the application to remind the user in the best way where they have been and which possible financial activities were picked, it offers the user these "waiting" items in the form of: date; time; address where the user was (e.g. Hradecka 1249/6, Hradec Kralove); and category where this ascertained item probably belongs (based on the previous financial activity at this location).

The location is controlled by the mobile phone in regular time intervals (e.g. every 10 min) so that the activity of the user would be mapped in the best possible way and that way the possible financial activities would be predicted. The control whether the device is located in a known location (that has previously been described by some financial activity) is done based on a firmly set radius (for more see the Implementation of the solution, the paragraph IV).

4   Implementation of the Solution

The technical implementation of the solution can be divided according to the purpose into three basic parts:

Visual form: the GUI user environment is being solved through the standard activities with the corresponding layouts. The implementation of Google Maps Android API [8] is an inseparable part of it and with its help it is possible to show the location on the map where the financial activities have been made. Then, the application uses standard components like TextView, ListView, EditText, AutoCompleteTextView, RadioButton, etc.

In Fig. 2 there is the home screen (so called activity) of the application. The user can see the sum of expenses, incomes and the balance. Also, there are expenses for each category in the current month.

The tool for long-term data saving: in order to save the data in the phone memory for a long-term use, two tools are used. The first one is class SharedPreferences for simple records of the numerical or Boolean type [9]. The second tool is the class SQLiteDatabase that is used to save financial records and other objects into the programme database [10].

Regular control of the user location: the control of the location is provided by the tool GooglePlayServicesClient [11]. This tool has the advantage of being able to share the current location with the application using GMS that is without using the GPS satellites. This ensures the highest probability of getting the current location. This tool

Fig. 2. Initial activity of the application where it is possible to see the current total expenses, income, the remaining budget, and the expenses in the individual categories in the current month.

is run as a service (class type Service) so that the tool would be run on a long-term basis, not depending on Activity that starts it. This service runs in regular intervals (the default time is 10 min and this interval can be readjusted) using the tool AlarmManager. AlarmManager runs the service for the location control regularly, even while the application is closed and the mobile phone is inactive, for example, locked. This ensures the strict regular control of the current location of the mobile phone.

The control whether the mobile phone is currently in the area where the financial activity has already been saved is performed using beforehand set tolerance/margin (± 250 m) and it is done by comparing the saved and currently found GPS coordinates. Visually the control of the location is displayed in (Fig. 3).

Subsequently, the classes Calendar and SimpleDateFormat are used for the work with time and time data (comparison of the dates to produce statistics in the given month etc.)

The suggestion of the exact address from the tracked GPS coordinates is made using the class Geocoder [12]. Figure 4 illustrates the way the user is given information about the places where the financial activity could have been made. The user has the possibility to check the exact location on the map later by clicking the address column or to save the data by clicking on "Save".

Figure 5 illustrated the class diagram of a complete proposed application. It is composed of the main classes PendingPosition (the item suggested by the application is

Fig. 3. The control and comparison of the current location with the already known location [source: Google]

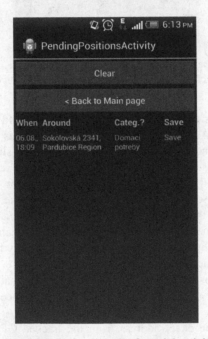

Fig. 4. Suggestion of selected locations where the financial activity could have been made.

saved and is waiting to be saved or deleted by the user), FinancialItem (classic financial activity, including category, sum of money, location, etc.), MainDatabaseAdapter, MainDatabaseHelper (classes for the work with database), Dates (the class for comparison, comparing and further work with dates), TableFragmentPendingPositions and TableFragment (classes, or rather fragments defining the form and structure of the financial items overview).

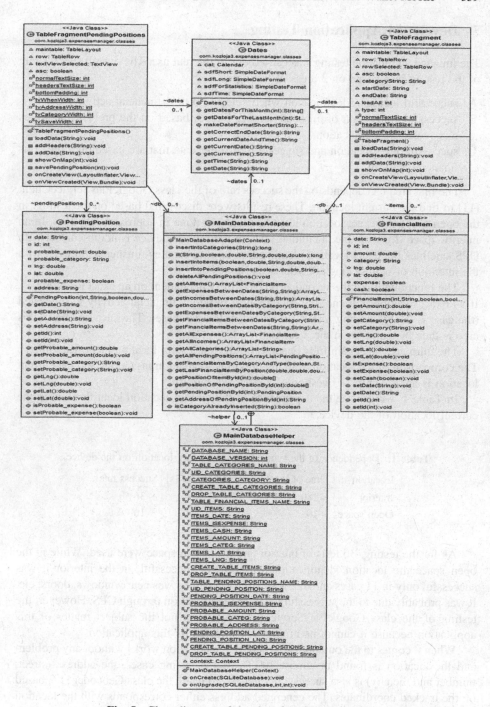

Fig. 5. Class diagram of developed testing application.

5 Developed Application Testing

The finished application testing was carried out in the real use. The overall success rate of the testing was based on 3 areas of testing:

A. successful location identification when entering a new financial activity,
B. successful suggestion of financial activity figures based on the previous activities discovered in this location,
C. successful identification and suggestion of these data that are based on a previous financial activity.

The first area (A) depends on the success rate of the class GooglePlayServiceClient [11] to find the current location. These results were discovered based on the testing: in the open space the exact location identification was done in approximately 10 s. In an interior space (for example, a building) where the mobile device is not in contact with GPS satellites the exact location identification is unfortunately unsuccessful even with the intention of using GooglePlayServicesClient [11].

The functionality of the second area (B) is fully dependent on an exact location (A). If an exact location is found, the data about a previous financial activity is suggested (the case is "only" finding a relevant record in the database). The success rate in this area is then the same as in the area A.

The third area (C) again fully depends on the successful location identification (A). The comparison of the location from the previous financial transactions and the current location is again "only" a question of a database inquiry.

In Table 1, we can see the dependence of the current location identification on the current location of the device.

Table 1. Dependence of the success rate of finding location on the device.

Location	Time of location identification [s]	Success rate
Interior	∼180 to ∞	∼36 %
Open space	∼10	∼100 %

As for the testing, 30 tests of interior and also open space were used. While in the open space the location identification was always successful, in the interior it was successful only in 11 cases and that was when the device was near windows, doors, etc. It was probably due to the successful location identification through GPS. However, the testing of the class GooglePlayServicesClient [11] is not the subject matter of this application because it cannot be in any way affected by this application.

When it comes to the outdoor use where the application works without any problem and the location is found in almost 100 % of the testing cases, the address (street, number and the city) is also successfully generated using the class Geocoder [12] based on the tracked coordinates. The generated address either corresponds with the location or differs in the street or house number.

The aim of the testing was not only to observe the success rate of right financial activity suggestions but also, for example, to measure the long-term battery life with every 10 min' location control. The regular location controls affected the battery life only slightly and the phone power has not lowered much (between 24 to 48 h, depending on the amount of other phone load). The testing was carried out on the device HTC Desire X.

6   Conclusions

The created application offers a new approach to the evidence of personal financial expenses. It exempts the user from the responsibility to remember to accurately enter everything. Rather, it actively invites the user to action, which is in this fast age more than desirable. This maximizes the probability that the user will always maintain their data updated.

The employment of the new method for location identification, class Geocoder [12] has not demonstrated much benefit, the exact location is found only when used in open space or when the device is inside of the building near to the window or door. The application can be then used with certainty only outside of the buildings and in the open space.

This automated tool can be alternatively used even in a wider use, such as, keeping record of tasks, visits, meetings and other entities of ordinary life that can be tied to a location. To prove that we can look at the other already designed applications, for example, from the engineering and transport fields [6, 7].

Acknowledgment. This work and the contribution were supported by project "Smart Solutions for Ubiquitous Computing Environments" FIM, University of Hradec Kralove, Czech Republic (under ID: UHK-FIM-SP-2016-2102). We also acknowledge the technical language assistance provided by Jirina Cancikova.

References

1. Duane, A., O'Reilly, P., Andreev, P.: Realising M-Payments: modelling consumers' willingness to M-pay using smart phones. Behaviour **33**(4), 318–334 (2014). doi:10.1080/0144929X.2012.745608
2. Mayrhofer, R.: An architecture for secure mobile devices. Secur. Commun. Netw. **8**(10), 1958–1970 (2015)
3. Wallet App - Budget Tracker, Android and iPhone. www.walletapp.net
4. My Wallet - Expense Manager, Android Application. https://play.google.com/store/apps/details?id=com.apps.balli.mywallet
5. My Wallets App. https://play.google.com/store/apps/details?id=my.wallets.lite
6. Jiang, H., Lin, P., Qiang, M., Fan, Q.: A labor consumption measurement system based on real-time tracking technology for dam construction site. Autom. Constr. **52**, 1–15 (2015)
7. Oliveira, R.R., Cardoso, I.M.G., Barbosa, J.L.V., da Costa, C.A., Prado, M.P.: An intelligent model for logistics management based on geofencing algorithms and RFID technology. Expert Syst. Appl. **42**(15–16), 6082–6097 (2015)

8. Behan, M., Krejcar, O.: Modern smart device-based concept of sensoric networks. EURASIP J. Wirel. Commun. Netw. **2013**(155), 13 pages (2013). http://link.springer.com/article/10.1186/1687-1499-2013-155

9. Krejcar, O.: Problem solving of low data throughput on mobile devices by artefacts prebuffering. EURASIP J. Wirel. Commun. Netw. **2009**, 8 (2009). doi:10.1155/2009/802523. Article ID 802523

10. Krejcar, O.: Threading possibilities of smart devices platforms for future user adaptive systems. In: Pan, J.-S., Chen, S.-M., Nguyen, N.T. (eds.) ACIIDS 2012, Part II. LNCS, vol. 7197, pp. 458–467. Springer, Heidelberg (2012)

11. Behan, M., Krejcar, O.: Adaptive graphical user interface solution for modern user devices. In: Pan, J.-S., Chen, S.-M., Nguyen, N.T. (eds.) ACIIDS 2012, Part II. LNCS, vol. 7197, pp. 411–420. Springer, Heidelberg (2012)

12. Benikovsky, J., Brida, P., Machaj, J.: Proposal of user adaptive modular localization system for ubiquitous positioning. In: Pan, J.-S., Chen, S.-M., Nguyen, N.T. (eds.) ACIIDS 2012, Part II. LNCS, vol. 7197, pp. 391–400. Springer, Heidelberg (2012)

13. Hustak, T., Krejcar, O., Selamat, A., Mashinchi, R., Kuca, K.: Principles of usability in human-computer interaction driven by an evaluation framework of user actions. In: Younas, M., Awan, I., Mecella, M. (eds.) MobiWIS 2015. LNCS, vol. 9228, pp. 51–62. Springer, Heidelberg (2015)

14. Kasik, V., Penhaker, M., Novák, V., Bridzik, R., Krawiec, J.: User interactive biomedical data web services application. In: Yonazi, J.J., Sedoyeka, E., Ariwa, E., El-Qawasmeh, E. (eds.) ICeND 2011. CCIS, vol. 171, pp. 223–237. Springer, Heidelberg (2011)

15. Maresova, P., Klimova, B.: Investment evaluation of cloud computing in the European business sector. Appl. Econ. **47**(36), 3907–3920 (2015)

16. Maresova, P., Klimova, B., Tuček, V.: Use of social networks in banking: a study in the Czech Republic. Applied Economics **47**(57), 6155–6169 (2015). https://ideas.repec.org/a/taf/applec/v47y2015i57p6155-6169.html

17. Machaj, J., Brida, P.: Performance comparison of similarity measurements for database correlation localization method. In: Nguyen, N.T., Kim, C.-G., Janiak, A. (eds.) ACIIDS 2011, Part II. LNCS, vol. 6592, pp. 452–461. Springer, Heidelberg (2011)

18. Machacek, Z., Hercik, R., Slaby, R.: Smart user adaptive system for intelligent object recognizing. In: Nguyen, N.T., Trawiński, B., Jung, J.J. (eds.) New Challenges for Intelligent Information and Database Systems. SCI, vol. 351, pp. 197–206. Springer, Heidelberg (2011)

19. Machaj, J., Brida, P., Majer, N.: Novel criterion to evaluate QoS of localization based services. In: Pan, J.-S., Chen, S.-M., Nguyen, N.T. (eds.) ACIIDS 2012, Part II. LNCS, vol. 7197, pp. 381–390. Springer, Heidelberg (2012)

Smart Automatic Control of GSM Alarm

Lukas Veselka, Jan Dvorak, and Ondrej Krejcar(⊠)

Center for Basic and Applied Research, Faculty of Informatics and Management,
University of Hradec Kralove, Rokitanskeho 62,
500 03 Hradec Kralove, Czech Republic
lukas.veselka@uhk.cz, dvorakj@gmail.com,
Ondrej@Krejcar.org

Abstract. This paper concerns with possibilities of automatic control of GSM alarms using a known location. It provides a compact look on an issue of input and output notification from a circle area identified by a given point and a radius. Consequently it describes a progress of an application for Android platform, which solves this problematic. It contains as well a comparison of the new solution with other mobile platforms and their deficits. The paper also mentions certain competition applications for Android platform and their interrelated comparison.

Keywords: Security · GSM · Alarm · Automation · Android

1 Introduction

A shed, a cottage, a garage, a garden, all of these realties are a property, which often means to us a lot more than just a material value. Often it may mean for example stored memories after grandmother in boxes in the shed's loft. All of us somehow protect these valuables before intruders, using either a common door lock, or complete safety measures such as safety locks, alarms etc. In fact, we are not present at these places all the time, may be that we travel there just for weekends or sometimes even just for vacation or holidays. This fact facilitates thieves' intentions and gives them easier ingress to our property. Generally the cabin areas are localized in the remote places [14], which doesn't make it easier to protect our property as well. But the thieves are not the only danger for our property – another threat can be also a fire, a gas leak and other threats. Even before these we have to protect ourselves. About the systems based on GSM technology you can read here [1], in the work its authors pay attention among other to use of GSM for temperature sensors, smoke sensors and alarm systems. Further authors of [2] occupy themselves with the use of GSM nets in the households in general [4].

Maybe most of us don't often realize this threat, or can even think in a way: "This can't happen to me", but the Sod's law speaks clearly, so we are being surprised afterwards. There are many possibilities how to protect our assets. Let's divide the secure elements into two main categories – active secure elements and passive secure elements. Among the passive secure elements let's categorize such elements, which prevent the unwanted incidents, and among the active secure elements those, which

© Springer International Publishing Switzerland 2016
M. Younas et al. (Eds.): MobiWIS 2016, LNCS 9847, pp. 363–375, 2016.
DOI: 10.1007/978-3-319-44215-0_31

somehow solve the certain situation when it already occurs. The more frequented are definitely the passive secure elements, such as doors, locks, window shutters, fences, in the case of a fire danger for example use of fireproof materials. In contrary to that the less often are the active secure elements, such as alarms, photo traps, smoke detectors, gas detectors etc. Among these active elements belong also various homemade traps and snares against the thieves (such as a bear trap), that became several times a subject of litigation here in the Czech Republic already.

This work deals particularly with the theme of alarms' possibilities. The alarms, or GSM alarms, are facilities, which contain a SIM card, the same one as we have in our mobile phones (out of this comes the name GSM - Global System for Mobile Communications). Therefore the device can be controlled by sending an SMS message with a respective text such as "#01#" for turning the alarm on. If the alarm then records the initializing event (fire, conflagration, gas …), it executes an ahead defined action according to set values – it can send an SMS with an information that there probably has started a fire, it can send an MMS with a photo of the place or it can make a phone call and mediate the sound of what is happening in the place.

According to a complexity of the GSM alarm it varies also its price, but the simplest models are available for a few hundred Czech crowns today. They are affordable for everyone and can save our property of much higher value. Then the more expensive models can include one main unit and one or more accessory units. The accessory units don't have the GSM module and therefore they can't contact the owner. So if the accessory unit sensors the initializing event, it activates the main unit (which includes the GSM module) and that one releases the alarm. The communication between the main and the accessory units can be wired or wireless (most often using radio waves). For more information about professional alarms see [3].

As it was mentioned supra, the GSM alarm control can be executed through the SMS orders. This possibility allows a complete control, including adding a telephone number contacted while initializing the alarm or setting the single sensors (the device can contain for example a movement sensor and infrared sensor, which both can be singularly turned on and off). The operations for alarm activation and deactivation can be controlled not only by the SMS orders, but mostly also by the wireless control using radio waves. The most remarkable disadvantage of the mentioned second type is the coverage of the waves, which is on the order of tens, maximally hundreds of meters.

The essential question is, if it is possible and how to automate obviously the most often action that we operate with the alarms, which is their activation and deactivation? Fundamentally there are two different possible directions how to find a solution. We can use either the radio waves control, which works just in a limited sphere, or deal with an issue, how to apply the control by the SMS messages. This is a division according to what the device provides us with. The next question is, if we don't want to control the GSM alarm manually, what impulse initiates its automatic activation or deactivation? The first possibility is a time aspect, we can say for example that we want to have the alarm activated during a week and want to turn it off for a weekend. But this possibility is supported natively by the most of the alarms, so it's not needed to deal with it. The second approach is to control the alarm in the relation with our location, and this is particularly what the next chapters concern with.

2 Problem Definition and Related Works

The previous chapter introduced the two possible approaches for the automated control. The first of them is using the radio controls delivered with the device; the second one is the control by the SMS messages. Then it was said that this control need to be executed according to tracking the owner's location. So if the owner's location changes towards the GSM alarm, he could react to such circumstance by deactivating the alarm, in contrary if he withdraws, the alarm is activated.

Now for the sake of completeness let's demonstrate a theoretically possible approach to handle the alarm by the radio control. It would be necessary to develop a specialized hardware including a GPS module, a radio transmitter and not least a controlling unit and a battery. The controlling unit would periodically detect a location from the GPS module and in the case the owner is close enough, it would transmit a signal for turning the alarm off (eventually on) using the radio transmitter. However this approach is theoretically possible, in the practice it wouldn't be much applicable. It would be always needed to carry the hardware with oneself, which would be probably too expensive.

The second and the last variant remains using the SMS orders for turning the alarm on and off. The mobile phone we have always with us, which makes the possibility clearly flexible. Moreover nowadays – in the time of smartphones – we have a possibility to track our location by using the integrated GSM modules in the phones [12]. So the obvious choice is to develop an application that would use our phone sensors for the automatic remote control of our GPS alarm.

Today it is possible to choose among three main mobile platforms – Android, iOS and Windows [12]. To select the appropriate alternative, it's necessary to consider the requirements that we expect the certain platform provides. Let's first draft a mind map (Fig. 1), which helped us to extract the single requirements.

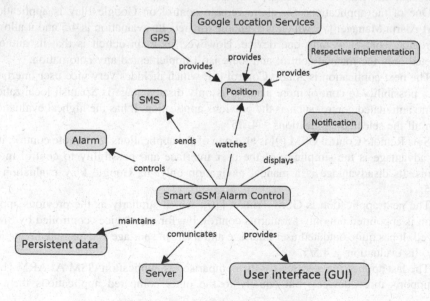

Fig. 1. Mind map of the requirements

The requirements are:

- providing a location,
- displaying notifications,
- user interface (GUI),
- server communication,
- persistent data storage,
- and sending SMS.

The platform has to accomplish the requirements for watching the position, because we need the position as a starter for the alarm activation/deactivation. The notifications is to be used to inform the user about such matter [13, 15]. The application include a graphic user interface and in the future it is considered an enhancement of the communication with the server. The persistent data storage is necessary for saving the information about the alarms statuses, the texts of SMS orders etc. The platform has to enable the program sending of SMS.

In the case of the Android and Windows platforms there wasn't any limit in the requirements, but while checking up on iOS there occurred a problem with sending the SMS messages [12]. The SMS can't be send without user's awareness, it is just possible to prepare the text of the message, which has to be sent manually then. This is a sufficient reason to refuse this platform as an alternative. The next aspect to select the right alternative is the share of the market of the certain platform. According to [1] the share of the market of the Android platform in the second quartile of 2015 was 82.8 %, which is a huge difference in comparison with Windows with 2.6 %. Therefore the best alternative for our requirements is definitely the Android platform. In the [5] or [6] you can find how to work effectively with the notifications for Android about entering and coming out of some area. Now let's have a look at similar solutions of an automated control for GSM alarms on Google Play and let's compare their possibilities.

One of the applications for alarm remote control on Google Play is application GSM Alarm Manager [7], which is available for free. Its evaluation is 4/5 and it allows the remote control of only one device. However, its main deficit is that its authors targeted only the manual control and there isn't implemented any automation.

The next application is Alarm Control [8], which includes very nice user interface and a possibility to control more alarms. Its only disadvantage is Spanish localization and no automated control such as the previous application. It has the highest evaluation from all the selected applications – 4.7/5.

Sms Remote Control GSM [9] is also one of the applications for remote control, it's key advantage is the simplicity of the user interface and possibility to control more alarms. Its disadvantage is a manual navigation only. Its Google Play evaluation is 3.9/5.

The next application is GSM Trinket [10], which similarly as the previous application is appointed not only for alarms control, but for any devices controlled by SMS as well. It has quite outdated user interface and its main shortage is a manual navigation only. Its evaluation is 4.5/5.

The last application selected for the comparison is application GSM ALARM [11]. It supports more devices, but equally to the other compared applications there is absence of the automatic control. It has simple navigation, but the design I would rather use for some kid's application. Its evaluation on Google Play is 4/5.

As we can see from the examples of already existing solutions for similar matters, it is difficult to find a direct competitor. None of the applications solve our problematic, which is automated alarm control. Moreover some of them are even not localized into English or there is missing a possibility of controlling more alarms.

To comment on the user interface (knowing it is only a subjective opinion) – except for the application Alarm Control, where the user interface was very nice (even though it was just in Spanish), the other applications' user interfaces looked quite outdated.

3   New Solution

In this first suggested version the application enable to activate and deactivate the GSM alarm using SMS. This is, equally to the applications mentioned in the previous chapter, enable the manual control (user's interaction needed [15]), but on the top of that it allow an automatic mode, which control the alarm independently (without user's interaction) according to a known alarm location and a current user's (device's) position [13]. The application let the user know about an accomplished activity through the notifications for the case that there happens an unwanted turning on/off. In such case the user can execute a manual correction. The communication using the SMS messages is realized only one way – from the application towards the alarm. These orders won't be checked neither by confirming SMS from the alarm side (which can be left off), nor by a delivering SMS from the operator.

On the mind map (Fig. 1) there are obvious the areas that we have to deal with during the implementation. Now let's describe the individual areas separately and contextualize them. As it was said already, sending the SMS serves for one-sided communication with the GPS alarm; displaying the notifications notify the user about the executed SMS commands. To save the setting for the individual alarms it is needed the persistent data storage, which is connected with the alarms' maintenance. All the necessary information is stored by SQLite into the database. Indeed the application provide a graphic user interface.

The most important element of the application and the core of the automatic control lie in watching the position, or more precisely watching the entering and the coming out of the certain area. Simply we need to gain the information about these events and react to them with some action (for example turning the alarm on).

The implementation by means of GPS rises as the first possibility, but right away in the beginning we encounter the problem, that in the background there would constantly have to run a service for checking up on the position regularly. That would be quite inappropriate in the terms of battery consumption, that's why we don't consider this alternative any more. A different approach could be a respective implementation that would just use even GPS, but primarily it would aim to employ different resources, such as WiFi nets, position according to GSM, but also for example a gyroscope, approach sensor etc.

The respective implementation could work as follows: Fist of all it's necessary to locate an approximate position for example by GSM; if we are far away enough, then it

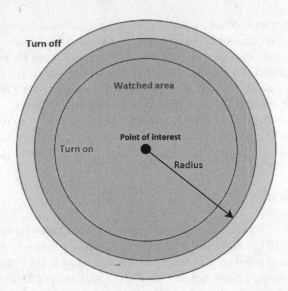

Fig. 2. Watching entering and coming out of the area (Color figure online)

is not necessary to have too precise position. But if we are closer to our point of interest, then we could turn the GPS on and in addition to that change the interval of restoring the position according as how close we are or which direction we're moving.

To anticipate turning on and off on the range of the watched area (the red circle), there are framed up two extra circles (Fig. 2). While achieving the smaller blue circle we would send out a signal to turn the alarm on, and in contrary to that if our distance become larger than radius of the green circle, we would turn the alarm off.

However in android it is possible to apply Google Location Services, which enable several functions and one of them is so-called proximity alert. Fundamentally it is an implementation of similar approach described supra, which is though maximally optimized and sufficient for our objective. A new point of interest can be added in as follows:

```
locationManager.addProximityAlert(
    LATITUDE,
    LONGITUDE,
    RADIUS,
    -1,
    proximityIntent);
```

The latitude and the longitude are coordinates of the point of interest (the alarm in our case), the radius is a radius of a circular area and the proximityIntent is an Intent, which we can capture by a BroadcastReceiver, in the case of entering or coming out of the area. For each alarm we can add a proximityAlert with a different Intent, This way we allocate an event to a certain alarm in the BroadcastReceiver. The BroadcastReceiver is defined in AndroidManifest.xml, so it's possible to capture the events even while the application is off. It is obvious that there is missing a specification, how often the system shall locate the position. If we wanted to make the system to actualize the position (and consequently to detect that it shall send us the necessary Intent), we could create a Service that would run continually and would take care of locating the position in regular intervals (for example every 5 min) [16–18]. There is no longer need to work with the location; the only objective is to initialize the position actualization.

```
locationManager.requestLocationUpdates(
        LocationManager.GPS_PROVIDER,
        LOCATION_REFRESH_TIME,
        LOCATION_REFRESH_DISTANCE,
        locationListener);
```

So if we capture an event in the BroadcastReceiver and detect to which alarm it belongs and if we shall turn it on or off, we react to it right away by several actions. First of all from SQLite we load a telephone number and an SMS text that has to be sent out. After that it is sent an SMS through a SmsManager, and a NotificationManager creates the notification for the user. While clicking the notification the application starts up and automatically it navigates to setting a certain alarm, where it's possible to execute a further action. The next figure (Fig. 3) shows a basic view of communication of the application with the system.

The application is implemented as an application with one activity and more fragments. While designing the application it is considered a recommendation of a consistent behavior of the applications by Google [10]. According to these recommendations the application have "left menu" implemented by a DrawerLayout. If some fragment refers to another one (a nested one), it is possible to return back in such tree hierarchy.

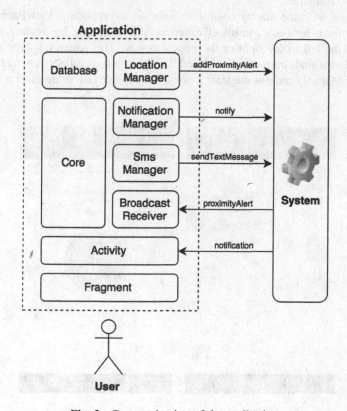

Fig. 3. Communication of the application

4 Implementation

According to the previous chapter the application consists of one activity; the particular screens are fragments, among which it's possible to navigate using the menu or navigation keys. The menu itself is made by a DrawerLayout and a NavigationView provided by Android SDK. The navigation among the fragments itself is accomplished by a FragmentTransation. This class includes a method addToBackStack, which simply allows us to navigate to the previous fragment then. The navigation back itself is processed using a method popBackStack in a class FragmentManager. However, for navigation back within the frame of the application it was used a respective class FragmentBackStack, which in contrary to the prepared solution manages to delete the whole fragment storage without calling a method onCreateView in every fragment in the storage - that would cause useless loading data, which are not needed.

The figure (Fig. 4) shows us two main screens of the application. On the left you can see the alarms control, which is a list of the alarms ordered alphabetically with an icon according to the fact, if the alarm is active or not (green – unlocked, red – locked). Next there is information if the automatic mode is activated. The alarms can be edited or deleted from the menu by passing across the item from the right to the left, added by clicking the blue icon on the right side or the user can go to the controlling screen by a single click on the item.

The screen with the alarms control is built on a component ViewPager, so it is possible to move between control of different alarms simply by passing across the screen from the left to the right or the opposite way. The screen displays a status in which the alarms finds currently (Unlocked, Locked), a possibility to change the mode (Automatic, Manual) and not the least a possibility to activate or deactivate the alarm.

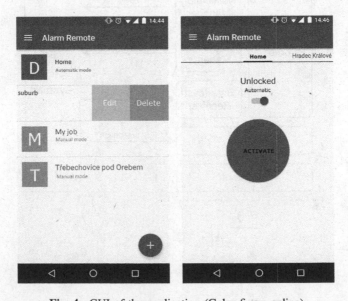

Fig. 4. GUI of the application (Color figure online)

The main functionality of the application is automated alarms control, so its integrated part is also their administration. For storing it is utilized the SQLite database, but the access to it is screened out from the rest of the application by a DAO layer. This way the application works everywhere with objects of a class AlarmEntity.

```
public class AlarmEntity {
private Long id;
private String name;
private Double latitude;
private Double longitude;
private Integer radius;
private String activateSms;
private String deactivateSms;
private String msisdn;
private boolean active;
private boolean autonomyEnabled;
...
}
```

From the previous chapters we know that the GSM alarms are controlled by the SMS orders – for this objective in the application exist a library class SmsUtils, which contains one method sendSms with one parameter AlarmEntity. This method transmits an SMS to a number msisdn with a message text activateSms or deactivateSms in order to what status the alarm just has (active).

For automation of the alarm activation and deactivation there are applied so-called proximity alerts by Google. Administration of these proximity alerts is covered by a class ProximityAlertManager, which has two methods - addProximityAlert and removeProximityAlert. In the case of entering or coming out of the area the system transmits an Intent, Which is captured by the BroadcastReceiver. In our application it is a ProximityReceiver, which actualizes the alarm status in the database, and then it transmits SMS order to the GSM alarm, displays the notification to the user and finally sends out another broadcast for GUI actualization, if the application is in the foreground.

The problem of proximity alerts is that their durability is given by a time of running the system. So if the system is restarted, the proximity alerts are forgiven and therefore there is no Intent that our ProximityReceiver could possibly capture. Therefore after restarting the phone it is necessary to renew all the proximity alerts. For this objective there was created a BootReceiver in the application, which is the BroadcastReceiver again, called when starting the system this time. It loads the alarms from the database and creates new proximity alerts.

For the case the application is running in the foreground and a proximity alert comes, it was necessary to deal with the GUI actualization. As it was mentioned, from the ProximityReceiver there is transmitted the broadcast, which engages with the task to notify the application that the GUI shall be actualized. The fragments that need to obtain the information inherit from an AbstractFragment. In this abstract fragment onto an event onResume it is registered the BroadcastRecevier, which then calls onto an onReceive a method onUpdateViewReceiver. This method can be rewritten in the

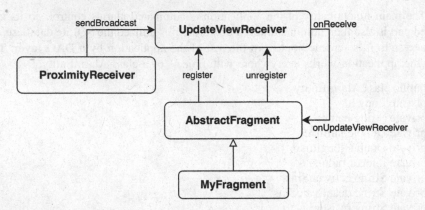

Fig. 5. Process of actualizing the GUI

subclasses. The AbstractFragment unregisters the BroadcastReceiver on an event onPause. A graphic illustration of the process is on the figure (Fig. 5).

5   Testing of Developed Application

In the range of the application we tested a mechanics of the automatic turning on and off the alarms. We qualified its correctness and completeness. By the correctness we mean a fact that the entering or coming out of the area is correctly interpreted. The completeness means that according to this event all the appropriate actions execute well.

The test were realized on a device LG Nexus 5, on which 4 alarms was set in the application, and we monitored, how the device reacts while everyday moving among these points. We noted down number of factual entries and coming-outs, number of undiscerned entries and coming-outs and number of mistakenly discerned entries and coming-outs. For completeness we noted down eventual occurred errors.

5.1   Results

The test of correctness took place during one week while everyday commuting to a job. The results are displayed in the table (Table 1).

Table 1.   Test results

	Factual		Undiscerned		Mistaken	
	Entry	Coming-out	Entry	Coming-out	Entry	Coming-out
1	5	5	0	0	2	4
2	10	10	0	0	0	0
3	10	10	0	0	0	0
4	5	5	0	0	3	2

In the first two columns there are numbers of the factual entries and coming-outs of the area. Then in the next two columns there are numbers of undiscerned entries and coming-outs. There weren't any. Therefore it didn't happen during all the testing time that some entry or coming-out would not be registered at all. In contrary to that several times occurred a case that some entry or coming-out was mistakenly discerned, even though in fact no entry or coming-out happened at all. This error occurred mostly on the range of the researched area. In the areas 2 and 3 there were not any mistakenly discerned entries or coming-outs, because it was entered or come-out directly. In contrary to that in the areas 1 and 4 it happened that we moved on the perimeter just in the range of the researched area. In these cases there occurred those mistaken discerns. These errors could be anticipated by a change of the radius value of the watched area, which is possible for each alarm individually.

The test of the completeness took place all the time during the application development. Through this time there were found several errors. It was for example the problem with durability of the proximity alerts described in the previous chapter. The next error was rewriting the proximity alerts and impossibility of watching more areas at one time, or not actualizing the GUI, which was also described in the previous chapter. All these problems were repaired and currently it's not known any error related to the completeness, as it was described in the introduction of this chapter.

Consequently let's have a look at a comparison of our solution with the solutions by other authors. We have compared it with the applications mentioned in the second chapter (Table 2).

Table 2. Comparison with the competition

	Automation	More devices	Appearance
GSM alarm manager	No	No	1/5
Alarm control	No	Yes	5/5
Sms remote control	No	Yes	3/5
GSM trinket	No	Yes	4/5
GSM ALARM	No	Yes	2/5
Alarm remote (our solution)	Yes	Yes	5/5

Indeed the largest advantage of our solution is the automatic control. Among the compared applications our application is the only one that manages to autonomously control the GSM device without a need of intervention of the user. The support for more devices we find at the majority of the applications – ours one in not an exception. The question of the appearance and the user friendliness is very subjective and could be a subject of a further analyze. Therefore the presented evaluation is just my subjective impression.

Except the application Alarm Control, which has only Spanish localization, all the other applications dispose with English localization as a minimum (including ours one). Our application is further localized into Czech language.

One of the compared applications turns quite aside the course, because it doesn't focus just on the GSM alarms control, but generally on control of any GSM devices.

It is application GSM Trinket. This adds to it a little advantage, but principally any of the compared applications could be used to control even different devices than just alarms.

So if we evaluate the applications in the objective of this work, which is automated control of the GSM alarm, our application has no competition there, simply because no other application offers this functionality.

6 Conclusions

As the objective of this work it was developed a new application for the Android platform, which deals with the automatic GSM alarm control. Its automation is executed on the basis of a current location of the mobile phone and a known position of the GSM alarm. The application watches entering and coming out of the area and according to that it transmits SMS orders into the device.

This new approach targets to simplify the GSM alarms control to the users. It can help saving one's time, but fundamentally gives the confidence that the user doesn't forget to turn the alarm on, because this application accomplishes the activation for him.

While testing it appeared that the automation is reliable. In several cases it came to mistakenly turning on/off the alarm on the range of the watched area. But the result end status of the alarm was right.

Acknowledgement. This work and the contribution were supported by project "Smart Solutions for Ubiquitous Computing Environments" FIM, University of Hradec Kralove, Czech Republic (under ID: UHK-FIM-SP-2016-2102). We also acknowledge the technical language assistance provided by Pavlina Simkova.

References

1. Wang, Y., Ren, X.: An intelligent fire alarm system based on GSM network. In: Zhao, M., Sha, J. (eds.) ICCIP 2012, Part II. CCIS, vol. 289, pp. 232–240. Springer, Heidelberg (2012)
2. Li, J.: Control system of GSM communication network based on remote household appliances. In: Zhong, Z. (ed.) Proceedings of the International Conference on Information Engineering and Applications (IEA) 2012. LNEE, vol. 218, pp. 105–112. Springer, Heidelberg (2012)
3. Huang, H., Xiao, S., Meng, X., Xiong, Y.: A remote home security system based on wireless sensor network and GSM technology. In: 2010 Second International Conference on Networks Security Wireless Communications and Trusted Computing (NSWCTC), Wuhan, Hubei, pp. 535–538 (2010)
4. Benikovsky, J., Brida, P., Machaj, J.: Proposal of user adaptive modular localization system for ubiquitous positioning. In: Pan, J.-S., Chen, S.-M., Nguyen, N.T. (eds.) ACIIDS 2012, Part II. LNCS, vol. 7197, pp. 391–400. Springer, Heidelberg (2012)
5. Bulut, M.F., Demirbas, M.: Energy efficient proximity alert on Android. In: IEEE International Conference on Pervasive Computing and Communications Workshops (PERCOM Workshops), San Diego, CA, pp. 157–162 (2013). doi:10.1109/PerComW. 2013.6529474

6. Krishnaprasad, N., Ravi, B.: Energy efficient proximity alert in Android through better sensor management. Int. J. Combined Res. Dev. **4**(4), 584–588 (2015). http://www.ijcrd. com/files/Vol_4_issue_4/5504.pdf
7. https://play.google.com/store/apps/details?id=btz.software.gsmalarmmanager
8. https://play.google.com/store/apps/details?id=com.alonsohnos.alarmcontrol
9. https://play.google.com/store/apps/details?id=nu.fdp.Sms_RC
10. https://play.google.com/store/apps/details?id=ru.zakharov.oleg.gsm.trinket
11. https://play.google.com/store/apps/details?id=com.qixinstudio.gsmalarm
12. Behan, M., Krejcar, O.: Modern smart device-based concept of sensoric networks. EURASIP J. Wirel. Commun. Netw. **2013**(155), 1–13 (2013)
13. Hustak, T., Krejcar, O., Selamat, A., Mashinchi, R., Kuca, K.: Principles of usability in human-computer interaction driven by an evaluation framework of user actions. In: Younas, M., Awan, I., Mecella, M. (eds.) MobiWIS 2015. LNCS, vol. 9228, pp. 51–62. Springer, Heidelberg (2015)
14. Machaj, J., Brida, P.: Performance comparison of similarity measurements for database correlation localization method. In: Nguyen, N.T., Kim, C.-G., Janiak, A. (eds.) ACIIDS 2011, Part II. LNCS, vol. 6592, pp. 452–461. Springer, Heidelberg (2011)
15. Behan, M., Krejcar, O.: Adaptive graphical user interface solution for modern user devices. In: Pan, J.-S., Chen, S.-M., Nguyen, N.T. (eds.) ACIIDS 2012, Part II. LNCS, vol. 7197, pp. 411–420. Springer, Heidelberg (2012)
16. Krejcar, O., Spicka, I., Frischer, R.: Implementation of full-featured PID regulator in microcontrollers. Elektron. ir Elektrotechnika **2011**(7), 77–82 (2011)
17. Tutsch, M., Machacek, Z., Krejcar, O., Konarik, P.: Development methods for low cost industrial control by WinPAC controller and measurement cards in matlab simulink. In: Proceedings of Second International Conference on Computer Engineering and Applications, ICCEA 2010, Bali Island, Indonesia, 19–21 March 2010, pp. 444–448 (2010)
18. Machacek, Z., Pies, M., Ozana, S.: Simulation of MIT rule-based adaptive controller of a power plant superheater. Adv. Intell. Soft Comput. **133**, 473–479 (2012)

Personalization and Social Networks

Impact of Individual Differences on the Use of Mobile Phones and Applications

Perin Ünal[✉], Tuğba Taşkaya Temizel, and P. Erhan Eren

Graduate School of Informatics, Middle East Technical University,
Ankara, Turkey
perinunal@gmail.com, {ttemizel,ereren}@metu.edu.tr

Abstract. Many studies examining the relation between mobile phone use and the personality traits of individual users have concluded that a significant relationship exists with extraversion standing out as a common trait in this context. In addition, innovativeness plays a key role in the users' adoption of technology and this has been studied within the domain of information systems including the adoption of mobile commerce. This study investigates the relationship between innovativeness, extraversion, mobile phone use and mobile applications, for the first time in the literature. A structured survey was administered to 343 university students. The results showed that mobile phone use features are predominantly related with the trait of extraversion whereas mobile application use features are mostly related with the innovativeness of the user.

Keywords: Mobile phones · Mobile applications · Individual differences

1 Introduction

The enriched functionality and interaction features including ubiquity, personalization, flexibility, dissemination, convenience, instant connectivity and location specific services have resulted in mobile phones becoming the primary communication device across the world. This development has been accompanied by the rapid increase in the use of mobile applications for communication, shopping, entertainment and utility purposes.

Previous studies have examined the relationship between the use of mobile phones and the Big-Five personality traits [1–3]. These studies concluded that extraversion is one of the most significant indicators in relation to mobile phone use. However, the relation between the use of mobile applications and personality traits has been relatively under-explored in the literature. Of the few studies that exist the relationship between installed applications and demographics information has been studied [4, 5] and also the relationship between mobile application usage and Big-Five traits [6].

In the mobile application domain, innovativeness is an important indicator that needs to be considered since it is related to individuals being willing and open to new experiences and making constructive use of the available information [7]. Perceived innovativeness has been analyzed in Technology Acceptance Models and Innovation Diffusion Theory, but not explored in the actual use of technology in the mobile domain.

© Springer International Publishing Switzerland 2016
M. Younas et al. (Eds.): MobiWIS 2016, LNCS 9847, pp. 379–392, 2016.
DOI: 10.1007/978-3-319-44215-0_32

The main contribution of this paper is to elaborate on the relationship between the use of mobile phones and applications, and extraversion and innovativeness as personality features of the users. We widened the mobile application categories to 17 whereas previous studies mainly focused on several application categories. Specifically, we have focused more on mobile applications in the communications category in terms of voice over IP communication (VoIP), instant messaging, e-mails and photograph sharing while the previous studies mainly placed emphasis on e-mail.

2   Literature Review

Understanding personality is a complex issue and has been the subject of numerous studies in social and psychological sciences. Personality has fundamental dimensions that are referred to as traits. There are several models that construct their theory on traits with Big-Five being the most known. This model consists of five personality traits: openness, conscientiousness, extraversion, agreeableness, and neuroticism. Extraversion is related with energy and enthusiasm [8] and associated with characteristics such as being active, assertive, energetic, enthusiastic, outgoing and talkative. Extraverts also enjoy the company of others [3].

In the literature, a limited number of studies investigated the relationship between extraversion and mobile phone use. Bianchi and Phillips [9] reported that mobile phone users are more likely to be extraverts. In another study by Butt and Phillips [1], extraverted people were found to receive more calls and spend more time on making and receiving calls. On the other hand, Chittaranjan et al. [2] did not find a significant relationship between extraversion and time spent on incoming and outgoing calls. Although not significant, it was found that extraverts spend more time on incoming calls. The duration of calls and the number of unique contacts who called were also found to be significantly higher for extraverts. Chittaranjan et al. [6] later found that extraverts spend more time on incoming calls and also receive more calls. The total duration of calls and the number of unique contacts in call logs and outgoing calls were also higher in extraverts. Oliveira et al. [10] reported that only the extraversion trait was significantly related with mobile phone use in terms of sending or receiving calls. Outgoing calls were not significantly explained by the personality traits in previous studies [1, 2, 6] inferring that extraversion is not a discriminative feature in outgoing calls. It was shown that personality was a fairly weak predictor of smartphone ownership and use, whereas extraversion was found to be the most consistent predictor [11].

The relationship between extraversion and SMS messaging has also been explored. Lane and Manner [11] found that extraverts reported a higher use of SMS messaging. In the study by Butt and Phillips [1], extraverts were reported to spend more time on writing and receiving messages using SMS. Similarly, Oliveira et al. [10] found that the only personality trait that was significantly related with sending and receiving SMS messages was extraversion. Although Chittaranjan et al. [2] showed that the extraversion trait negatively correlates with the number of SMS sent, in their later study [8], they found that users scoring high in extraversion are more likely to receive and send more SMS messages.

Recent studies have explored the relationship between the number of installed mobile applications and user attributes such as gender, religion, country and language [4, 5]. However, the relationship between mobile application use and personality features is a relatively unexplored field in the literature. Chittaranjan et al. [6] investigated this relationship by examining application logs but due to the sparse dataset obtained from Nokia N95 phones between October 2009 and February 2011, the authors could only obtain 11 applications. In the study by Chittaranjan et al. [6], basic applications that are mostly preinstalled in Nokia N95 phones were examined. The authors found that extraversion positively correlates with the use of office and calendar applications, e-mails only for males and negatively with internet, games and camera. Tan and Yang [3] also found that individuals high in extraversion tend to use internet applications in transaction, social networking, finance, games and online friends categories more frequently. In another study that measured the importance of six smartphone application categories (communications, games, multimedia, productivity, travel, and utilities), extraversion was found to be positively related to games and negatively related to productivity [12].

In the literature, innovation has been defined as "an idea, practice, or object that is perceived as new by an individual or other unit of adoption" and as the degree to which a person is early in adopting innovations when compared to others [13]. In the information systems domain, personal innovativeness has been explained as the inclination of an individual to try out any new information systems [14, 15]. Agarwal and Prasad [14] developed the personal innovativeness construct to understand the process by which new information technologies are adopted and they found that people with a higher degree of personal innovativeness were more likely to adopt new technologies.

Innovativeness was used as a personality construct to predict consumers' innovative tendencies to adopt a wide variety of technological innovations [16]. Nov and Ye [17] suggested that innovators are more promising customers than others. Innovativeness has also been found to be a very important indicator of consumer intention to use mobile commerce in the USA [18].

Mobile phones, mobile applications and evolving mobile communication modalities represent new and innovative forms of communication. It is obvious that mobile applications disrupt the traditional way of communication monopolized by service providers, namely traditional voice calls and SMS [19]. There is a fundamental shift in people's communication channels which characterized by a decline in the use of traditional communication services [20]. Mobile communication apps can be defined as applications to connect and communicate through mobile devices to share news, information and content [21]. These applications can be subdivided into the following categories [20]: (1) social networking (2) voice over Internet protocol (VoIP) (3) instant messaging (4) recommendation services. Examples of other forms of mobile communication modalities are photograph sharing applications like Instagram and of e-mails.

In our study, we investigate the use of mobile phones and applications, in particular communication applications, to determine users' adoption of mobile technologies. Furthermore, this study explores whether extraversion and innovativeness as personality features are determinants of mobile technology use. Extraversion is the most commonly used personality trait and has been reported to be effective in predicting the use of mobile phones and applications [1, 3, 11, 12]. However, traditional mobile phone use has been evolving and novel applications have started to substitute traditional methods. In this transition, innovativeness is a significant personality feature that is worthy of investigation.

3 Research Methodology

3.1 Participants

The empirical data was collected using a questionnaire that was e-mailed to the undergraduate and graduate university student lists of a well-known university in Turkey. The questionnaire was completed by 343 people, of whom 154 were female and 131 were male, and the remaining 58 students did not state their gender. The average age of participants was 21.7.

3.2 Materials

Measuring Extraversion. Within the framework of the Big-Five model, Gosling et al. [22] introduced the Ten Item Personality Inventory (TIPI), which contains ten questions to determine the Big-Five personality traits. In our study, we used TIPI to measure self-perceived personality. The relevant TIPI questions that were employed in the questionnaire were "extraverted, enthusiastic" and "reserved, quiet". Participants were asked to enter a number from 1 to 7, from strongly disagree to strongly agree. The scale reliability was considered to be sufficient since the Cronbach Alpha value was 0.7, which is compatible with the recommended values [23].

Measuring User Innovativeness. In the literature, innovativeness is used as a personality construct to predict consumer perceived innovativeness. The innovativeness index (INN) used in this study is a composite score of five innovativeness items which aim to measure users' openness to new technologies. The INN measure was adopted from Yang [17] who developed a 7-point Likert scale ranging from 1 (strongly disagree) to 7 (strongly agree). The scale reliability was measured using Cronbach's Alpha and found to be acceptable (0.82) [23].

Survey on Mobile Phone and Application Use. This survey consisted of three sections; demographic details, mobile phone use and mobile application use. In the demographics section, information on participants' age and gender was obtained. The mobile phone use section contained questions based on a 7-point Likert scale with 1 being no use to 7 being very frequent use. The questions were mainly based on the constructs in the study of Butt and Philips [2] but were further elaborated. In their study, the authors measured time spent per week on all calls (separating incoming and outgoing calls) and SMS messaging. In our study, we asked further questions regarding the time spent on all features of daily mobile phone use. More specifically, we represented the time spent on SMS using two variables; time spent on incoming messages and outgoing messages. In addition, the newly added questions concerned total time spent on using mobile phone, the number of incoming and outgoing calls, frequency of mobile application use and the number of people contacted for incoming and outgoing calls in a day. The third section of the survey contained questions regarding mobile application use patterns based on a Likert scale with responses graded from 1 to 5 with 1 being no use to 5 being very frequent use.

For the two most popular smartphone operating systems (iOS and Android), application categories were obtained from Apple Store and Google Play store. This method was based on the work of Hui-Yi and Ling-Yin [24], in which 12 major application categories were aggregated using three major mobile application platforms, Apple Store, Google Play Store and Windows Market.

In relation to the findings concerning the effect of personality features on mobile phone use and to investigate the shift from traditional mobile phone use to mobile communication applications use, applications in the communication category were prioritized in this study. Mobile applications in the communications category were presented in the sub categories of VoIP (e.g., Skype), instant messaging (such as Whatsapp and Viber), e-mails, and photograph sharing (e.g., Instagram and flickr). Then, the following most popular categories were added to the study: music/audio (such as radio and music player), video (e.g., Youtube, Vimeo) productivity, tools, weather, news, games, finance (e.g., banking, stock exchange), shopping (m-commerce), travel (navigation, maps i.e.), personal life (such as health, fitness and lifestyle), web browsers, and books/references.

3.3   Data Analysis and Results

Data was analyzed using SPSS. A total of 343 participants responded to the survey questions. The questions regarding extraversion and innovativeness were answered by 314 respondents. Among 314 respondents the questions concerning mobile applications use were answered by 285 respondents who stated that they used mobile applications in their mobile phones, These respondents were obviously using mobile applications with their smart phones. As a result, the analyses regarding mobile phone use comprised users who own mobile phones whereas the analyses with respect to mobile application use took into consideration the users using applications on their smartphones which is a total of 285 users.

For the features that were found to be positively skewed, a log transformation, log (feature + 1), was applied. For the features that were negatively skewed, the scale was inverted by subtracting it from its maximum value plus one before applying the log transformation. The features that were inversed were negated to ease interpretation. The assumption of normality was met after the data was transformed.

Analysis of the Independent Variables. The mean score for INN was 5.717 (SD = 0.916) whereas for extraversion feature it was 4.941 (SD = 1.397). The correlations between the independent variables were computed using Pearson's correlation coefficient. It was found that innovativeness is significantly correlated with extraversion

Table 1. Descriptive statistics for mobile phone use features

	N	Mean	SD	Skewness
Usage time [a]	343	4.297	1.770	0.064
Incoming calls time [a]	343	2.236	1.134	1.195
Outgoing calls time [a]	343	1.971	1.042	1.460
Incoming messages [a]	343	2.294	1,517	1.351
Outgoing messages [a]	343	2.233	1.496	1.430
Mobile app use [b]	343	3.580	1.904	0.362
Number of incoming calls [b]	343	3.076	1.090	0.913
Number of outgoing calls [b]	343	2.875	0.988	0.895
Number of contacts (incoming calls) [b]	343	3.000	0.970	0.946
Number of contacts (outgoing calls) [b]	343	2.834	0.970	1.132

[a] Likert scale with 1 being no use to 7 being very much use
[b] Likert scale with 1 being no use to 7 being very frequent use

Table 2. Descriptive statistics for mobile application use features [a]

	N	Mean	SD	Skewness
VoIP	285	2.270	1.311	0.764
Instant messaging	285	3.968	1.425	−1.128
E-mail	285	4.274	1.108	−1.622
Web browsers	285	4.039	1.469	−1.303
Video	285	3.779	1.223	−0.802
Photograph	285	2.649	1.639	0.320
Music/Audio	285	2.677	1.647	0.308
Productivity	285	2.804	1.562	0.140
Tools	285	1.898	1.314	1.231
Weather	285	3.551	1.328	−0.560
News	285	3.382	1.493	−0.457
Games	285	2.793	1.509	0.214
Finance	285	1.856	1.221	1.296
Shopping	285	2.137	1.210	0.888
Navigation	285	2.716	1.250	0.203
Personal life	285	1.825	1.153	1.334
Books/references	285	3.011	1.423	-0.011

[a] Likert scale with 1 being no use to 5 being very
frequent use

(p = 0.333). Although significant correlation exists it is below the selection criterion of 0.99 [25]. Hence, the assumption of no multi-collinearity is met.

Analysis of the Dependent Variables. Tables 1 and 2 present the descriptive statistics for mobile phone and mobile application use, respectively. Table 1 shows that the daily average time for total usage time is relatively higher than those found in the other constructs. The daily average time spent on incoming calls is higher than that spent on outgoing calls, which is consistent with the findings of Butt and Phillips [1]. Similarly,

Table 3. Correlations between independent variables and mobile phone use

	Extraversion	INN [a,b]
Usage time	0.261**	0.113*
Incoming calls time [b]	0.202**	0.020
Outgoing calls time [b]	0.144**	0.031
Incoming messages [b]	0.175**	0.133*
Outgoing messages [b]	0.148**	0.085
Mobile app use	0.159**	0.189**
Number of incoming calls	0.283**	0.226**
Number of outgoing calls	0.256**	0.170**
Number of contacts (incoming calls)	0.274**	0.213**
Number of contacts (outgoing calls) b	0.213**	0.193**

* Correlation is significant at the 0.05 level (2-tailed)
** Correlation is significant at the 0.01 level (2-tailed)
[a] Reverse is taken
[b] Log transformation is applied

the daily average time spent on incoming messages is greater than the time spent on outgoing messages. When the frequency of use is considered, the mean is higher for the daily number of incoming calls than the number of outgoing calls, and the number of contacts for incoming calls is higher than those for outgoing calls. The frequency of using mobile applications is higher than the number of incoming or outgoing calls. Table 4 shows that personal life categories are the least used whereas email and messaging are the most used categories.

Table 3 shows that mobile phone use features are mostly correlated with extraversion. Table 4 demonstrates that mobile application use features are mostly correlated with innovativeness. To test whether extraversion and innovativeness can be used to predict each mobile phone usage construct a total of ten multiple regression models were constructed. The results are given in Table 5. The standardized regression coefficient (β) and t − statistics are presented in Table 6. The regression analysis of mobile phone use showed that extraversion as an independent variable significantly predicted the features for usage time, time spent on incoming calls, time spent on outgoing calls and messages, the number of incoming and outgoing calls, and the number of contacts for incoming and outgoing calls. Innovativeness significantly predicted the frequency of mobile application use, the number of incoming calls and the number of contacts for incoming calls. The personality traits explained 9.8 % of the variance (F = 16.984, p = 0.00*) in predicting the number of incoming calls, which is the highest among all models. When the standardized regression coefficients were examined, the extraversion trait was found to be significant in predicting mobile phone use ($\beta = 0.251$, p = 0.00*) whereas innovativeness was significant in predicting mobile application use ($\beta = 0.159$, p = 0.00*).

A total of 17 multiple regression models were constructed to test whether extraversion and innovativeness can be used to predict each mobile application usage construct Table 7 presents the results regarding the R2 values and significance levels. The standardized regression coefficient (β) and t − statistics are presented in Table 8. This analysis showed that the independent variables significantly predicted the features

Table 4. Correlations between independent variables and mobile application categories

	Extraversion	INN [a,b]
VoIP	0.101	0.200**
Instant messaging [a,b]	0.181**	0.175**
Email [a,b]	0.216**	0.178**
WebBrowsers [a,b]	0.099	0.198**
Video	0.187**	0.245**
Photograph	0.189**	0.122*
Music	0.191**	0.118*
Productivity	0.075	0.215**
Tools [b]	0.074	0.224**
Weather	-0.022	0.159**
News	0.188**	0.298**
Games	0.072	0.221**
Finance [b]	0.143*	0.252**
Shopping	-0.005	0.137*
Navigation	-0.016	0.242**
PersonalLife [b]	0.069	0.050
Books/references	0.038	0.204**

* Correlation is significant at the 0.05 level (2-tailed)
** Correlation is significant at the 0.01 level (2-tailed)
[a] Reverse is taken [b] Log transformation is applied

Table 5. Regression analysis for mobile phone use

	F	p	R^2
Usage time	11.513	0.000**	0.069
Incoming calls time [b]	7.037	0.001**	0.043
Outgoing calls time [b]	3.342	0.037*	0.021
Incoming messages [b]	5.947	0.003**	0.031
Outgoing messages [b]	3.725	0.025*	0.023
Mobile app use	7.514	0.001**	0.046
Number of incoming calls	17.223	0.000**	0.100
Number of outgoing calls	11.277	0.000**	0.073
Number of contacts (incoming calls)	15.753	0.000**	0.092
Number of contacts (outgoing calls) [b]	10.323	0.000**	0.062

* Correlation is significant at the 0.05 level (2-tailed)
** Correlation is significant at the 0.01 level (2-tailed)
[a] Reverse is taken
[b] Log transformation is applied

Table 6. Standardized regression coefficient, t-value and significance for mobile phone use

	Extraversion			INN [a,b]		
	Beta	t	p	Beta	t	p
Usage time	0.251	4.334	0.000	0.029	0.502	0.616
Incoming calls time b	0.220	3.734	0.000	-0.053	-0.903	0.367
Outgoing calls time b	0.150	2.525	0.012	-0.019	-0.314	0.753
Incoming messages b	0.147	2.490	0.013	0.084	1.423	0.156
Outgoing messages b	0.135	2.272	0.024	0.040	0.670	0.503
Mobile app use	0.109	1.849	0.065	0.153	2.598	0.010
Number of incoming calls	0.234	4.104	0.000	0.148	2.591	0.010
Number of outgoing calls	0.224	3.868	0.000	0.096	1.656	0.099
Number of contacts (incoming calls)	0.229	3.991	0.000	0.137	2.395	0.017
Number of contacts (outgoing calls) b	0.168	2.883	0.004	0.137	2.354	0.019

[a] Reverse is taken
[b] Log transformation is applied

Table 7. Regression analysis for mobile application use

	F	p	R^2
VoIP	6.031	0.003**	0.042
Instant messaging [a,b]	7.053	0.001**	0.049
Email [a,b]	8.908	0.000**	0.054
WebBrowsers [a,b]	5.904	0.003**	0.041
Video	11.064	0.000**	0.074
Photograph	5.771	0.004**	0.040
Music	5.846	0.003**	0.034
Productivity	6.653	0.002**	0.039
Tools [b]	7.247	0.001**	0.043
Weather	4.304	0.014*	0.030
News	15.254	0.000**	0.093
Games	7.052	0.001**	0.049
Finance [b]	9.074	0.000**	0.055
Shopping	2.943	0.054*	0.014
Navigation	9.899	0.000**	0.060
Personal life [b]	0.756	0.047*	0.005
Books/references	6.083	0.003**	0.035

Correlation is significant at the *0.05 level
** 0.01 level (2-tailed)
[a] Reverse is taken
[b] Log transformation is applied

Table 8. Standardized regression coefficient, t-value and significance for mobile application use

	Extraversion			INN [a,b]		
	Beta	t	p	Beta	t	p
VoIP	0.046	0.740	0.460	0.187	3.021	0.003
Instant messaging [a,b]	0.142	2.301	0.022	0.133	2.153	0.032
Email [a,b]	0.179	2.922	0.004	0.125	2.043	0.042
Web browsers [a,b]	0.044	0.713	0.477	0.185	2.999	0.003
Video	0.125	2.065	0.040	0.208	3.424	0.001
Photograph	0.167	2.704	0.007	0.072	1.163	0.246
Music	0.171	2.773	0.006	0.067	1.089	0.277
Productivity	0.012	0.202	0.840	0.211	3.418	0.001
Tools [b]	0.009	0.144	0.885	0.221	3.591	0.000
Weather	-0.075	-1.213	0.226	0.181	2.911	0.004
News	0.109	1.819	0.070	0.266	4.441	0.000
Games	0.008	0.125	0.901	0.218	3.548	0.000
Finance [b]	0.080	1.307	0.192	0.213	3.484	0.001
Shopping	-0.050	-0.799	0.425	0.151	2.425	0.016
Navigation	-0.096	-1.575	0.116	0.271	4.441	0.000
Personal life [b]	0.061	0,969	0.334	0.028	0.437	0.663
Books & references	0.025	0.402	0.688	0.212	3.428	0.001

[a] Reverse is taken
[b] Log transformation is applied

of mobile application categories. As shown in Table 8, 14 of the 17 mobile application categories were significantly related with innovativeness: VoIP, instant messaging, e-mails, web browsers, tools, finance, video, productivity, weather, games, shopping, navigation, books/references and news whereas instant messaging, email, video, photograph, music categories were found to be significantly related with extraversion. Both personality traits explained the highest variance (1.03 %) (F = 15.728, p = 0.00*) in the model predicting the use of news applications. Furthermore, the innovativeness trait was found to be significant in prediction ($\beta = 0.201$, p = 0.001). In addition, the traits accounted for 7.5 % of the variance (F = 11.153, p = 0.00*) in predicting the use of video related application. Although both extraversion ($\beta = 0.124$, p = 0.044) and innovativeness ($\beta = 0.210$, p = 0.001) were significant predictors in this model, the effect of innovativeness feature was higher. The traits in the models predicting VoIP, instant messaging, web browsers, tools, finance, VoIP, photograph, productivity, games, navigation, books/references, and news explained 4.1 % to 6.9 % of the variance.

4 Discussion

In this study, we investigated the relationship between personality traits and mobile technology use, traditional communication channels such as voice calls and SMS messaging and various mobile application categories. To our knowledge, this was the first study to explore the relationship between different personality features and different aspects of mobile technology use. In addition, the frequency of mobile application use was analyzed for the first time in the literature.

Our results confirmed the results of the previous studies concluding that personality traits can be used to determine the patterns of mobile phone use [1]. People with high scores in extraversion trait were found to; (1) make longer incoming and outgoing calls, (2) spend more time using their mobile phones [1, 2], [6], [26], (3) send and receive a higher number of messages [1], [6], [10, 11], (4) make a higher number of incoming and outgoing calls, and (5) communicate with a higher number of different contacts [6].

In addition, our findings offer the following novel contributions: Individuals high in extraversion trait (1) spend more time in using mobile applications, (2) spend more time in applications that provide voice calling and sending messages, the reasons of which can be explained by our aforementioned findings: the extravert people spend more time in mobile phone use and (3) spend more time in using music applications. However in the literature, Chittaranjan et al. [6] found a slight negative relationship between the category of audio/music/video applications. Youtube on the other hand was found to be more likely to be used by extraverts. Using visual and audio multimedia may coincide with enthusiasm-seeking, active and energetic nature of extraverts. Previous research found positive relation between extraversion and use of office and calendar mobile applications and with e-mails only for males [6]. Internet applications in transaction category [3] are also found to be positively related with extraversion.

The use of mobile applications is significantly related to the innovativeness trait. People who are high in innovativeness trait spend more time in (4) communicating with others, (5) sharing media including video and photography (6) using music, news, weather, navigation, bookmarking, gaming, shopping, books and references type applications. However, people who are high in innovativeness trait tend to use Tools and Finance applications less frequently.

Innovativeness was found to significantly predict mobile application use, the number of incoming calls and the number of contacts for incoming calls. In other words, innovative people receive a higher number of incoming calls. According to the results of the regression analysis of mobile application use, the independent variables significantly predicted the features of mobile application categories. The positive relationship between innovativeness trait and the frequency of mobile application use suggests that innovative people are open to new experiences and technology. In particular, the use of e-mail, search, timetable and navigation services is significantly higher in innovative individuals. Furthermore, there is a positive relationship between gaming applications and innovativeness, which can also be attributed to innovative people being more open to information technology and applications. Our results show that innovativeness positively relates to the use of finance applications. In addition, there is a positive relationship between innovativeness and shopping applications.

The most significant positive relation was observed between innovativeness and news applications ($r = 0.304$, $p < 0.01$) suggesting that innovative people tend to download more news applications. This may be due to tendency towards increasingly accessing knowledge and information through news/information type applications. Similar discussions can explain the positive relationship between books/references and innovativeness. This is also supported by Kim et al. [27] who found that highly educated individuals were 13 % more likely to use literacy applications compared to individuals with a lower education level.

5 Conclusion and Future Work

This research investigated whether the extraversion and innovativeness of individuals are effective in the use of mobile phones and mobile applications, in particular those related to communication. In our study, mobile phone use features were found to be mostly correlated with extraversion. This is in line with previous research and social and outgoing nature of extraverts. Mobile application use features were mostly correlated with innovativeness. The relation between innovativeness and mobile phone and application use is explored for the first time to the best of our knowledge. It is not surprising to find that innovative people are more open to new experiences and technological innovations represented by mobile applications.

The major limitation of the study was the use of a convenience sample consisting of graduate and undergraduate university students since it does not completely represent the general consumer population who are likely to be less familiar with mobile applications. Another limitation of the study was the use of self-reporting method to collect data on the mobile phone and application use of individuals. In the questionnaires, the participants were asked to make an estimate based on their past behavior. However, this can result in bias and the use of log data would be more reliable. Future studies can resolve this issue by employing log data.

Mobile technology products should avoid one-size-fits-all approach to meet different needs of individuals. The findings of this study provide valuable information to improve personalization and recommendation services of mobile applications. People with similar personality features may be used to identify and cluster people with similar tastes and preferences. Understanding the patterns of mobile phone use is significant to reveal user preferences to improve the features of mobile phones and personalized mobile services. It can also help tailor for specific needs and specific populations and make predictions based on the available data. The identification of users who are innovators, early-adopter, leaders or users with a large number of friends is also important to determine the primary segment that should be targeted by marketing practitioners. Innovative individuals are potential primary market segment as being leaders and early-adopters in technology use. Extraverts are another target segment with their high potential in mobile phone and application use. The findings in this study provide useful insights for mobile technology designers, especially those designing for specific populations.

References

1. Butt, S., Phillips, J.G.: Personality and self reported mobile phone use. Comput. Human Behav. **24**, 346–360 (2008)
2. Chittaranjan, G., Blom, J., Gatica-Perez, D.: Who's who with big-five: analyzing and classifying personality traits with smartphones. In: 15th Annual International Symposium on Wearable Computers (ISWC), pp. 29–36. IEEE Press, New York (2011)

3. Tan, W.K., Yang, C.Y.: Internet applications use and personality. Telematics Inform. **31**, 27–38 (2014)
4. Seneviratne, S., Seneviratne, A., Mohapatra, P., Mahanti, A.: Predicting user traits from a snapshot of apps installed on a smartphone. ACM SIGMOBILE Mob. Comput. Commun. Rev. **18**, 1–8 (2014)
5. Seneviratne, S., Seneviratne, A., Mohapatra, P., Mahanti, A.: Your installed apps reveal your gender and more! In: ACM MobiCom Workshop on Security and Privacy in Mobile Environments (SPME 2014), pp. 1–6. ACM, New York (2014)
6. Chittaranjan, G., Blom, J., Gatica-Perez, D.: Mining large-scale smartphone data for personality studies. Pers. Ubiquit. Comput. **17**, 433–457 (2013)
7. Leavitt, C., Walton, J.: Development of a Scale for Innovativeness. In: Schlinger, M.J., Abor, A. (eds.), NA-Advances in Consumer Research. Association for Consumer Research pp. 545–554 (1975)
8. John, O.P., Srivastava, S.: The big five trait taxonomy: history, measurement and theoretical perspectives. In: Pervin, L., John, O.P. (eds.) Handbook of Personality: Theory and Research, 2nd edn, pp. 102–138. Guilford, New York (1999)
9. Bianchi, A., Phillips, J.: Psychological predictors of problem mobile phone use. Cyberpsychology Behav. **8**, 39–51 (2005)
10. Oliveira, R., Cherubini, M., Oliver, N.: Influence of personality on satisfaction with mobile phone services. ACM Trans. Comput. Interact. 20 (2013)
11. Lane, W., Manner, C.: The impact of personality traits on smartphone ownership and use. Int. J. Bus. Soc. Sci. **2**, 22–28 (2011)
12. Lane, W., Manner, C.: The influence of personality traits on mobile phone application preferences. J. Econ. Behav. Stud. **4**, 252–260 (2012)
13. Rogers, E.M.: Diffusion of Innovations. Simon and Schuster, New York (2010)
14. Agarwal, R., Prasad, J.: A conceptual and operational definition of personal innovativeness in the domain of information technology. Inf. Syst. Res. **9**, 204–215 (1998)
15. Chang, M.K., Cheung, W., Lai, V.S.: Literature derived reference models for the adoption of online shopping. Inf. Manag. **42**, 543–559 (2005)
16. Yang, K.C.C.: Exploring factors affecting the adoption of mobile commerce in Singapore. Telematics Inform. **22**, 257–277 (2005)
17. Nov, O., Ye, C.: Personality and technology acceptance: the case for personal innovativeness in IT, openness and resistance to change. In: 41st Hawaii International Conference on System Sciences (HICSS 2008), pp. 448. IEEE Computer Society, Washington (2008)
18. Dai, H., Palvi, P.C.: Mobile commerce adoption in china and the united states: a cross-cultural study. ACM SIGMIS Database **40**, 43–61 (2009)
19. Boase, J.: Implications of software-based mobile media for social research. Mob. Media Commun. **1**, 57–62 (2013)
20. Palekar, S., Weerasinghe, K., Sedera, D.: Disruptive innovation of mobile communication apps. In: 24th Australasian Conference on Information Systems (ACIS), pp. 1–10. RMIT University, Australia (2013)
21. Humphreys, L.: Mobile social media: future challenges and opportunities. Mob. Media Commun. **1**, 20–25 (2013)
22. Gosling, S.D., Rentfrow, P.J., William, B.S.: A very brief measure of the big-five personality domains. J. Res. Pers. **37**, 504–528 (2003)
23. Nunnally, J.C.: Psychometric Theory (McGraw-Hill Series in Psychology). McGraw-Hill, New York (1978)

24. Hui-Yi, H., Ling-Yin, S.: Uses and gratifications of mobile application users. In: International Conference on Electronics and Information Engineering (ICEIE), pp. 315–319. IEEE Press, New York (2010)
25. Tabachnick, B.G., Fidell, L.S.: Using Multivariate Statistics, 4th edn. Allyn & Bacon, Boston (2000)
26. de Montjoye, Y.-A., Quoidbach, J., Robic, F., Pentland, A(.: Predicting personality using novel mobile phone-based metrics. In: Greenberg, A.M., Kennedy, W.G., Bos, N.D. (eds.) SBP 2013. LNCS, vol. 7812, pp. 48–55. Springer, Heidelberg (2013)
27. Kim, Y., Briley, D.A., Ocepek, M.G.: Differential innovation of smartphone and application use by sociodemographics and personality. Comput. Human Behav. **44**, 141–147 (2015)

Smart Solution in Social Relationships Graphs

Ales Berger$^{(\boxtimes)}$ and Filip Maly

Faculty of Informatics and Management, University of Hradec Kralove,
Hradec Kralove, Czech Republic
{ales.berger, filip.maly}@uhk.cz

Abstract. The social relationships graph i.e. sociogram allows a transparent
view of people in their surroundings to whom we have a certain relationship. Such options have already depicted many tools. They generally use data
from social networks, e.g. Facebook or Google+. Certainly, not every such a
graph is entirely transparent and usable. A sociogram contains a large number of
vertices and edges when there are a larger number of people in their surroundings. Then it is not possible to simply work with the graph and subsequently describe it. In this article, we introduce options that will make the
sociogram transparent, thus offering easier work with it. We work with a software tool from the IHMC company, called CmapTools, which normally operates on desktop operating systems. In our case, we are working with a version
for the Android OS, which has been externally developed for the company for a
long time, but has not yet been publicly introduced.

Keywords: Social relationships · Sociogram · Graph theory · Anroid operating
system · CmapTools

1 Introduction

In autumn 2013, we completed a study internship at the American institution for science
and research IHMC (Institute for Human and Machine Cognition www.ihmc.us)
together with colleagues from the University of Hradec Kralove in Florida. Thanks to
our work experience with the development of mobile applications for the Android
operating system, we were assigned to the team for software development managing and
editing CmapTools concept maps. Our task was to prepare the cornerstone for the
subsequent development of a mobile version of CmapTools [1] especially for the
Android operating system. We prepared a partly usable version during the two-month
internship that the institution management liked and offered us an external collaboration.

After completing the course, Smart approaches to the creation of information
systems and applications, we chose just an extension of the CmapTools application.
The application is mainly used for creating and editing conceptual maps. [3] We chose
the solution of the problem in visualizing social relationships among people who use
the services on Facebook social network chosen by us in order to take advantage of the
options that the application offers, and because of our interest in social networks.

The main idea of the Facebook social network is to connect users and the dissemination of information. It is grounded in a virtual friendship. Each user can tag

M. Younas et al. (Eds.): MobiWIS 2016, LNCS 9847, pp. 393–405, 2016.
DOI: 10.1007/978-3-319-44215-0_33

someone else as their friend with their consent. This generates innumerable relationships among users. With one of the resulting friendships one can develop some more and so on.

For a transparent display of all our friendships, simply fill in the name or at first glance the unequivocal photo. If we are interested in a mutual friendship among our friends, it is no longer so simple. For a transparent display we will use graph theory and then draw our friendship as a graph.

Such a graph can be imagined as a simplification of the real world, where the studied problem will be illustrated by points, which are connected by lines thus describing the various characteristics. Such points in graph theory are called vertices (graph peaks). The lines that connect vertices are called edges [2].

The CmapTools application will simply be applicable for the representation of such a graph. In our case, when we need to represent users and relationships, we determine a user by using the vertices and edges will constitute the existing friendships of these users.

Obtaining information about friends and relationships among them from the Facebook social network cannot be performed as previously by using simple FQL queries to the Facebook SDK. The possibility of obtaining data from the social network was banned. Currently it is possible to obtain data in a similar manner by using the Graph API tool. The possibility of use is, however, significantly restricted. Information about friends can be obtained only from those with an application created by you, which will be using this data. Such a condition is not very acceptable and data retrieval will need to be resolved in a different manner [7].

The last part is a transparent representation of the obtained data in the CmapTools application. The simple depicting of vertices and edges in the graph would not be very transparent and usable. It is necessary to distribute individual vertices so that the graph clearly provides the information we need to find out. Since these days the average number of Facebook friends is approximately equal to the number 338 and its median is 200 [7], it is not possible to use a simple depiction. Our goal is to introduce perhaps the simplest algorithm suggested by us for the best positioning of vertices in the graph; furthermore, to minimize the number of edges necessary for the display of friendships and still retain all the information in the graph. Simply incorporate a community of friends dividing our social life on more parts.

The CmapTools application, graph theory, the possibility of obtaining data from Facebook social network and the algorithm for the transparent depiction of the sociogram and subsequent implementation are presented in more detail in this article.

2   Problem Definition

The easiest way to express the social network is as an undirected graph. The graph is the basic object of graph theory. The point is that this is a representation of a group of objects in which we want to represent that some of the elements have a certain relationship to another one. [2] Vertices will be assigned for the objects, in our case users, and their relationships will be represented by the edges among them. The relationship can be understood as a friendship, family or co-operation.

Graphs can be further divided into directed and undirected. A directed graph takes into account the order of vertices of each edge. It is not necessary to know from which vertex the edge proceeds concerning the edges of the undirected graph. [2] In our case it is sufficient to use an undirected graph in the sociogram. But there are also cases when it is necessary to depict relationships among the vertices by means of oriented graphs. This graph shows not only the relationship, but also determines the direction from which vertex is the relationship directed towards another relationship.

An undirected graph is the pair $G = <V, E>$, where V is a non-empty group of vertices and E the group of two-element groups of vertices $E \in \{ \{u, v\} | u, v \in V, u \neq v\}$. Each vertex can have some designation or name. The number of edges reaching the vertex is denoted as the degree of the vertex. This degree will be interesting for us. We will consider the number of friends and the user represented by the vertex have in common as the degree of vertex [2] (Fig. 1).

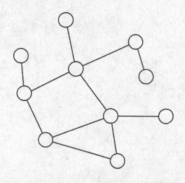

Fig. 1. Undirected graph

It is therefore necessary to define all the vertices and edges for our graph. The data will be drawn from Facebook social network. Information concerning our friends and the friends of our friends who are also our friends will be interesting for us. These users will therefore be presented by the vertices in the graph and the relationships between us and among the others will be presented by the edges.

A classical graph of social relationships has certain limitations. With visualization system with multiple objects, a great increase in the number of crossing edges representing their relationships occurs and thereby the graph becomes quite unclear. Therefore, it is necessary to first think about the exact location of all the vertices on the map, then define and create so-called communities and finally depict their relationships; as a community refers to a group of vertices, which have the most common relationships among themselves. It is not necessary to have all the vertices interconnected among themselves, which would represent already an arc of the graph, but it is sufficient that each vertex would be linked with most of the others. An arc of the graph is each maximal complete subgraph. All vertices of the arc are connected with all remaining by an edge [2, 4].

The location of vertices can be performed easily. One option may be to depict all vertices periodically according to the grid, for example sorted in ascending alphabetical order. Such a distribution would say anything to us after depicting all relationships. It would be impossible to recognize all relationships and the graph would be unusable.

It is therefore necessary to accurately calculate the location for each vertex. Individual vertices will be placed into a graph based on their grade. Approximately in the middle of the graph there will be vertices whose degree will be the largest. Conversely, the degree of vertices will be the smallest on the edge of the graph. It is also necessary to place vertices side by side so that adjacent ones would have relationships in common as much as possible. We need to minimize the number of edges, which will intervene through the entire graph and at the same time try to minimize the length of all edges in the graph.

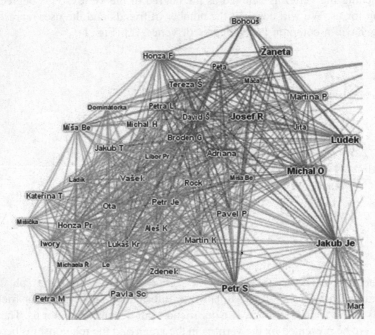

Fig. 2. Sociogram

On Fig. 2 there is a part of the graph that was created by TouchGraph (www. touchgraph.com). Data for the application will be provided, the same as in our case, Facebook. All vertices are already correctly located in the graph, but the result is not quite ideal. Even though it is clearly distinguishable which communities create our social relationships, it is not too clear who is with whom in the relationship, since the number of vertices and edges is very large.

Since our friends are also strongly linked to each other, it is necessary to propose a better solution for maximizing the clarity of the graph, that it be possible to work simply in the CmapTools application.

FQL (Facebook Query Language) was an ideal service for data provision and querying Facebook that was unfortunately stopped. FQL was a query language allowing the acquisition of user data from the Facebook social network. Working with it was carried out similarly to SQL language. Data returned to us in the JSON format and our application could work with them. However, this is not possible for newly created applications and therefore it is necessary to switch using The Graph API – a new platform for working with data on Facebook [7].

The proposed methods are described in more detail in the following chapter, which should make the graph more clear and facilitate the overall work with it.

3   New Solution

The standard solution for visualizing social relationships, for example the mentioned Touchgraph, displays users to whom the sociogram binds on the map of the graph. But this does not bring any benefit and we are only adding duty to depicting the vertex and just as many edges as many friends we have. The matter is that it concerns only our social relationships. It is therefore obvious that with each person in the graph there exists just one relationship with us. [4] We will save many edges in the graph only by not depicting ourselves. If we fail to do so, according to the rule we set in the previous chapter, the vertex with the highest degree will be in the middle, a vertex representing us would be in the middle. Thus, there will be one or more users who have the most common relationships with our friends over others in the middle.

In the graph, there is also the great possibility of the existence of one or more complete subgraphs, so-called arcs. Even the only two vertices which are linked can form an arc with two vertices. That one is just a little interesting for us. We will search for the maximum arc in each part of the graph. We will go through the graph by using the cycle and in every iteration we will try to add another vertex, which would meet the rules of the existing relationships with other vertices in the subgraph to the arc that is already created [2, 4].

Since the vertices in each arc are linked with each other, it is enough to clearly mark such a subgraph, and then there is no need to draw edges among vertices. This saves many edges and the graph will be clarified. We will mark the arcs by packing vertices into one larger area that will be color-marked only with a light color.

In case that some vertex was related to more than two thirds of the vertices of some arc, it can also be possible to include it in the group. There is also a possibility that some vertex will encounter this fact for more than just one arc. Then, this fact will be solved individually and we will include a vertex where there will be more common relationships. Within this defined group, we will depict some of the edges. However, it will not be the edges of the vertices, which are related to each other, but the edges of the vertices which do not have a relationship to each other. The edges of the missing relationship will be marked with a distinctive red color compared to standard edges. Thus it will not be too difficult to distinguish whether the edge indicates the presence or absence of the relationship between the vertices.

After creating all potential groups, we will begin to deal with the edges among vertices that will not fall into the same group. Again, we will try to save as many edges, or at least their length. Each should represent as many relationships as possible and not just one. We will test for all the vertices to see whether there exists multiple relationships for some of the already created groups. If so, we create such edges that are connected in one edge, and only those that will continue to the opposite vertex. Exactly through such a manner one edge may represent several existing relationships.

Another question is the already mentioned communities. The friends of each one us are divided into several groups. Some of our friends we know e.g. from primary school, some from high school, university, the place where we live or work. It would be good to divide our graph in such a manner to see how much our social life is divided. The solution offered by TouchGraph is very good and clear. We will simply highlight communities with specific colors. The only change will be that we will demonstrate the number of vertices in every community belonging to it.

It is necessary to define a new rule. How to determine that the vertex belongs to the community? Our goal for this moment will be coloring a simple undirected graph according to defined graph communities [6].

It will be necessary to use another group of cycles. In the first step we will look through vertices with the least degree of vertex and find such vertices that have a relationship with them and, if possible, the lowest degree at the same time. We will not deal with vertices having a degree of zero and they will not be incorporated in any of the communities. This will create the first small communities and we will try to decrease their number as much as possible. In the following steps, we will try to connect already existing communities. We will search for such a community for each community, whose vertices are related to all vertices of the second community. This described problem in Fig. 3 is depicted in the flow diagram [5].

When we come into a situation where it is not possible to continue and join any communities, it is necessary to start working individually. We will progressively set in each step certain coefficient k, for which we set the value 1 at the beginning. After each iteration, the coefficient will be reduced e.g. for a value of 0.05. The coefficient k will determine how many percent of vertices of communities it is necessary to have a relationship with to be able to unite the two communities into one. If the coefficient is equal to 0.5, we will stop with the iterations and the graph will be marked as resolved within the problems of the communities [5].

Furthermore, a situation will arrive in which it is necessary to choose colors according to the number of communities that are the most different from each other and each assign to a single community. We will mark all the vertices of a given community with the appropriate color. But the edges will remain marked by a standard black color; we will not deal with it as in TouchGraph, in which also the edges are colored according to their respective communities. The coloring of the edges would disclose nothing to us, and in our case when we have a relationship that does not exist marked with a red color, it would only create trouble.

Graph theory is resolved at the moment and it is now necessary to introduce options that will be used from the CmapTools tool. The whole application will run on the Android operating system. The CmapTools application standardly works on desktop operating systems. The application is totally free and it is possible to download from the Internet. In our case, we only use our proposed core of the application, the possibilities of depicting concepts and edges. The term concept is represented in the CmapTools application in the same way as the vertex in graph theory. However, it is possible to add additional information such as the URL address or image. We will use the supplementary information and each vertex will be marked with the abbreviated

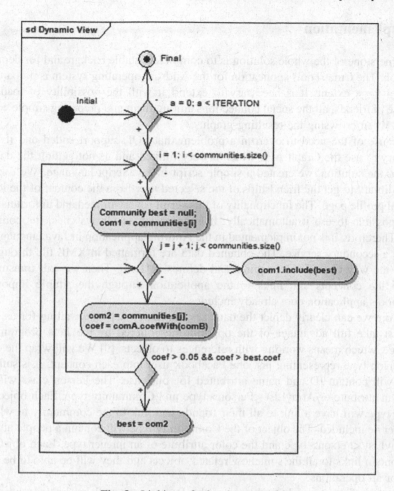

Fig. 3. Linking of related communities

name of the user (e.g. Thomas B.) and his additional information can be his full name, URL address on his Facebook profile or e.g. his profile photos. CmapTools allows modifying the visual characteristics of each concept separately and it is precisely the option which we need in our case [1].

The modified application will be called FaceTools, leaving it only original application possibilities, which are necessary for the functioning of our own. FaceTools will provide the possibility of importing relationships from the Facebook social network, a view of the entire generated social graph and the possibility of its simple editing. The menu will contain the possibility of changing the look of the vertices, their addition or removal and handling them. After finishing the development of the first version, the application will be tested by several Facebook users and compared with the output TouchGraph application.

4 Implementation

The cornerstone of the whole solution is to complete a stable background for depicting the graph. The CmapTools application for the Android operating system is prepared for use to a large extent. It is necessary to extend it with the possibility of loading a database of friends, all the social connections among them and preparing simple control options when browsing the resulting graph.

Because of the need to overrun a problem that FQL support ended and it being necessary to use the Graph API, which is very limited and us not getting the data we need for the solution, we created a simple script in JavaScript language. We used the jQuery library to get the friendships of the selected user from the content of the loaded personal profile page. The functionality of this script is very limited and unfortunately it is not possible to use it automatically. It is necessary to always check its course or result. Therefore, it is not implemented in the Android application in Java language, but only as a secondary service. The obtained data are formatted in XML file through the service the way CmapTools requires and defines it [1, 8]. Then we will transmit the data to the concepts and links to the application through the simple import the CmapTools application core already includes.

Before we can clearly depict the data, several major steps are waiting for us. First, we must take full advantage of the opportunities offered by the Java programming language, which means working with references to objects. [9] We will wrap the object of a Person type representing just one Facebook user into each concept. It is sufficient that it will contain ID and name attributed for our case. The Person class will also define an attribute of ArrayList <Person> type and Community type. Each object of a Person type will have a link to all their friends and link to the community to which it will later be included. The object of the Community type will contain a people attribute of ArrayList <Person> type and the color attribute of an integer type. Each object will then contain links to all the somehow related objects and they will be able to be easily used for all operations.

After the first step, when objects of the Person type will be created and all the necessary connections will be added to it, we will gradually cluster objects into individual communities. Our goal is to create as few communities as possible, so that in each of them will be people as much related as possible. After studying the algorithms clearly explained in [5], We chose for the communities to create successive iterations which we would cluster into one and so on within the next steps, based on relationships with users classified into those communities.

In the first step, We will create a community of two people who are friends while not having other friends. The next step will be clustering communities in which their members will be friends among themselves. Thus we will proceed until all clustering possibilities are exhausted.

The next step will be the connecting of two friends who have 2–10 friends and at least 60 % friends in common. After creating the first communities, we will do so not with people but with communities. We will therefore be uniting communities where it is valid that 60 % of friendships of all people of one community correspond to 60 % of friendships in the second community [5].

The last and also the most challenging step will be to combine people who are not in any community yet, which is the majority at this moment, so that there will exist as many friendships within individual communities and as less friendships of people who will be included between the two different communities. This will happen so that also the number of communities is the fewest.

In this step, the first task is to include all the people in their own newly created community. The final solution is presented through several embedded cycles, when we are trying to unite communities at every step so that their members (therefore only one member in the first step) have as many friends in common as possible. We can unite a community only with one more in each step of the cycle. The number of cycle steps is not numerically limited, but by reality, when the number of communities and their representation by the people in a given iteration have not changed. After certain steps of the cycle it is not possible anymore for the majority, therefore 60 % of community members selected by us, would be in a friendship with the majority of the second community. Therefore, it is necessary to choose another coefficient that would be for testing, in our case set to 5 %.

It is necessary that the number of existing friendships acquired at least 5 % of the value of all the possible existing friendships existing between all people from both communities so that a certain two communities could be mutually connected. A cycle is terminated when such a combination is no longer possible. So then we will get into a variable of List <Community> type optimally categorized people of the social networks into individual communities. Finally, the list must be sorted so that in the first positions there would be communities with the least number of members, in some cases just 1. In Fig. 4, there is shown, for the simplest possible idea, a class diagram consisting of the most important classes fulfilling the complete functionality of our application.

After the efficient sorting of the people it is necessary to calculate their position in the social graph. We are making an assumption from the simplest possible variant. A circle. We deploy an individual person, thus the vertices of the graph, on the coordinates according to the circle calculation. Subsequent friendships will be displayed as lines connecting two vertices. If we do not continue onwards, and leave the circle as the final solution for the calculation of the coordinates, our social network would look as follows.

When zooming into detail, it would be possible to recognize individual friendships, but it is not the result we want to achieve. Because we have people divided into separate communities, we will represent each community as their own subgraph.

We will mark each community, a subgraph, with its color, maximally different from all others. Every larger community will be depicted as a characteristic circle with its own embedded second circle. In each community there is a sort of a central core, or a group of people having the most common friends from the community. [4] Despite the fact that several relationships will be missing among these people, we will refer to this group of people as the near-arc of the graph. This arc will be embedded into the original circle, thus illustrating it also as a circle. Only a few friendships will be missing in this so-called arc of the graph, so we can depict it. We will circumscribe all communities having more than eight members by an imaginary circle and will fill the remaining space in the graph area with the remaining communities and totally secluded friends.

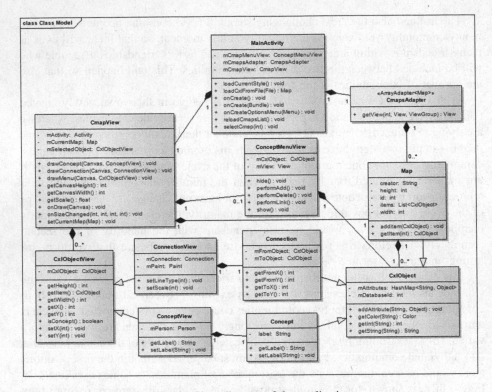

Fig. 4. Class diagram of the application

The result will look acceptable and clear despite a simple complexity and totally low algorithm intensity. Compared to other algorithms, with which the intensity shall not be compared, our result will not be that much simpler than the level of our algorithm.

5 Testing of the Developed Application

The main testing will be focused primarily on the speed of calculation and depicting the final location of the individual vertices of the social graph and all its edges. Another goal is to determine the number of edges representing friendship among the people, necessary for displaying the social graph in such a way that all the information will remain there, and it will capture all the defined friendships as a graph in Fig. 5. The testing of the application will take place in several mobile devices with the Android operating system. Unfortunately, due to the cancellation of a service for the simple possibilities of loading data from the Facebook social network, it is not possible to perform testing with multiple types of data, but only with data relating to one of our profiles.

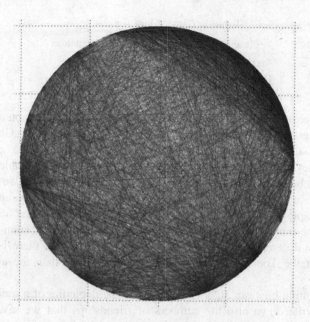

Fig. 5. The social graph - circle

5.1 Testing

Testing was carried out by us and several close friends who know the relationships on the Facebook social network after the quite successful implementation of solutions into the mobile application. We had the task of checking the performance of the application, its opportunities and proper functionality. Other testers, on the contrary, assessed the correctness of the social graph while trying to search for facts they did not know before testing. They evaluated the graphical result as quite clear and understandable.

The main shortcoming is the not very smooth handling with the entire social graph. This is due to the really great computational burden and not very optimal implementation of the components necessary for graph depicting. Unfortunately, even the core of the application has not yet been optimized for work with such a large amount of vertices and edges. The second problem and the biggest disappointment for testers was the possibility of working only and solely with some friends and interconnections with them. The really big problem is the very difficult data import from one's own profile on the Facebook social network, using the necessary script. The application thus loses its simple usability.

Consulting the possibilities and shortcomings of the application was followed by a simple measurement of the computational period. These data were selected for the possibility of comparing our application built for the Android operating system and for TouchGraph, the initial Internet application, from which we are making assumptions. All testing and measurement was performed for one social graph. Our social network on Facebook contains 216 friends and 1463 relationships among my friends. Based on this information, we arrived at the following results (Table 1).

Table 1. Time values for testing

Application	Average time of calculation
Android version	31 s
TouchGraph	17 s

The time measurement was carried out by testing the application on more than one device. When testing the mobile version, Google Nexus 7, Samsung Galaxy Tab Pro and Samsung Galaxy S3 mini devices were used. A measured test was carried out on each of these devices and the overall results were averaged. The Google Nexus 7 has the best results, but the differences were not substantial and therefore we could neglect the type of device on which the test was performed. The TouchGraph application was tested on two laptops with different high-performance and also lasted on both devices around the same time. The TouchGraph application and the application created by us use completely different methods and the results differ. Thus there is no negative conclusion that the TouchGraph application worked faster than the application we created.

After presenting how our algorithms facilitate the depicting of a social graph, it is necessary to write down also the numbers of friendships that we saved due to the defined algorithms and methods, but despite that we fully left out data concerning any relationships among friends in the graph.

We therefore gained a lot of information from Facebook at the beginning (Table 2).

Table 2. Amount of initial information

Number of friends	216
Number of relationships among friends	1463

After the successful information import into the application execution of the algorithms, all clustering and all calculations, we got these interesting numbers. The resulting social graph is therefore composed of such amounts of the building elements of the graph (Table 3).

Table 3. The amount of the resulting graph elements

Number of edges – "friendship"	1142
Number of edges – "zero friendship"	19
Number of communities (members > = 10)	4

5.2   Testing Evaluation

The original number of edges is greater than the number of edges which we gained. This is really a very interesting test result. Definitely, algorithms could be sorted or invented in another way and it is possible that it would result in better and more interesting results. Our solution is more than adequate for the first demonstration.

The calculation speed is not acceptable so far, however, only a simple optimization of the calculations was performed for the implementation of the solution. A more complicated optimization is very necessary for normal use, and if our application will be further developed, it is necessary to assign a very high priority to such optimization.

6   Conclusions

The proposed solution for displaying social relationships on Facebook is theoretically very interesting and its idea has been verified. However, we face the problem and limitations of the Facebook social network. The data and relationship retrieval of a particular user has already been limited for some time and therefore it is not practical to implement the idea completely and easily. We have tried to maximally circumvent these limitations and thus create at least partially corresponding solutions in this work.

Overall, we have to assess the outcome of this work negatively and unfortunately practically design it as not very useful.

Working on this project, however, gave us a very interesting insight for using information from social networks such as Facebook in this case. An interesting possibility of using our work would be if we could draw data e.g. from some private social network or the university system of students and teachers.

Acknowledgements. This work was supported by the SPEV project, financed from the Faculty of Informatics and Management, University of Hradec Kralove.

References

1. Novak, J.D., Cañas, A.J.: The theory underlying concept maps and how to construct and use them.   http://www.swwhs.org/site/wp-content/uploads/2013/06/2013-APPsychologySummer Readings.pdf
2. Wilson, R.J.: Introduction to Graph Theory, 4th edn. Prentice Hall, Harlow (1996)
3. RuizPrimo, M.A., Shavelson, R.J.: Problems and issues in the use of concept maps in science assessment. J. Res. Sci. Teach. **33**(6), 569–600 (1996). doi:10.1002/(SICI)1098-2736 (199608)33:6<569:AID-TEA1>3.0.CO;2-M
4. Ugander, J., Karrer, B., Backstrom, L., Marlow, C.: The Anatomy of the Facebook Social Graph. http://arxiv.org/pdf/1111.4503.pdf
5. Agarwal, G., Kempe, D.: Modularity-Maximizing Graph Communities via Mathematical Programming. http://arxiv.org/pdf/0710.2533.pdf
6. Girvan, M., Newman, M.E.J.: Community structure in social and biological networks. Proc. Natl. Acad. Sci. **99**(12), 7821–7826 (2002). doi:10.1073/pnas.122653799
7. FACEBOOK. The Graph API. https://developers.facebook.com/docs/graph-api
8. IHMC. An XML-Based Language for Describing the Content of Cmaps. http://cmap.ihmc.us/ xml/
9. Johnson, R.: Professional Java Development with the Spring Framework. Wiley, Indianapolis (2005). ISBN 0764574833

A Context-Based Personalization for Mobile Applications' Network Access

Yaser Mowafi[1](✉), Tareq Alaqarbeh[2], and Rami Alazrai[2]

[1] Department of Information Systems, Sultan Qaboos University, Muscat, Oman
mowafi@squ.edu.om
[2] School of Computer Engineering and Information Technology,
German Jordanian University, Amman, Jordan
{tareq.alaqarbeh, rami.azrai}@gju.edu.jo

Abstract. In this paper, we propose a context-based framework for eliciting context information and adapting this information with mobile applications network access decision mechanism. The framework leverages the execution of mobile applications inside a sandbox to control the communication between mobile applications and mobile device resources. Applications' access requests are analyzed based on user's context information collected from the mobile device sensors and the application network access configuration. We validate our proposed framework in Android Operating System running on handheld smartphone devices. Preliminary results revealed the efficacy of our proposed context-based framework in providing network access control management based on users' context information at run-time.

Keywords: Context awareness · Mobile computing · Recommendation system · AHP

1 Introduction

Significant advancements in mobile technologies have shifted personal computing to pervasive and ubiquitous sphere. Many use their mobile devices for their most daily tasks such as emails, text messaging, documents viewing, mapping, as well as for entertainment. Such value-added services typically require collecting not only users' personal information, such as location or identification [1], but also gathering and transmitting trust sensitive information [2].

Today, nearly 70 % of the network usage actions generated by third party mobile applications' services have become invisible to the users [3]. According to [4], most of the current existing mobile platforms (i.e., Android, Apple and iOS) typically leave it to users to specify the permission of mobile applications' access to users' personal information. More critically, survey studies report a lack of users' awareness of privacy breach and security risks associated with installing third party mobile applications [5]. That said, ensuring users' awareness of trust and security controls needs to start from the mobile devices. For example, [6] proposes leveraging the level of privileges of mobile devices' owners in terms of trust and security controls, commonly set by default at low levels throughout the installation lifecycle of applications on these devices, to

© Springer International Publishing Switzerland 2016
M. Younas et al. (Eds.): MobiWIS 2016, LNCS 9847, pp. 406–415, 2016.
DOI: 10.1007/978-3-319-44215-0_34

protect users' information from malicious attacks and/or intrusions. In addition, [7] suggests a framework to shadow users' personal data in places that users wants to keep private to block network transmissions that contain such data. Similarly, [8, 9] propose just-in-time notifications that appear when users' personal data is subject to sharing and displays a visual summary of the shared subject data. However, such security control measures and much of the existing security management mechanisms do not take into account the nature of users' context in mobility.

As research and practice on context-based mobile computing have achieved remarkable success, context-based network access in mobility is still at infancy. The main challenge that renders context-based solutions of ubiquitous computing systems compared to traditional information access systems is that the later handles access threats based on set scenarios of specific protection needs and policies in accordance to those needs. In ubiquitous computing environments, network access alternatives should be supported in the situation where and when the decision is required. Hence, current context needs to be considered to effectively control a given situation. In order to address the aforementioned deterrents, we propose a context-based network access framework for eliciting context information and adapting this information with mobile applications' network access measure. The network access measure is determined based on both the context information collected from the mobile device sensors and the user's settings of the mobile application network access. The user settings provide a mechanism to prioritize the importance of contexts towards the network access control of each mobile application. We implement the proposed framework in the Android Operating System (OS) for mobile devices. The remainder of this paper is structured as follows. In Sect. 2, we describe the context-aware network access framework architecture. Section 3 presents the AHP method. In Sect. 4, we present a prototype and evaluation of our network access control mechanism. Section 5 reviews related work. We conclude the paper with final comments.

2   Architectural Design

Our proposed framework extends an earlier proposed architecture [10] that aims to control the communication among mobile applications and mobile device resources at run-time. The framework consists of a mobile application sandbox and a context shadow application. To avoid any changes to mobile OS, the framework component is implemented as a shadow application. The sandbox is built inside the mobile OS. Mobile application data, code execution, and network access are all concealed within the sandbox. Any network access can only go through the sandbox.

When a running mobile application attempts to get a network access, the application sends TCP SYN request as part of a TCP handshake. This triggers a checking request in the sandbox, which in turn triggers a request in the shadow application. The shadow application examines the request based on both the context information collected from the mobile device sensors, and the user configuration of the mobile application network access settings using the Analytic Hierarchy Process method, discussed in Sect. 3, to provide the appropriate network access of allow or restrict recommendation decision. This decision will then be returned to the sandbox.

3 Analytic Hierarchical Process Method

Given that context dynamically combines a variety of heterogeneous context measures. While some measures are tangible and objectively measured, other measures are intangible and subjectively measured. To model the inherent interdependency of such various criteria measures of comprehended sub-problems into a single integrated decision problem, each of which can be evaluated independently. Hence, from a decision making perspective it will be necessary to consolidate these context measure into single integrated decision problem. Such consolidation allows for establishing a multi-criteria decision making (MCDM) [11]. A common methodology for dealing with MCDM problems is the Analytic Hierarchy Process (AHP) method [12]. One advantage of the AHP method that (a) it enables to breakdown unstructured complex decision problems into smaller constituent components in order to construct an integrative hierarchy, and (b) its capability of handling both tangible and intangible criteria that entails a systematic procedure in the thought process. AHP has been widely used in a variety of policy selection and decision making [13], adaptive learning [14], and recommendation and feedback systems [15].

When applied in decision problems, the AHP method assists in describing a general decision operation by decomposing the decision problem into a multi-level hierarchic structure. We apply the AHP method to perform a paired comparison among the contexts (i.e., location, time, and network) to determine the relative weights of the mobile application network access decision alternatives, secure and insecure network access (Fig. 1). The AHP structure represents the problem decision goal (context network access); the decision problem alternatives (secure and insecure) $A_1 \ldots A_i$; and the decision criteria (Location, Time, Network) C_i and Sub-criteria $C_{i,j}$. The weights ω_i and ω_{ij} are determined through a pair-wise comparison of C_i and $C_{i,j}$, respectively. In determining the relative weights of the decision problem alternatives, the AHP applies eigenvalue method to determine a ranking weight for each criterion and its sub-criteria variables using a pair-wise comparison among each alternative, and then consolidate the weighted values of the hierarchy alternatives to create an overall priority value for each alternative relative to the overall decision goal [16].

Consolidating the weighted values is performed via component measure priorities assigned by the decision maker to create an overall decision value for each alternative. For example, a pair-wise comparison of q elements' weights, $\omega_1, \omega_2, \ldots \omega_q$ is performed via composing the following comparison matrix, every element a_{ji} of each trial is the result of a paired comparison denoting the dominance of element i relative to element j. A comparison is also being made of the j th element with the i th element. This results in the comparison matrix being a reciprocal matrix satisfying $a_{ji} = 1/a_{ij}$. The matrix diagonal represents the self-comparisons on the matrix elements.

$$\begin{pmatrix} \frac{w_1}{w_1} & \frac{w_1}{w_2} & \frac{w_1}{w_3} & \cdots & \frac{w_1}{w_q} \\ \frac{w_2}{w_1} & \frac{w_2}{w_2} & \frac{w_2}{w_3} & \cdots & \frac{w_2}{w_q} \\ \cdots & & & & \\ \frac{w_q}{w_1} & \frac{w_q}{w_2} & \frac{w_q}{w_3} & \cdots & \frac{w_q}{w_q} \end{pmatrix}$$

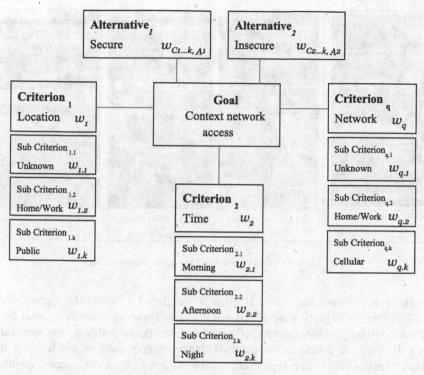

Fig. 1. The AHP structure

The association of the overall weighting for each element relative to its immediate above level is attained via priority vector (PV), which represents the eigenvector of the paired comparison matrices' components. The priorities assigned to the matrix elements reflect the order of their importance with respect to each alternative.

4 Implementation and Evaluation

We developed a prototype application of our proposed network access control mechanism in the Android OS on mobile devices. The application features prompt the execution of the mobile device applications inside a shadow application that controls the network access of these applications. The shadow application utilizes the AHP algorithm to determine the network access decision alternatives, namely secure or insecure. The calculated the AHP network access decision tallies the contexts' relative weights (location, network type, and time) with respect to the relative weights of their corresponding current states.

The application offers a network access setting interface for the users to prioritize the contexts towards the network access control of the running mobile application, such as Facebook that is used here for illustration (Fig. 2A). This is performed through a series of pair-wise comparisons among the contexts, as conferred in Sect. 2. The lowest

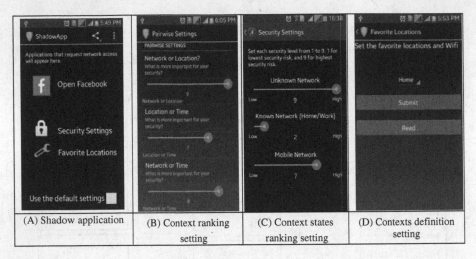

| (A) Shadow application | (B) Context ranking setting | (C) Context states ranking setting | (D) Contexts definition setting |

Fig. 2. Screenshot of the shadow application settings

network access control alternative is given a weight of 1, while the highest access control alternative is given a weight of 9 (Fig. 2B). These values will be used by the AHP analysis to provide eigenvector for the contexts. In addition, the application allows the users to prioritize the contexts' states with respect to the level of their network access control. The lowest alternative in terms of network access control is given a weight of 1, while the highest alternative is given a weight of 9 (Fig. 2C). The application settings allow users to add and/or to edit the definition of the contexts' states of their set locations and Wi-Fi networks (Fig. 2D).

Table 1. The pair-wise comparison matrix of the contexts criteria prioritization

Context	Location	Network	Time
Location	1	1/3	5
Network	3	1	7
Time	1/5	1/7	1

Table 1 illustrates the pair-wise comparison matrix of constructed contexts' security prioritization towards network access. These relative weights are then normalized and aggregated in order to calculate the priority weights defined from the AHP method (Table 2). Similar analysis is performed for the rest of the context sub-criteria states. For example, Table 3 presents the AHP matrix and the priorities for each alternative with respect to the different states of the Network criterion. Similar analysis is performed for the rest of the contexts' sub-criteria states.

The application uses the relative weights of the contexts along with the current user's context states to calculate the decision values of the context network access at run time. The overall weight of the decision values of the context network access is obtained from the sum-product of the normalized priority weights of each context criterion (Table 2) and the corresponding normalized priority weights of the assessed

Table 2. The normalized weight values for each context criterion

Context	Location	Network	Time	Priority
Location	0.238	0.385	0.226	**0.283**
Network	0.714	0.538	0.677	**0.643**
Time	0.048	0.077	0.097	**0.074**
Total	1	1	1	1

Table 3. The normalized weight values with respect to the network context states

Unknown	Priority	Home	Priority	Work	Priority	Cellular	Priority
Secure	**0.10**	Secure	**0.90**	Secure	**0.83**	Secure	**0.75**
Insecure	**0.90**	Insecure	**0.10**	Insecure	**0.17**	Insecure	**0.25**

context states (Table 3). Hence, the obtained higher priority value of each alternative of secure or insecure determines the recommended AHP network access level.

For example, Fig. 3A shows a scenario of a network access attempt of launching a mobile application, via the shadow application, at different context states. In this context, location is Public, Wi-Fi network type is Unknown, and time is Afternoon. The shadow application calculates the overall relative weight of the AHP context network access level. This yields a higher relative weight of an "insecure" network access that prompts the user, if decided to continue, to turn the mobile device location (geo-tracking) services off prior to launching the mobile application (Fig. 3B) — a feature that uses GPS along with crowd-sourced Wi-Fi hotspot and cell tower locations to determine user's approximate location.

Alternatively, Fig. 3C presents another scenario of network access attempt that is triggered with the launching a mobile application. The user's location is determined to be at Work, network type is Work, Wi-Fi, and time is Evening. The shadow application

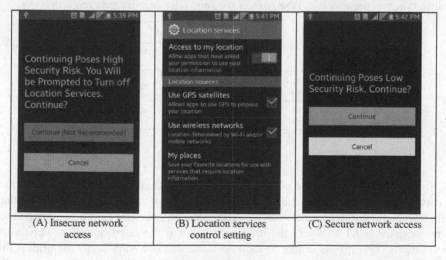

| (A) Insecure network access | (B) Location services control setting | (C) Secure network access |

Fig. 3. Screenshots of the shadow application network access

recalculates the overall relative weight of the AHP context network access level. This yields a higher relative weight of "secure" network access in this case.

In order to examine our network access control framework performance, we used the general cross-validation evaluation technique to test the power of accuracy of the network access control mechanism alternatives and their associated contexts. The validation of our framework draws on a dataset of nine undergraduate university students affiliated participants (5 males and 4 females). Participants' age ranged from 19 to 22 years old with a mean age of 21. The participants have been considered as frequent mobile devices users who own the Android mobile devices for an average of more than two years, and considered themselves as frequent users of mobile applications. After installing the framework shadow application on their mobile devices, participants were informed about the shadow application functionality and the network access control mechanism setting. Participants were then instructed to run the logging application at various times and places over a week time period. The application logs this information, along with participants' feedback options of whether they think that the mobile application launching of network access is secure or not– relevant to the shadow application network access control mechanism recommendation.

The collected data resulted into 118 observations of network access of mobile applications launching attempts via the shadow application, with an average of eight different mobile application network access logged attempts per user per day. The collected data were divided into 80 % of training data, and the remaining 20 % for testing. Table 4 presents the cross validation confusion matrix of network access options accuracy, in pursuit of the context states. The rows present the generated case values and the columns present the predicted values. The results showed a classification accuracy of 91 % with an average Euclidian distance of 0.006. Euclidian distance ranges from 0 for the perfect classifier and square root of 2 for incorrect classification.

Table 4. Confusion matrix of network access alternatives (TP, TN, FP, and FN represent true positive rate, true negative rate, false positive rate, and false negative rate, respectively)

		Predicted	
		Secure Network Access	Insecure Network Access
Actual	Secure Network Access	TP= 45.7%	FN= 4.1%
	Insecure Network Access	FP= 4.8%	TN= 45.4%

Finally, in order to test the possibility and the hypothesis of whether the difference in network access decision values could be resulted from random variation rather than from significant differences between the AHP decision alternatives; we use Analysis of Variance (ANOVA) to assess the differences among the decision values across the observations. Test results (Table 5) indicate that there is a statistically significant difference in the decision values (P-value <0.001).

Table 5. ANOVA test results ANOVA Test

ANOVA Test

Source of Variation	SS	df	MS	F	P-value	F crit
Between Groups	0.928026	1	0.438053	1123.14	3.6E-96	2.8248
Within Groups	0.060813	116	0.000614			
Total	0.996156	117				

5 Related Work

The wide spread use of mobile devices and their integration with personal computing in different domains have shifted the paradigm of how security needs to be handled. For example, [17] proposes TaintDroid to provide real-time analysis of more than 20 mobile applications access to users' private information. The authors found considerable instances of potential misuse of such applications towards users' private information. Similarly, [18] investigates how permissions and privacy could play a role in users application selection decisions. The study found that presenting privacy information in a clearer fashion could assist users in choosing applications that request less permission. In addition, [19] proposes a real-time taint aware analysis to detect mobile applications' vulnerabilities of exchanging data between a single application or among several applications. Earlier, [20] explores retrofitting the Android permissions model to determine third party application extra permissions network access beyond the applications needs.

Various research initiatives have explored the use of security relevant context with focus on delegation of context-based access control rights. For example, [21] proposes an ontology-based frame work that utilizes context information to derive access control measures of mobile devices' assets, such as messages, based on the confidentiality level of these assets. Others focus efforts on context-based authentication and authorization policies for augmenting network access control in mobile environments. For example, [22] explores context-aware scalable authentication (CASA) as a way of balancing security and usability for authentication by enabling easy access in commonplace everyday situations, such as home; while requiring more secure authentication in less common unidentified places. In addition, [23] proposes a context profiling framework using location Wi-Fi and Bluetooth to infer appropriate access and sharing policies for sensitive data on the mobile device. In our proposed framework, the network type is included along with other contexts to continuously perform network access control measures. In addition, our framework provides a generalized infrastructure that can be configured for different applications.

Finally, [24] proposes a context-aware usage control that takes into account context information, such as the spatial and time data to enforce ongoing policy defined by users during runtime to data access (i.e., data and files) and resource usage (i.e., CPU utilization and battery power). Similarly, [25] explores an access control mechanism that allows users to set configuration policies over applications' usage of mobile device resources and services when using the device at public places, and re-gain their original privileges when the device is used at private place. In addition, [26] proposes location-based access control mechanism among specified sub-areas via modifying the Android operating system to enforce access control restrictions within the specified locations.

6 Conclusions

In this paper, we proposed a context-based framework that incorporates users' context, collected from mobile device sensors, with network access control decisions. The framework applies the analytic hierarchy process (AHP) method to dynamically evaluate users' context, and to provide the appropriate network access control decision in run-time. We validate our proposed framework in the Android OS running on mobile devices. Evaluation results have illustrated the capability of our framework in providing network access control features based on real-time assessment of users' context.

References

1. Fischer, G.: Context-aware systems—the 'Right' information, at the 'Right' time, in the 'Right' place, in the 'Right' way, to the 'Right' person. In: AVI 2012, Capri Island, Italy (2012)
2. Almuhimed, H., et al.: Your location has been shared 5,398 times! A field study on mobile app privacy nudging. In: Proceeding CHI 2015 Proceedings of the 33rd Annual ACM Conference on Human Factors in Computing Systems. ACM, New York (2015)
3. Tu, G.-H., et al.: Accounting for roaming users on mobile data access issues and root causes. In: Proceeding of the 11th Annual International Conference on Mobile Systems, Applications and Services. ACM (2013)
4. Fu, H., et al.: A field study of run-time location access disclosures on android smartphones. In: USEC 2014. Internet Society (2014)
5. Ferreira, D., et al.: Securacy: an empirical investigation of android applications' network usage, privacy and security. In: WiSec 2015, New York (2015)
6. Distefano, A., et al.: Securemydroid: enforcing security in the mobile devices lifecycle. In: Proceedings of the Sixth Annual Workshop on Cyber Security and Information Intelligence Research, ser. CSIIRW 2010. ACM, New York (2010)
7. Hornyack, P., et al.: These aren't the droids you're looking for: retrofitting android to protect data from imperious applications. In: Proceedings of the 18th ACM Conference on Computer and Communications Security, ser. CCS 2011. ACM, New York (2011)
8. Balebako, R., et al.: Little brothers watching you: raising awareness of data leaks on smartphones. In: Proceedings of the Ninth Symposium on Usable Privacy and Security, ser. SOUPS 2013. ACM – Association for Computing Machinery (2013)
9. Rastogi, V., Chen, Y., Enck, W.: Appsplayground: automatic security analysis of smartphone applications. In: Proceedings of the Third ACM Conference on Data and Application Security and Privacy. ACM (2013)
10. Mowafi, Y., et al.: A context-aware adaptive security framework for mobile computing applications. In: the 4th International Workshop on Context Aware Middleware for Ubiquitous Environments (PerCAM 2014), UAE, Dubai (2014)

11. Dyer, J.S., et al.: Multiple criteria decision making, multiattribute utility theory: the next ten years. Manag. Sci. **38**(5), 645–654 (1992)
12. Rosenbloom, E.S.: A probabilistic interpretation of the final rankings in AHP. Eur. J. Oper. Res. **96**(2), 371–378 (1997)
13. Koumoto, Y., Nonaka, H., Yanagida, T.: A proposal of context-aware service composition method based on analytic hierarchy process. In: Nakamatsu, K., Phillips-Wren, G., Jain, L. C., Howlett, R.J. (eds.) New Advances in Intelligent Decision Technologies. SCI, vol. 199, pp. 65–71. Springer, Heidelberg (2009)
14. Cocea, M., Magoulas, G.: Context-dependent personalised feedback prioritisation in exploratory learning for mathematical generalisation. In: Houben, G.-J., McCalla, G., Pianesi, F., Zancanaro, M. (eds.) UMAP 2009. LNCS, vol. 5535, pp. 271–282. Springer, Heidelberg (2009)
15. Chen, D.-N., et al.: A Web-based personalized recommendation system for mobile phone selection: design, implementation, and evaluation. Expert Syst. Appl. **37**(12), 8201–8210 (2010)
16. Saaty, T.L.: Decision Making for Leaders: The Analytic Hierarchy Process for Decisions in a Complex World. RWS Publications, Pittsburgh (1999)
17. Enck, W., et al.: Taintdroid: an information-flow tracking system for realtime privacy monitoring on smartphones. In: Proceedings of the 9th USENIX Conference on Operating Systems Design and Implementation, ser. OSDI 2010. USENIX Association, Berkeley (2010)
18. Kelley, P.G., Cranor, L.F., Sadeh, N.: Privacy as part of the app decision-making process. In: CHI 2013 Proceedings of the SIGCHI Conference on Human Factors in Computing Systems. ACM, New York (2013)
19. Arzt, S., et al.: Flowdroid: precise context, flow, field, object-sensitive and lifecycle-aware taint analysis for android apps. In: Proceedings of the 35th Annual ACM SIGPLAN Conference on Programming Language Design and Implementation (PLDI 2014) (2014)
20. Felt, A., et al.: Android permissions: user attention, comprehension, and behavior. In: SOUPS 2012 Proceedings of the Eighth Symposium on Usable Privacy and Security. ACM, New York (2012)
21. Fischer, K., Karsch, S.: Modelling security relevant context an approach towards adaptive security in volatile mobile web environments. In: International Conference on Web Science, Germany, Koblenz (2011)
22. Hayashi, E., et al.: CASA: context-aware scalable authentication. In: Proceedings of the Ninth Symposium on Usable Privacy and Security, ser. SOUPS 2013. ACM, New York (2013)
23. Gupta, A., et al.: Intuitive security policy configuration in mobile devices using context profiling. In: Proceedings of the 2012 ASE/IEEE International Conference on Social Computing and 2012 ASE/IEEE International Conference on Privacy, Security, Risk and Trust, ser. SOCIALCOM-PASSAT 2012. IEEE Computer Society, Washington (2012)
24. Bai, G., Gu, L., Feng, T., Guo, Y., Chen, X.: Context-aware usage control for android. In: Jajodia, S., Zhou, J. (eds.) SecureComm 2010. LNICST, vol. 50, pp. 326–343. Springer, Heidelberg (2010)
25. Prakash, S., et al.: A proposed approach for mobile devices with context based access control mechanism. Int. J. Adv. Res. Comput. Sci. Technol. (IJARCST) **3**(1–2), 149–150 (2015)
26. Shebaro, B., Oluwatimi, O., Bertino, E.: Context-based access control systems for mobile devices. IEEE Trans. Dependable Secure Comput. **12**(2), 150–163 (2015)

Group Assist Recommendation Model Based on Intelligent Mobile Terminals—GARMIT

Lansheng Han[1], Changhua Sun[1(✉)], Mengxiao Qian[1], Shuxia Han[1], and Hamza Kwisaba[2]

[1] Huazhong University of Science and Technology, Wuhan, Hubei, China
{hanlansheng,sunchanghua}@hust.edu.cn
[2] Huawei Technologies Co., Ltd., Shenzheng, China

Abstract. Existing recommendations are more inclined to publish favorable information regarding the items. This asymmetry of item's information can not make an objective assessment of the recommended items. To overcome this shortcoming, the paper proposes group assist recommendation model based on intelligent mobile terminals (GARMIT). That invites ordinary users in all kinds of social network group to recommend what they think is the right items. The score of each of the recommended items consists of all the evaluated scores by users with each of his or her credibility, the number of participants and contextual information of requester. The new model shows best performance in content size, accuracy and satisfaction, except that time consumption is a bit longer. Since the item information is supplied by the ordinary users, items are somehow updated automatically in our new model.

Keywords: Recommendation systems · Group assist · Intelligent mobile terminal · Content-aware

1 Introduction

With the rapid development of information technology, the severe problem of "information overload" brings great information burden for normal people. Thus, recommender systems have been one of the most effective methods for having to deal with the problem of "information overload" [1,2].

Recommender Systems help users to select most interesting items from masses of information, then provide users with customized recommendations to satisfy their personalized requirements [3,4]. Currently, the greatest progress of recommender systems has been made in many fields such as e-commerce on mobile devices (Amazon, Alibaba, etc.), information retrieval (Google, Baidu, etc.), mobile applications [5], tourism e-commerce [6], network advertisement and so on [7].

However, the 3 recommendation systems mainly benefit the recommenders, in terms of recommended items somehow, they are unequal to the needs of users, mostly unnecessary, and some even fraud. Thanks to the current rapid popularity

M. Younas et al. (Eds.): MobiWIS 2016, LNCS 9847, pp. 416–430, 2016.
DOI: 10.1007/978-3-319-44215-0_35

of smart mobile terminals and the popularity of 4G networks [8,9], all kinds of social groups by Skype, Facebook, Twitter, etc. are coming into being especially in China by QQ or Weichat [10,11], such as classmates-group, friends-group, relatives-group, and all kinds of interesting groups. Large amounts of data show that there are more than 1000 million of all kinds of groups in China, almost every person of age between 15 and 55 in China take part in average two groups [12]. Those groups are almost nonprofit and across geographical, occupational, but playing an increasingly important role in social events, incidents, and in some fields do better than the governments do [13,14]. In those groups everyone can publish information, the information asymmetry is being changed and there are always some members who are always willing to help others. That is why we propose group assist recommendation model based on intelligent mobile terminals (GARMIT).

The organization of this paper is as follows: In Sect. 1, traditional recommender systems are introduced. In Sect. 2, we analyze the theories and technologies of the traditional recommender systems and point out their pros and cons. In Sect. 3, GARMIT is presented in details. Section 4 presents the recommended system architecture and main process. By applying GARMIT into the actual use, we compare GARMIT with the main typical recommender systems in four key factors and also present efficiency analysis.

2 Related Work

In this section, we introduce several main traditional recommender systems, mobile context-awareness recommendation method and social-network-based recommendation as well as some relative concepts and then point out shortcomings of each.

2.1 Traditional Recommender Systems

Traditional recommender systems are established based on the relationship between users and items. They predict users potential interest and investigate personal choice and the similarities between items. Those recommender systems are usually classified into the following three categories:

(1) Collaborative recommendation: The user is recommended items that people with similar tastes and preferences liked in the past. The advantage is that this method can explore the potential interest of user while its disadvantage is the sparsity of the matrix and the difficulty to mine and manage complex users similarities and interest database [15].
(2) Content-based recommendation: The user is recommended items similar to the ones which he was preferred in the past [16]. Its advantage is that the preferences of users to different items can be easily predicted and it is easy to comprehend the recommendation result while its disadvantage is that the user is limited to being recommended items similar to those already rated.

(3) Hybrid recommendation: This method combines collaborative and content-based recommendation [17,18]. Hybrid recommendation has the advantages of both collaborative and content-based recommendation and as a result it is superior to both. The hybrid recommendation on the other hand needs bigger storage space and the algorithm takes much time.

However, the 3 categories of recommender systems above don't take contextual information of users into consideration. To make up for the shortcomings of traditional recommender systems, some experts have proposed a context-awareness recommendation system.

2.2 Context-Awareness Recommendation and Social Network-Based Recommendation

The notion of "context" has not been definitely defined, but what is quoted most is the definition given by Doctor A.K. Dey: "Context is any information that can be used to characterize the situation of an entity. An entity is a person, place, or object that is considered relevant to the interaction between a user and an application, including the user and application themselves" [19].

Under a context-awareness system, the contexts include location, time, weather, emotion, devices and so on [20–22]. What is used most is several-dimension recommendation whose contexts include location, time, and weather and so on. For example, [23] considers time, location and personal information of users and provides recommendations based on hierarchical model. In terms of algorithmic paradigms, context-awareness recommendation systems are classified in 3 categories: pre-filtering, post-filtering and contextual modeling [24]. However, recent statistical report shows that the satisfaction of users to the recommendations is still low [25].

Faced with the emergence of the current social networks, there are many scholars have put forward the idea of social networks based on the recommended [26,27]: some discussed dynamics of social networks based recommended [28]; some talked about the multidimensionality of social networks recommendation [29]; others explored the uncertainty and classification of the social networks recommendation [30–32].

2.3 Shortcomings of Existing Recommender Systems

From the above discussions, we can find the following shortcomings of the existing recommender systems.

1. Traditional recommender systems [25,33] need to mine and manage the classification of items, similarities of users and their interests, and thus require big storage space.
2. The context-awareness recommendation takes user's contextual needs into consideration, but it doesn't improve the management technologies for items [34].

3. Most information of items is from owners of the items who are inclined to publish the favorable information rather than bad information about the items, so there may be fraud. This information asymmetry can not supply ordinary users an objective assessment and also causes items information update lagged.

In comparison with the current popular use of smart mobile devices, previous Internet devices are almost fixed and didn't enjoy much popularity [35]. News or information providers are mostly owners of the news, most of users are the audience that is why the existing recommender systems are asymmetric for ordinary users. Current social network-based recommendation can take use of social network but there is many uncertainty factors and the purpose of the vast majority of social networks is not for recommendation.

Mobile devices have the advantage of small size, fast network speed, and widespread use, the internet is gradually becoming accessible for everyone, thus the publisher and recipient of the news can be everybody, which alleviates the asymmetry [18,36].

Thus taking full advantage of mobile smart devices, our new model invites ordinary users (named volunteers) in all kinds of groups to recommend what they think is right to the customer (named asker) who wants to get the recommended items. Our new model can be called Group assist recommendation model based on intelligent mobile terminals (GARMIT).

3   New Model Construction

The recommender systems on mobile devices should not only consider the quality of items but also whether items suit for asker's context. Therefore, in this paper, the rank of items is calculated based on the scores given by volunteers and the asker's context.

3.1   Concepts

A recommendation is initiated by askers noted by $a_s(s = 1, 2 \dots)$. The web server receives the request and sends it to other users noted by $U_i(i = 1, 2 \dots m)$. Some users (called volunteers) then recommend items noted by $C_j(j = 1, 2 \dots n)$ to the asker. The total scores of items rely on two parts: the context scores of items noted by $A_j(j = 1, 2 \dots n)$ based on asker's contexts, the volunteers' scores of items noted by $S_j(j = 1, 2 \dots n)$ based on volunteers' recommendation. To simplify the description of model's algorithm, below we give the explanation of related symbols in Table 1.

Table 1. Symbols explanation

Symbol	Explanation
$a_s(s = 1, 2\ldots)$	Asker as well as askers contexts ·
$C_j(j = 1, 2\ldots n)$	Items recommended as well as the items contexts
$U_i(i = 1, 2\ldots m)$	The ith user
$T_i^{(k)}(i = 1, 2\ldots m)$	The credibility of U_i
$R = (R_{ij})_{m*n}$	Score matrix given by users where R_{ij} represents the score of C_j given by U_i
$A_j(j = 1, 2\ldots n)$	The context score of items based on askers contexts
$S_j(j = 1, 2\ldots n)$	The score of items based on users recommendation
$W_j(j = 1, 2\ldots n)$	The total score of item C_j

3.2 Construction of the Model

The construction of the model consisting of three main parts will be given in order based on symbols above: recommendation by volunteers, evaluation from asker's context and trust level of each volunteer.

Recommendation by Volunteers. Every volunteer could recommend several items based on volunteer's preference. We use a V-point scale, for item C_j, the score given by U_i is called R_{ij}, thus all the scores R_{ij} could form a matrix R with n rows and m columns, the score R_{ij} could be determined by the equation following:

$$R_{ij} = \begin{cases} 0, & if\ U_i\ didn't\ grade\ for\ C_j \\ R_{ij}, & if\ U_i\ graded\ for\ C_j \end{cases}$$

While different people have different preferences. To evaluate volunteers' recommendations and to avoid malignant recommendations, the credibility of users T_i is set to represent how much the volunteer can be believed by the feedback of the group. The credibility T_i can be adjusted itself to increase the flexibility of the system, the method of modulating will be given later in section "Sum of the Evaluation". $T_i^{(k)}$ represents the credibility in the kth time recommendation of U_i.

In a recommendation task, for a different number of volunteers grading for different items, we set γ_j as the total number of volunteers grading for C_j. The product $T_I^{(k)} * R_{ij}$ of volunteer's credibility and the score of C_j given by the volunteer U_i can be seen as the objective score of C_j, then the sum of all users' the objective score divided by the number of volunteers grading for C_j, can be seen as the average score $\overline{R_j}$ of C_j:

$$\overline{R_j} = \frac{\sum_{i=1}^{m}(T_i^{(k)} R_{ij})}{\gamma_j} \tag{1}$$

To eliminate the dimension and calculate with other factors which influence the score of item. We normalize the average score and use the min-max method.

$$\overline{r_j} = \frac{\overline{R_j} - \overline{R}_{\min}}{\overline{R}_{\max} - \overline{R}_{\min}} \tag{2}$$

In the Eq. (2), $\overline{r_j}$ is the average score of C_j after normalization, $\overline{R}_{\max}$ represents the maximum score of item C_j given by volunteers while $\overline{R}_{\min}$ represents the minimum score of C_j.

The value of one item relies on its average score but it is also related to the times it is recommended by volunteers. The more times it is recommended, the more popular it is. Thus, the score S_j based on user recommendation has a positive correlation with the average score $\overline{r_j}$ and the proportion of people recommending the item. So we have the Eq. (3) to denote the recommendation score by volunteers.

$$S_j = \overline{r_j} + \alpha * \frac{\gamma_j}{m} \tag{3}$$

Where S_j is the score based on user recommendation, $\overline{r_j}$ is the average score after normalization, $\frac{\gamma_j}{n}$ is the proportion of number of volunteers recommending C_j to total number and α is the variable depending on correlation between the average score and number of volunteers recommending the item.

Evaluation of Context of Asker. The contexts mainly refer to the asker's time and location [37]. The more similar the item's time and location contexts are to the asker's contexts, the higher the score of the item based on contexts. Thus the similarity $cntsim(a_j, c_j)$ of the set of item's contexts and the set of asker's contexts can be used as the score A_j based on contexts:

$$A_j = cntsim(a_i, c_j) = \frac{\sum_{tng \in c_j} \max(sim(tag, ctx))}{|c_j|} \tag{4}$$

Where a_i refers to the set of asker's contexts while c_j refers to the set of contexts of C_j, $cntsim(a_j, c_j)$ is the similarity of the two sets, ctx is one context of a_i while tag is one context of c_j, $|c_j|$ represents the number of contexts in c_j, sim represents the similarity of two sets, whose calculation is according to [23].

Sum of the Evaluation. The total score W_j of C_j is the weighted sum of the score S_j based on volunteer's recommendation and the score A_j based on contexts.

$$W_j = (1 - \beta)S_j + \beta * A_j \tag{5}$$

Where W_j is the total score of C_j, S_j is the score based on volunteer recommendation, A_j is the score based on contexts, β is a weighting coefficient which depends on the importance of volunteer recommendation and contexts.

Trust Level of Volunteers. The initial credibility of volunteers is set as 0.8, after one recommendation task, the credibility will change according to the deviation of the score given by volunteer from the average score. Thus, the credibility of volunteer D_i can be calculated by 1 minus the deviation.

$$D_i = 1 - \frac{\sum\limits_{C_j \in I_i} |\frac{R_{ij} - \overline{R_j}}{V}|}{|I_i|} \tag{6}$$

Where D_i refers to the credibility U_i gets this time, I_i is the set of items U_i recommends this time, namely $I_i = \{C_j | R_{ij} > 0, 1 < j \leq m\}$, $|I_i|$ refers to the number of items U_i recommends. Whats more, D_i should be between 0 and 1, thus the deviation should be normalized. To simplify the normalization, the normalization is the deviation divided by the max score V. Based on what is discussed above, the credibility of volunteers can change itself after one recommendation task, thus, the credibility of volunteers is not only dependent on the recommendation this time but also on the accumulated credibility previously. After this recommendation task, the credibility $T_i^{(k+1)}$ of volunteer is the weighted sum of the credibility D_i got this time and the credibility $T_i^{(k)}$ got previously.

$$T_i^{(k+1)} = \frac{1}{k+1} D_i + \frac{k}{k+1} T_i^{(k)} \tag{7}$$

Where $T_i^{(k+1)}$ refers to the credibility of user in $(k+1)$th time (next time), D_i refers to the credibility user gets this time while $T_i^{(k)}$ refers to the credibility user gets in previous k times. In this way, the system can avoid malignant recommendation.

4   Recommended System Implementation, Effect Analysis and Comparison

We spent six months to develop a GARMIT system. After another three months of use, we got some necessary data to do analysis, comparison and verification. We do not use data of MovieLens [38] because MovieLens don't have corresponding sample data to the group-assistant recommendation in GARMIT. We want to demonstrate the advantage of our model is that it can update the items' information automatically.

4.1   Design and Development of System

The system uses Mobile terminal and Server mode, namely M-S mode. We regard one recommendation as a task and the procedure of accomplishing the task is as follows. (1) The task is initiated by the asker who sends a request to the server; (2) The server records the request then sends it to volunteers; (3) Volunteers recommend items and then send them to the server; (4) The server accumulates

the items and computes based on the model then returns the result to the asker;
(5) Server updates the credibility of volunteers thus accomplishes the task.

Considering efficiency and utility of the system, we optimize the system under the following regulations:

1 It is an optional process for users to recommend;
2 The maximum time for recommendation of users is T_{wait};
3 The number of users recommending is M (generally $M = 20$). Within time T_{wait}, if the number of users is above M, we just receive the first M users' items; when the time gets T_{wait}, but the number of users doesn't reach M, then we receive all items within T_{wait}.

4.2   The Analysis of Effectiveness and Time Complexity

The development on mobile device is based on the Android version above 4.0. The CPU in use is an Intel Pentium and the operating system is Windows Server 2012 R2.

We choose a common recommendation task to show the efficiency and utility of the model. John planed to watch movies nearby, so he used the system to choose a cinema. The recommendation was on a 10-point scale, and the result was that there are 32 volunteers who recommended 7 cinemas for John. The cinemas are listed as follows and the list is used in mathematical formula. First of all, the system calculates the average scores of the cinemas based on the score matrix, volunteers' credibility and the Eq. (1). For convenience, the abbreviations and the result are as shown in Table 2.

Table 2. The abbreviations of cinema names

Cinema	Abbreviation in formula	Abbreviation in figures	Average score	Number of volunteers
China Micro Cinema	C_1	CMC	5.17	6
CGV Star Gathering Cinema	C_2	CGV	6.08	12
Tianhe International Cinema	C_3	THC	5.00	29
Star International Cinema	C_4	SIC	5.18	11
Universal Fable Cinema	C_5	UFC	4.75	4
IMAX Cinema	C_6	IMAX	6.53	19
Huaxia International Cinema	C_7	HIC	4.69	13

The score of cinema based on volunteers' recommendation is calculated based on Eq. (3). Especially, value of $\overline{r_j}$ and $\frac{\gamma_j}{m}$ are shown as Table 3. We set α as 1, then calculate and get the result as Fig. 1.

From Qinyuan where the asker resides, the system can get the distance to every cinema and the time to cinemas by bus, the result is as shown in the Table 4.

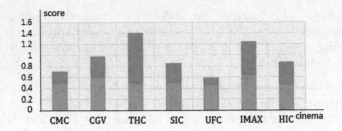

Fig. 1. Scores based on volunteers recommendation

Table 3. Values of $\overline{r_j}$ and $\frac{\gamma_i}{m}$

C_j	C_1	C_2	C_3	C_4	C_5	C_6	C_7
$\overline{r_j}$	0.1875	0.357	0.9062	0.3437	0.125	0.5937	0.4062
$\frac{\gamma_i}{m}$	0.517	0.608	0.5	0.518	0.475	0.653	0.469

Table 4. Contexts of asker

Cinema	C_1	C_2	C_3	C_4	C_5	C_6	C_7
Distance (km)	2.189	2.765	2.637	2.713	2.781	2.934	2.918
Time (min)	34	35	36	35	37	38	39

We set β as 0.5, and then calculate with the distance and time as contexts based on Eq. (5), which gives us the score based on the asker's context. We then add the scores from volunteers' recommendation and scores from asker's context, and get the total scores as shown in Table 5.

Table 5. Total scores

	CMC	CGV	THC	SIC	UFC	IMAX	HIC
Total scores	0.4476	0.5317	0.7477	0.3259	0.475	0.6296	0.4391

Meanwhile after the recommendation, the credibility of every volunteer will change according to Eqs. (6) and (7).

The Analysis of Time Complexity. According to the procedure design in 4.1, time consumptions include following 6 parts: (1) Asker sends the request to the server; (2) Server sends the request to every volunteer online. Suppose that the network speed is v, thus the time taken from asker's sending request to users' receiving request is $O(1/v)$.

(3) Suppose there are m users recommending with n items recommended, then the items are sent to the server. Therefore the time consumption in (3) is $O(m * n)_m + O(1/v)$. (4) The server calculates the average scores of the items.

There are n items with every item calculated according to the score from m users, thus the time complexity is $O(m*n)_s$. The server then computes the scores based on user recommendation. The complexity is $O(n)$ because there are n items.

Next, the server computes the scores based on context. The number of items is n. Taking the network speed and different time consumption of different locations into consideration, the time consumption for the system to get the contexts will be $O(n) + O(1/v)$ and the time complexity for calculating the scores based on contexts is $O(n)$.

According to the model, the server needs to sum up the score based on volunteer recommendation and the score based on contexts by linear weighting and then sort the scores. The time complexity is $O(n)$.

(5) After the calculation is done, the server sends the result to the asker, time consumption is relative to the network speed and time complexity and is computed as $O(1/v)$.

(6) Finally, the model needs to adjust the credibility of every volunteer. There are volunteers, the credibility of every volunteer is related to the items they recommended, thus the time complexity is $O(m*n)_s$.

Based on the discussion above, the total time can be got after adding the maximum waiting time T_{wait}:

$$T_{all} = \min(T_{wait}, O(n*m)_m + O(1/v)) + O(m*n)_s + O(n)$$
$$+ O(n) + O(1/v) + O(n) + O(n) + O(m*n)_s + O(1/v) \qquad (8)$$

The equation is got by simplification:

$$T_{all} = 4O(1/v) + \min(T_{wait}, O(m*n)_m + O(1/v)) + 2O(n*m)_s + 4O(n) \quad (9)$$

It can be seen from the Eq. (9) that the total time is relative to three factors: (1) the maximum waiting time T_{wait} given by asker or system; (2) the scale of recommendation, namely the number of users m and number of items n; (3) the network speed $O(v)$.

In the interest of comparison, we carried out another experiment. The items recommended are the restaurants around Qinyuan within 5 km, the users recommending were basically the same individuals who took part in the cinema experiment. We calculate related factors when the number of users reaches 10,

Table 6. Number of the volunteers and total time

$n = 20$	$O(m)$	$O(m*n)$	$O(m*n)_s + 4O(n)$	$T_{wait}(s)$	$T_{all}(s)$
$m = 10$	6.2	5.6	4.12	5	5.21
$m = 15$	6.5	6.1	4.12	5	5.23
$m = 20$	6.7	6.3	4.13	10	10.6
$m = 25$	7.1	6.5	4.13	10	10.8
$m = 30$	7.2	6.6	4.14	20	17.1
$m = 40$	7.3	6.7	4.14	20	18.9

Table 7. The number of items recommended and total time

m = 15	$O(m)$	$O(m*n)$	$O(m*n)_s + 4O(n)$	T_{wait}(s)	T_{all}(s)
n = 10	6.2	6.4	4.11	10	6.4
n = 15	6.2	6.7	4.11	10	6.7
n = 20	6.4	7.5	4.12	10	7.5
n = 25	6.7	8.2	4.13	10	8.2
n = 30	6.7	9.3	4.13	10	9.3
n = 40	7.1	10.2	4.13	10	10

15, 20, 25, 30 and so on. The Tables 6 and 7 is about the relation of users, items recommended and time consumption. The time consumption $O(1/v)$ by network speed is generally 3 to 5 s based on 3G-4G of China Mobile Communication Corp.

We can get some results and suggestions from the tables above:

(1) Of the total time consumed by the server, about 60 % of the time is spent on adjusting of credibility. Since the adjustment for credibility is after the recommendation for the asker, which does not affect the quality of services. Our advice is that trust level adjustment can be done after the recommendation returned to the asker.

(2) Of the total processing time including the server and mobile device, about 80 % of the total time is consumed by the mobile device. After analysis, we find that most of volunteers usually recommend 1 or 2 items with no respect to how many items are there. Thus we come up with the equation $O(m*n) = O(m)$. Since T_{wait} can not be too small if we increase T_{wait} properly, the time consumption will not increase propositional to the number of items.

(3) The network speed $O(v)$ is an important component of total time but out of the scope of the paper.

4.3   Comparison with Other Recommender Systems

The aim of recommender systems is to provide personalized service for the asker within a limited time while keeping the cost of the asker as low as possible. Based on the above statement, we can use several factors to evaluate recommender systems:

(1) Time: the total time of a whole recommendation task. Apparently the less time the better. Some systems only set the first return of recommendation webpage as the end [39], which is improper. In reality, the asker usually browses deep webpages for several times and then selects an item.

(2) Information content: This entails all the content the system provides for the asker in the recommendation routine. The larger the quantity of information, the higher the cost of network flow. Here we use the webpage's size to denote the information content of the webpage.

(3) Precision: Precision is the proportion of the number of items the asker selects to the total number of items recommended to the asker. The general recommender systems will recommend as many items as possible to make the precision more than zero [40], but this strategy makes the precision lower in turn.

(4) Satisfaction: the satisfaction of askers or customers is the overall feeling taking the above factors into consideration. It may be subjective but necessary because the factors above are not very comparable. For example, Google has a superior search service but its recommendations don't match its searching prowess. Likewise the advertisement recommendations of Taobao don't take the user's search queries into consideration. Therefore, this paper proposes satisfaction indicator has some significance. We developed a review module following the recommendation that require the asker to evaluate the result. While satisfaction with other systems can be estimated from the statistics got by the Web Crawler for the posts following the forum.

The traditional recommender systems based on items' relevance include elong travel website, Xiecheng travel website Douban, Baidu, Netflix movie and Google news'. In order to increase the comparability, we used their apps in several locations in order to neutralize the factor of network speed.

Table 8. The comparison of recommender systems

Model	Information content	Precision	Time	Satisfaction
Elong	270 k	12 %	3.1 s*3.2	43
Baidu	120 k	11 %	2.7 s*3.7	32
Netflix	50 k	25 %	3.42 s*2.1	53
Google	113 k	48 %	8.6 s*1.8	64
GARMIT	20 k	96 %	22.3 s*1.0	91

It can be seen from Table 8 that the time consumption by GARMIT is more than rest, but its precision is highest and thus yields the highest satisfaction of 91 %. However, another advantage of GARMIT has not been shown, which is that as time going by, the users (volunteers) will increase, GARMIT can update the items' information automatically.

5   Summary

After analyzing the drawbacks of exiting recommendation systems, the paper proposed group assist recommendation model based on intelligent mobile terminals (GARMIT). Besides considering asker's contexts, GARMIT pays more consideration on the recommendations by volunteers using mobile intelligent devices in all kinds group. As the items information is supplied by the volunteers who are the ordinary users, the information asymmetry of the traditional recommender systems is completely overcome. Furthermore, as the mobile intelligent devices are widely used in volunteers and all kinds of groups emerge, items information can update automatically.

References

1. Adomavicius, G., Tuzhilin, A.: Toward the next generation of recommender systems: a survey of the state-of-the-art and possible extensions. IEEE Trans. Knowl. Data Eng. **17**(6), 734–749 (2005)
2. Resnick, P., Varian, H.R.: Recommender systems. Commun. ACM **40**(3), 56–58 (1997)
3. Kurkovsky, S., Harihar, K.: Using ubiquitous computing in interactive mobile marketing. Pers. Ubiquit. Comput. **10**(4), 227–240 (2006)
4. Zhang, X., Li, Y.: Use of collaborative recommendations for web search: an exploratory user study. J. Inf. Sci. **34**(2), 145–161 (2008)
5. Han, J., Lee, H.: Adaptive landmark recommendations for travel planning: personalizing and clustering landmarks using geo-tagged social media. Pervasive Mob. Comput. **18**, 4–17 (2014)
6. Kim, J.W., Lee, B.H., Shaw, M.J., et al.: Application of decision-tree induction techniques to personalized advertisements on Internet storefronts. Int. J. Electron. Commer. **5**(3), 45–62 (2001)
7. Abowd, G.D., Mynatt, E.D.: Charting past, present, and future research in ubiquitous computing. ACM Trans. Comput.-Hum. Interact. (TOCHI) **7**(1), 29–58 (2000)
8. Kibria, M.R., Jamalipour, A.: On designing issues of the next generation on mobile network. IEEE Netw. **21**(1), 6–13 (2007)
9. IEEE standard for local and metropolitan area networks Part 21: media independent handover. In: IEEE STD 802.21-2008, pp. C1–C301 (2009)
10. Lee, J., Kim, S.: Exploring the role of social networks in affective organizational commitment: observation of strains: network centrality, strength of ties, and structural holes. Am. Rev. Public Adm. **41**(2), 205–223 (2011). doi:10.1177/0275074010373803
11. Gao, H., Tang, J., Liu, H.: Modeling geo-social correlations for new check-ins on location-based social networks. In: Proceedings of the 21st ACM International Conference on Information and Knowledge Management (CIKM 2012), pp. 1582–1586 (2012)
12. http://www.xue163.com/1282/1/12821424.html
13. Yan, Z., Chen, Y.: AdChatRep: a reputation system for MANET chatting. In: Proceedings of 1st International Symposium on From Digital Footprints to Social and Community Intelligence, New York, USA (2011)
14. de Nooy, W.: Graph theoretical approaches to social network analysis. In: Meyers, R.A. (ed.) Computational Complexity: Theory, Techniques, and Applications, pp. 2864–2877. Springer, New York (2012). doi:10.1007/978-1-4614-1800-9-176. ISBN 978-1-4614-1800-9
15. Goldberg, D., Nichols, D., Oki, B., et al.: Using collaborative filtering to weave an information tapestry. Commun. ACM **61**(10), 1–10 (1992)
16. Mooney, R.J., Roy, L.: Content-based book recommending using learning for text categorization. In: Proceedings of the Fifth ACM Conference on Digital Libraries, pp. 195–204. ACM (2000)

17. Burke, R.: Hybrid recommender systems: survey and experiments. User Model. User-Adap. Interact. **12**(4), 331–370 (2002)
18. Ricci, F.: Mobile recommender systems. Inf. Technol. Tourism **12**(3), 205–231 (2010)
19. Dey, A.K.: Providing architectural support for building context-aware applications. Georgia Institute of Technology (2000)
20. Henricksen, K., Indulska, J.: Developing context-aware pervasive computing applications: models and approach. Pervasive Mob. Comput. **2**(1), 37–64 (2006)
21. Abowd, G.D., Atkeson, C.G., Hong, J., Long, S., Kooper, R., Pinkerton, M.: Cyberguide: a mobile context-aware tour guide. Wirel. Netw. **3**(5), 421–433 (1997)
22. Yu, Z., Zhou, X., Zhang, D., Chin, C.Y., Wang, X., Men, J.: Supporting context-aware media recommendations for smart phones. IEEE Pervasive Comput. **5**(3), 68–75 (2006)
23. Han, J., Schmidtke, H.R., Xie, X., Woo, W.: Adaptive content recommendation for mobile users: ordering recommendations using a hierarchical context model with granularity. Pervasive Mob. Comput. **13**, 85–98 (2014)
24. Adomavicius, G., Tuzhilin, A.: Context-aware recommender systems. In: Ricci, F., Rokach, L., Shapira, B., Kantor, P.B. (eds.) Recommender Systems Handbook, pp. 217–253. Springer, New York (2011)
25. Friedrich, G., Zanker, M.: A taxonomy for generating explanations in recommender systems. AI Mag. **32**(3), 90–98 (2011)
26. Bródka, P., Musial, K., Kazienko, P.: A method for group extraction in complex social networks. In: Lytras, M.D., De Pablos, P.O., Ziderman, A., Roulstone, A., Maurer, H., Imber, J.B. (eds.) Communications in Computer and Information Science, pp. 238–247. Springer, Heidelberg (2010)
27. Yin, H., Cui, B., Sun, Y., et al.: LCARS: a spatial item recommender system. ACM Trans. Inf. Syst. **32**(3), 11 (2014)
28. Sellami, K., Ahmed-Nacer, M., Tiako, P., Chelouah, R.: From social network to semantic social network in recommender system. Int. J. Comput. Sci. Issues **9**(4) (2012)
29. Kazienko, P., Musial, K., Kajdanowicz, T.: Multidimensional social network and its application to the social recommender system. IEEE Trans. Syst. Man Cybern. Part A: Syst. Hum. **41**(4), 746–759 (2011)
30. Lopez-Vargas, J., Piedra, N., Chicaiza, J.: Recommendation of OERs shared in social media based-on social networks analysis approach. In: IEEE Frontiers in Education Conference (2014)
31. Sim, B.S., Kim, H., Kim, K.M.: Type-based context-aware service recommender system for social network. In: International Conference on Computer, Information and Telecommunication Systems C (2012)
32. Desrosiers, C., Karypis, G.: A comprehensive survey of neighborhood-based recommendation methods. In: Ricci, F., Rokach, L., Shapira, B., Kantor, P.B. (eds.) Recommender Systems Handbook, pp. 107–144. Springer, New York (2011)
33. Jannach, D., Zanker, M., Felfernig, A., Friedrich, G.: Recommender Systems: An Introduction. Cambridge University Press, Cambridge (2010)
34. Bronsted, J., Hansen, K., Ingstrup, M.: Service composition issues in pervasive computing. IEEE Pervasive Comput. **9**(1), 62–70 (2010)
35. Conti, M., Das, S.K., Bisdikian, C., Kumar, M., Ni, L.M., Passarella, A., Roussos, G., Tröster, G., Tsudik, G., Zambonelli, F.: Looking ahead in pervasive computing: challenges and opportunities in the era of cyber-physical convergence. Pervasive Mob. Comput. **8**(1), 2–21 (2012)

36. Zambonelli, F., Viroli, M.: A survey on nature-inspired metaphors for pervasive service ecosystems. J. Pervasive Comput. Commun. **7**, 186–204 (2011)
37. Cabri, G., Leonardi, L., Mamei, M., Zambonelli, F.: Location-dependent services for mobile users. IEEE Trans. Syst. Man Cybern. A **33**(6), 667–681 (2003)
38. http://grouplens.org/datasets/movielens/
39. Fong, A., Zhou, B., Hui, S., Hong, G., Do, T.A.: Web content recommender system based on consumer behavior modeling. IEEE Trans. Consum. Electron. **57**(2), 962–969 (2011). http://dx.doi.org/10.1109/TCE.2011.5955246
40. Han, J., Xie, X., Woo, W.: Context-based local hot topic detection for mobile user. In: Adjunct Proceedings of the 8th International Conference on Pervasive Computing, pp. 5–8. Springer (2010)

A Smart Arduino Alarm Clock Based on NREM and REM Sleep Stage Detection

Adam Drabek, Ondrej Krejcar(✉), and Kamil Kuca

Center for Basic and Applied Research, Faculty of Informatics and Management,
University of Hradec Kralove, Rokitanskeho 62,
500 03 Hradec Kralove, Czech Republic
{adam.drabek, kamil.kuca}@uhk.cz, Ondrej@Krejcar.org

Abstract. The article describes a development of a small-budget smart alarm clock, which is based on Arduino platform. A human organism can be found in three basic function stages during a sleep time. Vigilance or a light sleep, NREM sleep and REM sleep. The point of the smart alarm clock is to detect these stages and try to adapt a set alarm and wake a subject up in the best moment possible according to its sleeping cycle, which means during the vigilance or the light sleep. To detect the sleeping stages, the Arduino smart alarm clock uses a movement infra sensor and a noise sensor, which can enable the alarm clock to evaluate the impulses and adjust the set awaking time. For a better functionality the alarm clock is enhanced with a LCD LED display, a real-time clock, a sensor of temperature and humidity and a photosensitive sensor for switching the LED display off in the night. The alarm clock will be ready to use for better and more effective awakening.

Keywords: Smart alarm clock · Arduino · Sensors · Sleep · REM · NREM

1 Introduction

Sleeping – the time between falling asleep and awaking – can be divided into several phases that may alternate during the night. The two most frequent phases are **REM** (rapid eye movement) and **NREM** (opposite to REM). The NREM phase is characteristic by a rundown of brain activity, a physical calmness and a relaxation [1].

Consequently, these phases split into further four stages according to the depth of the sleep – from the deepest sleep far to the light sleep [10]. The second stage, REM, is characteristic with a brain activity on the level of vigilance, with rapid eye movements and a loss of tonus of mostly all the muscles controlled by our will. It is the most difficult to wake up someone, who is in this stage. These stages normally shift in a specific cycle four or five times a night [2, 10].

Next common stage is a **Dreaming**, which takes place during REM sleeping stage, according to the article [3]. Along with the theories the sleep and the dreaming have a regenerative function for our body and brain and while dreaming our brain reorders, categorizes and restores the saved information [8].

© Springer International Publishing Switzerland 2016
M. Younas et al. (Eds.): MobiWIS 2016, LNCS 9847, pp. 431–442, 2016.
DOI: 10.1007/978-3-319-44215-0_36

To complete the list of the stages let's add another stages, such as **Falling asleep** (hypnagogium) – passing from the vigilance into the sleep and **Waking up** (hypnexagogium) – passing from the sleep into the vigilance.

On the waking-up stage we have to focus now. The best efficiency of waking up is during the light sleep, when the sleeping person is not far from waking up. Indications of this stage are sudden body movements for changing the position of the sleeping person.

There exist plenty of solutions that aspire to increase the awakening efficiency and to accommodate themselves to people. They detect the sleep stages or they at least try to and then they adapt the waking time in a set time window. These solutions are usually in the form of various applications for mobile phones, tablets or directly for computers with external sensors [20]. However, the market offers even hardware solutions, which run mostly on Arduino, Raspberry Pi and other similar solutions [14].

However, most of these solutions work only as alarm clocks with enhancements. But the smart alarm clock applications available at Google Play or Apple Store are even principally limited by the hardware facilities of the phones or tablets they are installed on.

The sample application can be found for example at the web site [5]. Indeed, nowadays the mobile phones dispose with a large number of sensors and detectors [20], but they are limited by their functionality. If we wanted to use for example a built-in accelerometer for movement detection, we would have to fix the device on the subject, which even principally is not an ideal solution. It's possible to use a built-in camera of course, but there's a problem particularly with a night scanning, when it would be necessary to light the scene on for the movement detection [18]. But the light is a very disruptive element for sleep, so this solution has to be refused as well. Therefore, the mobile phone sensors are not sufficient for smart alarm clock use.

As it was mentioned already, there exist even better solutions based for example on Arduino platform [7, 14]. These smart alarm clocks dispose with an advantage of an option to be connected with various extern sensors that are not available in mobile devices [20]. For example, we can mention an infrared movement sensor, which deals with a problem of detecting movements of people in the dark. However, the existing solutions are not adequate solutions that would detect movement, noise and further factors and consequently the waking time. Usually they apply only a LCD display, an Ethernet shield and basic alarm clock functionality. When connected to a network they communicate most often through Google Services calendar and gmail services. The principal of the smart solution is an option to set the waking time by internet, a detailed description with the implementation can be found at the web site [6]. These solutions are not adequate solutions of the approach to improve the waking-up efficiency and they do not apply any sensors, or just their fragment.

Therefore, an objective of this project is to design a respective solution of the approach to smart alarm clocks and to enhance them with the accessory sensors such as movement infra detectors, sensors of noise, temperature and a light intensity. The result solution shall manage to react to the users' impulses in the period close to waking-up and to find a moment close to vigilance in a set time window and wake the user up then. Or if the solution doesn't find such moment, then it shall find at least a point close to the light sleep.

2   Existing Solutions and a Definition of the Problem

Everyone has to get up in the morning at a certain time, which they set up ahead on their mobile devices or classic alarm clocks. But the time they set up is definitive and when the alarm clock draws close to this value for a minimum interval, the alarm clock simply rings. No one cares whether you are just in the deep sleep or whether you got up already. Therefore, it can happen you are woken up in the wrong sleeping stage, which is a problem. This problem can chase you all the day afterwards – you feel more tired and have an impression as that you have slept less hours than usually. So the question is: how to avoid this precisely and reliably? Is it even possible to detect and recognize the single sleeping stages and wake the person up on time?

In the literature we can read, that closely before and after REM phase the sleeping person moves more than during the other phases. Additionally, these movements can be followed by making noises. All these signals can be detected and on their basis we can analyze the processing sleeping phases [19].

As the most optimal sensor for detecting movements not only in the dark it seems to be an infrared movement sensor, see Fig. 1, which shall dispose with at least basic setting possibilities. The advantage of these sensors is their small purchase cost, high availability, small consumption (<50 µA), high observation angel and sensing distance in order of meters. The sensing distance is adequate for utilization in the room.

As an additional sensor of sound sensing it can be used a classic microphone with a sufficient sensitivity. For output from the microphone into Arduino an analog signal is ideal, because it provides recording and interpreting of a whole scale of sound volume. It is very important to strain away noise of the surroundings for the best accuracy possible. If we used a microphone with a digital output, we could interpret only two statuses – quiet and noise. It would depend on the microphone sensitivity as well, but it would be a problem, which can be solved simply by using the analog output.

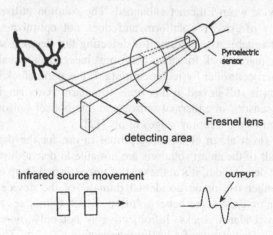

Fig. 1. PIR motion sensor [13]

In the night there arises another problem – redundant wasting of energy by lighting the display, which also is a disturbing element. For the best sleep possible it is necessary to minimize all the lighting disrupting elements. Therefore, it shall be used a photo resistor as well, which adjusts together with daytime the display backlighting and in the case of detecting a darkness/night the display simply turns off.

Next problem of a bad sleep occurs in overheated rooms. It is suitable to connect a sensor of an inside temperature to the intelligent alarm clock for checking on the temperature for basic orientation. All these sensors together with the elementary equipment of the function alarm clock create the smart alarm clock concept.

The smart alarm clock shall dispose with the basic functionality of the classic alarm clocks and minimally common sensors for the movement or noise detection. Ideally it shall dispose with the combination of both variants for the most precise results possible. Nowadays (2014) there exist several commercial or open source solutions throughout different platforms, which try to apply various detectors for the best and most comfortable ease possible while either waking up or reacting to different situations. For example, let's mention several solutions currently available on the market.

SleepTracker is a watch that monitors sleep in the night and according to the gathered sleeping information it rings right in the moment of the light sleep, so-called "almost a vigilance moment". The disadvantage of this solution is that the person has to sleep with the watch on and with the wristlet tighter than usually, which can influence the circulation system in a negative way [9].

Sleep Cycle is one of many applications for Android and iOS, which utilizes built-in sensors in phones or tablets. According to a producer recommendation it's necessary to place the phone/tablet on one's bed, where it detects movements using accelerometer. For an additional analyze it uses a microphone and it records sounds or noises in the background. There arises a possible problem of damaging the device while sleeping, therefore it can't be classified as a sufficient solution.

S.M.A.R.T. Alarm Clock is a solution based on Arduino platform. It uses a google calendar through an extern service Temboo [11]. The alarm clock accepts a waking time from this service when Ethernet enhanced. The solution utilizes just the fundamental functionality of Arduino platform and does not optimize the waking time. Therefore, it is not suitable as a solution for detecting the sleeping stages [6].

iWakeUp – An alarm clock for smart bedrooms based on a visual contact with the person. It uses a microcontroller for its functioning. If the alarm clock is set for a certain time and the person is still in bed at this time, the alarm starts ringing. The solution applies 3 pressure sensors, one thermal sensor and one optical sensor. But it does not deal with a problem of the sleeping stages at all [12].

None of these smart alarm clocks are optimal to use for the detection of human sleeping cycles. Half of the smart solutions are not able to detect these cycles. Though the second half can detect them, it's at the cost of uncomforted sleep or potential health problems while longer use or an accidental damage of the device. Therefore, it is necessary to design and test some better solution, which eliminates the insufficiencies of the existing smart alarm clocks. Its objective is not only more precise impulse detection, but also safer use out of a health perspective [20, 21]. The implementation and testing of this enhanced smart alarm clock are presented in the next chapters.

3   New Tiny Budget Smart Solution

A prototype of the smart alarm clock is built on a electronic prototypic Arduino platform, to be precise it applies Arduino Uno R3 model, which uses a microcontroller ATmega328. It works on a frequency 16 MHz and it contains 32 KB of a flash memory. The working frequency and the memory capacity are fully sufficient for the functionality of a smart alarm clock [7]. Visual output of the alarm clock is provided by a 2 line LCD 1602 I2C display. It displays not only actual time and information about the alarm, but also a room temperature.

To retain the actual time even in the case of a disconnection or power outage the alarm clock uses a DS3231 module with integrated temperature compensated crystal oscillator. This module is very precise (2 ppm) on condition of operation temperature in interval 0–40 °C. The module service is provided by a memory chip AT24C32. More information including a connection diagram can be found on the web site [13].

The alarm signalization was solved out by a breadboard set up with LED diodes for a light signalization and with buzzers connected serially for a sound signalization. While powered with 5 V the buzzers start to pipe harshly, but not too loudly to wake up a further neighbourhood. The alarm is not as loud as for example loud-speaker of a mobile phone, but the buzzer is greatly able to wake someone up in the stage of the light sleep.

To detect the room temperature, it was applied a DHT11 sensor with income voltage 3.3–5 V. The range of measured values is 20–90 % for humidity ($\pm$ 5 %) and 0–50°C for temperature ($\pm$ 2°C). The resolution is 1 % for the humidity and 1°C for the temperature. The temperature sensor is not a key attribute of the smart alarm clock, that's why these values are yet in the tolerance range. A more detailed technical specification and a connection diagram can be found on the web [15]. As an additional sensor to the alarm clock it was suggested a photosensitive resistor that detects intensity of coming light. Consequently, a computing unit of the alarm clock determines daytime and according to this time it adjusts display backlighting, or possibly it switches the display completely off. While sleeping it's entirely useless, if the LCD display emits the light and disturbs the sleep this way.

The most important sensors of the smart alarm clock are movement passive infra sensors and modules for sound detection. The Passive infrared sensor (PIR) is an electronic sensor. It measures infrared rays that are emitted from objects in its field of view [15]. All the objects with temperature above the absolute zero emit their thermal energy in the form of a radiation. For a human eye this radiation is invisible, because it is radiated in infrared spectrum, which can't be recognized by a human eye. But it can be detected by electric devices suggested for this objective. In this case "passive" means, that PIR devices don't radiate any energy for the purposes of detecting these rays. PIR sensors neither measure any heat; they detect only the emitted or reflected infrared radiance from the object. The PIR sensor consists of a sensor made from pyro electric material – the material that generates energy while incurred to the radiated heat. [16] Therefore the PIR movement sensors manage to detect people's movement, animals' movement or of another objects' by detecting a change of amount of the infrared radiance in the scanned field of view. So if for example a person enters this field, the sensor detects change of amount of the radiated heat from a lower temperature of a wall to a higher temperature of a human. This movement is consequently recorded by change of the outcome voltage, which the electronics assigns in the movement sensor, and the result is interpreted as a detected movement. However, the sensor detects also a simple change of the object's surface. Radiated sample, although with the same amount of heat, is different and is detected as a movement as well [17].

As the movement sensor it was used a HC-SR501 sensor, which works with income voltage 3.3–5 V. It scans 100° space of a cone into distance of up to 7 meters. This sensor disposes with two possibilities of a detection setting. The first setting facilitates to the following approach: from when the first movement was captured, the sensor scans continually until the subject in the scanning field of the sensor stops moving. So we can measure the lengths of the individual movements and according to their length we can react to the events. While a longer movement we can establish, that the detected person woke up at the activated alarm and therefore it is not necessary to let the alarm on any more. The second setting detects only a single-shot change in the field of view and a next movement isn't detected until a next pre-set interval. The interval can be set from 0.5 s to 60 s.

For the solution of the movement detection it is required to use two sensors with different settings. The first sensor will scan continually after the movement detection and will be activated just in the alarm period. After the pre-set time segment it will postpone or cancel the alarm and will suppose a successful awakening of the person. The second sensor will be activated continually. Its objective will be to detect a movement during the night and to detect the sleeping cycles. The movements of the person occur close before or close after the REM sleep stage. The sensor setting will be as the detector of the single-shot movement with 30 s delay. In half a minute the person shall be able to stop moving and pass over to another sleeping stage. The setting of the delay and the scanning can be still regulated later according to the measured values while testing this prototype. For higher accuracy of these phases the alarm clock will be supplied with a microphone module connected to the analogue input of Arduino. By using these data from the microphone it will be possible to work with the environment of the alarm clock and to react to the events.

The last part will be utilization of a touch sensor for manual switch-off of the alarm clock in the case the alarm clock will have to be cancelled immediately. Instead of touch sensor it is possible to use also a classic button.

Setting of the waking time is solved by connection to a computer USB port via serial virtual port. To the alarm clock it's sent out the time of the alarm activation in the format of numbers divided by commas. After evaluating the sensors data in the pre-defined time window (typically 30 min) the alarm is activated in the period of the light sleep, or if it doesn't detect any, then in the accurate set time.

This solution is new in the sense of using Arduino platform and eliminating the insufficiencies of the existing solutions. It is just a prototype.

4   Implementation Based on Arduino UNO R3

As it was said in the previous chapter, the solution of the smart alarm clock is based on the prototype Arduino platform. Connection of the individual components including their links is illustrated on a connection diagram in the figure (Fig. 2).

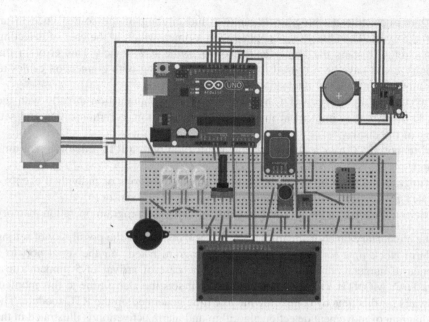

Fig. 2. Connection diagram of the components

The only difference versus the real connection is connection of the LCD display through an interface LCD 1602 Adapter Board w/IIC/I2C, which simplifies the final display connection especially by lowering the number of needed I/O ports to Arduino. It contains also a potentiometer for display brightness regulation and easier access to backlighting intensity. In comparison with the diagram the real connection does not have practically any influence on a different functioning of the alarm clock. A summary of all the used alarm clock components:

- Arduino Uno R3
- LCD 1602 I2C + Adapter Board w/IIC/I2C
- HC-SR501 PIR – a movement detector
- Photo resistor – regulation of the display brightness according to the surrounding light
- TTP223B – a capacity touch sensor
- DS3231 – a real time clock with integrated memory and an additional power supply, a battery
- D19 microphone
- DHT11 – a sensor of the surrounding temperature and humidity
- Breadboard – a prototype breadboard for components connection
- Buzzer + LED diodes for the alarm signalization

For development of the alarm clock source code it was used a development environment Arduino version 1.0.6 and libraries mentioned below:

- <Wire.h> - a communication with IC2 devices, in this case with the LCD display. The library was modified because of problems with connecting/disconnecting an

IC2 device while the program is running and circling of the source code in an infinite cycle. The library was supplied with a timer, which in the case of detecting the circling restarts the library and reconnects the IC2 device. This error in the library could have been caused for example by moving with connection cables to Arduino, eventually by fluctuating of the voltage.

- <LCD.h>, <LiquidCrystal_I2C.h> - libraries for communication directly with the LCD display, they implement functions for initialization, communication and setting of the display.
- <virtuabotixRTC.h> - a library for communication with a RTC circuit, a real time clock
- <Timer.h> - a timer library, it implements timing functions of individual events
- <DHT.h> - a library for communication with a DHT11 sensor
- <MemoryFree.h> - a library for debugging of using the program operation memory

The elementary functionality of the alarm clock consists in the possibility of setting the alarm clock time for a certain time. The program listens on the serial port to a sequence of numerals divided by commas. In the case of arrival of 5 numerals in a format DAY,MONTH,YEAR,HOUR,MINUTE, it sets the alarm time to this moment and awaits for this time by comparing the real time generated on the RTC module. The flow diagram of movement detection algorithm and alarm activation is illustrated in the following figure (Fig. 3).

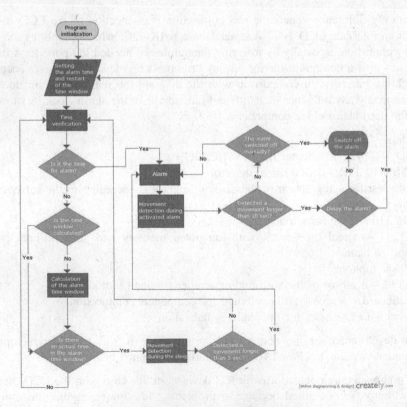

Fig. 3. Flow diagram of the alarm algorithm

The PIR detector that detects the movement in the sensor's field of view sends out the movement information into the computing unit of the alarm clock. In the case of a long enough movement > 3 s it records the movement of the subject and saves to a variable, that the movement was detected. Movement longer than 3 s was chosen by a reason of eliminating short moves that could be incorrect, such as "wince" while falling asleep. In the alarm clock there is preset default time window for 30 min, in this time window the alarm can ring after detecting this movement. Because a person moves most often before/after the REM stage, the alarm tries to activate itself before/after the REM stage. 30 s after detecting this movement the variable of the movement is restarted, because the movement can be detected out of the time window and the sensor searches another possible move. Therefore, the alarm activation can occur in two possible situations.

1. It's not detected any movement in the set time window (30 min back in time from the set alarm), the alarm is activated in the accurate time of the user's set alarm
2. In the time window there is detected a movement by PIR sensor, which is longer than 3 s, the alarm is activated.

When the alarm is activated, it initiates the light and sound signalization. If the display is in the mode of backlighting switched off (in the night), then the backlighting is turned on. To switch the alarm clock off there is the touch capacity button; the alarm clock detects other movements during the activated alarm. If it classifies that the subject gets up, the alarm clock is delayed for a pre-set number of minutes; a default value is 5 min. All the times are adjustable in the program definitions header and they can be arbitrarily changed without changing functionality of the alarm clock.

The next possibilities of enhancement the alarm clock consist in adding a SD card reader for saving the waking times, saving the time setting for the case of the power outage or recording a detected event for easier program optimization. It would be suitable to further enhance the alarm clock with a better touch LCD display, Ethernet or WiFi shield for setting the time through a network. Another improvement could be also replacing the buzzer with a speaker that would enable to record a personal melody for the alarm.

5 Testing of Developed Solution

Testing of the smart alarm clock application lies in a simulation of various waking times and verification of the assumption, that the application is stable and able to activate the alarm in the right time even after several days of operating. Therefore, the alarm activation shall be as the latest in the accurate set alarm time. The next assumption of the application's correct functionality is verification of the precise time calculations in the set time window and their application on the prior alarm activation. It's also required testing of all the sensors, if they provide correct information about their environment (light intensity, movement, sound).

The basic testing will take place in a window of a serial monitor of Arduino development environment, while switching the application on in so-called debug mode, where the individual statuses and important variables will be presented.

The more advanced testing of the sleeping cycle detection will proceed on a sample of 5 measurements, which will have the alarm set to the ultimate waking time possible and it will be tested, if the program manages to record the person's movement and activate the alarm in advance, in the 30 min time window. The consequent results will be displayed in a table (Table 1).

Table 1. The alarm times and their prior activation

Experiment nr.	Alarm time	Alarm activation
1	10:10	9:48
2	7:10	7:01
3	8:00	7:49
4	9:30	9:21
5	6:50	6:50

5.1 Results

While basic testing of the alarm clock functionality it was revealed, that the microphone module does not work correctly and does not forward the right information. Because it was the additional sensor to the movement sensor, the sound verification was removed and for the detection of the sleeping cycles it was used just the movement sensor. This discovered defect shall not have any radical influence on the functionality.

Further basic tests did not reveal any significant problem and there were tested the advanced functions for the movement detection while sleeping. For testing the functionality correctness there were realized 5 experiments with different alarm times, the values including the alarm clock activation are showed in the following table (Table 1).

Out of the sample with 5 experiments it's obvious, that in 1 experiment the alarm clock software did not find in the time window −30 min from the alarm time any

Fig. 4. Final setting of developed prototype solution of Smart Alarm on the Arduino platform

crossover from NREM stage to REM or the opposite and therefore it didn't activate the alarm in prior. In the other 4 experiments this crossover was detected and the activation processed entirely right, it means in the time window interval.

A comparison with a different existing solution is not possible; because both of the solutions are closely associated while the alarm activation. If one application found a moment close to awakening and activated its alarm, the second application would activate its alarm immediately as well, because it would detect movement while waking up, eventually the times would differ by maximum of a minute. Therefore, the experiments would have to be effected separately, which would have no predicative value – every day, or every morning the crossover times are different.

Proposed application (Fig. 4) was also tested for stability and reliability. Reliability testing was realised by application run within seven days, while the application run reliably without the slightest signs of a slowdown, the shortage of memory or jam/restart alarm (assuming a constant source of alarm). The application is also able to handle all instruction up to 160.15 Hz, which is for required purposes and properties (scanning sensors in real time) better than requested value [4].

6   Conclusions

The result of this work is the full-fledged alarm clock, which can detect crossovers between the sleeping cycles and activate the alarm in the best time possible, which means the time close to waking up. Regarding the activation of the alarm clock in the right time, the impression is quite subjective and therefore it's not possible to say with an accuracy, how proper the result is. Since the alarm signalization is provided by the pair of LED diodes and one buzzer, which is not that loud such as for example a speaker, therefore the waking moment has to be timed up for the right moment of the light sleep. On the sample of 5 experiments it was achieved to wake the subject up in every case, even when the right moment was not found, which can be considered as a very good result.

Acknowledgement.   This work and the contribution were supported by project "Smart Solutions for Ubiquitous Computing Environments" FIM, University of Hradec Kralove, Czech Republic (under ID: UHK-FIM-SP-2016-2102). We also acknowledge the technical language assistance provided by Pavlina Simkova.

References

1. Krejcar, O., Jirka, J., Janckulik, D.: Use of mobile phones as intelligent sensors for sound input analysis and sleep state detection. Sensors **11**(6), 6037–6055 (2011). doi:10.3390/s110606037
2. Polysomnography. http://www.nlm.nih.gov/medlineplus/ency/article/003932.htm. Accessed 17 Dec 2015
3. Maquet, P., et al.: Functional neuroanatomy of human rapid-eye-movement sleep and dreaming. Nature **383**(6596), 163–166 (1996)

442   A. Drabek et al.

4. Drabek, A., Krejcar, O., Selamat, A., Kuca, K.: A smart arduino alarm clock using hypnagogia detection during night. In: Fujita, H., et al., (eds.) IEA/AIE 2016. LNAI, vol. 9799, pp. 1–13 (2016). DOI:10.1007/978-3-319-42007-3_45
5. Smart Alarm for Android. http://sport.com/smart_alarm_android.html. Accessed 16 Dec 2015
6. S.M.A.R.T Alarm Clock. http://makezine.com/projects/s-m-a-r-t-alarm-clock/. Accessed 16 Dec 2015
7. Arduino [cit. 2014-12-16]. http://www.arduino.cc
8. Crick, F., Mitchinson, G.: The function of dream sleep. Nature 304(5922), 111–114 (1983)
9. SleepTracker. http://www.sleeptracker.cz. Accessed 18 Dec 2015
10. Cerny, M., Penhaker, M.: The HomeCare and Circadian rhythm. In: International Conference on Information Technology and Applications in Biomedicine 2008, Shenzhen, pp. 245–248 (2008). DOI 10.1109/ITAB.2008.4570546
11. Temboo. https://temboo.com. Accessed 18 Dec 2015
12. Liao, W.H., et al.: iWakeUp: a video-based alarm clock for smart bedrooms. J. Chin. Inst. Eng. 33(5), 661–668 (2010)
13. How Infrared motion detector components work. http://www.glolab.com/pirparts/infrared.html. Accessed 19 Dec 2015
14. Horalek, J., Sobeslav, V.: Measuring of electric energy consumption in households by means of Arduino platform. Proc. Adv. Comput. Commun. Eng. Technol. ICOCOE 2015, 819–830 (2016)
15. Machacek, Z., Slaby, R., Vanus, J., Hercik, R., Koziorek, J.: Non-contact measurement system analysis for metallurgical slabs proportion parameters. Elektron. ir Elektrotechnika 19(10), 58–61 (2013). ISSN: 1392-1215
16. Krejcar, O., Frischer, R.: Non destructive defects detection by performance spectral density analysis. Sensors 11(3), 2334–2346 (2011). doi:10.3390/s110302334
17. PIR sensor technology [cit. 19 December 2014]. http://www.ecosirius.com/technology.html
18. Augustynek, M., Pindor, J., Penhaker, M., Korpas, D.: Detection of ECG significant waves for biventricular pacing treatment. In: Proceedings of 2010 Second International Conference on Computer Engineering and Applications, ICCEA 2010, vol. 2, pp. 164–167 (2010). DOI:10.1109/ICCEA.2010.186
19. Aserinsky, E., Kleitman, N.: Two types of ocular motility occurring in sleep. J. Appl. Physiol. 8(1), 1–10 (1955)
20. Cerny, M., Penhaker, M.: Wireless body sensor network in health maintenance systems. Elektron. ir Elektrotechnika 9, 113–116 (2011)
21. Cimler, R., Matyska, J., Sobeslav, V., Cloud based solution for mobile healthcare application. In: Proceedings of the 18th International Database Engineering & Applications Symposium, pp. 298–301. ACM (2014)

Author Index

Printed in the United States
By Bookmasters